Big
Book of
Everything

Big Book of Everything

BARNES & NOBLE

NEW YORK

This 2007 edition published by Barnes & Noble, Inc.
by arrangement with Miles Kelly Publishing Ltd.

Publishing Director Anne Marshall
Editorial Director Belinda Gallagher
Art Director Jo Brewer
Editors Rosalind McGuire, Teri Putnam, Stephen Setford
Assistant Editor Hannah Todd
Editorial Assistant Caroline Tate
Proofreaders Teri Putnam, Jenni Rainford
Designers Jo Brewer, Venita Kidwai, Sally Lace, Peter Radcliffe
Indexer Helen Snaith
Picture Research Manager Liberty Newton
Picture Researcher Laura Faulder
Production Elizabeth Brunwin
Reprographics Anthony Cambray, Stephan Davis, Liberty Newton, Ian Paulyn
Planners, Authors and Consultants Sue Becklake, Stuart Cooper, Camilla de la Bedoyere, Fiona MacDonald, Rupert Matthews, Stephen Setford, Clint Twist, Brian Williams
Americanization Bethanie Bourne

www.mileskelly.net
info@mileskelly.net

ISBN-13: 978-0-7607-9037-3
ISBN-10: 0-7607-9037-X

Printed and bound in China

10 9 8 7 6 5 4 3 2 1

CONTENTS

UNIVERSE 10–69

PLANET EARTH 70–129

LIFE ON EARTH 130–189

PEOPLE 190–249

COUNTRIES 250–309

HISTORY 310–369

SCIENCE & TECHNOLOGY 370–429

ARTS & CULTURE 430–489

INDEX 490

UNIVERSE 10–69

The Big Bang	12	The Moon	32	Asteroids and Meteors	52
Stars	14	Mercury	34	Astronomy	54
Constellations	16	Venus	36	Telescopes and Observatories	56
Galaxies	18	Mars	38	Space Probes	58
The Milky Way	20	Jupiter	40	Artificial Satellites	60
Nebulae	22	Saturn	42	Man on the Moon	62
Black Holes	24	Uranus	44	The Space Shuttle	64
The Solar System	26	Neptune	46	Space Stations	66
The Sun	28	Pluto	48	Glossary	68
The Earth	30	Comets	50		

PLANET EARTH 70–129

The Formation of Earth	72	Volcanoes	92	Forests	112
Spinning Earth	74	Earthquakes	94	The Atmosphere	114
Ages of the Earth	76	Landscapes	96	Clouds	116
Inside the Earth	78	Mountains	98	Weather	118
Rocks	80	Glaciers and Ice Ages	100	Climate	120
Gemstones	82	Rivers	102	Global Warming	122
Fossils	84	Lakes	104	Resources	124
Continents	86	Oceans and Seas	106	Maps and Mapmaking	126
Islands	88	Caves	108	Glossary	128
Drifting Continents	90	Deserts	110		

LIFE ON EARTH 130–189

Origins of Life 132	Fish 152	The Human Body 172
The Plant Kingdom 134	How Animals Feed 154	Bones and Joints 174
Parts of a Plant 136	Amphibians 156	Muscles and Moving 176
Food Factory 138	How Animals Breed 158	Lungs and Breathing 178
Plant Reproduction 140	Reptiles 160	Eating and Digestion 180
How Plants Grow 142	Dinosaurs 162	Heart and Blood 182
Plants on our Planet 144	Communication 164	The Nervous System 184
The Animal Kingdom 146	Birds 166	Reproduction 186
Invertebrates 148	Mammals 168	Glossary 188
How Animals Move 150	Animals in Danger 170	

PEOPLE 190–249

Ancient Myths 192	Eternal Life and Paradise 206	Team Sports 220
Gods of Egypt 194	Religious Buildings 208	Solo Sports 222
Greek Myths 196	Epic Tales 210	Track and Field Events 224
Norse Myths 198	Heroes 212	Olympic Games 226
Native American Beliefs 200	Magic and Witchcraft 214	Sporting Records 228
Hindu Deities 202	Mythical Creatures 216	Famous People 230
Religious Founders 204	Sport and Leisure 218	

COUNTRIES 250–309

The World	252	Africa	262	Oceania	274
North America	254	Africa People and Places	264	Oceania People and Places	276
North America People and Places	256	Asia	266	Antarctica	278
South America	258	Asia People and Places	268	Factfile	280
South America People and Places	260	Europe	270	Dependencies	302
		Europe People and Places	272	World Flags	306

HISTORY 310–369

The Ancient World	312	The Americas	332	The Age of Revolutions	352
The Fertile Crescent	314	New Learning	334	Europe in Revolution	354
Ancient Greece	316	Age of Explorers	336	Europe Supreme	356
The Roman Empire	318	Religion and Wars	338	World Wars	358
China and Japan	320	Beyond Europe	340	The Cold War	360
The Barbarians	322	1600–1800	342	The Changing World	362
New States	324	Expanding World	344	History Timeline	364
Feudal Europe	326	Asia in Decline	346	Glossary	366
Indian Empires	328	A Europe of Ideas	348		
Medieval Asia	330	The Industrial Revolution	350		

SCIENCE & TECHNOLOGY 370–429

Atoms and Molecules	372	Light	390	History of Air Transport	410
Solids, Liquids, and Gases	374	Sound	392	Computers	412
The Periodic Table	376	Air and Water	394	Telecommunications	414
Chemicals and Materials	378	Early Inventions	396	The Internet	416
Carbon Chemicals	380	Machine Power	398	Sound and Vision	418
Electricity and Magnetism	382	Construction	400	Power	420
Energy	384	Bridges	402	Medicine	422
Force and Motion	386	History of Rail Transport	404	Numbers and Shapes	424
Heat and Temperature	388	History of Road Transport	406	Glossary	428
		History of Water Transport	408		

ARTS & CULTURE 430–489

The First Artists	432	Modern Theater	454	Home Entertainment	472
Old Masters, New Ideas	434	Moving to Music	456	The First Films	474
Art Techniques	436	Ballet	458	Making Movies	476
Art around the World	438	Dance	460	Special Effects and Superstars	478
Modern Art	440	Words and Writing	462	Buildings Great and Small	480
Making Music	442	Scriptures and Sacred Writing	464	Modern Architecture	482
Classical Music	444	Poems and Novels	466	History of Culture	484
Musical Instruments	446	Printing and Publishing	468	Glossary	486
Popular Music	448	Beginnings of Broadcasting	470		
The Origins of Drama	450				
World Theater	452				

UNIVERSE

The Big Bang

The Universe is everything that we can ever know—all of space and all of time. It is almost entirely empty, with small clusters of matter and energy. The Universe is about 15 billion years old, but estimates vary. The Big Bang explosion is how scientists think the Universe began 15 billion years ago.

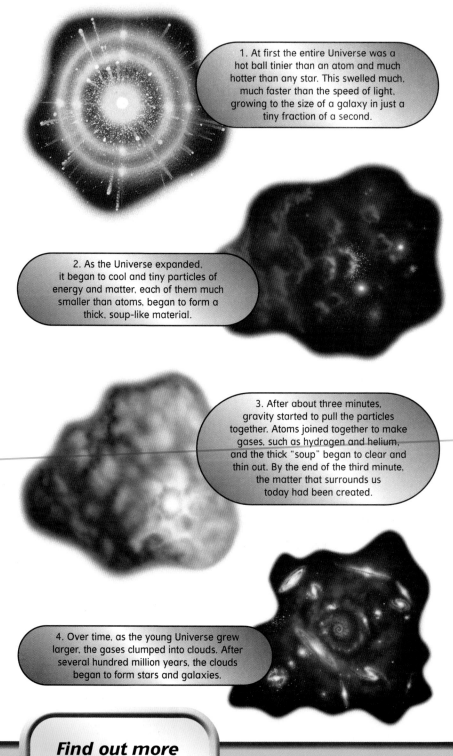

1. At first the entire Universe was a hot ball tinier than an atom and much hotter than any star. This swelled much, much faster than the speed of light, growing to the size of a galaxy in just a tiny fraction of a second.

▶ *The Universe after the Big Bang. Although the Big Bang took place in just a fraction of a second, the explosion was strong enough to send energy and matter flying out at great speed in all directions. No one is able to explain yet what might, if anything, have come before the Big Bang.*

2. As the Universe expanded, it began to cool and tiny particles of energy and matter, each of them much smaller than atoms, began to form a thick, soup-like material.

○ First there was a hot ball tinier than an atom. This grew to football size and cooled to about 340 billion billion°F.

○ A split second later, a superforce swelled the infant Universe a thousand billion billion billion times. Scientists call this inflation.

3. After about three minutes, gravity started to pull the particles together. Atoms joined together to make gases, such as hydrogen and helium, and the thick "soup" began to clear and thin out. By the end of the third minute, the matter that surrounds us today had been created.

○ As it mushroomed out, the Universe was flooded with energy and matter, and the superforce separated into forces such as electricity and gravity.

○ There were no atoms at first, just tiny particles, such as quarks, in a dense soup a trillion trillion trillion trillion trillion times denser than water.

○ There was also antimatter, the mirror image of matter. Antimatter and matter destroy each other when they meet, so they battled it out. Matter won—but the Universe was left almost empty.

4. Over time, as the young Universe grew larger, the gases clumped into clouds. After several hundred million years, the clouds began to form stars and galaxies.

Find out more

Galaxies pp. 18–19

The Universe is expanding, with all the galaxies rushing away from each other. Astronomers do not know if this will go on forever. If it stops, and the Universe starts to contract, the galaxies would rush towards each other. Then the Universe might end in a Big Crunch, the opposite of the Big Bang. This might set off another Big Bang and a brand new Universe.

○ After three minutes, quarks started to fuse (join) to make the smallest atoms, hydrogen. Then hydrogen gas atoms fused to make helium gas atoms.

○ After one million years, the gases began to curdle into strands with dark holes between them.

○ After 300 million years, the strands clumped into clouds, and then the clouds clumped together to form stars and galaxies.

○ The afterglow of the Big Bang can still be detected as microwave background radiation coming from all over space.

○ The Universe may have neither a center nor an edge, because according to Einstein's theory of relativity, gravity bends all of space-time around into an endless curve.

○ The furthest galaxies yet detected are about 13 billion lightyears away.

Amazing

Scientists believe that because both space and time began with the Big Bang, there may possibly be no time "before" it occurred.

Lightyears and parsecs

Earth distances are measured in miles or kilometers, but these units are too small to be useful in space. Scientists measure the Universe in lightyears or parsecs. Light is the fastest thing in the Universe, so by measuring in lightyears scientists are able to get a better idea of such great distances. A lightyear is the distance that light travels in one year— about 6 million million mi. A lightyear is roughly 3.25 parsecs. Light from even the closest star takes years to reach us. The nearest star is over four lightyears away, so this means that when astronomers look at it through a telescope, they are actually looking back into the past—seeing the star as it was four years ago. Light from the most distant galaxies takes about 10,000 million years to reach us. The Universe may go on expanding forever. Or it may eventually stop and collapse in on itself to possibly even start all over again.

Hot ball

Scientists have calculated that the hot ball before the Big Bang must have swelled at a much faster rate than even the speed of light. The hot ball would have grown to the size of a galaxy within a fraction of a second.

History of the Universe

Time after Big Bang	Era	Description
10^{-43} seconds	Planck era	Temperatures and pressures too high for scientists to understand
10^{-6} seconds	Hadron era	Fireball in which protons and neutrons formed from quarks
1 second	Radiation era	First atoms of hydrogen and helium form as fireball cools
30,000 years	Matter era	Matter dominates over radiation
300,000 years	Decoupling era	Particles and radiation no longer interact. Background radiation starts to cool
1 million years	Formation of galaxies	Ripples in the Universe result in galaxy formation
1 billion years	Formation of stars	Stars and galaxies bring light to the Universe and create the elements from which people and planets are made

Stars

A star is a ball of gas so hot that it burns and glows. The temperatures of stars range from 3,812°F to about 90,032°F. The color of a star is an indication of how hot it is. White stars are hotter than red ones, but some stars become even hotter and shine with a blue light.

1. A nebula formed from cloud and dust

2. A star is born when nuclear reactions begin

4. Dust swirling round a new star may form planets

3. A star burns steadily

Stars begin in giant clouds of dust and gas, where material gathers into clumps called nebulae, each containing evaporating gas globules or ECGs, which are the beginnings of stars.

Find out more

The Milky Way pp. 20–21

Clusters

A swarm or large cluster of stars known as M80 (Nac 6093) is found in the Milky Way galaxy. This swarm, 28,000 lightyears from Earth, contains hundreds of thousands of stars, "attracted" to each other by gravity.

○ Stars are balls of mainly hydrogen and helium gas.

○ Nuclear reactions in the heart of stars, like those in atom bombs, generate heat and light.

○ The center of a star reaches 28,800,032°F. A grain of sand this hot would kill someone 93 mi away.

○ The gas in stars is in a hot state called plasma, which is made of atoms stripped of electrons.

○ Stars twinkle because we see them through the Earth's atmosphere.

○ In the core of a star, hydrogen nuclei fuse (join together) to form helium. This nuclear reaction is called a proton-proton chain.

○ Astronomers work out how big a star is from its brightness and temperature.

○ The size and brightness of a star depends on its mass—that is, how much gas it is made of. Our Sun is a medium-sized star, and no star has more than 100 times the Sun's mass or less than 6–7 percent of its mass.

○ The few thousand stars visible to the naked eye are just a tiny fraction of the trillions in the Universe.

Amazing

It is estimated that there are about 50,000 billion billion stars in the Universe, more than all the grains of sand on all the beaches of the Earth.

○ The coolest stars, such as Arcturus and Antares, glow reddest. Hotter stars are yellow and white. The hottest are blue-white, like Rigel and Zeta Puppis.

○ The blue supergiant Zeta Puppis has a surface temperature of 72,032°F.

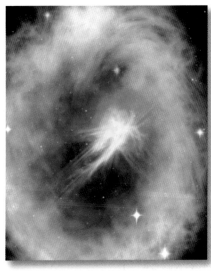

Life cycle of a star

The "life cycle" of a star: gases and dust collect (1) and form a hot core, a new star (2). A "main sequence" star (3), like our Sun, shines for 10 billion years. This cools to a red giant (4), which leaves a smaller, hotter white dwarf (5).

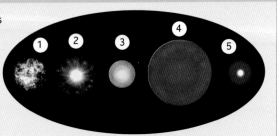

⒜ Once a supergiant's core turns to dense iron at the end of its life, gravity squeezes it so hard that it collapses in just a few seconds, then blows itself to bits in a gigantic explosion called a supernova (plural supernovae). Gases are thrown out thousands of miles in a fraction of a second and huge amounts of light, heat, and X rays radiate out. Supernovae rarely last for more than a few months, but in that brief time they can burn brighter than a billion suns.

Brightest stars

	Star of constellation	Apparent magnitude	Distance
Sirius	Alpha Canis Major	−1.46	8.6 lightyears
Canopus	Alpha Carinae	−0.72	110 lightyears
	Alpha Centauri	−0.01	4.37 lightyears
Arcturus	Alpha Bootis	−0.04	36 lightyears
Vega	Alpha Lyrae	+0.06	26 lightyears
Capella	Alpha Aurigae	+0.08	45 lightyears
Rigel	Beta Orionis	+0.12	850 lightyears
Procyon	Alpha Canis Minoris	+0.38	11.4 lightyears
Achernar	Alpha Eridani	+0.46	118 lightyears

Note: the lower the magnitude, the brighter the star.

Not all of these stars can be seen in the Northern Hemisphere

Constellations

Constellations are patterns of stars in the sky that astronomers use to help them pinpoint individual stars among the thousands in the night sky. Astronomers today recognize 88 different constellations that are visible at some time during the year from each hemisphere (half) of the world.

○ In the middle of the constellation of Orion (the Hunter), a row of three bright stars mark his belt and the smaller row is his sword.

○ Seven bright stars in the constellation of the Great Bear in the northern sky make a familiar shape called the Plow or Big Dipper.

○ Most of the constellations were identified long ago by the stargazers of ancient Babylon and Egypt.

○ Constellations are simply patterns—there is no real link between the stars.

○ Southern Hemisphere constellations are different from those in the Northern Hemisphere.

○ Heroes and creatures of Greek myth, such as Orion the Hunter and Perseus, provided the names for many constellations, although each name is usually written in Latin form, not Greek.

○ The stars in each constellation are named after Greek alphabet letters.

○ For thousands of years, sailors used the stars to navigate. Studying the constellations could tell them which way was north, for example.

Amazing

The three great pyramids of ancient Egypt at Giza are positioned in such a way as to mirror the pattern of the three bright stars in the constellation Orion.

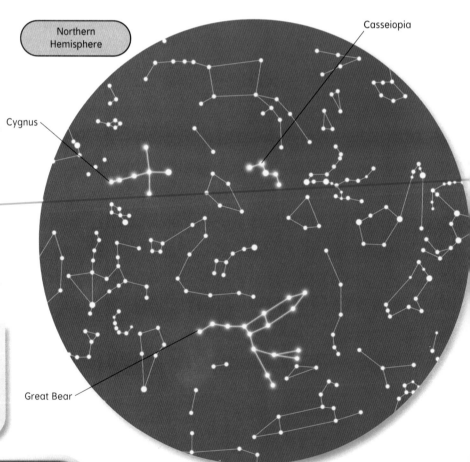

Northern Hemisphere

Casseiopia

Cygnus

Great Bear

Find out more
Astrology p. 55

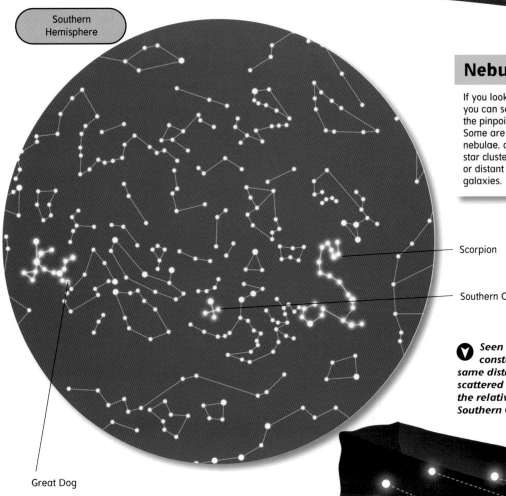

Southern Hemisphere

Great Dog

Scorpion

Southern Cross

Nebulae

If you look at the sky through binoculars, you can see some fuzzy patches between the pinpoint stars. Some are nebulae, others star clusters, or distant galaxies.

▼ *Seen from Earth, the stars in a constellation appear to be the same distance away. In fact, they are scattered in space. This diagram shows the relative distances of stars in the Southern Cross constellation.*

Same star pattern seen side on

Arrow indicates view seen from Earth

◀ ▲ *The star groups seen in the Northern Hemisphere are not the same as those seen south of the Equator, in the Southern Hemisphere. Stars are best seen on a clear, moonless night away from the glare of city lights.*

Constellation shapes

The patterns the stars make in the sky do not change from night to night. We see the same constellations that the ancient Greeks did thousands of years ago. However, the constellations appear to move slowly across the sky from east to west during the night. This is because the Earth is always spinning around.

❍ The brightest star in each constellation is called the Alpha star, the next brightest Beta, and so on.

❍ Different constellations become visible at different times of the year, as the Earth travels around the Sun.

Galaxies

Galaxies are giant groups of millions or even trillions of stars. Our own local galaxy is the Milky Way. There may be 20 trillion galaxies in the Universe.

○ Only three galaxies are visible to the naked eye from Earth besides the Milky Way—the Large and Small Magellanic Clouds, and the Andromeda Galaxy.

○ Although galaxies are vast, they are so far away that they look like fuzzy clouds. Only in 1916 did astronomers realize that they are huge star groups.

○ Spiral galaxies are spinning, pinwheel-shaped galaxies with a dense core and spiraling arms.

○ Irregular galaxies are galaxies with no obvious shape. They may have formed from the debris of galaxies that crashed into each other.

○ Elliptical galaxies are vast, very old, egg-shaped galaxies, made up of as many as a trillion stars.

○ Barred spiral galaxies have just two arms. These are linked across the galaxy's middle by a bar from which they trail like water from a spinning garden sprinkler system.

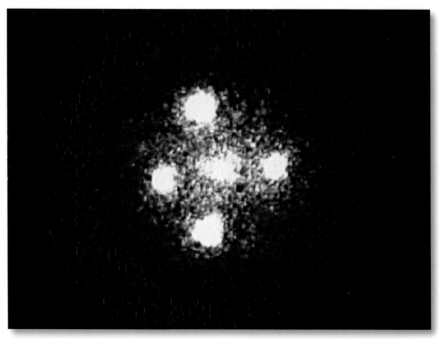

▲ *Quasars are luminous objects at the center of some distant galaxies. Most are the size of the Solar System and glow with the brightness of 100 galaxies.*

▶ *Galaxies are incredibly vast. Even traveling at lightspeed, a spacecraft would take 100,000 years to cross the Milky Way.*

Sucked in

Spiral galaxies may have a giant black hole at the center, which sucks in stars like water spiraling down the drain.

▼ *The main galaxy shapes are spiral, irregular, oval, and elliptical. A very ordinary galaxy contains a million stars, while the supergalaxies are giants with as many as a billion stars. There are about 200,000 million stars in our own galaxy, the Milky Way.*

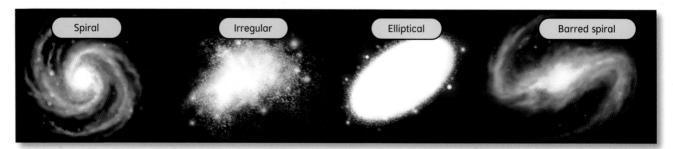

Spiral　　Irregular　　Elliptical　　Barred spiral

Find out more

The Milky Way pp. 20–21

Magellanic clouds

In the night sky of Earth's Southern Hemisphere, two blurry shapes can be seen with the naked eye. These are the Magellanic Clouds—small galaxies lying relatively near to our own galaxy, the Milky Way. The Magellanic Clouds are irregular galaxies, having no distinct pattern or shape.

Amazing

When galaxies get too near, they pull each other into weird shapes, often with a long tail or a bright ring. Large galaxies swallow up small ones that get too close.

Some galaxies in the Local Group

The Milky Way is part of a group of galaxies held together by gravity, called the Local Group.

	Type	*Distance*
Milky Way	Spiral	–
Andromeda	Spiral	2.2 million lightyears
Triangulum	Spiral	2.7 million lightyears
Large Magellanic Cloud	Irregular spiral	160,000 lightyears
Small Magellanic Cloud	Irregular	200,000 lightyears

Plus at least 20 other very small galaxies

The Milky Way

*T*he Milky Way is the faint, hazy band of light that you can see stretching right across the night sky. It is the galaxy we live in. Looking through binoculars, you would see that the Milky Way is made up of countless stars.

○ A galaxy is a vast group of stars.

○ There are billions of galaxies located in space. The centers of regular-shaped galaxies are believed to contain vast black holes.

► *We cannot see the spiral shape of the Milky Way Galaxy because we are inside it. We see it as a hazy band so faint that you can only see it on very clear nights.*

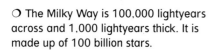

○ The Milky Way is 100,000 lightyears across and 1,000 lightyears thick. It is made up of 100 billion stars.

○ All the stars are arranged in a spiral (like a giant pinwheel), with a bulge in the middle.

○ Our Sun is just one of the billions of stars on one arm of the spiral.

○ The Milky Way's stars are all whirling rapidly around the center. Our Sun is moving at 497,000 mi/h.

○ The Sun travels around the galaxy once every 200 million years—a journey of about 170,000 lightyears.

○ The huge bulge at the center of the Milky Way is about 20,000 lightyears across and 3,000 thick. It contains only very old stars and little dust or gas.

○ There may be a huge black hole in the very middle of the Milky Way.

▲ *If you could fly out of the Milky Way Galaxy in a spaceship and see it from the side, it would look like this—very flat with a bulge in the middle.*

○ In the spiral arms are mostly young stars, and clouds of dust and gas where new stars are born.

Factfile

Diameter	100,000 lightyears
Thickness (disc)	1,000 lightyears
Mass	140 billion solar masses
Age	About 12 billion years
Distance of Sun from center	26,000 lightyears

Find out more

Black holes pp. 24–25

A *The word galaxy comes from the ancient Greek word for milk, gala. The Greeks saw a hazy belt in the night sky, which reminded them of a trail of spilt milk. They made up a story to explain that the heavenly milk had been spilt by the baby Heracles (Hercules). The galaxy came to be known as the "road of milk," or Milky Way. The center of the Milky Way is the core or nucleus of the galaxy, with a dense mass of stars. The Sun is about halfway out from the center, on one of the spiral arms of the galaxy.*

Round or elongated?

The Milky Way looks different seen from above (showing the spiral arms) and from sideways on, when it looks like a flying saucer.

Black hole

A two-week observation through the optic eye of the Chandra X-Ray Observatory revealed a stunning explosion occurring in the supermassive black hole at the Milky Way's center, known as Sagittarius A. Huge lobes of 36,000,032°F gas flank both sides of the black hole and extend over dozens of lightyears, indicating that enormous explosions have occurred several times over the last 10,000 years.

Amazing

If the Sun were the size of a baseball, the density of the stars in the Milky Way would be comparable to scattering 80 baseballs across the USA.

Nebulae

Nebula (plural—nebulae) was the word once used for any fuzzy patch of light in the night sky. Today nebulae are giant clouds of dust and gas where new stars are born and old ones die.

Nebulae types

There are three main types of nebula—glowing, reflection, and dark nebulae. Out in space are huge invisible clouds of dust and gas. Nebulae are the parts of these clouds that we can see, as they either glow or reflect starlight, or block out light.

○ Many nebulae are gigantic clouds of gas and space dust.

○ Glowing nebulae are named because they give off a dim, red light, as the hydrogen gas in them is heated by radiation from nearby stars.

○ The Great Nebula of Orion is a glowing nebula just visible to the naked eye.

○ Reflection nebulae have no light of their own. They can only be seen because starlight shines off the dust in them.

○ Not only do dark nebulae not have any light of their own, they also soak up all other light. They can only be seen as patches of darkness, blocking out light from the stars that are sitting behind them.

▲ *This is a glowing nebula called the Lagoon Nebula, which glows as hydrogen and helium gas in it are heated by radiation from stars.*

Amazing

The Crab Nebula is the remains of a supernova that exploded in AD 1054.

Find out more

Stars pp. 14–15

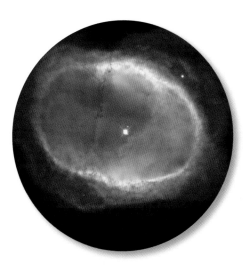

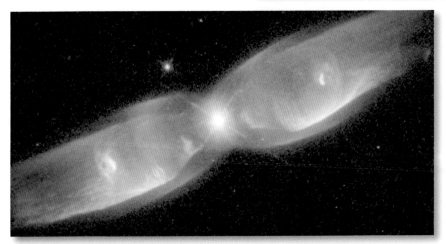

Pictures of planetary nebulae, as observed by the Hubble Space Telescope.

The Horsehead Nebula in Orion is the best-known dark nebula. As its name suggests, it is shaped like a horse's head.

An example of a "butterfly" or a bipolar planetary nebula. If the nebula is sliced across a star, each side of it appears like a pair of exhausts from a jet engine. Because of the nebula's shape and the velocity of the gas, in excess of 656 ft/sec, astronomers believe that the description as a supersupersonic jet exhaust is very suitable.

❍ Planetary nebulae are thin rings of gas cloud, which are thrown out by dying stars. Despite their name, they have nothing to do with planets.

❍ The Ring Nebula in Lyra is the best-known of the planetary nebulae.

❍ Inside nebulae, gravity creates dark clumps called dark nebulae, each clump containing the seeds of a family of stars.

Orion's nebula

The Great Nebula of Orion is the nearest star formation region to Earth, about 1,500 lightyears away. It is visible to the naked eye as a fuzzy patch of light near the center of Orion's sword, in the same spiral arm of the Milky Way as the Sun. With a cloud that spans some 30 lightyears, it is one of the most visually stunning objects in space.

Black Holes

Black holes are places where gravity is so strong that it sucks everything in, including light. Black holes form when a star or galaxy gets so dense that it collapses under the pull of its own gravity.

○ Black holes may exist at the heart of every galaxy.

○ Gravity shrinks a black hole to an unimaginably small point called a singularity.

○ Around a singularity, gravity is so intense that space-time is bent into a funnel.

▶ *No light is able to escape from a black hole. Scientists know where they are because they swallow gas from nearby stars and give out X rays.*

▼ *This X ray image shows the central part of the Andromeda Galaxy. The blue dot in the center shows a supermassive black hole. The gas swirling into it has a temperature of 1,800,032°F.*

Amazing

If you were sucked into a black hole, your body would be stretched out like a piece of spaghetti.

○ Matter spiraling into a black hole is torn apart and glows so brightly that it creates the brightest objects in the Universe—quasars.

○ The swirling gases around a black hole turn it into an electrical generator, making it spout jets of electricity billions of miles out into space.

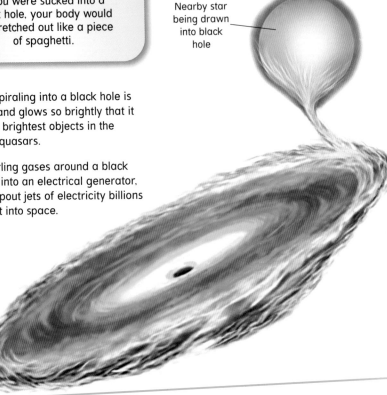

Nearby star being drawn into black hole

Find out more

Galaxies pp. 18–19

White holes and wormholes

Some scientists believe in the existence of white holes, which are the opposite of black holes because they spray out matter and light rather than sucking it in. Some also think that black holes and white holes may join to form tunnels called wormholes—and these may be the secret to time travel. However, white holes have not been proved to exist, and they may violate one of the fundamental laws of physics.

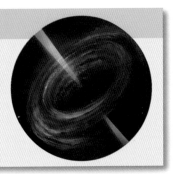

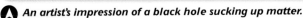 An artist's impression of a black hole sucking up matter.

A supermassive black hole blows bubbles of hot gas into space. Known as the peculiar galaxy because of its unusual shape, NGC4438 is 50 million lightyears from Earth. One bubble rises from a dark band of dust while another emanates from below the band of dust showing up as dim red blobs in the close-up. These exceedingly hot bubbles are caused by the voracious eating habits of black holes.

A Boeing Delta II rocket was launched in 1999 from Cape Canaveral Air Station, carrying the Stardust spacecraft. The Swift observatory that it carried was sent to monitor gamma-ray bursts that are thought to occur when a black hole forms.

Black holes and electricity

An artist's impression of what a black hole might look like, with jets of electricity shooting out from either side.

The Solar System

The Solar System is made up of the Sun, the nine planets and their 135 known moons, asteroids, comets, dust, and gas. The planets, asteroids, and comets travel around the Sun, the center of our Solar System.

○ Most of the bodies in the Solar System travel around the Sun along nearly circular paths or orbits, and all the planets travel around the Sun in a counterclockwise direction (when viewed from above).

○ Solar System formation began billions of years ago, when gases and dust began to come together to form the Sun, planets, and other bodies of the Solar System.

○ The Sun is a medium-sized star measuring 864,972 mi across—100 times the diameter of the Earth.

○ Mercury is the nearest planet to the Sun—during its orbit it is between 28.5 and 43.3 million mi away.

○ Venus is the nearest of all the planets to Earth in size, measuring 7,521 mi across its diameter.

○ Mars is the nearest planet to Earth after Venus, and its temperature is the closest of any of the planets to the Earth's, although it is much colder.

○ Jupiter is the biggest planet in the Solar System—twice as heavy as all the other planets put together.

○ Saturn is the second biggest planet in the Solar System—815 times as big in volume as the Earth, and measuring 74,567 mi around its equator.

○ Uranus is the seventh planet out from the Sun. Its orbit keeps it a distance of 1,109 million mi away on average and takes 84 years to complete.

○ Neptune is the eighth planet out from the Sun, varying in distance from 2,768 to 2,819 million mi.

○ Pluto was the last of all the planets to be discovered. Astronomers were searching for a giant planet beyond Neptune, but found tiny Pluto.

Saturn

Uranus

Neptune

Pluto

▲ The inner Solar System is composed of Mercury, Venus, Earth, Mars, and the asteroid belt. The outer Solar System contains Jupiter, Saturn, Uranus, Neptune, and Pluto.

Find out more

The Earth pp. 30–31

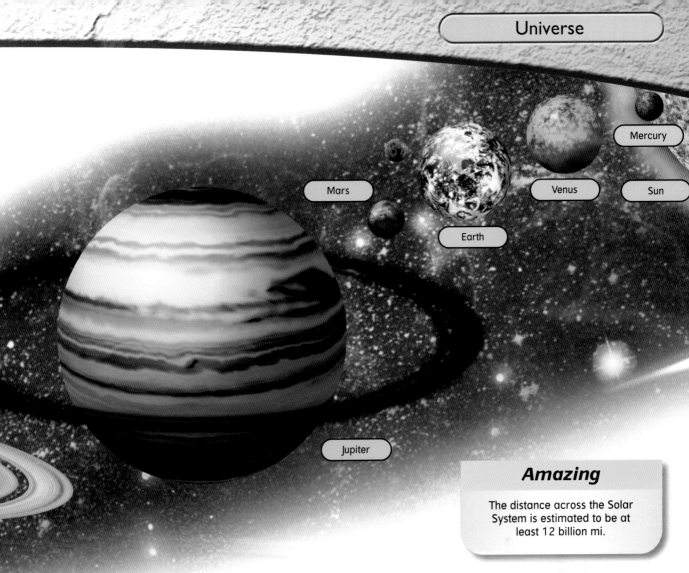

Mercury

Mars

Venus

Sun

Earth

Jupiter

Amazing

The distance across the Solar System is estimated to be at least 12 billion mi.

Moons in our Solar System

To date, there are 135 known natural moons orbiting planets in our Solar System.

Planets in the Solar System

	Discovered	Distance from Sun	Diameter
Mercury	Ancient times	36 million mi	3,032 mi
Venus	Ancient times	67.2 million mi	7,521 mi
Earth	–	93 million mi	7,926 mi
Mars	Ancient times	141.6 million mi	4,222 mi
Jupiter	Ancient times	483.8 million mi	88,849 mi
Saturn	Ancient times	890.7 million mi	74,900 mi
Uranus	1781	1,784.9 million mi	31,764 mi
Neptune	1846	2,793.2 million mi	30,776 mi
Pluto	1930	3,647.5 million mi*	1,485 mi

*Pluto has an unusual orbit, which at times brings it closer to the Sun than Neptune

Venus

Venus is the hottest of the Sun's nine planets, even hotter than Mercury. Temperatures on Venus can reach 878°F, which is hot enough to melt some metals.

The Sun

The Sun is the Earth's nearest star, about 93.2 million mi away. It is a medium-sized star, and belongs to a group of star types that astronomers call "main sequence" stars. Most of these, including the Sun, will burn for about ten billion years before expanding and cooling to become red giants, ultimately using up all their fuel. The Sun is about halfway through its lifetime.

○ The Sun weighs 2,000 trillion trillion tons—about 300,000 times as much as the Earth—even though it is made almost entirely of hydrogen and helium, the lightest gases in the Universe.

○ The Sun's interior is heated by nuclear reactions to temperatures of 27 million°F.

○ The visible surface layer of the Sun is the photosphere. This sends out the light and heat we see and feel on Earth.

○ Above the photosphere is the chromosphere, a layer through which dart flames called spicules, making the chromosphere look like a flaming forest.

○ Above the chromosphere is the Sun's halo-like corona.

○ The Sun gets hot because it is so big that the pressure in its core is huge—enough to force the nuclei of hydrogen atoms to fuse to make helium atoms. This nuclear fusion releases huge amounts of heat.

Photosphere is a mass of hot gas, radiating heat and light into space

Radiating zone

Core of the Sun reaches 27 million°F

Chromosphere is a layer of gas. Bursts of heat-like energy called spicules flame through it

Sun's outer "skin" is the corona, a halo-like layer of boiled-off gases

Giant tongues of hot gas, known as prominences, burst out from the chromosphere

Ⓐ *This cutaway of the Sun shows its different parts. The energy that is created inside the core takes ten million years to pass through its many layers and reach the surface.*

Factfile

Diameter	865,302 mi
Mass	333,000 times Earth's mass
Volume	1.3 million times Earth's volume
Density	49,723 ft³ (1.4 times density of water)
Average rotation period	25.4 Earth days
Surface temperature	10,832°F
Distance from Earth	93 million mi

Find out more

Lunar eclipses p. 32

When the Moon passes between the Earth and the Sun, it causes a solar eclipse that blocks out the light from the Sun momentarily.

Earth

Moon

Light rays passing from Sun to Earth

Sun

○ The heat from the Sun's interior erupts on the surface in patches called granules and in gigantic, flamelike tongues of hot gases called solar prominences.

○ Halfway out from its center to its surface, the Sun is about as dense as water. Two-thirds of the way out from its center, it is as dense as air.

○ The nuclear fusion reactions in the Sun's core send out billions of light photos every single minute—but they take 10 million years to reach its surface.

○ Space observatories like SOHO (Solar and Heliospheric Observatory) have revealed a great deal about the Sun to astronomers.

○ Never ever look directly at the Sun. It can damage your eyes.

Tilting Earth

As the Earth tilts on its axis and spins around the Sun, the Sun warms different parts of the planet. The Earth is the third planet out from the Sun, on average 93 million mi away. On January 3, at the nearest point of its orbit (called the perihelion), the Earth is 91,402,335 mi away from the Sun. On July 4, at its furthest (the aphelion), it is 94,509,440 mi away.

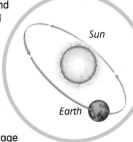

Sun

Earth

Sunspots

Astronomers viewing the Sun through special filters can detect dark spots called sunspots on the Sun's surface. The sunspots are caused by changes to the magnetic field surrounding the Sun. As the Sun spins round, the magnetic field becomes tangled. Sunspots develop in places where the magnetic force has become up to 3,000 times stronger than normal. The Sun's surface is cooler at these places, so the sunspots appear darker than the surrounding surface.

Sunspots

Solar eclipses

	Type of eclipse	Visible from where in the world
April 8, 2005	Annular/total	New Zealand, North and South America
October 3, 2005	Annular	Europe, Africa, Asia
March 29, 2006	Total	Africa, Europe, Asia
September 22, 2006	Annular	South America, Africa, Antarctica
March 19, 2007	Partial	Asia, Alaska
September 11, 2007	Partial	South America, Antarctica
February 7, 2008	Annular	Antarctica, Australia, New Zealand
August 1, 2008	Total	North America, Europe, Asia
January 26, 2009	Annular	Africa, Antarctica, Asia, Australia
July 22, 2009	Total	Asia, Pacific Ocean, Hawaii
January 15, 2010	Annular	Africa, Asia
July 11, 2010	Total	South America

Amazing

The temperature at the Sun's surface is 10,832°F. Each centimeter of the Sun's surface burns with the brightness of 250,000 candles.

The Earth

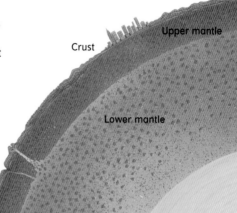

Crust

Upper mantle

Lower mantle

Outer liquid core

Inner solid core

The Earth is the fifth largest planet in the Solar System, with a diameter of 7,920 mi and a circumference of 24,869 mi at the Equator.

○ The Earth is one of four rocky planets, along with Mercury, Venus, and Mars. It is made mostly of rock, with a core of iron and nickel.

○ No other planet in the Solar System has water on its surface, which is why Earth is uniquely suitable for life. Over 70 percent of Earth's surface is under water.

○ The Earth's atmosphere is mainly nitrogen and life-giving oxygen, and it is over 435 mi deep. The oxygen has been made and maintained by plants over billions of years.

○ The Earth formed 4.65 billion years ago from clouds of spacedust whirling around the Sun. The planet was so hot that it was molten at first. Only slowly did the surface cool into a hard crust.

○ The Earth's orbit around the Sun is 584,018,333 mi long and takes 365.242 days.

○ The Earth is tilted at an angle of 23.5°. Even so, it orbits the Sun in a level plane, called the plane of the ecliptic.

○ The Earth is made up of the same materials as meteorites and the other rocky planets— mostly iron (35 percent), oxygen (28 percent), magnesium (17 percent), silicon (13 percent), and nickel (2.7 percent).

Central Sun

Polish scientist Nicolaus Copernicus realized in the 1500s that the Universe must work with the Sun at the center of the Universe and that all the planets in the Solar System moved around it.

Amazing

Because the Earth rotates and is more flexible than you might think, it bulges in the middle like a pumpkin. The bulge was lessening for centuries, but now, suddenly, it is growing again because of accelerated melting of the glaciers.

Factfile

Diameter	7,926 mi
Planetary mass	6×10^{24} kg
Average distance from Sun	93 million mi
Length of day	23 h 57 min
Length of year	365.242 Earth days
Number of moons	1
Planetary ring system	0
Average temperature	59°F
Atmospheric composition	21% oxygen, 78% nitrogen, many other minor trace elements

▲ *Scientists call planet Earth the geosphere. The outer rocky part on which we live is the biosphere. Surrounding this is the atmosphere in layers. The inside of the Earth is also in layers. At the center is a solid inner core made of an alloy of nickel and iron squeezed together under pressure. The rocks surrounding the core are hot and liquid.*

Find out more

Asteroids and Meteors pp. 52–53

Life planet

Earth is the only planet we know of that can support life because of a remarkable set of conditions. The Sun is a stable star with a constant temperature. Earth's temperature is high enough for liquid water to occur, and for oxygen-producing organisms to thrive in the liquid oceans, but not so hot that all the water vapor evaporates (as in the case of Venus). The presence of the Moon helps to preserve liquid water. Large gas giants in the Solar System help to draw a lot of earthbound asteroids away from our planet.

Viewed from space, the Earth, which is mainly covered by oceans, appears mostly blue. Cloud formations swirl above the familiar shapes of the continents. The Earth is protected from the Sun's radiation by a magnetic field that stretches 37,282 mi out into space.

UFO sightings

Who?	When?	Where and what?
Betty and Barney Hill	September 1961	From New Hampshire, USA, the couple reported a close sighting with a UFO. They underwent hypnosis and claim to have been abducted and probed.
Frederick Valentich	October 1978	Australian pilot disappeared over the Bass Strait between Tasmania and Australia after he saw a UFO. The place was never found.
Travis Walton	November 1975	Woodcutter who disappeared for a few days and claimed to have been abducted and probed at a secret UFO base.
Airmen	December 1980	Airmen at a USAF base in Suffolk, England, claimed to have had encounters with a UFO.
Linda Cortile	November 1989	Cortile claims to have been beamed from her apartment in New York and transported to a UFO that plunged into the Hudson River, near Brooklyn Bridge.

The Moon

○ Only the side of the Moon lit by the Sun is bright enough to see. And because we see more of this side each month as the Moon orbits the Earth, and then less again, the Moon seems to change shape.

○ During the first half of each monthly cycle, the Moon waxes (grows) from a crescent-shaped New Moon to a Full Moon. During the second half, it wanes (dwindles) back to a crescent-shaped Old Moon.

○ A lunar month is the time between one Full Moon and the next. This is slightly longer than the time the Moon takes to orbit the Earth because the Earth is also moving.

○ The Moon has no atmosphere and its surface is simply gray dust, pitted with craters created by meteorites smashing into it early in its history.

○ On the Moon's surface are large, dark patches called seas—because that is what people once believed they were. They are, in fact, lava flows from ancient volcanoes.

○ One side of the Moon is always turned away from us and is called its dark side. This is because the Moon spins around on its axis at exactly the same speed that it orbits the Earth.

The Moon is 238,885 mi from the Earth and about 25 percent of Earth's size. The Moon orbits the Earth once every month and each orbit takes 27.3 days. It spins once on its axis every 720 hours.

▲ *The Moon may have formed when a smaller, newly formed planet collided with the Earth early on in the formation of the Solar System.*

○ The Moon is the brightest object in the night sky, but it does not give out any light itself. It shines only because its light-colored surface reflects sunlight.

Lunar eclipses 2005–2010

Each eclipse of the Moon can be seen from about half of the Earth's surface.

April 24, 2005	Penumbral	August 16, 2008	Partial
October 17, 2005	Partial	February 9, 2009	Penumbral
March 14, 2006	Penumbral	July 7, 2009	Penumbral
September 7, 2006	Partial	August 6, 2009	Penumbral
March 3, 2007	Total	December 31, 2009	Partial
August 28, 2007	Total	June 26, 2010	Partial
February 21, 2008	Total	December 21, 2010	Total

Monthly Full Moons

January	Moon after Yule
February	Wolf moon
March	Lenten moon
April	Egg moon
May	Milk moon
June	Strawberry moon
July	Hay moon
August	Green corn moon
September	Harvest moon
October	Hunter's moon
November	Beaver's moon
December	Moon before Yule

Find out more

Solar eclipses p. 29

▶ *The Moon is **relatively close to the Earth and therefore seems much larger than the stars.***

Amazing

The Moon's gravity is 17 percent of the Earth's, so astronauts in space suits can jump 13 ft high.

◆ *The changes from New to Full Moon and back again are called the phases of the Moon. The full cycle from New to Full and back to New again takes one month.*

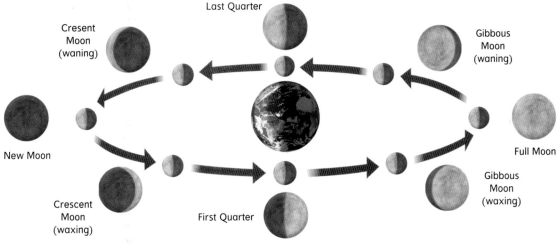

Last Quarter

Cresent Moon (waning)

Gibbous Moon (waning)

New Moon

Full Moon

Crescent Moon (waxing)

First Quarter

Gibbous Moon (waxing)

10 seas on the Moon

Sea of Cleverness
Sea of Clouds
Sea of Islands
Sea of Moisture
Sea of Nectar
Sea of Serenity
Sea of Showers
Sea of Tranquility
Sea of Vapors
Sea of Waves

Moon crater names

All moon craters are named after people

Aldrin	Edwin (Buzz) Aldrin	**Morse**	Samuel Morse
Babbage	Charles Babbage	**Newton**	Sir Isaac Newton
Cook	Captain James Cook	**Oppenheimer**	Robert Oppenheimer
Darwin	Charles Darwin	**Pasteur**	Louis Pasteur
Edison	Thomas Alva Edison	**Quetelet**	Adolphe Quetelet
Freud	Sigmund Freud	**Rutherford**	Ernest Rutherford
Gagarin	Yuri Gagarin	**Scott**	Robert Falcon Scott
Harvey	William Harvey	**Tereshkova**	Valentina Tereshkova
Icarus	Greek mythological character	**Urey**	Harold Urey
		Van de Graaff	Robert van de Graaff
Jenner	Edward Jenner	**Watt**	James Watt
Kepler	Johannes Kepler	**Xenophon**	Greek historian
Lindberg	Charles Lindberg	**Young**	Thomas Young

Mercury

Mercury, named after the Roman messenger god, is the second smallest planet in the Solar System, and the closest to the Sun. This makes observations very difficult as it is lost in the Sun's glare at least half of the time. It can be observed for only a brief period in the morning or early evening.

○ Mercury is the fastest orbiting of all the planets, traveling around the Sun in just 88 days.

○ Mercury takes 58.65 Earth days to rotate once, but from sunrise to sunrise is 176 Earth days, so a "day" on Mercury is twice as long as its year.

○ Temperatures on Mercury range from −292°F at night to over 806°F during the day (enough to melt lead).

○ The crust and mantle are largely rock, but the core (75 percent of its diameter) is solid iron.

○ Mercury's dusty surface is pocketed by craters made by space debris crashing into it.

○ With barely 20 percent of Earth's mass, Mercury is so small that its gravity is too weak to hold on to a permanent atmosphere.

○ Mercury is so small that its core has cooled and solidified. As this happened, Mercury shrank, and its surface wrinkled like the peel of an old apple.

○ Craters on Mercury discovered by the USA's *Mariner* space probe have names like Bach, Beethoven, Wagner, Shakespeare, and Tolstoy.

Mercury is a tiny planet with a thin atmosphere and a solid core.

Sunrise, sunset

If you could stand on the surface of Mercury in certain places you would see the Sun rise about halfway, then reverse and set, then rise again, all within the same day.

○ Mercury's surface is wrinkled by long, low ridges, which probably formed as the core cooled and shrunk.

○ The largest feature on Mercury is a huge impact crater called the Caloris Basin, which is about 808 mi across and 1 mi deep.

Amazing

Twice during its orbit, Mercury gets very close to the Sun and speeds up so much that the Sun seems to go backward in the sky.

Find out more

Space probes p. 58

Mercury in close-up

The **Mariner** *mission explored Venus in February 1974 before moving on to three encounters with Mercury in March and* *September 1974, and March 1975. The spacecraft took more than 7,000 photos of Mercury, Venus, the Earth, and the Moon.*

Discovery Rupes scarp

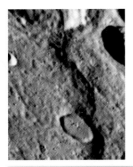

In this image, the Sun is low to the horizon, highlighting the topographic features with heavy shadows. The prominent scarp that snakes up the image was named Discovery Rupes and is thought to have been formed as the planet compressed, possibly caused by cooling of the planet.

Kuiper crater

A conspicuous bright crater (top center) on the rim of a larger older crater, named "Kuiper."

Mercury's South Pole

This image shows the South Pole of Mercury, located on the right-hand edge of the large crater that has only its rim sticking up in the light (Chao Meng Fu crater). When this photo was taken, *Mariner 10* was about 51,578 mi from Mercury.

Mariner Mission

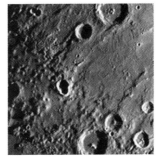

The *Mariner 10* spacecraft flew past Mercury three times. However, each time it flew past, the same side of the planet was facing the probe so it sent back pictures of only about half of the planet's surface.

Messenger

On August 3, 2004, a *Boeing Delta II* rocket took off on a NASA mission named *Messenger*—its destination Mercury. After a journey of seven years, the spacecraft will reach Mercury and onboard cameras and sensors will take images. This information should help scientists to understand how Mercury was formed, how it evolved, and the planet's interaction with the Sun.

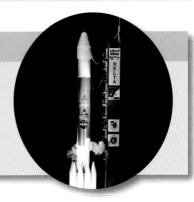

Factfile

Diameter	3.032 mi
Mass	0.33×10^{24} kg
Time to spin once	58.65 days
Average distance from Sun	36 million mi
Time for one orbit	88 days
Average temperature	333°F
Length of year	88 Earth days
Number of moons	0
Ring system	No

Venus

Venus is named after the Roman goddess of love and beauty. It orbits at a distance of between 66.7 and 67.7 million mi and is the second planet from the Sun. Venus is also known as the Evening Star, because it can be seen from Earth in the evening, just after sunset. Venus can also be seen before sunrise.

○ Venus shines like a star in the night sky because its thick atmosphere reflects sunlight amazingly well. This planet is the brightest object in the sky, after the Sun and the Moon.

○ Venus's cloudy atmosphere is a thick mixture of carbon dioxide gas and sulfuric acid.

Almost three-quarters of the surface of Venus is covered by plains. These were mostly formed by volcanic processes and are marked by impact craters and flows of lava. They have features that have been sculpted by the winds on Venus. Ridges rise for several hundred feet and can stretch for hundreds of miles across the Venus plains.

This is what Venus would look like if you could see through the thick clouds that hide the surface. Space probes have mapped the whole of Venus using radar that can penetrate the clouds, to reflect off the volcanoes and craters on the surface.

○ Venus is the hottest planet in the Solar System, with a surface temperature of over 878°F.

○ Venus is so hot because the carbon dioxide in its atmosphere works like the panes of glass in a greenhouse to trap the Sun's heat. This overheating is called a runaway greenhouse effect.

○ Venus's thick clouds hide its surface so well that until space probes detected the very high temperatures some people thought there might be rainforests beneath the clouds.

Find out more

Space probes pp. 58–59

Pressured planet

The pressure at the surface of Venus is so strong that the first spacecraft that tried to land there was crushed before it even reached the surface.

Maat Mons

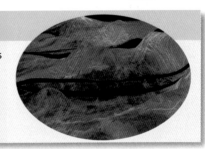

This is a view of a 4 mi-high volcano on Venus's surface called Maat Mons. It is not an actual photograph but was created on computer from radar data collected by the *Magellan* orbiter, which reached Venus in the 1980s. The colors are what astronomers guess them to be from their knowledge of the chemistry of Venus.

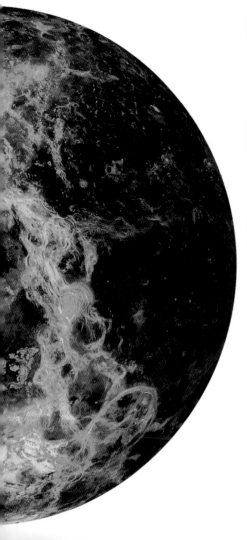

○ Venus's day (the time it takes to spin round once) lasts 243 Earth days—longer than its year, which lasts 224.7 days. But because Venus rotates backward, the Sun actually comes up twice during the planet's yearly orbit—once every 116.8 days.

○ Venus is the nearest of all the planets to Earth in size, measuring 7,521 mi across its diameter.

○ Pressure on the surface of Venus is 90 times greater than that on Earth.

○ Periodically the planet Venus passes directly between the Earth and the Sun, appearing as a small black dot on the Sun's disk. These "transits of Venus" may help astronomers to measure the Solar System, but they are extremely rare. Only several transits occurred between 1631, when astronomers first became aware of them, and 2004. Another one is due to take place on June 6, 2012.

Amazing

All the planets in the Solar System rotate counterclockwise, except Venus. It is the only planet that rotates clockwise.

Factfile

Diameter	7,521 mi
Mass	4.87×10^{24} kg
Time to spin once	243 days retrograde
Average distance from Sun	67 million mi
Time for one orbit	224.7 Earth days
Average temperature	867°F
Number of moons	0
Ring system	No

Mars

Mars, named after the Roman god of war, is the fourth planet out from the Sun, and the nearest planet to Earth after Venus. Its temperature is closer to Earth's than any other planet and a Martian day is almost the same as an Earth day.

❍ Mars is called the red planet due to its rusty red color. This comes from oxidized (rusted) iron in its soil.

❍ Mars orbits the Sun at an average distance of 142 million mi. It takes 687 days to complete its orbit.

❍ Mars is 4,221 mi in diameter and spins around once every 24.6 h— almost the same time as the Earth takes to rotate.

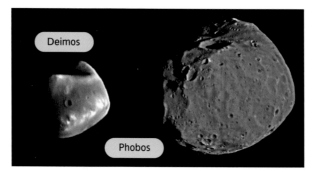

Deimos

Phobos

◀ Deimos and Phobos are the two satellites (moons) that orbit Mars. They are named after the two companions of the Roman god, Mars.

❍ Mars's volcano Olympus Mons is the biggest in the Solar System. It covers the same area as Ireland and is three times higher than Mount Everest.

❍ In the 1880s, the American astronomer Percival Lowell was convinced that the dark lines he could see on Mars's surface through his telescope were canals built by Martians.

Amazing

Two rovers called *Spirit* and *Opportunity* landed on Mars in 2004 and spent over a year exploring. They analysed the rocks, looking for evidence of a watery past.

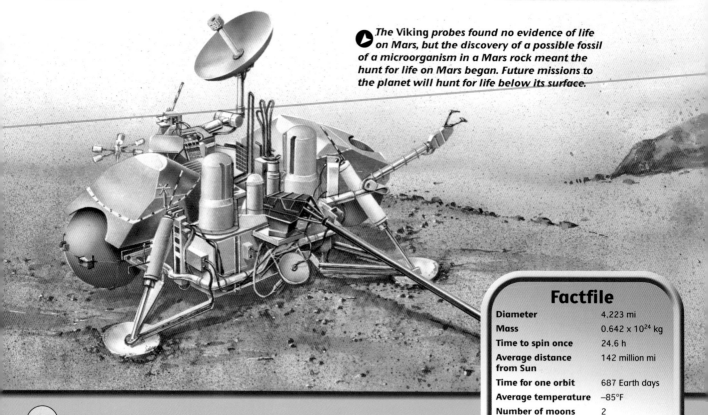

▶ The Viking probes found no evidence of life on Mars, but the discovery of a possible fossil of a microorganism in a Mars rock meant the hunt for life on Mars began. Future missions to the planet will hunt for life below its surface.

Factfile

Diameter	4,223 mi
Mass	0.642×10^{24} kg
Time to spin once	24.6 h
Average distance from Sun	142 million mi
Time for one orbit	687 Earth days
Average temperature	−85°F
Number of moons	2
Ring system	No

○ The evidence is growing that Mars was warmer and wetter in the past, although scientists cannot say how much water there was, or when and why it dried up.

○ Mars has two tiny moons called Phobos and Deimos. Phobos is just 17 mi across, while Deimos is just 9 mi across and has so little gravity that you could reach escape velocity riding a bicycle up a ramp!

○ The 1997 Mars *Pathfinder* mission showed that many of the rocks on Mars's surface were dumped in their positions by a huge flood at least two billion years ago.

Life on Mars?

Because it has an atmosphere, surface water, and a similar temperature to Earth, some people think that life may exist, or may once have existed, on Mars. Researchers claim that a certain rock that is believed to have originated on Mars—meteorite ALH84001 (shown in this illustration against a dice to give an idea of scale)—contains evidence of past life. Also, traces of the gas methane in the Martian atmosphere are thought to indicate biological activity. However, none of the probes that have been to Mars have so far found any solid proof of life on the planet.

Giant valley

Mars's surface is cracked by a valley called the Vallis Marineris—so big that it makes the Grand Canyon look tiny. It appears to cut Mars in half. Dark areas cover about one-third of the planet. They have historically been called *maria* (meaning seas), even though they do not contain any amount of water that can be measured. These *maria* change color at different times of the year. During the Martian fall and winter parts of them become lighter or disappear. In spring and summer they become darker and larger.

▶ *Winds on Mars whip up huge dust storms that can cover the whole planet. Mars is very dry, like a desert, and covered in red dust. It has giant volcanoes, valleys, ice caps, and dried-up riverbeds.*

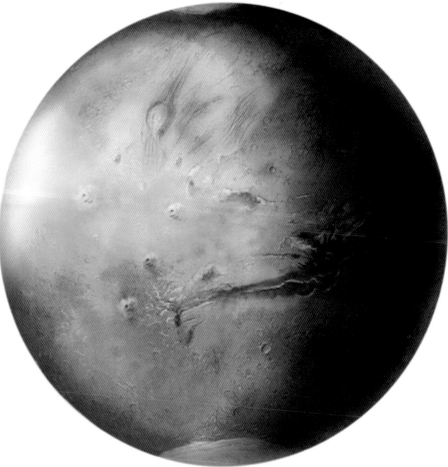

Find out more
Space probes pp. 58–59

Jupiter

Named after the Roman god of the skies and the supreme ruler of all the gods, Jupiter is the biggest planet in the Solar System. It is twice as heavy as all the other planets put together and has over 60 known moons. Jupiter is the fifth planet out from the Sun.

Jupiter is a gigantic planet, 88,846 mi across. Its orbit takes 11.86 years and varies between 460.3 and 506.8 million mi from the Sun. Its surface is often rent by huge lightning flashes and thunderclaps, and temperatures here plunge to −238°F. Looking at Jupiter's surface, all you can see is a swirling mass of red, brown, and yellow clouds of ammonia, including the Great Red Spot.

○ Towards Jupiter's core, immense pressure turns the hydrogen to solid metal.

○ The ancient Greeks originally named the planet Zeus, after the king of their gods. Jupiter was the Romans' name for Zeus.

○ Jupiter spins right around in less than ten hours, which means that the planet's surface is moving at nearly 31,068 mi/h.

○ Jupiter's speedy spin makes its middle bulge out. It also churns up the planet's metal core until it generates a hugely powerful magnetic field, ten times as strong as the Earth's.

○ Jupiter has a Great Red Spot—a huge swirl of red clouds measuring more than 24,854 mi across. The scientist Robert Hooke first noticed the spot in 1644.

○ Jupiter's four biggest moons were first spotted by Galileo in the 17th century. Their names are Ganymede, Callisto, Io, and Europa.

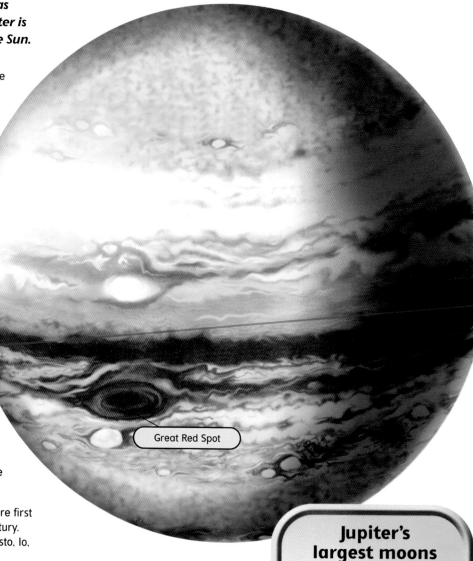

Great Red Spot

Jupiter's largest moons

Metis	Leda
Adastrea	Himalia
Amalthea	Lysithea
Thebe	Elara
Io	Ananke
Europa	Carme
Ganymede	Pasiphae
Callisto	Sinope

plus at least 47 other smaller moons

Find out more
Space probes pp. 58–59

○ Jupiter also has at least 59 other smaller moons. Most are tiny and some have been discovered so recently that they have not yet been named.

○ Jupiter is so massive that the pressure at its heart makes it glow very faintly with invisible infrared rays. Indeed, it glows as brightly as four million billion 100-watt lightbulbs. But it is not quite big enough for nuclear reactions to start, and make it become a star.

Life on Europa?

Jupiter's moon Europa may have oceans of water beneath its icy surface, and it is a major target in the search for life in the Solar System.

○ Jupiter's rings consist of three different types. The inner halo is a faint ring about 12,000 mi thick that is thought to extend down to the top of the clouds. The second is the main ring, 4,849 mi wide and about 19 mi thick. The third is the gossamer ring that extends out to 132,973 mi.

Amazing

Jupiter has a hurricane that has lasted for at least three centuries and affects an area twice the size of planet Earth.

Ganymede

Callisto

Io

Europa

A *The largest of Jupiter's Galilean moons is Ganymede, with a diameter of 3,273 mi. It is bigger than the planet Mercury and is the largest moon in the Solar System. Callisto (2,986 mi in diameter) is scarred with craters from bombardments in the Solar System's early life. Io's surface (2,263 mi diameter) is a mass of volcanoes, caused by Jupiter's massive gravity. Europa, the smallest Galilean moon (1,949 mi in diameter), is covered in ice.*

Gas planet

Jupiter has no surface for a spacecraft to land on because it is made mostly from helium gas and hydrogen. The massive pull of Jupiter's gravity squeezes the hydrogen so hard that it is liquid.

Factfile

Diameter	88,846 mi
Mass	1899 x 10^{24} kg
Time to spin once	9.9 h
Average distance from Sun	484 million mi
Time for one orbit	11.86 Earth years
Average temperature	−166°F
Number of moons	63
Ring system	Yes

Saturn

Saturn is the second biggest planet in the Solar System after Jupiter, and is easily recognized by its distinctive, shimmering rings. The sixth planet out from the Sun, it was named after Saturnus, the Roman god of seed sowing, who was celebrated in the Roman's wild festival of Saturnalia.

○ Saturn takes 29.42 years to travel around the Sun, so Saturn's year is 29.46 Earth years. The planet's complete orbit is a journey of more than 2.8 billion mi.

○ Winds ten times stronger than a hurricane on Earth constantly swirl around Saturn's equator, reaching up to 684 mi/h.

○ Saturn is not solid, but is made almost entirely of gas—mostly liquid hydrogen and helium. Only in the planet's very small core is there any solid rock.

○ Because Saturn is so massive, the pressure at its heart is enough to turn hydrogen solid. That is why there is a layer of metallic hydrogen around the planet's inner core of rock.

○ Saturn is one of the fastest spinning of all the planets. Despite its size, it rotates in just 10.7 hours—which means it turns around at over 6,000 mi/h.

○ Saturn's surface appears to be almost completely smooth, though *Voyager 1* and *2* did photograph a few swirling storms when they flew past.

▼ *Saturn is almost as big as Jupiter, and made largely of liquid hydrogen and helium. Saturn is stunningly beautiful, with a smooth, pale-butterscotch surface (clouds of ammonia) and a shimmering halo of rings. Telescopes have never pierced its upper atmosphere, and data from the fly-bys of the Voyager probes focused on its rings and moons. The* **Cassini** *probe went into orbit around Saturn in 2004 for a four-year study of the planet and its moons and rings.*

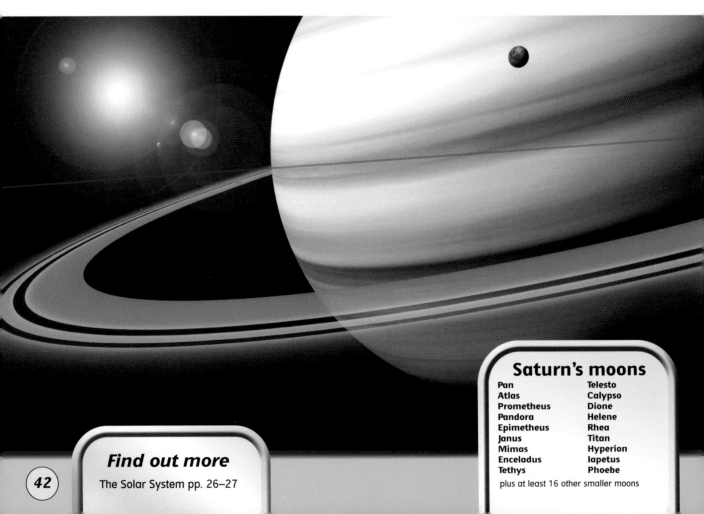

Saturn's moons

Pan	Telesto
Atlas	Calypso
Prometheus	Dione
Pandora	Helene
Epimetheus	Rhea
Janus	Titan
Mimas	Hyperion
Enceladus	Iapetus
Tethys	Phoebe

plus at least 16 other smaller moons

Find out more

The Solar System pp. 26–27

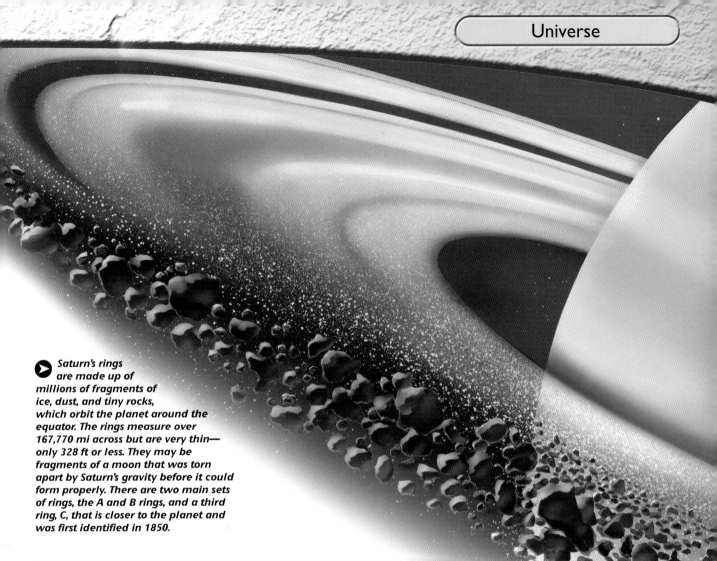

▶ *Saturn's rings are made up of millions of fragments of ice, dust, and tiny rocks, which orbit the planet around the equator. The rings measure over 167,770 mi across but are very thin—only 328 ft or less. They may be fragments of a moon that was torn apart by Saturn's gravity before it could form properly. There are two main sets of rings, the A and B rings, and a third ring, C, that is closer to the planet and was first identified in 1850.*

Amazing

Saturn is so low in density that if you could find a bathtub big enough, you would be able to float the planet in water.

Saturn's rings

Saturn's rings may be fragments of a moon that was torn apart by Saturn's gravity before it formed properly. In the 1980s, space probes revealed many other rings and 10,000 or more ringlets, some just 33 ft wide.

Factfile

Diameter	74,897 mi
Mass	568×10^{24} kg
Time to spin once	10.7 h
Average distance from Sun	891 million mi
Time for one orbit	29.42 Earth years
Average temperature	−220°F
Number of moons	34
Ring system	Yes

Titan

Saturn has more than 18 moons—new tiny ones are still being discovered. One of its moons, Titan, is one of the few moons with no atmosphere. Its sky is a mass of yellowish clouds.

Uranus

Uranus is the seventh planet out from the Sun and is the third largest in the Solar System. It is only just visible from Earth, looking like a star, but a telescope shows it as a small greenish spot. Uranus was named after the Greek god of the heavens.

○ When Herschel first spotted Uranus in 1781 he thought he had found a new comet, even though it had no tail. However, astronomers soon realized that its orbit was round like a planet's and not long and thin like a comet's.

○ Uranus tilts so far on its side that it seems to roll around the Sun like a gigantic bowling ball. The angle of its tilt is 98°, so its equator runs top to bottom. This tilt may be the result of a collision with a meteor or another planet a long time ago.

○ In summer on Uranus, the Sun does not set for 20 years. In winter, darkness lasts for over 20 years. In the fall, the Sun rises and sets every nine hours.

○ Because Uranus is so far from the Sun, it is very, very cold, with surface temperatures dropping to −346°F. Sunlight takes just eight minutes to reach Earth, but 2.5 hours to reach Uranus.

○ Uranus's icy atmosphere is made of hydrogen and helium. Winds whistle around the planet at more than 1,242 mi/h—ten times as fast as hurricanes on Earth.

○ Uranus's surface is an ice-cold ocean of liquid methane (natural gas), thousands of miles deep, which gives the planet its beautiful color. If you were to fall into this ocean even for a fraction of a second, your body would freeze so hard that it would shatter like glass.

A *These two images of Uranus were put together from pictures taken by Voyager 2 in 1986 when the spacecraft was 11 million miles from the planet. The image on the left shows Uranus as the human eye would see it from the spacecraft. The image on the right is an exaggerated false-color view, obtained by using different color filters, that shows details not visible to the human eye. The blue-green appearance of Uranus is a result of the methane in the atmosphere.*

Uranus's moons
All named after Shakespeare characters

Ariel	Oberon
Belinda	Ophelia
Bianca	Portia
Caliban	Puck
Cordelia	Rosalind
Cressida	Sycorax
Desdemona	Titania
Juliet	Umbriel
Miranda	

plus at least 10 other smaller moons

Find out more
Space probes pp. 58–59

Moons

Uranus has 27 moons, all named after characters in William Shakespeare's plays. There are five large moons—Ariel, Umbriel, Titania, Oberon, and Miranda. The smaller ones were discovered by the *Voyager 2* space probe in 1986. Uranus's moon Miranda (shown here) is the weirdest moon of all. It seems to have been blasted apart, then put itself back together again.

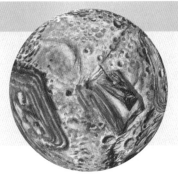

In 2002, the Hubble Space Telescope peered deep into Uranus's atmosphere to see clear and hazy layers created by a mixture of gases, and identified features of three different atmospheric layers. The red rim around the planet's edge represents a very thin haze at a high altitude. The haze is so thin that it can only be seen by looking at the edges of the disk, and is similar to looking at the edge of a soap bubble. The yellow near the bottom is another hazy layer. The deepest layer, the blue near the top of Uranus, shows a clear atmosphere. Image processing was used to brighten Uranus's rings. In reality, the rings are the color of black lava or charcoal.

Uranus is the third largest planet in the Solar System—31,765 mi across and with a mass 14.54 times that of the Earth's. The planet spins round once every 17.2 h, but because it is lying almost on its side, this has almost no effect on the length of its day. Instead, this depends on where the planet is in its orbit of the Sun. Like Saturn, Uranus has rings, but they are much thinner and were only detected in 1977. They are made of the darkest material in the Solar System.

Amazing

Uranus's 11 narrow rings were discovered when an astronomer saw a star "wink" on and off on either side of the planet when the star went behind Uranus.

Factfile

Diameter	31,763 mi
Mass	86.8×10^{24} kg
Time to spin once	17.2 h retrograde
Average distance from Sun	1,785 million mi
Time for one orbit	83.75 Earth years
Average temperature	-319°F
Number of moons	27
Ring system	Yes

Studying the night sky

Uranus was not discovered until 1781. It was identified by the English astronomer William Herschel who, using a telescope, made a thorough study of the night sky.

Neptune

Neptune is the fourth largest planet, and the eighth out from the Sun. Like its neighbor Uranus it has a surface made up of icy blue liquid methane, an atmosphere of hydrogen and helium, and a thin layer of rings. It is named after the Greek god of the ocean.

○ Neptune was discovered in 1846 because two mathematicians, John Couch Adams in England and Urbain le Verrier in France, worked out that it must be there because of the effect of its gravity on the movement of Uranus.

○ Neptune is so far from the Sun that its orbit lasts 163.7 Earth years. Indeed, it has not yet completed one orbit since it was discovered in 1846.

○ Like Uranus, Neptune has a surface of icy cold liquid methane (−373°F), and an atmosphere of hydrogen and helium.

○ Unlike Uranus, which is almost perfectly blue, Neptune has white clouds, created by heat inside the planet.

○ Neptune has the strongest winds in the Solar System, blowing at up to 2,296 ft/sec.

○ The *Voyager 2* encounter confirmed that Neptune has three distinct rings, with a diffuse ring of material.

○ Neptune's moon Triton is the coldest place in the Solar System, with surface temperatures of −393°F.

○ Triton is the only moon to orbit backward.

Great Dark Spot

🅰 *At 30,775 mi across, Neptune is slightly smaller than Uranus—but it is actually a little heavier. Like Uranus, its oceans of incredibly cold liquid methane make it a beautiful shiny blue, although Neptune's surface is a deeper blue than that of Uranus. Again like Uranus, Neptune has a thin layer of rings. But Neptune's are level, and not at right angles to the Sun. Neptune's swirling storm, the Great Dark Spot, had disappeared when the Hubble Space Telescope looked at the planet in 1994.*

Factfile

Diameter	30,775 mi
Mass	102 x 10^{24} kg
Time to spin once	16.1 h
Average distance from Sun	2,793 million mi
Time for one orbit	163.7 Earth years
Average temperature	−328°F
Number of moons	13
Ring system	Yes

Find out more
Space probes pp. 58–59

Magnetism

Neptune and Uranus are unusual planets because, unlike other planets' magnetic fields, theirs are at right angles to their axis of rotation (the angle at which they spin).

Neptune's biggest moon is Triton, with a diameter of 1,677 mi. It looks like a green melon, while its icecaps of frozen nitrogen resemble pink ice cream. Triton is gradually spiraling towards Neptune and in 10 million to 100 million years time it will break up and form rings around the planet. Triton's geysers shoot out freezing nitrogen gas.

Amazing

Neptune has the strongest winds in the Solar System, blowing at up to 1,242 mi/h.

Aerial view

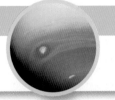

The Great Dark Spot, and the little white tail of clouds, named Scooter by astronomers, are clearly visible in photographs of Neptune, taken from orbiting spacecraft.

Neptune's largest moons

Despina	Nereid
Galatea	Proteus
Larissa	Thalassa
Naiad	Triton

plus at least five other smaller moons

Pluto

Pluto is the furthest planet from the Sun, at an average distance of 3,647 million mi. If you could stand on Pluto's surface, the Sun would look no bigger than a star in Earth's sky. Pluto is also the smallest planet and is no bigger than the Earth's moon. It was named after the Roman god of the Underworld.

○ Pluto was the last of all the planets to be discovered, and it was only found because astronomers thought there was another planet disturbing the orbits of Uranus and Neptune.

○ Pluto's orbit makes its distance from the Sun vary from 2,939 to 4,583 million mi.

○ Pluto's orbit is so far from the Sun that it takes 248 Earth years just to travel right around once. This means that a year on Pluto lasts almost three Earth centuries. A day, however, lasts just under a week.

○ Pluto has a strange elliptical (oval) orbit which actually brings it closer to the Sun than Neptune for a year or two every few centuries.

○ Unlike all the other planets that orbit on exactly the same plane (level) as the Earth, Pluto's orbit cuts across diagonally.

○ While studying a photograph of Pluto in 1978, American astronomer James Christy noticed a bump. This turned out to be a large moon, which was later named Charon.

○ Charon is about half the size of Pluto and they orbit one another, locked together like a weight lifter's dumbbells.

○ Charon always stays in the same place in Pluto's sky, looking three times as big as our Moon.

○ Unlike the other outer planets, Pluto is made from rock, which is covered in water and ice.

○ Daytime temperatures on Pluto's surface are −364°F or less, so the surface is thought to be coated in frozen methane.

○ Pluto is god of the Underworld in Roman mythology. The planet got its name from the fact that it is so far from the Sun that it is in perpetual darkness.

○ Pluto is the only planet in the Solar System that has not been visited by a spacecraft. A possible mission is being planned. The Hubble Space Telescope can make out only the largest features on its surface.

▶ *This picture of Pluto is entirely imaginary, since it is so small and so far away that even photographs from the Hubble Space Telescope show just fuzzy dark and light patches on Pluto's surface, with no detail at all. However, a twinkling of starlight around the edge of the planet shows that it must have some kind of atmosphere.*

Amazing

When Pluto was discovered in 1930, many names were considered for the planet. The name Pluto was a suggestion submitted by Venetia Burney, an 11-year-old schoolgirl from Oxford, England.

Factfile

Diameter	1,485 mi
Mass	0.0125 x 10²⁴ kg
Time to spin once	6.39 days
Average distance from Sun	3,647 million mi
Time for one orbit	248 Earth years
Average temperature	−373°F
Number of moons	1
Ring system	No

Find out more

Space probes pp. 58–59

Clyde Tombaugh

Pluto was discovered by the American astronomer Clyde Tombaugh (1906–1997). He was looking for a Planet X, which was thought erroneously to exist because of its effect on the orbits of Neptune and Uranus (see right). He made the discovery by analyzing different photographs taken of a section of the sky. Tombaugh also discovered 14 asteroids, including one that was named after him.

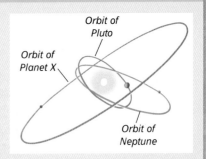

Orbit of Pluto

Orbit of Planet X

Orbit of Neptune

Tiny Pluto

Pluto is tiny in comparison to the Earth. This made it exceedingly hard to find. Earth is five times bigger and 500 times as heavy. This illustration shows the relative size of the two planets—Earth and Pluto.

Pluto's moon, Charon, was named after the mythological figure who ferried the dead across the River Aceron into the Underworld. Pluto and Charon orbit with the same side always facing each other. This means that you could never see Charon from the far side of Pluto and you would not know that Pluto existed from the far side of Charon.

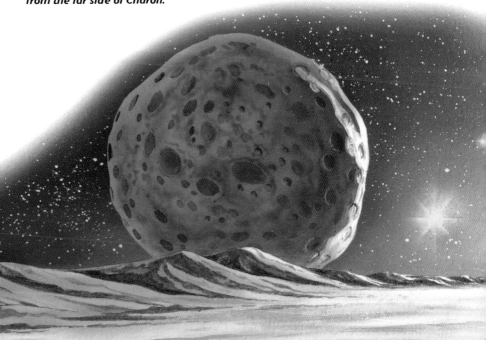

Comets

Comets are bright objects with long tails, which we sometimes see streaking across the night sky. They may look spectacular, but a comet is actually just a dirty ball of ice a few miles across.

○ Many comets orbit the Sun, but their orbits are very long and they spend most of the time in the far reaches of the Solar System. We see them when their orbit brings them close to the Sun for a few weeks.

○ A comet's tail is made as it nears the Sun and begins to melt. A vast plume of gas millions of miles across is blown out behind by the solar wind. The tail is what you see, shining as the sunlight catches it.

◀ This photograph of Halley's Comet was taken when it last came close to Earth in 1986. The comet comes back close to Earth within visible range roughly every 76 years.

▲ The Kohoutek Comet was first seen on March 7, 1973, by Czech astronomer Luos Kohoutek. The period when it could be seen with the naked eye was from the end of November 1973 until late January 1974. Initially labeled the "Comet of the Century" it actually proved to be disappointing in putting on a poor display.

Comet orbits

	Orbital period
Encke	3.30 years
Grigg-Skjellerup	5.09 years
Honda-Mrkos-Pajd	5.28 years
Wirtanen	5.46 years
Wild 2	6.17 years
Kohoutek	6.24 years
Giacobini-Zinner	6.52 years
Crommelin	27.89 years
Temple-Tuttle	32.92 years
Chiron	50.7 years
Halley	76.1 years
Hale-Bopp	4000 years
Hyakutake	65,000+ years

Find out more

The Solar System pp. 26–27

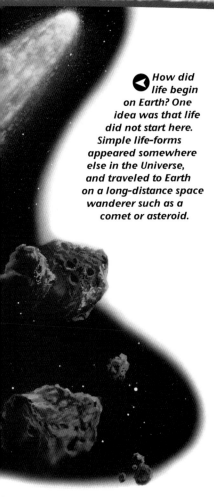

How did life begin on Earth? One idea was that life did not start here. Simple life-forms appeared somewhere else in the Universe, and traveled to Earth on a long-distance space wanderer such as a comet or asteroid.

What is a comet?

The nucleus of a comet (resembling an eye in this diagram) is usually just a few miles across. Jets of gas burned off by the Sun form the coma, or curved front, and the tail.

Ancient comet

The most famous comet is named after the British scientist Edmund Halley (1656–1742). He accurately predicted that this particular comet would be seen in the night sky in 1758, which was 16 years after his death. He was the first person to predict when a comet would arrive. Halley's comet orbits the Sun every 76 years. It was last seen in 1986 and its next visit will be in 2062. The Chinese described a visit from the comet as long ago as 240 BC.

King Harold of England saw it in 1066, and it is embroidered on the Bayeux Tapestry, which shows Harold's defeat by William the Conqueror.

○ Some comets are bright enough to be seen with the naked eye, while others can only be seen with the aid of a telescope. You will not be able to see comets moving, but over a period of time their progress can be charted.

○ Comets called periodics appear at regular intervals.

○ Some comets reach speeds of 1,243 million mi/h as they near the Sun.

○ Far away from the Sun, comets slow down to 621 mi/h or so—that is why they stay away for so long.

○ The visit of the Comet Hale-Bopp in 1997 gave the brightest view of a comet since 1811, visible even from brightly lit cities.

○ The Shoemaker-Levy 9 Comet smashed into Jupiter in July 1994, with the biggest crash ever witnessed.

Comets travel through the inner Solar System and after about 100 orbits usually lose all their gas and dust, and die. However, sometimes comets die more spectacularly, as these seen being pulled apart by Jupiter's gravity. In July 1994, 21 pieces crashed into Jupiter's atmosphere.

Halley's Comet

1682	British astronomer Edmund Halley saw it and worked out that the comet (now named after him) would return in 76–77 years.
1759	Great excitement: the comet returned as predicted.
1835	Comet was seen again, but was not so bright.
1910	Despite scientific progress, some superstitious people still feared that the reappearance of the comet heralded the end of the world.
1986	Several spacecraft flew close to the comet.
2062	Next time Halley's Comet is due to return.

Asteroids and Meteors

Asteroids are lumps of rock that orbit the Sun. They are sometimes called the minor planets. Meteors are chunks of stone and iron that break away from asteroids and comets, and sometimes enter the Earth's atmosphere. Meteroids are chunks of rock and dust zooming through space. When they hit the atmosphere, they burn up, leaving a streak called a meteor or shooting star.

❍ Most asteroids travel within the Asteroid Belt, which lies between Mars and Jupiter.

❍ Some distant asteroids are made of ice and orbit the Sun beyond Neptune.

❍ A few asteroids come near the Earth. These are called Near Earth Objects (NEOs).

❍ The first asteroid to be discovered was Ceres in 1801. It was detected by Giuseppi Piazzi, one of the Celestial Police whose mission was to find a "missing" planet.

❍ Ceres is the biggest asteroid— 584 mi across, and 0.0002 percent the size of the Earth.

❍ The *Galileo* space probe took close-up pictures of the asteroids Ida and Gaspra in 1991 and 1993.

❍ The Trojan asteroids are groups of asteroids that follow the same orbit as Jupiter. Many are named after warriors from the ancient Greek tales of the Trojan Wars.

A *This crater in Arizona, measuring 0.7 mi in diameter, is the first to be identified as an impact crater, proved to be such by the discovery of fragments of the Canyon Diablo meteorite. Between 20,000 and 50,000 years ago this small asteroid, about 82 ft in diameter, hit Earth.*

Amazing

Once every 50–100 million years the Earth is hit by an asteroid measuring over 6 mi in diameter.

Largest asteroids in the Asteroid Belt

These are still much smaller than the Moon. Collectively, the asteroids probably only weigh about one-twentieth of the Moon's weight.

	Discovered	Discoverer	Diameter	Distance from Sun
Ceres	1801	G. Piazzi	580 mi	257.2 million mi
Pallas	1802	H. Olbers	327 mi	257.6 million mi
Vesta	1807	H. Olbers	317 mi	219.6 million mi
Hygiea	1849	A. de Gasparis	254 mi	292.2 million mi
Davida	1903	R. Dugan	203 mi	295.4 million mi
Interamnia	1910	V. Cerulli	196 mi	284.7 million mi
Europa	1858	H. Goldsmith	188 mi	287.9 million mi
Juno	1804	K. Harding	167 mi	248.2 million mi
Sylvia	1866	N. Pogson	162 mi	324.0 million mi
Euomnia	1851	A. de Gasparis	159 mi	245.8 million mi
Euphrosyne	1854	J. Ferguson	159 mi	293.4 million mi
Psyche	1852	A. de Gasparis	158 mi	271.6 million mi
Cybele	1867	E. Tempel	149 mi	318.8 million mi
Bamberga	1892	J. Palisa	143 mi	249.4 million mi
Patentia	1899	A. Charlois	140 mi	284.7 million mi
Doris	1857	H. Goldschmidt	138 mi	289.3 million mi
Camilla	1968	N. Pogson	138 mi	324.2 million mi
Herculina	1904	M. Wolf	138 mi	257.7 million mi
Eugenia	1857	H. Goldschmidt	133 mi	253.0 million mi

Earthbound

Most meteors burn away in the atmosphere, but some come crashing down to Earth.

Small asteroids are burnt up by the Earth's atmosphere every day. The chances of a big one colliding with us and destroying the Earth, like in this illustration, are remote.

○ A meteor that strikes Earth is called a meteorite. It can create a huge hole or crater.

○ Scientists believe that a huge meteorite, possibly the size of an asteroid, crashed to Earth 65 million years ago and sent up a huge dust cloud that caused the extinction of the dinosaurs.

Meteors are mostly caused by dust smaller than a grain of sand, much too small to be seen, even with a telescope.

10 largest meteorite craters on Earth

		Diameter
Vredefort	South Africa	186 mi
Sudbury	Ontario, Canada	155 mi
Chicxulub	Yucatan, Mexico	105 mi
Popigai	Russia	62 mi
Manicouagan	Quebec, Canada	62 mi
Acraman	Australia	55 mi
Chesapeake Bay	Virginia, USA	55 mi
Puchezh-Katunki	Russia	49 mi
Morokweng	South Africa	43 mi
Kara	Russia	40 mi

The Asteroid Belt

More than half a million asteroids can be found in the Asteroid Belt, which lies between the orbits of Mars and Jupiter. They range in size from Ceres, which is about one-quarter the diameter of our Moon, to bodies that are less than 0.6 mi across. Spacecraft that have traveled through the Asteroid Belt have found that it is actually quite empty and that asteroids are separated by large distances.

Find out more

The Earth pp. 30–31

Astronomy

***A**stronomy is the study of the night sky—from the planets and moons to the stars and galaxies. It is the most ancient of sciences, dating back thousands of years. The word astronomy comes from the Greek* astro, *meaning "star" and* nomia, *meaning "law."*

❍ The ancient Egyptians used their knowledge of astronomy to work out their calendar and to align the pyramids. The great Egyptian pyramids at Giza are said to have been positioned to align with certain stars.

❍ Astronomers use telescopes to study objects far fainter and smaller than can be seen with the naked eye.

❍ Space objects give out other kinds of radiation besides light, and astronomers have special equipment to detect this.

❍ Professional astronomers study photographs and computer displays instead of staring through telescopes, because most faint space objects only show up on long-exposure photographs.

▶ *Most astronomers work far from city lights in observatories where they can get a very clear view of the night sky and sights such as this supernova.*

Amazing

In 2003, NASA's WMAP satellite took images of the most distant parts of the Universe observable from Earth. Nearly 14 billion lightyears away, it showed the Universe long before the stars and galaxies formed.

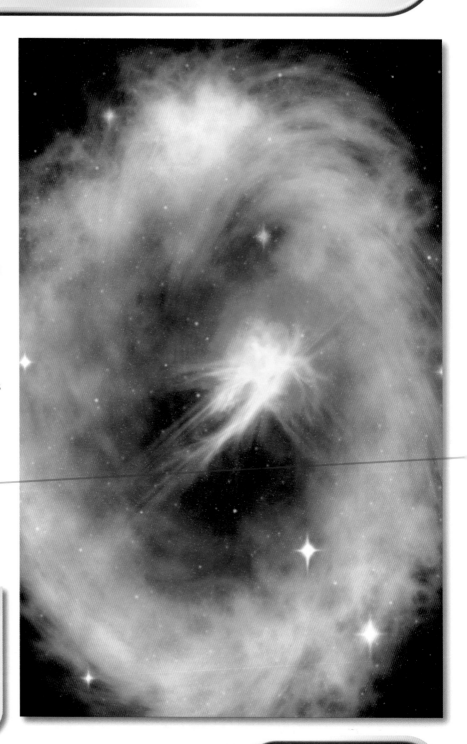

Find out more

Telescopes/observatories pp. 56–57

Astrology

The Zodiac is the band of constellations the Sun appears to pass in front of during the year, as the Earth orbits the Sun. It lies along the ecliptic, which is the plane (level) of the Earth's orbit around the Sun. The Moon and all planets but Pluto lie in the same plane. The ancient Greeks divided the Zodiac into 12 parts, named after the constellation they saw in each part. These are the signs of the Zodiac. The Zodiac signs are imaginary symbols that ancient astronomers linked to star patterns. Astrologers believe that the movements of planets and stars have an effect on people's lives. They are not scientists, like astronomers. A 13th constellation, Ophiuchus, now lies within the Zodiac but astrologers ignore it.

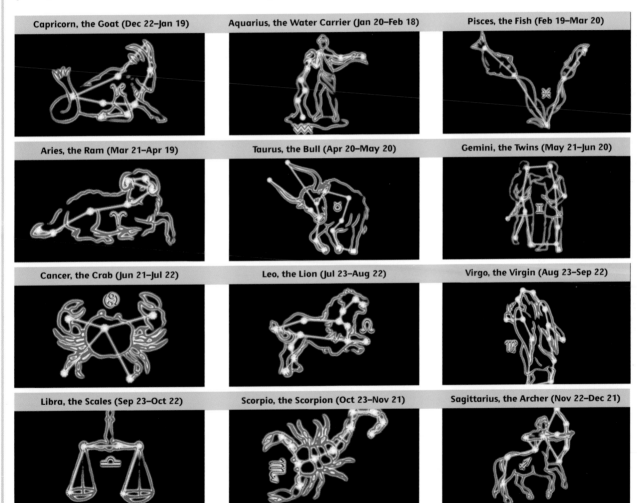

Capricorn, the Goat (Dec 22–Jan 19)

Aquarius, the Water Carrier (Jan 20–Feb 18)

Pisces, the Fish (Feb 19–Mar 20)

Aries, the Ram (Mar 21–Apr 19)

Taurus, the Bull (Apr 20–May 20)

Gemini, the Twins (May 21–Jun 20)

Cancer, the Crab (Jun 21–Jul 22)

Leo, the Lion (Jul 23–Aug 22)

Virgo, the Virgin (Aug 23–Sep 22)

Libra, the Scales (Sep 23–Oct 22)

Scorpio, the Scorpion (Oct 23–Nov 21)

Sagittarius, the Archer (Nov 22–Dec 21)

Telescopes and Observatories

The most important tool for studying the skies is the telescope. Today, there are several different types of telescope, ranging from simple ones used by amateur star-gazers to immensely powerful space telescopes that allow astronomers to see into the furthest reaches of the Universe. Observatories are special places where astronomers study space and, to give the best view of the night sky, most are built on mountain tops far from city lights.

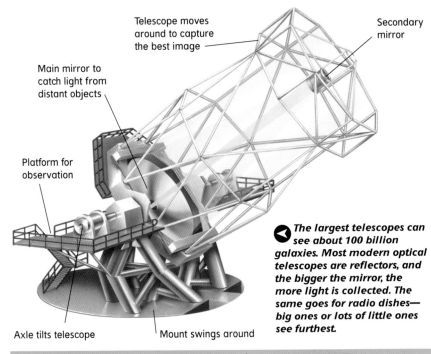

Telescope moves around to capture the best image

Secondary mirror

Main mirror to catch light from distant objects

Platform for observation

Axle tilts telescope

Mount swings around

○ Optical telescopes magnify distant objects by using lenses or mirrors to refract (bend) light rays so they focus (come together).

○ Other telescopes detect radio waves, X rays, or other kinds of electromagnetic radiation.

○ Refracting telescopes are optical telescopes that use lenses to refract the light rays.

○ Reflecting telescopes are optical telescopes. They work by refracting light rays that are reflected off curved mirrors.

○ Because the light rays are folded, reflecting telescopes are shorter and fatter than refracting ones.

○ Most professional astronomers do not gaze at the stars directly, but pick up what the telescope shows with light sensors called Charge Coupled Devices (CCDs).

The largest telescopes can see about 100 billion galaxies. Most modern optical telescopes are reflectors, and the bigger the mirror, the more light is collected. The same goes for radio dishes—big ones or lots of little ones see furthest.

Galileo Galilei

The great Italian mathematician and astronomer, Galileo Galilei(1564–1642), studied the skies through his telescope, which he demonstrated to members of the Venetian senate. Learning of the invention of the telescope, Galileo made his own to look at the Moon, Venus, and Jupiter. Through his telescope, he discovered four of Jupiter's moons and studied the phases of Venus.

○ In most observatories, telescopes are housed in a dome-roofed building that turns around so they can keep aiming at the same stars while the Earth rotates.

○ Modern observatories use gigantic reflector dishes made up of hexagons of glass or coated metal.

○ The highest observatory on the Earth is 14,107 ft above sea level, at Denver, Colorado, in the USA.

○ The lowest observatory is 1 mi below sea level, in Homestake Mine, Dakota, USA. Its "telescope" is actually tanks of cleaning fluid, which trap neutrinos from the Sun.

○ The first photographs of the stars were taken in 1840. Nowadays, most observatories rely on photographs rather than on the naked eyes of astronomers.

Find out more

Astronomy pp. 54–55

Observatories

The most powerful optical telescopes are housed in observatories—specially designed buildings that allow astronomers to study space in comfort. To give the best view of the night sky, most observatories are built on mountaintops far away from city lights. They generally have domed roofs that can turn around in order to aim at the same stars, as the Earth rotates. The oldest existing observatory is the Tower of the Winds in Athens, Greece, which dates from 100 BC. One of the largest observatory complexes (shown here) is 13,779 ft above sea level, in the crater of the extinct Hawaiian volcano, Mauna Kea.

Amazing

Telescope dishes have to be made accurate to within 2 billionths of a millimeter.

❍ Observatory photographs are made using sensors called Charge Coupled Devices (CCDs), which give off an electrical signal when struck by light.

❍ Astronomers can spot new objects in the night sky by laying a current photograph over an old one and looking for differences.

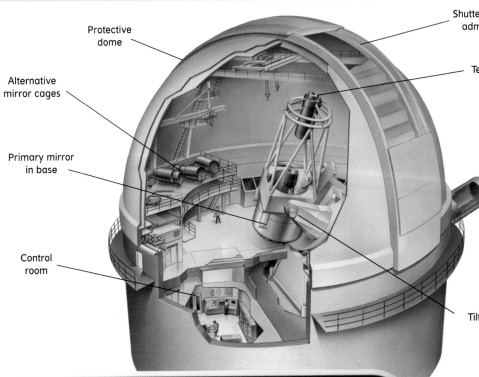

Shutter door to admit light

Telescope

Protective dome

Alternative mirror cages

Primary mirror in base

Control room

Tilt mechanism

A huge dome protects this large telescope. It opens to let the telescope point at the sky, and both the dome and telescope can turn to look at any part of the sky.

Major radio telescopes

		Size of array
Australia Telescope	New South Wales, Australia	199 mi
Effelsberg Radio Telescope	Effelsberg, Germany	328 ft
Arecibo Observatory	Puerto Rico	1,000 ft diameter
Green Bank Telescope	West Virginia, USA	328 x 361 ft
JCMT (James Clerk Maxwell Telescope)	Mauna Kea, Hawaii	49 ft diameter

Space Probes

Space probes are used to explore space. They are unmanned computer-controlled spacecraft. Most probes are "fly-bys," which spend just a few days passing their target and beaming data back to Earth, although some actually land on the surface of planets, moons, and asteroids.

○ *Viking 1* and *2* were launched and landed on Mars in 1976.

○ The Soviet probe *Mars 3* was the first probe to make a soft landing on Mars, on December 2, 1971, and sent back data for 20 seconds before it unexpectedly fell silent.

○ *Voyager 1* was launched into space on September 5, 1977. It flew past Jupiter in March 1979 and Saturn in November 1980, then headed onward on a curved path that will take it out of the Solar System altogether.

○ *Voyager 2*, also launched in 1977, has flown over 4 billion mi and is heading out of the Solar System after passing close to Jupiter (1979), Saturn (1980), Uranus (1986), and Neptune (1989).

○ To save fuel on journeys to distant planets, space probes may use a nearby planet's gravity to catapult them on their way. This technique is called a slingshot.

○ In the first ten years of the 21st century, more than 50 space probes will be sent off to visit planets, asteroids, and comets, as well as to observe the Moon and the Sun.

Galileo space probe

The *Galileo* space probe has circled Jupiter for more than six years. It arrived there in 1995 and dropped a small probe into Jupiter's clouds. *Galileo* sent back pictures of the planet and its largest moons. Through this. it was discovered that two of them may have water hidden under ice thicker than the Arctic ice on Earth. When *Galileo* has finished sending back pictures of Jupiter and its moons, it will plunge into Jupiter's swirling clouds.

Probes to the planets

MERCURY		
Mariner 10	November 3, 1973	Three fly-bys March and September 1974 and March 1975
MESSENGER	August 3, 2004	Orbit from March 2011
VENUS		
Venera 4-16	1967–1983	Series of entry probes, landers, and orbiters. *Venera 7* was first successful lander
Pioneer Venus	May/August 1978	One orbiter and four atmospheric probes
Magellan	May 4, 1989	Orbiter—radar mapped surface
MARS		
Mariner 9	May 30, 1971	Orbiter—first to orbit another planet
Viking	August/September 1975	Two orbiters with two landers—tested soil for life
Mars Global Surveyor	November 7, 1996	Orbiter
Mars Pathfinder	December 4, 1996	Lander with *Sojourner* rover
Mars Odyssey	April 7, 2001	Orbiter
Mars Express	June 1, 2003	Orbiter with *Beagle 2* lander (failed)
Mars Exploration Rovers	June/July 2003	Rovers *Spirit* and *Opportunity* explored surface for over one year
JUPITER		
Voyager 1	September 5, 1977	Fly-by March 1979
Voyager 2	August 20, 1977	Fly-by July 1979
Galileo	October 18, 1989	Orbited December 1995 – September 2003
		Dropped small probe into atmosphere
SATURN		
Voyager 1	September 5, 1977	Fly-by November 1980
Voyager 2	August 20, 1977	Fly-by August 1981
Cassini	October 15, 1997	Orbiter plus *Huygens* probe that landed on Titan January 2005
URANUS		
Voyager 2	August 20, 1977	Fly-by January 1986
NEPTUNE		
Voyager 2	August 20, 1977	Fly-by August 1989
PLUTO		
New Horizons	January 2006	Fly-by 2015

Find out more
Mars pp. 38–39

Amazing

In January 2005, the *Huygens* probe, launched from the *Cassini* spacecraft, landed on Saturn's moon, Titan. It is the furthest from Earth a spacecraft has ever landed, about 0.8 billion mi away.

○ Space probes will bring back samples from Mars, comets, and asteroids early in the 21st century.

○ NASA's Terrestial Planet Finder (TPF) may be used to detect planets circling nearby stars in 2009.

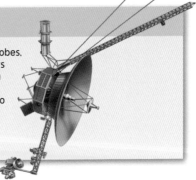

The first successful planetary probe was the USA's Mariner 2, *which flew past Venus in 1962.* Mariner 10 *reached Mercury in 1974.*

Voyagers

The Voyagers are a pair of unmanned US space probes, launched to explore the outer planets. The Voyagers used the "slingshot" of Jupiter's gravity to hurl them on towards Saturn. The probes revealed volcanoes on Io, one of Jupiter's Galilean moons. *Voyager 2* also found ten unknown moons around Uranus and six unknown moons and three rings around Neptune. *Voyager 2* will beam back data until 2020 as it travels beyond the edges of the Solar System.

On September 5, 1977, Voyager 1 was launched aboard the Titan III/Centaur. It was sent to join its sister spacecraft, the Voyager 2, on a mission to the outer planets.

Probes to comets and asteroids

Vega 1	December 15, 1984	Russian probe flew past Comet Halley
Vega 2	December 21, 1984	Russian probe flew past Comet Halley
Sakigake	January 8, 1985	Japanese probe flew past Comet Halley
Suisei	August 18, 1985	Japanese probe flew past Comet Halley
Giotto	July 2, 1985	Flew past Comet Halley, closest approach 1986
NEAR	February 17, 1996	Orbited asteroid Eros then landed on it, 2001
Deep Space 1	October 24, 1998	Flew past asteroid Braille July 1999 Flew past Comet Borrelly September 2001
Stardust Return	January 7, 1999	Flew past Comet Wild 2, collected sample. to Earth January 2006
Genesis	August 8, 2001	Collected sample of solar wind. Crash landed on return to Earth, some samples saved
Hayabusa	May 9, 2003	Sample return from asteroid Itokawa 2005
Rosetta	March 2, 2004	Orbit Comet Churyumov-Gerasimenko, drop lander 2014
Deep Impact	January 12, 2005	Launch impactor at Comet Tempel 1, July 2005

Artificial Satellites

***N**atural satellites are objects, such as moons that orbit planets and other bodies in space. Artificial satellites are devices that are launched to orbit around the Earth. The signals they transmit are picked up by radio telescopes and other equipment, providing us with useful information about the Earth and space, and enabling us to communicate over long distances.*

○ The first artificial satellite, *Sputnik 1*, was launched on October 4, 1957.

○ About 100 artificial satellites are now launched every year. A few of them are space telescopes.

○ **Communications satellites beam everything from TV pictures to telephone calls around the world.**

○ Observation satellites scan the Earth and are used for purposes such as scientific research, weather forecasting, and spying.

○ Navigation satellites, such as the Global Positioning System (GPS), are used by people, such as airline pilots, to work out exactly where they are.

○ Satellites are launched at a particular speed and trajectory (path) to place them in just the right orbit.

○ A geostationary orbit is 22,236 mi above Earth. Satellites in geostationary orbit over the Equator always stay in exactly the same place above the Earth.

○ Polar orbiting satellites circle the Earth from pole to pole about 528 mi up, covering a different strip of the Earth's surface on each orbit.

○ Geostationary orbit gets crowded, so when a geostationary satellite fails, it is pushed into another orbit to make room for others.

Weather satellites look down at the clouds and give warning when a violent storm is approaching

Communications satellites can beam TV programs directly to your home through your own aerial dish

Satellite telescopes let astronomers look far out into the Universe and discover what is out there

Pictures of the Earth taken by satellites can help make very accurate maps

Find out more
Space probes pp. 58–59

The most famous space telescope is the Hubble, launched from a space shuttle in 1990. The diameter of its main light-gathering mirror measures 94 in. It is controlled by NASA and transmits data by radio waves to astronomers on the ground. The Hubble orbits about 379 mi above the Earth, thus escaping the effects of the Earth's atmosphere, which bends light from the stars and thus blurs images. The Hubble produces much sharper images.

Modern navigation instruments use signals from several satellites to pinpint their position. A handheld instrument, called a GPS receiver, receives signals from satellites in space. It shows your position within a few feet. These receivers can be built into cars, planes—even laptop computers.

Sputnik

Sputnik was the world's first artificial satellite, sent into orbit by the USSR on October 4, 1957. Sputnik, which means "fellow-traveler" in Russian, weighed 185 lb and was about the size of a basketball. It took about 98 minutes to orbit the Earth on its elliptical path, and transmitted a "beep-beep" signal for 23 days before the chemical (silver-zinc) batteries ran down. The launch of Sputnik marked the start of the space age and the battle for dominance in space exploration between the United States and Russia, which was known as the "space race."

Satellite orbit

Global Positioning Satellite (GPS)

Satellite speed

The lower a satellite's orbit, the faster it must fly to avoid falling back to Earth. Most satellites fly in low orbits, 310 mi above the Earth.

Amazing

About 4,000 satellites have been launched since Sputnik 1, by a total of nine countries: Australia, China, France, India, Israel, Japan, Russia, UK, USA.

Satellite orbits

	Earth-observation/ navigation	Communication/ weather	Space telescopes
Orbit	Low Earth	Geostationary	High Earth
Height	93–621 mi	22.369 mi	63.137 mi+
Speed of satellite	16,777 mi/h	6.835 mi/h	Variable
Time to orbit Earth	Once every 90 min	Once a day	Variable

Man on the Moon

As the largest object in the night sky, the Moon has held a fascination for man since the earliest times. It was not until the late 1960s, however, that the technology was developed to send a man to the Moon.

○ The first unmanned Moon landing was the Soviet probe *Lunar 9*, which touched down on the Moon in 1966.

○ The first men to orbit the Moon were the astronauts onboard the US *Apollo 8* in 1968.

○ On July 20, 1969, the manned American mission, *Apollo 11*, landed on the Moon. Astronauts Neil Armstrong and Edwin (Buzz) Aldrin stepped from the *Eagle* landing craft and became the first men ever to walk on the Moon.

○ When the first astronauts landed on the Moon they found a landscape of cliffs and plains, completely covered in many places by a fine white dust.

○ Twelve men landed on the Moon between 1969 and 1972.

Space suits protect astronauts outside their spacecraft. The suits are also called EMUs (Extravehicular Mobility Units). The outer layers of a space suit protect against harmful radiation from the Sun and bullet-fast particles of spacedust (micrometeoroids). The clear, plastic helmet also protects against radiation and micrometeoroids. Oxygen is circulated around the helmet to stop the visor misting.

○ The Moon astronauts brought back 838 lb of Moon rock.

○ A mirror was left on the Moon's surface to reflect a laser beam, which measured the Moon's distance from Earth with amazing accuracy.

○ Laser measurements showed that, on average, the Moon is 233,806 mi away from the Earth.

○ Gravity on the Moon is so weak that astronauts can leap high into the air wearing their heavy space suits.

○ Temperatures reach 243°F at midday on the Moon, but plunge to −259°F at night.

Apollo 13

On April 11, 1970, the third Apollo mission, *Apollo 13*, blasted off and started its journey to the Moon. However, halfway there disaster struck. A big explosion onboard the spacecraft left the three astronauts with little air or power. Landing on the Moon was out of the question. The problem now was devising a way to get the crew back to Earth. To save energy, they turned the heating off and traveled in the cramped Lunar Module. They had to go round the Moon before they could swing back to Earth, but eventually they landed safely on April 17.

The 12 men who have walked on the Moon

Neil Armstrong
Edwin "Buzz" Aldrin
Charles Peter Conrad
Alan Bean
Alan Shepard
Edgar Mitchell
David Scott
James Irwin
John Young
Charles Duke
Eugene Cernan
Harrison Schmitt

Find out more
The Moon pp. 32–33

On July 20, 1969, the American astronauts Neil Armstrong and Edwin (Buzz) Aldrin (seen here) became the first men ever to walk on the Moon. When Neil Armstrong stepped on the Moon for the first time, he uttered these now famous words: "That's one small step for a man; one giant leap for mankind."

An astronaut's footprint left on the Moon will remain there for centuries because there is no wind or erosion to disturb it.

Amazing

Even though only 12 people have walked on the Moon, 24 people have actually traveled to it.

Neil Armstrong

Before becoming an astronaut, Neil Armstrong flew over 78 combat missions over Korea as a Navy fighter pilot, then joined NASA as a civilian test pilot. He was accepted into the astronaut corps in 1962 and piloted the *Gemini 8* mission, launched in 1966. Named commander for the *Apollo 12* mission, he was the first to step onto the Moon's surface.

Apollo missions to the Moon

Mission	Dates	Time on Moon	Rock collected
Apollo 11	July 16–24, 1969	22 h	49 lb
Apollo 12	November 14–24, 1969	32 h	77 lb
Apollo 14	January 31–February 9, 1971	34 h	93 lb
Apollo 15	July 26–August 7, 1971	67 h	172 lb
Apollo 16	April 16–27, 1972	71 h	216 lb
Apollo 17	December 7–19, 1971	76 h	253 lb

The Space Shuttle

The space shuttle is a reusable craft, able to land on a runway and then blast off again on another mission. Since the first shuttle, Columbia, was launched in 1981, astronauts from many countries have worked together on missions to launch, repair, and retrieve satellites, take photographs of the Earth and deep space, and carry out experiments.

❍ The space shuttle is made up of a 122 ft-long orbiter, two big Solid Rocket Boosters (SRBs), three main engines, and a tank.

❍ The shuttle orbiter is launched into space upright on the SRBs, which fall away to be collected for reuse. When the mission is over, the orbiter lands like a glider.

▶ The biggest problem when launching a spacecraft is overcoming the pull of Earth's gravity. To escape Earth's gravity, a spacecraft must be launched at a particular velocity (speed and direction). A spacecraft cannot use wings to lift it off the ground, as wings only work in the lower atmosphere. Instead, launch rockets must develop a big enough thrust to power them straight upward, overcoming gravity with a mighty blast of heat. Three rocket engines and two huge booster rockets are used to launch the spacecraft.

❍ The orbiter can only go as high as a near-Earth orbit, some 186 mi above the Earth.

❍ The maximum crew is eight, and a basic mission is seven days, during which the crew work in shirtsleeves.

❍ Orbiter toilets use flowing air to suck away waste.

❍ The orbiter can carry up to a 55,115 lb-load in its cargo bay.

Amazing

The shuttle orbiter is covered with 27,500 special tiles that protect it from temperatures that can reach 3002°F when it reenters the Earth's atmosphere.

Landing

Unlike other spacecraft, the space shuttle can land like an airplane ready to be used again for another mission. The shuttle lands back on Earth on a long runway. It does not use any engines for the landing, unlike an aircraft. It touches down so fast, the pilot uses a parachute as well as brakes to stop it on the runway.

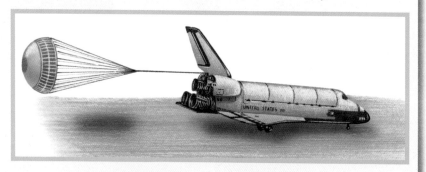

Orbiter factfile

Length 122.17 ft

Height 56.66 ft

Wingspan 78.05 ft

Capacity of cargo bay 55,093 lb

Crew size 2–8

Endurance up to 16 days in space

Power 3 main engines plus 44 smaller rockets for orbital maneuvring

Fuel supercold liquid oxygen and liquid hydrogen

Capacity of external fuel tank 50,060 gal

Speed in orbit about 17,579 mi/h

Maximum landing speed 257.8 mi/h

Cost to build *Endeavour*, built in 1991, cost approximately $1.7 billion

Find out more
Space stations pp. 66–67

❍ The first four orbiters were named after old sailing ships—*Columbia*, *Challenger*, *Discovery*, and *Atlantis*.

❍ The three main engines are used only for liftoff. In space, the small Orbital Maneuvring System (OMS) engines take over. The Reaction Control System (RCS) makes small adjustments to the orbiter's position.

❍ In 1986, the shuttle program suffered a major setback when the *Challenger* space shuttle exploded shortly after launch, killing its crew of seven. Tragedy struck again in 2003, when the shuttle *Colombia* broke up as it returned from a 16-day mission, killing the seven astronauts on board.

❍ In recent years, the space shuttle has played an important part in the development of the International Space Station (ISS), delivering parts, and transporting crew to-and-from the station.

Orbiter crew place satellite in space

Main fuel tank falls away 80 mi up

Orbiter goes into orbit around the Earth

Orbiter positions itself to reenter the Earth's atmosphere

⚠ *Powerful rockets are needed to boost a spacecraft to the speed it needs to break away from the Earth's gravity. But once it is out in space, these rockets are no longer needed, so spacecraft are launched by a series of rockets or stages that drop away once their task is done and their fuel is spent.*

Solid fuel rocket burners fall away 28 mi up

Orbiter lands like a glider

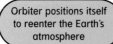

Shuttle blasts off using its own engines and two solid rocket boosters

Cargo bay

The entire center section of the orbiter is a cargo bay, which can be opened in space so that satellites can be placed in orbit.

Firsts in space

Man in space	Yuri Gagarin	1961
American in space	Alan Shepard	1961
American to orbit the Earth	John Glenn	1962
Woman in space	Valentina Tereshkova	1963
Space walk	Alexei Leonov	1965
American woman in space	Sally Ride	1983
Woman to pilot a spacecraft	Eileen Collins	1995

Space Stations

A space station is a structure designed for human beings to live on in outer space, for periods of weeks, months, or even years. They are used to study the effects of long-term space flight on the human body and to carry out scientific experiments in space. Space stations do not have a major propulsion system and are unable to land back on Earth. Instead, other vehicles are used to transport crew, equipment, and supplies to-and-from the station.

○ The first space station was the Soviet *Salyut 1*, launched in April 1971. Its low orbit meant it stayed up for only five months.

○ The first US space station was *Skylab*. Three crews spent 171 days in it in 1973–1974.

○ All the air, food, and water that the astronauts need to live on a space station must be supplied regularly by spacecraft from Earth.

○ A robot arm mounted on the outside of the International Space Station helps astronauts build the space station and keep it in good repair.

○ There is neither an up nor a down in a space station, but *Mir* had carpets on the "floor," pictures on the "wall" and lights on the "ceiling."

○ Cosmonaut Valery Polyakov spent a record 437 consecutive days in space onboard *Mir*.

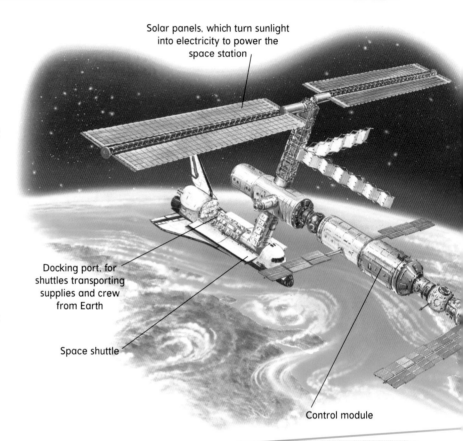

Solar panels, which turn sunlight into electricity to power the space station

Docking port, for shuttles transporting supplies and crew from Earth

Space shuttle

Control module

○ The giant International Space Station (ISS) is being built in stages and is due for completion in the early 21st century.

○ The first crew went aboard the ISS in November 2000.

○ The ISS will be 354 ft long and 295 ft wide, and weigh 450 tons.

Amazing

Weightlessness can make an astronaut grow several centimeters taller during a long mission in space.

International Space Station factfile

Length	357 ft
Width	288 ft
Weight	454 tons
Living space	15,009 ft³ (a bit bigger than a three-bedroom house)
Average altitude	219 mi
Speed	16,603 mi
Time to orbit Earth	Once every 90 min
Power	Electricity (110 kilowatts) provided by four giant solar arrays
Crew number	3–7
Crew changeover	Every 90 days
Ground crew	More than 100,000 people in 16 countries
Cost	$28 billion

Find out more

The space shuttle pp. 64–65

▶ *The first US space station was Skylab. It orbited the Earth for months on end. People spent long periods of time onboard, being replaced at intervals. Skylab was launched in 1973 and lasted until 1979.*

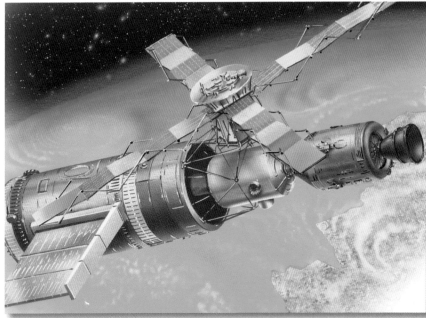

Living module, where crew live on board for several months at a time

Soyuz ferry, for ferrying people to-and-from the space station.

Mir

Mir was a Russian space station, and the largest serving station ever. It was launched in 1986 and made more than 76,000 orbits of the Earth. The last crew left it in 1999. *Mir* was built in stages. It weighed 125 tons and had six docking ports and two living rooms, plus a bathroom, and two small cabins. It was crashed into the Pacific Ocean in March 2001.

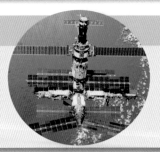

▲ *The International Space Station (ISS) is being built in space. This is the latest and largest space station. Sixteen countries are helping to build it, including the USA, Russia, Japan, Canada, Brazil, and other European countries. It is built up from separate sections called modules that have been made to fit together like a jigsaw. Each part is launched from Earth and added to the ISS in space. There they are fitted by astronauts at the ISS using the shuttle's robot arm. When all the pieces have been put into place, the ISS will look like this as it circles the Earth.*

Life onboard

Some inhabitants of the *Mir* space station spent more than a year on board. The station experienced power failures and crashes with ferry craft bringing supplies. The large panels shown here are solar cells used to make electricity from sunlight.

Most experienced in space

Sergei Avdeyev	USSR/Russia	747.59 days	3 missions
Valery Poliakov	USSR/Russia	678.69 days	2 missions
Anatoli Solovyov	USSR/Russia	651.44 days	5 missions
Viktor Afanasyev	USSR/Russia	545.92 days	3 missions
Musa Manarov	USSR/Russia	541 days	2 missions

Glossary

Antimatter Atomic particles that are the exact opposite of normal particles. If a particle meets its antiparticle they cancel each other out, releasing huge amounts of energy.

Asteroid Small rocky body circling the Sun, usually in a region between Mars and Jupiter called the Asteroid Belt.

Atmosphere Layer of gas around a planet, moon, or star. Usually a mixture of different gases thinning out further from the planet until it merges into space.

Atom The smallest particle of any element that can exist on its own.

Big Bang The event that happened at the beginning of the Universe when time and space began, and the Universe started expanding.

Black hole An object that has a pull of gravity so strong that nothing, not even light, can escape, so it cannot be seen.

CCD (charge coupled device) A computer chip that can detect light falling on it and convert it into an electrical signal. Telescope cameras use CCDs to produce an image instead of photographic film.

Chromosphere The region of the Sun's atmosphere just above its visible surface made of very hot gas.

Cluster A group of stars or galaxies that are all held together by the pull of gravity between them.

Comet A tiny icy body that circles the Sun in a long thin orbit, bringing it from the Solar System edge to swing close by the Sun. Near the Sun it forms a huge glowing tail that astronomers can see.

Constellation A pattern made by stars in the night sky.

Corona The thin outer atmosphere of the Sun, made of very hot gas. It can be seen as a glowing halo during an eclipse of the Sun.

Eclipse This happens when one body passes in front of another, hiding it from view. During an eclipse of the Sun, the Moon hides the Sun. In an eclipse of the Moon, the Earth blocks the sunlight that would fall on the Moon.

Galaxy A huge family of stars, gas, and dust held together by gravity.

Geostationary orbit An orbit above the Earth's Equator where a satellite moves around the Earth at the same pace as the Earth spins, so the satellite appears to stay fixed in the sky always above the same point on the Earth.

Gravity A force that pulls bodies toward each other. The Earth's gravity pulls us all down onto the ground and the Sun's gravity holds everything in the Solar System in orbit around it.

Jet A thin stream of high-speed particles and radiation coming from a galaxy, quasar, or young star.

Lightyear The distance that light travels in one year, used to measure the vast distances in space. One lightyear is 5.9 million million miles.

Local Group of galaxies The small cluster of galaxies that contains the Milky Way Galaxy. There are about 30 members, mostly very small.

Magellanic Clouds The two small galaxies closest to the Milky Way galaxy. They are called the Large Magellanic Cloud and the Small Magellanic Cloud. They can be seen from the Southern Hemisphere as faint, fuzzy patches.

Meteor A streak of light seen in the night sky when a small piece of space rock burns up in the atmosphere.

Meteorite A space rock that falls to the ground because it is too large to burn up when it hits the atmosphere. A meteorite often forms a crater when it lands.

Meteoroid A small rock speeding through space.

Micrometeoroid A tiny particle of dust speeding through space.

Microwave background radiation Weak radio waves that come from all directions in the sky. Astronomers think this is a residue of the Big Bang.

Milky Way Galaxy The galaxy that the Sun belongs to. It is a spiral galaxy, but we see it as a very faint band of light across the sky.

Moon An object that circles around a planet. Most of the planets in the Solar System have moons and the Earth has one, called the Moon.

Near Earth Object An asteroid that does not orbit in the Asteroid Belt but comes nearer the Sun. Some pass quite close to the Earth.

Nebula A cloud of gas and dust in space where new stars are born. A planetary nebula is a shell of gas thrown off by a dying star. The gas reflects starlight or glows when heated by nearby stars, making the nebula visible through a telescope.

Observatory A place or site where telescopes are built and astronomers study the Universe. They are mostly on mountaintops above the clouds to get a clearer view of the Universe.

Orbit The path of a planet around the Sun, or a moon, or satellite around a planet. An orbit can be almost circular like a planet or very long and thin like a comet, or anything in between.

Parsec A measure of distances in space. One parsec is 3.26 lightyears or 19 million million miles.

Phases Changing shape of the Moon during a month. As the Moon orbits the Earth we see different amounts of its sunlit side, from a tiny crescent increasing to a whole disk at Full Moon and then back to nothing at New Moon.

Photosphere The surface of the Sun that gives out the heat and light that reaches the Earth. It is hot, churning gas with no solid surface.

Planet A large body circling the Sun or another star. Some are small and rocky like the Earth, others are large and made of gas and liquid with no solid surface, like Jupiter.

Planetary rings Flat rings stretching round the equator of a large planet, made of millions of icy or dusty particles all orbiting the planet.

Prominence A huge loop or tail of hot gas reaching out from the Sun's surface. These prominences can last for a few days or months.

Quasar A very bright but very distant object that looks like a star but is probably the center of a young energetic galaxy.

Radar Radio waves bounced off an object, like the surface of a planet, to map its landscape.

Radiation Particles or energy like heat or light that travel through space. X rays, gamma rays, radio waves, infrared, and ultraviolet radiation are all types of radiation similar to light.

Radio telescope A telescope that collects radio waves from distant objects in space, often using a large metal dish. It produces an image of the Universe as seen in radio waves.

Retrograde Movement along an orbit in a clockwise direction as seen from above, meaning in the opposite direction to most planets and moons in the Solar System. It also applies to the spin of a planet or moon.

Satellite Anything that circles around another object in space. Moons are called natural satellites. Artificial satellites are manufactured objects usually circling the Earth.

Shooting star A popular name for a meteor.

Singularity A point with temperatures and pressures too enormous for scientists to explain. The Universe is thought to have started from a singularity, and there is a singularity at the center of a black hole.

Solar System The family of planets, moons, comets, and asteroids orbiting the Sun, held together by the Sun's pull of gravity.

Space probe Robot spacecraft sent to explore other planets and moons. A probe can fly past, go into orbit, or land on the surface of the planet or moon.

Space shuttle Reusable spacecraft that carries astronauts into Earth orbit or to a space station and returns to Earth for repeat trips.

Space station A home and workplace for astronauts, usually in orbit around the Earth, containing everything needed to keep them alive and well.

Space telescope A telescope launched into space to orbit the Earth or the Sun. Most collect radiation like X rays that cannot get through the atmosphere to telescopes on the ground.

Star A ball of hot, glowing gas. Nuclear reactions in its center make the energy that it gives out as light and heat.

Sun The nearest star to the Earth, an ordinary star of average size and temperature. It is made mostly of hydrogen and helium, and has many layers. It has a core where most heat is made.

Sun spot A darker area on the Sun that is cooler than the rest of the surface.

Supernova Explosion of a giant star that has collapsed at the end of its life. It shines very brightly for a short time then may leave a glowing nebula with a tiny neutron star or a black hole at the center.

Telescope An instrument that collects light or other radiation and forms images of stars, galaxies, or nebulae.

Universe Everything that exists out in space and here on Earth.

Weightlessness Floating in space and feeling as if you weigh nothing when in an orbiting space station or shuttle.

PLANET EARTH

The Formation of Earth

The story of the Earth began about 4.6 billion years ago when dust whirling around the newborn Sun started to clump into lumps of rock called planetesimals. Pulled together by their mutual gravity, these planetesimals then clumped together to form the Earth and other planets.

○ When the Earth first formed, it was little more than a red-hot ball of churning molten rock.

○ After 50 million years a giant rock crashed into the newborn Earth. The impact melted the rock into a hot splash, which cooled to become our Moon.

○ The Earth was so shaken by the impact that all the elements in it separated. The dense metals, iron, and nickel, collapsed to the center to form the Earth's core.

○ The molten rock formed a thick mantle about 1,864 mi thick around the metal core. The core's heat keeps the mantle warm and churning, like boiling porridge.

○ After about 100 million years the surface of the mantle cooled and hardened to form a thin crust.

○ An atmosphere containing poisonous gases, such as methane, hydrogen, and ammonia, soon wrapped around the planet, rising from fierce volcanoes on the surface.

○ After about 1 billion years, the air began to clear as water vapor that had gathered in the clouds fell as rain, to create the oceans.

◄ *When the Earth formed from a whirling cloud of stardust, the pieces rushed together with such force that the young planet turned into a fiery ball. It slowly cooled down, and the continents and the oceans formed.*

Find out more
Earth's Interior pp. 78–79

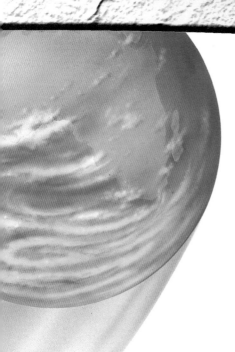

Early volcanoes

A mass of erupting volcanoes and smoke appeared on the young Earth. Streams of lava (molten rock) turned the Earth's surface into churning, red-hot oceans.

Watery planet

The Earth is unique in the Solar System because it is the only planet with running water on the surface, and life. Seen from space, the Earth is a planet of oceans. Only about 29 percent is land. Earth is home to a huge variety of living things that can only survive here because of all this water.

❍ The Solar System was created when the gas cloud left over from a giant supernova explosion started to collapse in on itself and spin.

❍ About 4.5 billion years ago, a rock the size of Mars crashed into Earth. Splashes of material from this crash clumped together to form the Moon.

The Moon was also hit by rocks in space. These made huge craters, and mountain ranges of up to 16,404 ft high.

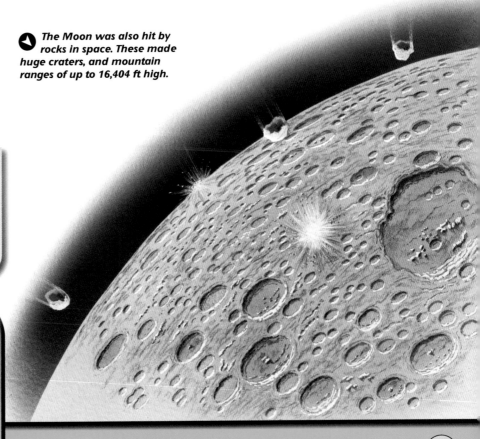

Amazing

Earth's first atmosphere would have been poisonous to animals. Early microscopic plants gradually converted carbon dioxide gas into oxygen gas for animals to breathe.

History of the Earth

4,600 mya	Sun formed
4,600–4,500 mya	Earth formed
4,500 mya	Moon formed
3,500 mya	Life appeared in oceans
400 mya	Life started on land
2 mya	Humans appeared

mya approximate million years ago

Spinning Earth

Though it seems perfectly still, the Earth is actually spinning around at an average speed of more than 994 mi/h. We are unaware of this rapid movement because we are locked firmly to the ground by gravity.

○ As the Earth spins and whirls through space, the view of the Sun from different places on the Earth is constantly changing, bringing not only day and night but all the seasons, too.

○ At any one time, half the Earth is facing towards the Sun and is brightly lit, while the other half is facing away from the Sun and is in darkness.

○ As the Earth turns, the dark and sunlit halves move around the world, bringing day and night to different parts of the world.

○ Because the Earth turns eastward, we see the Sun rising in the east as the Earth turns our part of the world toward it, and setting in the west as it turns us away from the Sun.

○ The Earth turns completely around once every 24 hours, which is why there are 24 hours in every day.

○ The Earth does not spin upright, but is tilted at an angle, which always remains the same.

○ When the Earth is on one side of the Sun, and the Northern Hemisphere (the world north of the Equator) is tilted toward it, it receives more sun, bringing summer.

○ At the same time, the Southern Hemisphere is tilted away from the Sun, bringing winter.

○ Six months later when the Earth is on the other side of the Sun, the Northern Hemisphere tilts away from the Sun and so there is less sunlight and it is winter here.

○ The Southern Hemisphere now gets more heat and light from the Sun and has its summer time.

○ The part of the Earth close to the Equator is never tilted far away from direct sunlight so it is always hot and there is little change in the seasons.

○ In between, as the Earth moves around the Sun and neither hemisphere is tilted more toward it, we have spring and fall.

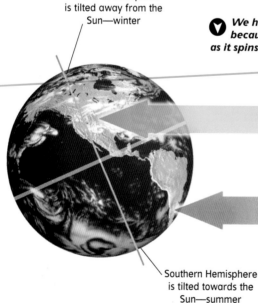

Northern Hemisphere is tilted away from the Sun—winter

Southern Hemisphere is tilted towards the Sun—summer

▼ **We have different seasons because the Earth is tilted as it spins round.**

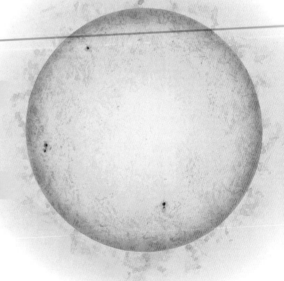

Find out more

Weather pp. 118–119

❍ The Earth takes 0.242 days longer than a calendar year to complete its orbit. To make up for this, an extra day is added to the end of February every four years. This is called a leap year.

Time zones

As the Earth rotates, the Sun rises in one place and sets in another, so time is not the same everywhere. So that noon is always at the middle of the day wherever you are, the world is divided into 24 time zones, one for each hour of the day. So at noon in London, it is 7 a.m. in New York. Some countries like Russia are so large that they have several time zones. The western side of Russia can be up to 11 hours different from the eastern side.

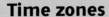
Axis

North Pole

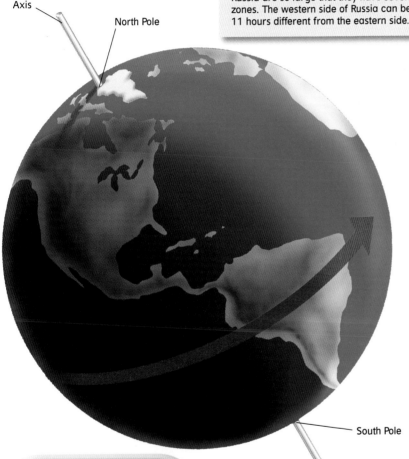

South Pole

❍ Near the North and South poles the Earth's tilt means that the Sun never rises in the middle of winter, and night can last for several weeks.

❍ In the middle of summer at the poles the Sun never sets and there is daylight all the time.

Amazing

The spin of the Earth is very gradually slowing down, but only by less than two thousands of a second in every hundred years.

❍ Around March 21 and September 21, the night is exactly 12 hours long all over the world. These times are called the vernal (spring) equinox and the autumnal equinox.

◀ *The Earth spins on its axis—an imaginary line between the poles.*

What's the time?

When it is 12 noon Greenwich Mean Time (GMT) in London, the time in other cities is:

3 p.m.	Moscow, Russia
5 p.m.	Karachi, Pakistan
8 p.m.	Beijing, China
9 p.m.	Tokyo, Japan
10 p.m.	Sydney, Australia
12 a.m.	Auckland, New Zealand
4 a.m.	Los Angeles, USA
6 a.m.	Mexico City, Mexico
7 a.m.	New York, USA
9 a.m.	Buenos Aires, Argentina

Earth speed

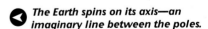

As the Earth spins around every 24 hours, places near the poles barely move at all, while places at the Equator whizz around at more than 994 mi/h. The extra speed of the Earth at the Equator flings it out in a bulge.

Ages of the Earth

The Earth was formed 4,570 million years ago (mya) but the first animals with shells and bones appeared less than 600 mya. It is mainly with the help of their fossils that geologists have learned about Earth's history. We know very little about the 4,000 million years before, known as Precambrian Time.

○ Just as days are divided into hours and minutes, so geologists divide the Earth's history into time periods. The longest are eons, thousands of millions of years long. The shortest are chrons, a few thousand years long. In between come eras, periods, epochs, and ages.

○ The years since Precambrian Time are split into three eras: Palaeozoic, Mesozoic, and Cenozoic.

○ Different plants and animals lived at different times, so geologists can tell from the fossils in rocks how long ago the rocks formed. Using fossils, they have divided the Earth's history since Precambrian Time into 11 periods. Layers of rock form on top of each other, so the oldest rocks are usually at the bottom and the youngest at the top, unless they have been disturbed. The order of layers from top to bottom is known as the geological column.

▶ *Experts use clues about fossils of particular animals or plants to divide the last 590 million years of the Earth's history into 11 units of time called Periods, each lasting many millions of years.*

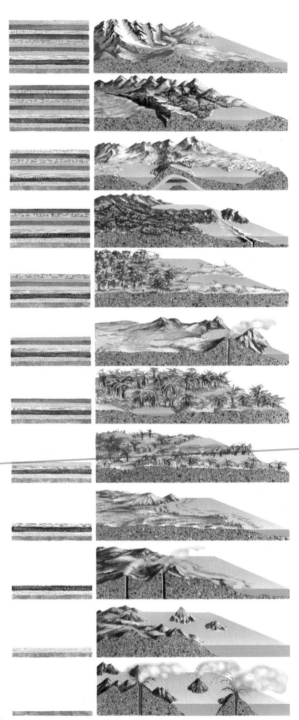

Quaternary 0–2 mya
Many mammals die out; humans evolve

Tertiary 2–65 mya
First large mammals appear; birds thrive; grasslands spread

Cretaceous 65–144 mya
Dinosaurs die out; first flowering plants

Jurassic 144–213 mya
Age of the dinosaurs; some dinosaurs evolve into birds

Triassic 213–248 mya
Mammals and seed-bearing plants appear

Permian 248–286 mya
Conifers appear, but many animals die out as deserts spread

Carboniferous 286–360 mya
Reptiles evolve; vast areas of swampy fern forests

Devonian 360–408 mya
Insects and amphibians evolve; ferns and mosses as big as trees

Silurian 408–438 mya
Plants appear on land and fish in rivers

Ordovician 438–505 mya
Sahara is covered in ice; fishlike creatures evolve in the sea

Cambrian 505–590 mya
No life on land but shellfish thrive in the oceans

Precambrian Time before 590 mya
First microorganisms appear, give atmosphere the oxygen larger animals need to breathe

Find out more

Fossils pp. 84–85

Amazing

The earliest evidence of living things on Earth are tiny threadlike fossils in rocks from 3.5 billion years ago, visible only under a microscope.

▲ **Megazostrodon** *probably fed like the shrews of today.*

○ By looking for certain fossils geologists can tell if one layer of rock is older than another, and so place it within the geological column.

○ Fossils can only show if a rock is older or younger than another; they cannot give a date in years. Also, many rocks, such as igneous rocks, contain no fossils. To give an absolute date, geologists may use radiocarbon dating.

○ Radiocarbon dating allows the oldest rocks on Earth to be dated. After certain substances such as uranium and rubidium form in rocks, their atoms slowly break down into different atoms. As atoms break down they send out rays, or radioactivity. By assessing how many atoms in a rock have changed, geologists work out the rock's age.

○ Breaks in the sequence of the geological column are called unconformities. They help to create a picture of the geological history of an area.

Long tail with tail backbones

▼ **Archaeopteryx** *could probably glide well, swoop, and turn as it chased flying prey, such as dragonflies. However, its long, strong legs suggest that it was also an able walker and runner. So it may have chased victims, such as baby lizards and cockroaches on the ground.*

Three clawed "fingers," midway along front of wing

Flight feathers suited to agile maneuver in the air

Teeth in long, light, jaws (all birds lack teeth today)

▼ **Indricotherium** *was three times bigger than elephants of today.*

▲ *The ammonite's body was covered by a spiral shell. The body rotted while the shell became a fossil.*

Inside the Earth

T he Earth is not a solid ball. Vibrations from earthquakes and volcanic explosions have revealed a complex internal structure. The Earth's crust rests on a layer of hot, partly molten rock called the mantle, which in turn surrounds the two cores, one inside the other.

The main layers inside the Earth from the boiling hot core to the hard rocky surface.

○ The Earth's crust is a thin, hard, outer shell of rock which is a few dozen miles thick. Its thickness in relation to the Earth is about the same as the peel on an apple.

○ There are two kinds of crust: oceanic and continental.

○ Oceanic crust is the crust beneath the oceans. It is much thinner—just 4 mi thick on average. It is also young, with none being more than 200 million years old.

○ Continental crust is the crust beneath the continents. It is up to 31 mi thick and mostly old.

○ The mantle makes up the bulk of the Earth's interior. It reaches from about 6–56 mi to 1,796 mi down.

○ Temperatures in the mantle climb steadily as you move through the mantle, reaching 8,132°F.

○ Mantle rock is so warm that it churns slowly around like very, very thick syrup boiling on a stove. This movement is known as mantle convection currents. Beneath the mantle is a core of hot iron and nickel. The outer core is so hot— climbing from an amazing 8,132°F to 10,832°F—that it is always molten. The inner core is even hotter (up to 12,632°F) but it stays solid because the pressure is 6,000 times greater than on the surface.

Continental crust (0–31 mi)

Oceanic crust of cold hard rock (0–6 mi)

Lithosphere, asthenosphere, and mesosphere (0–248 mi)

Mantle of soft, hot rock where temperatures climb steadily to 8,132°F (6–1,795 mi)

Outer core of liquid iron and nickel where temperatures climb to 10,832°F (1,795–3,200 mi)

Inner core of solid iron and nickel where temperatures climb to 12,632°F (below 3,200 mi)

Find out more
Earthquakes pp. 94–95

Earth's weight

The inner core contains 1.7% of the Earth's mass, the outer core 30.8%; the core-mantle boundary 3%; the lower mantle 49%; the upper mantle 15%; the ocean crust 0.099%, and the continental crust 0.374%.

Earthquake waves

Our knowledge of the Earth's interior comes mainly from studying how earthquake waves vibrate right through the Earth. Analysis of how earthquake waves are deflected reveals where different materials occur in the interior. S (secondary) waves pass only through the mantle. P (primary) waves pass through the core as well. P waves passing through the core are deflected, leaving a shadow zone where no waves reach the far side of the Earth. Love, or Q, waves shake the ground from side to side in a jerky movement. Rayleigh, or R, waves shake the ground up and down, often making it seem to roll.

S-waves move rocks up and down or side to side

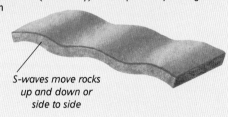

▲ Hot material from the Earth's interior often bursts on to the surface from volcanoes.

Amazing

In 1983 scientists in Russia drove the deepest borehole into the Earth's crust. It was 40,226 ft deep. The temperature of the rocks at the bottom was 410°F.

❍ The only time we see the hot molten rock of the mantle is when it bursts out through the crust in a volcanic eruption.

❍ Hot spots are places on Earth's crust where the hot mantle rock wells up nearer to the surface and breaks through to form volcanoes.

Rocks

Rocks are the hard mass of the Earth's surface. Some are just a few million years old. Others formed almost 4 billion years ago when the Earth was young, but they are always being added to as new rock forms.

❍ There are three main kinds of rock: igneous rock, sedimentary rock, and metamorphic rock.

❍ Igneous rocks are formed from molten rock called magma, deep inside the Earth.

❍ Magma is so hot, over 1,832°F, that it is molten rock. It is also crushed by enormous pressure. When magma gets pushed to the surface by volcanic action it cools to form igneous rocks.

▶ **Rocks are continually broken down and then remade in the rock cycle.**

❍ Sedimentary rocks such as shale and sandstone are made by the action of wind and water, which grind other rocks into sand and mud, carried by rivers until they are deposited as sediments.

❍ Sediment piles up in layers, and is squeezed hard by the pressure of layers on top, until it becomes rock.

❍ Metamorphic rocks are rocks that are formed when other rocks are changed by extreme heat and pressure, such as limestone, which hot magma turns to marble.

❍ Limestone and chalk are sedimentary rocks made mainly from the remains of sea creatures. All rocks are made of tiny crystals or grains of naturally occurring chemicals called minerals. Some rocks are made from just one mineral; others contain six or more.

❍ There are more than 2,000 different kinds of mineral, but only 30 or so occur commonly.

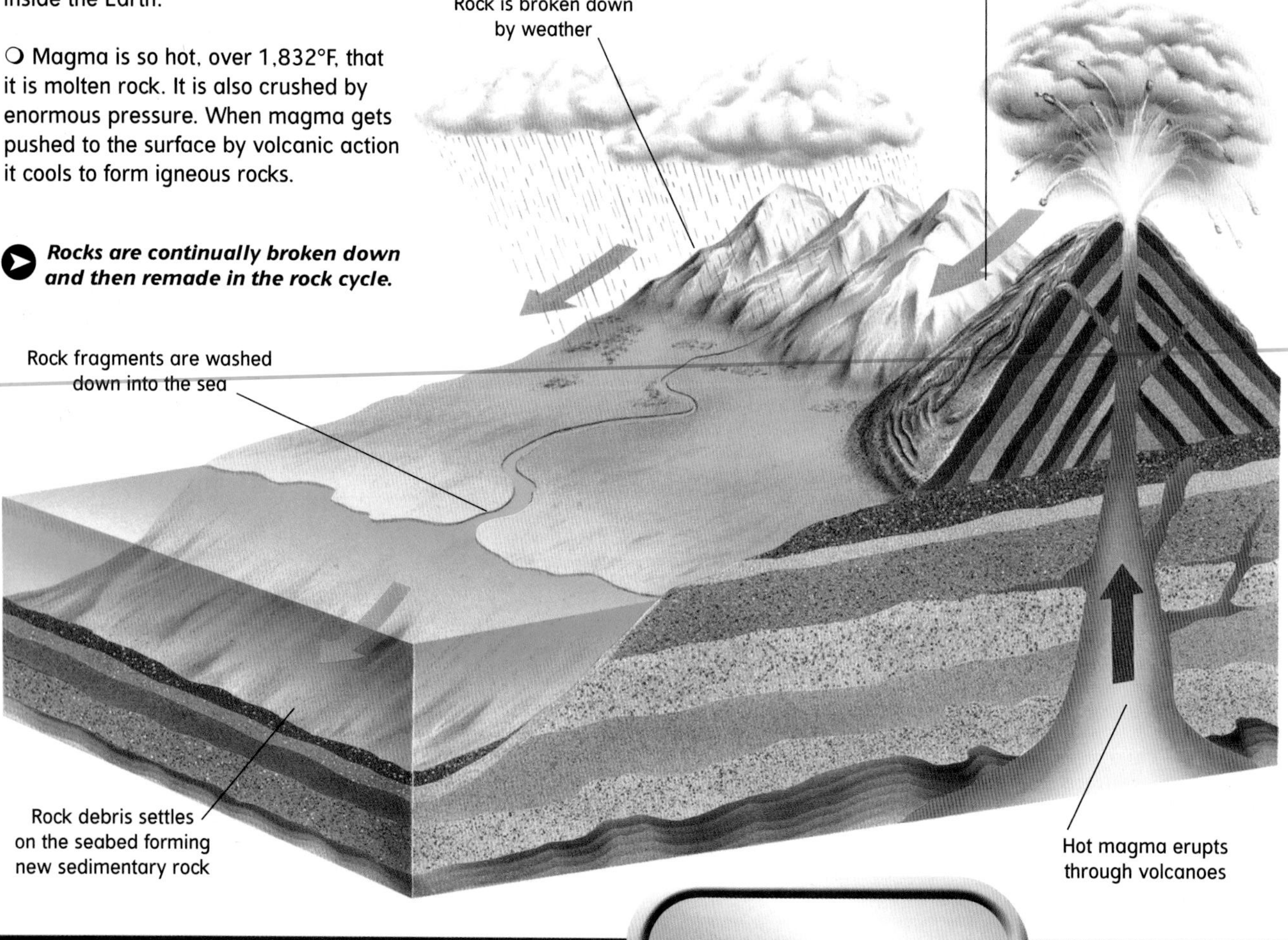

Lava cools to form igneous rock

Rock is broken down by weather

Rock fragments are washed down into the sea

Rock debris settles on the seabed forming new sedimentary rock

Hot magma erupts through volcanoes

Find out more

Weathering p. 96

Rock cycle

Rocks are continually recycled. Whether they form from volcanoes or sediments, all rocks are broken down into sand by weathering and erosion. The sand is deposited on seabeds and riverbeds where it hardens to form new rock. This process is the rock cycle.

◀ *The rich range of colors in each layer is evidence of traces of different minerals within the rocks. Many minerals found in rocks contain useful materials like metals.*

▲ *Most chalk was formed at the time of the dinosaurs but chalk is still forming in some places today.*

▲ *Scientists study the Earth's history to understand how it has changed, and is still, as natural forces reshape it.*

Chemical elements

Most of the Earth is made from just four chemical elements: iron, oxygen, silicon, and magnesium. Much of its rocky crust is made from combinations of two of these elements: oxygen and silicon, known as silicates. But there are small quantities of many other elements, such as aluminum and calcium.

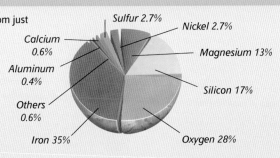

Sulfur 2.7%
Nickel 2.7%
Calcium 0.6%
Magnesium 13%
Aluminum 0.4%
Silicon 17%
Others 0.6%
Iron 35%
Oxygen 28%

Amazing

The oldest rocks found on Earth are 3,962 million years old, discovered in Canada. Some older crystals of zircon, 4,276 million years old, have been discovered near Perth, Australia.

Gemstones

The Earth is full of natural riches. Most metals are found in rocks called ores—mixtures of different substances, of which metal is one. Beautiful crystals grow in lava bubbles. There are more than 100 kinds of gemstone—colored rocks that are cut and polished. Gems, such as topaz, emerald, and garnet, formed in hot rocks that rose to the Earth's crust and cooled. Most are found as small crystals. Some are associated with different months of the year and are known as "birthstones."

▲ Silver forms branching wires in rock. It does not shine in its natural state like jewelry, but is covered in a black coating called tarnish.

▲ Quartz is a very common mineral. Occasionally it forms beautiful purple amethyst. Minute traces of iron in the rock turn the quartz to amethyst.

▲ This is bauxite, which is the ore of aluminum. Heat, chemicals, and electricity are used to get the metal out of the rock. Aluminum is used to make all kinds of things, from kitchen foil to airplane parts.

▲ A number of color varieties of beryl are known, many of which are gemstones. Emerald is the rich green variety of beryl, heliodor is yellow, morganite is a pink form, and aquamarine is greenish blue.

▲ Gold forms in small grains or large nuggets or veins in rocks. It can be melted and molded to form all kinds of jewelry.

Gemstones

Name	Type	Hardness	Color
Diamond	Carbon	10	Colorless
Ruby	Corundum	9	Red
Sapphire	Corundum	9	Blue
Emerald	Beryl	7.5–8	Green
Aquamarine	Beryl	7.5–8	Greenish blue
Garnet	Garnet	6.5–7.5	Dark red
Jade	Jade	6.5–7	Green
Lapis lazuli	Lapis lazuli	5–6	Deep blue
Opal	Opal	5.5–6.5	Milky white, blue, or green
Peridot	Peridot	6.5–7	Olive green
Amethyst	Quartz	7	Purple, violet
Topaz	Topaz	8	Yellow, brown
Tourmaline	Tourmaline	7–7.5	Pink, green + wide range
Zircon	Zircon	7.5	Green, brown
Turquoise	Turquoise	5–6	Blue-green
Amber	Fossilized resin	2–2.5	Orange, brown
Pearl	Oyster shells	3–4	White, cream

Amazing

Quartz is thought to have great healing properties. This may stem from its ability to vibrate consistently. A perfect quartz crystal can allow meditation at a deep level.

Birthstones

For nearly 2,000 years, crystals and precious stones have been linked with months of the year. Different religious and cultural groups have associated different stones with different months. Those popular in western culture today are shown here, together with their different characteristics. According to tradition, a person's birthstone brings them good luck. Gemstones also correspond to the signs of the Zodiac, although the birth dates for each month do not exactly match the beginning and end of each month. Birthstones may originate from a story in the Bible about Aaron, first high priest of the Israelites, whose breastplate is described as being decorated with 12 precious stones.

January, Garnet, Constancy

February, Amethyst, Sincerity

March, Aquamarine, Courage

April, Diamond, Innocence

May, Emerald, Love

June, Pearl, Health

July, Ruby, Contentment

August, Peridot, Married happiness

September, Sapphire, Clear thinking

October, Opal, Hope

November, Topaz, Faithfulness

December, Turquoise, Wealth

Fossils

Fossils are the remains of once-living things that have been preserved in rocks and turned to stone, usually over millions of years. Many kinds of living things from prehistoric times have formed fossils, including dinosaurs, mammals, birds, lizards, fish, insects, and plants such as ferns and trees.

▶ *Fossils are usually formed when an animal's remains were quickly covered by sediments, such as sand, silt, or mud, especially along the banks of a river or lake, or on the seashore.*

❍ When an animal dies, its soft parts rot away quickly. If its bones or shell are buried quickly in mud, they may turn to stone over time.

❍ When a shellfish dies and sinks to the seabed, its shell is buried. Over millions of years, water trickling through the mud may dissolve the shell, but minerals in the water fill its place to make a perfect cast.

❍ Fossil formation is a very long process and extremely prone to chance and luck. Only a tiny fraction of animals that ever lived have left remains preserved by this process.

❍ Because of the way fossils are formed, animals that died in water or along banks and shores were most likely to become fossilized.

❍ It is very rare to find all parts of an animal arranged as they were in life. Much more often, parts have been separated, jumbled, broken, crushed, and distorted.

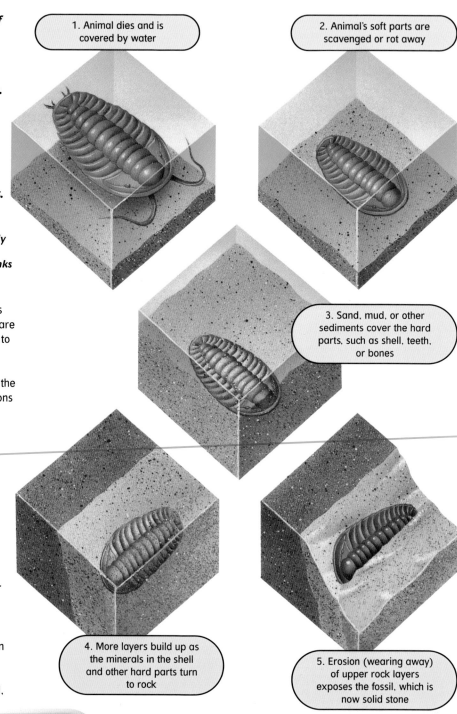

1. Animal dies and is covered by water

2. Animal's soft parts are scavenged or rot away

3. Sand, mud, or other sediments cover the hard parts, such as shell, teeth, or bones

4. More layers build up as the minerals in the shell and other hard parts turn to rock

5. Erosion (wearing away) of upper rock layers exposes the fossil, which is now solid stone

Find out more

Ages of the Earth p. 76

○ Many insects have been preserved in amber, the solidified sap of ancient trees.

○ Certain widespread, short-lived fossils are very useful for dating rock layers. These are known as index fossils. They include ancient shellfish such as trilobites, graptolites, crinoids, belemnites, ammonites, and brachiopods.

This fossil ammonite is a mollusc that swam in prehistoric seas. The soft body parts decayed millions of years ago but the impression of the animal's shell is preserved.

Fossilized footprints

Thousands of fossilized dinosaur footprints have been found all over the world. Some dinosaurs left footprints when they walked on the soft mud or sand of riverbanks. Then the mud baked hard in the sun, and was covered by more sand or mud, which helped preserve the footprints as fossils. Some fossil footprints were made when dinosaur feet left impressions in soft mud or sand that was then covered by volcanic ash, which set hard. The relative positions of footprints indicate how a dinosaur stood or moved.

○ "Trace" fossils were not actual parts of bodies, but other items or signs of their presence. Trace fossils include egg shells, footprints, and marks made by claws and teeth.

○ Not all fossils are composed of stone. Mammoths have been preserved by being frozen in the permafrost of Siberia.

Fossil of a Tyrannosaurus rex skull, a dinosaur that lived on Earth about 65–70 million years ago.

Amazing

The largest dinosaur footprints were found near Salt Lake City in the USA. They are 4.46ft long and 32 in wide.

Fossil discoveries

Sometimes scientists find a whole skeleton, which can be removed bone by bone and carefully reconstructed for scientific analysis or exhibition.

Continents

Emerging above the Earth's oceans are seven masses of land. These are the continents of North and South America, Oceania, Antarctica, Africa, Asia, and Europe. The continents are made of very old rocks, dating back some 3,800 million years.

The seven continents include Antarctica, which has land beneath its thick ice, but not the Arctic, which is mostly frozen ocean.

❍ Africa is a vast, warm, fairly flat continent covered in savannah, desert, and tropical forest.

❍ Africa is the world's warmest continent. It lies almost entirely within the tropics or subtropics. The very hot temperatures in the Sahara Desert are the highest on Earth, often soaring to over 122°F.

❍ Oceania is a vast region that includes islands spread over much of the Pacific Ocean as well as Australia and New Zealand. Australia is the only large land mass in Oceania.

❍ Oceania is mostly tropical, with temperatures averaging 86°F in the north of Australia, and slightly lower on the islands where the ocean keeps the land cool.

❍ Europe is the smallest continent, with an area of just 4,015,754 sq mi. For its size Europe has an immensely long coastline. Europe is joined to Asia and some people think that they should be one continent, Eurasia.

❍ North America is the oldest continent on Earth. It has rocks that are almost 4,000 million years old.

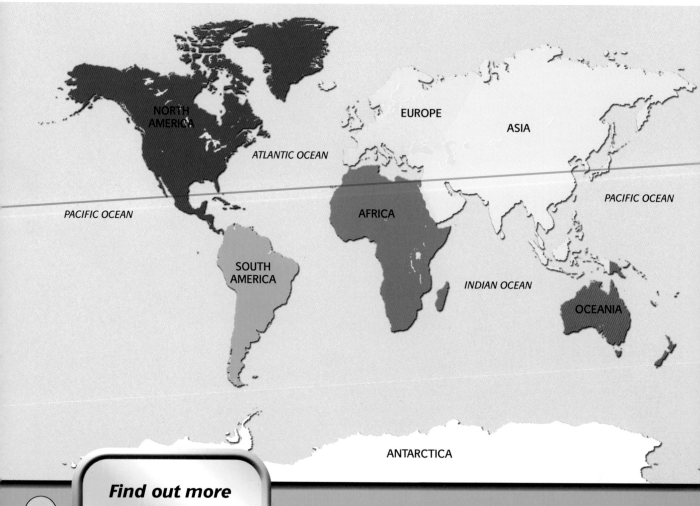

NORTH AMERICA

EUROPE

ASIA

ATLANTIC OCEAN

PACIFIC OCEAN

PACIFIC OCEAN

AFRICA

SOUTH AMERICA

INDIAN OCEAN

OCEANIA

ANTARCTICA

Find out more
Drifting continents pp. 90–91

○ The north of North America lies inside the Arctic Circle and is icebound for much of the year. Death Valley, in the southwestern desert in California and Nevada, is one of the hottest places on the Earth.

○ The heart of South America is the vast Amazon rainforest around the Amazon River and its tributaries. No other continent reaches so far south. South America extends to within 621 mi of the Antarctic Circle.

Asia

Asia is by far the biggest continent. The total land area of Asia is 16,989,728 sq mi, which is four times bigger than Europe and nearly twice as big as North America. Asia includes the biggest country by land area (Russia) and the two biggest by population (China and India).

▲ This tree in the Namib Desert of southwestern Africa manages to survive, even growing in such a hostile, dry environment.

◀ *Many penguins such as the emperor, the world's largest penguin, live on the ice floes of the Southern Ocean. Antarctica is so cold that no land animals live there, only sea creatures like penguins.*

Antarctica

Antarctica is the ice-covered continent at the South Pole. It is the coldest place on Earth. Even in summer, temperatures rarely climb over −13°F. On July 21, 1983, the air at the Vostok science station plunged to −128°F. Antarctica is also one of the driest places on Earth, with barely any rain or snow. It is also very windy. Antarctica does not belong to any one nation. Under the Antarctic Treaty of 1959, 12 countries agreed to use it only for scientific research.

Amazing

The continents are made of very old rock, some over 4,000 million years old. They are much older than the rocks that are found underneath the oceans.

▶ *The spectacular Iguacu Falls lie on the border between Brazil and Argentina in South America. Water thunders over 275 falls cascading 269 ft down into a gorge formed 100 million years ago. The horseshoe shape of the Falls is 2 mi wide.*

The seven continents

Asia	16,993,204 sq mi
Africa	11,678,894 sq mi
North America	9,351,687 sq mi
South America	6,885,473 sq mi
Antarctica	5,400,417 sq mi
Europe	4,032,357 sq mi
Oceania	3,300,254 sq mi

Islands

Islands are made in different ways. Some are the tops of undersea mountains or volcanoes. Others, such as the British Isles, were once part of a large landmass, but became surrounded by sea when the water level rose.

○ A chain of islands is called an archipelago. The world's biggest archipelago is Indonesia, with more than 13,000 islands.

○ New islands can appear out of the ocean. Surtsey Island off Iceland rose from the waves following a volcanic eruption as recently as 1963.

▶ *Surtsey Island, off Iceland, grew to a height of 557 ft in three years as lava and ash from repeated volcanic eruptions piled up above sea level.*

○ Reefs are made from the bodies of millions of tiny coral animals. In warm waters they often form rings around small islands.

○ Coral is the skeletons of tiny sea animals called polyps. Some polyps can grow to be 12 in across.

○ A coral reef is a rich habitat for wildlife. It provides food and shelter for all kinds of tropical fish.

○ There are thousands of tiny islands in the Pacific Ocean. Many are ringed by coral reefs.

Ⓐ *When volcanoes erupt under the sea, new islands may appear.*

Molten rock breaks through Earth's crust

As more lava is deposited on the seabed, a cone shape builds up

5 largest islands in the world

Greenland	Atlantic/Arctic Ocean	849,486 sq mi
New Guinea	Pacific Ocean	317,012 sq mi
Borneo	Indian Ocean	287,280 sq mi
Madagascar	Indian Ocean	226,658 sq mi
Baffin	Arctic Ocean	183,797 sq mi

Great Barrier Reef

The biggest coral reef on Earth is the Great Barrier Reef off eastern Australia. It is 1,243 mi long, and is made from over 400 different corals. The reef has taken more than 2 million years to form.

Amazing

The newest island on the Earth is a volcanic island that appeared in the Tongan group of islands in the South Pacific Ocean in 1995.

▲ *Sometimes a volcanic island sinks, and all that is left is a ring of coral, called an atoll.*

When this breaks the water's surface, a new island appears. The volcano may go on erupting

Greenland

The biggest island in the world is Greenland, at 1,659 mi long and 752 mi wide. It is owned by Denmark, but is 50 times bigger. Greenland is 85 percent covered by ice and has very little greenery!

▶ *The Indian Ocean is scattered with thousands of tropical islands such as the Seychelles and Maldives. Many of the Indian Ocean's islands have shining coral beaches.*

Different types of islands

Volcanic islands	Islands that appear when an undersea volcano grows tall enough to emerge above the surface of the ocean
Archipelago	Group of islands close together or an area of the ocean that has many islands in it
Coral islands	Islands in warm tropical waters that have built up from coral reefs
Freshwater islands	Islands in inland lakes or rivers where the water is fresh, rather than salty

Drifting Continents

Slowly, slowly, the Earth's surface is moving around beneath our feet. About 220 million years ago (mya) all the world's continents were joined together in one huge landmass that geologists call Pangaea. Pangaea gradually split up into today's continents.

▼ *The continents drifted to where they are today (continental drift) and are still moving.*

○ Continental drift is the name for the slow movement of the continents around the world.

○ It is not just the continents that are moving. The ocean beds are also moving. In fact, the whole of the Earth's surface is on the move.

○ The Earth's crust is made of curved rocky plates, which float like pieces of a gigantic jigsaw puzzle on the molten layer of hot rocks in the mantle.

Amazing

Scientists know that the continents were once all joined up because identical fossils of prehistoric plants and reptiles have been found in Africa, India, South America, and Antarctica. These continents have now moved away from each other to form separate continents.

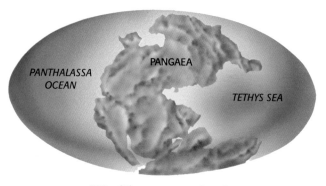

220 million years ago (mya)
There was just one giant land mass, called Pangaea (meaning "all Earth"), and one giant ocean, known as Panthalassa. But a long arm of the ocean, the Tethys Sea, stretched into the heart of Pangaea

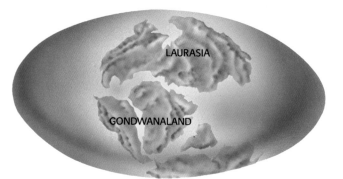

200 mya
Pangaea split either side of the Tethys Sea. To the north was Laurasia, including North America, Europe, and most of Asia. To the south was Gondwanaland, including South America, Africa, Australia, Antarctica, and India

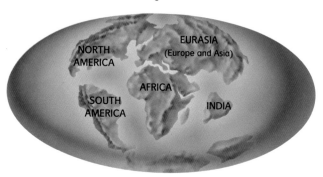

135 mya
The South Atlantic Ocean opened up between the continents of Africa and South America. India broke off from Africa and drifted toward Asia. Europe, and North America were still joined

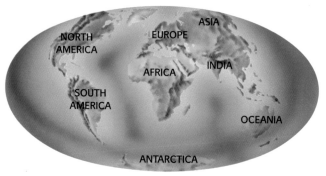

Today
North America and Europe are widely separated, having split 60 mya. India has crunched into Asia, Australia is moving into the tropics, and Antarctica has moved to the South Pole

Find out more
Continents pp. 86–87

○ Over millions and millions of years, the continents that rest on top of these plates also move.

○ There are seven large plates and some 20 smaller ones, and they move very slowly (between 0.5 and 4 in every year) on currents circulating within the mantle.

○ Strong evidence of continental drift has come from similar ancient fossils found in separate continents, such as the Glossopteris fern found in both Australia and India; the Diadectid insect found in Europe and North America; and Lystrosaurus, a tropical reptile from 200 million years ago, found in Africa, India, China, and Antarctica.

▶ *The jagged boundaries between the plates of the Earth's surface. Along these boundaries where the plates push together or slide past each other earthquakes and volcanoes occur.*

○ Rates of continental drift vary. India drifted north into Asia very quickly. South America is moving 9 in farther from Africa every year. On average, continents move at about the same rate as a fingernail grows.

○ Some tectonic plates have moved so far, they have traveled half way around the globe.

Major tectonic plates

Pacific plate
North American plate
South American plate
Antarctic plate
African plate
Eurasian plate
Indian plate

Tectonic plates

In some places, tectonic plates are crunching together. Where this happens, one of the plates—typically the one carrying a continent—rides over the other and forces it down into the Earth's interior. This process is called subduction. Where one plate dives beneath the other, there is often a deep trench in the ocean floor.

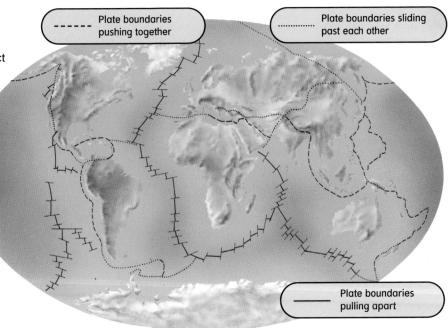

Plate boundaries pushing together

Plate boundaries sliding past each other

Plate boundaries pulling apart

Diverging plates

In some places, usually in the midocean on the seabed, tectonic plates move apart or diverge. As they move apart, hot molten magma from the Earth's interior wells up through the gap and solidifies on the exposed edges. So the seabed grows wider and wider. The floor of the Pacific Ocean is becoming wider by about 9 in every year.

Volcanoes

Volcanoes are places where hot molten rock or magma wells up to the surface from deep within the Earth's interior. When a volcano erupts, molten magma explodes from the main vent. Ash and lava pour out and flow down the side of the volcano. Gas, dust, and rock "bombs" are thrown into the sky.

▶ *The biggest volcanic eruptions are powered by a combination of steam and carbon dioxide gas. They remain dissolved in the magma inside the volcano because of the extreme pressure. But as the plug of magma breaks, the pressure is suddenly released, creating an explosion big enough to send chunks of rock the size of houses many thousands of feet up into the air.*

Amazing

The most active volcano in the world is Kilanea on Hawaii in the Pacific Ocean. It has erupted continuously since 1983 and produces lava at a rate of 176 cu ft every second.

❍ Eruptions begin with a build up of pressure in the magma chamber beneath the volcano.

❍ Bubbles of steam and gas form and swell rapidly inside the magma, and burst out like the foam from a violently shaken bottle of soda.

❍ As the steam and gas jet out, they carry with them clouds of ash and larger fragments of the broken plug of magma, called rock bombs or tephra.

❍ With the volcanic plug out of the way, magma surges up and out of the volcano, and flows down as lava.

❍ All the magma does not gush up the central vent. Some exits through branching side vents, often forming their own smaller cones on the side of the main one.

❍ Successive eruptions can build up such a huge cone of ash and lava around the volcano that it becomes a mountain.

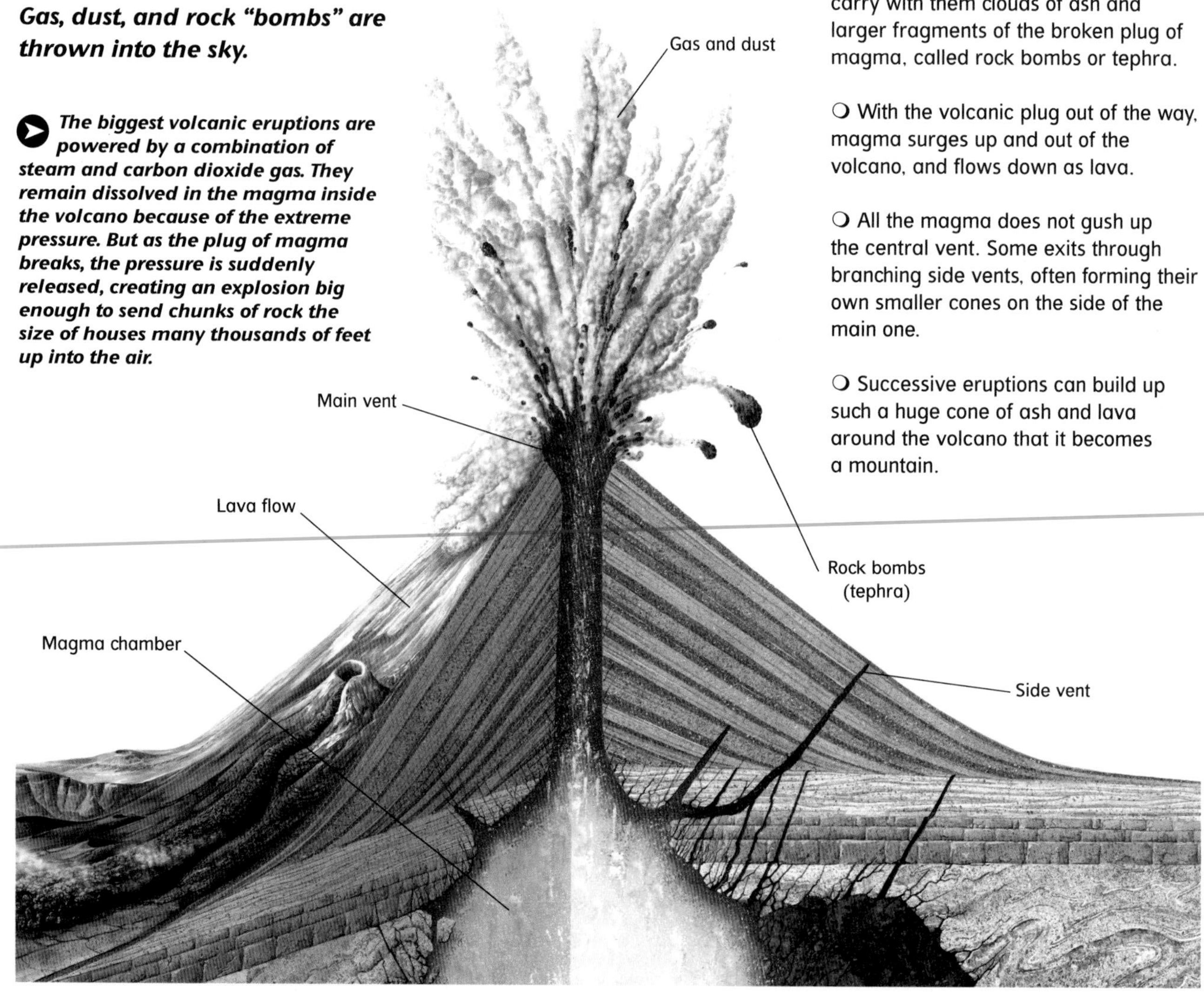

Gas and dust

Main vent

Lava flow

Magma chamber

Rock bombs (tephra)

Side vent

Find out more

Volcanic mountains p. 98

○ Where the magma is runnier, it reaches the surface easily and floods out steadily as lava to form a gentle slope that looks like an upturned shield, known as a "shield" volcano. Kilauea volcano on the island of Hawaii is a typical shield volcano.

A *Every now and then, mantle rock melts into floods of magma, which collects along the edges of tectonic plates. It then rises to the surface and erupts as a volcano.*

○ If the level of magma in the magma chamber drops, the top of the volcano's cone may collapse into it, forming a giant crater called a caldera.

Geysers

Geysers are spouts of steam and hot water. They are found in volcanically active regions. In 1903 a New Zealand geyser spurted to 1,509 ft high—the highest ever measured. The tallest geyser "blowing" today is Steamboat Geyser in Yellowstone National Park, USA (see above). Hot steam rises to a height of 377 ft.

○ The lava that gushes from the Hawaiian volcanoes in the Pacific is very runny. Because of this, the explosive gases leak out, and so the lava rarely bursts out in a huge explosion. Instead, it tends to spray out frequently in fiery fountains, or well out in slower streams of molten rock.

○ Active volcanoes erupt often. Dormant volcanoes do so only occasionally. Extinct volcanoes are safely dead and will not erupt again.

○ The biggest volcano is Mauna Loa in Hawaii, with a crater 6 mi wide and 590 ft deep. More than 80 per cent of this volcano is beneath the ocean.

○ There are more than 800 active volcanoes in the world. The country with the most is Indonesia, which has about 200.

A *Volcanoes in the Pacific spray out fiery lava fountains.*

Ring of Fire

Most volcanoes occur near cracks between the giant tectonic plates that make up the Earth's surface. Around the Pacific there is a ring of explosive volcanoes called the Ring of Fire. It includes Mount Pinatubo in the Philippines and Mount St Helens in Washington State, USA. There are about 60 major volcanic eruptions a year, including two or three huge, violent eruptions.

Major volcanic eruptions

Location	Date	Casualties
Tambora, Indonesia	1815	92,000
Santorini, Greece	c.1500 BC	Unknown, but probably destroyed the Minoan civilization
Krakatoa, Indonesia	1883	50,000 (the eruption was heard 2,485 mi away)
Mount Pelée, Martinique	1902	30,000
Mount St Helens, USA	1980	over 100

Earthquakes

Earthquakes are a shaking of the ground. Some are slight tremors that barely rock a baby's crib. Others are so violent they can tear down mountains and cities. Small earthquakes may be set off by landslides, volcanoes, or even just heavy traffic. Bigger earthquakes are set off by the grinding together of the vast tectonic plates that make up the Earth's surface.

○ Tectonic plates are moving all the time, radiating minor tremors as they grind past each other.

○ Every now and then they get jammed. Then the pressure builds up until they suddenly lurch on again, sending out vibrations, called shock waves, in all directions and creating major earthquakes.

○ Tectonic plates typically slide 1.5 in past each other in a year. In a slip that triggers a major quake they can slip more than 3 ft in a few seconds.

○ In an earthquake, shock waves radiate out in circles from its origin or hypocenter (focus).

○ Shock waves vibrate throughout the ground, but it is at the surface that they do most damage.

○ Damage is most severe at the epicenter—the point on the surface directly above the focus—where the shock waves are strongest. But they can often be felt up to thousands of miles away.

◀ During an earthquake, shock waves radiate in circles outward and upward from the focus of the earthquake. The damage caused is greatest at the epicenter, where the waves are strongest, but vibrations may be felt 621 mi away.

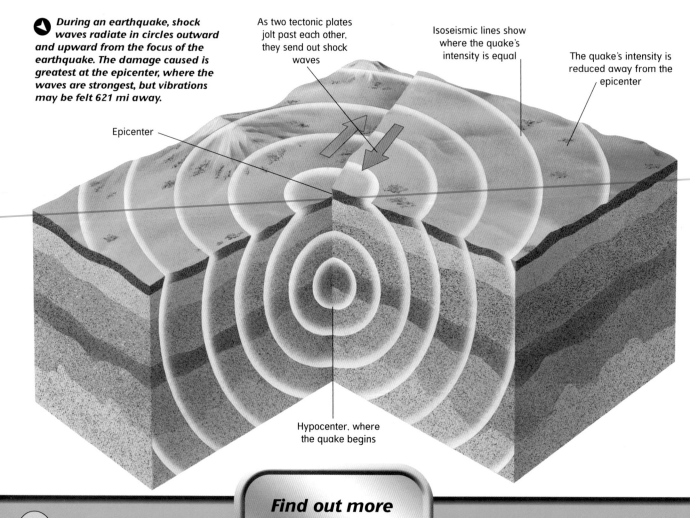

As two tectonic plates jolt past each other, they send out shock waves

Isoseismic lines show where the quake's intensity is equal

The quake's intensity is reduced away from the epicenter

Epicenter

Hypocenter, where the quake begins

Find out more

Drifting continents pp. 90–91

Richter scale

This scale indicates how much energy an earthquake has and thus how big it is.

1	Instrumental
2	Feeble
3	Slight
4	Moderate
5	Rather strong
6	Strong
7	Very strong
8	Destructive
9	Ruinous
10	Disastrous
11	Very disastrous
12	Catastrophic

Seismometer

Seismologists (scientists who study earthquakes) measure the strength of the shock waves with a device called a seismometer. They then grade the severity of the quake on the Richter scale, from 1 (slight tremor) to over 9 (devastating quake). Experts also rate an earthquake on the Mercalli scale, which assesses the damage on a scale of 1 (barely noticeable) to 12 (total destruction).

Tsunamis

Undersea earthquakes can produce huge waves, called tsunamis. These waves move at up to 497 mi/h but may not be noticed in the open ocean. In shallow waters however, the wave builds into a colossal wall of water up to 98 ft high, which rushes inland, drowning everything in its path.

A shift in the seabed sends out a pulse of water

As the pulse moves into shallow water it rears into a giant wave

Amazing

Each year around 800,000 earthquakes are detected by sensitive instruments worldwide. About 40,000 to 50,000 can be felt but don't do any damage, and less than 1,000 actually cause damage.

 In 1906, San Francisco in California, USA, was shaken by an earthquake that lasted three minutes. The earthquake started fires that burned the city almost flat. The earthquake was so strong that its effects were detected thousands of miles away. More than two-thirds of San Francisco's population were left homeless.

○ In most quakes a few minor tremors (foreshocks) are followed by an intense burst lasting just one or two minutes. A second series of minor tremors (aftershocks) occur over the next few hours. While aftershocks are less powerful than the main quake they can often add to the damage.

▲ *The Richter scale tells us how much energy an earthquake has— but the damage it does to somewhere depends on how far the place is from the center of the earthquake.*

Major earthquakes of the 20th century

Place	Date	Richter scale
San Francisco, USA	1906	8.3
Gansu, China	1920	8.6
Kanto Plain, Japan	1923	8.3
Assam, India	1950	8.6
Aleutian Islands, USA	1957	9.1
Tangshan, China	1976	8.2

Landscapes

The Earth's surface changes all the time. Most changes take millions of years. The surface is distorted and reformed from below by the huge forces of the Earth's interior. The landscape is molded from above by waves, weather, water, ice, wind, and other agents of erosion.

◐ Rivers are one of the most powerful agents of erosion. The Colorado River in the USA has worn away tons of rock, creating a huge canyon that extends for 277 mi.

Weathering

Weathering is the gradual breakdown of rocks when they are exposed to the air. Weathering works chemically and mechanically. Chemical weathering is when gases dissolve in rain to form weak acids that corrode rocks, such as limestone. The main form of mechanical weathering is frost shattering—when water expands as it freezes in cracks in the rocks and so shatters the rock. The landscape is shaped by the weather often into formations like this rock arch.

Amazing

The Grand Canyon shows the power of flowing water that has cut through rock to a depth of 5,249 ft in places and to a width of 9 mi.

Find out more

Weather pp.118–119

○ Mountains are made by movements of the Earth's rocky crust, pushed up by enormous pressure deep inside the Earth.

○ The Earth's landscape is changing all the time because of erosion, which is the wearing away of rocks and soil by "scouring" forces, such as wind, water, ice, and frost.

○ Most landscapes, except deserts, are molded by running water, which explains why hills have rounded slopes. Dry landscapes are more angular, but even in deserts water often plays a major shaping role.

○ Over thousands of years a river carves out a course through the rocks and soil, as it flows towards the ocean or into lakes. These river courses create valleys and canyons.

○ In winter, water trapped in cracks in rock freezes, expands, and causes chunks of rock to split off.

▼ *Cold conditions have a dramatic effect on the landscape.*

Glaciers

Glaciers move slowly but their sheer weight and size give them enormous power to shape the landscape. Over tens of thousands of years glaciers carve out winding valleys into huge, straight U-shaped troughs. Glacier lakes are created by glacial erosion, which deepens the valley floor. Water fills these valleys and moraine debris falls from the glacier to form a dam to keep the water in.

▲ *The desert heat means that both the chemical and the mechanical weathering of the rocks is intense.*

○ When water freezes in cracks in rocks, it expands and splits the rock with an estimated force of 6,613 lbs on an area the size of a postage stamp.

○ Heavy rain can quickly wash soil down a slope, especially if there are no trees on the slope to "bind" the soil.

○ The wind can make a mountain of sand. The Dune of Pilat on the French Atlantic coast has been created by wind and waves piling up sand from the bay over the last 200 years. The dune is 344 ft high, 1,640 ft wide and nearly 1.8 mi long.

▲ *The contours of hills in damp places have often been gently rounded over long periods by a combination of weathering and erosion by running water.*

Mountains

Mountains look solid and unchanging, but they are being built up, then worn away by the weather, all the time. The Himalayas, for instance, were built up in the last 40 million years, and are still growing.

○ All the world's great mountain ranges, such as the Andes and Rockies, were made by the crumpling of rock layers as tectonic plates pushed against each other. Such mountains are called fold mountains.

○ A few mountains, such as Washington's Mount St Helens, are volcanoes—tall cones built up by successive eruptions of lava and ash.

○ Fault block mountains are made when a section of rock tilts or is pushed up during a tremor. This happens along faults or breaks in the Earth's crust.

○ The Himalayan range in Asia has the world's 20 highest mountains, including Mount Everest, which rises to 29,078 ft.

○ The most ancient mountain ranges have long been worn flat, or reduced to hills, such as New York's Adirondacks, which are now over 1 billion years old.

○ The Andes is the longest mountain range, stretching for 4,498 mi along the western side of South America. The highest peak is Mount Aconcagua in Argentina. It is 22,834 ft high.

○ One side of a mountain range is often very wet. Approaching winds rise over the mountains, cooling and dropping rain on the windward side. The other side gets very little rain and often becomes a desert.

◀ *The highest mountain in the world, Mount Everest, is surrounded by other mountains that are almost as tall.*

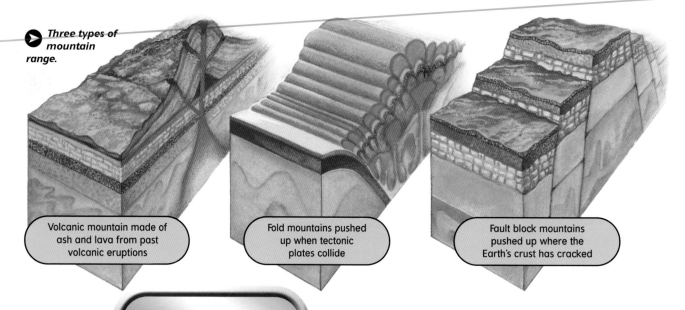

▶ *Three types of mountain range.*

Volcanic mountain made of ash and lava from past volcanic eruptions

Fold mountains pushed up when tectonic plates collide

Fault block mountains pushed up where the Earth's crust has cracked

Find out more

Atmosphere pp. 114–115

10 highest mountains

Everest	29,078 ft
K2	28,251 ft
Kangchenjunga	28,169 ft
Lhotse	27,939 ft
Makalu	27,762 ft
Cho Oyu	26,906 ft
Manaslu	26,758 ft
Nanga Parbat	26,656 ft
Annapurna	26,545 ft

Thin air

The air is thinner on mountains, so the air pressure is lower. Climbers may need oxygen masks to breathe. Temperatures drop 33°F for every 328 ft you climb, so mountain peaks are very cold and often covered in snow.

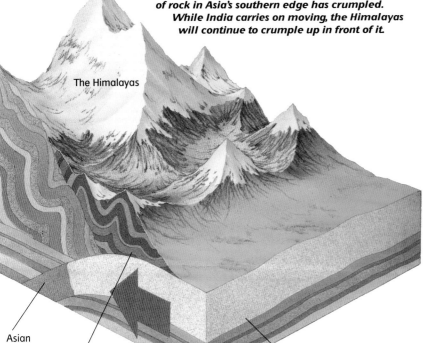

▼ *The Himalayas were thrown up by the collision between India and the rest of Asia. India has been plowing relentlessly north into Asia for the last 40 million years. As it does so, layer upon layer of rock in Asia's southern edge has crumpled. While India carries on moving, the Himalayas will continue to crumple up in front of it.*

The Himalayas

Asian plate

Folded rock layers

India moving north

Fold mountains

Most rocks form in flat layers called strata. Fold mountains build up where the movement of the Earth's crust tilts, crumples, and squeezes, and lifts these flat layers.

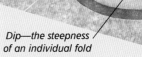

Strike—the direction of the folding movement

Dip—the steepness of an individual fold

Amazing

The tallest mountain measured from its base under the sea is Mauna Kea in Hawaii. From base to tip it measures 33,780 ft but only 13,795 ft is above the sea.

10 longest mountain ranges

The Andes	4,498 mi
Rocky Mountains	2,999 mi
Himalayas	2,399 mi
The Great Dividing Range	2,249 mi
The Transantarctic Range	2,199 mi
Brazilian Coastal Range	1,899 mi
Sumatra-Java Range	1,799 mi
Aleutians	1,599 mi
Tien Shan	1,399 mi
New Guinea Range	1,249 mi

▲ *The Andes mountain range is being pushed up along the western side of South America.*

Glaciers and Ice Ages

Glaciers are rivers of slowly moving ice. Today, glaciers only form in the highest mountains and in polar regions. But in the past, in cold periods called ice ages, glaciers were far more widespread.

❍ Glaciers begin in small hollows in the mountain called cirques, or corries. They flow downhill, gathering huge piles of debris called moraine on the way.

❍ Glaciers form when new snow, or névé, falls on top of old snow. The weight of the new snow compacts the old snow into denser snow called firn.

❍ In firn snow, all the air is squeezed out so it looks like white ice. As more snow falls, firn gets more compacted and turns into glacier ice that flows slowly downhill.

❍ When a glacier goes over a bump in the rock below it, or round a corner, the ice often breaks making deep cracks in the ice. These cracks are called crevasses.

❍ Ice ages are periods lasting millions of years when the Earth is so cold that the polar ice caps grow huge.

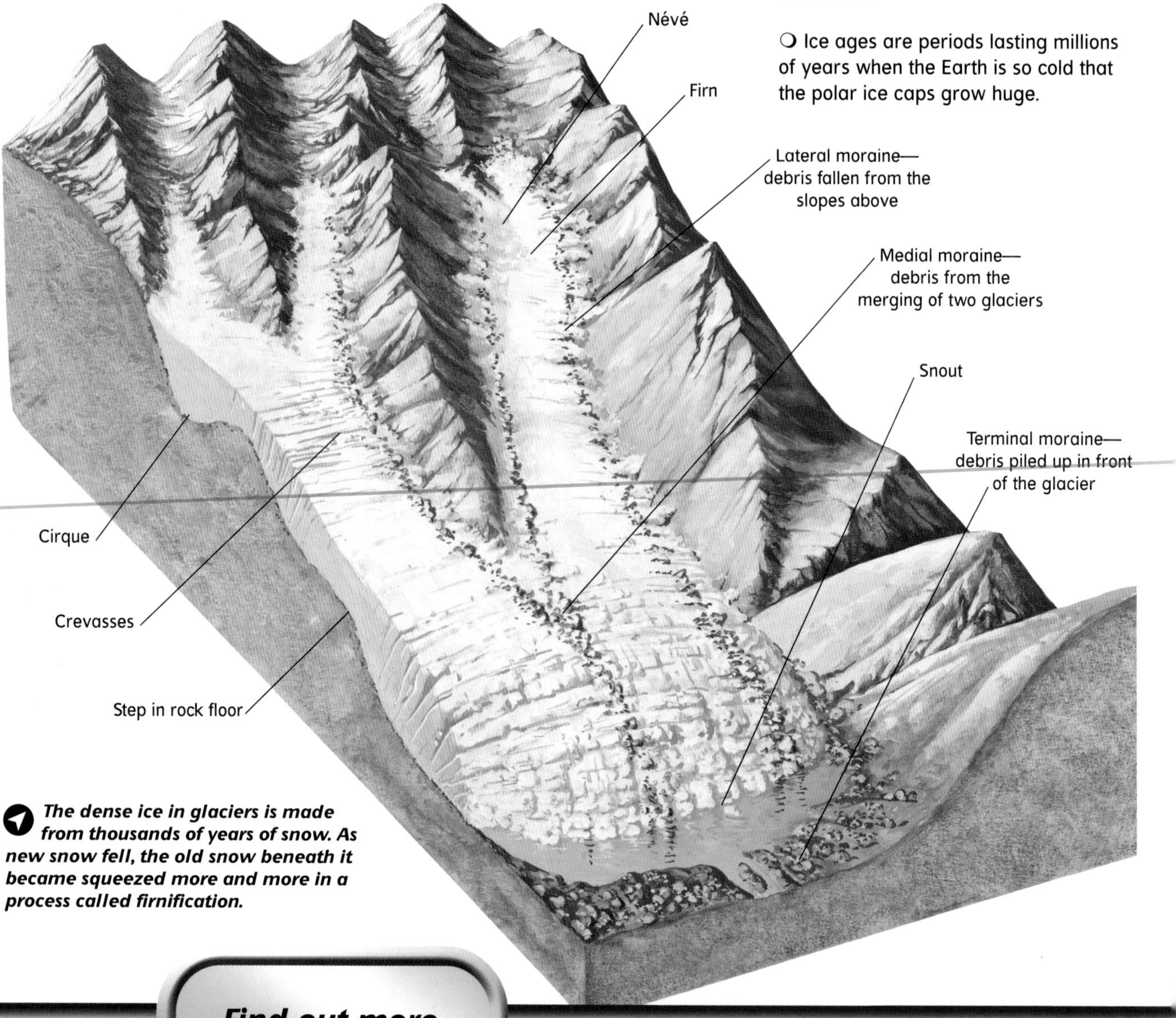

Névé

Firn

Lateral moraine—
debris fallen from the
slopes above

Medial moraine—
debris from the
merging of two glaciers

Snout

Terminal moraine—
debris piled up in front
of the glacier

Cirque

Crevasses

Step in rock floor

➤ *The dense ice in glaciers is made from thousands of years of snow. As new snow fell, the old snow beneath it became squeezed more and more in a process called firnification.*

Find out more

Landscapes pp. 96–97

Longest glaciers

Lambert-Fisher, Antarctica	320 mi
Novaya Zemlya, Russia	259 mi
Arctic Institute, Antarctica	224 mi

○ There have been four ice ages in the last 1,000 million years, including one which lasted 100 million years.

○ The most recent ice age—called the Pleistocene Ice Age—began about 2 million years ago.

○ Ice covered 40 per cent of the world and glaciers spread over much of Europe and North America 18,000 years ago. Ice caps grew in Tasmania and New Zealand. About 18,000 years ago there were glaciers in Hawaii.

○ Where Washington, USA, and London, England, are today, the ice was 0.9 mi thick 18,000 years ago.

Snowflake crystals

Snowflakes are made of masses of tiny crystals. These crystals grow together in an infinite variety of shapes and no one has ever found an identical pair. They fall from clouds in cold weather when the air is too cold to melt ice or rain.

▲ Around 15,000 icebergs calve each year in the Arctic.

Floating ice

Icebergs are big lumps of floating ice that calve, or break off, from the end of glaciers or polar ice caps. This often occurs when tides and waves move the ice up and down. Arctic icebergs vary from car-sized ones called growlers to mansion-sized blocks. The biggest Arctic iceberg, 7 mi long, was spotted off Baffin Island in 1882. Antarctic icebergs are much bigger than Arctic ones. The biggest Antarctic iceberg, 186 mi long, was spotted in 1956 by the icebreaker USS *Glacier*. About 11 per cent of a tall iceberg shows above water, the rest is submerged.

▲ Icebergs float out to sea where they can be a danger to shipping because nine-tenths of the iceberg is hidden beneath the water.

Amazing

The fastest flowing glacier is the Columbia Glacier in Alaska, USA. It moves at 114 ft per day and has doubled its speed in the last 20 years.

Sizes of icebergs

Category	Height	Length
Growler	Less than 3ft	Less than 16 ft
Bergy Bit	3–13ft	16–45 ft
Small	16–49 ft	49–196 ft
Medium	52–147ft	200–400 ft
Large	150–246 ft	403–698 ft
Very large	over 246 ft	over 698 ft

Rivers

Rivers are filled with water from rainfall running directly off the land, from melting snow or ice, or from a spring bubbling out water that is soaked into the ground. Whenever there is enough rain or melting snow to keep them flowing, rivers run down to the ocean or to lakes.

Amazing

The world's rivers carry about 8,000 million tons of sediment, tiny particles of rock and debris, into the oceans every year.

▼ *A river changes in many ways as it flows from its source high up in the hills downward to the ocean.*

○ High up in mountains near their source (start) rivers are usually small. They tumble over rocks through narrow valleys, which they carved out over thousands of years.

○ All the rivers in a certain area flow down to join each other, like branches on a tree. The branches are called tributaries. The bigger the river, the more tributaries it is likely to have.

○ As rivers flow downhill, they are joined by tributaries and grow bigger. They often flow in smooth channels made not of big rocks but of fine debris washed down from higher up. River valleys are wider and gentler lower down, and the river may wind across the valley floor.

In its upper reaches, a river tumbles over rocks through steep valleys

The neck of a meander may in time be worn through to leave an oxbow lake

In its lower reaches, a river winds broadly and smoothly across flat floodplains

Over flat land, a river may split into branches

In its middle reaches, a river winds through broad valleys

Find out more

Floods p. 118

Longest rivers

Nile, Africa	4,144mi
Amazon, South America	4,001mi
Yangtze-Kiang, China	3,914mi
Mississippi-Missouri, USA	3,740mi
Yenisey/Angara, Russia	3,442mi

○ Rivers wear away their banks and beds, mainly by battering them with bits of gravel and sand and by the sheer force of the moving water.

○ Every river carries sediment, which consists of large stones rolled along the riverbed, sand bounced along the bed, and fine silt that floats in the water.

○ In its lower reaches a river is often wide and deep. It winds back and forth in meanders across broad floodplains made of silt from higher up.

○ A river slows down as it flows into the ocean, so it can no longer carry the load of silt it has collected along the way. Often, the silt is dumped in a fanlike shape, or a delta.

○ The Amazon River carries more water than any other river. It pours 203 billion gallons of water into the Atlantic Ocean every hour.

○ Oxbow lakes form when a river meanders (changes course) cutting off patches of water before linking back up.

○ The discharge of a river is the amount of water flowing past a particular point each second.

○ The world's rivers wear the entire land surface down by an average of 3 in every 1,000 years.

10 highest waterfalls

Angel Falls	Venezuela
Tugela	South Africa
Utigord	Norway
Monge	Norway
Mutarazi	Zimbabwe
Yosemite	USA
Espelands	Norway
Mara Valley	Norway
Tyssestrengene	Norway
Cuquenan	Venezuela

Waterfalls

Waterfalls occur when a river flows over a band of hard rock, and then over softer rock, which is more quickly worn away by the water. The hard rock forms a step over which the river pours, creating a waterfall. The highest falls are the Angel Falls in Venezuela, South America, with a drop of 3,212 ft.

⊙ *Near its source, the river tumbles over the rocks wearing them away to smooth pebbles.*

Water cycle

All the water on Earth is constantly recycled. The warmth of the sun makes water in the oceans "evaporate" or turn into water vapor in the air. The water vapor is blown over land by the wind. As the moist air rises over hills, it cools and turns into water droplets that fall as rain or snow. The rainwater finds its way into streams and rivers, which return it to the oceans.

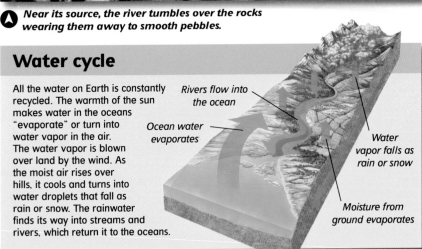

Rivers flow into the ocean

Ocean water evaporates

Water vapor falls as rain or snow

Moisture from ground evaporates

Lakes

A lake is a big expanse of water surrounded by land. Some lakes are so big they are called inland oceans. Most lake water is fresh rather than salt, but in some lakes so much water evaporates that the remaining water tastes very salty.

O Most of the world's great lakes lie in regions that were once glaciated. The glaciers carved out deep hollows in the rock in which water collected. The Great Lakes of the USA and Canada are partly glacial in origin.

O The world's deepest lakes are often formed by faults in the Earth's crust, such as Lake Baikal in Siberia and Lake Tanganyika in East Africa.

O Most lakes last only a few thousand years before they are filled in by silt or drained by changes in the landscape.

V *Many of the world's great lakes were formed by glaciation, and will eventually disappear.*

A *A salt island of crystal formations in the Dead Sea, a saltwater lake, in Israel. It is almost impossible to sink in the Dead Sea because of the amount of salt produced by scorching temperatures and high evaporation.*

Salt and freshwater

There is a huge amount of water in the world—over 207 million cubic mi—but 97 per cent is saltwater in the ocean. The other 3 per cent is freshwater, but most of this is frozen in ice sheets at the poles, or deep underground. Only a very tiny portion moves round in the water cycle.

Find out more

Underground lake p. 108

Amazing

The Aral Sea, a large lake in central Asia, is rapidly shrinking because the rivers that feed it have been diverted to irrigate farmland. The water level has dropped by over 39 ft since 1960 and its area has shrunk by one-third.

O Lake Baikal in Siberia, Russia, is about 25 million years old. It is 5,370 ft deep and contains about one-fifth of all the world's freshwater. The water is carried there by 336 rivers that flow into it.

O The Dead Sea in Israel and Jordan is well-named. This saltwater lake is the lowest lake on Earth—about 1,312 ft below sea level. In summer, scorching heat causes high evaporation, making the water so salty that a person cannot sink, and any fish entering the lake from the Jordan River die instantly. Only bacteria can survive.

O The Caspian Sea is the biggest lake in the world. But it is getting smaller because more water is being taken out for irrigation than flows into it from rivers.

O High in the Andes Mountains of Peru, straddling the border with Bolivia, is Lake Titicaca—the highest navigable lake in the world. It is 12,500 ft above sea level.

O The largest underground lake in the world is Drauchen-hauchloch, which is inside a cava in Nambia.

O The construction of dams creates large artificial lakes called reservoirs.

O Some lakes, called crater lakes, form as water collects in the hollow of an old volcano, like Crater Lake in Oregon, USA, which is 6 mi across.

▲ *Lake Titicaca is a vast expanse of blue water surrounded by snow-capped peaks. It is home to the native Indians, who live in floating villages made from huge reed rafts.*

Great Lakes

Canada and the United States share the five Great Lakes, so named because they are the biggest group of freshwater lakes in the world. They are: Lake Superior (the world's biggest freshwater lake), Lake Huron (the fourth largest lake in the world), Lake Michigan (the fifth largest lake), Lake Erie and Lake Ontario. Canada has the most freshwater (by area)—twice as much as any other country.

Lake Superior

Lake Huron

Lake Michigan

Lake Erie

Lake Ontario

Largest lakes

Caspian Sea, Asia	143,563 sq mi
Superior, USA/Canada	31,797 sq mi
Victoria Nyanza, Africa	26,836 sq mi
Huron, USA/Canada	23,013 sq mi
Michigan, USA	22,395 sq mi
Aral Sea, Asia	15,445 sq mi
Tanganyika, Africa	12,703 sq mi
Great Bear, Canada	12,278 sq mi
Baikal, Russia	11,776 sq mi
Malawi, Africa	11,429 sq mi

O During the colder winter months, powerful icebreakers are used to keep the Great Lakes free of ice so that the shipping routes remain navigable throughout the icy period.

Oceans and Seas

Viewed from space, the Earth looks like a planet of blue ocean—more than 70 per cent is water. About 97 per cent of all the Earth's water is in the oceans, which cover more than 139 million sq mi of the planet.

Surveys undertaken with sound equipment and computerized underwater craft have revealed a hugely varied landscape on the seabed, with high mountains, wide plains, and deep valleys.

❍ There are five oceans, which all connect to make one vast body of water. The three biggest oceans are the Pacific, Atlantic, and Indian oceans. They meet in the Southern or Antarctic Ocean. The Pacific and the Atlantic also meet in the smaller Arctic Ocean.

❍ Seas, such as the Baltic Sea, are smaller areas of saltwater, but most seas are joined to an ocean, such as the Mediterranean Sea, which is linked to the Atlantic Ocean at the Strait of Gibraltar.

❍ The Pacific is the world's largest ocean. It is twice as large as the Atlantic (the next largest) and covers an area of 70 million sq mi—one-third of the world.

❍ Around the edge of the ocean is a shelf of shallow water called the continental shelf.

❍ At the edge of the shelf, the seabed plunges steeply to the deep ocean floor—the "abyssal plain."

❍ This plain is vast, but not completely flat. In the Pacific especially, it is dotted with huge mountains, called seamounts.

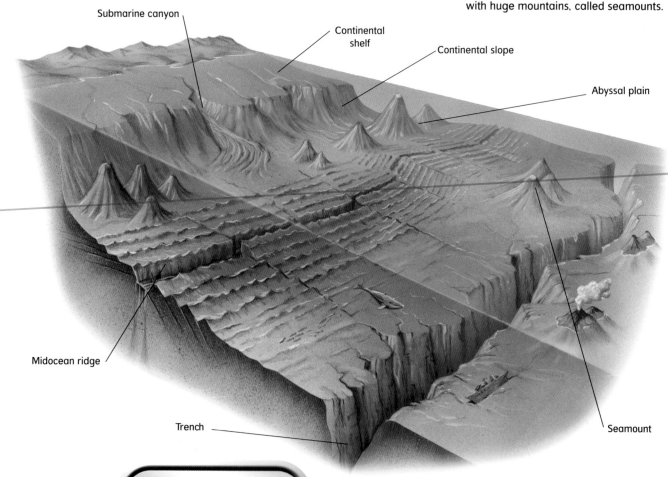

Submarine canyon

Continental shelf

Continental slope

Abyssal plain

Midocean ridge

Trench

Seamount

Find out more

Diverging plates p. 91

10 largest seas

South China Sea
Caribbean Sea
Mediterranean Sea
Bering Sea
Gulf of Mexico
Arabian Sea
Sea of Okhotsk
Sea of Japan
Hudson Bay
East China Sea

▶ *Where the ocean meets the land, waves batter the coast wearing it away and forming strange rock shapes. When a sea arch collapes, it leaves behind tall pillars called stacks.*

Amazing

Deep under the ocean where sunlight never reaches are black smokers, springs of water heated by volcanic rocks. Strange tube worms and blind crabs live there.

▶ *Some maps name the North and South Pacific, and the North and South Atlantic separately, but the Pacific and Atlantic are each one ocean.*

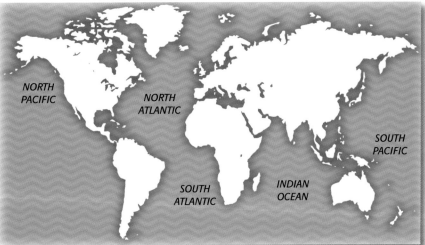

NORTH PACIFIC

NORTH ATLANTIC

SOUTH PACIFIC

SOUTH ATLANTIC

INDIAN OCEAN

Arctic Ocean

Most of the Arctic Ocean is permanently covered with a vast floating raft of sea ice. Temperatures are low all year round, averaging −22°F in winter and sometimes dropping to −94°F. During the long winters, which last more than four months, the Sun never rises above the horizon. The seal is one of the few creatures that can survive the bitter cold of the Arctic winter.

Tides

All around the world, the ocean rises and falls slightly twice every day in "tides." Tides are caused by the pull of the Moon's gravity on the oceans' waters as the Earth spins around. Spring tides (high tides) happen twice a month. They occur as the Moon and Sun line up with each other, combining their gravitational pull.

The sea moves or "flows" upward and inland as the tide rises

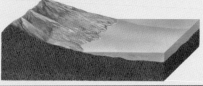

The ocean ebbs, sinking, and retreating, as the tide drops

Ocean depths

	Deepest point
Pacific	35,797 ft
Atlantic	30,246 ft
Indian	24,458 ft
Caribbean Sea	22,788 ft
South China Sea	16,456 ft

Caves

Caves are holes in the ground, usually hollowed out by water. Rainwater trickles down through the ground and dissolves the minerals in rocks, such as limestone, forming hollows and tunnels.

Amazing

The longest underwater cave system in the world is the Nohoch Nah Chich system in Mexico. Over 32 mi of underwater passages have been mapped by cave diving teams.

Cave animals

Cave animals include bats, birds, and even fish. Bats roost in caves, often in huge numbers, sleeping upside-down by day and leaving the cave at dusk to feed. Rarely disturbed by people, some caves have been home to bat colonies for thousands of years. Many cave species are blind and so rely on smell, touch, or echolocation (using echoes from sound to judge distances and obstacles) to find their way around in the darkness.

○ Soft rock in limestone caves is worn away by "chemical weathering". In the limestone, calcium carbonate reacts with rainwater to form a weak acid, which gradually dissolves rock. Water seeping down the rock forms cracks and potholes that open into caverns.

◑ *Limestone caverns and cave systems are eroded (worn away) by chemical weathering.*

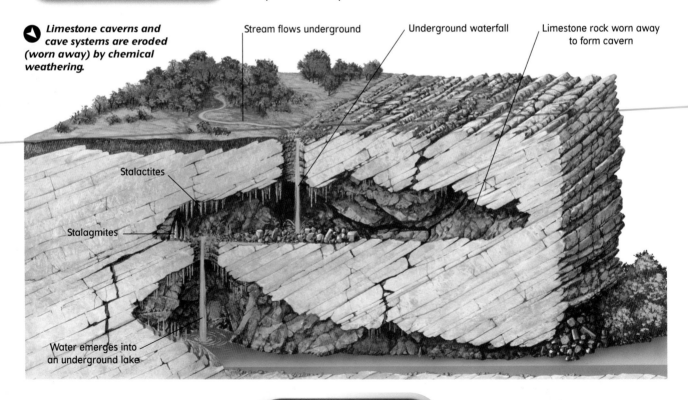

Stream flows underground

Underground waterfall

Limestone rock worn away to form cavern

Stalactites

Stalagmites

Water emerges into an underground lake

Find out more

Weathering p.96

Prehistoric cave paintings

Prehistoric people lived in caves, and some caves contain pictures of animals made by these cave dwellers. Stone Age people drew cave paintings of hunting scenes at Lascaux in France more than 15,000 years ago.

O Some caves are very long passages, and some caves are huge open spaces called caverns.

O Much more common are "potholes," which are deep, narrow passages, sometimes leading to caverns. Explorers crawl through potholes, or even swim through flooded sections of a cave, using flashlights to penetrate the gloom.

O Stalactites hang down like huge icicles from the roofs of caves. They form as water drips down and deposits calcium carbonate.

O Stalagmites grow up from the floors of caves as water drips down from the roof and deposits calcium carbonate.

O The world's longest caves are the Mammoth Caves of Kentucky in the USA, first explored in 1799. This system has 348 mi of caves and passages, with underground lakes and rivers.

O The biggest cave chamber is called the Sarawak Chamber, in a cave system in Sarawak, Malaysia. It is 2,296 ft long, has an average width of 984 ft and is about 229 ft from floor to roof.

O One of the longest stalactites on record measured more than 39 ft long. It was in a cave in Brazil.

▲ *Some cave systems contain huge caverns, large enough for people to stand in. Others are cramped and narrow, and can only be crawled through by cave explorers.*

▼ *A stalagmite more than 98 ft tall— higher than a house— was measured inside a cave in Slovakia.*

Deep caves

Krubera, Georgia, Asia	5,610 ft
Reseu Jean Bernard, France	5,225 ft
Shakta Pantujhina, Georgia	4,947 ft
Sistema Huautla, Mexico	4,839 ft
Sistema del Trava, Spain	4,727 ft
Vercors, southeast France	4,169 ft
Gunung Mulu, Borneo	1,541 ft
Carlsbad Cavern, USA	1,036 ft

Deserts

Dry desert, where the land gets less than 250 mm of rainfall in a year, covers almost one-eighth of the Earth's surface. Many are hot, but one of the biggest deserts is Antarctica.

○ The driest place on Earth is the Atacama Desert in Chile, South America. Intervals between showers may be as long as 100 years, and in some areas it has not rained for more than 400 years!

○ The biggest desert is the Sahara in north Africa, at 3,106 mi across and up to 1,398 mi north to south.

○ The vast Sahara takes in 11 countries of northern Africa, including Algeria and Tunisia, where there are "seas of sand," called ergs.

○ The Sahara Desert has the world's biggest sand dunes, some more than 1,312 ft high.

○ In the Arabian Desert is the world's biggest area of sand dunes—the Rub' al-Khali, which means "Empty Quarter" in Arabic.

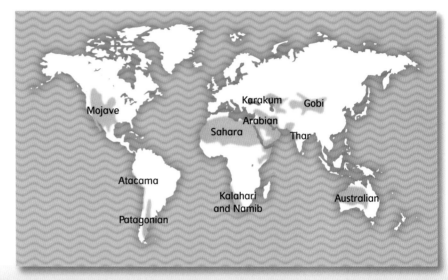

Mojave
Karakum   Gobi
Arabian
Sahara   Thar
Atacama
Kalahari and Namib   Australian
Patagonian

▲ *Hot dry deserts occur in warm areas where cool air sinks, warms up and absorbs moisture from the land. The world's biggest deserts are shown here.*

Amazing

Dallol in Ethiopia is called the hottest place on Earth with an average temperature of 93°F. But the hottest temperature ever measured was 136°F in the shade, in Libya in 1922.

▼ *Wind and sand have eroded, or worn away, these famous desert rocks in Monument Valley, Arizona, USA, giving them strange shapes.*

Find out more

Climate pp. 120–121

Temperatures in the desert can be scorching hot by day and near freezing at night.

○ Only about 20 percent of the Earth's deserts are sandy. The rest are rocky, stony, covered by scrub and bush, or ice-covered.

○ An oasis is a green "island" in the desert, a haven for thirsty travelers. Plants can grow there by tapping water from a well or underground spring. Even beneath the Sahara Desert a lot of water is trapped deep in the rock strata (layers).

Sand dunes

Loose sand is blown by the wind and piles up in wave-shaped formations called dunes. Sand is made up of tiny mineral grains, less than 2 mm across. Like waves of water, sand is blown up, rolls over the crest of the wave and down the steeper far side. Dunes move across the desert in this way.

Desert animals

Desert animals are able to go for days without water, getting most of the moisture they need from their food. These animals include mammals, such as antelope, camels, foxes, and rodents, as well as birds and insects. Other animals, such as desert frogs, go into a state of suspended animation in burrows until the next rain.

Largest deserts

Sahara North Africa, 3.4 million sq mi
Australian Australia, 1.5 million sq mi
Arabian Southwest Asia, 0.5 million sq mi
Gobi Central Asia, 0.4 million sq mi
Kalahari Southern Africa, 200,787 sq mi

Forests

Many trees covering an area of land create a forest. A wood is a smaller area of trees. There are different types of forest around the world, depending on the climate in the world's vegetation zones.

Amazing

Although tropical rainforests cover less than 8 per cent of the Earth's surface they contain half the world's growing wood and provide a home for 40 per cent of all plant and animal species.

○ In the warm tropics there are rainforests, seasonal forests, (where trees lose leaves during the dry season) and savanna (warm grassland) forests.

○ Rainforests are abundant with wildlife. There are more species of animals and plants in the Amazon rainforest than anywhere else on Earth.

○ Tropical rainforests grow luxuriantly because the rainfall is heavy and regular—often more than 2,000 mm of rain in a year.

○ A rainforest has different levels, like floors in a building. The thickest part is the main canopy, about 98 ft high, where most animals live. Taller trees emerge from the canopy.

○ The world's biggest rainforest is the Amazon rainforest of South America, which stretches from the foothills of the Andes Mountains in the west to the Atlantic Ocean in the east.

○ Rainforests also grow in cooler zones, where there is a lot of rainfall.

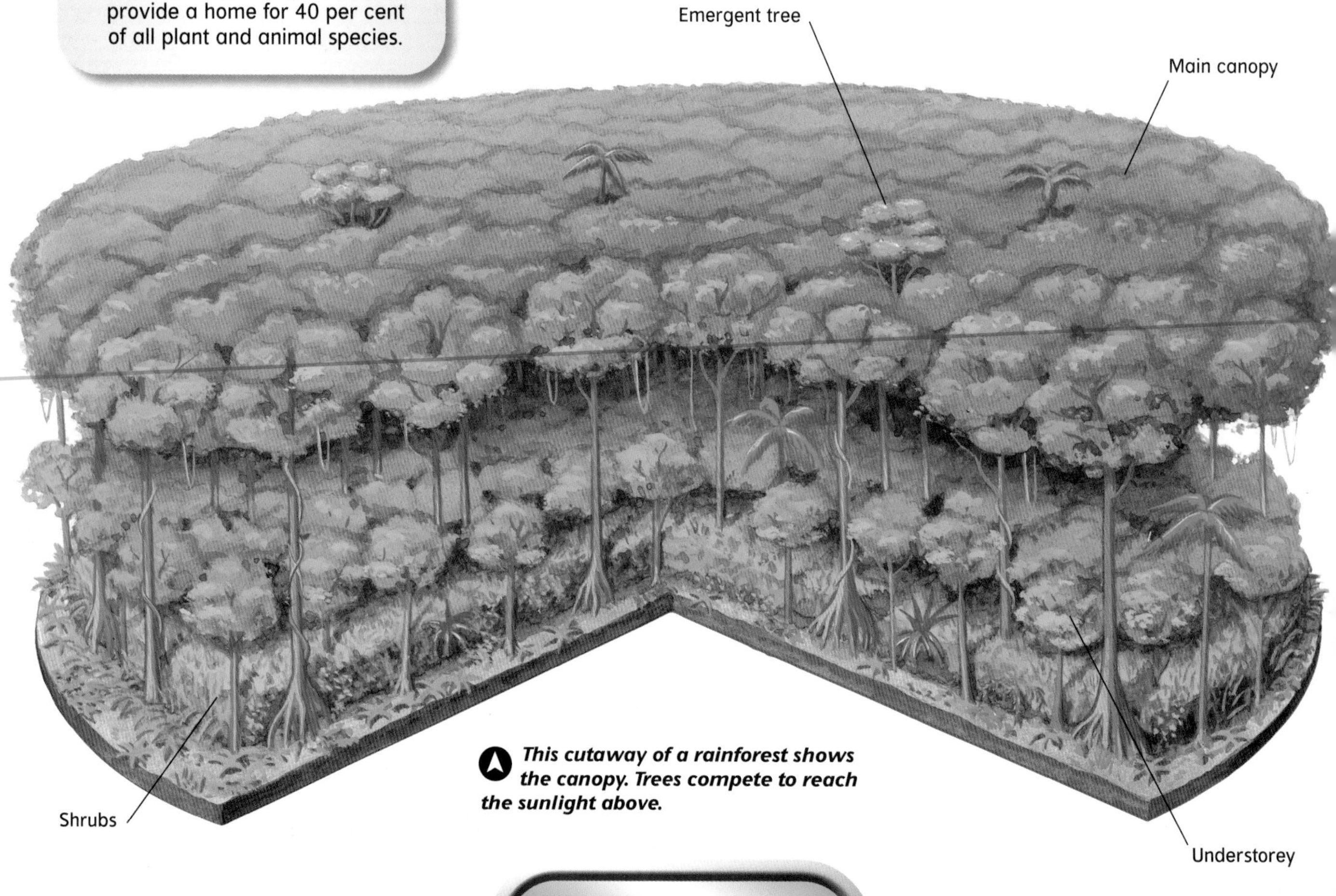

Emergent tree

Main canopy

Shrubs

▲ This cutaway of a rainforest shows the canopy. Trees compete to reach the sunlight above.

Understorey

Find out more

Forestry p. 125

Forest fires

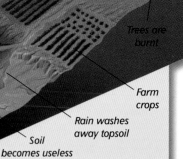

Forest fires can begin naturally, when vegetation is very dry after months without any rain. Often humans are responsible for starting the fires carelessly. Many forest trees and other plants regenerate quickly after a fire, but wildlife can be seriously affected. Forest fires can spread rapidly. Firefighters often cut trees to create a firebreak (strip of open ground) to stop flames spreading.

❍ In cooler zones, there are forests of mixed deciduous trees (which shed their leaves before winter), and of evergreen conifers, such as fir and pine.

❍ Trees in a deciduous forest shed their leaves to save water, because their roots cannot soak up water very well from cold soil. Deciduous forests grow in countries with warm summers and cool winters.

▲ *With high temperatures and heavy rain the rainforest air is always moist and misty. Vegetation and plants thrive in this atmosphere, growing rapidly. The different levels within the rainforest support many animals.*

Tropical rainforests

Many tropical rainforests are being destroyed to clear the land for farming and ranching. Felled trees are not replaced, leaving a wasteland littered with stumps. Widespread deforestation can have devastating effects on the landscape. Tropical soil rapidly loses fertility. Rain washes off the topsoil, and once lush forest becomes scrubland or desert.

Natural forest

Trees are burnt

Farm crops

Rain washes away topsoil

Soil becomes useless

Types of forest

Tropical rainforest Hot and wet regions, supporting a huge variety of plant and animal species

Deciduous forest Regions with warm summers and colder winters; trees lose their leaves in winter

Evergreen forest Cold climates; trees such as pines with narrow needles that lose less moisture and shed snow; supports fewer different species

The Atmosphere

The atmosphere is the layer of gases that surround the Earth. It is held in place by the Earth's gravity, which keeps most of the gases in the atmosphere close to the ground.

○ The atmosphere contains oxygen, nitrogen, and tiny amounts of other gases—argon, carbon dioxide, carbon monoxide, hydrogen, ozone, methane, helium, neon, krypton, and xenon.

○ The most important gas in the atmosphere is oxygen, because people and animals need to breathe it. When we breathe, we take in oxygen and breathe out carbon dioxide. Green plants, such as trees, take in carbon dioxide and give off oxygen during their food-making process (photosynthesis).

○ The atmosphere can be divided into five main layers: troposphere (the lowest), stratosphere, mesosphere, thermosphere, and exosphere.

Amazing

The atmosphere protects the Earth from space rocks. About 100 tons of rocks and dust enters the atmosphere every day but almost all of it burns up when it hits the atmosphere at high speed.

▶ *The atmosphere absorbs the Sun's warmth, yet shields the Earth from its most harmful rays. It gives us fresh, clean water to drink and provides us with the air that we, and most other animals, need to breathe.*

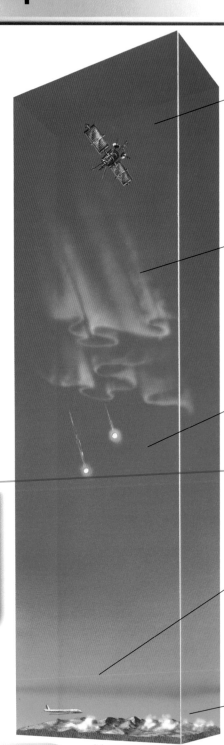

Exosphere 310–497 mi
Contains hardly any gas; low level satellites orbit here

Thermosphere 50–310 mi
Becomes roasted by the Sun to up to 3,272°F, but is so thin in gases that it contains little real heat

Mesosphere 31–50 mi
Is too thin to soak up much heat, but is thick enough to stop meteorites that burn up leaving fiery trails in the sky

Stratosphere 6–31 mi
Contains the ozone layer and becomes hotter higher up; little water and no weather; airliners cruise here in the still air

Troposphere 0–6 mi
Contains three-quarters of the atmosphere's gases and nearly all its water; temperatures drop by about 44°F every mile further down

Find out more

Hole in the ozone layer p. 123

In the Northern Hemisphere, winds spiral clockwise away from areas where the air pressure is high.

Winds spiral counterclockwise in toward low-pressure areas where the air is rising. In the Southern Hemisphere the directions are reversed.

○ At the bottom is the troposphere—only 6 mi thick, but containing over 70 per cent of the atmosphere's gases by weight.

○ All of Earth's weather, including clouds, is produced in the lowest layer of the atmosphere, called the troposphere.

Northern Lights

The Aurora Borealis, or Northern Lights, makes the night sky glow green, gold, red, or purple. The effect is caused by solar wind—radiation from the Sun—hitting Earth's atmosphere.

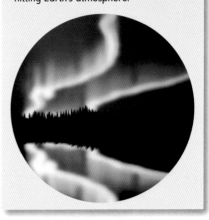

○ In the upper levels of the atmosphere is a layer of ozone (a form of oxygen), which forms a protective layer blocking out harmful ultraviolet rays from the Sun.

○ The gases become thinner and thinner with each layer, until at about 497 mi up, they are so thin or "rarified" that it is hard to tell where the atmosphere ends and where empty space begins.

○ Air pushes in all directions at ground level with a force of over 2 lb per sq in— that is the equivalent of an elephant standing on a coffee table.

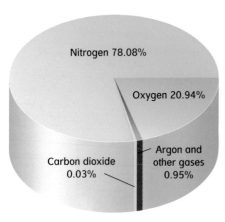

Nitrogen and oxygen together make up about 99 percent of the Earth's atmosphere.

Nitrogen 78.08%

Oxygen 20.94%

Carbon dioxide 0.03%

Argon and other gases 0.95%

Blue sky

The sky looks blue because light from the Sun is scattered by tiny particles of dust and moisture in the air. This breaks up the sunlight into its rainbow colors. The blue rays scatter most, so we see blue more and the sky looks blue.

Clouds

Clouds are dense masses of water drops and ice crystals that are so tiny they float high in the air. Most clouds eventually turn to rain, which falls back to the ground. This is called precipitation.

○ There is a large variety of clouds, but only two main shapes: fluffy, heaped "cumulus" that form clouds when air moisture billows upward; and flat "stratus" clouds that form when a layer of air cools down enough for its water content to condense.

○ Strong updrafts create huge cumulonimbus, or thunder, clouds. Cumulonimbus thunder clouds are the tallest clouds, often over 6 mi high.

○ Cumulus clouds are fluffy white clouds. They pile up as warm, moist air rises. Once the air reaches about 6,561 ft the air cools to the point where water vapor condenses and clouds are able to form.

○ Stratus clouds are vast shapeless clouds that form when a layer of air cools to the point where moisture condenses. They often bring long periods of light rain.

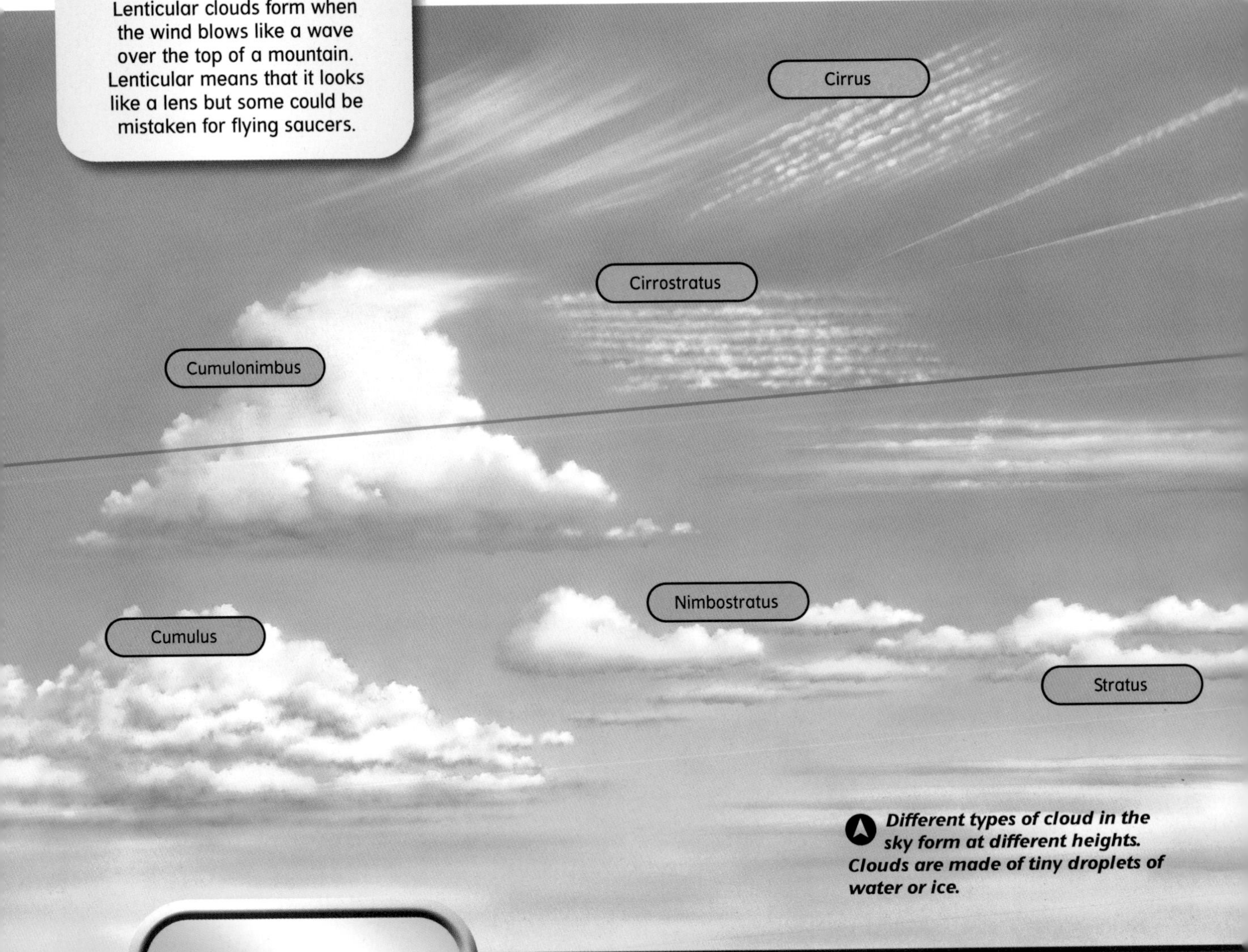

Amazing

Lenticular clouds form when the wind blows like a wave over the top of a mountain. Lenticular means that it looks like a lens but some could be mistaken for flying saucers.

Cirrus

Cirrostratus

Cumulonimbus

Cumulus

Nimbostratus

Stratus

Different types of cloud in the sky form at different heights. Clouds are made of tiny droplets of water or ice.

Find out more

Tropical storms p. 121

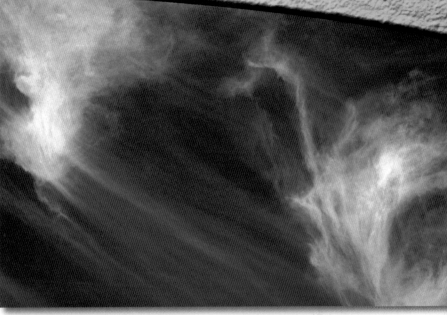

A ⬤ Cumulus clouds build up in fluffy piles as warm, moist air rises. Once it reaches about 6,561 ft, the air cools enough for clouds to form.

○ Cirrus clouds are wispy clouds that form so high up they are made entirely of ice. Strong winds high up blow them into "mares" tails.

○ Hailstones form when water droplets freeze inside a storm cloud then grow as more water freezes around them.

○ The highest clouds are the rare "mother of pearl" nacreous clouds, which can be found at 258,333 ft.

A ⬤ Feathery cirrus clouds high up in the sky are a clear warning that a warm front is on its way, bringing steady rain. When there is a warm front, a cold front is likely to follow, bringing heavy rain, strong winds, and perhaps even a thunderstorm.

○ The lowest clouds are stratus clouds, from 3,608 ft to ground level.

○ Contrails are trails of ice crystals left by jet aircraft.

Mist

Like clouds, mist is billions of tiny water droplets floating on the air. Fog forms near the ground. Meteorologists define fog as a mist that reduces visibility to less than 0.6 mi.

Rain clouds

Rain starts when water drops or ice crystals inside clouds grow too large for the air to support them. Cloud drops grow when moist air is swept upward and cools, causing lots of drops to condense. This happens when pockets of warm, rising air form thunderclouds. In the tropics raindrops grow in clouds by colliding with each other. In cool places, they also grow on ice crystals.

Types of cloud

Cirrus	Feathery white clouds
Cirrocumulus	Small patchy white clouds
Cirrostratus	Thin white sheets of clouds
Cumulus	White puffy clouds
Stratus	Low gray clouds
Nimbus	Dark heavy rain clouds

Weather

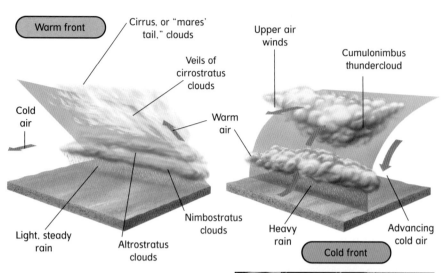

Warm front

Cirrus, or "mares' tail," clouds

Veils of cirrostratus clouds

Cold air

Warm air

Light, steady rain

Altrostratus clouds

Nimbostratus clouds

Upper air winds

Cumulonimbus thundercloud

Heavy rain

Cold front

Advancing cold air

At a warm front, warm air rises over cold giving rain. At a cold front, cold air pushes warm air upward giving heavy showers.

Winter weather is cold because the days are too short to give much heat. The Sun always rakes across the ground at a low angle, spreading out its warmth. Black ice forms when rain falls on a very cold road. Rime is a thick coating of ice that forms when moisture cools well below 32°F before freezing onto surfaces.

A satellite view of a large hurricane approaching Florida, USA. The yellow eye is the center of the storm.

Amazing

There have been many reports of frogs raining down from the sky. This is probably caused by a tornado sucking up frogs from ponds and streams then dropping them from clouds like rain.

The more of the Sun's energy there is in the air, the windier it is. This is why the strongest winds may blow in the warm tropics.

A flood is when a river or the ocean rises so much that it spills over the surrounding land. Small floods are common—big floods are rare. So flood size is described in terms of frequency. A two-year flood is a smallish flood that is likely to occur every two years. A 100-year flood is a big flood that is likely to occur once a century. A flash flood occurs after a small stream changes to a raging torrent after heavy rain in a dry spell. Even when no one drowns, a flood can destroy homes and wash away soil from farmland, leaving it barren.

Rainbow mnemonic

Richard **O**f **Y**ork **G**ave **B**attle **I**n **V**ain
Red, Orange, Yellow, Green, Blue, Indigo, Violet

Find out more
Climate pp. 120–121

10 types of lightning

Anvil
Ball
Bead
Cloud to air
Cloud to cloud
Cloud to ground
Forked
Ribbon
Sheet
Staccato

A tornado starts deep inside a thundercloud, where a column of strongly rising warm air is set spinning by high winds roaring through the cloud's top. As air is sucked into this column, or mesocyclone, it corkscrews down to the ground.

Fresh snow can contain up to 90 percent air, which is why snow can actually insulate the ground and keep it warm, protecting plants.

Without sunshine, the Earth would be cold, dark, and dead.

Hailstones can be as big as melons. These chunks of ice can fall from thunderclouds. The biggest ones ever fell in Gopaljang, Bangladesh, in 1986 and weighed 2 lb each.

A drought is a long period when there is little or no rain. During a drought the soil dries out, streams stop flowing, groundwater sinks, and plants die. Drought bakes the soil so hard that it shrinks and cracks. It will no longer absorb water even when rain comes.

Rainbows are caused by sunlight passing through falling raindrops. The water acts like a glass prism, splitting the light. White light is made up of seven colors—red, orange, yellow, green, blue, indigo, and violet—so these are the colors, from top to bottom, that make up the rainbow.

Beaufort Scale

		Wind speed
0	Calm	under 1 mi/h
1	Light air	1–3 mi/h
2	Light breeze	3–7 mi/h
3	Gentle breeze	7–11 mi/h
4	Moderate breeze	12–18 mi/h
5	Fresh breeze	19–24 mi/h
6	Strong breeze	25–31 mi/h
7	Moderate gale	32–38 mi/h
8	Fresh gale	39–46 mi/h
9	Strong gale	47–54 mi/h
10	Storm	55–63 mi/h
11	Violent storm	63–72 mi/h
12–17	Hurricane	73 mi/h and above

Climate

The nearer a place is to the Equator, the warmer the weather, or climate, tends to be. The effect is to give the world three broad climate bands which fall either side of the Equator: the warm tropics, the cold polar regions, and a moderate "temperate" zone in between.

○ Climates are warm near the Equator, where the Sun climbs high in the sky. Tropical climates are warm climates in the tropical zones on either side of the Equator. Average temperatures of 80°F are typical.

○ The climate is cool near the Poles, where the Sun never climbs high in the sky. Average temperatures of −22°F are typical.

The warmth of a region's climate depends on how close it is to the Equator. But oceans and mountain ranges have a huge influence too, so the pattern of climate is complicated, with many local variations.

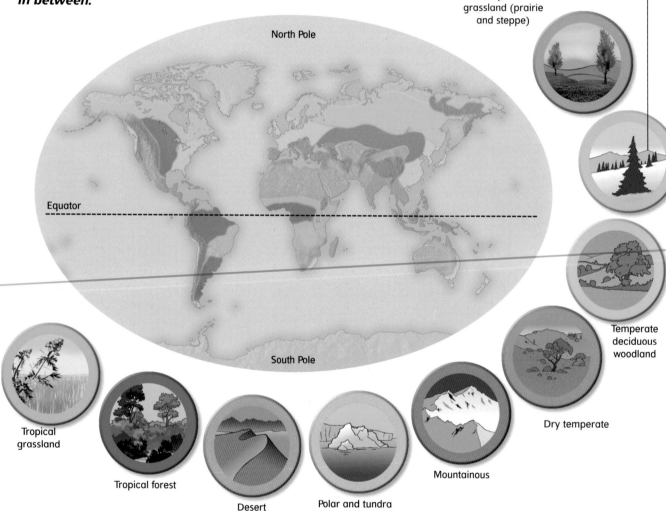

Cool conifer forest (taiga)

Temperate grassland (prairie and steppe)

North Pole

Equator

South Pole

Temperate deciduous woodland

Dry temperate

Mountainous

Polar and tundra

Desert

Tropical forest

Tropical grassland

Find out more
Rainforests pp. 112–113

Monsoons

A monsoon climate is a climate with one very wet and one very dry season. This climate is typically found in countries such as India and Southeast Asia. Hot air rising over the land pulls in warm moist winds off the sea bringing heavy rain. Then the winds change, blowing cool dry weather from the mountains.

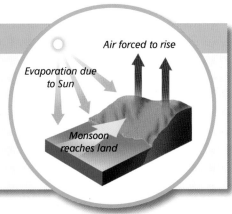

Air forced to rise

Evaporation due to Sun

Monsoon reaches land

Amazing

Volcanic eruptions can send enough dust into the atmosphere to change the world's climate for a short time. After Mount Pinatubo erupted in the Philippines in 1991 many parts of the world had cooler weather in 1992.

❍ Antarctica has the coldest climate. It is so cold that almost nothing grows and nobody lives there.

❍ Temperate climates are mild climates in the temperate zones between the tropics and the polar regions. Summer temperatures may average 73°F, and winter 54°F.

❍ An oceanic climate is a wetter climate near oceans, with cooler summers and warmer winters.

❍ A continental climate is a drier climate in the center of continents, with hot summers and cold winters.

◀ *California, USA, may have looked something like this 18,000 years ago when it was on the fringes of an ice sheet.*

❍ One of the most pleasant climates in the world is Quito in Ecuador. It rarely drops below 46°F at night, nor rises above 72°F during the day, and 100 mm of rain falls reliably each month of the wet season.

❍ One of the world's hottest places is Dallol in Ethiopia, Africa, where typical temperatures are on average 93.9°F.

❍ One of the world's wettest places is Tutunendo in Colombia, which gets about 461 in of rain every year.

Tropical storms

Some tropical places are warm and dry, including hot deserts such as the Sahara; some are warm and wet. Where it is wet, it tends to be very wet indeed, since the warm air takes up huge amounts of moisture. Large thunderclouds often build up in the morning heat, then unleash torrents of rain in the afternoon. Steamy rainforests flourish in this hot, moist climate.

Global Warming

Global warming is the general increase in average temperatures around the world. This increase has been between 32.5°F and 33.4°F over the last 100 years. Most scientists now think that global warming is caused by human activities, which have resulted in an increase in the Earth's natural greenhouse effect. Humans have added carbon dioxide gas to the air by burning coal, oil, and gas at an increasing rate in the demand for electricity and car travel.

▲ *Increase in global temperatures may turn some places into deserts, while others could become wetter as well as hotter.*

○ The greenhouse effect is the way that certain gases in the air—notably carbon dioxide—trap some of the Sun's warmth like the panes of glass in the walls and roof of a greenhouse.

○ When heat from the Sun reaches the Earth, some of it penetrates the atmosphere and reaches the ground. Much of this heat is then reflected back into space. Certain gases in the air trap heat reflected from the ground.

○ In the past, this natural "greenhouse effect" has kept the Earth comfortably warm.

○ The gases pumped into the air by the burning of coal and oil in factories and cars, for example, have trapped much more heat.

○ Scientists believe that this is causing global (worldwide) warming of the climate, which could have devastating effects in years to come.

▼ *The greenhouse effect keeps the Earth warm by trapping heat.*

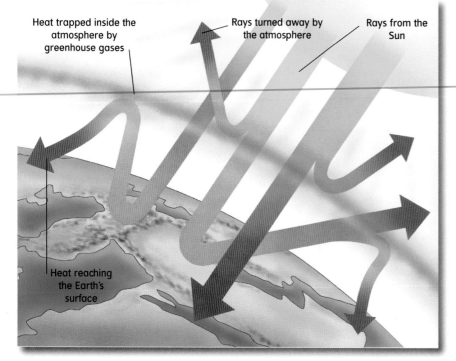

Heat trapped inside the atmosphere by greenhouse gases

Rays turned away by the atmosphere

Rays from the Sun

Heat reaching the Earth's surface

Find out more

The atmosphere pp. 114–115

Amazing

The greenhouse effect keeps the Earth at a reasonable temperature. Without any greenhouse effect the average temperature would be 91°F lower and the Earth would be covered in ice. It would be lifeless.

▶ *The lush vegetation of the world's rainforests absorbs carbon dioxide from the atmosphere. When the rainforest is cut down and burnt, not only does it stop absorbing, but the burning releases even more carbon dioxide to add to global warming.*

Cattle contribution

Cattle produce large amounts of methane gas digesting their food as they graze. This methane gas is an effective greenhouse gas. Rice fields also produce high levels of methane. It is estimated that methane is responsible for up to 20 per cent of global warming.

○ Global warming is bringing stormier weather by trapping more energy inside the atmosphere.

○ Many experts have predicted that there will be a 39°F rise in average temperatures over the next 100 years.

○ Global warming may melt much of the polar ice caps, flooding low-lying countries, such as Bangladesh.

○ Many countries have agreed to try and reduce global warming by limiting the amount of carbon dioxide their factories and cars produce.

Hole in the ozone layer

Life on Earth depends on the layer of ozone gas in the air, which shields the Earth from the Sun's ultraviolet (UV) rays. In 1982 scientists in Antarctica noticed a 50 percent loss of ozone over the Antarctic every spring. The loss of ozone is caused by manufactured gases, notably CFCs (chlorofluorocarbons), which drift up through the air and combine with the ozone. CFCs are used in many things, from refrigerators to aerosol sprays. CFCs were banned in 1996, but the hole is still growing. The levels of ozone are now constantly monitored by satellites looking down from space.

Greenhouse gases

Carbon dioxide Normally balanced—animals breathe it out but plants use it up. Increased by burning fuels in cars, factories, and power stations

Water vapor Naturally present in the atmosphere

Methane From animal waste, swamps, oil, and gas rigs—increasing

Nitrous oxide From car exhausts and chemical fertilizers—increasing

CFCs Used in fridges, aerosols, and foam packaging—now mostly banned

123

Resources

The Earth has many natural resources that sustain life. The planet has air, water, forests, minerals, and a range of environments that living things can use.

○ Some of these resources, such as the Sun's energy, are limitless.

○ Others are renewable, such as plants, which means that they can be regrown.

○ We cut trees for firewood and timber to make homes and furniture.

○ But some, like coal and oil, are nonrenewable resources. Once used, they are gone for ever.

○ Fossil fuels are oil, coal, and natural gas. Fossil fuels were made from the remains of plants and animals that lived millions of years ago. The remains were changed into fuel by intense heat and pressure.

○ Coal is made from plants that grew in huge warm swamps 300 million years ago in the Carboniferous Period.

○ Oil and natural gas were made from the remains of tiny plants and animals that lived in warm seas.

○ Metals, like coal, are mined from deep underground, but most have to be extracted from rock by fierce heating in a furnace with other chemicals.

A The Earth's surface contains an enormous wealth of mineral resources, from clay for bricks to precious gems, such as rubies and diamonds.

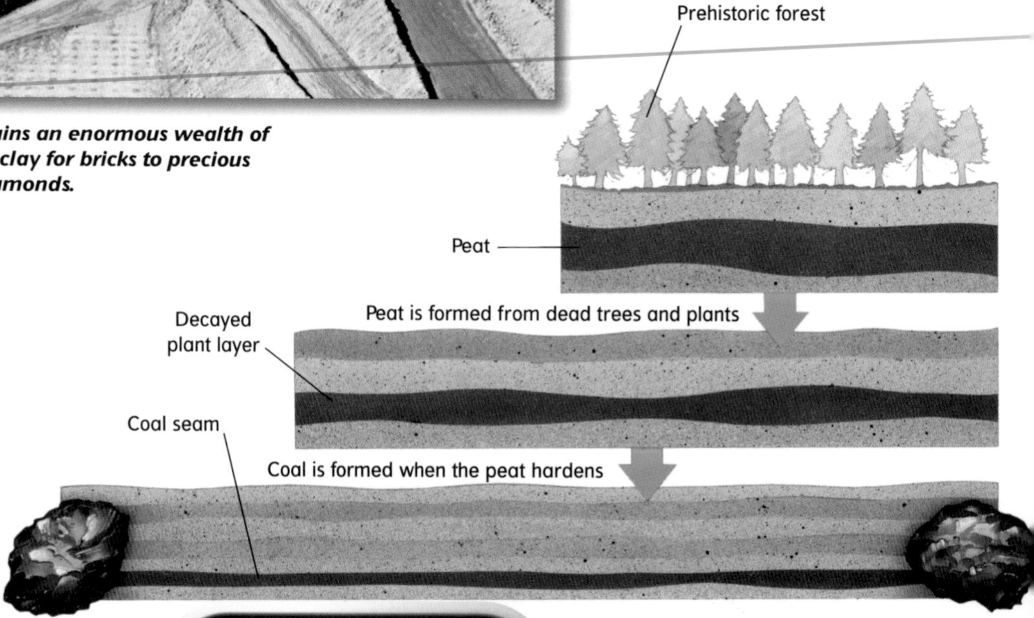

▶ This diagram shows how coal seams are formed over millions of years. Much of the coal lies deep beneath rock layers, called strata. The pressure of the topmost layer squeezes the layers below, turning sand and mud into hard rock, and plant remains from peat into coal.

Prehistoric forest

Peat

Peat is formed from dead trees and plants

Decayed plant layer

Coal seam

Coal is formed when the peat hardens

Find out more
Gemstones pp. 82–83

Oil is an extremely valuable natural resource that we use in our homes and for transport. It is found deep in the ground or below the seabed, pumped out by oil rigs that float in the sea, anchored to the seabed.

○ Ores are the minerals from which metals are extracted. Bauxite is the ore for aluminum; chalcopyrite for copper; galena for lead; hematite for iron; sphalerite for zinc.

○ Bulk materials, such as cement, gravel, and clay, are taken from the ground in huge quantities for building.

Amazing

Almost all energy on Earth came originally from the Sun. Coal and oil were made from the bodies of living plants and animals that grew using the Sun's energy.

Recycling

To save resources, much of our "rubbish" can be recycled—used again—in a variety of ways. Materials, such as glass, paper, and metals can be treated and processed in a factory to be reused in the same form.

Wind power

Wind power is one method of generating electricity without using up precious resources. The wind is a renewable resource because in many parts of the world it seldom stops blowing. Wind turbines with spinning blades are grouped in wind farms, which supply electricity to the grid system.

Managed forestry means replacing trees that are cut by loggers with new saplings (young trees) that will grow and ensure the forest survives.

Maps and Mapmaking

Geographers (scientists who study the Earth and its features) rely on maps. A map is a small picture of a large area, and is drawn to scale. For example, 1 in on the map might represent 1,000 mi of land on the ground.

Amazing

Satellites are now used to make very accurate maps, providing pictures of remote areas that are difficult to get to. They can accurately measure the heights of mountains and the depths of the oceans.

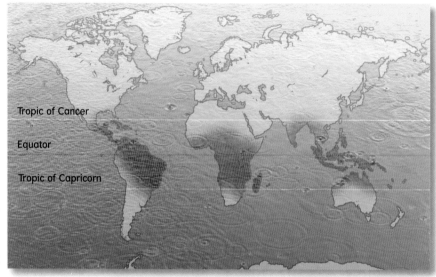

Tropic of Cancer

Equator

Tropic of Capricorn

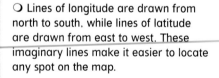

▲ The Equator is an imaginary line around the middle of the Earth, with the tropics north and south of it.

▼ The first reasonably accurate maps were made in Europe in the 1500s.

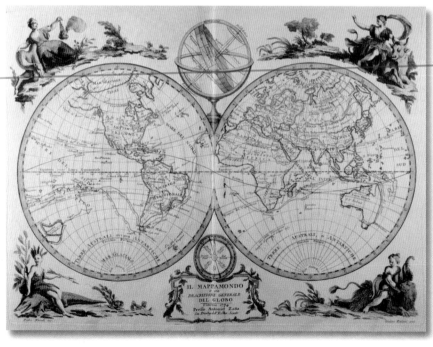

○ Early navigators used a sextant to measure the height of the Sun above the horizon to help them work out latitude. Finding longitude became possible in the 1750s with the invention of accurate clocks for use at sea.

○ Lines of longitude are drawn from north to south, while lines of latitude are drawn from east to west. These imaginary lines make it easier to locate any spot on the map.

○ A flat map of a sphere like the Earth cannot be accurate unless certain adjustments are made. If you peel an orange carefully, you will discover that the peel won't lie flat on a table without breaking (see Mercator maps box).

○ Maps are drawn such that one feature (such as land area) is accurate, but another feature (for example, shape) less so. These different ways of mapmaking are known as projections.

○ The Equator is the line of 0° latitude.

Find out more

Spinning Earth pp. 74–75

Mercator maps

One map projection is named Mercator after a Flemish mapmaker named Gerardus Mercator (1512–1594). This projection shows the correct direction between two points, because the lines of latitude and longitude are correct. It makes landmasses look wrong though —Greenland looks the same size as North America, which is actually really much larger. If the Earth were an orange and could be "unpeeled," this is what you would see. The curved surface cannot be transformed into a flat map unless some features are distorted.

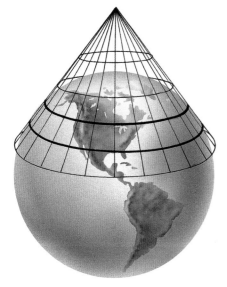

A *A conic projection of a globe projects the lines of latitude and longitude into a cone shape, which can then be flattened to give a picture of the wide landmasses, such as the USA and Russia, as accurately as possible.*

❍ The line of 0° longitude runs through Greenwich in London, England, and is known as the prime meridian.

❍ The tropics are the regions of the Earth that lie immediately north and south of the Equator.

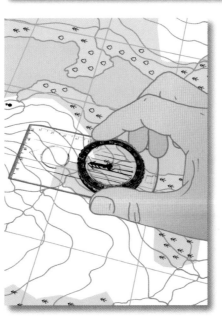

❍ The northern region is the Tropic of Cancer, the southern region is the Tropic of Capricorn.

❍ About 5,000 years ago people in Egypt and Babylonia made drawings to show who owned which bit of land and where rivers were. The oldest map in existence is a clay tablet found in present-day Iraq, which has what may be a river valley scratched on it.

◀ *The spinning Earth acts like a magnet. At the center of the Earth is liquid iron. As the Earth spins, it makes the iron behave like a magnet with a North and South Pole. These act on the magnet in a compass to make the needle point to the North and South poles.*

Global positioning systems

Global positioning system (GPS) satellites in orbit around the Earth can inform travelers where they are, to within a few feet. The satellites send out radio signals that are picked up by a computer on an airplane, ship, or car; three or more "fixes" give a precise position.

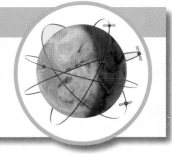

Glossary

Abyssal plain The broad plain on the deep seabed, 16,404 ft down and covered in ooze.

Atmosphere The thick layer of gases surrounding the Earth.

Aurora Spectacular displays of colored lights in the night sky above the North and South poles.

Black smoker Chimney-like vent on the deep seabed churning out superheated water that looks black because of the minerals dissolved in it.

Chlorofluorocarbons (CFCs) Man-made chemicals that probably damage the ozone layer in the atmosphere.

Climate Weather conditions that are normal for any particular place, e.g. deserts have a very dry climate and rainforests a very wet climate.

Continental drift The process whereby continents move slowly around the world, over millions of years.

Continental shelf A wide strip of seabed surrounding a continent or land mass. The sea here is much shallower than in the middle of the ocean.

Core The dense hot center of the Earth.

Crater A circular rocky shape surrounding a hollow often found at the top of a volcano or left after a volcano has erupted.

Crevasse A deep crack in a glacier.

Crust The solid outer shell of the Earth, varying from 3 to 50 mi thick.

Deciduous Trees that drop their leaves in winter and grow new ones in spring.

Deforestation Clearing a forest by cutting down the trees without replacing them. The cleared area is often used for farming.

Delta A flat piece of land, which has built up from material such as silt that has been deposited by a river as it flows to the sea.

Earthquake A brief, violent shaking of the Earth's surface, typically set off by the movement of tectonic plates.

Element A material made of only one type of atom. There are more than 100 elements on Earth.

Epicenter The place on Earth's surface directly above an earthquake's center. This is where most damage occurs.

Equator An imaginary line around the middle of the Earth dividing it in two equal halves.

Erosion The gradual wearing away of land and rocks, usually by wind, rain, ice, rivers, or waves.

Eruption The explosion of a volcano when it throws out rocks, lava, ash, and gases.

Fault A fracture in rock where one block of rock slides past another.

Firn Snow that has been packed down hard to make the ice in a glacier.

Fold mountains Mountains formed when the Earth's crust is squeezed into folds by the collision of two tectonic plates.

Fossil The preserved remains of a creature or plant long dead, usually turned to stone.

Fossil fuels Fuels such as coal, oil, and gas made from the remains of plants and animals that have been gradually squashed beneath the ground for millions of years.

Geologist A scientist who studies the structure of the Earth.

Geyser A fountain of hot water and steam that shoots out of a hole in the ground. The water is heated by hot underground rock.

Glaciation The molding of the landscape by glaciers and ice sheets.

Global warming The gradual increase in temperature of the Earth.

Gravity The pulling force that holds down everything on the Earth and stops it floating away.

Greenhouse effect The way certain gases in the atmosphere trap the Sun's heat like the panes of glass in a greenhouse.

Hemisphere Half of the Earth. The Southern Hemisphere is the half south of the Equator.

Hot spot A place where hot molten rock from the Earth's mantle pushes up through the crust to form volcanoes.

Ice age A long cold period when huge areas of the Earth are covered by ice sheets.

Iceberg An enormous chunk of ice broken from the end of a glacier and floating in the sea.

Igneous rock Rocks created as hot magma from the Earth's interior cool and solidify.

Latitude Distance in degrees north or south of the Equator. Lines of latitude are imaginary lines round the Earth parallel to the Equator.

Lava Hot molten rock emerging through volcanoes, known as magma when underground.

Longitude Distance round the world measured in degrees from a north to south line through Greenwich, England. Lines of longitude are imaginary lines between the North and South poles.

Magma Hot molten rock in the Earth's interior. It is known as lava when it emerges to the surface of the Earth.

Mantle The warm layer of the Earth's interior below the crust. Every now and then parts of the upper mantle melt to form magma.

Meander A bend or loop in a river.

Metamorphic rock Rocks created by the alteration of other rocks by heat or pressure.

Methane A gas given off by rotting material and cows passing wind that adds to the greenhouse effect.

Mid-ocean ridge A ridge down the middle of the sea floor where tectonic plates meet.

Mineral A material (not living) found naturally in the Earth. Rocks mostly contain a mixture of minerals.

Monsoon A season with heavy rain and winds that happens in southern Asia including India.

Moraine Sand and gravel deposited in piles by a glacier or ice sheet.

Oasis An area in a desert where there is water, and plants can grow.

Oceanic trench A deep underwater trench formed where one tectonic plate is pushed under another.

Ore Rock that contains a useful material like a metal. Metals and other materials are extracted from ore that has been dug out of the ground.

Ozone "hole" Part of the ozone layer over the Antarctic with much less ozone than normal. The "hole" appears each spring.

Ozone layer A layer of ozone (a form of oxygen gas) high in the stratosphere that protects us from the Sun's radiation.

Pangea A single huge continent that scientists think existed millions of years ago before it split up into the continents of today.

Planetesimal One of the small lumps of rock circling the early Sun which later clumped together to form the planets.

Poles The North and South poles are the two points on Earth's surface furthest away from the Equator.

Precipitation Rain, snow, or hail falling from clouds in the sky.

Projection A way of flattening out the Earth's round shape to draw it as accurately as possible on a flat map.

Seamount A mountain under the sea.

Sediment Small particles of sand and rock that are carried along by fast flowing water in rivers. They are dropped when the river slows as it reaches the sea.

Sedimentary rock Rock made from sand, mud, and remains of creatures laid down underwater and gradually squashed into hard rock.

Seismologist A person who studies earthquakes.

Silt Fine grains of sand and clay carried by rivers and dropped when the flow of water slows at a river mouth.

Stalactite Stone column hanging from the roof of a cave, slowly built up by dripping water.

Stalagmite Stone column growing up from the floor of a cave, slowly built up by water dripping onto the ground.

Strata Layers of sedimentary rock.

Subduction The bending of a tectonic plate beneath another as they collide.

Tectonic plate The 20 or so giant rock slabs that make up the Earth's surface.

Tides The regular rise and fall of the sea along the shore caused by the pull of the Moon's gravity.

Tremor A shaking movement of the Earth's surface that is usually caused by an earthquake.

Tributary A smaller river or stream that joins a larger river.

Tropics Regions of the Earth on either side of the Equator with a hot climate.

Tsunami A giant wave moving out in all directions from an undersea earthquake or volcano.

Weathering The breakdown of rock when exposed to the weather.

LIFE ON EARTH

Origins of Life

Life began on Earth a very long time ago. The earliest fossils (remains) of life that have been found are of simple single-celled creatures called bacteria. They are about 3.8 billion years old. It is thought that these microscopic creatures are the ancient ancestors of all life on Earth.

▶ The "panspermia theory" suggests that life did not begin on Earth but came from outer space on comets. Long ago, comets often crashed into the Earth's surface and some carried the chemicals that are essential to life.

▼ The science of grouping animals is called taxonomy. It is important in many ways, for example when making a decision about which creatures today are the closest relatives of the dinosaurs.

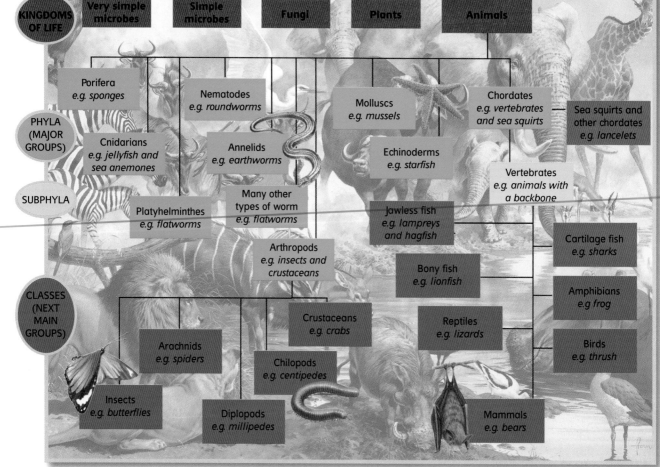

KINGDOMS OF LIFE

| Very simple microbes | Simple microbes | Fungi | Plants | Animals |

PHYLA (MAJOR GROUPS)

Porifera
e.g. sponges

Nematodes
e.g. roundworms

Molluscs
e.g. mussels

Chordates
e.g. vertebrates
and sea squirts

Sea squirts and
other chordates
e.g. lancelets

Cnidarians
e.g. jellyfish and
sea anemones

Annelids
e.g. earthworms

Echinoderms
e.g. starfish

SUBPHYLA

Platyhelminthes
e.g. flatworms

Many other
types of worm
e.g. flatworms

Vertebrates
e.g. animals with
a backbone

Jawless fish
e.g. lampreys
and hagfish

Arthropods
e.g. insects and
crustaceans

Cartilage fish
e.g. sharks

Bony fish
e.g. lionfish

CLASSES (NEXT MAIN GROUPS)

Amphibians
e.g frog

Crustaceans
e.g. crabs

Reptiles
e.g. lizards

Birds
e.g. thrush

Arachnids
e.g. spiders

Chilopods
e.g. centipedes

Insects
e.g. butterflies

Diplopods
e.g. millipedes

Mammals
e.g. bears

Amazing

Almost two million species, or types, of animal have been identified by scientists so far.

❍ Scientists do not agree about the way life began on Earth. Some believe that a mixture of chemicals was sparked into life by a source of energy, such as lightning. Others think that life first came to our planet from outer space, on a comet or by some similar means.

❍ However life began, it appears that early life-forms were very simple and remained so for an extremely long time. The first multicelled creatures, such as sponges and jellyfish, did not appear until about 700 million years ago.

Corals may look like plants, but they contain many tiny animals called polyps.

❍ Since this explosion in growth, animal and plant life has continued to develop and change (evolve) and has resulted in the huge variety of life that exists on our planet today.

❍ To make sense of the different types (species) of animals and plants on Earth, scientists put them into categories. They do this by looking at the physical characteristics of each creature; those that are similar are put in the same category, or group.

❍ Life-forms are divided into groups or kingdoms, which are then split into smaller groups. The Animal Kingdom, for example, is divided into phyla (single: phylum) and each phylum is split into smaller groups.

❍ Animals or plants that are in the same group do not just share similar physical characteristics, such as appearance. They are also likely to be closely related to one another, and have evolved from common ancestors.

Disappearing species

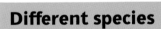

Many, many more species of animal have come and gone than are alive today. This birdlike reptile, *Archaeopteryx*, lived in the trees, hunting insects. It had feathers, but scientists believe it would not have been able to fly very well.

❍ About 600 million years ago life on Earth underwent an explosion in growth, and many new varieties of different animals and plants appeared in a relatively short time.

Different species

Animals of the same species can only breed with one another. Dogs, for example, can breed with other dogs and they therefore belong to the same species. A dog cannot breed with a cat, and they are therefore different species. Each species is given a Latin name that is used by scientists all over the world, no matter what their own language. Humans belong to the species *Homo sapiens*, which means "wise man."

Numbers of species

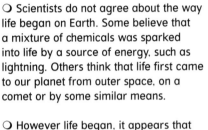

1,000,000	Insects
375,000	Plants
110,000	Arachnids
100,000	Roundworms
50,000	Molluscs
27,000	Fish

The Plant Kingdom

There are millions of different kinds of living things on Earth, so scientists group them to make them easier to study. One of the largest groups is the plant kingdom, which includes more than 400,000 different kinds of plants.

These plants grow in damp, shady places. They do not make seeds or have vessels to carry water. Mosses can survive for weeks without water, then soak it up like a sponge when it rains.

There are more than 50,000 different types of fungi, including mushrooms, toadstools, yeast, and molds. Fungi do not have chlorophyll, but feed either from other plants and animals, or from dead matter that has rotted in the soil.

Lichens can survive in many places where other plants would die, such as the Arctic, on mountaintops and in deserts. Some Arctic lichens are over 4,000 years old.

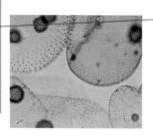

Algae are simple organisms that live in oceans, lakes, rivers, and damp mud. Algae vary from single-celled microscopic organisms to huge fronds of seaweed that can grow to over 196 ft long.

Phytoplankton is made up of tiny floating plants, such as diatoms, that live in water.

MOSSES

LIVERWORTS

FUNGI

LICHENS

ALGAE AND SEAWEEDS

MICROSCOPIC PLANTS

BROADLEAVED TREES AND BUSHES, FLOWERS, AND HERBS

Trees, bushes, flowers, and herbs that grow wide, flat leaves. Broadleaved trees can be evergreen or deciduous.

The flowering plant group contains more than 250,000 different species, including flowers, herbs, grasses, vegetables, and trees (except conifers). Flowering plants are also known as angiosperms.

FLOWERING PLANTS

GINGKOS

Also known as maidenhair trees, gingkos are an ancient type of plant with fan-shaped leaves and fleshy yellow seeds.

CONIFERS

Conifer trees have needle-like leaves that make their seeds in cones rather than in flowers. Conifers, cycads, and gingkos are also known as gymnosperms.

CYCADS

FERNS

These are mostly short, stubby, palmlike trees. Some are thousands of years old. Cycads have fernlike leaves growing in a circle around the end of the stem. New leaves sprout each year and last for several years.

CLUB MOSSES

HORSETAILS

These are amongst the world's most ancient plants and were common at the time of the dinosaurs. Horsetails once grew as tall as trees, but they are similar in lifestyle to mosses and ferns.

Ferns live in damp, shady places around the world. They are an ancient group of plants and have been found as fossils in rocks 400 million years old. Coal is made largely of fossilized ferns, horsetails and club mosses.

Parts of a Plant

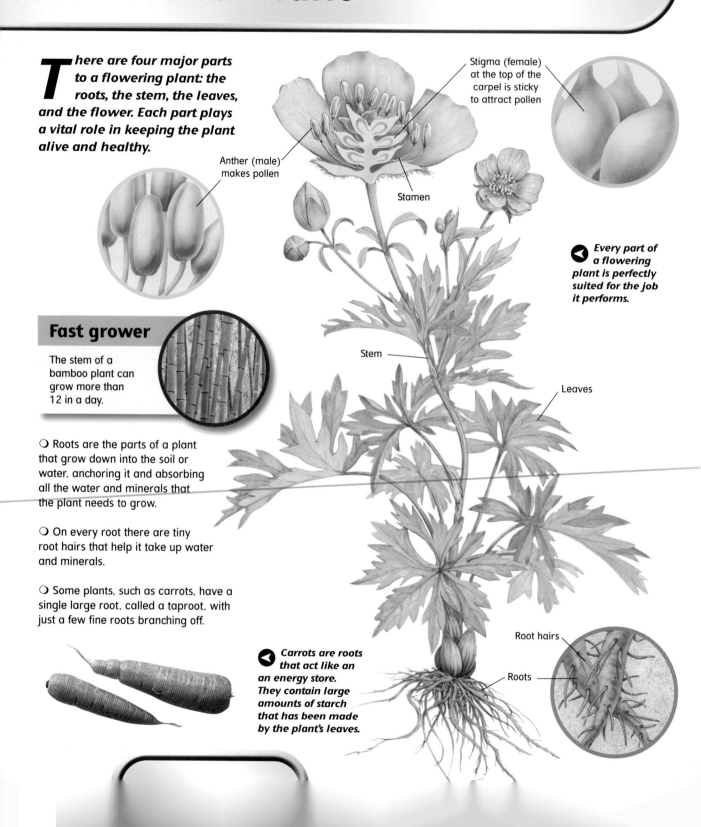

There are four major parts to a flowering plant: the roots, the stem, the leaves, and the flower. Each part plays a vital role in keeping the plant alive and healthy.

Stigma (female) at the top of the carpel is sticky to attract pollen

Anther (male) makes pollen

Stamen

Every part of a flowering plant is perfectly suited for the job it performs.

Fast grower

The stem of a bamboo plant can grow more than 12 in a day.

Stem

Leaves

❍ Roots are the parts of a plant that grow down into the soil or water, anchoring it and absorbing all the water and minerals that the plant needs to grow.

❍ On every root there are tiny root hairs that help it take up water and minerals.

❍ Some plants, such as carrots, have a single large root, called a taproot, with just a few fine roots branching off.

Carrots are roots that act like an an energy store. They contain large amounts of starch that has been made by the plant's leaves.

Root hairs

Roots

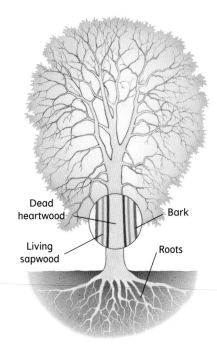

Dead heartwood
Bark
Living sapwood
Roots

A *A tree trunk includes living sapwood, dead heartwood, and a thick, protective layer of bark.*

○ Some plants, such as grass, have lots of small roots, called fibrous roots, branching off in all directions.

○ The flowers are the plant's reproductive organs. In gymnosperms (conifers, cycads, and gingkos) the flowers are often small and hidden. In angiosperms (flowering plants) they are usually much more obvious.

○ The stem of a plant supports the leaves and the flowers. It also carries water, minerals, and food up and down between the plant's leaves and roots.

○ Trees have one tall, thick, woody stem called a trunk. Trunks are at least 4 in thick to help the tree stand up.

Amazing

There are thousands of poisonous plants around the world. Every part of the deadly nightshade is poisonous and eating a single berry can kill you.

Water carriers

If you break open a celery stalk you will see fibers sticking out of the end. These fibers are from groups of tubes, called xylem vessels, which carry water through the plant.

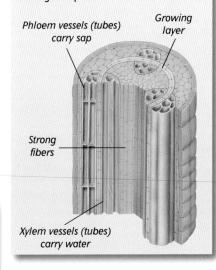

Phloem vessels (tubes) carry sap
Growing layer
Strong fibers
Xylem vessels (tubes) carry water

○ Most desert plants have tough waxy leaves to cut down on water loss. They also have very few, or very small, leaves. For example, cactus spines are tiny leaves that lose very little water.

○ The leaves of green vegetables are rich in many essential vitamins including Vitamin A, Vitamin E, and folic acid (one of the B vitamins).

○ Root vegetables are parts of a plant that grow underground in the soil.

○ Turnips, rutabaga, beets, carrots, parsnips, and sweet potatoes are the actual roots of the plant. Potatoes and cassava are tubers or storage stems.

◄ *Plants in the desert are specially adapted so they can survive for months, or even years, without rain.*

Food Factory

Unlike animals, plants are able to make their own food. Each green plant is a remarkable chemical factory, taking in energy from the Sun and using it to combine carbon dioxide, from the air, with water to make sugary food. This process is called photosynthesis.

○ Plants are made from tiny blocks of living matter called cells. The surface of a leaf is made from flat cells that are transparent to allow sunlight through.

○ Most plant leaves contain a chemical called chlorophyll. This traps the energy in sunlight. During photosynthesis, plants spread out their leaves so the sunshine can reach as much chlorophyll as possible.

Life-giving plants

After great activity, the body breathes faster and deeper, to replace the oxygen used by the muscles for energy. The oxygen in the air, on which we depend for life, was all made by plants during photosynthesis.

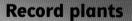

Sun's rays carry light energy to leaf

▼ Photosynthesis, as shown in this tulip plant, is a process whereby simple chemicals are changed into food using sunlight.

Carbon dioxide is taken from air into leaves

Oxygen is given off from leaves

Stem

Bulb

Roots

Record plants

Tallest sunflower	25.4 ft
Slowest growing tree	White cedar 4 in in 155 years
Longest seaweed	Giant kelp 197 ft
Oldest plant	Creosote plant and Antarctic lichen 12,000 years
Largest seed	Giant fan palm, weighs up to 44 lb

Amazing

All green plants make sugar. Much of the sugar we eat comes from sugar cane, which is a tropical grass.

○ **A** *While a poppy is growing toward sunlight, the plant uses food that is stored in its bulb. Without heat and light energy from the Sun, there would be no life on Earth.*

○ The leaf draws in air, which contains the gas carbon dioxide, through holes called stomata. It also draws up water from the ground, through the stem and leaf veins.

○ When the Sun is shining, chlorophyll soaks up its energy and uses it to split water into hydrogen and oxygen. The hydrogen combines with carbon dioxide to make sugar, and the oxygen is released through the stomata.

○ Sugar is transported around the plant to where it is needed. Some sugar is burned up instantly, leaving carbon dioxide and water. This process is called respiration.

○ Some sugar is combined into substances called starches, which are easy for the plant to store. The plant breaks these starches down into sugar again, when it needs fuel.

○ Unlike other living things, plants cannot move to find sunlight—but they can grow toward it. Plant stems have tips that are sensitive to light to ensure that they grow in the right direction.

○ **◀** *This is a hugely magnified slice through a leaf, showing the different layers. Leaves are thin and flat so they can catch the maximum amount of sunlight. The flat part of a leaf is called a blade, the stalk is called a petiole.*

Sugar producers

Together all of the world's plants produce about 150 billion tons of sugar each year by photosynthesis.

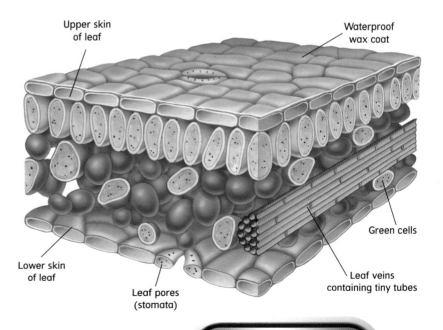

Upper skin of leaf

Waterproof wax coat

Lower skin of leaf

Leaf pores (stomata)

Green cells

Leaf veins containing tiny tubes

Find out more

How plants grow pp. 142–143

Plant Reproduction

Every plant has a life cycle. It begins when a seed germinates, and continues as the new plant grows and forms flowers. The flowers are pollinated, and in turn, produce their own seeds.

▼ Biennial plants take two years to grow from seed to a mature plant. The young plant must be able to survive through a cold or dry season, then it continues to grow and change the year after and makes flowers and seeds.

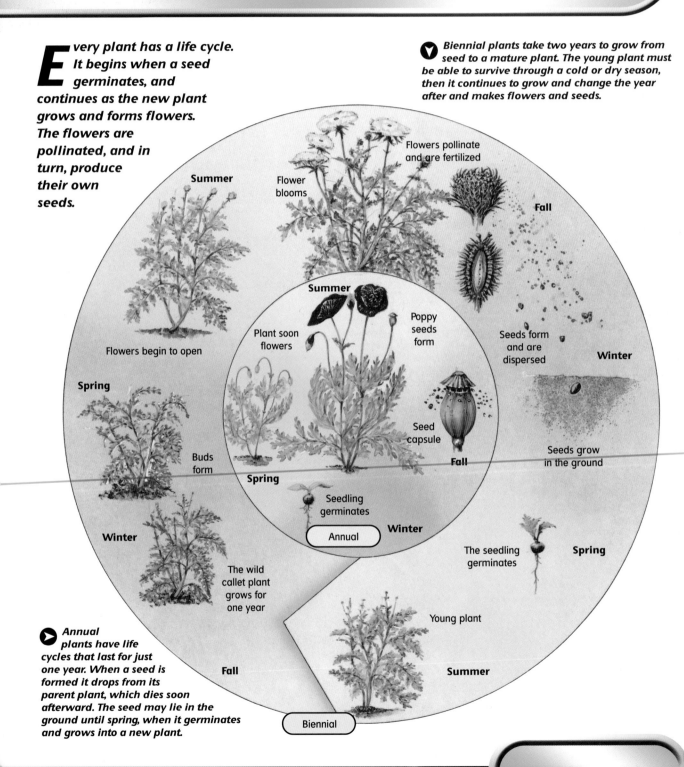

Summer

Flower blooms

Flowers pollinate and are fertilized

Fall

Flowers begin to open

Summer

Plant soon flowers

Poppy seeds form

Seeds form and are dispersed

Winter

Spring

Buds form

Seed capsule

Fall

Seeds grow in the ground

Spring

Seedling germinates

Winter

Annual

Winter

The wild callet plant grows for one year

The seedling germinates

Spring

Young plant

▶ **Annual** plants have life cycles that last for just one year. When a seed is formed it drops from its parent plant, which dies soon afterward. The seed may lie in the ground until spring, when it germinates and grows into a new plant.

Fall

Summer

Biennial

Find out more

Parts of a plant pp. 136–137

Daisy

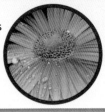

The name "daisy" comes from "day's eye" since these eyelike flowers open by day and close up at night.

○ Flowers have both male parts, called stamens, and female parts, called carpels. Seeds for new plants are made when pollen grains from the stamens join with eggs inside the carpels.

○ The carpel contains the ovaries, where the flower's eggs are made. A carpel usually looks like a short, thick stalk in the center of a flower. The top of the carpel is sticky. This part is called the stigma.

○ Stamens normally appear as spindly stalks that surround the carpels. Pollen is made in the anthers, at the top of the stamens.

○ Before a flower can make seeds, it must be pollinated. The pollen has to be transferred to the stigma of another flower of the same type. This process is called pollination.

Amazing

Orchids produce the world's smallest seeds. A single gram of orchid seed contains an unbelievable 992 million seeds.

⬤ *Pollen grains reach an ovule by traveling down a pollen tube. In some flowers, pollen tubes can be more than 4 in long and grow in one or two days.*

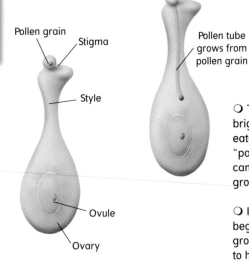

Pollen grain
Stigma
Style
Ovule
Ovary

Pollen tube grows from pollen grain

Male pollen nucleus
Female ovule

○ There are several ways in which pollen can travel: it can be carried by insects or other animals, by wind, or by water. Flowers that are pollinated by animals often have bright colors to attract insects. Wind-pollinated flowers are often dull in color.

○ When a pollen grain lands on a stigma it grows a long, thin tube that reaches down into the ovary. Inside the ovary are one or two egg-shaped ovules. The pollen tube seeks out an ovule to fertilize.

○ After fertilization, the ovule turns into a seed and the ovary turns into a fruit. Meanwhile, parts of the flower, such as the petals and stamens, fall away.

○ The fruit may swell up and become brightly colored and juicy, so it gets eaten—or it may dry up and form "parachutes" or "wings" in order that it can be carried away by the wind to grow into a new plant.

○ Inside a seed a plant embryo (the beginnings of a plant) is waiting to grow. The seed contains a store of food to help this growth.

○ When the seed settles in the soil it takes in water, swells up, and breaks open so the new plant can grow out. This process is called germination.

Recycling seeds

When an animal eats the seeds in a sweet, juicy fruit they are not entirely digested. Instead, they leave the animal's body in the droppings, so the seeds have a supply of manure to help the new plants grow.

Plant families

Angiosperms	Have enclosed seeds and easily seen flowers
Gymnosperms	Wind-pollinated, "naked seeds" in cones
Pteridophytes	Simple plants, such as ferns, horsetails, and clubmosses
Bryophytes	Liverworts and mosses, the simplest true land plants
Algae	Most live in water—they range from singlecelled diatoms to giant seaweeds

How Plants Grow

When tiny plants start to grow they change food, stored in the seeds, into substances that build their root, stem, and leaves. If the seeds are kept in warm conditions, such as a greenhouse, the changes take place quickly and the seeds soon sprout.

Spores

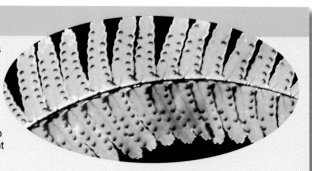

Spores are special cells that grow into new organisms. In seed plants, the spores develop into seeds. In plants, such as ferns and mosses, and in fungi, spores develop directly into a new plant called a gametophyte.

▶ *Stages of germination of a bean seed as it grows from a seed into a plant.*

1. The seed lies dormant until conditions are right

3. The shoot bursts into the air and grows cotyledons (seed leaves)

Amazing

Rice grains are seeds of a type of grass. They are a popular source of food and more than 6,000 tons or rice is eaten every second worldwide.

2. The seed sends a root down and a shoot up

▼ *Coconuts are the fruit of the coconut palm tree. The seed is contained in a brown woody shell called a husk.*

○ Not all seeds germinate in the same way. Coconuts, for example, often fall into the ocean and may be swept away, eventually washing up on another warm beach where they can grow into new coconut palms.

4. The stem and roots grow longer, and the plant soon begins to grow new leaves

Super giants

Tallest grass	Bamboo	82 ft
Tallest cactus	Saguaro	59 ft
Biggest fern	Norfolk Island tree fern	66 ft
Biggest seed	Coco-de-mer	66 lb

○ A seed does not always sprout as soon as it forms. It may spend some time before germination, being inactive or dormant.

○ An embryo inside a seed contains a seed store (cotyledon) that is protected by the seed's tough outer casing (testa). As the growing plant increases in size the seed case breaks open.

○ The young plant that grows out of a seed is called a seedling.

○ The root is the first part to appear and it grows downward. Later, the shoot appears and grows upward.

○ The shoot grows toward the light, so its first leaves can make food by the process of photosynthesis.

▲ *Plants can even get all their needs—sunlight and water—in a crack in a sidewalk as rainwater carrying minerals seeps in.*

▶ *This bristlecone pine from the USA has a long lifespan because it grows very slowly and in cool, dry areas, such as Nevada, Utah, and California.*

▶ *Trees grow tall as they compete for space and light. Branches spread out so that their leaves can reach the sunlight needed for photosynthesis. Deciduous trees lose their leaves in the winter and plants living beneath them often bloom in spring when most light reaches them.*

○ Once the store of food in the seed has been used, the plant relies on photosynthesis. The roots absorb water and minerals and grow strong enough to keep the plant anchored in the soil.

How old is a tree?

If a tree is sawn across you can see the annual growth rings. These show how much the tree has grown each year; new rings are made just beneath the bark and the oldest rings are found at the center of the trunk. Counting the rings gives the age of the tree.

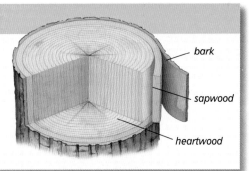

bark

sapwood

heartwood

○ There are two kinds of trees: evergreen, which hold onto their leaves all year round, and deciduous, which usually lose their leaves in the fall and grow new ones in the spring.

○ Wood is a particularly long-lasting and tough plant material. Woody plants can live for a long time. The bristlecone pine of North America is one of the oldest species of tree in the world— almost 5,000 years old.

○ When trees grow together in large groups they form forests. There are three main types of forest: coniferous, temperate, and tropical. Each kind of forest grows in different places, depending on weather conditions. Coniferous forests, for example, grow where winters are long and cold.

Find out more

Food factory pp. 138–139

Plants on our Planet

Plants are vital to life on our planet because they make oxygen and help provide food that animals and people eat. Plants also provide us with useful materials, such as wood, cotton, paints, rubber, and medicines.

This illustration shows the typical sequence of events in a grain farmer's year, from plowing and sowing the seed through to harvest the following fall.

Harvest time in late summer when the wheat is harvested

A few days after harvesting, the soil is cultivated to get rid of unwanted weeds

The seeds sprout before winter sets in, but don't begin to ripen until the following spring

After cultivation, the soil is prepared by plowing and harrowing

About six weeks after the harvest, seeds are sown in the prepared soil

Wood

Every year the world uses 10 billion cu ft of wood—a pile as big as a soccer stadium and as high as Mount Everest (29,028 ft).

❍ Plant leaves, stems, flowers, and sap have been used since earliest times for medicinal purposes and, even today, plant-based remedies are popular across the world.

❍ Since about 3000 BC rice has been cultivated, and it is now the basic food for about half of the world's population. Rice grows in purposely flooded areas, called paddy fields.

Flower meanings

Basil	Hatred
Cactus	Maternal love
Daffodil	Deceit
Daisy	Affection
Geranium	Melancholy
Honeysuckle	Bonds of love
Hyacinth	Benevolence
Larkspur	Levity
Laurel	Glory
Lavender	Distrust
Lily	Pride
Lily of the valley	Return of happiness
Narcissus	Selfishness
Nettle	Cruelty
Rose	Beauty
Saffron	Abuse

Amazing

Bacteria in flooded rice fields produce methane gas that scientists believe may add to the problem of global warming.

❍ Wood was probably the first material from a plant to be used by people. It was used to make shelters and weapons. About 5,000 years ago people began to weave cotton—a fiber that grows on the seeds of the cotton plant— to make clothes.

❍ The first crops were probably root crops like turnips. Grains and green vegetables were probably first grown as crops later.

❍ Corn was probably first grown about 9,000 years ago from the teosinte plant of the Mexican highlands.

❍ Farmers usually put fertilizers on their fields to improve the soil. While the plants are growing they are treated with chemicals to prevent disease and insects from destroying the crop.

❍ Rubber comes from the sap of rubber trees. Natural rubber is very soft, but it can be toughened by adding chemicals. This is called vulcanizing.

❍ Algae may be tiny, but they are a vital food source for many creatures, from shrimps to whales, and they provide most of the oxygen that water creatures need for life.

Healing plants

For almost 50,000 years people have used plants to treat illness. Aspirin, for example, was originally made from willow bark. Many modern medicines are still made from plants.

◀ The bitter-tasting century plant was once used to help people with fevers and digestion problems.

▼ Rice is grown in paddy fields. Once the grains of rice have been harvested, the plant stalks can be used to make mats, hats, and shoes.

The Animal Kingdom

There are millions upon millions of different kinds, or species, of animals. They can be divided into two large groups: the invertebrates and the vertebrates. Invertebrates, such as worms and insects, do not have backbones. Vertebrates, such as lizards, birds, and humans, do have backbones.

Crabs and lobsters are part of an enormous group of shelled invertebrates called crustaceans.

Worms are long, wriggling tubelike animals. The bodies of earthworms are divided into segments.

Crabs and lobsters are decapods, which means they have ten legs—although the first pair are often strong pincers that are used to hold and tear food.

Snails and slugs are small, squidgy, slimy, soft-bodied crawling creatures. They belong to a group of animals called molluscs.

Spiders are small scurrying creatures which, unlike insects, have eight legs not six, and bodies with two parts not three.

Octopuses and squid belong to a group of molluscs called cephalopods. They are sea creatures with eight arms, or tentacles.

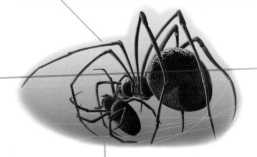

Insects may be tiny, but there are more of them than all other animals put together— over 1 million species.

Spiders belong to a group of 70,000 creatures called arachnids, which also includes scorpions, mites, and ticks.

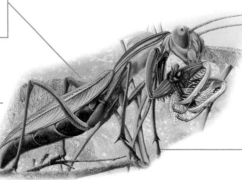

Flies, butterflies, moths, beetles, ants, grasshoppers, dragonflies, fleas, earwigs, bees, and wasps are all types of insect.

Insects have six legs and a body divided into three sections: the head, thorax (middle), and abdomen.

Find out more

Origins of life pp. 132–133

Fish are mostly slim, streamlined animals that live in water. Many are covered in tiny, shiny plates called scales.

Amphibians live both on land and in water. They include frogs, toads, newts, and salamanders.

Frogs and toads begin life as tadpoles, hatching into water from huge clutches of eggs called spawn.

Record-breakers

Tallest land mammal
Giraffe

Largest mammal
Blue whale

Heaviest land mammal
African elephant

Largest fish
Whale shark

Largest land carnivore
Polar bear

Largest feline
Siberian tiger

Largest deer
Alaskan moose

Largest rodent
Capybara

Largest butterfly
Queen Alexandra's Birdwing

Largest bird
Ostrich

Longest snake
Reticulated python

Smallest horse
Falabella

Smallest bird
Bee hummingbird

Fastest land mammal
Cheetah

Slowest land mammal
Three-toed sloth

Most poisonous fish
Stonefish

Most poisonous snake
Gaboon viper

Most poisonous jellyfish
Australian sea wasp

Loudest insect
African cicada

Most fish have bony skeletons and a backbone but sharks have skeletons of rubbery material called cartilage.

Crocodiles, alligators, lizards, snakes, turtles, and tortoises are all types of reptile.

Reptiles are scaly-skinned vertebrates that live in many different habitats, especially warm places.

Not all birds can fly, but they all have feathers.

Mammals have furry bodies and feed their young on milk.

Instead of teeth, birds have a hard beak or bill.

Unlike humans, birds do not give birth to babies. Instead they lay eggs.

Mammals are able to keep their body temperature constant, which means that they can survive in very hot or very cold weather.

Invertebrates

*I**nvertebrates, despite their size, are a very important group of animals. They are found all over the world, in many different habitats, especially oceans. They account for 97 per cent of all animal species.*

❍ Insects were the first creatures to live on land—nearly a quarter of a billion years before the first dinosaurs—and the first to fly.

❍ An insect's body is encased in such a tough shell (its exoskeleton) that it has no need for bones. Insects grow by getting rid of their old exoskeleton and replacing it with a bigger one. This is called molting.

➤ *Tropical coral reefs are the habitat of an amazing range of marine plants and creatures. Over millions of years the polyp skeletons pile up to form huge wall-like structures called reefs. One such reef, the Great Barrier Reef, can be seen from space. It is over 1,200 mi long and is the largest structure ever built by living creatures.*

❍ Jellyfish are sea creatures with bell-shaped, jellylike bodies and long stinging tentacles. The bell of one giant jellyfish was found to measure 7.51 ft across and was over 118 ft long.

❍ At least 250,000 species of beetle have been identified. They are found worldwide, except in the oceans. They have a pair of thick, hard front wings, called elytra, which form an armor-like casing over the beetle's body.

❍ Coral reefs are the undersea equivalent of rainforests and teem with fish and other sea life. The reefs are built by invertebrates called polyps.

❍ Octopuses belong to a family of sea molluscs called cephalopods. An octopus has a round, soft boneless body, three hearts and eight long tentacles that are covered in suckers.

❍ Snails and slugs are gastropods. Gastropod means "stomach foot" and these animals seem to slide along on their stomachs. Most gastropods live in the ocean, for example, limpets and whelks.

❍ Spiders are hunters and most of them feed mainly on insects. They have eight eyes, but most have poor eyesight and hunt by feeling vibrations with their legs. Many of them use silken webs to catch their prey.

Intriguing insects

The average lifespan of a dragonfly is 24 hours.

The praying mantis is the only creature on the planet that is born with one ear.

A cockroach can survive for up to a week minus its head.

A caterpillar has over 2,000 muscles in its body.

The butterfly was originally called a flutterby.

You are more likely to be bitten by a mosquito if you have blond hair, wear blue clothes, and eat bananas.

The ant has the largest brain in the animal kingdom in proportion to the size of its body.

The hum of a housefly is in the key of F.

The heaviest insect in the animal kingdom is the Goliath beetle weighing over 4 oz.

○ Despite their name, starfish are not fish but belong to a group of sea invertebrates called echinoderms. They have five strong "arms" that they use to prise open their prey. They eat shellfish, such as oysters.

Long jumpers

Grasshoppers are insects with powerful back legs, which allow them to leap huge distances. Some grasshoppers can leap more than 10 ft.

Useful invertebrates

Invertebrates play an important role in the survival of all animals. Many of them are food for other animals, such as birds and reptiles. Insects, such as bees, wasps, and butterflies (such as this Monarch butterfly), pollinate flowers. Without them plants, including those we eat, would quickly die out.

○ Many invertebrates are parasites; this means that they live on or in other animals' bodies. Tapeworms live in animals' guts and eat their food. Other invertebrates spread diseases. Mosquitoes, for example, carry malaria.

The caterpillars of Death's head hawk moths reach 5 in when fully grown and make a clicking sound if they are disturbed.

Horse flies are among the fastest flying insects, reaching maximum speeds of 24 mi/h. Unlike most other flies, their flight can be silent, allowing females to sneak up on their prey.

If the Bhutan glory butterfly is disturbed it quickly opens and shuts its wings, exposing its bright orange markings.

Springtails are also called snow fleas as they can survive in extreme cold. They are active even in freezing weather.

Spittlebug nymphs produce "cuckoo spit" by giving off a sticky liquid and blowing this into a frothy mass of white bubbles. As well as hiding the nymph from predators, these bubbles also protect the young bug from the drying effects of the sun.

Water boatmen are not buoyant enough to float, so when they stop swimming, they sink to the bottom. This is useful because they feed on the bottom of ponds, canals, and ditches, using their shovel-like front legs to scrabble up food.

How Animals Move

Movement defines what an animal is. Creatures travel to find food and shelter and avoid predators. Most land animals, from bugs to bears, use their legs for moving, or locomotion. Others fly, crawl on their bellies, wriggle, swing, slide, swim, or slither.

○ Burrowing animals use various methods of movement. Moles shovel soil using their powerful front legs. Earthworms contract their muscles to make their bodies hard so that they can force their way between grains of soil.

○ Monkeys move through trees by swinging from their arms. A gibbon's arms are twice as long as its legs and it has hook-shaped hands to hang from the branches.

○ Movement through water is much more difficult than movement through air—it needs extra muscle power. More than four-fifths of a fish is muscle.

○ The African fringe-toed lizard has to dance across the hot sand in the desert to keep its feet cool.

○ Hummingbirds and nectar-sipping bats flap their short, broad wings quickly, almost 100 times a second, so they can hover. An albatross, however, soars on the winds above the ocean, and can travel for many miles without flapping its wings once.

▲ *Cheetahs are the world's fastest land animal. Within two seconds of starting, a cheetah can reach speeds of 47 mi/h, reaching a top speed of about 65 mi/h. Their spines are so bendy that they can bring their hind legs forward between their front paws when they run. Unlike most cats, they do not have retractable claws on their feet. When they run, their claws stick into the ground like the spikes on an athlete's shoes.*

Fast flier

Fastest of all animals is the peregrine falcon, which has been recorded traveling at 167 mi/h when it dives or "stoops" to catch its prey.

Fastest land animals

Cheetah	65 mi/h
Pronghorn antelope	56 mi/h
Springbok	49 mi/h
Ostrich	43 mi/h
Racehorse	43 mi/h

▶ *The paws of big cats have soft pads that are surrounded by tufty fur to muffle the sound of every footstep. Each claw on this lion's paw is curved and very sharp.*

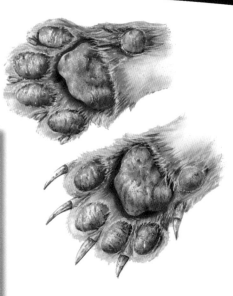

Muscles

Muscles get shorter, or contract, and pull different body parts to allow movement. In vertebrates the muscles are joined to bones, which make up the skeleton, as seen here in the bear. In insects and spiders the muscles are joined to a hard outer body casing (an exoskeleton).

▼ *The earthworm wriggles between soil grains, munching humus as it tunnels. The stiff hairs along its body help to grip the sides of the burrow, so the worm can thrust forward its front end to move onward.*

○ Fliers and swimmers both use broad pushing surfaces—wings through air, and fins, flippers, and tails through water. These surfaces produce propulsion (forward movement). Other body parts control steering and slowing down.

○ Water is very dense so streamlining (a smooth body shape) enables fish, dolphins, seals, and other sea creatures to easily move through it.

○ One of the most adaptable movers has no limbs at all. The golden tree snake can slither fast, swim well, burrow, climb trees, and even launch itself from a branch, and flatten its body, to glide for many feet.

○ Jellyfish float about freely, moving by squeezing water out from beneath their bodies. When a jellyfish stops squeezing, it slowly sinks.

○ To escape a predator, the ostrich can hurtle over the African grasslands at 43 mi/h—faster than a racehorse can run. If it tires it can still deliver a massive kick with its muscular legs.

○ Penguins can leap high out of the water to land on an ice bank, but on land they can only waddle clumsily or toboggan along on their bellies.

Cat landings

Some cats spend a lot of their time in trees. When a cat, such as this caracal, falls out of a tree, it can twist its body round so that it lands on its feet.

1. The caracal may lose its footing as it chases prey along branches

2. It has a superb sense of balance and quickly begins to right itself

3. A flexible spine helps the falling caracal twist its body

4. Cats' muscles are very strong and their joints are very flexible so they can absorb the shock of hitting the ground with a soft landing

Fish

Fish were the first vertebrate (backboned) animals to evolve on Earth, over 500 million years ago. They breathe using gills instead of lungs and their bodies are usually covered in scales. Fish live in freshwater (lakes and rivers) or salt water (sea and oceans). A few species can live in both types of water.

▼ *Some fish pack so closely in a shoal, that they are almost touching. They twist and turn as one whirling mass. This confusing sight makes it difficult for a predator to pick out and attack a single individual.*

Amazing

A jellyfish has no brain, no eyes, no ears, no bones, no heart, and comprises of 95 percent water.

○ There are over 21,000 species of fish. Fish are cold-blooded vertebrates that breathe through gills—rows of feathery brushes inside each side of the fish's head.

○ To get oxygen, fish gulp water into their mouths and draw it over their gills. As water passes into the gills it is cleaned by sieve-like structures and the oxygen passes into the fish's blood.

○ Salmon are river and sea fish that are caught or farmed in huge quantities for food. All salmon are born in rivers and lakes far inland, then swim downriver and out to sea. Years later they return to their birthplace to spawn (lay eggs).

○ Deep-sea anglerfish live deep in the ocean where it is pitch-black. They lure prey using spines with lights at the tip.

○ Sharks have a reputation as the most fearsome predatory fish of the seas. They have a skeleton made of rubbery cartilage—most other kinds of fish have bony skeletons.

Freshwater fish

Rivers, lakes, and other freshwater habitats are home to all sorts of fish, including bream and trout. Some fish feed on floating plant matter, while others take insects from the surface of the water. Pikes, such as this northern pike, are the sharks of the river—deadly hunters that lurk among weeds for unwary fish, rats, and birds.

Biggest fish

The world's biggest fish is the whale shark, which can grow to over 12 m in length. Unlike most other sharks, the whale shark eats plankton and is completely harmless.

○ Gulper eels can live more than 24,600 ft deep in the Atlantic Ocean. Their mouths are huge to help them catch food in the dark, deep water. They can swallow fish that are larger than themselves.

○ Nearly 75 per cent of all fish live in the seas and oceans. The biggest and fastest fish, such as swordfish, live near the surface of the ocean, far from land. They often migrate (travel) large distances to spawn or find food.

○ Flat fish start life as normal-shaped fish, but as they grow older, one eye slowly slides around the head to join the other. The pattern of scales changes so that one side is the top, the other is the bottom.

○ Many colorful fish species live in warm seas around coral reefs. They are often very bright, which makes them instantly recognizable to their own kind.

A *The world's biggest predatory, or hunting, fish is the great white shark. It measures up to 20 ft in length and weighs more than 1 ton. It has 50 or more teeth and each one is 2 in long. The teeth are slim and razor-sharp like blades to "saw" lumps of food from its victim. Sometimes they snap off but new teeth are always growing just behind, ready to move forward and replace them.*

○ Rays have flat diamond-shaped bodies. They mostly live on the seafloor, feeding on oysters and other shellfish.

Sea creatures

Dolphins always sleep with one eye open.

The pupil of the octopus's eye is rectangular.

The starfish has no brain and can turn itself inside out.

Oysters change sex annually.

Large electric eels can produce shocks in excess of 650 volts of electricity.

The heart of a shrimp is located in its head.

Sharks

Cleaner wrasse gather around the mouth and gill slits of this white-tip reef shark.

The epaulette shark can leave the water and move over dry land. It drags itself between rock pools using its strong pectoral fins.

The sand tiger has a huge appetite for many kinds of prey.

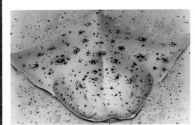

The angel shark has a wide flat body the same color as sand. It lies in wait on the seabed for prey.

How Animals Feed

Animals that mainly eat other animals are called carnivores. Some are active predators that hunt down prey, while others use stealth or ambush methods. More than three-quarters of all animals in the world are herbivores (plant eaters).

○ Meat eaters range from killer whales and sharks in the sea, big cats and wild dogs on land, and eagles and hawks in the air, to much smaller—but equally deadly—shrews, bats, frogs, dragonflies, spiders, and even sea anemones.

○ Some animals that may not seem to be carnivores actually are. A starfish might prey on a shellfish that is clamped to a rock, and spend most of a day prising it off and devouring the flesh.

The leopard has a very varied diet that ranges from dung beetles to large mammals, such as this gazelle, which should provide the cat with enough food for two weeks. Leopards drag their prey up into trees where it is out of the reach of other hungry predators and scavengers. They have large heads and powerful jaws to kill and take apart their prey.

Super-eater

An elephant can consume 330 lb of food daily—the weight of two average-sized adult people.

The giraffe feeds by using its very long, black, powerful tongue to grasp leaves, pulling them into its mouth. It jerks its head away and the teeth strip leaves from the branch. The giraffe can extend its tongue by as much as 17 in to gather shoots and leaves from branches. As the world's tallest animal, males measuring nearly 20 ft to the tips of their horns, it is able to reach the uppermost branches when feeding.

Vicious eaters

Many carnivores have bodily weapons to jab into their prey, wound, and tear it apart to eat. These include strong, sharp, pointed teeth of sharks, alligators, and big cats, fanglike mouthparts in spiders, sharp beaks of birds of prey, and claws of many birds and mammals.

❍ Rodents, such as rats, mice, and squirrels, use their long, continuously growing front teeth to crack open the toughest seeds and nuts. Parrots achieve the same effect using their sharp and powerful bills.

❍ Foods, such as flesh, blood, and eggs, contain large amounts of nourishment and energy compared to plant foods, so carnivores can spend much less time eating than herbivores do.

▼ *Rather than spinning a web to catch its prey, the spitting spider squirts a gluelike chemical from its fangs, which turns into sticky threads as it flies through the air and traps the spider's victim.*

❍ In any habitat, there are always more herbivores than carnivores, as the carnivores must feed on the plant eaters. Plant eaters range from elephants and hippopotamuses to many kinds of bugs, beetles, moths, and caterpillars.

❍ Deer, most gazelles, giraffes, and the black rhino are browsers, eating leaves from trees and shrubs. Zebras, cattle, and the white rhino are grazers, eating leaves or grasses from the ground.

Amazing

Wild horses and ponies can graze for up to 16 hours daily on grass, flowers, fruits, and berries.

❍ The open ocean contains billions of microscopic animals and plants, called plankton. Plankton is eaten by whales and fish, and also by tiny animals, such as copepods, that are then eaten by larger animals.

❍ As darkness falls, birds of prey, such as hawks, rest while owls come out of tree holds, cliff crevices, or quiet buildings. These nocturnal hunters catch a range of prey from beetles and mice, to young rabbits and squirrels.

Find out more

Huge appetite p. 161

Amphibians

Amphibians first appeared on land around 370 million years ago. They spend at least part of their lives in water and even when they are on land they usually prefer damp habitats. Frogs, toads, newts, and salamanders are amphibians.

▶ *There are about 3,500 species of frog and toad. Frogs are superb jumpers with long back legs to propel them into the air. Most also have suckers on their fingers to help them land securely on slippery surfaces.*

Amazing

Not all tadpoles are left to fend for themselves. The male reen poison-dart frog looks after the eggs while they develop on leaf litter, and then gives the tadpoles a piggyback ride to the nearest pool of water.

Green tree frog

Arum lily frog

Malaysian horned frog

Natal ghost frog

African clawed toad

○ Most frogs and toads live near water, but some live in trees and others live underground. Amphibians are particularly unusual because they can breathe both in water and in air.

○ Frogs are mostly smaller and better jumpers than toads. Toads are bigger, with wartier skin that hold on to moisture better, allowing them to live on land for longer.

○ Newts and salamanders are amphibians with tails. They are not so common as frogs and toads but they can be found in tropical forests as well as lakes and forests in cooler climates.

Poisonous frogs

Arrow-poison frogs of Central America produce deadly poison in their skin. People from the rainforests use the poison to tip their arrows and spears.

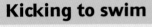

Kicking to swim

Many frogs move by leaping, which enables them to escape from predators quickly. They have toes that are joined with flaps of skin, called webbing, to make a broad surface area for kick swimming.

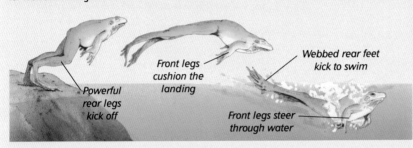

Front legs cushion the landing

Webbed rear feet kick to swim

Powerful rear legs kick off

Front legs steer through water

○ Amphibians have moist skin, which they normally keep covered in mucus to prevent it from drying out. Many amphibians are patterned or colored so they can hide from predators. This is called camouflage.

○ Although most amphibians prefer to stay near water, or in a wet habitat, there are some species of toad that manage to survive in deserts. They coat themselves in a thick layer of mucus and burrow underground during the hottest, driest spells of weather.

○ Some amphibians are able to breathe through their thin skin. Oxygen from the air passes directly into their bloodstream.

○ Some salamanders are lungless. They absorb oxygen through their skin and the lining of their mouth. This means the skin must always stay moist. If it dries, oxygen cannot pass through.

○ Newts and salamanders tend to be well camouflaged, with patterns and colors that enable them to hide. However, some species are brightly colored, often to indicate to predators that they are toxic (poisonous).

○ Frogs and toads are meat eaters, or carnivores. They catch fast-moving insects by darting out their long, sticky tongues.

○ The Goliath frog of West Africa is the world's largest frog, growing to more than 10 in long. The biggest toad is the cane toad of Queensland, Australia— one weighed 5.7 lb and measured 20 in in length with its legs outstretched.

1. Frog spawn floats on top of freshwater

4. The froglet loses its tail and grows into an adult frog

Toads hibernate on land during the winter

2. Tadpoles hatch from the eggs

3. Tadpoles grow legs and change into froglets

Newts swim by lashing their tails

◀ *Amphibians go to water when it is time to lay their eggs. Females usually lay their eggs in or near a pond or stream. Most frogs lay between 1,000 and 20,000 eggs in a mass of jelly. This large cluster of eggs is called spawn. Like many amphibians, frogs go through different stages before becoming adults. This change is called metamorphosis.*

How Animals Breed

Breeding or reproduction—making more of the same kind—is essential for all living things. Some animals can reproduce by themselves, but others need a mate. Some animals lay eggs, others give birth to live young.

Some sharks lay eggs. Each egg has a strong case with the developing embryo inside. The case, known as a "mermaid's purse," has long threads that stick to seaweed or rocks. This cat shark embryo develops slowly. At 50 days it is smaller than its store of food, the yolk. It gradually develops and finally hatches eight months later.

○ Small and simple creatures may reproduce asexually. This means that they clone themselves by simply growing identical offspring as "stalks" on their own bodies. Animals made of just one cell can halve that cell to reproduce.

○ Most animals reproduce sexually, when a male and female mate. The male's sperm joins with (fertilizes) the female's eggs.

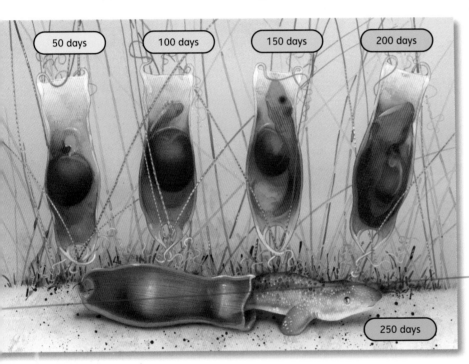

50 days | 100 days | 150 days | 200 days | 250 days

Mating alone

Some aphids, flatworms, leeches, and other smaller animals reproduce by parthenogenesis. This means that they can make eggs and produce offspring without a male's sperm. If a female stick insect reproduces by parthenogenesis her offspring will all be female; if she mates with a male her offspring will be a mixture of males and females.

Young animals

Animal	Young
Antelope	Calf
Badger	Kit
Bat	Pup
Bear	Cub
Beaver	Kitten
Camel	Calf
Cat	Kitten
Cod	Codling
Cow	Calf
Cranefly	Leatherjacket
Crocodile	Crocklet
Deer	Fawn
Dog	Puppy
Duck	Duckling
Eagle	Eaglet
Eel	Elver
Elephant	Calf
Fish	Fry
Frog	Tadpole
Giraffe	Calf
Goat	Kid
Goose	Gosling
Hamster	Pup
Hare	Leveret
Hawk	Eyas
Hippopotamus	Calf
Hog	Shoat
Horse	Foal
Jellyfish	Ephyra
Kangaroo	Joey
Lion	Cub
Llama	Cria
Mosquito	Nymph
Ostrich	Chick
Otter	Whelp
Owl	Owlet
Oyster	Spat
Pig	Piglet
Pigeon	Squab
Pilchard	Sardine
Rabbit	Kit
Rhinoceros	Calf
Sheep	Lamb
Snail	Spat
Spider	Spiderling
Squirrel	Kitten

○ Animals that live in water often reproduce by simply releasing their eggs and sperm into the water, and leaving fertilization to chance. This is called external fertilization.

○ On land, a female and male animal usually mate when the sperm pass into the female's body to fertilize the eggs. This is called internal fertilization.

○ Courtship is an essential part of male and female animals getting together to mate. Animals use courtship to check that a possible mate is fit, healthy, and strong; this means that their offspring will have a better chance of survival.

○ For some animals breeding depends on owning a territory. This is an area that the animal occupies, and defends from intruders. Usually males defend a territory and perform courtship displays.

Amazing

The tadpole of the South American frog is three times bigger than the adult. Unlike most living things, it actually gets smaller as it grows.

○ The female Nile crocodile lays her eggs in nests that she digs in sandy riverbanks. She covers the eggs to keep them at a steady temperature. When the babies hatch they make loud piping calls and the mother digs them out and carries them to the river, one by one.

○ Larger animals, such as elephants and apes, usually produce just one offspring at a time and care for it over several years.

Putting on a show

A peacock is chosen by a female (peahen) according to how magnificent his brightly colored tail feathers are, and how proudly he displays them.

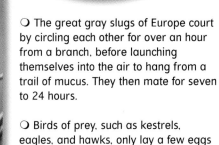

Many male birds, such as frigatebirds, put on amazing courtship displays as they puff out their red throat pouch to attract a mate. These birds can form colonies of thousands of pairs during breeding time.

○ The great gray slugs of Europe court by circling each other for over an hour from a branch, before launching themselves into the air to hang from a trail of mucus. They then mate for seven to 24 hours.

○ Birds of prey, such as kestrels, eagles, and hawks, only lay a few eggs at a time. This makes them vulnerable to human egg collectors—one reason why many are endangered species.

Many animals mate with different partners each year, either one or several. However, some larger birds, such as swans, are monogamous—they mate for life. Each spring, pairs of swans renew their relationship by twining their necks together and calling to each other. A female swan lays up to eight eggs, which she cares for until they hatch, then both parents look after them.

Find out more

Prolific breeders p. 168

Reptiles

It is believed that reptiles evolved from amphibians, around 340 million years ago. While amphibians have bare skins and lay their eggs in water, reptiles have a scaly skin and lay their eggs on land. They include lizards, snakes, crocodiles, alligators, tortoises, and turtles.

○ Reptiles are cold-blooded, but this does not mean that their blood is cold. Cold-blooded animals cannot keep the temperature of their bodies steady; it changes according to the temperature around them. They control their temperature by moving between hot and cool places.

Lizards cannot control their own body heat, and so rely on sunshine for warmth. This is why they live in warm climates and bask in the sun for hours each day.

Amazing

A 13–16 ft long African rock python was once seen to swallow an entire 132 lb impala, a kind of antelope, whole—horns and everything.

Pythons are tropical snakes that live in moist forests in Asia and Africa. They are the world's biggest snakes, rivaled only by giant anacondas. Pythons are one long tube of muscle, well able to squeeze even big victims to death. They usually eat animals about the size of domestic cats, but occasionally they go for really big meals, such as wild pigs and deer.

Crocodiles

Crocodilian species lived alongside the dinosaurs 200 million years ago, and they are the nearest we have to living dinosaurs today. Crocodiles are hunters that lie in wait for animals coming to drink at the water's edge. This dwarf crocodile, measuring only 5–7 ft in length, is one of the smallest crocodiles. It is so small that a frog, fish, or baby water bird is more than enough of a meal.

○ Reptiles bask in the sun to heat their blood. When they are warm, reptiles' bodies work more efficiently and they can hunt for food. For this reason reptiles are often less active at cool times.

○ A reptile's skin looks slimy, but it is dry and, unlike an amphibian's skin, it retains moisture well. Reptiles can live in very hot, dry places.

○ Although reptiles grow for most of their lives their skin does not, so they slough (shed) it every now and then.

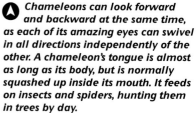

Chameleons can look forward and backward at the same time, as each of its amazing eyes can swivel in all directions independently of the other. A chameleon's tongue is almost as long as its body, but is normally squashed up inside its mouth. It feeds on insects and spiders, hunting them in trees by day.

Huge appetite

The Komodo dragon of Sumatra is the biggest lizard, weighing up to 330 lb. It can catch deer and pigs and swallow them whole.

○ Lizards move in many ways; they can run, scamper, slither, and even glide. Their legs stick out sideways rather than downward.

○ Most lizards lay eggs, although a few give birth to live young. Mother lizards do not look after their young.

○ Crocodiles, alligators, caimans, and gharials are large reptiles that form a group called crocodilians. There are 14 species of crocodile, seven alligators and caimans, and one species of gharial.

○ Constrictors are snakes that squeeze their victims to death before swallowing them whole. They have special jaws that allow their mouths to open wide, and can spend days digesting a meal.

○ Two kinds of poisonous snake are dangerous to humans: vipers and elapids, such as cobras and mambas. In India, cobras kill more than 7,000 people every year.

Tortoises and turtles are like armored tanks—slow but well protected by their shells. The hawksbill turtle lives in warm seas all around the world. Its beautiful shell means that it has been hunted so much that it has nearly died out.

Dinosaurs

For about 160 million years dinosaurs were the most successful animals on Earth. There were giant land dinosaurs that were much bigger than elephants. Enormous flying reptiles took to the air and reptile monsters ruled the oceans.

Amazing

Scientists study fossilized animal dung called coprolite to find out what ancient animals ate.

Spinosaurus

Ankylosaurus

▲ Some dinosaurs, such as **Maiasaura** were careful parents. They made nests, guarded their eggs against predators, and stayed with the young until they were able to fend for themselves.

◯ Dinosaurs lived from about 225 million to 65 million years ago. This period is known as the Age of the Dinosaurs or the Mesozoic Era.

◯ No one knows exactly how dinosaurs evolved, or what type of animal they evolved from. It is thought that they probably evolved from a group of reptiles called thecodonts.

◯ Some thecodonts resembled sturdy lizards, others evolved into true crocodiles, which are still around today.

▶ **Spinosaurus** preyed on weaker dinosaurs, but some victims put up a fight, like this **Ankylosaurus.**

◯ Most of the information we have about dinosaurs comes from fossils. These are the remains of previously living things that have been preserved in rocks and turned to stone, over millions of years.

Studying dinosaurs

Paleontologists are people who study fossils. They study fossilized dinosaur remains and modern reptiles, birds, and mammals, to try and understand how dinosaurs may have lived.

◯ When animals are fossilized their soft tissues (such as muscle or skin) are rarely preserved. Hard tissues, such as bones, teeth, and claws, are much more likely to be preserved.

Biggest dinosaurs

	Weight	Length
Seismosaurus	50–80 tons	164 ft

Find out more

Animals in danger pp. 170–171

Dino defenses

Plant-eating dinosaurs were preyed on by the fierce meat eaters, but they had effective defences in the form of armor plating, shields, spikes, and club-tails. Neck frills and horns protected the slow-moving Ceratopsians or "horn-faced" dinosaurs from predators' teeth.

Triceratops was the largest of the Ceratopsians

Styracosaurus had frilled horns with bony centers that weighted heavily on the neck

Chasmosaurus had large bumps called tubercules scattered among its scales

◯ Dinosaurs laid eggs, like most other reptiles. There is evidence that some dinosaurs protected their eggs and looked after their young when they emerged from eggs.

◯ Some dinosaurs, such as *Velociraptor*, were fierce hunters who preyed on other dinosaurs. Others, such as *Diplodocus*, were plant eaters. It is now believed that *Tyrannosaurus rex* was both a predator and a scavenger; it hunted but also ate animals that had died naturally or been killed by another hunter. It had both monstrous jaws to rip off large chunks of flesh and sharp, savage claws.

▶ **Dinosaurs were all land-living reptiles. They are divided into two groups, Ornithischians and Saurischians, according to the shape of their skeletons. Ornithschians had hips shaped like birds' hips, while Saurischians had hips shaped like reptiles' hips.**

What happened to the dinosaurs?

The most likely explanation for the extinction of the dinosaurs is that a comet, asteroid, or meteorite hit the Earth. There have been other extinctions in Earth's history, but the disappearance of the dinosaurs around 65 million years ago was a cataclysmic event. Dust-clouds flung up by the impact caused climate change: plants died, eggs failed to hatch, and mature animals died of starvation or cold.

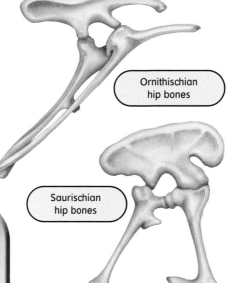

Ornithischian hip bones

Saurischian hip bones

◯ Amongst the biggest land animals of all times were prehistoric reptiles, such as *Seismosaurus* and *Brachiosaurus*. These 50-ton reptiles were as big as houses.

◯ Dinosaurs were well-equipped for both defending themselves and attacking others. Some had horns on their heads; others had spikes or bony plates on their tails and spines. Meat-eating dinosaurs had large, pointed teeth with serrated edges for slicing through flesh.

◯ Dinosaurs lived on land, but other giant reptiles lived in the air and the seas. Plesiosaurs lived in the oceans and used paddle-shaped limbs to swim. They had large bodies, long necks, and small heads. Pterosaurs were flying reptiles with beaks and large batlike wings.

Meaning of dinosaur names

Brachiosaurus	Arm lizard
Brontosaurus	Thunder lizard
Diplodocus	Double beamed
Ichthyosaurus	Fish lizard
Pterodactyl	Wing finger
Scelidosaurus	Limb lizard

Communication

Communication means passing on messages and information. Animals use sound, sight, and movement to communicate, as well as a range of methods including scent, taste, touch, and the emitting of electrical signals.

○ Some messages are understood only by an animal's own kind, for example when a frog croaks to attract a female of the same species. Other messages can be understood by a wide variety of creatures—these are often about matters of life and death.

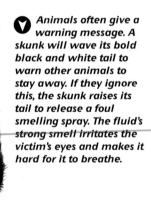

▼ *Animals often give a warning message. A skunk will wave its bold black and white tail to warn other animals to stay away. If they ignore this, the skunk raises its tail to release a foul smelling spray. The fluid's strong smell irritates the victim's eyes and makes it hard for it to breathe.*

Color warning

Yellow and black is one of the most common color combinations to be used as a warning. It tells predators that an animal is venomous or tastes foul. Spiders, wasps, frogs (like this arrow-poison frog), and snakes all use this code. After an animal has had an unpleasant encounter with another bearing these colors, it will avoid others with this color combination in the future.

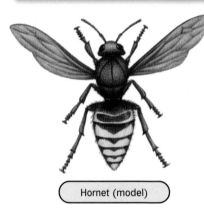

Hornet (model)

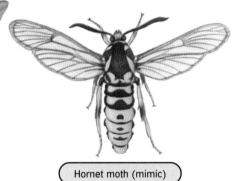

Hornet moth (mimic)

▲ *Some insects pretend to be what they're not—especially other insects. The hornet moth is a mimic of the hornet. A hornet has a very painful sting and few other creatures dare to try and eat it. The hornet moth is harmless but few other creatures dare to eat it either.*

○ One method of communication is widely understood in the animal world —rearing or puffing up to make oneself appear bigger. This type of threatening behavior makes other animals think twice before attacking. Cobras, for example, raise their heads, spread their hoods and hiss at an attacker. A scared or angry cat hisses and spits while its hair stands on end.

○ The male orangutan burps to warn other males to keep away.

○ Honeybees indicate to each other the site of a rich food source, such as nectar laden flowers, by "dancing." The bee flies in a figure of eight and shakes its body to indicate the direction of the food source.

Brain power

	Brain weight
Sperm whale	275 oz
Dolphin	60 oz
Human	49 oz
Camel	24 oz
Giraffe	24 oz
Horse	19 oz
Cow	18 oz
Chimpanzee	15 oz
Lion	8 oz
Baboon	5 oz
Sheep	5 oz
Dog	3 oz
Kangaroo	2 oz
Racoon	1.3 oz
Cat	1 oz

Wolves are intelligent animals that communicate with body language. They use facial expressions and howl at each other. The howls of a hunting pack of wolves can be heard for about 6 mi, telling other wolves to keep their distance. Coyotes use their ears and mouths to express feelings and will bare their teeth to show fear and anger.

Sudden danger needs a short, sharp message to warn others in the group. Rabbits thump the ground and many birds make a loud "seep" or "tic" noise. Meerkats will give a shrill shriek, while the first beaver to notice a predator nearby will slap its flat tail hard on the water's surface.

▼ *The male white rhinoceros sprays urine to mark his home range. The center of his territory needs to be marked in this way to a distance of about 0.5 sq mi. Scent has an advantage over sights or sounds—it lasts after the sender has gone. Foxes, sheep, and other animals spray strong smelling urine or leave droppings around their territory. This gives information about the age, sex, and health of the animal.*

Amazing

Lemurs have different calls to warn members of their troop whether danger is coming from above, along the ground, or is hidden in the undergrowth.

▶ *Cobras raise their heads, spread their hoods and hiss at an attacker. The extended hood reveals a pattern that is on the rear of the hood, but shows through the stretched skin and thin, transparent scales. Some cobras spit, spraying venom out of tiny apertures in their fangs. The venom does not kill but can cause blindness.*

Identifying strangers

Wolves and wild dogs smell each other's rear ends so if they find droppings later they will know if a pack member left them, or a stranger.

Crows use at least 300 different croaks to communicate with each other. Crows from one area, though, cannot understand those from another.

A gorilla named Coco was trained so that she could use over 1,000 different signs to communicate. She made the signs with her hands and each sign stood for a word. Coco called her cat "soft good cat cat" and herself "fine animal gorilla." Using sign language, she took an IQ test and scored 95.

Many insects communicate using the smell of chemicals called pheromones, which are released from special glands. The tropical tree ant uses ten different pheromones, combining them with different movements to send 50 different kinds of message.

Female glow worms communicate with males through a series of flashes.

Birds

Birds *probably evolved from dinosaurs. The earliest known fossil of a bird is 150 million years old. Called* **Archaeopteryx,** *this creature had feathers and large eyes, like a bird, but a snout and teeth, like a reptile.*

▼ *The lungs of the respiratory system and the heart from the circulatory system take up much of the front part of the body in the pigeon's chest. The digestive, excretory, and reproductive systems fill the rear part of the body.*

Chickens

All domestic chickens are descended from the wild red jungle fowl of India. They were first tamed 5,000 years ago, and there are now more than 200 different breeds.

○ Birds have four kinds of wing feather —large primaries, smaller secondaries, coverts, and contours. Every kind of bird has its own formation, pattern, and color of feathers, called its plumage.

○ Feathers are light, but they are linked by hooks called barbs to make them strong enough for flight. Birds fly in two ways—by gliding with still wings or by flapping their wings up and down.

○ All birds lay hard-shelled eggs, in which their young develop. If a mother bird had young that developed inside her body instead, she would be too heavy to fly.

○ Owls are nocturnal birds and hunt by night. They have huge eyes that allow them to see in almost pitch darkness, and their hearing is four times sharper than a cat's.

○ Penguins cannot fly, but they are superb swimmers. They use their wings as flippers to push them through the water and steer with their webbed feet. Their feathers are waterproofed with oil and they have thick layers of fat to survive at temperatures of −76°F.

○ Swifts are among the fastest flying birds. Spine-tailed swifts of eastern Asia have been recorded flying at 149 mi/h. They use their short, gaping bills to catch insects on the wing and can fly for thousands of miles without stopping.

○ Ratites are big, but flightless, birds. They include ostriches, emus, and kiwis. The emu is the biggest living bird, towering up to 9 ft in height and weighing more than 330 lb.

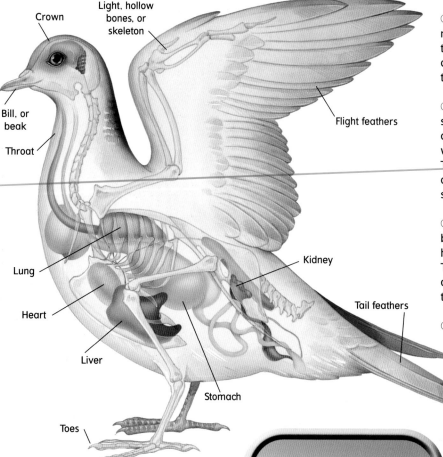

Crown

Light, hollow bones, or skeleton

Bill, or beak

Throat

Flight feathers

Lung

Heart

Liver

Kidney

Tail feathers

Stomach

Toes

10 flightless birds

○ Birds of rivers and lakes include birds that dive for fish (such as kingfishers), small wading birds (such as avocets and curlews), large wading birds (such as herons and flamingos), and waterfowl (such as ducks and geese).

○ A game bird is a bird that is hunted for sport, for example pheasants, grouse, and partridges. They spend most of their time on the ground looking for seeds. They only fly in emergencies.

○ Migration is when animals move from one place to another to avoid the cold or find food and water. Migrating birds are often brilliant navigators. Bristle-thighed curlews, for example, find their way from Alaska to tiny Pacific islands 5,592 mi away.

Perching birds

More than 70 percent of all bird species—over 5,000 species altogether—are perching birds or passerines, for example sparrows and starlings, and this song thrush shown here. They have feet with three toes pointing forwards and one backward, to help them cling to a perch. They build small, neat cup-shaped nests and they sing a sequence of musical notes.

Ⓐ *All birds have wings of varying shapes. They beat them to improve the airflow past their wings, thus helping them to fly. Wings are the birds' front limbs. Birds that soar in the sky for hours, such as hawks and eagles, have long broad wings. Small fast flying birds, such as swifts, have slim, pointed wings.*

In an eggshell

A bird's egg protects the developing chick inside. The yellow yolk in the egg provides the chick with food while it is growing. Layers of egg white, called albumen, cushion the chick and keep it warm, while the hard shell protects it. The shell is porous so that the chick can breathe.

1. The chick starts to chip away at the egg

2. The chick uses its egg tooth to break free

3. The egg splits wide open

4. The chick wriggles free. Its parents will look after it for several weeks until it can look after itself

○ Eagles are among 280 species of raptor (birds of prey). Birds of prey include kestrels, falcons, buzzards, and vultures. Most are hunters and feed on birds, fish, and small mammals. Most kill with their talons rather than their bill.

Amazing

Ostrich eggs are the largest eggs in the world and would take 40 minutes to hard-boil.

Bird oddities

Emus are unable to walk backward.

The bones of a pigeon weigh less than its feathers.

Mammals

There are about 4,500 species of mammals alive today that are probably descended from reptiles. Humans are also mammals. They have hairy bodies, a large brain, and special mammary glands for feeding their young with milk.

The duck-billed platypus lives along rivers and billabongs. At night it noses in the mud for worms, shellfish, and other small animals. The male has a spur on his rear ankle, which he uses to jab poison into his enemies.

Prolific breeders

One single rabbit could have more than 33 million offspring in just three years, if they all survived to breed.

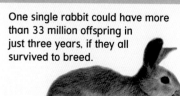

○ There are two main mammal groups: the placentals and the marsupials. Animals in these groups give birth to live young. A third group, the monotremes, lay eggs. The duck-billed platypus and spiny anteater are both monotremes.

○ When marsupials are born they are undeveloped and small. They usually move into a protective pouch for months, feeding from a teat.

○ Giraffes are the tallest mammals, growing to more than 16 ft. Their height allows them to reach and eat the leaves, twigs, and fruit at the tops of trees.

○ Apes are our closest relatives in the animal world. The great apes are gorillas, chimpanzees, and orangutans. Gibbons are called lesser apes. Like us, apes have long arms, and fingers, and toes for gripping. They are clever and can use sticks and stones as tools.

○ All mammals have three tiny bones in their ears that transfer sound vibrations to the inner ear from the eardrum.

○ Bats are the only flying mammals. Most bats feed on insects or fruit, but vampire bats feed on blood, sucking it from animals, such as cattle and horses.

○ Lions (along with tigers) are the biggest members of the cat family, weighing up to 507 lb. Male lions may be as long as 10 ft. Lions usually live in grasslands or scrub, in families (prides).

○ Mammals have a variety of teeth shapes: chisels for gnawing, fangs for fighting and killing prey, sharp-edged slicers, and flat-topped crushers.

○ Whales, dolphins, and porpoises are large mammals called cetaceans that live mostly in the sea and ocean. Dolphins and porpoises are small whales. The blue whale is the largest creature ever and can grow to be more than 98 ft long.

○ Elephants are the largest living animals on land—they can be as tall as 13 ft and weight up to 10 tons. They are intelligent animals, with the biggest brain of all land animals. They have very good memories.

Find out more

How animals move pp. 150–151

Mammals on Earth

Newborn kangaroo

When they are first born, kangaroos are naked and look like tiny jellybeans with two arms. They haul themselves up through the fur on their mother's belly and into her pouch. Here the baby kangaroo (called a joey) sucks on teats and grows for six to eight months.

Amazing

Bats that hunt at night do not need to use their eyes. Instead, they find prey by echolocation: they make high-pitched squeaks and use the echoes to find their way in the dark.

The snow leopard has thick fur and can survive extreme cold. Its gray coat helps to camouflage it in snow.

The puma is a great athlete. It has long hind legs packed with muscles.

The caracal lives in dry places. Its gold color makes it difficult to spot among the brown plants and sandy soil. It can jump four times its own body length.

Jaguars can feed on turtles because they have large, heavy teeth and immensely powerful jaws.

Lions live on vast grasslands called savannah. Their pale fur blends in with the dried grasses of the open plains.

The world's most mysterious cat is the clouded leopard. It sleeps all day and only hunts at night.

Record-breaking mammals

Tallest land mammal	Giraffe	up to 20 ft
Largest mammal	Blue whale	up to 110 ft
Heaviest land mammal	African elephant	more than 6 tons
Fastest land mammal	Cheetah	62 mi/h
Slowest land mammal	Three-toed sloth	crawls at 7 ft a minute

Animals in Danger

In the next few hours, somewhere in the world, a species of animal will become extinct—disappear and be gone for ever. The species may be a rare kind of bird or mammal, or an insect, such as a beetle.

Extinct animals

The giant panda now lives only in south and west China. There are less than 1,000 left in the wild and they may become extinct. There are many other species that will disappear from the planet—forever—before we have discovered them. It is estimated that there are 20 million different species of animal on Earth, but scientists have not named even two million yet.

Amazing

In prehistoric times several mass extinctions happened. The largest extinction took place 240 million years ago when about 96 percent of living things vanished. The mass extinction of 65 million years ago saw the disappearance of the dinosaurs.

▼ The rare river dolphins of the Amazon, Ganges, and other great waterways face many problems. Their survival is threatened by water pollution from chemicals and they must compete with fishermen for food supplies. They also have to avoid boats with slashing propellers that may harm them and noisy engines that disrupt their sound-sonar communication system.

▲ The dodo lived on the island of Mauritius in the Indian Ocean until European sailors arrived in the 1500s. Sailors killed the birds for food, and rats and cats ate the eggs. By 1680 the dodo was extinct.

❍ The biggest threat to animals is the destruction of their habitat. For example, this occurs when a forest is cut down for timber or when houses, factories, or roads are built through the countryside.

❍ Tigers are often killed for their teeth, which are used in eastern medicines, and for their luxurious fur by people who enjoy hunting wildlife. Tigers are an endangered species, which means that they are at risk of extinction.

❍ As people in poor countries struggle to feed themselves, some turn to hunting wild animals, or sell them as pets or to eat. This trade affects apes, monkeys, tropical birds, lizards, and snakes.

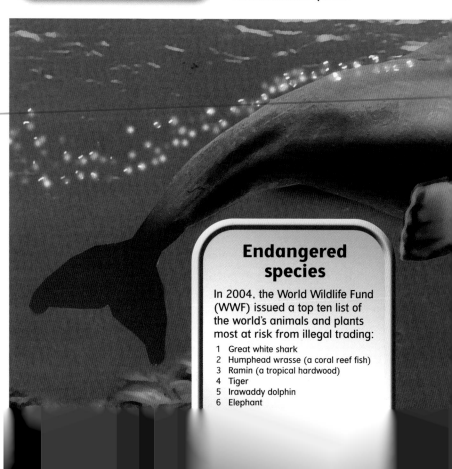

Endangered species

In 2004, the World Wildlife Fund (WWF) issued a top ten list of the world's animals and plants most at risk from illegal trading:

1 Great white shark
2 Humphead wrasse (a coral reef fish)
3 Ramin (a tropical hardwood)
4 Tiger
5 Irawaddy dolphin
6 Elephant

❍ Great white sharks are caught so often, both for "sport" and because they are sometimes considered a threat to the safety of human swimmers, that they are now in danger of becoming extinct.

❍ The North American buffalo, or bison, had a narrow escape. Two hundred years ago millions of buffalo wandered the Great Plains, but hunters in the 1800s killed most of them and by 1881 only 551 were left. Now protected, numbers have increased and there are more than 30,000 in the USA and Canada.

▶ *When an animal such as the golden lion tamarin's natural habitat disappears it has nowhere to find food or breed, so its numbers decline until it dies out altogether. Animals at risk can be bred in captivity.*

Disappearing forests

Nearly half of the world's tropical rainforests have been destroyed over the last 50 years to clear the way for farmland or buildings.

❍ Power stations and vehicles send fumes up into the air; factory pipes pour poisons into rivers, lakes, and seas; pesticides and herbicides (insect and weed killers) leaks into water supplies. These factors all affect the natural environment, for the worst.

❍ Zoos and wildlife parks are extremely valuable for conservation (saving wildlife for the future). Animals can be studied safely and bred in these places and will, hopefully, one day be released back into the wild.

❍ In many parts of the world animals will remain under threat, particularly in areas where humans live in poverty. It is difficult for poor people to look after their own wildlife when they are struggling to survive.

❍ Ecotourism can help share the wealth of the world more evenly. People pay to see rare animals in their natural habitats, through such activities as going on safari. Money raised from these schemes can be used to support local people and conservation projects.

Find out more

Dinosaurs pp. 162–163

The Human Body

There are more than six billion human bodies in the world, and each one of those bodies has unique characteristics. Inside, however, they are all made and work in much the same way.

The body's biggest internal organ is the liver.

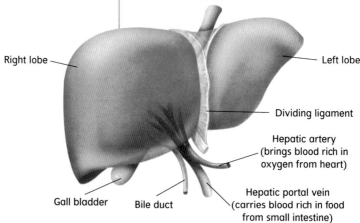

Right lobe

Left lobe

Dividing ligament

Hepatic artery (brings blood rich in oxygen from heart)

Gall bladder

Bile duct

Hepatic portal vein (carries blood rich in food from small intestine)

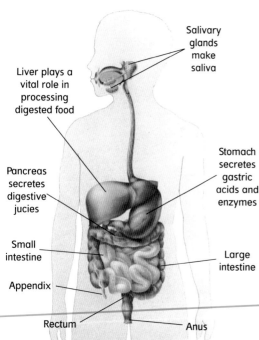

Salivary glands make saliva

Liver plays a vital role in processing digested food

Stomach secretes gastric acids and enzymes

Pancreas secretes digestive jucies

Small intestine

Large intestine

Appendix

Rectum

Anus

Cells are the body's building blocks. They vary in size and shape, according to the job that they do. Different organelles (special parts of a cell) keep it working properly. Instructions come from the nucleus in the cell's control center.

Mitochondria "power stations" change chemical fuel supplied by the blood as glucose into "energy packs" of the chemical ATP

Endoplasmic reticulum, the main chemical factory where proteins are built under instruction from the nucleus

The digestive system is a passageway looped and coiled within the body. Foods passing along the tract are broken down and digested.

Ribosomes, individual chemical assembly lines where proteins are put together from basic chemicals called amino acids

Nucleus, the cell's control center sending out instructions via a chemical called messenger RNA whenever a new chemical is needed

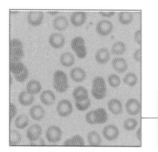

Lysosomes, the cell's dustbins, breaking up any unwanted material

The whole body contains more than 50 billion billion cells.

Golgi bodies, the dispatch center where chemicals are bagged up inside tiny membranes to send where needed

Find out more

DNA p.187

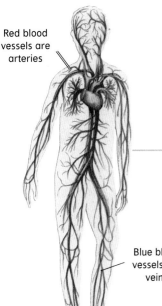

Red blood vessels are arteries

Blue blood vessels are veins

Tissues are groups of cells that are all similar and work to do a particular job. Brain cells, for example, make brain tissue.

The heart, blood vessels, and blood all work together to transport gases and food around the body. They make the circulation system.

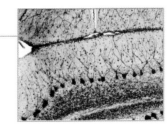

The outer layer of the skin is called the epidermis. It is hard-wearing and tough. Below the epidermis is the dermis. This skin layer contains the cells that sense touch, heat, pain, and movement. Hair grows from its root, which is found in the skin's dermis. This cross section of skin, hugely magnified shows all these parts.

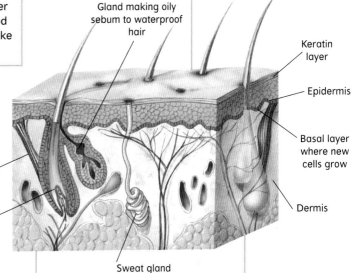

Gland making oily sebum to waterproof hair

Keratin layer

Epidermis

Basal layer where new cells grow

Dermis

Hair erector muscle

Hair follicle (root)

Sweat gland

A nail has its root under the skin and grows along the nail bed, which is the skin underneath it. The paler crescent-like area is the lunula or "little moon." Nails grow about 0.5 mm a week.

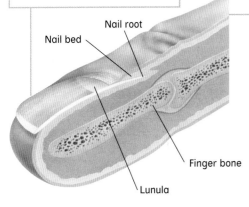

Nail root

Nail bed

Finger bone

Lunula

Fingernails and hair are both made from a protein called keratin. A hair is alive and growing only at its root, down in the base of the follicle. The shaft that sticks out of the skin is dead and is made of flattened cells stuck firmly together. An average person has between 100,000 and 120,000 hairs on the scalp.

Skin is the body's protective coat. It shields the body from infection, protects organs and tissues from damage, and helps the body maintain a constant and steady temperature.

Humans have...

206 bones

300 bones as babies

33 vertebrae

An average pulse rate of 70 to 80 beats a minute

3,000 taste buds on the tongue

230 joints

100,000 hairs on an average scalp

23 pairs of chromosomes

Bones and Joints

Bones provide the strong framework that supports the whole body and holds its parts together. All of the bones together are called the skeleton, and this gives protection to organs, such as the brain, as well as providing an anchor for muscles.

▶ *The 206 bones of the human skeleton includes 32 bones in each arm, 31 in each leg, 29 in the head, 26 in the spinal column and hips, and 25 in the chest.*

Skull bones

The skull, or cranium, is the hard bone that protects the brain. It is made up of 22 separate bones, cemented together along rigid joints called sutures.

◀ *Bones contains threads of the tough, slightly bendy substance called collagen. It also has hard minerals, such as calcium and phosphate. Together, the collagen and minerals make a bone strong and rigid, yet able to bend slightly under stress. Bones have blood vessels for nourishment and nerves to feel pressure and pain. Inside the tough casing of most bones is a soft, jellylike core called the marrow, which can be either red or yellow.*

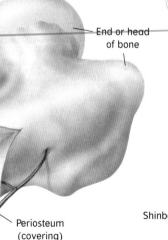

Nerves and blood vessels

Marrow

Spongy layer

Hard bone layer

Periosteum (covering)

End or head of bone

Neck bones (cervical vertebrae)

Breastbone

Ribs

Hipbone (pelvis)

Shinbone (tibia)

○ An adult's skeleton has 206 bones, joined together by rubbery cartilage. A baby's skeleton has 300 or more bones but some of these fuse (join) together as the baby grows.

○ Most women and girls have smaller and lighter skeletons than men and boys. Women's pelvises, or hip bones, are bigger than men's because the opening has to be wide enough to allow a baby to be born.

○ Weight for weight, bone is five times stronger than steel, but bones are so light that they only account for 14 percent of body weight.

○ Marrow is the soft, jellylike tissue in the middle of certain bones. It contains special cells that make new blood cells—up to five million every day.

○ Body joints are places where bones meet. Joints allow bones to move. There are several different kinds of joints, such as synovial joints that allow movement, and suture joints that do not.

○ Synovial joints are found throughout the body, especially in the shoulder, elbow, hip, and knee. These allow various kinds of movements, depending on their design. The elbow and knee are hinge joints, which allow only a to-and-fro movement. The shoulder and hip are ball-and-socket joints, which enable more flexibility, such as twisting.

X rays

In 1895 the German physicist Wilhelm Rontgen discovered X rays and how they pass through flesh, but not through bone. X rays are invisible waves of energy (called electromagnetic radiation). Doctors use X rays to examine bones without the need for surgery.

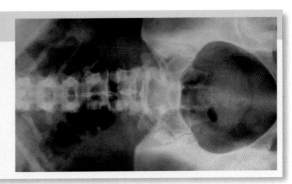

○ Cartilage is a tough but flexible material that is used in many joints to cushion the bones against impact. It gives strength to the skeleton but allows movement. Unborn babies' skeletons are mostly made of cartilage that eventually hardens to bone.

○ The backbone, or spine, extends from the base of the skull down to the hips. It is not a single bone, but a column of drum-shaped bones called vertebrae (single: vertebra).

○ The backbone supports the body and contains and protects the spinal cord, which carries messages between the brain and parts of the body. The cord is about 17 in long, and 31 pairs of main peripheral nerves branch from it.

○ Tendons are cords that tie a muscle to a bone, or a muscle to another muscle. They are made from collagen. Ligaments are strong cords of tough collagen and stretchy elastin that strengthen joints.

▶ *Strap-shaped ligaments crisscross the outside of the knee joint to hold the bones in place.*

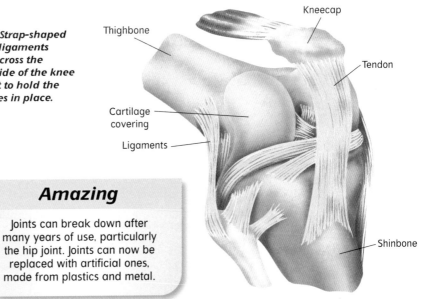

Kneecap

Thighbone

Tendon

Cartilage covering

Ligaments

Shinbone

Bone facts

The upper arm bone is called the humerus or, jokingly, the funny bone.

The smallest bones are the three tiny ossicles inside each ear.

The longest bone is the thighbone or femur, making up about one-quarter of the body's total height.

The broadest bone is the hipbone or pelvis.

Amazing

Joints can break down after many years of use, particularly the hip joint. Joints can now be replaced with artificial ones, made from plastics and metal.

Muscles and Moving

Every movement, every breath, every mouthful you chew—all of these actions and more are carried out by the body's muscles. By working together, the body's muscles carry out thousands of different activities every day.

○ Muscles are special fibers that contract (shorten) and relax (lengthen) to move parts of the body.

○ Voluntary muscles are those that you control by thinking, such as moving an arm. Involuntary muscles are those that work automatically, such as those that move food through your intestine.

○ There are about 640 voluntary muscles in the human body and they make up over 40 percent of the body's entire weight. Men usually have more muscle than women.

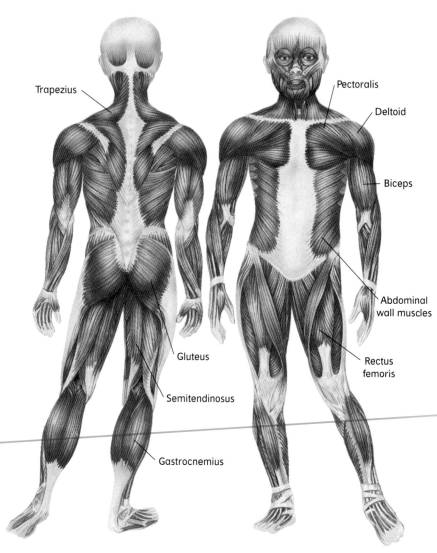

Trapezius

Pectoralis

Deltoid

Biceps

Abdominal wall muscles

Gluteus

Rectus femoris

Semitendinosus

Gastrocnemius

Working together

Muscles are controlled by the brain, which sends messages to them along stringlike nerves. When a muscle contracts for a long time, its fibers "take turns." Some of them shorten powerfully while others relax, then the contracted ones relax while others shorten, and so on.

Ⓐ *The muscles shown here are just beneath the skin. They are called superficial muscles. Underneath them is another layer, the deep muscle layer. In some areas there is an additional layer, the medial muscles.*

○ Most muscles are firmly anchored at both ends and attached to the bones either side of a joint, either directly or via tough fibers called tendons.

Muscle power

An elephant has an estimated 40,000 muscles in its trunk.

The tongue is the only muscle in the human body not attached at both ends.

It takes 17 muscles to smile and 43 to frown.

A caterpillar has over 2,000 muscles in its body.

Pulling together

If all of the muscles in your body could pull together, they would have enough combined strength to lift a bus.

❍ Most muscles are arranged in pairs because although muscles can shorten themselves, they cannot forcibly make themselves longer. So the flexor muscle that bends a joint is paired with an extensor muscle to straighten it again.

❍ The brain controls muscles by sending nerve signals along nerves to the muscles, telling them when to contract, by how much and for how long. We learn to do many activities, such as walking, when we are young and they soon become automatic—this means we can do them without having to think about them.

▼ *Most muscles are arranged in opposing or antagonistic pairs to pull a bone one way and then the other, like the biceps and triceps in the upper arm.*

Biceps

Triceps

1. To lift something, the biceps muscle gets shorter

2. The hinge joint of the elbow moves

3. To move the arm back down, the triceps shortens and the biceps gets longer

❍ Muscles use a lot of energy, and they need food and oxygen to work. Muscles get tired when the blood cannot bring these essential supplies fast enough. During exercise you breathe hard and fast to get more oxygen to your muscles.

❍ The body's smallest muscle is the stapedius. It is about the same size as this letter "I" and is attached to the tiny bones in the ear that enable us to hear.

❍ The body cannot make new muscles, but the ones it has can grow. Exercise can make muscles grow larger and more efficient.

❍ The heart muscle is a unique combination of skeletal and smooth muscle. It has its own built-in rhythm of contractions of 70 beats a minute, and special muscle cells that work like nerve cells for transmitting the signals for waves of muscle contraction to sweep through the heart.

❙ *Inside a muscle are bundles of myofibers, each about as thick as a human hair. Every myofiber is made of even thinner myofibrils, which contain numerous strands of the substances actin and myosin. These slide past each other to make the muscle contract.*

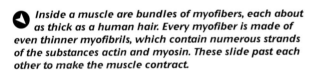

Fascicle (bundle of fibers)

Myofibers

Myofiber

Myofibril

Epimysium (covering)

Actin strand

Myosin strand

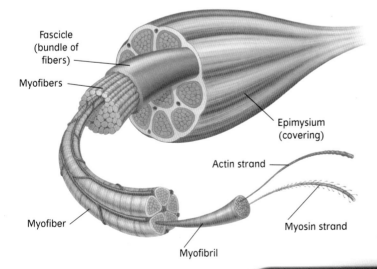

Amazing

The body's biggest muscles are the ones you sit on—the gluteus maximus muscles in the buttocks.

Lungs and Breathing

*T*he human body is constantly active, even when it appears to be at rest. One process that never stops, day or night, is breathing. Breathing is concerned with the movement of two gases (oxygen and carbon dioxide) into and out of our bodies.

Breathing muscles

0.1 gal of air passes in and out of the lungs each time you breathe. Breathing uses the diaphragm below the chest and the intercostals between the ribs. To breathe in, both muscle sets contract. The diaphragm changes from a domed shape to a flatter shape, pulling down the bases of the lungs. The intercostal muscles force the ribs up and out pulling on the lungs. Both these actions stretch the spongy lungs to suck in air. To breathe out, both muscle sets relax. The stretched lungs spring back to their smaller size, blowing out air.

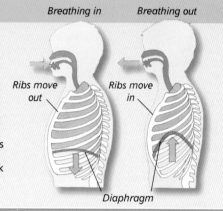

Breathing in   Breathing out

Ribs move out   Ribs move in

Diaphragm

Muscles in wall of bronchus

Right bronchus

Windpipe

Upper lobe of left lung

Air space inside bronchus

Right lung

Left bronchus

Left lung

◀ *Air flows to and from the lungs along the windpipe, which branches at its base into two bronchi, one to each lung. The heart fills the space located between the lungs. Breathing in is called inspiraton and breathing out is called expiration. No matter how much you breathe out, about 0.1 gal of air stays in your lungs.*

○ You breathe because every single cell in your body needs a continuous supply of oxygen to burn glucose, the high-energy substance from digested food that cells get from blood. As the cells burn glucose they make carbon dioxide, a waste gas.

Lower lobe of right long

Space for heart

Lower lobe of left long

Capillaries

Alveoli

Blood vessel

View along inside of bronchus

▶ *The bubble-like alveoli are in groups or bunches at the ends of the narrowest air tubes. They make up about one-third of the space taken up by the lungs.*

Air space inside alveoli

Bronchiole

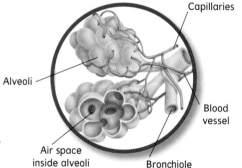

Breathe in, breathe out

If you live to the age of 80 you will have taken well over 600 million breaths.

○ Scientists call breathing "respiration." Cellular respiration is the way that cells use oxygen to burn glucose.

○ When you breathe in, air rushes in through your nose or mouth, down to your windpipe and into millions of tiny branching airways in your lungs.

○ The two biggest airways in the lungs are called bronchi (single: bronchus), and they branch into smaller airways called bronchioles. At the end of each bronchiole are bunches of minute air sacs called alveoli (single: alveolus).

○ Huge quantities of oxygen seeps across the cells walls of the alveoli and into the blood. Carbon dioxide moves from the blood into the alveoli and can then be breathed out.

○ The surface of the airways is protected by a slimy film of mucus that gets thicker to protect the lungs when you have a cold.

○ 0.1 gal of air passes in and out of the lungs each time you breathe. Deeper breathing can increase this by up to six times!

○ Yawning happens after the body has been at rest, and shallow breathing. A yawn is an extra-deep breath that brings in more oxygen. It prepares the body for action, rather than showing that a person is bored.

Amazing

Some people open their mouths to yawn so wide when they yawn forcefully that they dislocate or "detach" their jaws and cannot close the mouth again. Yawning happens when the body has been still for a time, breathing shallowly, so more oxygen is needed.

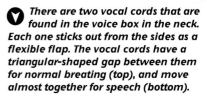

There are two vocal cords that are found in the voice box in the neck. Each one sticks out from the sides as a flexible flap. The vocal cords have a triangular-shaped gap between them for normal breating (top), and move almost together for speech (bottom).

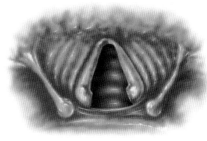

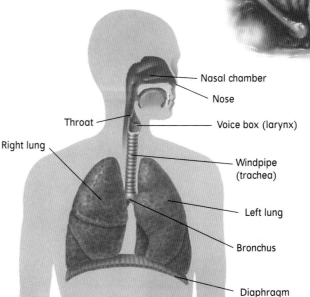

- Nasal chamber
- Nose
- Throat
- Voice box (larynx)
- Right lung
- Windpipe (trachea)
- Left lung
- Bronchus
- Diaphragm

The respiratory system includes the parts of the body specialized to take in oxygen from the air. Some parts have other uses too, such as smell in the nose and speech in the ` voice box (larynx).

Find out more

Heart and blood pp.182–183

Eating and Digestion

T he human body needs food and water. Food provides substances that are essential for the body to grow and repair itself. It also provides energy for life itself. Water is needed for the body to carry out all of its processes and has to be continually replaced.

▶ *The digestive system includes the mouth, teeth, tongue, throat, gullet, stomach, the small and large intestines, which together form a long tube, the digestive tract, the liver and the pancreas.*

Amazing

When your stomach is empty it holds barely 0.1 gal, but after eating a big meal it can stretch to more than 1 gal.

▼ *Semi-digested food moves from the stomach to the small intestine, which is 20 ft long, but tightly coiled. Here enzymes are added to the food, breaking it down so it can be absorbed. The intestine wall is covered with finger-like projections, called villi, which increase the surface area.*

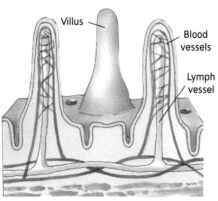

Villus
Blood vessels
Lymph vessel

Water for life

Your body is mainly made of water—more than 60 percent. You can survive for weeks without food, but only a few days without water.

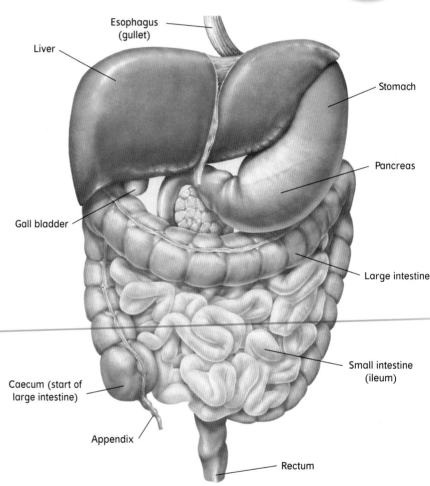

Esophagus (gullet)
Liver
Stomach
Pancreas
Large intestine
Gall bladder
Small intestine (ileum)
Caecum (start of large intestine)
Appendix
Rectum

Digestion timeline

0 hour	Food is chewed and swallowed.
1 hour	Food is churned with acids and juices in the stomach.
2 hours	Partially digested food begins to flow into the small intestine for further digestion and absorption.
4 hours	Most food has left the stomach and passed to the small intestine.
6 hours	Leftover and undigested foods pass into the large intestine, which takes the water and returns it to the body.
10 hours	Leftovers begin to collect in the last part of the system, the rectum, as feces.
16–24 hours	Feces pass through the last part of the system, the anus, and out of the body.

○ Digestion is the process by which your body breaks down the food you eat into substances that it can absorb (take in) and use.

○ Your digestive tract is basically a long winding tube called the alimentary canal, or gut. It starts at your mouth and ends at your anus. If you could lay your gut out straight it would be six times as long as you are tall.

○ When you eat you chew your food to break it into small lumps. They are coated in saliva (spit), which softens the food with special chemicals called enzymes.

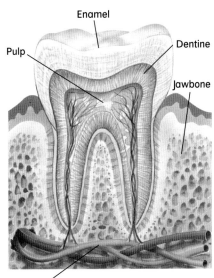

Enamel

Pulp

Dentine

Jawbone

Nerves and blood vessels

A *In each side of the jaw, the adult set of teeth includes two incisors at the front for biting, one taller canine for tearing, and two broad premolars, plus three wider molars for crushing and chewing. In the center of a tooth is a soft pulp of blood vessels and nerves. Around this is tough dentine. On the outside of the top part, the crown, is even harder enamel. The roots fix the tooth into the jawbone.*

▶ *The kidneys, ureters, bladder, and urethra form the urinary system. The kidney has two layers—the cortex and medulla. The space where urine collects is the renal pelvis. Blood enters each kidney and filters through over a million nephrons (filtration units). The body has two kidneys, placed on either side in the small of the back.*

○ When you swallow, food travels down your esophagus and into your stomach where more enzymes work on it and it is broken down into a mush called chyme. From here it travels into your small intestine.

○ Chyme is further broken down by enzymes in your small intestine and the goodness is absorbed across the intestine wall into blood vessels that transport it around the body. Waste moves into the large intestine.

○ Waste products and food that you cannot digest are pushed out of the large intestine through the anus when you go to the lavatory. This is called excretion.

○ Nutrients from your food are taken to your liver to be turned into glucose, the main energy-giving chemical for body cells. The liver helps keep levels of glucose steady in the bloodstream.

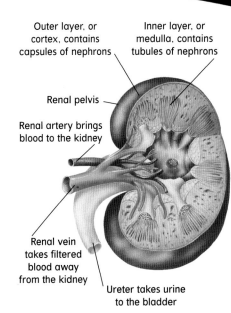

Outer layer, or cortex, contains capsules of nephrons

Inner layer, or medulla, contains tubules of nephrons

Renal pelvis

Renal artery brings blood to the kidney

Renal vein takes filtered blood away from the kidney

Ureter takes urine to the bladder

○ Your body needs a balance of different food types to work properly. Carbohydrates, proteins, fat, fiber, vitamins, and minerals are all essential for a healthy body.

○ Kidneys are the body's filters. They take goodness and water out of the blood, and return them to the body while removing excess water and waste products. This excess water and waste is sent to the bladder, where it is stored as urine.

Hormones

The process of digestion is, like other body processes, controlled by hormones. These are natural chemicals that work to keep the body in harmony. Hormones are made in special places called endocrine glands and they travel all round the body in the blood. Female and male bodies have much the same hormone-making glands, except for the reproductive parts—ovaries (seen here) in the female and testes in the male.

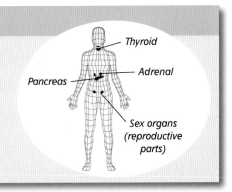

Thyroid

Adrenal

Pancreas

Sex organs (reproductive parts)

Heart and Blood

The circulatory system is a complex network of blood vessels, such as arteries, veins and capillaries, and the heart. These all work together to transmit blood to every cell in the body, bringing oxygen and nutrients or removing waste products.

○ Blood is the reddish liquid that circulates around your body. It carries food and oxygen to your body cells and removes waste. It also carries hormones and special cells that fight infections.

○ The heart is a muscular bag that never stops pumping blood round the body. It is divided into two pumps. One pump sends blood to the lungs, to collect oxygen. It returns to the heart, where the other pump sends it to the rest of the body.

Taking your pulse

Your pulse is the powerful high-pressure surge, or wave, that runs through your body and vessels every time the heart pumps blood out. You can feel your pulse by pressing two fingertips on the inside of your wrist, below your thumb.

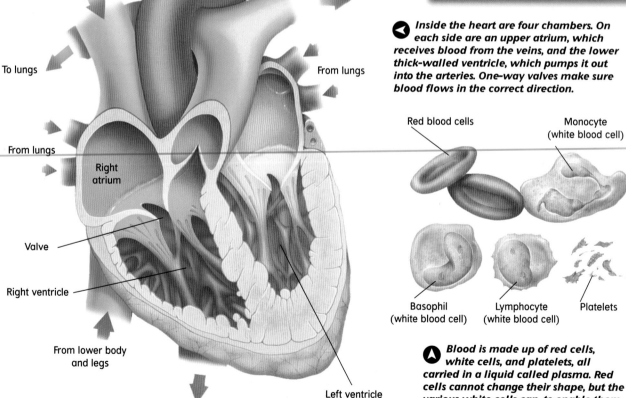

Aorta (main artery) with branches to head and brain

Vena cava (main vein) from head and brain

To lungs

To lungs

From lungs

From lungs

Right atrium

Valve

Right ventricle

From lower body and legs

To lower body and legs

Left ventricle

Inside the heart are four chambers. On each side are an upper atrium, which receives blood from the veins, and the lower thick-walled ventricle, which pumps it out into the arteries. One-way valves make sure blood flows in the correct direction.

Red blood cells

Monocyte (white blood cell)

Basophil (white blood cell)

Lymphocyte (white blood cell)

Platelets

Blood is made up of red cells, white cells, and platelets, all carried in a liquid called plasma. Red cells cannot change their shape, but the various white cells can, to enable them to attack germs invading the body.

Amazing

At any moment about 66 percent of all the body's blood is in the veins, 29 percent in the arteries, and 5 percent in the capillaries.

A blood vessel wall has several layers and blood itself contains different types of cells. Red cells are the most numerous and have a rounded, dish shape. White cells can change their shape as they surround and attack germs. Platelets are much smaller, resembling pieces of cells.

○ White blood cells are essential in the fight against infection. There are different types of white blood cell and they work together to kill invading organisms, such as viruses or bacteria.

○ Arteries are tubelike blood vessels that carry blood away from the heart. Most arteries contain blood that carries oxygen to the body parts.

○ Veins are blood vessels that carry blood back to the heart. Most veins carry blood that has had the oxygen and nutrients removed. It contains carbon dioxide, which is released into the lungs.

○ Capillaries are the smallest of all your blood vessels. They are only one cell thick, so chemicals can easily pass through them and into your cells. The largest capillary is still thinner than a human hair.

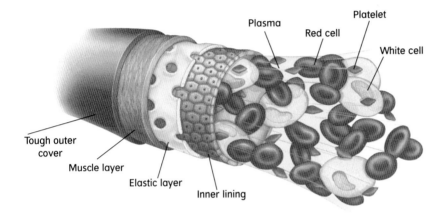

Plasma
Red cell
Platelet
White cell
Tough outer cover
Muscle layer
Elastic layer
Inner lining

○ Your blood has two main types of cell, white cells and red cells. It also contains platelets, which help to form blood clots to stop any bleeding. Blood also carries substances that fight infection and hormones.

○ Red blood cells are button-shaped and they contain a red protein called hemoglobin. This protein combines with oxygen to carry it around the body. In each red blood cell there are about 250 million hemoglobin molecules

Arteries carry blood away from the heart. They have thick walls to withstand the surge of high-pressure blood with each heartbeat. Capillaries are the smallest blood vessels, less than 1 mm long and far too thin to see. Oxygen and nutrients seep from blood through their walls into surrounding tissues. Veins are wide, thin-walled and floppy and take blood back to the heart.

Body full of blood

The amount of blood in your body depends on your size. An adult weighing 176 lb has about 1.3 gal of blood, a child weighing 88 lb has half that amount.

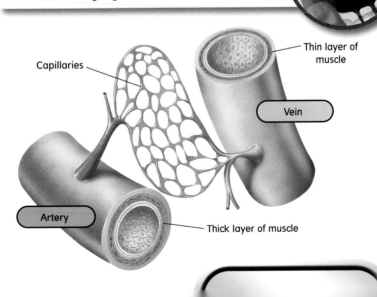

Capillaries
Thin layer of muscle
Vein
Artery
Thick layer of muscle

The Nervous System

The nervous system is your body's control and communication system. It is made up of nerves and the brain. It is your nervous system that controls everything you do, everything you see, and everything you feel. It is the body's central "computer."

○ Nerves are your body's hot lines, carrying instant messages from the brain to every organ and muscle—and sending back an endless stream of data to the brain about what is going on both inside, and outside, your body.

○ Nerves are made of very specialized cells called neurons. Neurons are spider-shaped, with lots of branching threads called dendrites and a winding tail called an axon. An axon can be up to 3 ft long.

○ Neurons link up, like beads on a string, to make up your nervous system. Nerve signals are electrical pulses and they travel down neurons at great speed—3–6 ft each second.

○ Sensory nerves carry information to your brain about your body's experience of the world. Eyes, ears, tongue, and nose all have sensory nerves. Your skin is covered with sensory nerve endings, called receptors.

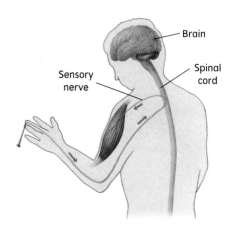

Brain

Sensory nerve

Spinal cord

▲ *If you touch a sharp pin, a message goes along a sensory nerve to your spinal cord. A motor nerve moves your hand away at once. This immediate response is called a reflex action. The message carries on to your brain, which knows about the pain after your hand has moved, so then you feel it.*

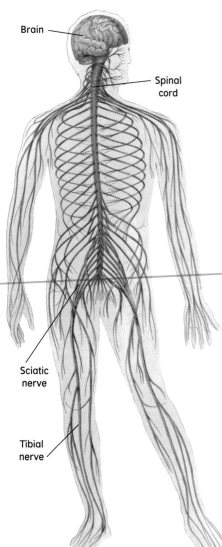

Brain

Spinal cord

Sciatic nerve

Tibial nerve

Amazing

The left half of your brain controls the right-hand side of your body, and the right half of your brain controls the left-hand side of your body.

◄ *Nerves branch from the brain and spinal cord to every part of the body. All nerve signals are similar, but there are two main kinds, depending on where they are going. Sensory nerve signals travel from the sensory parts (eyes, ears, nose, tongue, and skin) to the brain. Motor nerve signals travel from the brain out to the muscles, to make the body move about.*

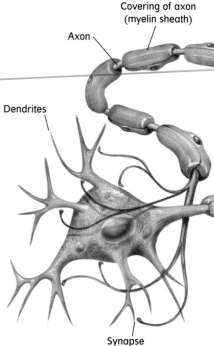

Covering of axon (myelin sheath)

Axon

Dendrites

Synapse (junction between nerve cells)

○ Information about light, taste, touch, heat, smell, and sound are all sent to the brain where it is processed.

○ The brain is an extremely complicated organ, and very little is known about how it works. Nerves from around the body bring information to the brain, where it is stored (as memory) or acted upon.

MRI scanners

Brain and nervous tissue do not show up well on X rays, so doctors use special scanning equipment to investigate these areas. MRI (Magnetic Resonance Imaging) scans are commonly used in hospitals to examine brains for possible injuries and damage.

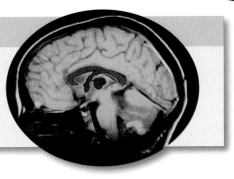

Nerve cells

There are hundreds of billions of nerve cells in the body. The brain alone contains 100 billion nerve cells.

▼ *About nine-tenths of the brain is the large dome of the two cerebral hemispheres. The outer cerebral cortex is where conscious thoughts happen.*

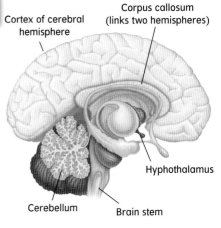

Cortex of cerebral hemisphere

Corpus callosum (links two hemispheres)

Hyphothalamus

Cerebellum

Brain stem

▼ *The brain and nerves are made of billions of specialized cells, nerve cells, or neurons. Each has many tiny branches (dendrites) to collect nerve messages, and the axon or fiber is a longer, thicker branch that passes on these messages.*

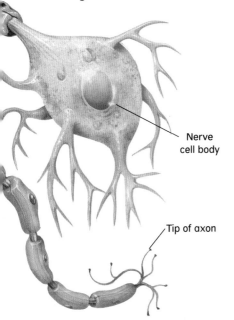

Nerve cell body

Tip of axon

Spinal cord

Vertebra (backbone)

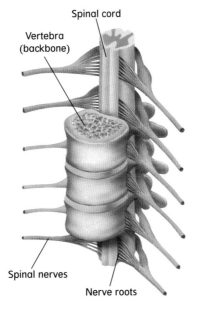

Spinal nerves

Nerve roots

▲ *The brain is "wired" into the body by the spinal cord. It extends from the base of the brain down inside the backbone (spinal column). Thirty-one pairs of nerves branch from it on each side out into the body. The spinal cord is protected inside a tunnel, which is formed by a row of holes through the vertebrae (backbones).*

○ The brain is divided into different regions, which perform different tasks. They are all linked and work together.

○ The hypothalamus and brain stem are involved with automatic processes, such as breathing and digestion. The cerebral cortex is involved in thinking, making decisions, and learning.

○ The brain sends messages out to the muscles via motor nerves. The nerves instruct the muscles to contract and relax. The brain coordinates all your muscles so they produce smooth, flowing movements.

Reproduction

In the beginning, a human body begins as a single cell, which is a fertilized egg. This egg grows, over a period of about nine months, into a baby that is ready to be born. A newborn baby needs constant care to survive.

○ The process of making a new human being is called reproduction. Humans are mammals and reproduce in a very similar way to other mammals: they give birth to live young and feed them with milk that is made in special glands in the mother's body.

○ A baby grows from an egg cell that has been fertilized by a sperm cell. Egg cells are made by females, in special places called ovaries. Every month a woman's body instructs an egg to ripen, ready for fertilization.

○ Sperm cells are made by a man's body, inside special places called testes. Millions of sperm cells are made every day and they are stored inside a coiled tube called the epididymis. Unused sperm are reabsorbed by the body.

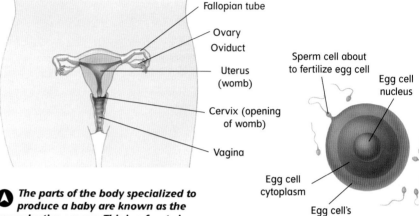

Fallopian tube
Ovary
Oviduct
Uterus (womb)
Cervix (opening of womb)
Vagina

Sperm cell about to fertilize egg cell
Egg cell nucleus
Egg cell cytoplasm
Egg cell's outer coat

The parts of the body specialized to produce a baby are known as the reproductive organs. This is a front view of the inside of a female reproductive system showing the two ovaries and fallopian tubes, which join to the uterus. In the woman, egg cells are contained in the two ovaries. Each month the menstrual cycle causes one egg to ripen and pass along the oviduct into the womb, where a sperm cell may join with it.

The female egg cell passes along the woman's fallopian tube. At fertilization, tiny sperm cells swarm around the egg until one sperm manages to push its head on to the surface of the egg. The sperm head and egg membrane join, and fertilization takes place.

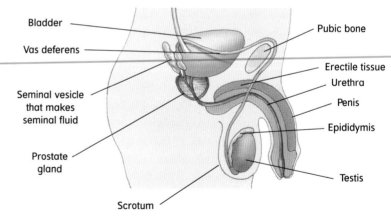

Bladder
Vas deferens
Seminal vesicle that makes seminal fluid
Prostate gland
Scrotum

Pubic bone
Erectile tissue
Urethra
Penis
Epididymis
Testis

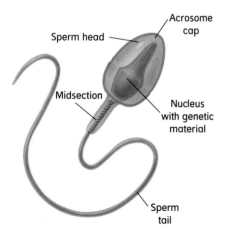

Sperm head
Acrosome cap
Midsection
Nucleus with genetic material
Sperm tail

A mature sperm cell consists of a head, where genetic information is stored, a midsection and a tadpole–like tail, which allows it to swim rapidly toward the female egg cell.

This is a side view of the inside of the male reproductive organs. In a man, sperm are made in the two testes. During sex they pass along the vas deferens tubes, which join and continue as the urethra, to the outside.

○ During sexual intercourse (sex), sperm cells enter the woman's vagina and may meet up with an egg. If a sperm enters the egg, and joins with it, then the egg is fertilized and might grow into a baby.

○ A fertilized egg implants in the woman's womb. This is the place where babies grow during pregnancy.

○ The fertilized egg divides into two, then each new cell divides again and this continues until lots of new cells have been created. The cells grow and become specialized; some become brain cells, some muscle cells. Each have a role to play in the new body.

Life begins when the fertilized egg divides into two cells, then four, eight, and so on. After a few days there are hundreds of cells, and after a few weeks, millions. These cells build up the various body parts. An unborn baby develops "head-first," starting with the brain and head, then the main body, then the arms and legs. At first, the tiny baby has plenty of room in the womb and can float about freely. But as it grows it becomes cramped and has to bend its neck, back, arms, and legs.

Ultrasound scans

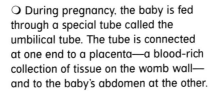

Pregnant women can find out how their babies are growing, and check they are well by having ultrasound scans.

○ During pregnancy, the baby is fed through a special tube called the umbilical tube. The tube is connected at one end to a placenta—a blood-rich collection of tissue on the womb wall—and to the baby's abdomen at the other.

Amazing

Every single person is unique. Not just because of genes inherited from parents, but because experiences and learning changes us.

DNA—the structure of life

Children often look like their parents because all of our cells, including egg and sperm cells, contain DNA (deoxyribonucleic acid). DNA holds information about special structures called genes. Genes make us tall or short, fair, or dark, healthy or likely to get particular illnesses and so on. Genes are passed on to children through sexual reproduction. Half of your genes are from your mother and half from your father. No one has the same mix of genes except identical twins. Inside a single cell of your body, there are over 30,000 individual genes.

○ When the baby is ready to be born the mother begins "labor." During this process her body prepares itself to deliver the baby. The mother's womb has to push the baby out with strong muscular contractions. Once born, the umbilical cord is cut and the baby breathes on its own.

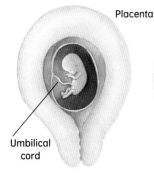

Placenta

Umbilical cord

Two months
All main body parts are formed and baby is now called a fetus

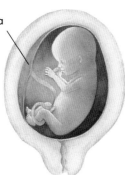

Three months
First hairs grow on skin

Five months
Hands and fingers can grip the umbilical cord

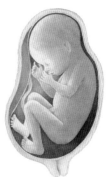

Seven months
Eyelids open, body is slim and skin wrinkled

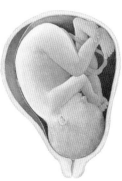

Nine months
Baby has "turned" and is head-down, ready to be born

Glossary

Alveoli Microscopic air spaces inside the lungs, with more than 300 million in each.

Annual A flowering plant that completes its life cycle in one year.

Anther The tip of a stamen, where pollen is made.

Artery Blood vessel that normally carries blood with oxygen.

Biennial A flowering plant that takes two years to complete its life cycle.

Bladder A bag-like organ in mammals that stores urine.

Broadleaved tree A tree that grows leaves that are wide and flat. It may be an evergreen or deciduous tree.

Camouflage Pattern or color that blends in with the surroundings.

Capillary Tiny blood vessels.

Carbon dioxide A gas that plants need to photosynthesize, and that animals make as a waste product from respiration.

Carnivore Animal that mostly or totally eats meat.

Carpel The female part of a flower.

Cartilage A rubbery substance that is similar to bone.

Cell The basic building block of animals and plants. The cells have different shapes to perform different tasks to keep the plant alive.

Chlorophyll Chemical found in green plants essential for photosynthesis.

Chromosomes Lengths of the genetic material DNA that have been coiled up very tightly to resemble microscopic threads.

Clone An offspring that is identical in every way to its parent.

Conifer Trees and plants that produce cones, not flowers.

Cortex The outer region or layer of a body part such as the kidney, brain, or lymph node.

DNA Deoxyribonucleic acid, a chemical that makes up the instructions or genes for how the body grows and functions.

Deciduous Plants or trees that lose their leaves in the fall.

Digestion The process of taking the goodness out of food.

Endangered An animal or plant species that is in danger of becoming extinct.

Enzyme A chemical substance that causes other chemical reactions to occur, or speeds them up.

Evergreen Plants that keep their leaves all year.

Evolution The gradual process by which animals and plants adapt and develop to survive in a changing world.

Excretion Removal of wastes, by-products and other unwanted substances from the body—by the excretory or urinary system.

Exoskeleton The tough outer coat of an insect.

Extinction When an animal or plant species completely dies out.

Fertilization The process by which a male sex cell and a female sex cell join together, for example sperm and egg in mammals, pollen and ovule in flowering plants.

Fossil The process by which the remains of an animal or plant become preserved as rock, over millions of years.

Genes Instructions or information, in the form of the chemical DNA, for how the body develops, grows and functions.

Germination The process by which a seed begins to produce a seedling.

Gills Organs used for breathing (respiration) by many animals that live in water, such as fish.

Glucose A type of sugar that is used as an energy supply by plants and animals.

Habitat The place that an animal or plant lives.

Herbivore An animal that only eats plants.

Hormone A chemical substance that is transported around a plant or animal to make an organ or tissue respond in a particular way.

Hydrogen Gas that combines with oxygen to make water.

Invertebrate Animals without backbones.

Joint The place where two or more bones meet.

Ligament Strong and flexible tissue that joins bones.

Lung Special organ used for breathing by animals that breathe on land (and mammals that live in water).

Marrow Soft, jellylike substance in the middle of many bones, which makes new cells for the blood (red marrow) or stores energy and nutrients as fat (yellow marrow).

Migration Movement by animals to find better conditions, such as food or weather.

Mimicry When one animal looks like another (the model) to gain an advantage, for example pretending to be a poisonous animal when it is not itself poisonous.

Neurons Nerve cells, specialized to receive and pass on information in the form of tiny electrical signals called nerve impulses.

Nocturnal Active at night rather than during the day.

Nucleus The central region or control centre of a cell, containing the genetic material DNA.

Organ A collection of tissues that perform a particular job, for example lung, stomach, or heart.

Organism Any living thing.

Ovary Place where eggs are made in females.

Ovule An egg.

Oxygen A gas that animals breathe. It combines with hydrogen to make water.

Perennial A plant that lives for many years.

Photosynthesis Process by which plants combine carbon dioxide with water to make food, using sunlight as a source of energy.

Plankton Tiny animals and plants that drift in the water of seas, oceans, and large lakes.

Plasma The liquid part of blood without the microscopic cells (red cells, white cells, and platelets).

Pollen Tiny capsules made by the stamens. To reproduce, plants must pass pollen between flowers. Pollen is carried by the wind or other insects to other plants.

Pollination The process by which pollen is transferred to the female part of a flower.

Predator An animal that hunts, or preys, on other animals.

Prey An animal that is hunted upon by another.

Reproduction The process of creating new life, or offspring.

Respiration Another word for breathing, or releasing energy from food and gases.

Sap The liquid that moves through the root and stem of a plant.

Seed A capsule, which forms from the ovule after fertilization, and contains a tiny plant with a foodstore.

Sepal A small leaf that forms part of the covering of the flower bud.

Species A type of animal or plant.

Spore A tiny capsule made by nonflowering plants such as mosses and fungi. It contains a piece of the parent plant or fungus, which can break out and grow into a new plant.

Stamen A male part of the flower that bears the anther.

Stem Part of the plant that supports the leaves and flowers and carries water and minerals and food made in the leaves to other parts of the plant.

Stigma The top of the carpel.

Stomata Tiny holes in a leaf through which gases can pass.

Synapse The junction or connection between two nerve cells or neurons.

Temperate forest A forest that grows in a region with warm summers and cool winters.

Tendon Special tissue that connects muscles to bones.

Territory An area or place where an animal lives and feeds, and which it defends by chasing away others of its kind.

Tissue A collection of similar cells that perform a particular task.

Tropical rainforest A forest that grows where the weather is always hot and wet.

Vein Main blood vessel or tube that carries blood towards the heart.

Vertebrate An animal with a backbone.

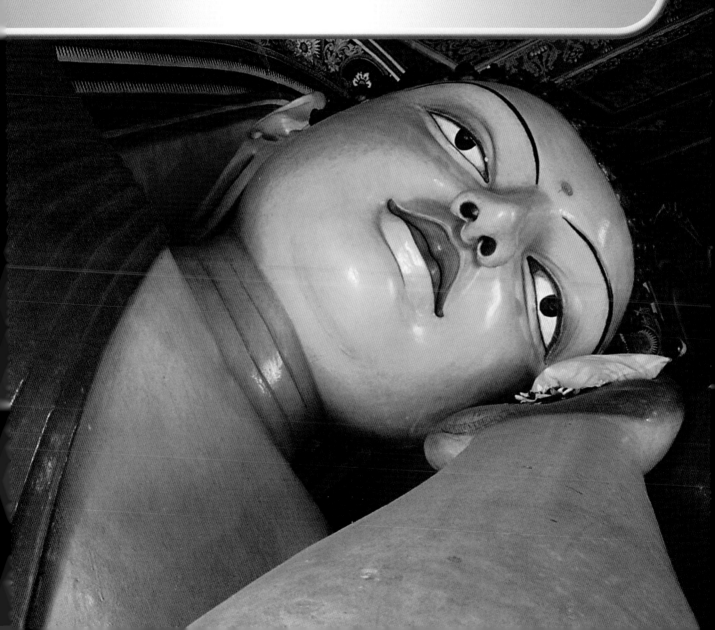

Ancient Myths

Myths and legends existed in civilizations all over the world for thousands of years before writing was developed. They were told as entertainment by professional poets trained to remember the long works and perform them. This is called the oral tradition of literature.

❍ Myths from the Middle East are the oldest recorded mythology in the world, dating from 2500 BC.

❍ The Babylonian creation myth grew from the Sumerian creation myth. It is called the Enuma Elish.

❍ The Enuma Elish says that in the beginning the Universe was made of salt waters (Mother Tiamat), sweet waters, (Father Apsu), and a mist (their son Mummu).

❍ The waters gave birth to new young rebellious gods who overthrew Apsu and Mummu.

❍ Tiamat and her followers (led by a god called Kingu) were conquered by a male Babylonian god, Marduk, in a battle of powerful magic.

❍ The Babylonians pictured Marduk with four eyes and four ears, so he could see and hear everything. Fire spurted from his mouth and haloes blazed from his head.

❍ Marduk became the new ruler. He made Tiamat's body into the earth and sky. He appointed gods to rule the heavens, the earth, and the air in between.

Origins of Enuma Elish

Enuma Elish, the Babylonian creation myth, was written in a language called cuneiform on seven clay tablets discovered by archeologists excavating Nineveh in AD 1845. It grew out of the Sumerian creation myth. The Sumerians of Mesopotamia are famous for their ziggurats— massive stepped temples of mud bricks that were built around 2100 BC.

▼ *Aborigines believe that their ancestors had magical powers of creation. Aboriginal myths say that people were carved out of animals and plants by their ancestors who then went back to sleep in rocks, trees, or underground—where they are to this day.*

Find out more

Norse myths pp. 198–199

▶ *One Chinese creation myth says that in the beginning, the Universe was an egg containing chaos. The first being, a dwarflike creature called Panku, pushed open the egg. The chaos separated to form the Earth and sky.*

Amazing

Most religions have just one creation myth, but the ancient Egyptians had four. Each myth was linked to a city and its god—Heliopolis (Atum), Memphis (Ptah), Hermopolis (Thoth), and Esna (Khnum).

▲ *Some Polynesian myths say that the creator god, Tangoroa, formed the world by throwing rocks into a watery waste. He made people from the leaves of a vine.*

❍ Human beings were created out of Kingu's blood. Marduk made them build a temple to himself and the other gods at Babylon.

❍ Every spring, Babylon was in danger of flooding from the rivers Tigris and Euphrates. Historians believe that the Enuma Elish might have been acted as a pantomime to please Marduk so he kept order and prevented the flooding.

❍ The mythology of ancient Egypt may go back as far as 4000 BC, when the land was populated by farming peoples.

❍ Egyptians had fewer myths than most ancient peoples. Almost all of their stories are about creation, life, and death.

❍ One story told how the Sun god Ra-Atum traveled across the sky and was reborn every day at dawn.

❍ Egyptian myths were written down in hieroglyphic writing. This was invented around 3000 BC, when Upper Egypt and Lower Egypt united into one kingdom.

❍ Hieroglyph means "sacred carving." Each picture stands for an object, an idea, or a sound.

Hieroglyphs decoded

It was not until the 1820s that experts decoded hieroglyphs. Before that, what we knew about ancient Egyptian mythology came from old writings in other languages. The Rosetta Stone, found in 1799 but dating from 197 BC, provided the key. It was inscribed with the same text in three languages: two understood, the other hieroglyphs.

Gods of Egypt

People in each area of Egypt originally worshiped their own gods. Their stories spread and merged, so there are many versions and some gods are known in different forms. The mythology of ancient Egypt may go back as far as 4000 BC, when the land was populated by farming peoples.

○ The ancient Egyptians believed that if they preserved a dead body from decay by mummifying it, its spirit would live forever.

○ Egyptian myths say that in the beginning the Universe was filled with dark waters.

○ The first god was Re-Atum. He appeared from the waters as the land of Egypt appears every year out of the flood waters of the Nile.

Sacred eye

An amulet was a piece of jewelry thought to have magical powers. Many amulets were in the shape of an eye—either the Sun god's or Horus's. The ancient Egyptians believed the sacred eye had healing powers and could ward off evil.

Horus

○ Re-Atum spat and the spittle turned into the gods Shu (air) and Tefnut (moisture).

○ The world was created when Shu and Tefnut gave birth to two children: Nut—the sky, and Geb—the Earth.

○ Humans were created when Shu and Tefnut wandered into the dark wastes and got lost. Re-Atum sent his eye to find them. On reuniting, Re-Atum's tears of joy turned into people.

○ The ancient Egyptians believed that part of the spirit of a god could live on Earth in the body of an animal. This is why their gods are pictured as humans with animal heads.

○ Hathor or Sekhmet was the daughter and wife of Re-Atum. She could take on the form of a terrifying lioness or cobra to attack and punish enemies of the Sun god.

○ The most important Egyptian myth was the story of Osiris and Isis.

▼ *On the left of this scene is Sobek, god of the Nile, with a crocodile's head. Bastet, goddess of musicians, dancers, and cats, is in the center, while the moon god Thoth is on the right, with the head of an ibis. Sometimes Thoth was represented as a baboon.*

Sobek, god of the Nile

Bastet, goddess of musicians, dancers, and cats

The moon god Thoth

Find out more

Egyptian gods p. 207

A pharaoh called Amenhotep IV changed his name to Akhenaten, after the god Aten. During his reign, the pharaoh worshiped only Aten and he made Aten the king of all the gods.

Amazing

In ancient Egypt, cats were sacred to the goddess Bastet. When a pet cat died, the family had it mummified—just like a dead human.

Scarab beetle

The Sun god, Re-Atum, often appeared as a scarab beetle, as can be seen on this amulet. This was because a scarab beetle rolls a ball of dung before it, as the ball of the Sun rolls across the sky.

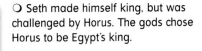

○ Osiris was the son of Re-Atum. He became king of Egypt and, later, ruler of the underworld Kingdom of the Dead.

○ Osiris was a good ruler, but he was doomed to be killed by his wicked brother.

○ Osiris's brother, Seth, represented evil in the Universe. He hatched a wicked plot to murder Osiris and take the crown of Egypt for himself.

○ Osiris's sister and wife was called Isis. She was a powerful mother goddess of fertility.

○ After killing Osiris, Seth tore his body into pieces, but Isis rescued most of the pieces for burial beneath temples.

○ Horus was Osiris's son. He inherited the throne of Egypt. Ancient Egyptians believed that all pharaohs were descended from Horus.

○ Seth made himself king, but was challenged by Horus. The gods chose Horus to be Egypt's king.

○ Seth was banished to the desert, a place of evil, and became the god of terrible storms.

○ Osiris was mummified by Anubis and became god of the dead. Later pharaohs were believed to be gods themselves.

The dwarf god, Bes, was the ancient Egyptian god of children and the home.

Gods of Egypt

Nut	The sky
Geb	The Earth
Shu	The air and sky
Tefnut	Moisture
Thoth	The moon
Re-Atum	The Sun
Isis	Mother goddess
Osiris	Death and afterlife

Greek Myths

T*he stories about Greek and Roman gods, spirits, and heroes are known as Classical mythology. The gods and goddesses of ancient Greece were adopted by the Romans, under new names. Hence Zeus became Jove, Hera became Juno, Poseidon became Neptune and so on.*

❍ We know about Greek mythology from works of art and writings from as early as 800 BC.

❍ The earliest ancient Greeks were Bronze Age farmers who worshiped a Mother Earth goddess called Gaia.

❍ Myths say that Gaia emerged out of an emptiness called Chaos.

❍ Gaia, the Earth mother, gave birth to Ourea (Mountains), Pontus (Sea), and Uranus (Father Sky).

Chief among the Greek gods, Zeus would hurl thunderbolts from the skies to show his displeasure.

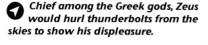

1	**Ares** god of war	6	**Pan** god of wild nature
2	**Aphrodite** goddess of love	7	**Poseidon** god of the sea
3	**Athene** goddess of wisdom	8	**Hermes** messenger of the god
4	**Hades** god of the Underworld	9	**Zeus** king of the gods
5	**Artemis** goddess of nature	10	**Hera** wife to Zeus

Find out more

Greek temples p. 208

The Cyclops

The Cyclops were one-eyed giants who gave Zeus the gift of thunder and lightning, and Poseidon his trident, with which he could stir up the sea into terrible storms.

○ The next rulers were the children of Gaia and Uranus: 12 immortals called the Titans. They were gigantic rulers of the Earth.

○ The children of two Titans, Oceanus and Tethys, lived as spirits called nymphs in all the springs, rivers, and seas of the world.

○ Another two Titans, Cronus and Rhea, had children who overthrew them. These were the next immortal rulers: the Greek gods and goddesses.

○ Three Greek gods divided the Universe between them: Zeus ruled the Earth, Poseidon the sea, and Hades ruled the underworld kingdoms of the dead.

🅐 *The Greeks built impressive temples to Zeus and their other gods and goddesses. You can see the ruins of many of them on Greek islands today. One of the most famous Greek temples is the Parthenon in Athens.*

○ Some myths say that the most intelligent Titan, Prometheus, created the first man out of clay and water.

○ Other myths say that the chief god, Zeus, has created five races of human beings. The Gold Race lived in harmony with the gods and died peacefully. The Silver Race were quarrelsome and disrespectful, so Zeus wiped them out. The Bronze Race loved weapons and war, so brought death upon themselves. The Race of Heroes were so noble that Zeus took them to live on islands of the blessed. The Race of Iron is our own. Myths predict that we show no respect for the earth we live on, so Zeus will destroy us.

Titans facts

The Titans were 12 immortals in Greek and Roman mythology.

The strongest of the Titans was Atlas—he held up the Earth.

The cleverest Titan was Prometheus.

A Titan called Epimetheus is said to have married the first mortal woman, Pandora.

The Titan Helios became god of the Sun. Selene became goddess of the Moon.

Oceanus became god of the river that the Greeks believed surrounded the Earth.

A prophecy said that the youngest Titan, Cronus, would be overthrown by his own son. So when Cronus's children were born, he ate them. However, his wife hid one child away—this was Zeus.

Zeus and his brothers and sisters fought against the Titans for ten years. The Titans were finally overthrown and hurled into an underworld realm of punishment called Tartarus. There, they were bound in chains for ever.

There were also three one-eyed Cyclopes and three Hekatonchires (100-headed monsters)—they were also children of Uranus and Gaia.

Atlas

Amazing

After the war between the gods and the Titans, Zeus punished Atlas by commanding him to hold up the heavens and Earth on his shoulders for eternity.

Norse Myths

The ancient Norse peoples who lived in Scandinavia in the Bronze Age told stories about a race of gods and goddesses called the Aesir. The Norse peoples were ancestors of the Vikings—the seafaring warriors from Norway, Sweden, and Denmark who invaded other parts of Europe—to whom they passed on their mythology.

❍ The gods built themselves a heavenly homeland called Asgard.

❍ A rainbow bridge links the realm of the gods to the world of humans. The god Heimdall was sent as watchman to make sure that only gods and goddesses could cross.

❍ The Norse gods do not take much notice of humans. They are more concerned with battling giants and dealing with other magical creatures.

❍ Odin, the chief of the warrior gods, has a high throne called Lidskialf, from which he can see anything happening in the Universe.

❍ Odin occasionally likes to disguise himself as a traveler and wander undetected through the world of humans—almost like taking a vacation.

❍ Norse gods and goddesses are not immortal. They can be killed by cunning magic or simple bravery, just like humans.

❍ The most important warrior goddesses are Odin's wife, Frigg (a mother goddess with fertility powers), and the beautiful Freyja (goddess of love).

❍ The daughters of Odin were beautiful spirits called Valkyries. They flew over battlefields and took warriors who had died bravely to live happily in a place in Asgard called Valhalla.

❍ Two days of the week are named after Norse warrior gods. Wednesday means Woden's Day—Woden was another name for Odin, the father of the gods. Thursday means Thor's Day, after the Norse god of thunder.

◀ *Odin rode an eight-legged horse. Two ravens, called Thought and Memory, flew by his side.*

Amazing

The Norse world had three levels: Asgard, home of the gods; Alfhelm, home of the elves; and Midgard, the land of men.

Find out more
Greek myths pp. 196–197

Njord

Norse stories said that the god of the sea, Njord, married the giantess Skadi, who watched over snowy mountains.

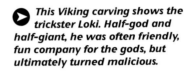

▶ *This Viking carving shows the trickster Loki. Half-god and half-giant, he was often friendly, fun company for the gods, but ultimately turned malicious.*

Ragnarok

Norse myths tell of Ragnarok, which means "the doom of the gods." This will be a terrible time, when the forces of good will clash with the powers of evil. The gods will fight against giants and monsters— and lose. The world will come to an end, but a new Universe will be born from the ruins of the old.

❑ The Aesir once fought against gods and goddesses called the Vanir (or "shining ones"). They finally made a peaceful alliance against the giants.

❑ The ruler of the Vanir was the fertility god Njord, ruler of the winds and the sea.

❑ Loki was a famous trickster in Norse mythology who enjoyed stirring up trouble between the gods and the giants.

◀ *The beautiful Freyja rode in a chariot pulled by cats. She and her brother Frey, the farmer's god, brought pleasure and fertility.*

Native American Beliefs

Native American myths come from the first people to live in North America. They arrived there from Asia around 15,000 years ago when the two continents were linked by ice. Native Americans settled in many different tribes. Each tribe had its own myths and legends, although they shared many beliefs. The stories were passed down through generations by word of mouth. Most tribes believed that everything is part of one harmonious creation. Harming anything can upset the balance of the world.

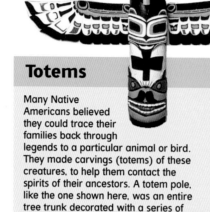

Totems

Many Native Americans believed they could trace their families back through legends to a particular animal or bird. They made carvings (totems) of these creatures, to help them contact the spirits of their ancestors. A totem pole, like the one shown here, was an entire tree trunk decorated with a series of spirit carvings.

○ The Iroquois believed that Mother Earth fell into a lake from a land beyond the sky. The animals helped to create the Sun, the Moon, and stars.

○ According to the Algonquian, the Earth was created by Michabo the Great Hare, from a grain of sand from the bottom of the ocean.

○ The Maidu tribe believed that the gods Kodoyanpe and Coyote floated on a vast expanse of water and one day decided to create the world.

○ The Navajo people believed that the first man and woman were created when four gods ordered the winds to blow life into two ears of corn.

○ Four sky spirits were important to the Pawnee: the North Star (their creator), the Morning Star (their protector), the South Star (the underworld leader of enemy forces), and the Evening Star (bringer of darkness).

○ South Eastern tribes, including the Cherokee, built earth mounds in the shape of sacred animal spirits, around which all tribal ceremonies were held.

◄ *The Iroquois (an Algonquian tribe) lived in an eastern area of North America now known as New York State.*

Amazing

Many tribes believed that they would be punished by the animal spirits of their ancestors if they hunted or fished for more food than they needed.

○ Shamans or "medicine men" were holy men who knew how to contact spirits. They sometimes used herbs and chanting to sink into a trance. This then allowed a spirit to enter them and speak.

○ Many Native American myths say that when the world was created, humans and animals lived together.

▲ *European settlers in North America fought Native American tribes for their land. By 1890, the tribes had been pushed onto reservations far from their homes.*

○ In the late 19th century, many Native American tribes performed ghost dances to ask the spirits of their animal ancestors to drive European settlers from their lands.

▲ *Many Native American myths involve the coyote, a wily trickster with decidedly human characteristics, but who is also often tricked himself.*

Thunderbird

Several Native American tribes told stories about the Thunderbird—a powerful spirit in the form of a bird who could create terrible storms. Lightning was said to flash from its beak and the beating of its wings brought on thunder.

Hindu Deities

Hinduism is the main religion of India. It originated about 1500 BC among the Aryan people of the northwest of the country. Hindus believe that one great spirit is in everything. This is Brahma, whom they worship as thousands of different gods. About 1000 BC, the first Hindu books, the **Veda**, were written down.

Brahma

Hindu mythology says the world is created, destroyed and recreated in cycles that go on for ever, thanks to Brahma, the creator god. In scriptures, Brahma is shown looking in all directions with four heads, to symbolize that he has knowledge of all things.

❍ People have lived in India for thousands of years. Myths are still an important part of their culture and religions today.

❍ The earliest Indians were farmers who thought that Prithivi, the Earth and Dyaus, the sky, were the parents of all gods and humans.

❍ A warrior race called the Aryans then invaded India. They believed a god called Varuna created the world by picturing everything in his eye, the Sun.

❍ Aryans believed that the storm god Indra later took over as chief god, supported by human beings. He rearranged the Universe by organizing the heavens and the seasons.

❍ Hindus believe that one day in the life of the spirit Brahma, is equivalent to 4,320 million years on Earth.

❍ Brahma created the world. He emerged from a lotus flower floating on the floodwaters of chaos and thought everything into being.

❍ The god Vishnu preserves a balance of good and evil in the Universe by being born on Earth as a human from time to time to help men and women.

◀ *Hindu deities on the front of the Sri Veeramakaliamman Temple in Sri Lanka. Hindus believe that gods and goddesses are present in their shrines and temples. The picture or statue that represents the god or goddess living there is called a murti.*

Find out more

Hindu temples p. 209

Amazing

In 1995, thousands of people in India reported that statues of Hindu gods were drinking milk. Some people believed this was a miracle. Others said that the statues were made of porous stone, which was soaking up the liquid.

❍ The god Shiva is the destroyer god. He combats demons and keeps the Universe moving by dancing.

❍ The fire god, Agni, acts as a link between people and the heavens, because the smoke from his sacred flames rises up into the skies.

▲ The Hindu god of learning is Hanuman, who is half-human, half-monkey.

Hindu life

Like people from many different religions, Hindu families mark important stages in each individual's life, such as weddings and funerals, with prayers and religious ceremonies. They also believe that ordinary, everyday actions have a religious meaning. Each good deed takes a person closer to their spiritual goal, which is freedom from life in this world and union with Brahma, the supreme God.

❍ The wife of the mighty destroyer god, Shiva, is a very important goddess. She has three forms: the gentle Parvati, the brave demon fighter Durga, and the bloodthirsty Kali.

❍ When Hindus worship at a shrine or temple, they leave the god or goddess a small offering of food or flowers. The Hindu word for worship is "puja."

❍ In Hindu art, gods and goddesses are often painted blue—the Hindu color of holiness.

❍ Hindu gods and goddesses are often pictured with several heads or arms, to depict their special characteristics.

❍ After each 1,000 Great Ages, Shiva destroys the world by fire and flood. He preserves the seeds of all life in a golden egg, which Brahma breaks open to begin the rebirth of creation.

❍ Hindus believe that there is a set, correct way for everyone to behave, according to their role in society. Myths say that the god Vishnu set this code of good behavior on Earth, known as "dharma."

▼ *Ganesha, derived from Shiva, is the popular Hindu god of wisdom. He is pictured with an elephant's head.*

Religious Founders

Some religions, such as Hinduism, developed gradually over centuries, but others, including Islam and Buddhism, were founded by specific people whose life and teachings won them many followers. Most faiths recall the deeds of key figures, often referred to as prophets.

Amazing

Many Christian stories tell how Mary, the mother of Jesus, has appeared throughout history in visions to young people, such as to St Bernadette at Lourdes.

○ The earliest prophet of any world religion was Zoroaster, who was born in northeast Persia (modern day Iran) around 1200 BC.

○ Legend says that the founder of Sikhism, Guru Nanak, once disappeared into a river. Days later he emerged, saying that he had been with God.

○ Christians follow the teachings and life of Jesus, believed to be the son of God. Jesus respected the teachings of Judaism, but added his own message: the most important thing is to love God and to behave well towards other people.

○ The Indian prince Siddhartha Gautama (563–483 BC) left behind all his riches, and wandered the world until he found the secret of true happiness. He became known as the Buddha. The Buddha taught that people should aim to achieve absolute peace and enlightenment—a state called nirvana.

◄ *This painting shows God creating the first man and woman, Adam and Eve. According to Jewish tradition, Adam was made from earth, and Eve was made from a rib bone in Adam's side.*

○ An Old Testament Bible story tells how God asked Abraham to offer him his only son, Isaac, as a sacrifice. God stopped Abraham just in time, once he had tested his obedience. Abraham is an important figure in Judaism, Christianity, and Islam.

○ Daoism is based on the writings of Lao-Tse, who lived in China about the same time as Confucius. Lao-Tse described many gods, nature spirits, and magical practices.

▼ *Lao-Tse taught that there is a great power, known as Dao (the Way), that guides the Universe. His followers, called Daoists, try to live in harmony with Dao. Lao-Tse encouraged meditation and spiritual harmony.*

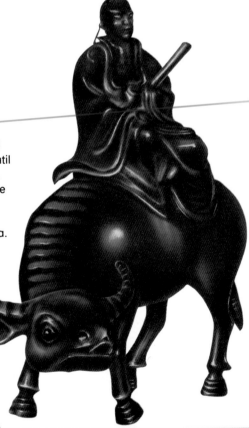

Find out more

Religious buildings pp. 208–209

A scattered people

For almost 2,000 years, Jewish people were forced to live outside their traditional homeland in the Middle East. Some settled in Europe, but were often persecuted. During the 19th century, many Jewish people emigrated to the United States, where they hoped to find religious freedom. Today, there is a Jewish state in Israel, and Jewish communities all around the world.

▲ *Buddhists do not worship the Buddha as a god, but rather as a guide who shows them the best way to live. There are many huge, splendid statues of the Buddha, beside which Buddhists leave offerings of flowers, incense, and candles.*

▼ *Moses was a Jewish leader who lived about 1200 BC. God parted the waters of the Red Sea so that he could lead the Jews out of captivity in Egypt. They were chased by Egyptian soldiers but, according to Jewish scriptures, when the Jews had crossed to safety the waters ran back and the Egyptians were drowned.*

❍ The Chinese "way" of Confucianism was founded by Kongfuzi, or Confucius. He was not concerned with worshiping gods, or with hopes of life after death. Instead, he taught his followers to live a good life, encouraging self control, hard work, and respect for families.

❍ Islam began in Arabia in the 7th century AD when the Prophet Muhammad (AD c.570–632) received a series of revelations from God. These were written down to form a holy book, the Koran, which is honored as a guide and inspiration by Muslims today.

❍ Bahá'u'lláh, the Founder of the Bahá'i Faith, taught that there is one God, who progressively reveals his will to humanity through his messengers, including Moses, Krishna, Buddha, Zoroaster, Jesus, the Prophet Muhammad, and Bahá'u'lláh himself.

The Christmas story

Christians believe that Jesus was born in a stable in Bethlehem, to Mary, the virgin, and her future husband Joseph, a carpenter. Three shepherds came to honor the newborn child, whose birth was announced to them by angels.

▲ *Muslim traders, scholars, and soldiers traveled long distances across the desert by camel. They carried the faith of Islam with them to many parts of Asia, North and West Africa, and the Middle East.*

Eternal Life and Paradise

Throughout history, people have been fascinated with the idea of living for ever—eternal life. In most mythologies and religions, there are stories of life after death, and of a special place where those who are good, brave, or wise can go.

○ The ancient Egyptians believed that people could enjoy life after death by preserving the body through mummification, putting food and personal possessions in their tomb, and following elaborate funeral rites. Each mummy had a mask so every spirit could recognize its body.

○ In Medieval Europe, early scientists, called alchemists, strove to create an elixir (magical potion) of life that would cure all illnesses.

○ The Celtic god Govannon is a blacksmith who also brews a mead of eternal life.

○ The mischievous Chinese spirit, Monkey, was once appointed Guardian of the Garden of Immortal Peaches— but he ate all the heavenly fruit and became immortal himself.

○ In Arabic, "khuld" means eternal life. Islamic stories teach that all souls are immortal—some will go to heaven and others will go to hell.

▶ *The Bible tells how the first man and woman lived in a paradise on Earth called the Garden of Eden. When the first woman, Eve, was tempted into eating forbidden fruit, the couple were cast into the world of sin and suffering.*

Find out more

Adam and Eve p. 204

Taoist beliefs

The Chinese religion, Taoism, teaches belief in eight immortals who discovered a magical elixir of life that allowed them to live for ever. The symbol at the center of this Taoist shrine is Yin Yang. It represents the balance of calm, female forces in life (Yin) with active, male forces (Yang).

❍ Christian stories say that Jesus could raise people from the dead. He brought one man back to life called Lazarus, who had been in his tomb for four days.

❍ In some Classical myths, Elysium is a happy realm at the ends of the Earth for heroes. In others, it is portrayed as being a peaceful place in the Underworld where good souls rest before being reborn.

❍ Islamic stories say that paradise is a beautiful garden, where the souls of the blessed will live in splendid palaces.

❍ Chinese Buddhists believe in a heavenly paradise where souls appear as flowers before an enlightened spirit.

❍ Tillan-Tlapaallan is one of three Aztec heavens, reserved for those who share in the wisdom of the god Quetzalcoatl.

▲ The Celts believed that various "otherworlds" existed. Tir Nan Og (or Tir inna Beo) was an earthly paradise, only far more beautiful, and without illness, old age, or death.

❍ In Roman mythology, Jupiter punished a traitor called Janus by giving him immortality but taking away his freedom to move. Janus was made to stand for ever as Heaven's gatekeeper.

❍ In Greek myth, ambrosia was the food of the gods. Anyone who ate it became immortal.

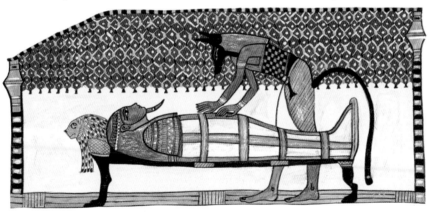

▲ In ancient Egyptian mythology, the jackal-headed embalmer god, Anubis, brought the souls of the dead into an underworld courtroom to be judged good or bad.

Mountain goddess

Sengen is the Japanese goddess of blossom and the sacred mountain Fujiyama. She guards the secret Well of Eternal Youth. Mount Fuji is the highest mountain in Japan. In summer, hundreds of pilgrims climb to the Shinto shrine at Mount Fuji's summit.

Amazing

Part of mummification in ancient Egypt involved removing the internal organs into pots called canopic jars.

Religious Buildings

Followers of most great religions use special buildings for worship. These buildings have different names, such as church (Christian), mosque (Islam), synagogue (Judaism), and temple (Hinduism, Sikhism, and Buddhism). Some buildings built for worship date back to ancient times.

The Dome of the Rock in Jerusalem is believed by Muslims to stand on the spot from where Muhammad ascended into heaven.

The Golden Temple at Amritsar in India is the holiest shrine for Sikhs. Guru Nanak founded the Sikh religion in the late 1400s.

The ancient Greeks built beautiful temples as shrines to their gods; this is the temple of Apollo at Delphi in Greece.

Inside St Paul's Cathedral in London. This great church was built by Sir Christopher Wren to replace an older one burned down in 1666.

Jews pray at the Western Wall in Jerusalem, all that remains of the ancient second Temple. The first Temple was built by King Solomon.

The Mayan people of Central America built pyramid temples with steps leading to a temple on top. This is the temple at Palenque, Mexico.

Find out more

Buddhists p. 205

Buddhists put statues of Buddha inside and outside their temples. This statue, approached by steps, is on Samu Island in Thailand.

The world's biggest Hindu temple is Angkor Wat in Cambodia. It was built in the 1100s but abandoned in the mid 1400s.

Hindu temples are often decorated inside and out with statues and carvings of gods and goddesses, that are brightly painted.

An Islamic mosque has minarets, tall towers from which the muezzin, or crier, calls people to pray.

St Peter's Basilica in Rome was built between 1506 and 1614 and is the biggest Christian church in Europe. The dome measures 138 ft across.

Amazing

St Peter's Basilica dominates the Vatican—a tiny district of Rome that is the center of the Roman Catholic Church and the world's smallest independent country.

In Japan, Shinto shrines are entered through a sacred gateway called a torii, like this one at Miyajima.

Epic Tales

An epic is an adventure story in the form of a long poem that follows the brave deeds of human heroes as they struggle against magical dangers. Most epic poems were passed on by the oral tradition before they were written down. Epic poetry provided early peoples with standards and goals for how to live a good life.

Daedalus and Icarus

One of the enduring Greek stories is that of Daedalus and Icarus. Daedalus made feathered wings so the two could fly away and escape from King Minos of Crete. But Icarus flew too close to the Sun, melting the wax that held his wings together. The boy fell into the sea and drowned.

Beowulf was the hero of an Anglo-Saxon epic poem of the same name. He had to battle three ferocious monsters—Grendel, Grendel's mother, and a dragon. Here, he descends to the bottom of a murky lake to fight Grendel's mother. The Beowulf story, an oral tale of ancient Danish warrior heroes, was later written down in Old English.

○ Different versions of the legend of the warrior hero Sigurd the Volsung exist in Norse, British, and German mythologies.

○ The earliest existing written version appears as part of the Norse epic poem, *Beowulf*, where a storyteller recites the saga as entertainment for warriors.

○ The most detailed version of the myth is known as *The Volsunga Saga* (written around AD 1300 by an unknown author).

○ The most famous greek epic poems are the *Iliad* and the *Odyssey*. Some historians think these were written by a blind man called Homer around 750 BC. Others think they were composed gradually in the oral tradition by several poets.

○ Archeologists have found written fragments of the *Iliad* and the *Odyssey* dating from the 4th century BC. However, the oldest complete manuscripts date from much later—the 10th century AD.

Amazing

Hindus believe that Rama, hero of the epic poem the *Ramayana*, was one of the ten human forms of the god Vishnu.

Find out more

Greek myths p. 196

○ The Indian epic poem the *Ramayana* focuses on the battle between the forces of good and evil. Historians think it was written between 200 BC and AD 200 by a poet called Valmiki.

○ Like the Greek epic the *Odyssey*, the *Ramayana* follows a hero (Prince Rama) on a long and difficult journey.

○ Prince Rama's enemy is the demon, Ravana. He can work powerful magic, but is not immortal and can be killed.

Achilles's heel

The greatest Greek warrior in the *Iliad* is Achilles. He was protected by divine armor—except for a small spot on his heel, which is where he finally received his death wound.

○ The demon Ravana's followers are known as Rakshasas. They can change shape and disguise themselves so they do not appear evil. They can thus tempt good people to do the wrong thing.

▼ The **Iliad** *tells the story of a ten-year war between the ancient Greeks and the Trojans. The Trojan War ended when Greek warriors secretly entered the city of Troy by hiding inside a huge wooden horse. This is a replica of the wooden horse in Turkey.*

▲ *In the* **Ramayana,** *Rama rescues queen Sita from the demon Ravana, aided by the god Hanuman.*

○ An epic poem from Sumeria tells of Gilgamesh, who was a real king of the city Uruk, around 2700–2500 BC. In the poem, King Gilgamesh is a man of mighty strength who is loved dearly by the gods. Experts think that *Gilgamesh* was first written down on clay tablets in an ancient language called cuneiform.

Heroes

Many heroes of myths, legends, and epic poems possess superhuman powers and are helped by gods or spirits. They usually possess at least one magical weapon or object with magical properties.

○ The *Odyssey* is an adventure story that follows the Greek hero, Odysseus, after the Trojan War, on his long and difficult sea voyage home.

○ Odysseus and his men have to face many magical dangers on their journey, including monsters and giants.

○ By the time Odysseus finally reaches his palace in Ithaca, he has been away for 20 years. Disguised as a beggar, only his faithful old dog recognizes him.

○ The *Aeneid* is an epic poem that follows the adventures of a Trojan prince, Aeneas, also after the end of the Trojan War.

○ The *Aeneid* was not composed in the oral tradition. The Roman author, Virgil, wrote it down in Latin.

○ The Celtic legend of Finn McCool might be based on a warrior hero who lived in Ireland in the 3rd century AD.

○ In the legend, Finn McCool has an argument with a giant in Scotland. They throw rocks across the sea at one another, which creates the rock formation now known as the Giants' Causeway. In reality, it was formed when lava from a volcano cooled and set.

Romulus and Remus

The story of Romulus and Remus tells how twin boys grew up to build the foundations of the mighty city of Rome. As babies, the twin boys were cast out by their evil great-uncle, who had stolen the king's crown from their grandfather. They survived because a wolf found them and let them drink her milk. A bird also fed them by placing crumbs in their mouths.

▶ *After 20 years at war, Odysseus returns to his kingdom disguised as a beggar. He is greeted by his old dog, who then dies content.*

Find out more

Epic poems pp. 210–211

Theseus

There are many myths about a Greek hero called Theseus who slew a beast called the Minotaur, which had the body of a man and the head of a bull. Historians have proved that a real King Theseus did once exist.

▶ *Cuchulain was an Irish warrior hero supposed to have lived in the 1st century AD. Stories say that he was killed in battle. Despite being terribly wounded, he lashed himself to a stone so that he would die on his feet, fighting to the end.*

▲ *Virgil was the well-educated son of a farmer. The Roman Emperor, Augustus Caesar, became his patron. Virgil wrote the Aeneid and based it on the Greek epics the Iliad and the Odyssey. It explains how the gods instructed Aeneas to leave Troy and found a Roman dynasty.*

The labors of Heracles

To become immortal, the Greek hero Heracles was commanded by the gods to complete 12 tasks:

1. Kill the man-eating Nemean lion
2. Kill the nine-headed, poisonous swamp monster called the Hydra
3. Capture the golden deer sacred to the goddess Artemis
4. Capture the vicious Erymanthian boar
5. Capture a ferocious bull belonging to the god Poseidon
6. Capture some flesh-eating horses
7. Get rid of a flock of birds who shot their feathers like arrows at people
8. Steal the belt of the fearsome Amazon queen, Hippolyte
9. Steal a herd of cattle belonging to the giant, Geryon
10. Clean out the biggest, dirtiest stables in the world
11. Journey to the ends of the Earth to fetch some golden apples
12. Venture into the Underworld to bring back the three-headed guard dog, Cerberus

Amazing

Finn McCool had a magical "tooth of knowledge" that could tell him whatever he wanted to know.

Magic and Witchcraft

Belief in magic—the use of spells and rituals to harness supernatural forces or the powers of nature—dates back to earliest times. Sorcerers, such as witches and wizards, feature in the legends and mythologies of many cultures throughout history, as do magical beings such as fairies and elves.

○ Entertainers on the Indonesian island of Bali perform myths about a witch called Rangda. The character came from a wicked queen called Mahendradatta who lived 1,000 years ago.

○ The wizard Merlin was King Arthur's most trusted advisor. Merlin warned Arthur that Guinevere, his wife, would bring him grief—and she did. She fell in love with Sir Lancelot. Lancelot was banished from the alliance of the Knights of the Round Table. The weakened Arthur was killed in battle, and the remorseful Guinevere went to live in a convent.

○ Sikkim is a tiny kingdom in the Himalayas where belief in magic is still strong. Sir Tashi Namgyal—a maharaja who lived there—was believed to be able to control the weather.

▼ Mandrake root is famous for being a chief ingredient in witches' brews. According to legend, it was only safe to pull the plant out of the ground after performing a special chant and ritual in moonlight.

◄ The most famous fictional witch of recent times is the clever Hermione Granger, a character in J K Rowling's Harry Potter stories.

Find out more

King Arthur p. 230

A Banshees were fairy women who announced their presence with an eerie wail. Celtic peoples believed that anyone who heard the wail would soon die.

Faery Queen

The Queen of Faery has terrifying magical powers in the Scottish legend of Tam Lin. In the story, a brave girl wins a man captured by the Queen of Faery by holding him tight while the queen changes him into a succession of horrific creatures.

○ Greeks and Romans worshiped the goddess of darkness, Hecate, at crossroads. Today she is worshiped by those who practice black magic.

○ Stories from eastern Europe tell of a wicked witch called Baba Yaga. Her house scuttles about on chicken's legs. To reach it, travelers must cross a river of fire.

○ In 1487, James Sprenger and Henry Kramer wrote *The Malleus Maleficarum* —a book of rules for detecting witches. It was used by the church in Europe for 300 years to accuse people of black magic and condemn them to death.

○ Aztec sorcerers used black mirrors of polished obsidian to predict the future. Their patron was the god Tezcatlipoca— "lord of the smoking mirror."

▶ European folklore usually portrays witches as being evil, but in early medieval times they were considered wise women, skilled in the art of herbal healing.

○ In Greek mythology, an enchantress called Circe was the aunt of a beautiful young witch called Medea. They both knew powerful magic.

Merlin and the Lady of the Lake

Arthurian legend says that Merlin fell in love with the Lady of the Lake, who gave Arthur his magical sword Excalibur. Merlin taught the Lady of the Lake all the secrets of his sorcery. She repaid the wizard by imprisoning him in a glass tower.

Mythical Creatures

Myths and legends abound with strange creatures, from dragons and unicorns, to mermaids and trolls. They have magical powers sometimes, and often they are unpleasant and dangerous. Monsters and weird creatures not only make the myths in which they feature more exciting, but encountering them in stories also helped ancient peoples to confront their fears.

Norse myth said that a giant serpent called Jormungand lived in the sea, and would swim ashore at the end of the world to join a battle against the warrior gods.

In Greek mythology, the sphinx (the name means "throttler") was a cruel monster with a woman's face, a lion's body, and a bird's wings. It lay in wait outside the city of Thebes, and killed travelers who could not work out its riddles.

Amazing

In 1842 in America, the famous Phineas T Barnum's traveling circus show displayed a "real" mermaid. It turned out to be a hoax, created from a monkey's body and a fish's tail.

Dragons

Dragons are found in mythologies from all over the world, but play a particularly important role in traditional tales from China. According to Chinese myth there were five types of dragon: dragons who guarded gods, dragons who guarded emperors, dragons who controlled wind and rain, dragons that deepened rivers and seas, and dragons who guarded hidden treasure.

The bunyip

Myths from the Aborigines of Australia tell of a swamp monster called the bunyip who hunts children at night. Aboriginal artwork, such as this bunyip painting, can be found over sacred rocks and cliffs throughout tribal territories in Australia.

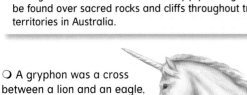

○ A gryphon was a cross between a lion and an eagle, and first appeared in myths of the Middle East.

○ A basilisk or cockatrice appears in the Bible, as well as Greek legend. It was a snake with a cockerel's wings and a dragon's tail. J. K. Rowling featured the monster in a *Harry Potter* story.

○ Medusa the Gorgon was a female monster in Greek myth who had writhing snakes for hair. Anyone who looked at her face was turned to stone.

Unicorns feature in the myths of many civilizations. They are rare, beautiful creatures with the body of a horse and a single, spiral horn.

○ In Greek myth, a centaur was half-man, half-horse. A satyr was half-man, half-goat.

○ The phoenix was a magical bird that lived for 500 years. It died by setting fire to itself, and was then born again from the ashes.

○ Philippine myths tell of alan— creatures who are half-human, half-bird. They live in forests and look after lost children.

○ In Chinese mythology, hsigo are monkeys with birdlike wings.

○ Many Scandinavian myths feature hairy, cruel creatures called trolls, who live inside the Earth and are expert metalworkers.

○ Greek stories said that a manticore had a lion's body, but a human face— with three rows of teeth. It shot poisoned spines from its tail.

○ In Greek myth, the chimaera was a fire-breathing monster with a lion's head, a goat's body, and a serpent's tail.

Greek myth tells how the hero Heracles tied up the three-headed hell hound Cerberus, dragged the beast to the court of King Eurystheus, then returned him to the Underworld.

In the Caribbean, mermaids are called water-mamas. People believe that if you find a water-mama's comb, she will grant you a wish.

Find out more

The Cyclops p. 197

Sport and Leisure

P eople have always enjoyed playing games. As town life began to develop more than 5,000 years ago, people played board games and games of chance, using dice or marked pieces, such as dominoes. The ancient Egyptians enjoyed chariot racing and wrestling, and Greek athletes took part in the Olympic Games more than 3,000 years ago. Rules for many modern games such as tennis, rugby, soccer, and baseball were established in the 1800s. Some professional sports stars today are among the highest paid people in the world.

Cricket has been played under "modern" rules since the 1800s, and is enjoyed at all levels from the village green to Test match arenas. The leading cricket countries are England, Australia, India, Pakistan, and South Africa.

In the game of snooker there are 22 balls on the table at the start of the game: 15 red, one yellow, one green, one brown, one blue, one pink, one black, and one white cue ball.

Amazing

The best quality badminton shuttlecocks are said to be made from the feathers of the left wing of a goose.

HARTLEY WINTNEY C. C.

Playing cards are thought to have originated in China after the invention of paper. Today, a standard pack excluding jokers contains 52 cards, 13 of each suit.

Referee's equipment

The items a soccer referee takes onto the pitch are: a whistle, a coin, a notebook, a pencil, a yellow card, a red card, a stop watch and a spare watch.

Find out more

Swimming p. 222

A golfer is allowed to take a maximum of 14 clubs onto the course. Completing a hole in one under par is called a birdie, two under par an eagle and three under par an albatross.

○ Sumo is a Japanese form of wrestling in which the competitors weigh up to 588 lb. Being fat is an advantage, since the object is to push the opponent out of the ring.

○ The first darts world championship was held in 1978 and was won by Leighton Rees of Wales.

○ Red Rum is the only horse to have won the UK Grand National three times, in 1973, 1974, and 1977. He is now buried beside the winning post at Aintree, Liverpool.

Swimming strokes

Of the four strokes in competitive swimming (breaststroke, backstroke, crawl, and butterfly), the crawl is the fastest, followed by the butterfly, shown here.

○ Polo is a four-a-side sport and is played on the largest pitch of any team sport. Polo originated in Persia more than 2,000 years ago. The game is divided into periods of play called chukkas, each lasting 7.5 min.

○ The game of badminton was named after the Gloucestershire home of the Duke of Beaufort, Badminton House.

○ Cycling was contested in the first modern Olympics of 1896 and the first road race took place over a distance of 54 mi.

○ In Rugby Union, the symbols representing each team are: red rose for England, shamrock for Ireland, thistle for Scotland, and fleur-de-lis for Wales.

○ In skiing, the slopes are graded by color for difficulty. A green run denotes a beginner's slope, blue an easy slope, red an intermediate or medium slope and black, a very difficult slope—the most demanding of all.

Sporting key dates

1299	Bowling club recorded in Southampton, England
1330	First known references to, and pictures of, hockey
1544	Earliest mention of billiards
1620	Mayflower pilgrims play darts
1657	Earliest known golf match played between Scotland and England
1744	First cricket rules were formed
1846	First recorded baseball game under modern rules
1860s	Badminton first played
1863	English Football Association (FA) formed
1865	Queensberry Rules for boxing established
1874	Lawn tennis invented, known as "sphairistike" (Greek for "ball")
1875	Earliest mention of snooker
1898	First international cross-country race

In tenpin bowling, knocking all the pins down with one ball is called a strike. Three consecutive strikes is known as a turkey, because bowling alley owners used to give a turkey to any player that achieved this feat. A perfect score in tenpin bowling is 300.

Team Sports

Most team sports involve hitting, kicking, or throwing balls. People probably first played ball games thousands of years ago. High schools and colleges did not begin organizing ball games as part of formal education until the 19th century, leading to the growth in professional ball sports across the world today.

○ An American football field is known as a gridiron because of the lines that cross the field at intervals of 15 ft.

○ In professional baseball there are nine players on each team. Each team bats for nine innings on a pitch called a diamond. "Home runs" are scored when the hitter makes a complete counterclockwise circuit of the four bases.

○ Brazil is the only country to have appeared in every soccer World Cup finals tournament.

○ Soccer originated from violent medieval football games, but was organized with rules, leagues, and professionals in the 19th century. It is now the world's most popular spectator sport.

○ The word "cricket" is derived from the French word criquet, meaning goalpost. The first cricket Test match in England took place at the Oval in 1880, when England played Australia.

▶ *A baseball hitter strikes at the ball. The catcher behind wears protective clothing to guard against the ball's impact.*

○ The game of volleyball was originally called mintonette and was devised in 1895 by William George Morgan of the United States.

○ Ice-hockey players skate around the rink at speeds exceeding 30 mi/h and the puck travels at speeds of over 93 mi/h.

Amazing

A gentleman by the name of Abner Doubleday is credited with inventing the game of baseball. Legend has it that he was also the person who fired the first shot in the US Civil War.

Find out more

Soccer p. 228

In beach volleyball, the ball must be cleanly hit, or "pop" off the hand.

Rugby

There are four ways of scoring in rugby: a try—worth five points; a conversion that follows a try—worth two points; a penalty goal—worth three points; and a dropped goal—worth three points. In Rugby Union there are 15 players in each team while in Rugby League there are only 13.

American football

An American football team can have as many as 45 players, but only 11 from either side are allowed on the field at any one time.

Hockey is one of the oldest stick-and-ball games, with versions of the game dating back to the Aztec civilization of Mexico.

❍ A basketball player cannot make more than two steps without passing or bouncing the ball. A violation of this rule is known as traveling.

❍ Netball was invented in 1891 by a Canadian called James Naismith, who adapted the rules of basketball for a female version of the game.

❍ Lacrosse players use a stick (the crosse) with a net on the end to throw and catch the ball. The game was first played by Native Americans in Canada, when as many as 1,000 players would take part in a game.

❍ Water polo takes place in a swimming pool. Two teams of players try to throw a ball into their opponents' goal.

❍ Since 1854 the Oxford and Cambridge boat race has been contested over a distance of 4 mi.

Soccer World Cup winners

2002	Brazil
1998	France
1994	Brazil
1990	Germany
1986	Argentina
1982	Italy
1978	Argentina
1974	West Germany
1970	Brazil
1966	England
1962	Brazil
1958	Brazil
1954	West Germany
1950	Uruguay
1938	Italy
1934	Italy
1930	Uruguay

Solo Sports

Success in team games involves cooperation, understanding, and coordination between players on the same side, but solo sports such as skiing, motor racing, or boxing rely on the skills, reactions, and strength of individuals. In some solo sports, especially racket sports such as tennis or badminton, versions of the game have been devised so that doubles matches can be played.

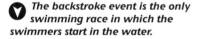
The backstroke event is the only swimming race in which the swimmers start in the water.

Amazing

On average, humans can reach a top speed of 5 mi/h swimming, whereas fish have an average top speed of 67 mi/h.

Speedway motorcyclists lean into a bend to increase their cornering speed as they race round a dirt track.

○ The tennis term "love" is derived from *l'oeuf*, the French word for egg, symbolizing a zero; "deuce" is from *deux*, the French word for two, because an advantage of two points is needed to win the game.

○ The four tournaments that make up the tennis Grand Slam are Wimbledon, the US Open, the Australian Open, and the French Open.

○ Major golf championships are contested over four rounds of 18 holes making 72 holes in total.

○ Participants in judo are awarded colored belts that indicate their level of achievement. Beginners wear white, followed by yellow, orange, green, blue, brown, black, and red.

Find out more
Tennis p. 229

Powerful new tennis rackets with larger heads have added power to the modern game. Top players can achieve speeds of up to 149 mi/h on their serve.

In judo, bouts usually last for five minutes, although in major championships, seven minutes are allowed.

Rallies and races

During a car rally, cars set off at intervals and are timed on each section. During a Grand Prix race, a number of cars start in ranks from a grid and race around a circuit. A drag racer, shown here, is a special car with huge rear wheels to get it moving, and an airfoil to keep the wheels on the ground as the car accelerates along a straight track.

❍ In slalom and giant slalom races, skiers travel downhill in the fastest possible time zigzagging through a series of gates marked by flags.

❍ An Olympic-size swimming pool is 164 ft long and has eight lanes.

❍ The game of squash originated during the 19th century at England's Harrow School.

❍ The balls used in a game of squash are marked with colored dots to indicate their speed. A yellow dot is superslow, a white or green dot is slow, a red dot is medium-fast, and a blue dot is fast.

Key motor sport dates

1895	First organized car race in France
1906	First Grand Prix race, at Le Mans, France
1911	First Indianapolis 500 in the USA
1920	Grand Prix races first held outside France
1923	First 24-hour race for sports cars at Le Mans
1936	First organized stock-car races in the USA
1960s	Rear-engined cars take over from front-engined cars in Grand Prix races

Ice skating

Ice skating is thought to have developed in Scandinavia where primitive skates dating back 2,000 years have been found. Speedskaters wear tight-fitting Lycra suits with aerodynamic hoods in order to reduce air resistance. Figure skating became an official Olympic sport in 1908.

Track and Field Events

The first people to take running seriously and compete against one another were the ancient Greeks. Track and field athletics as we know them began in the 19th century in schools and colleges in Europe and North America. Today these events play a big part in the Olympic Games, and there are also regular world and regional championships. Track races and some field events can also take place indoors.

Highland Games

Throwing events in Scotland's Highland Games include the shot, the hammer, the caber (a tree trunk), and sheaf-tossing. The latter involves the throwing of a heavy bag of hay over a bar using a pitchfork. The games date back to the 8th century.

▼ In the high jump there is a fan-shaped run-up area before the crossbar, and a cushioned landing mat beyond.

○ Field events include throwing and jumping. There are four throwing events: javelin, discus, shotput, and hammer. The jumping events are long jump, triple jump, high jump, and pole vault.

○ Pole-vaulting originated in ancient Greece where the Cretian people used long poles to vault over bulls.

Amazing

Stella Walsh won a 100-m women's gold medal at the 1932 Olympics. She was killed in 1980 during a robbery and an autopsy revealed that she was a man.

Find out more
Olympics pp. 226–227

○ High jumpers and pole-vaulters are allowed three attempts to clear each separate height.

○ The javelin is thrown overarm from behind a curved white line. Distances are measured from the throwing line to the nearest mark on the ground made by the javelin.

○ In the discus competition, the marked circle from which the competitor throws has a diameter of just 8.2 ft. The thrower releases the discus after one-and-a-half turns.

○ The rules of the IAAF (International Amateur Athletic Federation) state that the maximum number of spikes allowed on athletes' footwear is 11.

▼ *Javelins were made of wood until 1950, when an aluminum javelin was designed that enabled throwers to achieve greater distances.*

▼ *Athletes on the starting block preparing to sprint off at the start of the race.*

Hurdling

The heights of hurdles in athletics vary according to the distance of the race. The heights are: 1.06 m in the 110-m men's race; 0.91 m in the 400-m men's race; 0.83 m in the 100-m women's race; and 0.76 m in the 400-m women's race.

○ The athletics coaches George Breshnahan and William Tuttle invented starting blocks for sprinters in 1928.

○ In 1968 American sprinter Jim Hines became the first person to run 100 m in under 10 seconds with a time of 9.9 seconds.

○ Relays are team races, with four runners on each team. Each runner carries a baton that must be passed to the next in a 20-m changeover zone.

○ If the baton is dropped, only the runner that dropped it may pick it up.

○ In international competitions, the longest race that is contested solely on the track is the 10,000 m, which equals 25 laps of the track.

○ The longest running race takes place on roads—the 26.2 mi long marathon. The marathon is one of the few races that is not measured in metric distances.

Olympic Games

*T*he Olympic Games is the biggest event in the sporting calendar. The first Olympics were held at Olympia in ancient Greece in 776 BC, and consisted of one sprint race that was won by a chef called Corubus. The ancient Olympics were held in honor of the Greek god Zeus.

The Olympic flag is made up of five interlocking rings, each representing a continent.

The Olympic torch travels by runner to light the Olympic flame that burns throughout the Games.

1. Gaining height

2. Gaining momentum

3. Gaining speed

4. Landing on sand with feet as far forward as possible

The triple jump involves three stages: a hop, a step, and a two-footed jump. The competitor must jump from or behind a 8 in wide foul line. If a toe crosses the foul line a no jump, signalled by a red flag, is declared by the judges.

Ancient Olympians

Ancient Greek athletes competed naked in the original Olympic Games. This Greek vase depicts a discus thrower and an athlete with a javelin.

Eighteen Winter Olympics were held in the 20th century, the first in 1924 in France. Here, US alpine skier Sarah Schleper competes in the Ladies Giant Slalom during the 2002 Games, held in the USA. Norway has won the greatest number of Winter Olympic gold medals.

Gymnastics

Gymnastic events are performed on various pieces of apparatus, and each is scored by a panel of judges who can award a maximum mark of 10. The gymnasts are marked on their agility, timing, strength, and flexibility.

❍ The modern Summer Olympics are held every four years. The next games are to be held in 2008 in Beijing, China.

❍ At the first modern Summer Olympics held in 1896 in Athens, 311 male athletes took part but no females.

❍ In 1916, 1940, and 1944, the Summer Olympics were cancelled due to World Wars I and II.

Modern Olympic "gold" medals are made mostly of silver. They contain 7 oz of silver, which is then coated with just 0.03 oz of 24 carat gold. The last pure gold Olympic medals were awarded in 1912.

❍ The opening ceremony of the Olympics is always led by Greece, with the host nation marching out last.

❍ By tradition, prior to the Olympic Games, the Olympic torch is carried by a collection of runners from Athens to the city hosting the Games. Every two years the Olympic flame is rekindled using strong magnifying equipment and the Sun's rays.

❍ The Olympic Latin motto of "Citius, Altius, Fortius" means "swifter, higher, stronger."

❍ In 1900 Charlotte Cooper became the first woman to win an Olympic gold medal when she won the tennis tournament.

❍ Winter sports, such as skiing and ice-skating, are part of the Winter Olympics. These also take place every four years; the next Winter Olympics will be in 2006, hosted by the Italian city of Turin.

Modern Olympic venues

1896	Athens, Greece
1900	Paris, France
1904	St Louis, USA
1908	London, UK
1912	Stockholm, Sweden
1920	Antwerp, Belgium
1924	Paris, France
1928	Amsterdam, Netherlands
1932	Los Angeles, USA
1936	Berlin, Germany
1948	London, UK
1952	Helsinki, Finland
1956	Melbourne, Australia
1960	Rome, Italy
1964	Tokyo, Japan
1968	Mexico City, Mexico
1972	Munich, Germany
1976	Montreal, Canada
1980	Moscow, USSR
1984	Los Angeles, USA
1988	Seoul, South Korea
1992	Barcelona, Spain
1996	Atlanta, USA
2000	Sydney, Australia
2004	Athens, Greece
2008	Beijing, China

Find out more

Ancient Greece pp. 196–197

Sporting Records

Sport is popular throughout the world. Athletes and players compete to achieve amazing feats, and constantly break world records. Television and other media help promote sport and create successful sports stars that often become internationally recognized and acclaimed.

▶ *Fred Perry, the famous Wimbledon tennis champion of the 1930s, was also a table tennis star, winning the world title in 1929.*

○ The heaviest world boxing champion was Primo Carnera, who tipped the scales at 260 lb.

○ When Mark Spitz won seven swimming gold medals at the 1972 Olympics, he won all his races in world record times.

Olympic gold

Athletes who have won the most gold medals in the Summer Olympics:

10 Ray Ewry, jumping events for the USA, 1900–1908

9 Larissa Latynina, gymnastics for the USSR, 1956–1964

9 Paavo Nurmi, long-distance runner for Finland, 1920–1928

9 Mark Spitz, swimming for the USA, 1968–1972

8 Matt Biondi, swimming for the USA, 1984–1992

8 Carl Lewis, long jump/sprint for the USA, 1984–1982

8 Sawao Kato, gymnastics for Japan, 1968–1976

Carl Lewis

At the 2000 Sydney Olympics the American athlete Marion Jones became the first woman to win five medals at the same Games. She won gold in the 100 m, 200 m and 4 x 400 m relay, and two bronze medals in the long jump and the 4 x 100 m relay.

Amazing

At the age of 14, at the 1976 Olympics, Nadia Comaneci became the first gymnast ever to be awarded a perfect 10 by the panel of judges.

○ The 1996 Superbowl was the largest TV audience to watch a game of American football. The Dallas Cowboys beat the Pittsburgh Steelers 27–17, watched by 138.5 million TV viewers.

▶ *Aged 17 years and 111 days, Wayne Rooney became the youngest soccer player ever to play for England when he made his international debut against Australia in February 2003. In 2004, he also became the youngest goalscorer in the European Championships, scoring against Switzerland during the finals in Portugal.*

Find out more

Olympic Games pp. 226–227

Boxing champions

Only three fighters representing Britain have become world heavyweight champions. Bob Fitzsimmons won the title in the late 19th century, Frank Bruno won the WBC title in 1995, and Lennox Lewis won his first world title in 1992. At the 1988 Seoul Olympics Lennox Lewis won a boxing gold medal representing Canada's national team.

❍ In 2000 Manchester United were officially named as the world's richest football club when they became the first club to have a market value exceeding £1 billion.

❍ The highest test cricket batting average of 99.94 runs is held by the legendary Sir Donald Bradman of Australia. In his final Test appearance he needed just four runs to give him a career average of 100 but unfortunately he was out for a duck.

❍ Italian goalkeeper Dino Zoff holds the record in international matches for keeping the most consecutive clean sheets. In the 1970s he kept goal for almost 13 matches without conceding a goal.

❍ At the 2000 Sydney Olympics, British rower Sir Steve Redgrave collected his fifth consecutive Olympic gold medal.

❍ The oldest driver to become Formula One world motor racing champion was Argnetinian Juan Manuel Fangio. He won his fifth world title in 1957 at the age of 46.

▲ **Tiger Woods has become one of the world's most successful golfer since his professional debut in 1997.**

▲ **In 1990, at the age of 19, Pete Sampras became the youngest player to win the men's singles at the US Open. By the time he retired in 2003, he had won a further four US Open titles, two Australian Opens, and seven Wimbledon titles.**

▶ **In 2001, Britain's Ellen MacArthur became the fastest woman to sail solo round the world, taking just 94 days. In 2004/2005, she beat this time and set a new world record for circumnavigating the globe, completing a 27,030 mi voyage in 71 days and less than 15 hours.**

Famous People

Alcock, Sir John (1892–1919) **PILOT** Alcock had a distinguished career in the Royal Flying Corps (the forerunner of the Royal Air Force) during World War I. In 1919, he made the first nonstop flight across the Atlantic Ocean, together with Sir Arthur Whitten Brown. They flew from Newfoundland, Canada, to Ireland in 16 h 27 min. Alcock was killed in a flying accident soon afterward.

Sir John Alcock in flight

Alfred the Great (849–899; reigned 871–899) **KING** Alfred was ruler of Wessex, in southwest England. When he came to power, England was divided into several small, rival kingdoms, and a Viking army had invaded. He defeated the Vikings at the Battle of Edington, and they agreed to leave Wessex. Alfred then gave orders for burghs (fortified towns) to be built throughout Wessex, to defend it from further attack. Alfred was very interested in learning and invited many scholars to live at his court. He personally translated important religious books from Latin into Anglo-Saxon (the language spoken in England) so that English people would be able to understand them.

Anderson, Elizabeth Garrett (1836–1917) **DOCTOR** Because no university or hospital would accept women as medical students, Anderson worked as a nurse and studied to be an apothecary—the old name for a pharmacist. She qualified as an apothecary in 1865, becoming the first woman to be listed as a doctor in England. In 1866, she opened a dispensary (drugstore) for women in London, where she examined patients and gave advice, as well as selling medicines. It later became a major hospital, named in her honor.

Appleton, Sir Edward (1892–1963) **SCIENTIST** Appleton investigated the layers of gas that surround planet Earth. In 1925, he discovered the top layer of the ionosphere—a blanket of gases that stretches up into space from about 31 mi above sea level for 373 mi. Appleton found that its top layer, known today as the Appleton layer, reflected radio waves. His discovery was later used in the invention of radar.

Archimedes (c.287–c.212 BC) **GREEK SCIENTIST** Archimedes lived in Syracuse in Sicily (then ruled by the Greeks) and was the first to apply mathematics to science. He discovered the principle of liquid displacement as he saw the water level in his bath rise as more of his body became immersed. He is said to have jumped out of the bath and run naked through the streets shouting "Eureka!"—Greek for "I've got it!"

Archimedes in his bath

Aristotle (384–322 BC) **PHILOSOPHER** This ancient Greek thinker studied many areas of science and philosophy at Plato's academy in Athens and helped pioneer the study of animals (zoology) and plants (botany). He established a basic approach to science, showing how scientists must observe things closely, classify these observations, and use logical arguments to understand them. His ideas remained a key part of university education in Europe for more than 2,000 years.

Arkwright, Sir Richard (1732–1792) **INVENTOR** While apprenticed to a wig maker, Arkwright experimented with different ways of spinning and weaving thread. In 1767 he invented a water-powered machine that could spin fine cotton thread, strong enough to be used for weaving. Arkwright's invention meant that for the first time, pure cotton cloth could be woven by machine. This transformed the clothmaking industry.

Arthur (early 6th century) **KING** Legends about an extraordinary British king called Arthur have been popular for over 800 years, yet historians have never been able to prove whether he was a real figure in history. Arthur's knights went on many dangerous quests to test their bravery and honor. Some legends say that King Arthur was taken to a country of blessed souls called Avalon and will return when Britain falls into its greatest danger.

Attlee, Clement (Earl Attlee) (1883–1967) **POLITICIAN** Attlee trained as a lawyer, and became mayor of Stepney, East London, in 1920. He became a Labour MP in 1922, and held important posts in Churchill's wartime government. Attlee became prime minister in 1945—the first Labour Party leader to have an absolute majority in the House of Commons. He introduced many policies to reform British society, such as the welfare state.

Clement Attlee

Austen, Jane (1775–1817) **WRITER** Austen completed her first full-length novel, *Pride and Prejudice*, when she was only 21. She left her sixth and last book, *Sanditon*, unfinished at her death. One of Britain's greatest writers, Austen won little fame during her lifetime, and received hardly any money. Yet her skill at observing and describing people, her insights into character and feelings, her elegant use of language, and her sharp sense of humor, have delighted readers the world over.

Babbage, Charles (1792–1871) **SCIENTIST** As a child, Babbage was brilliant at math, and it became his lifelong career. Today, he is remembered as the inventor of the world's first computer—a "calculating engine" that he began to build in 1812. He spent the next 33 years trying to improve the design, but never completely succeeded.

Baird, John Logie (1888–1946) **ELECTRICAL ENGINEER** Born in Scotland, and trained as an electrical engineer,

Baird invented the first machine to transmit live pictures, in 1922. Four years later, he built the first television set. Baird's machines were supplied to the BBC in 1929, and used to make the first regular TV broadcasts in 1936. But in 1937, the BBC stopped using them, preferring a system that used a cathode-ray tube.

Beatles, The (founded late 1950s) **MUSICIANS** A pop group, formed in Liverpool in the late 1950s, which transformed the British music industry. The Beatles owed their early success to the shrewd management of Brian Epstein (1935–1967). Later, their records achieved worldwide fame. Original members were John Lennon (1940–1980), Sir Paul McCartney (born 1942), George Harrison (1943–2002). In 1962, they were joined by Richard "Ringo Starr" Starkey (born 1940).

Becket, St Thomas (à) (1118–1170) **RELIGIOUS LEADER** Becket began his career as a senior government official. King Henry II of England was so impressed by his skills that he invited him to become Archbishop of Canterbury. For many years, King Henry had been quarreling with the Pope in Rome and he was furious when Becket sided with the Pope. Becket fled to France. Four knights overheard Henry say "Will no one rid me of this meddlesome priest?," rushed to find Becket, and murdered him in Canterbury Cathedral. King Henry was disgraced and Becket became a saint.

Bede, St (673–735) **WRITER** Bede lived as a monk in the northeast of England. During his lifetime, he was respected as the most learned man in Europe, and his books are still read today, more than 1,000 years after his death. Bede's most famous work was *The*

Ecclesiastical History of the English Church and People. In it, he describes life in Anglo-Saxon England, and how the first Christian missionaries arrived there from Rome. Bede was the first person to divide the past into the periods "AD" and "BC."

Beethoven, Ludwig van (1770–1827) **COMPOSER** Born in Germany, Beethoven was a musical genius whose creativity was hampered in later life by increasing deafness. He was a passionate idealist, whose works include five symphonies, two masses, string quartets, an opera, songs, and piano solos. He worked most of his life in Vienna, Austria, where he became famous for his untidiness and bad temper. Beethoven did not make much money from his music during his lifetime, but it is now amongst the best loved and most played in the world.

The murder of St Thomas à Becket

Bell, Alexander Graham (1847–1922) **INVENTOR** Born and educated in Scotland, Bell emigrated in 1870 to Canada, then the USA. While working as a teacher of deaf people, he experimented with different machines for transmitting sound, especially speech. He invented the telephone, which he first displayed in public in 1876. The next year, he founded a telephone company, to profit from his invention and to fund future research.

Berners-Lee, Tim (born 1955) **SCIENTIST** The Internet is now a vast network linking many millions of computers around the world. It began in 1983 with networks that allowed American army computers and university computers to swap data. Then, in 1989, English scientist Tim Berners-Lee, who worked at the CERN laboratories in Switzerland, invented the World Wide Web. This allows computers to search and find data on any computer that is linked into the Internet.

William Blake

Blake, William (1757–1827) **WRITER** Artist, poet, and dreamer, Blake was one of Britain's most original thinkers. He began to write verses while still a child, and illustrated them with his own designs. After training as a print-maker, he opened a shop to sell decorative prints and his own unusual books and poems. Some of Blake's poems—most famously "Jerusalem"—have been turned into rousing hymns.

Boudicca (died AD 62) **QUEEN** Boudicca was the wife of Prasutagus, king of the Iceni tribe of eastern England. When he died in AD 60, Roman invaders put most of his family in prison or made them slaves. Boudicca joined with another threatened tribe, the Trinobantes, to attack Roman camps and forts. In AD 61, she led her army to attack London, where they destroyed buildings and killed many people. However, Boudicca's army was finally defeated by Roman soldiers, and she was trapped on the battlefield. Too proud to surrender, she killed herself by taking poison.

Boyle, Robert (1627–1691) **CHEMIST** Boyle developed ideas and experiments that became the basis of modern chemistry. Boyle wrote *The Sceptical Chymist*, which introduced the idea of chemical elements and compounds for the first time, and insisted that ideas should be proven with chemical experiments. Boyle is also remembered for an important physics law—Boyle's law—that shows how the volume of a gas changes if the pressure is changed.

Britten, Benjamin (Lord Britten) (1913–1976) **MUSICIAN** Born in Suffolk, Britten began to compose tunes while still a young child. Britten's most famous works include: *War Requiem*, which mourns those killed in the war; *Gloriana*, written for the coronation of Queen Elizabeth II; and *The Young Person's Guide to the Orchestra*, a witty piece in which different instruments take it in turns to perform.

Brontë Sisters, Charlotte (1816–1855); **Emily** (1818–1848); **Anne** (1820–1849) **WRITERS** Daughters of a clergyman, the Brontës lived in wild, remote countryside in northern England. All three worked as badly-paid school

teachers in small schools, then returned home. From childhood, each sister wrote poems and, later, novels. Charlotte's novel *Jane Eyre* was the first to be published. Next, Emily published *Wuthering Heights*, a passionate story of doomed love. The public was surprised and shocked to learn that it had been written by a woman, not a man. Anne's *Agnes Grey* and *The Tenant of Wildfell Hall* were printed soon after.

The Brontë Sisters

Brown, Lancelot "Capability" (1716–1783) **DESIGNER** Brown created a new form of "landscape" garden to surround great country houses. He wanted his gardens to look natural, rather than artificial. To achieve this, he dug out irregularly-shaped lakes, planted trees in clumps, and avoided straight paths or neat beds of flowers. His nickname came from his habit of telling landowners that their gardens "had capabilities for improvement."

Bruce, Robert the (Robert I) (1274–1329; reigned 1306–1329) **KING** Famous as a Scottish patriot who fought against English armies. Bruce lived at a time when rival nobles and warriors were claiming the right to be king of Scotland, and when English kings Edward I and Edward II had ambitions to conquer Scotland for themselves. After becoming king, Bruce led soldiers to recapture all the Scottish castles occupied by the English. He defeated Edward II at the Battle of Bannockburn (1314) and forced England to recognize Scotland as an independent nation.

Isambard Kingdom Brunel

Brunel, Isambard Kingdom

(1806–1859) ENGINEER Son of Sir Marc Brunel, a famous French-born engineer, Isambard Brunel also had a very successful career. He began by building bridges, including the daring Clifton Suspension Bridge at Bristol. Brunel then became chief engineer for the new Great Western Railway, surveying over 994 mi of track and designing tunnels, bridges, and stations. In 1838, he designed the *Great Western*, one of the first steamships to cross the Atlantic. In 1858, he built the *Great Eastern*, the largest ship ever made (until 1899).

Burns, Robert (1759–1796) WRITER
The son of a poor Scottish farmer, Burns was keen to be educated and read all he could. He also began to write poems and songs in standard English and in the Scottish dialect he spoke at home. Burns retold many traditional Scottish stories and legends. When his first book of poems was published, it became an overnight success. Burns died aged only 37, his birthday, January 25, is still celebrated by Scots today.

Carroll, Lewis (Charles Dodgson)
(1832–1898) WRITER Carroll spent most of his life as a mathematician at Oxford University, but he is remembered today as a writer of fantasy books for children. The best-known of these books is *Alice's Adventures in Wonderland*, which was published in 1865. Carroll also wrote nonsense verse for adults, and experimented with photography.

Caxton, William (c.1422–1491)
PRINTER The first printing press with movable type was built by Johan Gutenburg in Germany around 1455. Caxton learned the technique of printing whilst living in Bruges, Belgium, and printed his first book in English there in 1474. Two years later he moved to London, where he printed about 80 further volumes, including many books of poems and romances.

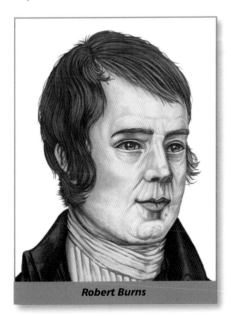
Robert Burns

Chaplin, Sir Charles "Charlie"
(1889–1977) ACTOR The son of music-hall performers, Chaplin grew up in an orphanage. In 1913, he traveled with a British theater company to America, where he was spotted by a Hollywood film director, who recognized his talent. From 1914 to 1940, Chaplin made a great many films, some featuring the character he created—a bowler-hatted tramp. Most of these films were silent (without words)—Chaplin was a brilliant mime. Some of his films, like *The Kid* (1921), were purely amusing; others, like *Modern Times* (1936), commented on social conditions.

Charlemagne (742–814) EMPEROR
Charles the Great, known as Charlemagne, was a warrior-leader of the Franks and became their king in 771. By conquest, he extended his rule from France into Germany and Italy, and in 800 Pope Leo III crowned him Emperor of the West—head of a new Holy (Christian) Roman Empire. Charlemagne could read but never learned to write, yet he was an enthusiastic patron of learning, inviting Europe's scholars to his court at Aachen.

Charles II (1630–1685) KING
Known as the "merry monarch," Charles became Britain's king in 1558, after the restoration of the monarchy following the English civil war and commonwealth (republic) of Oliver Cromwell. His father, King Charles I, had been executed by Parliament in 1649. Charles escaped after the battle of Worcester (1651) by hiding in an oak tree, and fled into exile. He was intelligent but lazy, witty, and interested in theater, science, sport, and women. He had many love affairs, one of his mistresses being the actress Nell Gwynn.

Sir Winston Churchill

Chaucer, Geoffrey (c.1340–1400) **WRITER** One of the first British poets to write in English as well as French and Latin, Chaucer worked as a government official and became famous for poems written to entertain members of the royal family at the courts of King Edward III and King Richard II. His best-known work is *The Canterbury Tales*. This describes a very mixed group of travelers riding on a pilgrimage to a holy site.

Chippendale, Thomas (1718–1779) **DESIGNER** Probably the greatest British furniture-maker, Chippendale made beautiful pieces from fine woods for wealthy families' stately homes. He also published a book of furniture designs—*The Gentleman and Cabinet-Maker's Director* (1754). This allowed his ideas and styles to be copied by many other craftworkers for less wealthy people to use and enjoy.

Churchill, John "Duke of Marlborough"(1650–1722) **SOLDIER** A professional soldier, Churchill led British armies to many victories against rival European nations, especially against France. He pioneered new, successful battle tactics; his most famous victories were at Blenheim (1704) and Ramillies (1706).

Churchill, Sir Winston (1874–1965) **POLITICIAN** Churchill was born into a famous political family (he was descended from John Churchill.) He served as a soldier and worked as a newspaper reporter in Africa before becoming a Conservative MP in 1900. Churchill changed his views to support the Liberal Party in 1904. He served as a government minister, but resigned in 1915 after a Navy attack he had authorized went badly wrong. From 1917 to 1922, he took various junior government posts, and also wrote a history of World War I. He rejoined the Conservative Party in 1924, served again as a government minister, then became prime minister in 1940, soon after the start of World War II. This war was (in words he himself made famous) "Britain's finest hour." Although old (almost 70) and unwell, he united the nation in a courageous war effort.

Columbus, Christopher (1451–1596) **EXPLORER** Columbus was the Genoese sailor who crossed the Atlantic and "discovered" North and South America for Europe. Columbus set sail on August 3, 1492 in three caravels—the *Santa Maria*, the *Niña*, and the *Pinta*. On October 12, a lookout spotted the Bahamas. Columbus thought he was in the Indies (hence the "West Indies"). He called the native peoples Indians.

Confucius (551–479 BC) **PHILOSOPHER** Confucius set out a "way of living" that has been followed in China for over 2,000 years. He traveled around China, discussing people's problems and how government should work. He became so famous he was put in charge of the city of Chung-lu for a time. His most famous saying is "What you do not want done to yourself, do not do to others."

Constable, John (1776–1837) **ARTIST** Pictures of the English countryside painted by John Constable are among Britain's best-known works of art. The son of a Suffolk miller, Constable was inspired by the gentle landscape around him. He was also interested in difficult new techniques, such as painting light and shadow.

Cook, Captain James (1728–1779) **EXPLORER** Cook joined the navy as an ordinary seaman, but was promoted to officer because of his navigation skills. Cook was chosen to command the ship *Endeavour* on a round-the-world voyage to collect scientific and geographic data. Between 1768 and 1771, he made the first scientific maps of the coasts of New Zealand, eastern Australia, and Hawaii. He also proved that there was no vast "Southern Continent," as earlier sailors had claimed. Cook made further voyages to explore the Pacific (1772–1775 and 1776–1779). He was killed by local people in Hawaii.

Captain James Cook

Cooper, Anthony Ashley (Lord Shaftesbury) (1801–1885) **CAMPAIGNER** Inspired by his Christian beliefs, Cooper campaigned for shorter working hours in factories, especially for women and children. Thanks to him, new laws—known as the Factory Acts—were introduced between 1833 and 1850. He also introduced laws protecting boys and girls from being sent underground to work in mines.

Copernicus, Nicolaus (1473–1543) SCIENTIST Until the 16th century, most people believed that the Earth was at the center of the Universe, and that the Moon, Sun, planets, and stars all revolved around it. But the Polish astronomer Copernicus developed the revolutionary new theory that the Sun, not the Earth, was at the center of the Universe.

Cromwell, Oliver (1599–1658) POLITICIAN A devout Puritan (Christian with strict, simple beliefs), Cromwell became an MP, and supported Parliament against King Charles I during the English Civil War (1639–1660). When the king was defeated in 1649, Cromwell helped to arrange his trial and execution. Cromwell was an excellent army commander. In 1649, he was sent to Ireland, to lead Parliament's soldiers against rebels there. In 1653, he was appointed "Lord Protector"—head of the government. He ruled sensibly and tolerantly, and refused to be called "king."

Curie, Marie (1867–1934) and **Pierre** (1859–1906) SCIENTISTS In 1897 French scientist Henri Becquerel (1852–1908) found that the new kinds of radiation being discovered did not always come from electricity. They seemed to appear around uranium atoms. His work influenced Polish–French scientist Marie Curie who, with her husband Pierre, showed that the radiation was coming directly from the atoms themselves. The Curies called this atomic radiation "radioactivity." Marie Curie was the first woman to win the chemistry Nobel prize in 1911 and the first person to win two Nobel prizes in two different subjects (chemistry and physics).

Darwin, Charles Robert (1809–1882) NATURALIST Darwin was appointed naturalist (biologist) on HMS *Beagle*, a ship making a pioneering voyage to South America from 1831 to 1836. On this voyage, Darwin saw and reported on many new species of plants and animals. His findings led him to work out a new theory of "evolution," in which he described how all life on Earth has developed and changed over millions of years. In 1859, Darwin published his ideas in a book, *On the Origin of Species by Means of Natural Selection*. This was followed by *The Descent of Man* in 1871.

Marie and Pierre Curie

Davies, Emily (1830–1921) CAMPAIGNER A clergyman's daughter, Davies worked to reform society and win rights for women, especially rights to education, and to vote on equal terms with men. She trained as a teacher and in 1866 set up the London Schoolmistresses' Association, so that women could work together to improve schooling for girls. In 1869, Davies founded a college for young women, which later became Girton College at Cambridge University—the first women's college at Oxbridge (Oxford and Cambridge universities).

Davy, Sir Humphry (1778–1829) SCIENTIST Born in Cornwall, the son of a wood-carver, Davy conducted pioneering experiments to investigate chemistry and electricity. In 1815, Davy invented a safety lamp, which was carried by coal miners working deep underground. Unlike earlier miners' lamps, it did not set fire to mine gases and cause dangerous explosions. Davy's invention saved many lives.

Descartes, René (1596–1650) PHILOSOPHER/MATHEMATICIAN The Frenchman Descartes is best known for his ideas on the nature of human existence. He is most famous for arguing that everything should be doubted before being believed. His most famous quote, "Cogito ergo sum" means "I think therefore I am." He also developed a kind of math called coordinate or analytical geometry. This enables scientists and mathematicians to show statistics using lines of geometry on a graph.

Dickens, Charles (1812–1870) WRITER Born into a poor family, 12-year-old Dickens was sent to work in a factory and was determined to make a better life for himself. After starting as a solicitor's clerk he worked at different reporting jobs. His first novel, *The Pickwick Papers*, was published in instalments in a popular magazine when Dickens was only 24. It was a great success, and he became famous. Dickens produced many more novels and short stories.

Disraeli, Benjamin (1809–1882) POLITICIAN Disraeli trained as a lawyer and worked as a journalist, but soon became active in politics. He was a keen, ambitious Conservative Member of Parliament. In 1852, he became chancellor of the exchequer, and was prime minister in 1868 and from 1874 to 1880. Disraeli believed in the idea of "one nation," in which rich and poor worked together for the country's good.

Sir Francis Drake

Drake, Sir Francis (c.1542–1596) EXPLORER Born in Devon to a seafaring family, Drake sailed with his cousin, Sir John Hawkins, to West Africa and the Caribbean. His pirate raids on Spanish ships off the coast of America were encouraged by Queen Elizabeth I. He also claimed California as a British colony. As a reward, Elizabeth knighted him on board his ship, *The Golden Hind*. From 1577 to 1580, Drake sailed around the world; only one ship had achieved this before. In 1588, he helped to defeat the Spanish Armada (armed fleet).

Edison, Thomas Alva (1847–1931) INVENTOR Edison is America's most famous inventor, with over 1,000 patents to his name. In 1876, he built a research laboratory at Menlo Park, New Jersey, and here he invented the carbon microphone, the phonograph (record-player), and the electric light bulb. He built a power station to light city streets by electricity for the first time.

Edward III (1312–1377) KING
If Edward I, his grandfather, was nicknamed the "hammer of the Scots," Edward III was the "scourge of the French." He ruled England firmly, after the disorder of his father Edward II's reign, and imposed his authority on the rulers of Scotland. With his son, Edward the Black Prince, he invaded France to take the crown. The English won the battles of Crécy (1346) and Poitiers (1356), but Edward failed in his ambition to become king of France as well as king of England.

Einstein, Albert (1879–1955) PHYSICIST In his theory of relativity German physicist Einstein overturned the old idea of time and was the first to show that time is relative. Time is not fixed but depends entirely on how you measure it—and you can only measure it relative to something else. Einstein showed that time does not run one way, but is a dimension, just like length, breadth, and depth, and that it can run backward as well as forward. Einstein's equation $E=mc^2$ showed just how much energy there was in an atom, and led to the development of the atomic bomb.

Thomas Edison

Elgar, Sir Edward (1857–1934) MUSICIAN One of the most important English composers, Elgar wrote many works for orchestras, choirs, and solo instruments that are still popular today. His music blended the rich "romantic" style of great European classical composers with gentler English themes. Many of Elgar's works were inspired by the beautiful countryside of the Malvern Hills where he lived. One of his tunes was later turned into the famous song "Land of Hope and Glory."

Eliot, George (pen-name of Mary Ann Evans) (1819–1880) WRITER Daughter of a wealthy landowner, Evans quarreled with her father, and became a writer. From 1854, Evans lived with scholar G H Lewes, who encouraged her to write fiction. As she wanted no publicity, she published under a man's name. Her major novels include *The Mill on the Floss* (1860) and *Middlemarch* (1871–1872).

Elizabeth I (1533–1603; reigned 1558–1603) QUEEN Elizabeth came to power at a time when the country faced many problems. At home, there were serious quarrels between Catholics and Protestants. Abroad, there were threats from rival nations, Spain and France, and from rival claimants to her throne, especially Mary Queen of Scots. A clever but cautious politician, Elizabeth arranged a moderate settlement to the religious quarrels, and worked with trusted advisers to defend England from foreign attack. She became tremendously popular after English sailors stopped the Spanish Armada (fleet of ships) from invading in 1588. During Elizabeth's reign, great achievements were seen in music, art and especially literature. She paid for many poets and writers—including Shakespeare—to perform their works at her court. She also encouraged explorers like Sir Francis Drake and Sir Walter Raleigh to seek treasure and claim new lands for England overseas.

Elizabeth I

Elizabeth II (born 1926; started reign 1952, crowned 1953) QUEEN When Elizabeth was born, her parents, the Duke and Duchess of York, did not expect to become king and queen. She was educated at their home in London and at Windsor Castle, and was a bright student, especially in history, music, and languages. During World War II, she volunteered to work as a driver for the ATS (the women's branch of the army). In 1947, she married a distant cousin, Prince Philip of Greece, and from 1951 began to undertake royal duties on behalf of her father, who was unwell. He died in 1952, and she was crowned queen the following year. Although she has no say in government policy, Elizabeth is admired by politicians for her knowledge and judgement. She performs many royal duties and has traveled more than any British ruler.

Faraday, Michael (1791–1867) SCIENTIST Faraday began his career as assistant to Humphry Davy, then started his own investigations. He won great respect among other scientists for the brilliant experiments he designed. Faraday made many important discoveries about electricity and magnetism, and also investigated the electrical properties of atoms. A unit of electrical measurement, the farad, is named after him.

Fawkes, Guy (1570–1606) ACTIVIST One of the leaders of the Gunpowder Plot in 1605. This was a conspiracy to murder the Protestant king, James I of England, by blowing him up with gunpowder, and to replace him with a Catholic ruler. The plotters believed this was the only way to win religious freedom for Catholics in England. The plotters were betrayed, and Fawkes was discovered on November 5, hiding with barrels of gunpowder under the Houses of Parliament. With seven others, he was hanged for treason.

Guy Fawkes and his conspirators

Fleming, Alexander (1881–1955) DOCTOR Born in Scotland, Fleming worked as a medical researcher. In 1928, he noticed that green mold growing on a dish in his laboratory was killing bacteria nearby. From this discovery, he helped create penicillin, one of the world's first antibiotic drugs. Penicillin was not widely available until 1940, when Sir Howard Florey found ways of mass-producing it. Fleming and

Florey were jointly awarded the Nobel Prize for medicine in 1945.

Franklin, Benjamin (1706–1790) STATESMAN AND SCIENTIST The American Franklin wondered if lightning consisted of electrical sparks. To test his idea, Franklin flew a kite in a thunderstorm, attaching a metal key to the string on a short silk thread. Electricity from the lightning flowed down the wet string to the key and made a huge electrical spark. Franklin had proved his point—but he was lucky to be alive.

Freud, Sigmund (1856–1939) PSYCHOLOGIST Few scientists have had such an impact on our way of thinking about ourselves as Austrian psychologist Sigmund Freud. He suggested that we have "conscious" thoughts, which we know about, and "unconscious" thoughts, which we do not—but which both influence our behavior. Freud believed that our childhood experiences play an important role in shaping our behavior as adults.

Fry, Elizabeth (1780–1845) REFORMER Married to a wealthy banker, Fry believed it was her duty to help others. She began to visit women in prison and was shocked at the conditions she found. Fry organized clean clothes, water, and fresh food. She set up prison schools and found work, such as sewing, that women could do to earn a little money. She spent hours talking or reading to them, believing most could be helped to live honest, useful lives.

Galileo (1564–1642) SCIENTIST Galileo the Italian scientist, helped us to understand how things move, by proving that nothing changes, stops or starts, goes faster or slower unless a force is applied. He also used the newly invented telescope to discover that Jupiter has four moons and that Venus goes through phases like our Moon. His observations led to the proof that Copernicus was right: that the Earth is not at the center of the Universe and that it does move around the Sun. This got Galileo into trouble with the Catholic Church.

Mohandas Gandhi

Gandhi, Mohandas (1869–1948) REFORMER Gandhi was the inspirational leader who led India's fight for independence in a remarkable campaign of nonviolent protest. This method of action was called Satyagraha. In 1920, Mahatma Gandhi became the leader of a movement demanding independence for India. Gandhi led a series of nonviolent protests against the British, such as boycotting British goods and refusing to pay taxes. He gained millions of supporters. In 1942, Gandhi launched his "Quit India" campaign to get rid of the British, who then jailed Indian leaders. Indian and British leaders agreed to partition (split) India and Pakistan. Pakistan became independent on August 14, 1947. India finally gained independence in the same year. Gandhi was assassinated on January 30, 1948, by a Hindu who hated his tolerance of Muslims and others.

Gates, Bill (born 1955) INDUSTRIALIST As boss of Microsoft Corporation, the world's biggest computer software maker, Bill Gates became one of the most powerful business leaders of his time. He set up his first software company at the age of 15, and in 1985 introduced the first Windows program for PCs. Bill Gates went on to become one of the richest men in the world.

Genghis Khan (c.1162–1227) CONQUEROR In 1180, a 13-year-old Mongol boy called Temujin was made khan (chief) of his tribe. He soon became a great leader, and in 1206 he was hailed as Genghis Khan (Chief of all Men). He was a brilliant and ruthless soldier. In just four years (1210–1214), Genghis Khan conquered northern China and much of India and Persia. His empire stretched through Asia from Korea to the Caspian Sea.

George III (1738–1820) KING Of the six English kings named George, George III reigned longest, from 1760 until his death. His reign saw great events, such as the French and American revolutions, the wars with Napoleon, and the start of the British Empire in India. After 1815, illness made George unfit to reign, and his son became Prince Regent.

Gladstone, William Ewart (1809–1898) POLITICIAN After serving as a Conservative government minister, Gladstone changed his political views and joined the Liberal Party. He campaigned for better working conditions in factories, religious tolerance, and a ban on slavery. He was prime minister four times between 1868 and 1894. He also believed strongly that Ireland should have the right to rule itself.

Glendower, Owen (c.1354–c.1417) REBEL AND SOLDIER Descended from Welsh princes, Glendower began his political career working for the English government. However, he became a rebel, fighting for independence. He won many Welsh supporters, and in 1400 they declared him "Prince of Wales"—a title claimed by the sons of English kings. For the rest of his life, Glendower led armies to attack the English. This was the last Welsh revolt against English rule, and it failed.

Halley, Edmond (1656–1742) ASTRONOMER Oxford mathematics professor, astronomer, and friend of astronomer Isaac Newton, Halley was one of the first scientists to study nebulae—mysterious clouds of glowing gas that appear in the night sky. He is best-known for his observations of a bright comet, now named after him, that travels at regular intervals (every 76 years) across the sky.

Hargreaves, James (c.1720–1778) INVENTOR Trained as a woodworker and maker of weaving-looms, Hargreaves invented a machine that could spin several strands of thread at once. It became known as a "spinning jenny," and played a great part in the Industrial Revolution that transformed Britain during the early 19th century. Machines meant goods could be made much more quickly and cheaply than in the old-fashioned way, by hand.

Harvey, William (1578–1657) DOCTOR Court physician (doctor) to kings James I and Charles I, Harvey was the first European to discover how the blood circulates around the body through veins and arteries, and how the heart works as a pump. He also studied how babies grow and develop in the womb, and how animals move.

Henry VIII

Hawking, Stephen (born 1942) **SCIENTIST** One of the youngest people ever elected to membership of Britain's prestigious Royal Society (an association of top scientists). Hawking has investigated the structure and origins of the Universe by combining the two most important—and challenging—theories of 20th-century mathematics and physics: relativity and quantum mechanics. He also studied mysterious objects in space such as black holes. His book on the Universe, *A Brief History of Time*, became a bestseller when it was published in 1988.

Henry VIII (1491–1547) **KING** Henry VIII became England's king in 1509, on the death of his father Henry VII, founder of the Tudor dynasty. His reign was notable for his quarrel with the Pope, which led to the formation of the Church of England. His six marriages produced three heirs: Edward VI, Mary I, and Elizabeth I.

Hippocrates (460–379 BC) **DOCTOR** The ancient Greek doctor Hippocrates is often called the father of medicine. He lived during a time when many believed that illness was caused by evil spirits or magic. Hippocrates showed that disease has physical causes, such as poor diet or dirt. Today, doctors still practice under an updated version of the "Hippocratic oath" undertaking to provide good care for their patients.

Hitchcock, Alfred (1889–1980) **FILM DIRECTOR** One of Britain's most successful film directors, Hitchcock worked in Hollywood—the center of the 20th-century film industry—as well as in the UK. He became famous for a series of horror films, including *Psycho* (1960) and *The Birds* (1963). Hitchcock's film work combines excitement, fear, and chilling thoughts about why some people's minds become twisted or evil.

Hitler, Adolf (1889–1945) **DICTATOR** Hitler turned Germany into a war machine and murdered six million Jews in the Holocaust. Hitler was so angry at the terms ending World War I that he joined the National Socialist (Nazi) party, becoming its leader. In the 1933 elections, the Nazis got 37 percent of the vote and President Hindenburg asked Hitler to become chancellor (chief minister). In 1938, Hitler invaded Austria, then in 1939 Czechoslovkia and Poland too, and so began World War II. As Germany faced defeat in 1945, he married his mistress Eva Braun on April 29 in their bomb shelter in Berlin. They shot themselves the next day.

Hobbes, Thomas (1588–1679) **PHILOSOPHER** Political philosopher Hobbes is remembered today for his book, *Leviathan*, published in 1651. In it he put forward his views on how society works. He believed that people were selfish by nature, and that strict laws and powerful rulers were necessary to run society. Without them, Hobbes believed, people could not be trusted to behave well.

Hodgkin, Dorothy (1910–1994) **SCIENTIST** Using newly invented X ray techniques Hodgkin studied the way crystals were made. She then used this information to find out more about how chemicals combine to form new compounds, making important discoveries that helped doctors and chemists formulate new drugs. Hodgkin was awarded the Nobel Prize for chemistry in 1964.

Hooke, Robert (1635–1703) **SCIENTIST** After working as assistant to Robert Boyle, Hooke began to make experiments of his own. He studied many different topics, including astronomy, optics (the science of light), cell biology, and the science of materials. He discovered a law (now named after him) that describes how materials bend and stretch. Hooke also invented new scientific machines, and suggested improvements to microscopes and telescopes.

Adolf Hitler

St Joan of Arc

similar but much more deadly human disease. He therefore used cowpox to infect patients deliberately so that they would be protected against smallpox.

Joan of Arc, St (c.1412–31) **NATIONAL HEROINE** A peasant girl who led France from defeat in the Hundred Years War and was burned at the stake for her beliefs. By the age of 13, Joan was having visions and believed that God had chosen her to help the French king Charles VII to beat the English. Joan was given armor and an army to rescue the town of Orléans from the English and succeeded in just ten days. In May 1430, Joan was captured by the English and accused of witchcraft. She was burned at the stake in Rouen on May 30, 1431.

John (1165–1216; reigned 1199–1216) **KING** John was nicknamed "Lackland," because as the youngest of Henry II's sons there had been nothing left over to give him. He was not a very successful king. His reign is remembered today for a very important document that he was forced (by angry nobles) to seal in 1215. Its name was Magna Carta ("great charter") and, for the first time ever, it introduced laws limiting the king of England's powers and guaranteeing rights to his subjects.

Johnson, Samuel (known as Dr Johnson) (1709–1784) **WRITER** Son of a bookseller in Lichfield, Staffordshire, Johnson began his career as a schoolmaster, but left to live and work in London. At first he wrote reports of debates in Parliament for newspapers, but in 1747 was commissioned to produce an English dictionary. This was a great success when it was published in 1755, and Johnson became respected for his scholarship, outspoken opinions, and wit.

James VI and I (1566–1625; reigned Scotland 1567–1625; England, and Ireland 1603–1625) **KING** Son of Mary Queen of Scots, he became king of Scotland while still a child. When Queen Elizabeth I of England died in 1603, he also inherited her throne. James became the first king ever to rule England, Scotland, and Ireland, although the nations were not legally united. James believed strongly that God had given kings a "Divine Right" to rule, and that they should be obeyed without question.

Jenner, Edward (1749–1832) **DOCTOR** Country doctor Jenner pioneered the medical technique of vaccination. This places dead or weakened germs inside a person's body, so that it will learn to fight against them and protect them from future disease. Jenner discovered that dairymaids, who often caught a rash called cowpox from the animals they milked, never got smallpox, a

Julius Caesar (101–44 BC) **POLITICIAN AND SOLDIER** Caesar came from an aristocratic Roman family and earned fame as a soldier—he conquered Gaul (France) and invaded Britain twice. He defeated his rival in a civil war and was so powerful he might have become king, had he wished. He was murdered by senators led by Brutus and Cassius.

Keats, John (1792–1821) **WRITER** One of Britain's best-loved poets, Keats was born in London, and gave up medical work to be a writer. In 1818 and 1819 he produced a series of brilliant poems, including "Ode to a Nightingale," "To Autumn," "The Eve of St Agnes," and "Ode to a Grecian Urn." However, Keats had tuberculosis and was already seriously ill. He died in Italy, aged only 25. Keats's work is admired for its rich language. He was inspired by nature, by traditional stories, and by ancient legends.

Kennedy, John F (1917–1963) **US PRESIDENT** Elected in 1960, John Kennedy was the youngest person and the first Catholic to be president. He came from a wealthy Boston family, and won the election as much by his charisma on TV as by his arguments for change. Kennedy's presidency promised much but was cut short in 1963 when he was assassinated in Dallas, Texas, supposedly by a gunman named Lee Harvey Oswald.

Kenneth I (Kenneth MacAlpine) (died c.859; reigned c.843–858) **KING** Kenneth lived at a time when Scotland was divided into several different kingdoms. A famous warrior, he became ruler of Dalriada, in the Highlands, around 841. Two years later, he conquered the other Scottish kingdoms and declared himself the first king to rule all Scotland.

Kingsley, Mary (1862–1900)
EXPLORER Kingsley spent the first 30 years of her life quietly at home with her parents. When they died, she decided to travel. She made two long journeys through West Africa, traveling along rivers by canoe and meeting dangerous animals along the way. She also climbed to the top of Mount Cameroon, the highest point in West Africa—becoming only the second-known climber to do so. Mary collected examples of West African wildlife on her journeys, and presented them, for study, to London museums.

Kipling, J. Rudyard (1865–1936)
WRITER Born in India, Kipling worked as a journalist in Lahore (now in Pakistan) and published many poems and stories there. His books described everyday life in the sub-continent, and among members of the British Raj (ruling class). From 1889, Kipling lived in Britain and earned his living as a full-time writer. His most successful works were for children, and included *The Jungle Book* (1894) and *Just So Stories* (1902). His poem "If" was voted the most popular poem in Britain at the end of the 20th century.

Rudyard Kipling

Lavoisier, Antoine (1743–1794)
CHEMIST About 250 years ago, most scientists mistakenly believed that flammable materials contained a substance called phlogiston, which dissolved in the air when it burned. The brilliant French chemist Lavoisier demonstrated that by burning tin inside a sealed container and weighing it before and after, the tin, far from losing phlogiston to the air, actually gained something. He had discovered the gas that we now know as oxygen. Lavoisier also named many chemicals and arranged them into groups.

Leakey, Louis (1903–1972)
ANTHROPOLOGIST Leakey was born in Tanzania to British parents, who were missionaries. After education in England, he returned to Africa to study Stone Age remains. In 1948, he discovered the skull of an early ancestor of modern apes, from 25–40 million years ago. In 1959, his wife, Mary, discovered another ancient skull, this time from a creature half-way between apes and humans (now known as *Australopithecus boiseii*). Leakey used this skull to prove that human beings had evolved from apes about a million years earlier than anyone had previously thought.

Lenin (1870–1924) LEADER OF THE COMMUNIST REVOLUTION IN RUSSIA Lenin's real name was Vladimir Ilyich Ulyanov. He took the name Lenin from the River Lena in Siberia when he became a revolutionary. Like Karl Marx (1818–1883), Lenin believed the world's workers would revolt and take over industry. Unlike Marx, he thought a small band of professionals like the Bolsheviks would lead the way. After the failed 1905 revolution Lenin lived in exile, but he returned to Russia when the Czar fell, in 1917. After the October revolution, Lenin ruled the country as head of the Bolsheviks (now the Communists). The Communists won the civil war that followed and in 1922 changed the Russian empire into a new nation, called the Union of Soviet Socialist Republics (USSR).

Lenin

Leonardo da Vinci (1452–1519)
ARTIST One of the first great anatomical artists was Italian Leonardo da Vinci (1452–1519). Leonardo had a great mind and contributed to science in countless ways. Human dissection allowed him to produce detailed anatomical drawings. He painted the *Mona Lisa* and also designed amazing machines, including a helicopter.

Lincoln, Abraham (1809–65)
US PRESIDENT America's 16th, and possibly greatest, president. He led the Union through the Civil War and the freeing of slaves. In 1863, after the terrible battle of Gettysburg, Lincoln made a famous speech called the Gettysburg Address, which summed up the spirit of democracy. He was shot dead at Ford's Theater, Washington by John Wilkes Booth, a fanatical southerner.

Lister, Lord Joseph (1827–1912)
DOCTOR Lister was a surgeon who pioneered a new technique that saved countless lives. In the past, many patients died from infections after operations. In 1865, Lister read that French chemist Pasteur had discovered that infection was caused by bacteria (germs). So he decided to try to kill any germs before they could infect his patients. He covered wounds with dressings soaked in strong disinfectant, and sterilized his operating theater with a fine mist of disinfectant sprayed in the air. Lister's technique—which he called "antisepsis"—worked well.

Lord David Lloyd George

Livingstone, David (1813–1873)
EXPLORER AND MISSIONARY Born in southern Scotland, Livingstone qualified as a doctor in 1840, then sailed for southern Africa. Here, he worked as a medical missionary, and made several long journeys of exploration. He explored the Zambezi River, and became the first European to see Lake Nyasa and the Victoria Falls. In 1865, he set off to search for the source of the river Nile. Nothing was heard of him for over five years, until American journalist H M Stanley went in search of the explorer, finding him in 1871 and greeting him with the now famous words, "Dr Livingstone, I presume?"

Lloyd George, Lord David (1863–1945) **POLITICIAN** Trained as a solicitor, Lloyd George aimed for a political career. He became Liberal Party MP, and was soon appointed to government posts. From 1908–1915, he was chancellor of the exchequer, and introduced many important social reforms. He provided government money to pay the first old age pensions, and started a National Insurance scheme (where working people contributed a share of their wages to pay for welfare benefits.) In 1916, Lloyd George became prime minister. He proved a strong, capable leader during World War I. Forced to resign in 1923, he continued as leader of the Liberal Party until 1931.

Llywelyn the Great (Llywelyn ap Iorwerth) (died 1240) **PRINCE** Prince of Gwynedd (north Wales), Llywelyn became the most powerful ruler in Wales. He was accepted as leader by all the other rulers of Welsh kingdoms, although he never claimed the title "Prince of Wales." In 1211–1212, he successfully led the fight against an invasion by English King John and kept English troops out of Wales for the next 20 years.

Luther, Martin (1483–1546)
REFORMER A poor miner's son from Saxony in Germany. As a monk at Wittenberg University, he earned a reputation for his great biblical knowledge. In 1517, Luther nailed a list of 95 grievances on the door of Wittenberg Castle's chapel, hoping to start a debate. The pope issued a papal bull (demand) that Luther go back on his views or face expulsion from the Church. Luther burned the bull—and the Church expelled him in 1521. Luther set up his own church, whose members soon came to be called Protestants— because of their protests.

Luther King, Martin (1929–1968)
REFORMER A Baptist preacher, King led the Civil Rights campaign for black rights in America, leading a huge march on Washington in 1963. King's "I have a dream…" speech galvanized support for the movement from all races and helped secure new civil rights legislation. He was assassinated in 1968 by a gunman, James Earl Ray.

Mackintosh, Charles Rennie (1868–1928) **DESIGNER** Creator of a distinctive new style, based on flowing lines and tall, slender shapes, he was one of the main exponents of the Art Nouveau style in Scotland. Mackintosh is seen today as one of the first truly modern artists in Britain.

Magellan (1480–1522) **EXPLORER** In 1519–1522, Magellan's ship *Victoria* sailed across the Atlantic, round the southern tip of South America, across the Pacific and back round Africa to

Magellan

Spain. Although this Portuguese explorer was killed in the Philippines, his crew and ship went on to complete the first around-the-world voyage.

Mandela, Nelson (born 1918) PRESIDENT In 1990, President de Klerk released Mandela, jailed since 1962, and repealed apartheid laws. In 1994, the ANC won the first open elections and Nelson Mandela became South Africa's first black president.

Marco Polo

Marco Polo (*c.*1254–1324) EXPLORER Polo was a famous Italian traveler, born in Venice. Marco's father Niccolo and uncle Maffeo were well-traveled merchants. The Polos took four years to reach China, traveling on foot and horse along the "Silk Road." Marco Polo spent many years in the court of Kublai Khan, emperor of China. The Polos arrived back in Venice in 1295, laden with jewels, silks, and spices.

Marlowe, Christopher (Kit) (1564–1593) WRITER Creator of several successful plays in blank (nonrhyming) verse, such as *Dr Faustus* and *Tamburlaine the Great*, Marlowe's lines are often still quoted today. He also wrote many poems, mostly about love. He died young, in a tavern brawl, so we do not know how his writing skills would have developed. Shakespeare himself borrowed ideas from Marlowe's work to use in his own early plays.

Marx, Karl Heinrich (1818–1883) POLITICAL THINKER Born in Prussia, north Germany, writer and thinker Marx worked as a radical journalist. He was expelled from Germany for his revolutionary ideas and moved to England in 1849, where he spent much of his adult life. His most famous texts were *The Communist Manifesto* and *Das Kapital* (about economics and the power of money). Marx's ideas inspired many revolutions and protest movements, notably in Russia (1917) and China (1948).

Mary, Queen of Scots (1542–1587; reigned 1542–1567) QUEEN Mary became queen of Scotland aged just six days old. She was sent to France to be educated, while her mother ruled Scotland on her behalf. As a child, Mary married the French crown prince. He became King Francois II in 1559, but died one year later, and Mary was sent back to Scotland in 1561. She was a Roman Catholic, but most Scots were Protestants. Mary wed her cousin, English nobleman Henry Darnley. Darnley was accused of planning the murder of her friend, musician David Rizzio. Soon afterwards, Darnley was found dead, in mysterious circumstances. Mary then scandalized Europe by eloping with one of the chief suspects—a violent Scots noble named

Bothwell. After this, the Scottish people no longer wanted Mary as queen. They locked her up in a castle, but she escaped, and fled to England in 1558. There, she became a serious problem for Queen Elizabeth, because England's enemies in Spain and France wanted Mary to be queen. Some Roman Catholics in England wanted this, too. For almost 20 years, Elizabeth kept Mary shut up in remote country houses. Mary was accused of taking part in several plots and was eventually executed.

Maxwell, James Clerk (1831–1879) SCIENTIST A physicist, Maxwell studied electricity and magnetism. He was the first to realize that electromagnetic radiation existed, and to realize that light is a form of electromagnetic energy. He worked out mathematical equations to describe how electromagnetic forces work. He was also a capable administrator, setting up and running the Cavendish research laboratory at Cambridge University for many years.

Mill, J S (1806–1873) PHILOSOPHER A civil servant and later an MP, Mill is remembered today for his writings on liberty, justice, women's rights, and economics. Mill campaigned for ordinary men and women to get the vote, and for workers to have the right to help run factories.

Milton, John (1608–1674) WRITER Milton's greatest work, *Paradise Lost* (1667), is a long epic that retells the Bible story of Adam and Eve. Milton went blind in middle age, but this did not stop him writing or studying as his wife and daughters read to him. During the civil war, he wrote poems and pamphlets calling for England to become a republic.

More, Sir (or St) Thomas

(1478–1535) POLITICIAN A famous scholar and government minister at the court of King Henry VIII. More was a Roman Catholic, who opposed Protestant church reforms. He resigned as chancellor when Henry announced his decision to seek a divorce from Catherine of Aragon, and was put in prison in 1534 for refusing to accept Henry's marriage to Anne Boleyn. Henry gave orders for More to be executed the next year. He is still remembered for his book *Utopia*, in which he discussed the best way of running society.

Sir Thomas More

Mozart, Wolfgang Amadeus

(1756–1791) COMPOSER Born in Salzburg, Austria, Mozart was a child prodigy and as a boy toured Europe with his father and his sister Maria, also a gifted musician. In a short creative life, he composed more than 40 symphonies, 21 piano concertos, and several operas. Despite his brilliance as a master of melody and technique, Mozart was never well paid and died from typhoid, in poverty, at the age of 35.

Mussolini, Benito (1883–1945)

POLITICIAN Fascist dictator of Italy from 1922–1943. Mussolini aimed to give Italy strong government and build a new "Roman Empire." His troops invaded Abyssinia (Ethiopia) and Albania, and fought alongside German armies in World War II until 1943. Mussolini was then overthrown, rescued by the Germans, but finally captured and executed by Italian resistance fighters.

Napoleon Bonaparte (1769–1821)

GENERAL Bonaparte, the greatest general of modern times, created for a short while a French empire that covered most of Europe. Napoleon was born on the island of Corsica. By 1794, at just 25, he was a brigadier general. By 1804, Napoleon's conquests had made him a hero in France, and he elected himself as Emperor Napoleon I. By 1812, Napoleon had defeated all the major countries in Europe but Britain, and decided to invade Russia. Napoleon's invasion of Russia ended in such disaster that it broke his power in Europe. He was finally defeated by Wellington's armies at Waterloo, Belgium in June, and then sent to the island of St Helena in the mid-Atlantic, where he died, aged 51.

Nelson, Lord Horatio (1758–1805)

SEAMAN Nelson joined the Navy aged 12, and served on ships sailing to the Arctic and the Caribbean. His skill as a seaman and leader was soon recognized, and he was given his first ship to command while still in his twenties. Although small and slight, he showed great physical courage. He lost his right eye fighting against the French in the Mediterranean Sea in 1793, and his right arm in 1797. The following year, he commanded British ships against the French at the Battle of the

Lord Horatio Nelson

Nile. He won a great victory, and became a national hero. His greatest success came at the Battle of Trafalgar in 1805, where his ships destroyed the French fleet. Nelson was killed in the fighting, but his victory made Britain the greatest sea power in the world.

Newcomen, Thomas (1663–1729)

ENGINEER Newcomen invented the first steam-powered engine that was strong and reliable enough for industrial use. Made to pump water out of deep coal mines, it was first installed in 1712. Newcomen's design was later adapted and improved by famous inventor James Watt.

Newton, Sir Isaac (1642–1727)

SCIENTIST Said by some to be the greatest British scientist of all time, Cambridge professor Newton was a mathematician and physicist. He made many key mathematical discoveries. He also discovered, and explained in mathematical terms, the natural laws that rule the Universe. Newton's "Laws of Motion" describe the forces at work when movement happens. His "Law of Gravitation" describes terms such as weight and mass, and explains why objects fall to Earth, and why the Earth orbits (moves around) the Sun. Newton also studied optics (the science of light and vision) and was the first to show that white light is made up of many different colors. In 1703, he was elected president of the Royal Society.

Nightingale, Florence (1820–1910) NURSE In 1854, British troops were sent to fight in the Crimea (southern Russia). Nightingale volunteered to lead a group of nurses there. Nightingale and her nurses found that conditions in army hospitals were dreadful, and set about improving them, with great success. Nightingale proved to be a brilliant, formidable organizer. She became known as "the Lady with the Lamp" (because of her habit of checking the wards every evening).

Offa (died 796) KING Warrior and ruler of the English kingdom of Mercia, in the West Midlands, Offa took control of weaker English kingdoms, and declared himself king of the English. He ordered the building of a massive earthwork (known as "Offa's Dyke"), to mark the boundary between his kingdom and Wales, and to display his wealth and power. Offa's Dyke was around 120 mi long and 25 ft high. Most of it still survives today.

Orwell, George (Eric Blair) (1903–1950) WRITER The son of a government official working in India, Orwell served in the British police force in Burma, then returned to England to become a writer. He sympathized with working-class protests, and fought on the Republican side, against Fascists, in the Spanish Civil War. But he strongly disliked communist governments. His two most famous books, *Animal Farm* (1945) and *Nineteen Eighty Four*

Florence Nightingale

(1949), attack governments that control their citizens.

Owen, Robert (1771–1858) REFORMER Remembered today as a pioneer of the cooperative movement (it encouraged workers to join together to improve their lives), Owen was the son of a Welsh draper (cloth seller). Owen took over cloth mills at New Lanark, in Scotland. He ran them as a model factory, building new houses, schools, shops, and water supplies for his workers.

Owen, Wilfred (1893–1918) WRITER One of the most important poets who took part in, and wrote about, World War I. Owen had already produced several fine poems by the time he was 21—he year the war began. He fought as a British soldier in France, turning his horrific experiences—and those of his comrades—into bleak, bitter verses, full of anger at the tragic waste of young men's lives. Owen was killed in action one week before the end of the war.

Pankhurst, Emmeline (1858–1928) CAMPAIGNER Leader of the Suffragette movement, which demanded votes for women, Pankhurst—and her daughters Christabel (1880–1958) and Sylvia (1882–1960)—are remembered today for taking direct, sometimes violent, action in their campaigns. They did this because they felt that peaceful, legal demands for women's right to vote would never succeed.

Pasteur, Louis (1822–1895) SCIENTIST French scientist Louis Pasteur discovered that liquids turn sour because they contain tiny organisms. He found that these organisms can be killed by heat in a process now known as "pasteurization" whereby a substance, such as milk, is heated to a certain temperature then rapidly cooled. Pasteur's greatest breakthrough was to find that germs, such as bacteria and viruses, carry disease from one person to another.

Peel, Sir Robert (1788–1850) POLITICIAN Son of a factory owner, Peel became a Conservative MP, home secretary (1834–1835), and prime minister (1841–1846). He is remembered today chiefly for founding the Metropolitan Police force, to combat crime in London. The police were nicknamed "bobbies" or "peelers" after Peel.

Pepys, Samuel (1633–1703) WRITER A senior government official who worked for the Royal Navy, Pepys is remembered today for the diary that he kept in a secret code—for privacy—between 1660 and 1669. In it he recorded many dramatic national events, including the Great Plague (1665) and the Great Fire of London (1666), and descriptions of new scientific discoveries.

Sir Walter Raleigh

Pitt, William (known as "Pitt the Younger") (1759–1806) **POLITICIAN** Son of Pitt the Elder, Pitt trained as a lawyer, then became an MP in 1781. Unlike his father, William supported the Conservative Party. Ambitious and clever, he was soon made a minister of government, then prime minister in 1783. He was only 24, and was the youngest man ever to be chosen for the job. The young prime minister reformed government finances —income tax was his idea—reduced the national debt, changed the way British merchants and soldiers ran their lands in India, and increased people's respect for Parliament.

Purcell, Henry (*c*.1659–1695) **MUSICIAN** Son of a singer in the royal chapel in London, Purcell also joined the choir but became more famous as an organist and composer. He wrote many works specially for the royal court, such as birthday odes (songs) for the queen, and impressive pieces for choir and organ to be performed at royal coronations. Purcell also composed many religious works, and music for the theater. He is remembered today as the composer of the first opera in English, in 1689, called *Dido and Aeneas*.

Raleigh, Sir Walter (1552–1618) **EXPLORER** Born in Devon, Raleigh fought as a soldier in France, then became a courtier, serving Queen Elizabeth I. He became one of her special favorites. However, he was restless at court, planned overseas voyages, and took part in wars in Ireland. He encouraged British explorer Humphrey Gilbert to explore Newfoundland, and organized his own (unsuccessful) voyage off the northeast coast of America.

Roosevelt, Franklin Delano (1882–1945) **US PRESIDENT** Roosevelt was elected president in 1932, during the economic depression. His New Deal policies helped America recover, and he was reelected in 1936 and 1940. During World War II, Roosevelt forged a friendship with Britain's war leader, Churchill. He was elected for a record fourth term in 1944. A polio victim since 1921, Roosevelt died suddenly in 1945, only weeks before World War II ended.

Franklin Delano Roosevelt

Scott, Sir Robert Falcon (1868–1912) **EXPLORER** Scott commanded the British National Antarctic Expedition of 1900–1904. In 1911, he led a second expedition, this time to the South Pole. He arrived there in 1912 but found that the Norwegian explorer, Roald Amundsen, had reached it before him. With all his team, Scott died on the return journey to base camp.

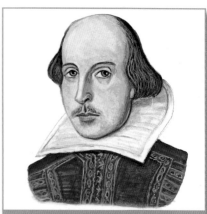

William Shakespeare

Shakespeare, William (1564–1616) **WRITER** The most famous English writer of all time, and, to many people, still the best. Shakespeare was born in the country town of Stratford-upon-Avon, in the English Midlands. He left home as a young man to work as an actor, then a writer, in London. He also became part-owner of two of London's most popular theaters, and staged performances at the royal court. His plays include love stories such as *Romeo and Juliet*, historical epics such as *Henry V*, and tragedies such as *Hamlet*.

Simpson, Sir James (1811–1870) **DOCTOR** Simpson began to study medicine aged 14. After qualifying as a doctor, he specialized in the care of mothers and young babies. There were no safe anesthetics, but in 1847 he pioneered the use of chloroform, which became widely used as an anesthetic for operations.

Smith, Adam (1723–1790) **PHILOSOPHER AND WRITER** Smith is famous today for his theories on economics. He was a professor at Glasgow University. Smith spent years traveling with pupils in Europe, meeting many famous writers and thinkers. In 1766, he returned to Scotland and spent the next ten years writing his most important book, *An Inquiry into the Nature and Causes of the Wealth of Nations*. In it, he discussed what made people and countries rich, and how wealth could be created.

Socrates (469–399 BC) **PHILOSOPHER** The Greeks called Socrates "the world's wisest man." He turned to ideas after soldiering in the Peloponnesian War. Among his pupils was the philosopher Plato. Socrates was accused of blasphemy by the authorities in Athens and sentenced to death. He killed himself by swallowing poison.

Stalin, Joseph (1879–1953) **DICTATOR** Stalin became dictator of the USSR after Lenin died in 1924, and remained so until he himself died, in 1953. Stalin was from Georgia and his real name was Joseph Vissarionovich Dzhugashvili. Stalin used terror to wipe out opposition and ensure the revolution survived. Russians lived in fear of the secret police NKVD (later the KGB), led by Beria, and millions went to their deaths in the Gulags (prison camps).

Stephenson, George (1781–1848) **ENGINEER** Stephenson began his working life in coal mines. He built his first steam locomotive in 1814, to haul coal trucks. Soon afterward, he became engineer to the pioneering Stockton and Darlington Railway Company and drove the world's first steam-powered train along its tracks in 1825. He worked closely with his son Robert (1803–1859) to build steam locomotives, including the famous *Rocket* in 1829.

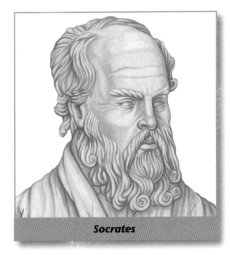

Socrates

Thomson, Sir William (Lord Kelvin) (1824–1907) **SCIENTIST** Born in Belfast to a famous family of scientists, Thomson began studying mathematics and physics at Glasgow University when he was only 11 years old. He became professor there aged 22. At 24, he developed one of his brightest ideas— a new scale for measuring temperature. It is still used, and is named after him.

Trevithick, Richard (1771–1833) **ENGINEER** One of the pioneers of railway transport, Trevithick worked as a mining engineer. He invented a steam-powered engine and used it in locomotives to transport miners and coal along roads. In 1802 he built a high-pressure steam engine that was dangerous but powerful. In 1803 he was the first person to design an engine that could run on rails.

Tull, Jethro (1647–1741) **INVENTOR** An Oxfordshire landowner, Tull invented some of the world's first farm machines. Before his inventions, almost all work on British farms, except plowing, was done using human muscle-power and hand-tools. Around 1701, Tull invented a seed drill (machine for planting seeds).

Turing, Alan (1912–1954) **INVENTOR** One of the inventors of modern computers, Turing designed a pioneering computing machine in 1937. During World War II (1939–1945) he belonged to a secret British government team of code-breakers, who worked to "crack" (spy on and translate) messages sent by German commanders to troops attacking Europe. After the war he worked on computers and on artificial intelligence (machines that could "think" for themselves).

Turner, J M W (Joseph Mallord William) (1775–1851) **ARTIST** Turner showed artistic talent even as a young child. He began to study at art college aged 14, then spent many years traveling and sketching in Britain and Europe. His early works were pictures of landscapes, in watercolors and oil paint. Towards the end of his life, Turner lost interest in accurately recording the views he saw, and became much more concerned with portraying dramatic effects of light and shade. In many of his works, such as the famous *Rain, Steam and Speed*, sunlight and clouds make beautiful abstract patterns.

The Grand Canal, Venice *by Turner*

Victoria (1819–1901; reigned 1837–1901) QUEEN Victoria was the longest-reigning British ruler, and one of the most successful. She became queen when she was only 18 years old. In 1840, she married her cousin Albert, a German prince. Extremely happy together, they had nine children. Victoria was devastated when he died young, in 1861, and withdrew from public life for some years. Persuaded to take up her duties again by prime minister Disraeli, she became a popular symbol of Britain's fast-growing power and prosperity. The 50th and 60th anniversaries of her accession (coming to the throne) were marked by splendid celebrations, and her death was widely mourned.

Wallace, Sir William (c.1274–1305) SOLDIER Wallace led the Scots to fight against King Edward I of England. He was appointed guardian of Scotland after his troops defeated the English at the Battle of Stirling Bridge in 1297. The next year, he lost a battle against the English at Falkirk and was forced to flee. He escaped to France but returned to Scotland in 1303. He was betrayed to the English and put in prison. Soon after, he was taken to London, tried for treason, and cruelly executed.

Wallis, Sir Barnes (1887–1979) ENGINEER Wallis created over 140 new designs, mostly for aircraft and weapons. He designed the R100 airship (in the 1930s) and the Wellington bomber plane (used throughout World War II). He also designed revolutionary "bouncing" bombs, to smash through massive concrete dams. After the war, Wallis helped to design missiles, supersonic jets, and swing-wing planes.

Walpole, Sir Robert (1676–1745) POLITICIAN Walpole came from a family

Queen Victoria

of country landowners. He was leader of the Cabinet for many years during the reigns of George I and George II. For this reason, he is often called "Britain's first prime minister" ("prime" = "first"). His policies aimed to increase British prosperity and maintain peace.

Washington, George (1732–1799) US PRESIDENT Washington had been a surveyor, soldier, and farmer before taking command of the American army against the British in the Revolutionary War (1775–1781). He proved an inspirational organizer and campaigner, and in 1789 was the popular choice to become the first president of the new United States.

Watt, James (1736–1819) ENGINEER Remembered today as one of the founders of the Industrial Revolution, Watt began his career as a scientific instrument-maker. In 1763, he saw a model of Newcomen's steam engine, and realized that it could be improved.

Around the same time, he also began experiments with steam and heat. He designed a new steam engine. In 1774, he began a business partnership with wealthy factory-owner Matthew Boulton. Together, they produced new steam-powered engines, used to power machines in many factories in Britain. Watt also invented the term "horsepower," to describe the power of a machine. Today, the Watt (another unit of power) is named after him.

Wellington, Duke of (1769–1852) SOLDIER A brilliant army commander, famous for his strict discipline (he was known as "the Iron Duke"). Wellington led British troops to fight against Napoleon's France. His most famous victory was the Battle of Waterloo (1815), which ended French hopes to take control of Europe. After he retired from active fighting, Wellington became a Conservative politician, serving as prime minister from 1828–1830, and in 1834.

Wesley, John (1703–1791) CHURCH LEADER A scholar at Oxford University, Wesley became leader of a small group with keen religious ideas. They became known as "methodists"—a name that is still preserved today in the church that Wesley founded.

A Watt steam engine

Wilberforce, William (1759–1833)
REFORMER Son of a wealthy merchant, Wilberforce served as a Liberal MP. He became convinced that slavery was wicked, and started to campaign against it. In 1807, he persuaded Parliament to ban the slave trade in Britain. After this great success, he continued to work for slavery to be abolished throughout the world.

William I "the Conqueror"

William I ("the Conqueror") (1027–1087) KING The son of Robert, Duke of Normandy, William was descended from Viking invaders who settled in northern France after AD c.900. After the English king, Edward the Confessor, died, William claimed the right to rule England, saying that Edward had promised it to him in return for his help. However, other rivals also claimed the throne, so William invaded England in 1066. Probably his most famous memorial is the *Domesday Book*, a massive survey of all England and its wealth.

Wolsey, Thomas (Cardinal) (1472–1530) PRIEST AND POLITICIAN Wolsey was an English Roman Catholic priest. Like many other churchman of his time, he held many senior positions, including lord chancellor. He helped shape England's relations with other European countries and with the leaders of the Roman Catholic Church in Rome. But after he failed to win King Henry VIII a divorce from his first wife, Catherine of Aragon, the king came to hate him, and accused him of treason. He died on his way to the trial.

Wordsworth, William (1770–1850)
WRITER One of Britain's most famous writers, Wordsworth's poems, such as "I wandered lonely as a cloud" (1815) are still popular today. He was born and raised in the Lake District, in northwest England, and spent most of his life there. Its magnificent mountain scenery is described in many of his works, and influenced his thoughts and feelings.

Wren, Sir Christopher (1632–1723)
ARCHITECT Trained as a scientist, Wren changed careers to become an architect. After the Great Fire of London (1666) he was asked to build many new London churches to replace the ones damaged in the Great Fire, including St Paul's Cathedral. This was a massive project, which took many years (1675–1711) to complete.

Wren's St Paul's cathedral

Orville Wright

Wright, Orville (1871–1948) **and Wilbur** (1867–1912) INVENTORS The Wright brothers were American bicycle makers, who became interested in flying. They read books, designed gliders, and then built a plane with an engine. On December 17, 1903, Orville piloted the *Flyer* on a 12-second flight at Kitty Hawk, North Carolina, USA. The age of powered flight had begun.

Yeats, William Butler (1865–1939)
WRITER Yeats was an Irish poet and dramatist. He was a keen supporter of Irish history, folklore, and traditional culture. While working as a poet and dramatist, he helped set up societies to study Irish literature, and was cofounder of the Irish National Theatre Company. His play, *The Countess Cathleen*, inspired many other writers to create works set in, or about, Ireland. From 1922–1928, Yeats served as a senator in the newly formed Irish Free State. He was awarded the Nobel Prize for Literature in 1923.

COUNTRIES

The World

Our world is a varied landscape with diverse countries and cultures. Mountains, rivers, deserts, seas, oceans, rainforests, grassland, and extreme weather are just some of the Earth's features. For over two million years humans have built towns and cities to live in, and worked the land.

○ More than 360,000 babies are born every day around the world.

○ Approximately 150,000 people die each day.

○ World population is growing by about 1.22 percent per year.

○ At the current rate, the population of the world will reach 7.5 billion by 2020.

○ The number of babies born to each woman varies from 1.11 in Bulgaria to 7.11 in Somalia.

○ In wealthy countries, such as Italy and Switzerland, there is on average one doctor for every 350 people; in most poor African countries there is one doctor for every 50,000 people.

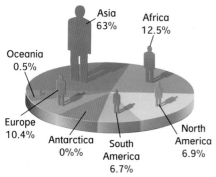

Asia 63%
Africa 12.5%
Oceania 0.5%
Europe 10.4%
Antarctica 0%%
South America 6.7%
North America 6.9%

▲ *Continents vary in population density. The size of the figures in this diagram shows the size of the population of each continent. The size of the segment the figure is standing on represents the area of the continent.*

Amazing

There are now more than twice as many farm animals in the world as humans— more than 14 billion.

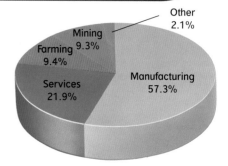

Other 2.1%
Mining 9.3%
Farming 9.4%
Services 21.9%
Manufacturing 57.3%

▲ *This diagram shows the proportions of different industries that make up world trade. The richest 30 countries control 82 percent of world trade, while the poorest 49 countries control just 2 percent. The World Trade Organization was founded in 1995 to police world trade. Many poor countries feel that the WTO is biased toward the richer nations.*

○ The world's richest countries contain less than one-quarter of the world's population, but have three-quarters of its wealth.

○ Most of the rich countries are in the Northern Hemisphere, and most of the poorest are in the Southern Hemisphere, so people talk about a North–South divide.

○ Half a billion people around the world are starving, or do not get enough to eat.

○ Life expectancy is higher in richer countries than poorer ones. In Andorra, for example, people live for an average of 83.5 years; in Mozambique, life expectancy is just 36.5 years.

◄ *Many of the world's towns and cities, such as Hong Kong, are growing very fast. The United Nations estimates that by 2007 half the world's population will live in urban areas.*

Find out more
Most populated countries p. 292

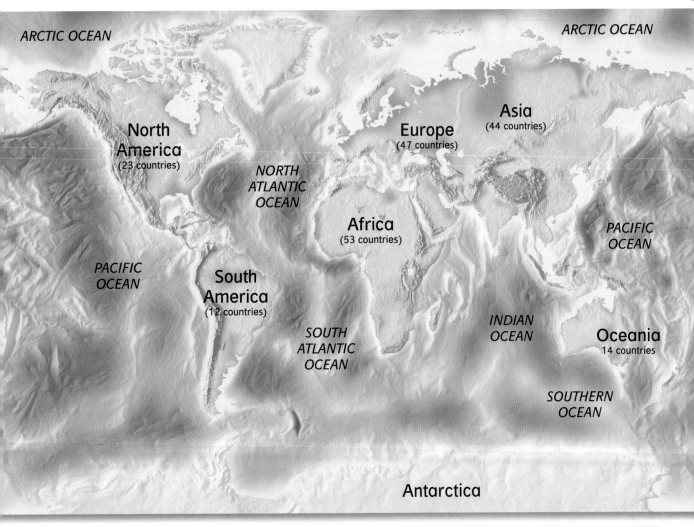

ARCTIC OCEAN

ARCTIC OCEAN

North America
(23 countries)

NORTH ATLANTIC OCEAN

Europe
(47 countries)

Asia
(44 countries)

Africa
(53 countries)

PACIFIC OCEAN

PACIFIC OCEAN

South America
(12 countries)

SOUTH ATLANTIC OCEAN

INDIAN OCEAN

Oceania
14 countries

SOUTHERN OCEAN

Antarctica

The land on the Earth's surface is split up into seven large land masses called continents. Some of these, such as Europe, are very crowded, while nobody at all lives permanently in Antarctica. Although most continents are big blocks of land, others, such as Oceania, are made up of many islands.

International organizations

Many countries and peoples of the world have joined together to create international organizations that provide law, order, aid, and support throughout the world. Foremost of these is the United Nations (UN), set up by governments in 1945 to promote peace and security. The UN now has agencies responsible for children (UNESCO), food and farming (FAO), health (WHO), science (UNICEF), and nuclear energy (IAEA). Some organizations have no links to governments. The Red Cross (Red Crescent in Islamic countries) is a worldwide humanitarian organization.

World population

1 billion	1804
2 billion	1927
3 billion	1960
4 billion	1974
5 billion	1987
6 billion	1999

North America

The third largest of the continents, North America extends from Greenland and Alaska in the Arctic north, through Canada and the United States, to Mexico and the countries of Central America in the south. It also encompasses the islands of the Caribbean Sea.

○ North America's hottest spot is Death Valley, California, where a temperature of 135°F was recorded in 1913.

○ North America's Great Lakes hold one-fifth of the world's freshwater.

○ Lake Superior is the largest body of freshwater in the world. About 200 rivers drain into the lake.

○ Canada has 10 percent of the world's forests. In the far north, the forest gives way to tundra—an almost treeless landscape of plains and moorland, where the subsoil never thaws out.

○ Yosemite National Park, in California, USA, sits on top of a volcanic hot spot. There are signs that Yellowstone may one day erupt as a "supervolcano"—an eruption on an unimaginable scale.

○ The San Andreas Fault, on the western coast of the USA, is the boundary between two huge continental plates. As it moves, it causes earthquakes in cities such as Los Angeles and San Francisco.

○ Powerful tropical storms, known as hurricanes, affect the Caribbean between May and October.

▶ Many animals live in the cold forests of Canada, including bears and moose. The American black bear can grow to a weight of 330 lb and eats berries, pine cones, and grass, as well as small animals.

▲ There are two falls on the Niagara River: the Horseshoe Falls on the Canadian side and the American Falls on the US side. The Horseshoe Falls are 2,598 ft wide and 167 ft high. The American Falls are 1,000 ft wide and about 177 ft high. The most water (about 85 percent) crashes over the Horseshoe Falls.

▶ Yellowstone National Park in California, USA, contains 300 geysers, the most famous of which is Old Faithful, shown here.

Rocky Mountains

Thousands of visitors flock to the Rocky Mountain range each year to see the vast array of fauna and wildlife, such as bears, deer, mountain lions, squirrels, and minks. The Rockies stretch more than 2,982 mi from Alaska to New Mexico. In the Canadian Rockies, the snowcapped mountains reach more than 2,236 mi above sea level and the tallest peak is Mount Robson, at 2,456 mi high. The Rockies are also a good source of lead, coal, silver, and zinc.

Find out more

Volcano records p. 289

Great Bear Lake

Great Slave Lake

Hudson Bay

ATLANTIC OCEAN

Mackenzie River

Lake Winnipeg

Missouri River

Lake Superior

St Lawrence River

R O C K Y

Lake Huron

Lake Ontario

Lake Michigan

Niagara Falls

Lake Erie

Great Salt Lake

Yosemite

Colorado River

Missouri River

M O U N T A I N S

Mississippi River

PACIFIC OCEAN

Rio Grande

Gulf of Mexico

Amazing

Pitch Lake, on the Caribbean island of Trinidad, is unusual because it contains no water and people can walk over it. The lake contains hot, sticky black tar, which covers about 57 ha to a depth of about 131 ft.

CARIBBEAN SEA

A *The North American landscape ranges from bleak polar regions, towering mountains, vast grassy plains or prairies (now plowed for cereal crops), forests, deserts, mighty rivers and enormous lakes. Parts of central America—the narrow part of the continent that links to South America— are covered by rainforest.*

Factfile

Area 9,072,901 sq mi
Population more than 505 million
Major cities Chicago (USA), Mexico City (USA), New York (USA), Philadelphia (USA), Toronto (Canada)
Largest country Canada 3,852,097 sq mi
Highest mountain Mount McKinley, USA, 20,321 ft
Longest river Mississippi, USA, 3,740 mi
Largest lake Lake Superior, Canada, 31,702 sq mi
Largest US state Alaska 579,195 sq mi
Main religion Christianity c. 250 million

North America People and Places

North America includes countries with diverse cultures and traditions. Canada and the United States have historic ties with Britain, and Canada also has a large French-speaking minority. Native Americans retain their traditional cultures and languages, as do those people of African, Asian, and European origin. In Mexico and Central America people speak Spanish —a legacy of the country's past.

Aztecs and Mayans

When the Spanish arrived in what is now Mexico in the 1500s, the region was part of an empire ruled by a warlike people called the Aztecs. Much of Central America was under the influence of the older Mayan culture. The Aztecs and Mayans worshiped a range of gods, performed religious rituals (including human sacrifice), and built steep-sided stone pyramid temples in their cities. The one shown here is at the sacred Mayan site of Chichén Itzá in Mexico. Both cultures were destroyed by Spanish invaders.

MAP KEY
1 Antigua & Barbuda
2 Aruba
3 Bahamas
4 Barbados
5 Belize
6 Bermuda
7 Dominica
8 Dominican Republic
9 El Salvador
10 Grenada
11 Guadeloupe
12 Haiti
13 Martinique
14 Montserrat
15 Puerto Rico
16 St Kitts–Nevis
17 St Lucia
18 St Vincent & the Grenadines
19 Trinidad & Tobago
20 Virgin Islands

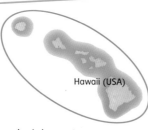

Hawaii (USA)

○ Canada is North America's largest country, but its population is only 11 percent that of the USA. Canada and the USA are rich in natural resources, making them wealthy countries, but many of the nations of Central America are very poor. Greenland belongs to the European country of Denmark.

Find out more

Biggest cities p. 280

In many US cities tall buildings, or "skyscrapers," create dramatic skylines, particularly in Chicago, along the shore of Lake Michigan, and in New York City, on Manhattan Island (shown here).

○ Disney World, in Florida, USA, is the world's largest theme park, covering 1,306,739,000 sq ft—the size of 17,250 soccer pitches.

○ The heads of four US presidents—George Washington, Thomas Jefferson, Theodore Roosevelt, and Abraham Lincoln—are carved into the side of Mount Rushmore, in South Dakota, USA. Each head is about 59 ft high and can be seen from almost 62 mi away.

○ The North American city with the greatest population is Mexico City, which has about 18.5 million people. Mexico City is close to an active volcano called Popocatépetl (Aztec for "smoking mountain").

Amazing

In the USA, 45,000 hamburgers are eaten every minute.

○ In 1999, the Canadian Inuit finally gained their own territory, called Nunavut ("Our Land"), providing both a homeland and a greater degree of self-rule.

○ The USA consumes more energy than any other country.

○ In the USA, 81 out of every 100 people own television sets; in Haiti, only five out of every 100 have TVs.

○ The first people to live in North America were the Native Americans and Inuit, whose ancestors came from Asia, probably before the last ice age. They were driven from their lands by European settlers in the 1500s.

○ Today, about one-fifth of Native Americans live on land known as reservations, which has been given back to them by the government.

The 50 mi-long Panama Canal provides a shipping short cut between the Atlantic and Pacific oceans, saving ships more than 7,456 mi traveling around the tip of South America. The Canal was dug across the isthmus (narrow neck of land) of Panama—the narrowest part of North America.

US states and zip codes

State	Code	State	Code
Alabama	AL	Montana	MT
Alaska	AK	Nebraska	NB
Arizona	AZ	Nevada	NV
Arkansas	AR	New Hampshire	NH
California	CA	New Jersey	NJ
Colorado	CO	New Mexico	NM
Connecticut	CT	New York	NY
Delaware	DE	North Carolina	NC
Florida	FL	North Dakota	ND
Georgia	GA	Ohio	OH
Hawaii	HI	Oklahoma	OK
Idaho	ID	Oregon	OR
Illinois	IL	Pennsylvania	PA
Indiana	IN	Rhode Island	RI
Iowa	IA	South Carolina	SC
Kansas	KS	South Dakota	SD
Kentucky	KY	Tennessee	TN
Louisiana	LA	Texas	TX
Maine	ME	Utah	UT
Maryland	MD	Vermont	VT
Massachusetts	MA	Virginia	VA
Michigan	MI	Washington	WA
Minnesota	MN	West Virginia	WV
Mississippi	MS	Wisconsin	WI
Missouri	MO	Wyoming	WY

South America

*T*he fourth largest continent, South America, is almost twice as big as Canada. It has the world's largest rainforest, the second-longest river, the Amazon, and the Andes Mountains. There are deserts and vast expanses of grassland, such as the pampas and Gran Chaco of the south, and the Llanos of the north. Volcanic eruptions and earthquakes are frequent.

▼ *Near the junction of the Iguaçu and Parana rivers, on the borders of Argentina and Brazil, is the spectacular Iguaçu Falls. The semicircular falls—really a complex of 275 linked cascades—measures 1.6 mi in diameter and some 262 ft high.*

○ The Amazon basin—the area that is drained by the Amazon and all of its tributaries—covers over 2.7 million sq mi and contains the world's largest tropical rainforest.

○ The temperatures in the Amazon rainforest remain at about 80°F all year round.

○ The Amazon rainforest contains more species of plant and animal than anywhere else in the world. There are more than 60,000 different plants, 1,550 kinds of bird, 3,000 species of fish, and two million insect species.

○ About 10 percent of the Amazonian rainforest has been lost for ever as trees are cut down by logging companies or to clear the way for mining and cattle ranching.

○ A desert is any place with an average annual rainfall of 250 mm or less. The Atacama Desert, along Chile's north coast, is one of the driest places on Earth. It hardly ever rains, and the average rainfall is less than 13 mm.

▼ *At 4,006 mi, the Amazon River is second only in length to the Nile, and it carries two-thirds of all the Earth's river water. In its upper reaches, it tumbles more than 16,000 ft in the first 621 mi.*

Find out more

Icebergs p. 278

Icy south

Patagonia is a cold, wind-blasted wilderness toward the southern tip of South America. Hundreds of huge glaciers on both the Chilean and Argentinian sides of the Andes form the Patagonian Ice Field. One of the most spectacular of these is Perito Moreno Glacier, in Argentina's Los Glaciares National Park.

South America contains the biggest rainforest in the world, covering an area ten times the size of France. Through this winds the mighty Amazon River. The continent has many other natural wonders, too, from stunning waterfalls and snowy mountaintops to smoking volcanoes and a staggering variety of wildlife.

Amazing

The sloth, an inhabitant of the Amazon rainforest, is the slowest mammal on Earth. It normally moves at just 0.16 mi/h—that's 15 seconds to travel 3 ft.

Lake Maracaibo

Negro River

Amazon River

Purus River

Tapajos River

São Francisco

ANDES

Lake Titicaca

Lake Poopo

GRAN CHACO

Paraná River

Uruguay River

ATACAMA DESERT

Paraná River

PAMPAS

PATAGONIA

ANDES

PACIFIC OCEAN

ATLANTIC OCEAN

Factfile

Area 6,900,533 sq mi
Population more than 350 million
Major cities Buenos Aires (Argentina), Lima (Peru), Rio de Janeiro (Brazil), Santiago (Chile), São Paulo (Brazil)
Largest country Brazil 3,286,724 sq mi
Highest mountain Cerro Aconcagua, Argentina, 22,831 ft
Longest river Amazon 4,006 mi
Largest lake Lake Maracaibo, Venezuela, 5,217 sq mi
Main religion Christianity c.474 million

South America People and Places

Before its conquest in the 16th century by the Portuguese and Spanish, South America was home to native peoples, including the Incas. Today, South Americans include American Indians, whites, blacks (whose ancestors were sent as slaves), and those of mixed race. Most speak Spanish or Portuguese, but some native languages survive.

○ South America is the fourth-largest continent, but it has one of the smallest populations. Much of the land is difficult to live on and is sparsely populated, and about 75 percent of the people live in cities (in Argentina and Uruguay, this figure is nearly 90 percent).

Amazing

The copper mine at Chuquicamata, in Chile, is the biggest artificial hole on Earth, measuring 2 mi wide and 2,460 ft deep.

Venezuela
Guyana
Suriname
French Guiana
Colombia
Ecuador
Peru
Brazil
Bolivia
Paraguay
Chile
Argentina
Uruguay

A With a population of more than 11 million, Argentina's capital, Buenos Aires, is famous for its broad streets and wide plazas, or squares. As in other South American cities, there is a wealthy elite, but many of the inhabitants of Buenos Aires are extremely poor and live in shanty towns on the outskirts of the city.

○ In the Amazon, some native tribes, such as the Yanomami and the Matses, still survive as they have done for thousands of years, hunting with spears or bow and arrow, and gathering fruit and roots.

○ Most people in South America are of mixed race. The largest mixed race groups are mestizos (people with both American Indian and white ancestors) and mulattoes (people with both black and white ancestors).

Find out more

Waterfalls p. 290

▶ *The Christ the Redeemer statue overlooks Rio de Janeiro. Founded by the Portuguese in 1565, this Brazilian city is a busy port, famous for its music, beaches, and vibrant, colorful carnivals.*

○ Mestizos are the majority in countries such as Venezuela and Paraguay; mulattoes are the majority in Brazil.

○ Most South Americans are Roman Catholics. During the European conquest, missionaries converted the local people to Christianity, but some traces of pre-Christian religions remain in local customs and rituals.

○ Argentina has the most educated population in South America, with more than one-third of all students going on to university.

○ The 149 million cattle on Argentina's pampas grasslands are herded by cowboys known as gauchos.

○ Brazil has one of the world's largest dams, the Itaipú, which dams the Paraná River to provide electricity.

○ Brazil is the world's largest coffee grower; Chile produces the most copper.

○ Chile is the world's longest country— about 2,672 mi from end to end. It is also one of the world's most volcanic countries, with more than 75 volcanoes.

○ The discovery of oil in Venezuela's Lake Maracaibo in 1917 brought much wealth to one of the poorest countries.

▲ *This Bolivian woman at a market is dressed in traditional clothes— blankets and a bowler hat. About 70 percent of Bolovia's population lives and farms on the Altiplano, a huge, near-treeless plateau in the Andes.*

Machu Picchu

One of the most amazing insights into South America's past is the lost city of Machu Picchu, built by the Inca people in the 1400s. This terraced city, 6,562 ft up in the Peruvian Andes, was one of the last refuges for the Incas after their empire was conquered by Spain in the 1500s. It had stone houses, a royal palace, and army barracks, and around it were fields cut into the mountain slopes. The city was abandoned and forgotten, until 1911 when it was rediscovered by an American archeologist.

Africa

Africa is a huge continent, covering about 20 percent of the Earth's land surface. Africa comprises 53 countries and over 600 different tribal or ethnic groups. Africa's landscape is varied, with the world's largest desert, the Sahara, and the longest river, the Nile. It has vast expanses of grasslands and rainforest.

○ The Okavango River in southwest Africa empties its water not into the ocean, like most rivers, but into the Kalahari Desert in Botswana, forming a vast inland swamp that provides a haven for thousands of birds and water-loving animals such as hippos.

Ⓐ Only one-third of the Sahara is covered by sand alone; the rest comprises mountains and stony plains.

○ Victoria Falls, on the border between Zambia and Zimbabwe, is Africa's most famous waterfall. Its African name, Mosi-oa-tunya, means "smoke that thunders," referring to the spray and noise as the Zambezi River tumbles over a 354 ft high rock wall.

○ About 40 percent of the African continent consists of desert, and about 40 percent savannah grassland.

River of life

The Nile runs nearly 4,349 mi km from its remotest headstream, the Luvironza River in central Africa, into the Mediterranean Sea on the Egyptian coast. The Nile drains 1,100,471 sq mi (about one-tenth of Africa), including parts of Egypt, Sudan, Ethiopia, Eritrea, Kenya, Uganda, Rwanda, Burundi, Tanzania, and the Democratic Republic of Congo. It is a major waterway for transport.

Ⓐ Male giraffes grow to almost 20 ft in height. Because of this they can keep a look out for danger, scanning the horizon for predators.

▶ At 19,340 ft high, Mount Kilimanjaro, a dormant volcano in Tanzania, is so high that, even though it is very near the Equator, its peak is always covered in snow. Its name in Swahili is Uhuru, which means "freedom."

○ The Sahara Desert is spreading slowly into the dry grasslands of the Sahel region to the south, because of drought, deforestation, and over grazing by farm animals.

○ Across the immense savannah grasslands, such as the Serengetti in Tanzania and Kenya, roam huge herds of wildebeest, zebra, and many other species of grazing animal. In their wake follow spectacular predators, such as lions and leopards.

▶ The Equator crosses the middle of Africa, and in most places it is hot all year round. There are great rivers and lakes in Africa but, in contrast, large areas of it are very dry and this has led to the spread of deserts. The Sahara stretches across north Africa; in southwest Africa are the smaller Namib and Kalahari deserts.

Find out more

Largest deserts p. 282

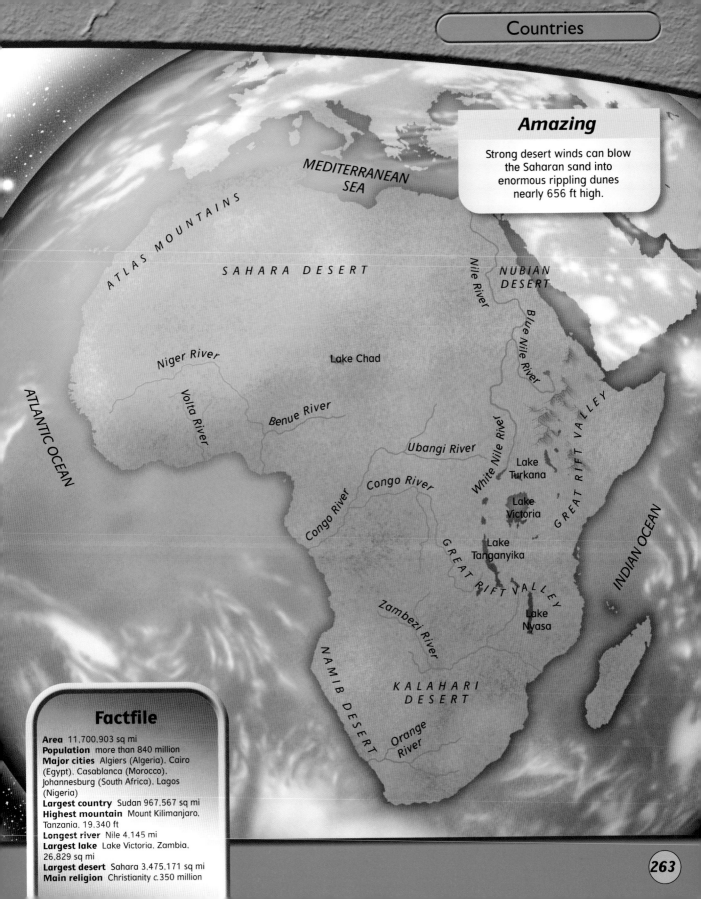

MEDITERRANEAN SEA

ATLAS MOUNTAINS

SAHARA DESERT

NUBIAN DESERT

Nile River

Blue Nile River

Niger River

Lake Chad

Volta River

Benue River

Ubangi River

White Nile River

Congo River

Congo River

Lake Turkana

Lake Victoria

GREAT RIFT VALLEY

ATLANTIC OCEAN

Lake Tanganyika

GREAT RIFT VALLEY

INDIAN OCEAN

Zambezi River

Lake Nyasa

NAMIB DESERT

KALAHARI DESERT

Orange River

Amazing

Strong desert winds can blow the Saharan sand into enormous rippling dunes nearly 656 ft high.

Factfile

Area 11,700,903 sq mi
Population more than 840 million
Major cities Algiers (Algeria), Cairo (Egypt), Casablanca (Morocco), Johannesburg (South Africa), Lagos (Nigeria)
Largest country Sudan 967,567 sq mi
Highest mountain Mount Kilimanjaro, Tanzania, 19,340 ft
Longest river Nile 4,145 mi
Largest lake Lake Victoria, Zambia, 26,829 sq mi
Largest desert Sahara 3,475,171 sq mi
Main religion Christianity c.350 million

Africa People and Places

By 1900 Europe ruled most of Africa. From the 1950s, Africans sought self-government and old colonial boundaries became those of independent African nations. In 1951, Libya was the first African country to win independence. Until the 1990s, a white minority ruled South Africa under the apartheid system.

○ Over 60 percent of Africans still live in villages.

○ In the northern countries such as Algeria, Morocco, and Egypt, people are mainly of Arabic descent.

○ In the south, most people are black Africans, belonging to more than 3,000 ethnic groups.

○ Over 1,000 different langauges are spoken in Africa.

Cape Town at the foot of Table Mountain was the first white settlement in South Africa. Founded in 1652, it is the country's capital city.

○ Most people in southern Africa speak English and one of more than 100 Bantu languages, such as Zulu or Swahili.

○ Liberia was founded as a land for freed African slaves from the USA.

○ Millet is an important crop in much of Africa. The seeds are ground into flour to make flatbread or a kind of porridge.

○ When European leaders split the countries of Africa between them, only Ethiopia and Liberia remained independent and ruled by Africans.

○ The world's biggest goldfield is in the Witwatersrand in South Africa.

Cairo, in Egypt, is Africa's largest city, with a population of more than 15 million people. All over Africa cities are growing rapidly, as people leave the countryside to look for work in towns. Cairo has grown into a large, modern city, but old mosques (Muslim places of prayer) remain.

Masai tribal custom

Many African countries have a mixture of tribal groups. The Masai are one of about 50 ethnic groups in Kenya. The Masai wear colorful headbands and beaded collars for tribal ceremonies. Many other traditional African costumes are now seldom seen except for tourist displays.

Find out more

Farmworkers by continent p. 287

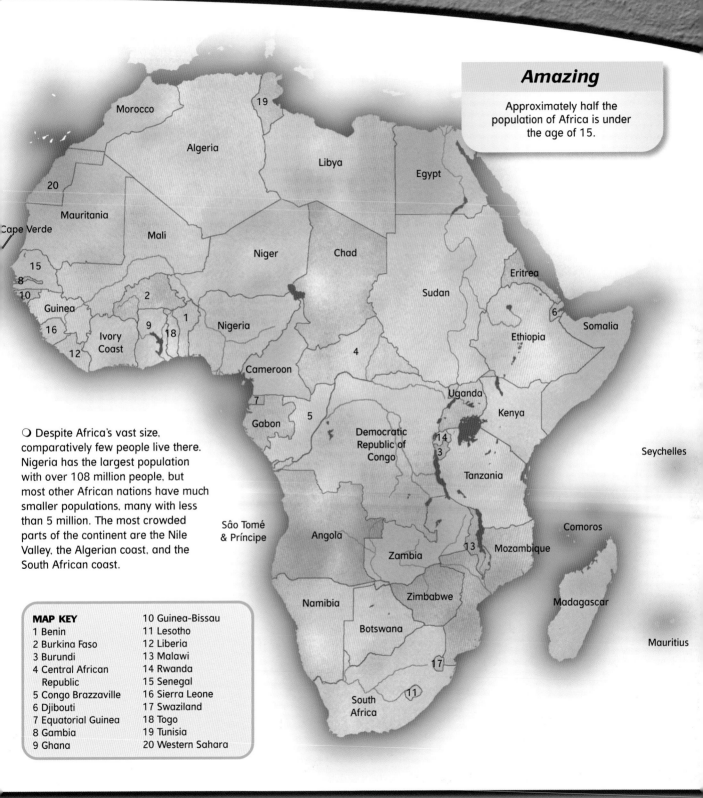

Amazing

Approximately half the population of Africa is under the age of 15.

○ Despite Africa's vast size, comparatively few people live there. Nigeria has the largest population with over 108 million people, but most other African nations have much smaller populations, many with less than 5 million. The most crowded parts of the continent are the Nile Valley, the Algerian coast, and the South African coast.

MAP KEY

1 Benin	10 Guinea-Bissau
2 Burkina Faso	11 Lesotho
3 Burundi	12 Liberia
4 Central African Republic	13 Malawi
5 Congo Brazzaville	14 Rwanda
6 Djibouti	15 Senegal
7 Equatorial Guinea	16 Sierra Leone
8 Gambia	17 Swaziland
9 Ghana	18 Togo
	19 Tunisia
	20 Western Sahara

Asia

Asia is the world's biggest continent, both in land area and in the number of people living there. It fills about one-third of the planet's area. About six in every ten people on Earth are Asian. Asia's terrain includes the world's highest mountain range, the Himalayas, as well as desert, steppe grassland, tundra, boreal (northern) forest, and rainforest.

Himalayas

The Himalayan mountain range separates the warmer, wetter countries of southern Asia from the rest of the continent. Mount Everest, on the border between China and Nepal, is the world's highest peak, at 29,028 ft. In fact, the Himalayas have the 20 highest mountains on the planet, all over 26,000 ft high. The mountain shown here is Machhapuchhare, in Nepal, which stands at 22,943 ft.

○ Japan and Indonesia are at particular risk from volcanoes. A ring of volcanoes called the Ring of Fire surrounds the Pacific Ocean.

○ Asia has the world's largest bat, the Bismarck flying fox from Indonesia, and the smallest bat, Kitti's hog-nosed bat from Thailand.

○ Garden plants that are native to Asia include tulips (Turkey) and rhododendrons (India).

○ Temperatures in Asia can range from −90°F in Verkhoyansk, Russia, to 129°F in Tirat Zevi, Israel.

○ Much of Bangladesh is low-lying and prone to flooding. Floods have devastated Bangladesh several times in the last 40 years.

⬆ *Cutting terraces into the side of hills, such as these rice terraces in Bali, Indonesia, enables farmers to produce crops on steep slopes that would otherwise be unsuitable for arable farming.*

○ The steppes are a vast expanse of temperate grassland stretching right across Asia.

○ Lake Baikal in Siberia, the northern region of Asia, is the world's oldest and deepest lake. It holds more than 20 percent of the world's unfrozen fresh water.

⬆ *The Li River, in China, winds through spectacular scenery known as karst, where limestone rock has been eroded away, leaving the landscape dotted with rocky pinnacles and verdant peaks.*

Holy river

To Hindus, the Ganges in India is the holiest of rivers. It was named after the goddess Ganga, the daughter of the mountain god Himalaya. Ganges water is used to cleanse places and objects for ritual purposes, and bathing in the river itself is thought to wash away sins. Hindu pilgrims gather in vast numbers for bathing festivals at sacred sites along the Ganges, such as the city of Varanasi, shown here.

Amazing

The Korowai people of Indonesia build their houses in trees. Their treehouses keep them away from the damp ground, and out of trouble if their neighbors become unfriendly.

Factfile

Area 17,140,088 sq mi
Population more than 3.8 billion
Major cities Kuala Lumpur (Malaysia),
Mumbai (India), Seoul (South Korea)
Largest country Russia*
6,593,309 sq mi
Highest mountain Mount Everest
29,028 ft
Longest river Chang Jiang 6380 km
Largest lake Caspian Sea
146,111 sq mi
Largest desert Arabian
482,662 sq mi
Main religion Islam *c.*807 million
* Russia is partly in Europe
Asiatic Russia is 5,065,866 sq mi

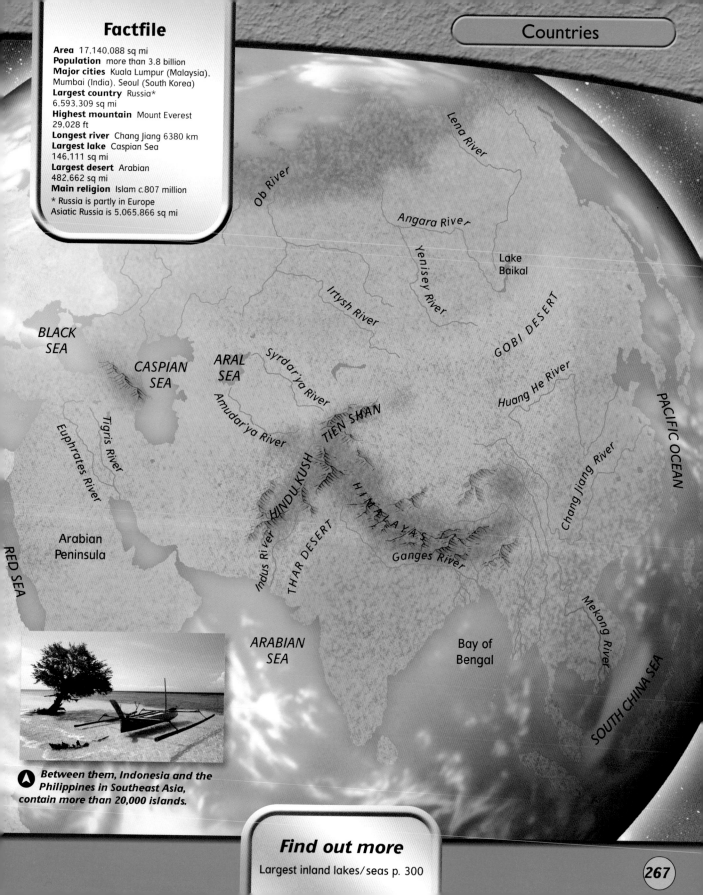

Lena River

Ob River

Angara River

Yenisey River

Lake
Baikal

Irtysh River

GOBI DESERT

BLACK
SEA

CASPIAN
SEA

ARAL
SEA

Syrdar'ya River

Huang He River

PACIFIC OCEAN

Amudar'ya River

TIEN SHAN

Tigris River

Euphrates River

HINDU KUSH

HIMALAYAS

Chang Jiang River

Arabian
Peninsula

Indus River

THAR DESERT

Ganges River

RED SEA

Mekong River

ARABIAN
SEA

Bay of
Bengal

SOUTH CHINA SEA

*Between them, Indonesia and the
Philippines in Southeast Asia,
contain more than 20,000 islands.*

Find out more

Largest inland lakes/seas p. 300

Asia People and Places

Asia was home to great ancient civilizations, such as those of the Tigris–Euphrates and Indus Valley regions. The greatest imperial power in Asia was China, but by the 1800s much of Asia was under European colonial rule. Japan was the first Asian country to "westernize" its industries, and by the 1950s it was a world leading economic power.

🄰 Japan's Akashi Kaikyo bridge stretches 1.2 mi across the strip of sea separating the islands of Shikoku and Honshu. This is the longest span of a bridge anywhere in the world.

MAP KEY

1 Armenia	15 Lebanon
2 Azerbaijan	16 Nepal
3 Bahrain	17 North Korea
4 Bangladesh	18 Oman
5 Bhutan	19 Qatar
6 Burma	20 Singapore
7 Cambodia	21 South Korea
8 Cyprus	22 Syria
9 Georgia	23 Tajikistan
10 Israel	24 Thailand
11 Jordan	25 Turkmenistan
12 Kuwait	26 United Arab
13 Kyrgyzstan	Emirates (UAE)
14 Laos	27 Uzbekistan
	28 Yemen

○ Much of Asia's wealth comes from its manufacturing nations, such as Japan, China, South Korea, Malaysia, and India; and its oil-producers, such as Saudi Arabia, Brunei, and Kuwait. The manufacturing countries have large populations, many of whom work for low wages, so the average income per person is less than in Europe or North America. The oil-rich states have smaller populations, so average incomes are higher.

Find out more

Largest oil reserves p. 288

To Hindus, the River Ganges, which flows through the city of Varnasi, is specially sacred. Hindus make pilgrimages to its banks to pray and worship.

Amazing

Nicknamed the Abominable Snowman by climbers, the Yeti is said to roam the snowy Himalayas of Asia. Photos of "Yeti footprints" were taken in 1951, but scraps of skin and droppings have not yet provided evidence.

○ India is a subcontinent and is home to about one-fifth of the world's population. The Indian subcontinent comprises India itself, which has more than one billion people, plus the countries of Pakistan, Bangladesh, Bhutan, Sri Lanka, Nepal, and the Maldives.

○ The Japanese call their country Nippon, meaning "source of the Sun." The red disc on the Japanese flag represents the Sun.

○ In some parts of China, couples have been limited to having only one child in an attempt by the Chinese government to control soaring population figures.

Many canals thread their way through Bangkok, the Thai capital. People use the canals to bring their goods into the city and sell them at floating markets.

Istanbul

Istanbul, in Turkey, is the only city to be situated on two continents. It lies on both banks of the Bosporus Strait, which separates Europe and Asia. It is known as the gateway between the two.

The Forbidden City

The Forbidden City in Beijing, China's capital, was once the Chinese emperor's private world, kept secret from ordinary Chinese people and foreigners. Only officials and nobles could gain entrance. One million workers took ten years to build the walled city, with its great halls, temples, pagodas, and gardens.

Europe

Europe is the most densely populated continent. It has the longest coastline of all the continents (more than 37,000 mi), with mountains in the north and south enclosing a central plain. There are 42 independent countries in Europe, some are large (Russia, Ukraine, France, and Spain) and others, such as Liechtenstein and Vatican City, are comparatively tiny.

Scandinavia

Scandinavia is a region of northern Europe with a shared geography and history. The countries of Scandinavia are Norway, Sweden, Denmark, Finland, and Iceland, which is an island in the Atlantic Ocean. The Scandinavian countries are famed for their landscapes of fjords (Norway), lakes (Sweden), forests (Finland), fishing ports (Denmark), and hot springs (Iceland).

The Rock of Gibraltar is a 1,397 ft high mass of limestone at the southern tip of Spain, where the Mediterranean Sea and Atlantic Ocean meet. Gibraltar is currently under British rule, but the Spanish government wants to reunite it with the rest of mainland Spain.

Europe is able to support such a large population because much of its land is very fertile. These French vineyards are producing grapes for the wine industry.

○ The Alps is the highest mountain range in western Europe, running through southeastern France, Switzerland, Italy, and Austria. The range started to form more than 15 million years ago.

○ The highest peak in the Alps is Mont Blanc, at 15,770 ft, but Mount Elbrus in the Caucasus mountain range is even higher, at 18,510 ft.

○ Less than 3 percent of mountainous Norway is cultivated.

The Netherlands

The name Netherlands means Low Countries, and this region is very low-lying. Sea walls or dykes have been built to stop the sea flooding the land, and water has been pumped (historically by windmills) from flooded parts to turn salt marshland into fertile agricultural land. The reclaimed land is known as polders. About 40 percent of the country has been reclaimed from the sea and 25 percent of this is used for housing and roads. It takes about eight years after draining the land for it to be suitable for farming and building on.

Europe has sea on three sides (north, west, and south), but it merges with the Asian landmass on the eastern side. There are natural land barriers forming a boundary between Europe and Asia. These boundaries include the Ural Mountains and the Caspian Sea, in Russia. Europe is separated from the continent of Africa by the Strait of Gibraltar, which lies between Morocco in Africa, and Spain in Europe.

The pointed summit of the Matterhorn, at 14,691 ft, is the third highest peak in the Alps. The Alps are the source of many of Europe's major rivers, such as the Rhone, Po, and Rhine.

BARENTS SEA

NORTH SEA

Lake Ladoga

Lake Onega

Volga River

Don River

BALTIC SEA

Rhine River

Elbe River

Vistula River

Dnepr River

Bay of Biscay

Loire River

Seine River

PYRENEES

ALPS

CARPATHIANS

Tagus River

Danube River

BLACK SEA

MEDITERRANEAN SEA

Factfile

Area 4,067,727 sq mi
Population more than 700 million
Major cities Berlin (Germany), London (UK), Madrid (Spain), Milan (Italy), Moscow (Russia), Paris (France)
Largest country Russia*
6,593,309 sq mi
Highest mountain Mount Elbrus, Russia, 18,510 ft
Longest river Volga, Russia, 2,194 mi
Largest lake Caspian Sea, Russia, 146,111 sq mi
Main religion Christianity c.552 million
* Russia is partly in Asia

Amazing

Europe's oldest national flag belongs to Denmark. It has been flown since 1219 when, according to legend, the Danish king saw a white cross in a red sky before winning a battle, and so adopted the flag.

Find out more

Biggest cities p. 280

Europe People and Places

Europe was the birthplace of ancient Greek and Roman culture, and later European ideas and technology were spread by explorers and empire-builders to other continents. In the 1700s, Europe experienced the Industrial Revolution and was also the cradle for two world wars, 1914–1918 and 1939–1945. Since 1950, the European Union has become an economic force.

MAP KEY
1 Albania
2 Andorra
3 Belgium
4 Bosnia-Herzegovina
5 Croatia
6 Estonia
7 Latvia
8 Liechtenstein
9 Lithuania
10 Luxembourg
11 Macedonia
12 Moldova
13 Netherlands
14 Serbia & Montenegro
15 Slovenia
16 Switzerland

Amazing

There is a fishing village in Norway whose name is simply one letter—A.

○ Europe is a wealthy continent, with many hi-tech industries. Today, Europe produces more manufactured goods than any other continent. However, several countries, especially those in the east, remain poor.

▲ Europe has many castles, a legacy of the conflicts that ravaged the continent for many centuries. This one is at Caelaverock, in Scotland.

Find out more
Deepest caves p. 299

Heart of an empire

The city of Rome, in Italy, was once the heart of the Roman Empire. The Romans conquered most of Europe over 2,000 years ago, and imposed their laws and culture on the peoples who lived under their rule. This had an enormous effect on later European history. The remains of some buildings from ancient Rome, such as the Pantheon and the great gladiatorial arena known as the Colosseum (shown here), can still be seen in Rome today.

◀ *Greek islands, such as Santorini (shown here), are popular with tourists, who enjoy the Mediterranean sunshine and beautiful old buildings.*

❍ Switzerland has long been a neutral country, staying out of all the major wars. This is why organizations such as the Red Cross and World Health Organization are based there.

Stonehenge

Stonehenge in England is a huge stone circle built by ancient Britons some 4,000 years ago. Some of the stones were brought from a quarry in Wales, 239 mi away. The stones were arranged so that the Sun would shine into the entrance way on the morning of the longest day of the year—the summer solstice.

❍ The most densely populated area in the world stretches from southeast Britain, through northern France and into the Netherlands, where there are approximately 410 people per sq mi. In the USA, by contrast, there are about 27 people per sq mi.

❍ St Petersburg, Russia's second-largest city, boasts the world's largest art gallery, the Hermitage Museum.

❍ France is the most visited country in the world.

▶ *St Basil's Cathedral, with its cluster of onion-shaped domes, is one of the key landmarks of Moscow, Russia's capital city.*

Countries that joined the EU in 2004

Cyprus	Lithuania
Czech Republic	Malta
Estonia	Poland
Hungary	Slovakia
Latvia	Slovenia

Oceania

Oceania is a continent containing the group of islands covering an enormous area in the Pacific Ocean. The biggest of these islands is Australia. Oceania also includes 14 other countries. Although Oceania spans vast tracts of the Pacific, it is the smallest continent in terms of population.

Great pebble

Ayers Rock is a reddish sandstone landmark in Australia's Northern Territory. The aboriginal people of Australia call Ayers Rock "Uluru," which means "great pebble." It is about 1.5 mi long, 0.9 mi wide and 5 mi around the base. It formed from a bed of coarse sand that was laid down in an inland sea some 600 million years ago. The rock rises 1,099 ft from the sandy plain on which it stands. Aboriginal people thought the rock was sacred, and made wall paintings in caves there.

❍ Melanesia ("black islands") includes New Guinea, the Solomons, New Caledonia, Vanuatu, and Fiji.

❍ Micronesia ("tiny islands") consists of about 2,000 islands to the north of Melanesia, including Guam, and the Marshall Islands.

▼ *Much of Australia's interior is desert, or semi-desert. The Pinnacles Desert, in western Australia, is named after the thousands of strange limestone spires that rise up out of the sand dunes. The spires were formed by erosion over thousands of years.*

❍ To the east of Micronesia and Melanesia is Polynesia ("many islands"). This a vast group of islands 8,000 km across. It includes Tahiti, Samoa, Tonga, Kiribati, and Easter Island.

❍ The world's oldest fossils, called stromatolites, are found in Shark Bay, Australia. These pizza-like mats were made by colonies of blue-green algae 3.6 billion years ago.

❍ The Pohutu geyser in New Zealand gushes up to 98 ft into the air, higher than any other in the world.

▲ *Like many Pacific islands that seem like paradise, Fiji has a booming tourist industry creating jobs, which brings money to the island.*

▶ *Oceania is made up of Australia, New Zealand, and Papua New Guinea, and the Pacific island groups of Melanesia, Micronesia, and Polynesia, which together contain at least 30,000 islands. Some of these islands are little more than rocks in the ocean, but others cover several thousand square miles. Much of what we call Oceania was isolated from the rest of the world for millions of years, so many unique animals are found there.*

Find out more

Marshall Islands p. 291

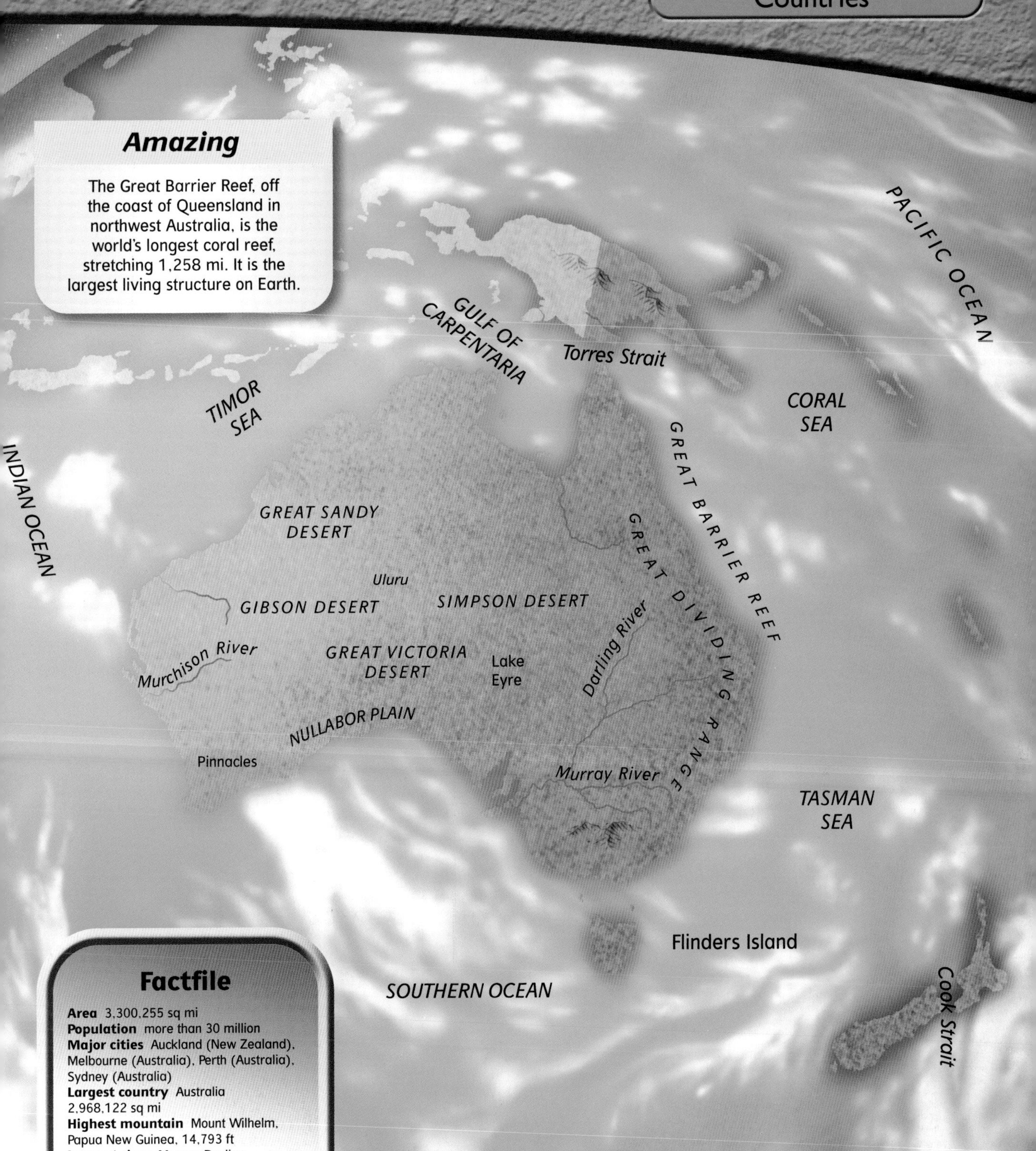

Amazing

The Great Barrier Reef, off the coast of Queensland in northwest Australia, is the world's longest coral reef, stretching 1,258 mi. It is the largest living structure on Earth.

PACIFIC OCEAN

GULF OF CARPENTARIA

Torres Strait

CORAL SEA

TIMOR SEA

INDIAN OCEAN

GREAT BARRIER REEF

GREAT SANDY DESERT

Uluru

SIMPSON DESERT

GIBSON DESERT

GREAT DIVIDING RANGE

GREAT VICTORIA DESERT

Murchison River

Darling River

Lake Eyre

NULLABOR PLAIN

Pinnacles

Murray River

TASMAN SEA

Flinders Island

SOUTHERN OCEAN

Cook Strait

Factfile

Area 3,300,255 sq mi
Population more than 30 million
Major cities Auckland (New Zealand), Melbourne (Australia), Perth (Australia), Sydney (Australia)
Largest country Australia 2,968,122 sq mi
Highest mountain Mount Wilhelm, Papua New Guinea, 14,793 ft
Longest river Murray-Darling, Australia, 1,703 mi
Largest lake Lake Eyre, Australia, 3,745 sq mi
Largest desert Australian 1,467,295 sq mi
Main religion Christianity c.24 million

Oceania People and Places

The majority of the people in Australia and New Zealand are descended from European settlers, although some are of Southeast Asian descent. There are still small populations in both countries of native peoples— the Aborigines in Australia and the Maoris in New Zealand. Most Pacific islanders still live in small traditional farming or fishing communities as they have for thousands of years, but western influences are changing the island way of life rapidly.

○ Aborigines were the first people to inhabit Australia. Aboriginal cave paintings and tools have been found in Australia dating back at least 45,000 years.

○ Today, Aborigines (or Kooris, as they prefer to be called) make up just 1.8 percent of Australia's population.

○ Only 6 percent of Australia is fit for growing crops, but there is rich pasture that is ideal for sheep-grazing.

Stone giants

The easternmost island in Polynesia is Easter Island, more than 3,728 mi from New Zealand. Easter Island is famous for its huge stone heads, called "moai," made between AD 900 and 1600. The largest of the heads weighs at least 75 tons, not including the 11-ton hat, called a pukao. Carved from single blocks of stone, the statues were moved great distances to their resting places, which were probably chosen to mark tombs. The eyes were made of coral.

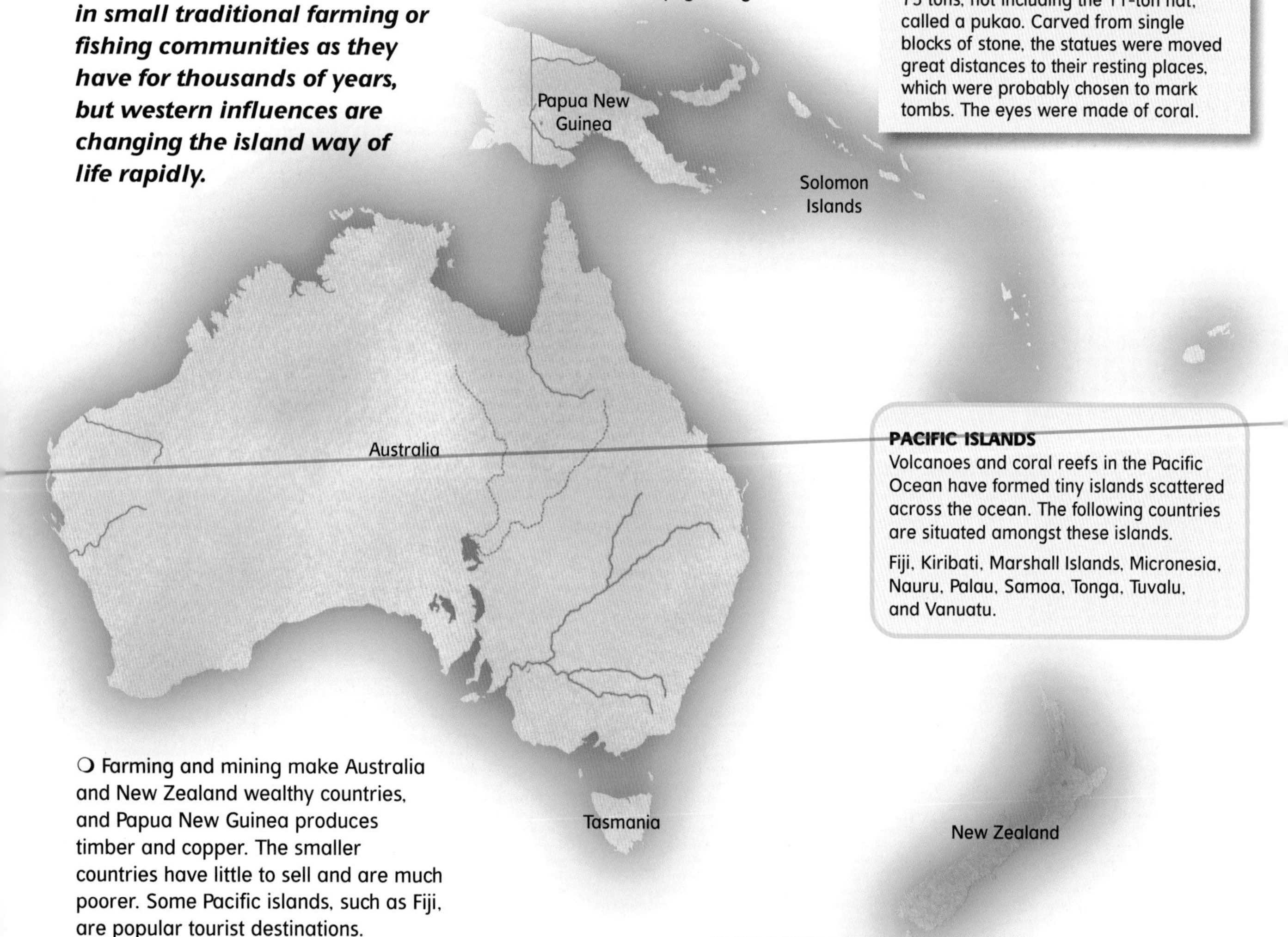

Papua New Guinea

Solomon Islands

Australia

PACIFIC ISLANDS
Volcanoes and coral reefs in the Pacific Ocean have formed tiny islands scattered across the ocean. The following countries are situated amongst these islands.

Fiji, Kiribati, Marshall Islands, Micronesia, Nauru, Palau, Samoa, Tonga, Tuvalu, and Vanuatu.

Tasmania

New Zealand

○ Farming and mining make Australia and New Zealand wealthy countries, and Papua New Guinea produces timber and copper. The smaller countries have little to sell and are much poorer. Some Pacific islands, such as Fiji, are popular tourist destinations.

Find out more

Papua New Guinea p. 294

The Sydney Opera House, which overlooks the harbor of this Australian city, is one of the world's most famous architectural landmarks. The building was completed in 1973.

Amazing

In the South Australian mining town of Coober Pedy, nearly half the people live in underground houses to escape temperatures that can exceed 122°F on summer days and plummet to 32°F on winter nights. The houses, or "dugouts," have superb natural insulation and remain at a constant temperature of around 73°F.

❍ More than one-quarter of the world's wool is shorn from sheep roaming the sheep stations of Australia. Some Australian sheep stations can reach up to 5,792 sq mi in size.

❍ Australia has huge amounts of iron, aluminum, zinc, gold, and silver. The Mount Goldsworthy mine in western Australia is thought to contain about 15 billion tons of ore.

❍ Papua New Guinea has more languages than any other country in the world—about 869. Each language is only spoken by about 4,000 people.

❍ About 34 percent of the world's diamonds come from Australia.

❍ About 14 percent of New Zealanders are Maoris, whose ancestors came from the eastern Pacific in about AD 850. The Maori traditions and language are still very much alive in New Zealand.

❍ The New Zealanders are nicknamed kiwis. The flightless bird of New Zealand called the kiwi has become one of New Zealand's national emblems, and a friendly nickname for its people.

When British settlers first arrived in Australia about 200 years ago they drove the native Aborigines from their land, destroying the traditional way of life. Now, 60 percent of Aborigines live in cities. After decades of hard campaigning, some aboriginal lands and sacred sites are being returned to them.

Farming nation

New Zealand farmers sheep-shear— shave the sheeps' coats for their wool. Agriculture is vital to New Zealand's economy, accounting for 60 percent of its exports. Around 64 pecent of the land in New Zealand is devoted to crops and pasture for sheep and cattle. New Zealand has some 58 million sheep and 8 million cattle— that's about 25 farm animals to every person.

Factfile

Afghanistan

Area 251,845 sq mi
Population 22,720,000
Capital Kabul
Main religions Sunni Muslim
Languages Pashto
Currency Afghani
Life expectancy 48 years
Highest point Nowshak 24,603 ft

Albania

Area 11,100 sq mi
Population 3,364,571
Capital Tirana
Main religions Muslim
Languages Albanian
Currency Lek
Life expectancy 69 years
Highest point Korab 9,025 ft

Algeria

Area 919,666 sq mi
Population 31,540,000
Capital Algiers
Main religions Sunni Muslim
Languages Arabic
Currency Algerian dinar
Life expectancy 69 years
Highest point Tahat 9,852 ft

Andorra

Area 181 sq mi
Population 66,000
Capital Andorra la Vella
Main religions Catholic
Languages Catalan, Spanish
Currency Euro, replaced franc/peseta

Did you know?

The Sahara Desert takes up over 80 percent of the area of Algeria.

Life expectancy 76 years
Highest point Coma Pedrosa 9,675 ft

Angola

Area 481,388 sq mi
Population 12,878,000
Capital Luanda
Main religions Catholic, Traditional beliefs
Languages Portuguese, Umbundu
Currency Kwanza
Life expectancy 48 years
Highest point Serra Moco 8,595 ft

Antigua & Barbuda

Area 169 sq mi
Population 70,000
Capital St John's
Main religions Anglican
Languages English
Currency East Caribbean dollar
Life expectancy 71 years
Highest point Boggy Peak 1,318 ft

Argentina

Area 1,057,599 sq mi
Population 36,260,000
Capital Buenos Aires
Main religions Catholic
Languages Spanish
Currency Argentine peso
Life expectancy 75 years
Highest point Cerro Aconcagua 22,831 ft

Armenia

Area 11,507 sq mi
Population 3,213,000
Capital Yerevan
Main religions Armenian Apostolic
Languages Armenian
Currency Dram
Life expectancy 67 years

Highest point Aragats 13,418 ft

Australia

Area 2,968,122 sq mi
Population 20,262,000
Capital Canberra
Main religions Catholic, Anglican
Languages English
Currency Australian dollar
Life expectancy 80 years
Highest point Mt Kosciuszko 7,316 ft

Austria

Area 32,376 sq mi
Population 8,065,000
Capital Vienna
Main religions Catholic
Languages German
Currency Euro, replaced the schilling
Life expectancy 77 years
Highest point Grossglockner 12,457 ft

Biggest cities (people)

1	**Mexico City** Mexico	10 million
1	**Cairo** Egypt	10 million
1	**Seoul** South Korea	10 million
1	**Mumbai** India	10 million
5	**São Paulo** Brazil	9.3 million
6	**Moscow** Russia	8.4 million
7	**Tokyo** Japan	8 million
7	**Manila** Philippines	8 million
9	**Shanghai** China	7.8 million
10	**New York City** USA	7.3 million

Tallest buildings

1 **Taipei 101 Tower** Taiwan 1,669 ft

2 **World Financial Centre** Shanghai, China 1,666 ft

3 **Petronas Towers** Kuala Lumpur, Malaysia 1,482 ft

4 **Sears Tower** Chicago, USA 1,450 ft

5 **Jin Mao Building** Shanghai, China 1,381 ft

6 **World Finance Center** Hong Kong 1,361 ft

7 **Empire State Building** New York, USA 1,250 ft

8 **T and C Tower** Taiwan 1,141 ft

Azerbaijan

Area 33,438 sq mi
Population 8,141,000
Capital Baku
Main religions Shia Muslim
Languages Azeri
Currency Manat
Life expectancy 63 years
Highest point Bazar-Dyuzi 14,652 ft

Bahamas

Area 5,382 sq mi
Population 302,000
Capital Nassau
Main religions Baptist, Nonreligious, Catholic
Languages English
Currency Dollar
Life expectancy 74 years
Highest point Mt Alvernia 206 ft

Bahrain

Area 267 sq mi
Population 651,000
Capital Manama
Main religions Shia Muslim
Languages Arabic
Currency Dinar
Life expectancy 75 years
Highest point Jabal al-Dukhan 439 ft

Bangladesh

Area 55,602 sq mi
Population 129,247,000
Capital Dhaka
Main religions Sunni Muslim
Languages Bengali
Currency Taka
Life expectancy 57 years
Highest point Keokradong 4,035 ft

Barbados

Area 166 sq mi
Population 269,000
Capital Bridgetown
Main religions Anglican, Pentecostal
Languages English
Currency Dollar
Life expectancy 75 years
Highest point Mt Hillaby 1,115 ft

Belarus

Area 80,160 sq mi
Population 9,951,000

Did you know?

Australia boasts the world's longest fence, extending over 3,346 mi and designed to keep dingoes away from sheep.

Capital Minsk
Main religions Nonreligious, Russian Orthodox
Languages Belarussian, Russian
Currency Rouble
Life expectancy 68 years
Highest point Dzyarzhynskaya 1,135 ft

Belgium

Area 11,780 sq mi
Population 10,310,000
Capital Brussels
Main religions Catholic
Languages Dutch (Flemish), French, German
Currency Euro, replaced the Belgian franc
Life expectancy 77 years
Highest point Botrange 2,276 ft

Belize

Area 8,865 sq mi
Population 242,000
Capital Belmopan
Main religions Catholic
Languages English, Creole

Most farm animals by country

Most chickens USA 1.3 billion
Most pigs China 485 million
Most cattle India 200 million
Most sheep Australia 120 million
Most goats China 60 million

Currency Dollar
Life expectancy 69 years
Highest point Victoria Peak 3,681 ft

Benin

Area 43,486 sq mi
Population 7,042,000
Capital Cotonou
Main religions Indigenous
Languages Fon
Currency CFA franc
Life expectancy 54 years
Highest point Atacora Massif 2,103 ft

Bhutan

Area 18,148 sq mi
Population 2,124,000
Capital Thimphu
Main religions Lamaistic Buddhist
Languages Dzongkha
Currency Ngultrum
Life expectancy 52 years
Highest point Khula Kangri 24,783 ft

Bolivia

Area 424,194 sq mi
Population 8,274,000
Capital La Paz (administrative), Sucre (legislative)
Main religions Catholic
Languages Spanish, Quechua, Aymara
Currency Boliviano
Life expectancy 61 years
Highest point Nevado Sajama 21,463 ft

Did you know?

Zoos were first invented in China, where they were called Parks of Intelligence.

Bosnia-Herzegovina

Area 19,782 sq mi
Population 3,989,000
Capital Sarajevo
Main religions Sunni Islam, Serbian Orthodox, Catholic
Languages Croatian, Serbian, Bosnian
Currency Convertible marks
Life expectancy 63 years
Highest point Maglic 922 ft

Botswana

Area 224,624 sq mi
Population 1,681,000
Capital Gaborone
Main religions Traditional beliefs, African churches
Languages English, Tswana
Currency Pula
Life expectancy 40 years
Highest point Mt Otse 4,885 ft

Brazil

Area 3,286,724 sq mi
Population 176,871,000
Capital Brasilia
Religions Catholic
Languages Portuguese
Currency Real
Life expectancy 65 years
Highest point Pico de Neblina 9,888 ft

Brunei

Area 2,228 sq mi
Population 333,000
Capital Bandar Seri
Main religions Sunni Muslim
Languages Malay
Currency Dollar
Life expectancy 72 years
Highest point Bukit Pagon 6,069 ft

Bulgaria

Area 42,825 sq mi
Population 7,974,000
Capital Sofia
Main religions Bulgarian Orthodox
Languages Bulgarian, Turkish, Romany, Macedonian
Currency Lev
Life expectancy 72 years
Highest point Musala 9,596 ft

Burkina Faso

Area 105,877 sq mi
Population 12,603,000
Capital Ouagadougou
Main religions Muslim
Languages Mossi
Currency CFA franc
Life expectancy 46 years
Highest point Mont Tema 1,555 ft

Burma

Area 261,989 sq mi
Population 45,611,000
Capital Yangon
Main religions Buddhist
Languages Burmese
Currency Kyat

Largest deserts

1 **Sahara** North Africa 3.4 million sq mi
2 **Australian** (comprising 10 deserts) Australia 1.5 million sq mi
3 **Arabian** Southwest Asia 502,000 sq mi
4 **Gobi** Central Asia 386,000 sq mi
5 **Kalahari** Southern Africa 201,000 sq mi

Weather records

Hottest place Death Valley, California, USA Above 120°F for 43 days (1917)

Hottest all-year-round Dallol, Ethiopia 93°F average (1960–1966)

Highest-measured windspeed New Hampshire, USA 230 mi/h (1934)

Coldest place Vostok base, Antarctica -128.5°C (1983)

Life expectancy 55 years
Highest point Hkakado Razi 19,295 ft

Burundi

Area 10,746 sq mi
Population 6,490,000
Capital Bujumbura
Main religions Catholic
Languages Rundi
Currency Franc
Life expectancy 46 years
Highest point Mont Hela 8,809 ft

Cambodia

Area 69,905 sq mi
Population 12,775,000
Capital Phnom Penh
Main religions Theravada Buddhist
Languages Khmer
Currency Riel
Life expectancy 48 years
Highest point Phnum Aural 5,948 ft

Cameroon

Area 183,581 sq mi
Population 15,746,000
Capital Yaounde
Main religions Catholic, Traditional beliefs
Languages Fang, Murri, French
Currency CFA franc
Life expectancy 51 years
Highest point Mt Cameroon 13,349 ft

Canada

Area 3,852,097 sq mi
Population 30,007,000
Capital Ottawa
Main religions Catholic, Protestant
Languages English, French
Currency Canadian dollar
Life expectancy 79 years
Highest point Mt Logan 19,524 ft

Cape Verde

Area 1,556 sq mi
Population 435,000
Capital Praia
Main religions Catholic
Languages Creole, Portuguese
Currency Escudo
Life expectancy 71 years
Highest point Mt Fogo 9,281 ft

Central African Republic

Area 240,551 sq mi
Population 3,577,000
Capital Bangui
Main religions Traditional beliefs, Baptist, Catholic
Languages Sango, French
Currency CFA franc
Life expectancy 47 years
Highest point Mont Gaou 4,658 ft

Chad

Area 495,790 sq mi
Population 7,651,000
Capital N'Djamena
Main religions Sunni Muslim
Languages Sara
Currency CFA franc
Life expectancy 48 years
Highest point Emi Koussi 11,204 ft

Chile

Area 292,280 sq mi
Population 15,116,000
Capital Santiago
Main religions Catholic
Languages Spanish
Currency Chilean peso
Life expectancy 75 years
Highest point Nevado Ojos del Salado 22,621 ft

Did you know?

Bolivia's capital La Paz is the highest capital city in the world.

China

Area 3,696,809 sq mi
Population 1,247,761,000
Capital Beijing
Main religions Atheist
Languages Mandarin Chinese
Currency Yuan Renminbi
Life expectancy 70 years
Highest point Mt Everest 29,028 ft

Colombia

Area 440,796 sq mi
Population 44,531,000
Capital Bogotá

Longest glaciers

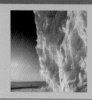

1. **Lambert–Fisher**
   Antarctica 320 mi

2. **Novaya Zemlya**
   Russia 259 mi

3. **Arctic Institute**
   Antarctica 224 mi

Main religions Catholic
Languages Spanish
Currency Colombian peso
Life expectancy 70 years
Highest point Pico Cristobal Colon 18,946 ft

Comoros

Area 719 sq mi
Population 509,000
Capital Moroni
Main religions Sunni Muslim
Languages Arabic
Currency Franc
Life expectancy 60 years
Highest point Mt Kartala 7,746 ft

Congo Brazzaville

Area 132,056 sq mi
Population 2,943,000
Capital Brazzaville
Main religions Catholic
Languages French, Monokutuba
Currency CFA franc
Life expectancy 47 years
Highest point Mont Berongou 2,962 ft

Congo, Democratic Republic of

Area 905,632 sq mi
Population 51,654,000
Capital Kinshasa
Main religions Catholic
Languages French, Lingala
Currency CFA franc

Life expectancy 49 years
Highest point Pic Marguerite on Mont Ngaliema (Mt Stanley) 16,765 ft

Costa Rica

Area 19,731 sq mi
Population 3,800,000
Capital San Jose
Main religions Catholic
Languages Spanish
Currency Colon
Life expectancy 76 years
Highest point Chirripo Grande 12,529 ft

Croatia

Area 21,830 sq mi
Population 4,437,000
Capital Zagreb
Main religions Catholic
Languages Croatian
Currency Kuna
Life expectancy 74 years
Highest point Dinara 6,007 ft

Cuba

Area 42,806 sq mi
Population 11,251,000
Capital Havana
Main religions Nonreligious
Languages Spanish
Currency Cuban peso
Life expectancy 76 years
Highest point Pico Turquino 6,476 ft

Cyprus

Area 3,571 sq mi
Population 786,000
Capital Nicosia
Main religions Greek Orthodox, Sunni Muslim
Languages Greek, Turkish
Currency Cypriot pound

Life expectancy 77 years
Highest point Olympus 6,400 ft

Czech Republic

Area 30,389 sq mi
Population 10,203,000
Capital Prague
Main religions Catholic
Languages Czech
Currency Koruna
Life expectancy 74 years
Highest point Snezka 5,255 ft

Denmark

Area 16,640 sq mi
Population 5,293,000
Capital Copenhagen
Main religions Evangelical/Lutheran
Languages Danish
Currency Krone
Life expectancy 76 years
Highest point Yding Skovhoj 568 ft

Djibouti

Area 8,494 sq mi
Population 638,000
Capital Djibouti
Main religions Muslim
Languages French
Currency Franc
Life expectancy 51 years
Highest point Musa Ali Terara 6,765 ft

Dominica

Area 290 sq mi
Population 71,000

Did you know?

Brazil covers 47.8 percent of South America.

Capital Roseau
Main religions Catholic
Languages French Creole, English
Currency East Caribbean dollar
Life expectancy 70 years
Highest point Morne Diablotin
4,747 ft

Dominican Republic

Area 18,817 sq mi
Population 8,562,000
Capital Santo Domingo
Main religions Catholic
Languages Spanish
Currency Peso
Life expectancy 70 years
Highest point Pico Duarte 10,417 ft

East Timor

Area 5,743 sq mi
Population 885,000
Capital Dili
Main religions Catholic
Languages Tetum
Currency Escudo
Life expectancy n/a
Highest point Mt Tatamailau
9,721 ft

Ecuador

Area 105,045 sq mi
Population 12,157,000
Capital Quito

Top chocoholics

1 **Britain** 35 lb
2 **America** 22 lb
3 **France** 20 lb
4 **Japan** 6 lb

Note: average
amount consumed per
person per year

Top 5 islands

1 **Greenland** Atlantic/Pacific Oceans
849,486 sq mi
2 **New Guinea** Pacific Ocean
317,012 sq mi
3 **Borneo** Indian Ocean 287,280 sq mi
4 **Madagascar** Indian Ocean
226,658 sq mi
5 **Baffin** Arctic Ocean
183,798 sq mi

Major cities San Lorenzo, Riobamba,
Loja, Cuencha
Main religions Catholic
Languages Spanish
Currency US dollar, replaced the
sucre
Life expectancy 72 years
Highest point Chimborazo 20,557 ft

Egypt

Area 385,258 sq mi
Population 64,650,000
Capital Cairo
Main religions Sunni Muslim
Languages Arabic
Currency Egyptian pound
Life expectancy 62 years
Highest point Mt Catherine
8,668 ft

El Salvador

Area 8,125 sq mi
Population 6,275,000
Capital San Salvador
Main religions Catholic

Languages Spanish
Currency Colon
Life expectancy 70 years
Highest point Volcan de Santa Ana
7,811 ft

Equatorial Guinea

Area 10,831 sq mi
Population 511,000
Capital Malabo
Main religions Catholic
Languages Fang, Spanish
Currency CFA franc
Life expectancy 57 years
Highest point Pico de Basile
9,868 ft

Eritrea

Area 46,846 sq mi
Population 4,362,000
Capital Asmara
Main religions Sunni Muslim
Languages Tigrinya
Currency Nakfa
Life expectancy 55 years
Highest point Ramlo 6,988 ft

Estonia

Area 17,464 sq mi
Population 1,370,000
Capital Tallinn
Main religions Lutheran,
Nonreligious, Estonian Orthodox
Languages Estonian, Russian
Currency Kroon
Life expectancy 69 years
Highest point Munamagi 1,043 ft

Did you know?

Bulgarian citizens nod their
head to indicate no and shake
their head for yes.

Ethiopia

Area 435,218 sq mi
Population 65,892,000
Capital Addis Ababa
Main religions Sunni Muslim, Ethiopian Orthodox
Languages Amharic, Oromo
Currency Birr
Life expectancy 41 years
Highest point Ras Dejen 15,157 ft

Fiji

Area 7,055 sq mi
Population 856,000
Capital Suva
Main religions Hindu, Methodist
Languages Fijan, English, Hindi
Currency Dollar
Life expectancy 68 years
Highest point Tomaniivi 4,672 ft

Finland

Area 130,137 sq mi
Population 5,206,000
Capital Helsinki
Main religion Evangelical/Lutheran
Languages Finnish, Swedish
Currency Euro, replaced the markka
Life expectancy 77 years
Highest point Haltiatunturi 4,357 ft

France

Area 211,224 sq mi
Population 59,080,000
Capital Paris
Main religions Catholic
Languages French
Currency Euro, replaced the franc
Life expectancy 78 years
Highest point Mont Blanc 15,771 ft

Gabon

Area 103,355 sq mi
Population 1,226,000
Capital Libreville
Main religions Christian, Indigenous
Languages French, Fang
Currency CFA franc
Life expectancy 57 years
Highest point Mont Iboundji 5,167 ft

Gambia

Area 4,363 sq mi
Population 1,365,000
Capital Banjul
Main religions Muslim
Languages Malinke
Currency Dalasi
Life expectancy 54 years
Highest point Unnamed location 174 ft

Georgia

Area 26,995 sq mi
Population 4,961,000
Capital Tbillisi
Main religions Georgian Orthodox
Languages Georgian
Currency Lari
Life expectancy 65 years
Highest point Kasbek 16,558 ft

Germany

Area 137,814 sq mi
Population 82,440,000
Capital Berlin
Main religions Catholic, Evangelical/Lutheran
Languages German
Currency Euro, replaced the Deutschmark
Life expectancy 77 years
Highest point Zugspitze 9,718 ft

Ghana

Area 92,107 sq mi
Population 18,845,000
Capital Accra
Main religions Indigenous
Languages Hausa
Currency Cedi
Life expectancy 57 years
Highest point Afadjato 2,904 ft

Famous walls

1 **Great Wall of China**, China
Averages 30 ft high, with 39 ft high watchtowers every 197 ft

2 **Hadrian's Wall**, England
Averages 20 ft high, with milecastles, or forts, at intervals

3 **Berlin Wall**, Germany
Was 16 ft high, 28 mi long, with electrified fences and watchtowers

Greece

Area 50,946 sq mi
Population 10,940,000
Capital Athens
Main religions Greek Orthodox
Languages Greek
Currency Euro, replaced the drachma
Life expectancy 78 years
Highest point Olympus 9,570 ft

Grenada

Area 131 sq mi
Population 101,000
Capital St George's
Main religions Catholic
Languages English
Currency East Caribbean dollar
Life expectancy 71 years
Highest point Mt St Catherine 2,756 ft

Guatemala

Area 42,045 sq mi
Population 11,237,000
Capital Guatemala City
Main religions Catholic
Languages Spanish
Currency Quetzal
Life expectancy 66 years
Highest point Tajumulco 13,845 ft

Guinea

Area 94,934 sq mi
Population 7,430,000
Capital Conakry
Main religions Muslim
Languages Fulani
Currency Franc
Life expectancy 46 years
Highest point Mont Nimba 5,748 ft

Guinea-Bissau

Area 13,947 sq mi
Population 1,361,000
Capital Bissau
Main religions Indigenous
Languages Portuguese
Currency CFA franc
Life expectancy 49 years
Highest point Unnamed location in the northeast corner of the country 984 ft

Guyana

Area 83,006 sq mi
Population 749,000
Capital Georgetown
Main religions Hindu, Protestant
Languages English, Creole
Currency Dollar
Life expectancy 62 years
Highest point Mt Roraima 9,088 ft

Did you know?

In Greek mythology, Hercules is said to have pulled Africa and Spain apart whilst holding Gibraltar and the Moroccan mountain of Jbel Musa. These two points are now known as The Pillars of Hercules.

Haiti

Area 10,715 sq mi
Population 7,820,000
Capital Port-au-Prince
Main religions Catholic, Voodoo
Languages Haitian Creole
Currency Gourde
Life expectancy 51 years
Highest point Pic La Selle 8,773 ft

Honduras

Area 43,281 sq mi
Population 6,480,000
Capital Tegucigalpa
Main religions Catholic
Languages Spanish
Currency Lempira
Life expectancy 65 years
Highest point Cerro Selaque 9,347 ft

Hungary

Area 35,922 sq mi
Population 10,197,000
Capital Budapest
Main religions Catholic
Languages Hungarian
Currency Forint
Life expectancy 71 years
Highest point Kekes 3,330 ft

Farmworkers

1 **Africa** 60 percent
2 **Asia** 58 percent
3 **Central/South America** 25 percent
4 **Europe** 8 percent
5 **USA and Canada** 2 percent
(percentage of population)

Iceland

Area 39,701 sq mi
Population 288,000
Capital Reykjavik
Main religions Evangelical/Lutheran
Languages Icelandic
Currency Krona
Life expectancy 79 years
Highest point Hvannadalshnukur 6,952 ft

India

Area 1,222 337 sq mi
Population 1,027,000,000
Capital New Delhi
Main religions Hindu
Languages Hindi
Currency Rupee
Life expectancy 63 years
Highest point Kanchenjunga 28,209 ft

Indonesia

Area 735,366 sq mi
Population 206,265,000
Capital Jakarta
Main religions Sunni Muslim
Languages Javanese
Currency Rupiah
Life expectancy 63 years
Highest point Puncak Jaya 16,503 ft

Iran

Area 632,506 sq mi
Population 65,540,000
Capital Tehran
Main religions Shia Muslim
Languages Farsi
Currency Rial
Life expectancy 68 years
Highest point Damavand 18,386 ft

Iraq

Area 167,988 sq mi
Population 27,072,000
Capital Baghdad
Main religion Shia Muslim
Languages Arabic
Currency Iraqi dinar
Life expectancy 67 years
Highest point Halgurd (on the mountain Hasarost) 12,228 ft

Ireland, Republic of

Area 27,137 sq mi
Population 3,917,000
Capital Dublin
Main religions Catholic
Languages English, Irish
Currency Euro replaced punt
Life expectancy 76 years
Highest point Carrauntuohill 3,415 ft

Longest tunnels

1 **Seikan** Japan 34 mi
2 **Channel Tunnel** UK-France 31 mi
3 **Dai-Shimizu** Japan 14 mi
4 **Shin-Kanmon** Japan 12 mi
5 **Great Belt** Denmark 5 mi
(all rail and underwater)

Israel

Area 7,877 sq mi
Population 6,631,000
Capital Jerusalem
Main religions Jewish
Languages Hebrew
Currency New Shekel
Life expectancy 78 years
Highest point Mt Hermon 7,297 ft

Italy

Area 116,314 sq mi
Population 56,306,000
Capital Rome
Main religion Catholic
Languages Italian
Currency Euro replaced lira
Life expectancy 79 years
Highest point Mont Blanc 15,771 ft

Largest oil reserves

1 **Saudi Arabia** 261 billion barrels
2 **Russia** 100 billion barrels
3 **Iraq** 98 billion barrels
3 **United Arab Emirates** 98 billion barrels
5 **Iran** 93 billion barrels

Ivory Coast

Area 124,512 sq mi
Population 14,786,000
Capital Abidjan (administrative), Yamoussoukro
Main religions Muslim

Languages French
Currency CFA franc
Life expectancy 46 years
Highest point Mont Nimba 5,748 ft

Jamaica

Area 4,243 sq mi
Population 2,607,000
Capital Kingston
Main religions Pentecostal, Nonreligious, Catholic
Languages English
Currency Jamaican dollar
Life expectancy 75 years
Highest point Blue Mountain Peak 7,402 ft

Japan

Area 145,893 sq mi
Population 126,926,000
Capital Tokyo
Main religions Shinto, Buddhist
Languages Japanese
Currency Yen
Life expectancy 80 years
Highest point Mt Fuji 12,388 ft

Jordan

Area 34,448 sq mi
Population 5,230,000
Capital Amman
Main religions Sunni Muslim
Languages Arabic
Currency Dinar
Life expectancy 73 years
Highest point Jabal Ramm 5,755 ft

Kazakhstan

Area 1,052,181 sq mi
Population 14,952,000
Capital Astana
Main religions Sunni Muslim, Nonreligious

Languages Kazakh, Russian
Currency Tenge
Life expectancy 64 years
Highest point Khan Tengri 22,949 ft

Kenya

Area 224,978 sq mi
Population 28,687,000
Capital Nairobi
Main religions Catholic, Protestant, Traditional beliefs
Languages Swahili
Currency Kenyan shilling
Life expectancy 48 years
Highest point Mt Kenya 17,057 ft

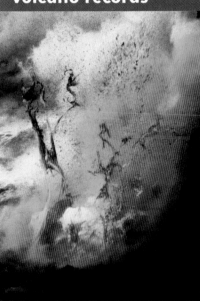

Volcano records

Biggest volcano Mauna Loa, Hawaii, crater 590 ft deep

Highest active volcano Ojos del Salado, South America, 22,595 ft high

Most restless volcano Kilauea, Hawaii, erupting since 1983

Did you know?

The Chilean city of Puntas Arenas is the most southerly city in the world.

Kiribati

Area 313 sq mi
Population 84,500
Capital Bairiki on Tarawa Island
Main religions Catholic
Languages English, Kiribati
Currency Australian dollar
Life expectancy 60 years
Highest point Unnamed point on Banaba 266 ft

Korea, North

Area 46,544 sq mi
Population 24,039,000
Capital Pyongyang
Main religions Nonreligious, Traditional beliefs
Languages Korean
Currency Won
Life expectancy 71 years
Highest point Paek-tu 9,002 ft

Korea, South

Area 38,026 sq mi
Population 48,517,000
Capital Seoul
Main religions Nonreligious, Buddhist
Languages Korean
Currency Won
Life expectancy 74 years
Highest point Halla-san 6,398 ft

Kuwait

Area 6,880 sq mi
Population 2,228,000

Capital Kuwait
Main religions Sunni Muslim
Languages Arabic
Currency Kuwaiti dinar
Life expectancy 77 years
Highest point Ash Shaqaya 948 ft

Kyrgyzstan

Area 76,647 sq mi
Population 4,699,000
Capital Bishkek
Main religions Sunni Muslim
Languages Kyrgyz
Currency Som
Life expectancy 64 years
Highest point Pik Pobedy 24,406 ft

Highest waterfalls

1 **Angel** Venezuela 3,212 ft
2 **Tugela** Africa 3,107 ft
3 **Utigård** Norway 2,625 ft
4 **Mongefossen** Norway 2,539 ft
5 **Yosemite** USA 2,425 ft
6 **Østre Mardøla Foss** Norway 2,152 ft

Laos

Area 91,435 sq mi
Population 5,777,000
Capital Vientiane
Main religions Buddhist
Languages Lao
Currency Kip
Life expectancy 54 years
Highest point Phou Bia 9,248 ft

Latvia

Area 24,751 sq mi
Population 2,346,000
Capital Riga
Main religions Lutheran, Nonreligious
Languages Latvian, Russian
Currency Lat
Life expectancy 67 years
Highest point Gaizinkalns 1,024 ft

Lebanon

Area 4,015 sq mi
Population 3,282,000
Capital Beirut
Main religions Muslim
Languages Arabic
Currency Lebanese pound
Life expectancy 71 years
Highest point Qurnat as-Sawda 10,131 ft

Lesotho

Area 11,719 sq mi
Population 2,158,000
Capital Maseru
Main religions Catholic, Traditional beliefs
Languages Sesotho
Currency Loti
Life expectancy 54 years
Highest point Thabana Ntlenyana 11,424 ft

Did you know?

In ancient Rome, Malta was known as Melita, which translates as "Island of honey."

Liberia

Area 38,253 sq mi
Population 3,154,000
Capital Monrovia
Main religions Traditional beliefs
Languages Creole
Currency Dollar
Life expectancy 60 years
Highest point Mt Wuteve 4,530 ft

Libya

Area 679,410 sq mi
Population 5,605,000
Capital Tripoli
Main religions Sunni Muslim
Languages Arabic
Currency Libyan dinar
Life expectancy 66 years
Highest point Bette Peak 7,500 ft

Liechtenstein

Area 62 sq mi
Population 34,000
Capital Vaduz
Main religions Catholic
Languages German
Currency Swiss franc
Life expectancy 78 years
Highest point Grauspitze 8,526 ft

Lithuania

Area 25,176 sq mi
Population 3,463,000
Capital Vilnius
Main religions Catholic
Languages Lithuanian

Currency Litas
Life expectancy 69 years
Highest point Juozapine 965 ft

Luxembourg

Area 999 sq mi
Population 440,000
Capital Luxembourg
Main religions Catholic
Languages Luxembourgish, French, German
Currency Euro, replaced the Luxembourg franc
Life expectancy 78 years
Highest point Buurgplaatz 1,833 ft

Macedonia

Area 9,782 sq mi
Population 2,022,604
Capital Skopje
Main religions Macedonian Orthodox
Languages Macedonian
Currency Denar
Life expectancy 73 years
Highest point Rudoka 9,015 ft

Madagascar

Area 226,673 sq mi
Population 15,692,000
Capital Antananarivo
Main religions Indigenous beliefs
Languages Malagasy
Currency Franc
Life expectancy 53 years
Highest point Tsaratanana 9,436 ft

Malawi

Area 45,748 sq mi
Population 11,549,000
Capital Lilongwe
Main religions Sunni Islam, Catholic, Presbyterian
Languages English, Chichewa

Longest bridges

1 **Akashi-Kaiko** Japan 6,528 ft
2 **Great Belt** Denmark 5,328 ft
3 **Humber Estuary** UK 4,625 ft
4 **Jiangyin** China 4,543 ft
5 **Tsing Ma** China 4,517 ft

Currency Kwacha
Life expectancy 37 years
Highest point Sapitwa Peak 9,849 ft

Malaysia

Area 127,325 sq mi
Population 23,275,000
Capital Kuala Lumpur
Main religions Sunni Muslim
Languages Malay
Currency Ringgit
Life expectancy 71 years
Highest point Mt Kinabalu 13,455 ft

Maldives

Area 116 sq mi
Population 270,000
Capital Male
Main religions Sunni Muslim
Languages Divehi
Currency Rufiyaa
Life expectancy 68 years
Highest point Unnamed point 13 ft

Mali

Area 428,109 sq mi
Population 11,234,000
Capital Bamako
Main religions Muslim
Languages Babara
Currency CFA franc
Life expectancy 47 years
Highest point Hombori Tondo 3,789 ft

Malta

Area 124 sq mi
Population 378,000
Capital Valletta
Main religions Catholic
Languages Maltese, English
Currency Euro, replaced lira
Life expectancy 78 years
Highest point Ta'Dmejrek 830 ft

Marshall Islands

Area 70 sq mi
Population 51,000
Capital Dalap-Uliga-Darrit
Main religions Congregational, Nonreligious, Catholic
Languages Marshallese, English
Currency US dollar
Life expectancy 66 years
Highest point Unnamed point 20 ft

Did you know?

In the Nazca Desert of Peru, ground art exists on a huge scale, its purpose a mystery. There are geometric patterns and drawings of fish, birds, spiders, and a monkey. They are visible properly only from the air.

Did you know?

Turkey is the only country to have territory in both Asia and Europe.

Mauritania

Area 397,983 sq mi
Population 2,508,000
Capital Nouakchott
Main religions Muslim
Languages Arabic
Currency Ouguiya
Life expectancy 50 years
Highest point Kediet Ijill 3,002 ft

Mauritius

Area 788 sq mi
Population 1,210,000
Capital Port Louis
Main religions Hindu
Languages English
Currency Rupee
Life expectancy 71 years
Highest point Piton de la Riviere Noire 2,709 ft

Mexico

Area 756,124 sq mi
Population 97,483,000
Capital Mexico City
Main religions Catholic
Languages Spanish

Currency Peso
Longest river Rio Grande
Life expectancy 72 years
Highest point Volcan Citlaltepetl (Pico de Orizaba) 18,405 ft

Micronesia

Area 271 sq mi
Population 107,000
Capital Kolonia (legislative), Palikir (administrative)
Main religions Catholic, Congregational
Languages English, Chuukese
Currency US dollar
Life expectancy 69 years
Highest point Mt Totolom 2,595 ft

Moldova

Area 13,012 sq mi
Population 4,248,000
Capital Chisinau
Main religions Romanian Orthodox
Languages Moldovian
Currency Leu
Life expectancy 64 years
Highest point Balaneshty 1,411 ft

Monaco

Area 0.75 sq mi
Population 32,000
Capital Monaco
Religions Catholic
Languages French, English, Italian
Currency Euro, replaced the franc

Life expectancy 79 years
Highest point Mont Agel 459 ft

Mongolia

Area 604,293 sq mi
Population 2,373,000
Capital Ulaanbaatar
Main religions Tibetan Buddhist
Languages Khalka Mongol
Currency Tugrik
Life expectancy 62 years
Highest point Huiten Peak 15,266 ft

Morocco

Area 177,131 sq mi
Population 30,367,000
Capital Rabat
Main religions Sunni Muslim
Languages Arabic
Currency Dirham
Life expectancy 69 years
Highest point Jebel Toubkal 13,665 ft

Mozambique

Area 309,517 sq mi
Population 18,083,000
Capital Maputo
Main religions Indigenous
Languages Portuguese, Makua
Currency Metical
Life expectancy 45 years
Highest point Monte Binga 7,992 ft

Namibia

Area 318,718 sq mi
Population 1,827,000
Capital Windhoek
Main religions Lutheran
Languages Ovambo, English
Currency Rand
Life expectancy 41 years
Highest point Konigstein 8,550 ft

Most populated countries

1 **China** 1,247,761,000
2 **India** 1,027,000,000
3 **USA** 288,369,000
4 **Indonesia** 206,265,000
5 **Brazil** 176,871,000

Did you know?

Sudan is Africa's largest country by area.

Nauru

Area 20 sq mi
Population 12,000
Capital Yaren
Main religions Congregational
Languages Nauruan
Currency Australian dollar
Life expectancy 61 years
Highest point Unnamed point 223 ft

Nepal

Area 56,831 sq mi
Population 23,078,000
Capital Kathmandu
Main religions Hindu
Languages Nepali
Currency Rupee
Life expectancy 58 years
Highest point Mt Everest 29,029 ft

Netherlands

Area 16,034 sq mi
Population 15,987,000
Capital Amsterdam
Main religions Catholic
Languages Dutch
Currency Euro, replaced the guilder
Life expectancy 78 years
Highest point Vaalserberg 1,053 ft

New Zealand

Area 107,745 sq mi
Population 4,009,000
Capital Wellington
Main religions Nonreligious, Anglican, Presbyterian
Languages English

Currency New Zealand dollar
Life expectancy 78 years
Highest point Mt Cook 12,316 ft

Nicaragua

Area 50,897 sq mi
Population 5,074,000
Capital Managua
Main religions Catholic
Languages Spanish
Currency Cordoba
Life expectancy 67 years
Highest point Pico Mogoton 6,913 ft

Did you know?

The most common family name in the world is probably Zhiang—1 in 10 Chinese are called Zhiang.

Niger

Area 496,938 sq mi
Population 10,790,000
Capital Niamey
Main religions Muslim
Languages Hausa
Currency CFA franc
Life expectancy 42 years
Highest point Mont Bagzane 6,634 ft

Nigeria

Area 356,695 sq mi
Population 111,506,000
Capital Abuja
Main religions Muslim
Languages Hausa
Currency Naira
Life expectancy 54 years
Highest point Chappal Waddi 7,936 ft

Norway

Area 125,190 sq mi
Population 4,552,000
Capital Oslo
Main religions Evangelical/Lutheran
Languages Norwegian
Currency Krone
Life expectancy 78 years
Highest point Galdhopiggen8,100 ft

Oman

Area 306,009 sq km
Population 2,331,000
Capital Muscat
Main religions Ibadhi Muslim
Languages Arabic

Longest rivers

1 **Nile** Africa 4,145 mi
2 **Amazon** South America 4,007 mi
3 **Chang Jiang (Yangtze)** China 3,964 mi
4 **Huang He (Yellow)** China 2,841 mi
5 **Congo (Zaire)** Africa 2,900 mi

Top annual global causes of death

1 **Heart attack** 7.2 million
2 **Stroke** 5.5 million
3 **Lower respiratory infections** 3.9 million
4 **HIV/AIDS** 2.9 million
5 **Chronic obstructive pulmonary disease** 2.7 million
6 **Diarrheal diseases** 2.0 million
7 **Tuberculosis** 1.6 million
8 **Childhood diseases** 1.3 million
9 **Cancer of trachea/bronchus/lung** 1.2 million
10 **Road accidents** 1.2 million
11 **Malaria** 1.1 million

Currency Rial Omani
Life expectancy 71 years
Highest point Jabal al-Akhdar 10,194 ft

Pakistan

Area 307,398 sq mi
Population 156,483,000
Capital Islamabad
Main religions Sunni Muslim
Languages Urdu
Currency Rupee
Life expectancy 59 years
Highest point K2 28,238 ft

Palau

Area 188 sq mi
Population 19,000
Capital Koror Island
Main religions Catholic, Traditional beliefs
Languages Palauan, English
Currency US dollar
Life expectancy 69 years
Highest point Makelulu 715 ft

Panama

Area 30,195 sq mi
Population 2,839,000
Capital Panama City
Main religions Catholic
Languages Spanish
Currency Balboa/US dollar
Life expectancy 75 years
Highest point Baru 11,401 ft

Papua New Guinea

Area 178,717 sq mi
Population 5,191,000
Capital Port Moresby
Main religions Catholic, Lutheran
Languages Pidgin English, English
Currency Kina
Life expectancy 63 years
Highest point Mt Wilhelm 14,793 ft

Paraguay

Area 157,058 sq mi
Population 5,206,000
Capital Asuncion
Main religions Catholic

Did you know?

Peru is home to Lake Titicaca, the world's highest navigable lake.

Languages Spanish, Guarani
Currency Guarani
Life expectancy 72 years
Highest point Cerro San Rafael 2,789 ft

Peru

Area 496,261 sq mi
Population 25,662,000
Capital Lima
Religions Catholic
Languages Spanish
Currency Neuvo Sol
Life expectancy 70 years
Highest point Nevado Huascaran 22,264 ft

Philippines

Area 115,839 sq mi
Population 76,499,000
Capital Manila
Main religions Catholic
Languages Filipino
Currency Philippine peso
Life expectancy 66 years
Highest point Mt Apo 9,692 ft

Poland

Area 120,736 sq mi
Population 38,199,000
Capital Warsaw
Main religions Catholic
Languages Polish
Currency Zloty
Life expectancy 73 years
Highest point Rysys 8,199 ft

Portugal

Area 35,675 sq mi
Population 10,318,000
Capital Lisbon
Main religions Catholic
Languages Portuguese

Currency Euro, replaced the escudo
Life expectancy 76 years
Highest point Pico Volcano 7,713 ft

Qatar

Area 4,416 sq mi
Population 599,000
Capital Doha
Main religions Sunni Muslim
Languages Arabic
Currency Riyal
Life expectancy 74 years
Highest point Dukhan 240 ft

Romania

Area 91,676 sq mi
Population 21,698,000
Capital Bucharest
Main religions Romanian Orthodox
Languages Romanian
Currency Leu
Life expectancy 71 years
Highest point Moldoveanu 8,346 ft

Russian Federation

Area 6,593,309 sq mi
Population 145,182,000
Capital Moscow
Main religions Russian Orthodox
Languages Russian
Currency Rouble
Life expectancy 65 years
Highest point Gora Elbrus 18,510 ft

Rwanda

Area 10,171 sq mi
Population 8,163,000
Capital Kigali
Main religions Catholic
Languages Rwanda
Currency Franc
Life expectancy 42 years
Highest point Mont Karisimbi 14,787 ft

St Kitts-Nevis

Area 104 sq mi
Population 46,000
Capital Basseterre
Main religions Anglican, Methodist
Languages English
Currency East Caribbean dollar
Life expectancy 68 years
Highest point Mt Misery 3,793 ft

St Lucia

Area 239 sq mi
Population 163,000
Capital Castries
Main religions Catholic
Languages English
Currency East Caribbean dollar
Life expectancy 72 years
Highest point Mt Gimie 3,146 ft

St Vincent & the Grenadines

Area 150 sq mi
Population 112,000
Capital Kingstown
Main religions Nonreligious, Anglican
Languages English
Currency East Caribbean dollar
Life expectancy 74 years
Highest point Mt Soufriere 4,049 ft

Highest dams

1 **Rogun** Tajikistan 1,099 ft
2 **Nurek** Tajikistan 1,083 ft
3 **Grand Dixence** Switzerland 935 ft

Samoa

Area 1,104 sq mi
Population 172,000
Capital Apia
Main religions Mormon, Congregational
Languages Samoan
Currency Tala
Life expectancy 69 years
Highest point Silisili 6,096 ft

San Marino

Area 23 sq mi
Population 27,000
Capital San Marino
Main religions Catholic
Languages Italian
Currency Euro, replaced the lira
Life expectancy 81 years
Highest point Monte Titano 2,425 ft

São Tomé & Príncipe

Area 371 sq mi
Population 138,000
Capital São Tomé
Main religions Catholic
Languages Portuguese
Currency Dobra
Life expectancy 64 years

Did you know?

The number 4 is regarded with great superstition in Japan. The Japanese word for 4 is "shi," the same as the word for death.

Did you know?

The republic of the Philippines is made up of 7,107 separate islands.

Highest point Pico de Sao Tome 6,640 ft

Saudi Arabia

Area 865,066 sq mi
Population 20,847,000
Capital Riyadh
Main religions Sunni Muslim
Languages Arabic
Currency Riyal
Life expectancy 70 years
Highest point Jabal Sawda 10,278 ft

Senegal

Area 75,755 sq mi
Population 9,802,000
Capital Dakar
Main religions Muslim
Languages Wolof
Currency CFA franc
Life expectancy 57 years
Highest point Fouta Djallon 1,906 ft

Serbia & Montenegro

Area 39,520 sq mi
Population 11,206,847
Capital Belgrade
Main religions Serbian Orthodox
Languages Serb, Albanian
Currency Yugoslav Dinar/Euro
Life expectancy 75 years
Highest point Deravica 8,714 ft

Seychelles

Area 176 sq mi
Population 77,000

Capital Victoria
Main religions Catholic
Languages English
Currency Rupee
Life expectancy 71 years
Highest point Morne Seychellois 2,972 ft

Sierra Leone

Area 27,700 sq mi
Population 4,854,000
Capital Freetown
Main religions Muslim
Languages Creole
Currency Leone
Life expectancy 49 years
Highest point Bintimani Peak 6,391 ft

Singapore

Area 250 sq mi
Population 4,064,000
Capital Singapore
Main religions Buddhist
Languages Chinese
Currency Dollar
Life expectancy 79 years
Highest point Bukit Timah 581 ft

Slovakia

Area 18,861 sq mi
Population 5,379,000

Capital Bratislava
Main religions Catholic
Languages Slovak
Currency Koruna
Life expectancy 73 years
Highest point Gerlachovka 8,711 ft

Slovenia

Area 7,821 sq mi
Population 1,948,000
Capital Ljubljana
Main religions Catholic
Languages Slovenian, Croatian
Currency Tolar
Life expectancy 75 years
Highest point Triglav 9,396 ft

Solomon Islands

Area 10,986 sq mi
Population 409,000
Capital Honiara
Main religions Anglican
Languages English, Pidgin English
Currency Dollar
Life expectancy 71 years
Highest point Mt Makarakomburu 8,028 ft

Somalia

Area 246,220 sq mi
Population 10,100,000
Capital Mogadishu

Religions with most followers

1 **Christianity** 1.97 billion
2 **Islam** 1.16 billion
3 **Hinduism** 800 million
4 **Buddhism** 356 million
5 **Traditional** 225 million
6 **Sikhism** 23 million
7 **Judaism** 14 million

Languages with most speakers

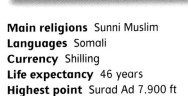

1 **Chinese** over 1 billion
2 **English** 510 million
3 **Hindustani** 500 million
4 **Spanish** 392 million
5 **Russian** 277 million

Main religions Sunni Muslim
Languages Somali
Currency Shilling
Life expectancy 46 years
Highest point Surad Ad 7,900 ft

South Africa

Area 471,044 sq mi
Population 44,820,000
Capital Cape Town (legislative),
Pretoria (administrative)
Main religions Traditional beliefs,
Local Christian Churches
Languages English, Zulu, Xhosa
Currency Rand
Life expectancy 56 years
Highest point Njesuthi 11,181 ft

Spain

Area 195,379 sq mi
Population 40,847,000
Capital Madrid
Main religions Catholic
Languages Spanish
Currency Euro, replaced the peseta
Life expectancy 78 years
Highest point Pico de Teide (located
on the island of Tenerife) 12,188 ft

Sri Lanka

Area 25,334 sq mi
Population 19,410,000
Capital Colombo
Main religions Buddhist
Languages Sinhali

Currency Sri Lanka rupee
Life expectancy 73 years
Highest point Pidurutalagala
8,280 ft

Sudan

Area 967,567 sq mi
Population 31,081,000
Capital Khartoum
Main religions Sunni Muslim
Languages Arabic
Currency Sudanese dinar
Life expectancy 56 years
Highest point Kinyeti 10,456 ft

Suriname

Area 63,044 sq mi
Population 417,000
Capital Paramaribo
Main religions Hindu, Catholic,
Sunni Muslim
Languages Dutch, Sranan, Hindu
Currency Suriname Guilder
Life expectancy 71 years
Highest point Juliana Top 4,035 ft

Swaziland

Area 6,704 sq mi
Population 1,008,000
Capital Lobamba
Main religions Local Christian
Churches, Traditional beliefs
Languages SiSwati
Currency Lilangeni
Life expectancy 39 years
Highest point Emlembe 6,112 ft

Sweden

Area 173,744 sq mi
Population 8,940,000
Capital Stockholm
Main religions Lutheran, Catholic
Languages Swedish
Currency Krona
Life expectancy 79 years
Highest point Kebnekaise 6,926 ft

Switzerland

Area 15,943 sq mi
Population 7,318,000
Capital Bern
Main religions Catholic
Languages German, French, Italian,
Romansch
Currency Swiss franc
Life expectancy 80 years
Highest point Dufourspitze,(also
known as Monte Rosa) 15,203 ft

Syria

Area 71,503 sq mi
Population 16,729,000
Capital Damascus
Main religions Sunni Muslim
Languages Arabic
Currency Syrian pound
Life expectancy 68 years
Highest point Mt Hermon
9,232 ft

Did you know?

The literary character of
Dracula was based on the
Romanian Prince of
Wallachia, Vlad the Impaler.

Tajikistan

Area 55,255 sq mi
Population 6,127,000
Capital Dushanbe
Main religions Sunni Muslim
Languages Tajik
Currency Somoni, replaced the tajik rouble
Life expectancy 65 years
Highest point Garmo 24,590 ft

Tanzania

Area 364,927 sq mi
Population 34,569,000
Capital Dar es Salaam (administrative), Dodoma (legislative)
Main religions Traditional beliefs, Sunni Muslim
Languages Swahili
Currency Shilling
Life expectancy 46 years
Highest point Mt Kilimanjaro 19,340ft

Thailand

Area 198,470 sq mi
Population 60,607,000
Capital Bangkok
Main religions Buddhist
Languages Thai
Currency Baht
Life expectancy 69 years
Highest mountain Doi Inthanon 8,516 ft

Togo

Area 21,929 sq mi
Population 5,429,000
Capital Lome
Main religions Indigenous
Languages Ewe
Currency CFA franc
Life expectancy 59 years
Highest point Mont Agou 3,235 ft

Tonga

Area 289 sq mi
Population 99,000
Capital Nuku'alofa
Main religions Free Wesleyan
Languages Tongan
Currency Pa'anga
Life expectancy 68 years
Highest point Kao 3,379 ft

Largest coal reserves

1 **Russia** 241 million tons
2 **USA** 240 million tons
3 **China** 114 million tons
4 **Australia** 91 million tons
5 **India** 69 million tons

Trinidad & Tobago

Area 1,981 sq mi
Population 1,262,000
Capital Port of Spain
Main religions Catholic, Hindu
Languages English
Currency Dollar
Life expectancy 71 years
Highest point Cerro del Aripo 3,084 ft

Tunisia

Area 63,175 sq mi
Population 9,990,000
Capital Tunis
Main religions Sunni Muslim
Languages Arabic
Currency Tunisian dinar
Life expectancy 73 years
Highest point Jebel ech Chambi 5,066 ft

Turkey

Area 301,405 sq mi
Population 67,804,000
Capital Ankara
Main religions Sunni Muslim
Languages Turkish
Currency Turkish lira
Life expectancy 73 years
Highest point Mt Ararat 16,854 ft

Turkmenistan

Area 188,469 sq mi
Population 4,495,000
Capital Ashgabat
Main religions Muslim
Languages Turkmen
Currency Manat
Life expectancy 61 years
Highest point Firyuza 9,652 ft

Tuvalu

Area 10 sq mi
Population 9600
Capital Fongafale
Main religions Church of Tuvalu
Languages Tuvaluan
Currency Australian dollar
Life expectancy 66 years
Highest point Unnamed point 20 ft

Uganda

Area 93,077 sq mi
Population 24,749,000
Capital Kampala
Main religions Protestant, Catholic
Languages Swahili, Ganda
Currency Uganda shilling
Life expectancy 43 years

Deepest caves

1 **Reseau Jean Bernard** France 5,256 ft
2 **Lamprechtsofen-Vogelshacht** Austria 5,043 ft
3 **Gouffre Mirolda/Lucien Bouclier** France 4,987 ft

Countries with most homes

1 **China** 277 million
2 **India** 195 million
3 **USA** 106 million
4 **Russia** 52 million
5 **Indonesia** 42 million
6 **France** 22 million
7 **UK** 22 million

Highest point Margherita Peak 16,765 ft

Ukraine

Area 233,107 sq mi
Population 48,416,000
Capital Kiev
Main religions Russian Orthodox, Nonreligious
Languages Ukrainian, Russian
Currency Hryvnia
Life expectancy 66 years
Highest point Mt Hoverla 6,762 ft

United Arab Emirates (UAE)

Area 32,002 sq mi
Population 4,041,000
Capital Abu Dhabi
Main religions Sunni Muslim
Languages Arabic
Currency Dirham
Life expectancy 75 years
Highest point al-Hajar 3,901 ft

United Kingdom

Area 94,532 sq mi
Population 58,789,000
Capital London
Main religions Anglican
Languages English
Currency Pound sterling
Life expectancy 77 years
Highest point Ben Nevis 4,406 ft

United States of America

Area 3,718,083 sq mi
Population 288,369,000
Capital Washington, DC
Main religions Catholic, Baptist
Languages English
Currency Dollar
Life expectancy 76 years
Highest point Mt McKinley 20,322 ft

Uruguay

Area 68,044 sq mi
Population 3,360,000
Capital Montevideo
Main religions Catholic
Languages Spanish
Currency Uruguayan peso
Life expectancy 76 years
Highest point Cerro Catedral 1,686 ft

Uzbekistan

Area 172,754 sq mi
Population 25,155,000
Capital Tashkent

Did you know?

Indonesia has the largest Muslim population in the world.

Largest inland lakes and seas

1 **Caspian Sea** Europe/Asia 146,112 sq mi
2 **Lake Superior** North America 31,798 sq mi
3 **Lake Victoria** Africa 26,829 sq mi
4 **Aral Sea** Asia 25,278 sq mi
5 **Lake Huron** North America 23,013 sq mi

Main religions Sunni Muslim
Languages Uzbek
Currency Som
Life expectancy 64 years
Highest point Bannovka 14,724 ft

Vanuatu

Area 4,707 sq mi
Population 187,000
Capital Vila
Main religions Presbyterian
Languages Bislama
Currency Vatu
Life expectancy 61 years
Highest point Mont Tabwemasana 6,165 ft

Vatican City

Area 0.17 sq mi
Population 860
Capital Vatican City
Main religions Catholic
Languages Italian, Latin
Currency Euro, replaced the lira
Life expectancy n/a
Highest point Unnamed 246 ft

Venezuela

Area 352,172 sq mi
Population 23,054,000
Capital Caracas
Main religions Catholic, Protestant
Languages Spanish
Currency Venezuelan bolivar
Life expectancy 73 years
Highest point Pico Bolivar 16,427ft

Vietnam

Area 127,253 sq mi
Population 76,325,000
Capital Hanoi
Main religions Buddhist
Languages Vietnamese
Currency Dong
Life expectancy 68 years
Highest point Fan si Pan 10,308 ft

Yemen

Area 207,302 sq mi
Population 18,862,000
Capital Sanaa
Main religions Muslim
Languages Arabic
Currency Rial
Life expectancy 60 years
Highest point Hadur Shu'ayb 12,336 ft

Zambia

Area 290,605 sq mi
Population 9,886,000
Capital Lusaka
Main religions Protestant, Traditional beliefs, Catholic
Languages English, Bemba

Did you know?

Norway has the longest coastline in Europe extending for 13,627 mi.

Currency Kwacha
Life expectancy 37 years
Highest point Unnamed location in Mafinga Hills 7,549 ft

Zimbabwe

Area 150,815 sq mi
Population 11,635,000
Capital Harare
Main religions Anglican, Traditional beliefs
Languages English, Shona
Currency Zimbabwean dollar
Life expectancy 39 years
Highest point Mt Inyangani 8,504 ft

World's highest peaks

1 **Everest** 29,029 ft
2 **K2** 28,248 ft
3 **Kanchenjunga** 28,209 ft
4 **Lhotse** 27,923 ft
5 **Makalu** 27,618 ft
(all are in the Himalayas, Asia)

Largest countries by land mass (sq mi)

1	Russian Federation	6,493,309
2	Canada	3,852,097
3	United States of America	3,718,083
4	China	3,696,809
5	Brazil	3,286,724
6	Australia	2,968,122
7	India	1,222,337
8	Argentina	1,057,599
9	Kazakhstan	1,052,181
10	Sudan	967,597
11	Algeria	919,666
12	Congo, Democratic Republic of	905,633
13	Saudi Arabia	865,067
14	Mexico	756,124
15	Indonesia	735,366
16	Libya	679,410
17	Iran	632,506
18	Mongolia	604,294
19	Niger	496,938
20	Peru	496,261
21	Chad	495,790
22	Angola	481,388
23	South Africa	471,044
24	Colombia	440,796
25	Ethiopia	435,218
26	Mali	428,110
27	Bolivia	424,195
28	Mauritania	397,984
29	Egypt	385,259
30	Tanzania	364,927
31	Nigeria	356,695
32	Venezuela	352,172
33	Namibia	318,718
34	Mozambique	309,518
35	Pakistan	307,398
36	Turkey	301,405
37	Chile	292,280
38	Zambia	290,605
39	Burma	261,989
40	Afghanistan	251,845
41	Somalia	246,220
42	Central African Republic	240,551
43	Ukraine	233,107
44	Madagascar	226,673
45	Kenya	224,978
46	Botswana	224,624
47	France	211,224
48	Yemen	207,302
49	Thailand	198,470
50	Spain	195,379
51	Turkmenistan	188,469
52	Cameroon	183,581
53	Papua New Guinea	178,717
54	Morocco	177,131
55	Sweden	173,744
56	Uzbekistan	172,754
57	Iraq	167,988
58	Paraguay	157,058
59	Zimbabwe	150,815
60	Japan	145,893
61	Germany	137,814
62	Congo Brazzaville	132,056
63	Finland	130,137
64	Malaysia	127,326
65	Vietnam	127,253
66	Norway	125,191
67	Ivory Coast	124,512
68	Poland	120,736
69	Oman	118,159
70	Italy	116,314
71	Philippines	115,839
72	New Zealand	107,745
73	Burkina Faso	105,877
74	Ecuador	105,045
75	Gabon	103,355
76	Guinea	94,934
77	United Kingdom	94,532
78	Uganda	93,077
79	Ghana	92,107
80	Romania	91,676
81	Laos	91,435
82	Guyana	83,006
83	Belarus	80,160
84	Kyrgyzstan	76,647
85	Senegal	75,755
86	Syria	71,504
87	Cambodia	69,905
88	Uruguay	68,044
89	Tunisia	63,175
90	Suriname	63,044
91	Nepal	56,831
92	Bangladesh	55,602
93	Tajikistan	55,255
94	Greece	50,946
95	Nicaragua	50,897
96	Eritrea	46,846
97	Korea, North	46,544
98	Malawi	45,749
99	Benin	43,486
100	Honduras	43,281

Did you know?

The Vatican City in Rome is the world's smallest independent state, with a land mass of only 0.17 sq mi.

Dependencies

A dependency is a country that is governed or controlled by another country. The following list includes all the world's dependencies. The country listed below each dependency is the country that governs that dependency.

Territory Administered by	Area sq mi	Population	Capital	Religion	Language	Currency
American Samoa USA	77	57,000	Fagatogo	Congregationalist	Samoan/English	US dollar
Anguilla UK	37	11,600	The Valley	Anglican	English	East Caribbean dollar
Aruba Netherlands	75	91,000	Oranjestad	Catholic	Dutch/ Papiamento	Aruban Florin
Bermuda UK	21	62,100	Hamilton	Anglican/Methodist	English	Bermuda dollar
British Indian Ocean territory UK	23	less than 10	–	–	English	US dollar
British Virgin Islands UK	59	21,000	Road Town	Methodist	English	US dollar
Cayman Islands UK	100	39,400	George Town	United Church	English	Cayman dollar
Christmas Island Australia	52	1500	The Settlement	Buddhist/Taoist	English/Chinese	Aus dollar
Cocos (Keeling) Islands Australia	5	620	West Island	Sunni Islam	English/Malay	Aus dollar
Cook Islands New Zealand	92	18,000	Avarua	Cook Islands Christian Church	English/Cook Islands Maori	NZ dollar
Coral Sea Islands Australia	3	less than 10	–	–	–	–
Europa Island France	11	less than 10	–	–	–	–
Faeroe Islands Denmark	540	47,000	Tórshavn	Evangelical Lutheran	Faeroese/ Danish	Danish krone
Falkland Islands UK	4,699	2,400	Stanley	Anglican	English	Falkland pound

Territory Administered by	Area sq mi	Population	Capital	Religion	Language	Currency
French Guiana France	33,402	181,000	Cayenne	Catholic	French/Creole	Euro
French Polynesia France	1,545	235,000	Papeete	Evangelical Church of Polynesia	French/Tahitian Pacific Franc	CFP franc
Gibraltar UK	2.5	25,000	Gibraltar	Catholic	English	Gibraltar pound
Glorieuses Island France	2	less than 10	–	–	–	–
Greenland Denmark	840,065	56,500	Nuuk	Evangelical Lutheran	Greenland Inuit/ Danish	Danish krone
Guadeloupe France	687	425,000	Basse–Terre	Catholic	French/Creole	Euro
Guam USA	209	155,000	Hagåtña	Catholic	English/ Chamorro	US dollar
Guernsey & Dependencies UK	31	62,700	St Peter Port	Anglican/Catholic	English	Pound
Isle of Man UK	221	76,300	Douglas	Anglican	English	Pound
Jan Mayen Norway	146	less than 10	–	–	–	–
Jersey UK	45	87,200	St Helier	Anglican	English	Pound
Johnston Atoll USA	1.1	500	–	–	English	–
Juan de Nova Island France	1.7	less than 10	–	–	–	–
Kerguelen Islands France	3,006	145	–	–	–	–
Martinique France	436	381,000	Fort-de-France	Catholic	French/Creole	Euro
Mayotte France	145	160,000	Dzaoudzi	Sunni Islam	French/ Mahorian	Euro

Territory Administered by	Area sq mi	Population	Capital	Religion	Language	Currency
Midway Islands USA	2	40	–	–	–	–
Montserrat UK	38	5,000	Plymouth	Anglican	English	East Caribbean dollar
Netherlands Antilles Netherlands	309	176,000	Willemstad	Catholic	Dutch/ Papiamento/ English	Netherlands Antilles guilder or Florin
New Caledonia France	7,173	208,000	Nouméa	Catholic	French	CFP franc
Niue New Zealand	100	1,800	Alofi	Congregational Niue Church	English/Niuean	NZ dollar
Norfolk Island Australia	14	2,000	Kingston	Anglican	English/ Norfolk Island	Aus dollar
Northern Mariana Islands USA	184	69,000	Capitol Hill	Catholic	English/ Chamorro/ Filipino	US dollar
Palmyra Atoll USA	5	20	–	–	–	–
Pitcairn Islands UK	18	47	Adamstown	Seventh–day Adventist	Pitkern	NZ dollar
Puerto Rico USA	3,515	3,859,000	San Juan	Catholic	Spanish/English	US dollar
Réunion France	969	699,000	St-Denis	Catholic	French/Creole	Euro
St Helena & Dependencies UK	159	7,000	Jamestown	Anglican/Baptist	English	St Helena pound
St Pierre & Miquelon France	93	6,300	St-Pierre	Catholic	French	Euro
South Georgia & South Sandwich Islands UK	1,579	less than 10	–	–	–	–

Territory Administered by	Area sq mi	Population	Capital	Religion	Language	Currency
Svalbard Norway	24,211	2,900	Longyearbyen	Evangelical Lutheran	Norwegian/ Russian/ Ukrainian	Krone
Tokelau New Zealand	5	1,500	–	Congregationalist	English/ Tokelauan	NZ dollar
Turks & Caicos Islands UK	166	20,000	Grand Turk	Baptist/Anglican	English	US dollar
Virgin Islands of the USA USA	136	109,000	Charlotte Amalie	Baptist/Catholic	English/Spanish	US dollar
Wallis & Futuna France	106	15,000	Mata'tu	Catholic	French/Wallisian/ Futunian	CFP franc

Disputed territories

The following are dependencies that are disputed. Various states claim them.

Territory	Area	Population	Capital	Religion	Language	Currency
Gaza and West Bank	2,416	3,040,000	–	Sunni Islam/ Christianity	Arabic	New Israeli shekel
Golan Heights	444	33,000	–	Sunni Islam/Jewish	Hebrew/Arabic	New Israeli shekel
Western Sahara (Morocco/ Polisario guerilla movement)	102,710	256,000	Laayoune	Sunni Islam	Arabic	Moroccan Dirham

World Flags

*E*very country in the world has its own flag. Also shown here are the flags for the states and provinces of the United States and Canada.

Afghanistan

Albania

Algeria

Andorra

Angola

Antigua & Barbuda

Argentina

Armenia

Australia

Austria

Azerbaijan

Bahamas

Bahrain

Bangladesh

Barbados

Belarus

Belgium

Belize

Benin

Bhutan

Bolivia

Bosnia-Herzegovina

Botswana

Brazil

Brunei

Bulgaria

Burkina Faso

Burma

Burundi

Cambodia

Cameroon

Canada

Cape Verde

Central African Republic

Chad

Chile

China

Colombia

Comoros

Congo, Democratic Republic of

Congo Brazzaville

Costa Rica

Croatia

Cuba

Cyprus

Czech Republic

Denmark

Djibouti

Dominica

Dominican Republic

East Timor

Ecuador

Egypt

El Salvador

Equatorial Guinea

Eritrea

Estonia

Ethiopia

Fiji

Finland

306

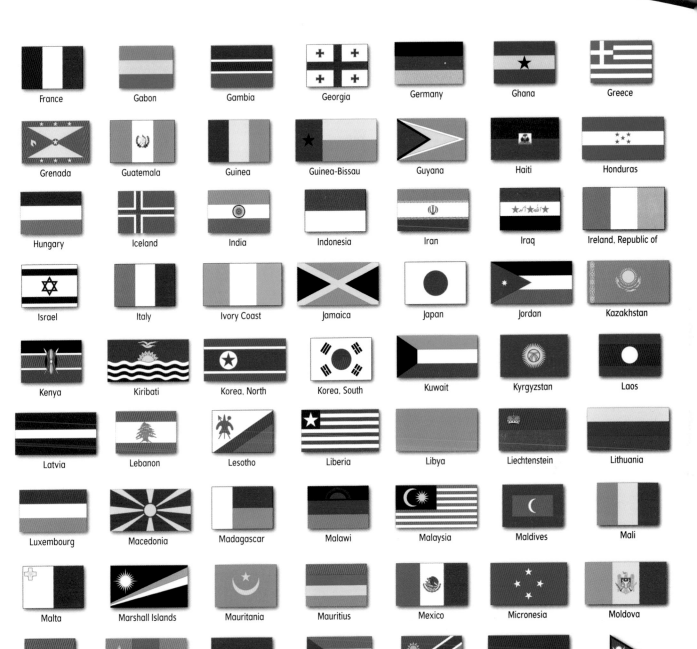

France

Gabon

Gambia

Georgia

Germany

Ghana

Greece

Grenada

Guatemala

Guinea

Guinea-Bissau

Guyana

Haiti

Honduras

Hungary

Iceland

India

Indonesia

Iran

Iraq

Ireland, Republic of

Israel

Italy

Ivory Coast

Jamaica

Japan

Jordan

Kazakhstan

Kenya

Kiribati

Korea, North

Korea, South

Kuwait

Kyrgyzstan

Laos

Latvia

Lebanon

Lesotho

Liberia

Libya

Liechtenstein

Lithuania

Luxembourg

Macedonia

Madagascar

Malawi

Malaysia

Maldives

Mali

Malta

Marshall Islands

Mauritania

Mauritius

Mexico

Micronesia

Moldova

Monaco

Mongolia

Morocco

Mozambique

Namibia

Nauru

Nepal

 Netherlands
 New Zealand
 Nicaragua
 Niger
 Nigeria
 Norway
 Oman

 Pakistan
 Palau
 Panama
 Papau New Guinea
 Paraguay
 Peru
 Philippines

 Poland
 Portugal
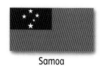 Qatar
 Romania
 Russian Federation
 Rwanda
 St Kitts-Nevis

 St Lucia
 St Vincent & the Grenadines
 Samoa
 San Marino
 São Tomé and Príncipe
 Saudi Arabia
 Senegal

 Serbia & Montenegro
 Seychelles
 Sierra Leone
 Singapore
 Slovakia
 Slovenia
 Solomon Islands

 Somalia
 South Africa
 Spain
 Sri Lanka
 Sudan
 Suriname
 Swaziland

 Sweden
 Switzerland
 Syria
 Tajikistan
 Tanzania
 Thailand
 Togo

 Tonga
 Trinidad and Tobago
 Tunisia
 Turkey
 Turkmenistan
 Tuvalu
 Uganda

 Ukraine
United Arab Emirates (UAE)
United Kingdom
United States of America
Uruguay
Uzbekistan
Vanuatu

Vatican City
 Venezuela
 Vietnam
 Yemen
 Zambia
 Zimbabwe

US State Flags

 Alabama
 Alaska
 Arizona
 Arkansas
 California
 Colorado
 Connecticut
 Delaware

 District of Columbia*
 Florida
 Georgia
 Hawaii
 Idaho
 Illinois
 Indiana
 Iowa

 Kansas
 Kentucky
 Louisiana
 Maine
 Maryland
 Massachusetts
 Michigan
 Minnesota

 Mississippi
 Missouri
 Montana
 Nebraska
 Nevada
 New Hampshire
 New Jersey
 New Mexico

 New York
 North Carolina
 North Dakota
 Ohio
 Oklahoma
 Oregon
 Pennsylvania
 Rhode Island

 South Carolina
 South Dakota
 Tennessee
 Texas
 Utah
 Vermont
 Viriginia
 Washington

 West Virginia
 Wisconsin
 Wyoming

*District of Columbia is a federal district, not a state

Canada
Province/Territory Flags

 Alberta
British Columbia
Manitoba
New Brunswick
Newfoundland and Labrador

Northwest Territories
Nova Scotia
Nunavut
Ontario
Prince Edward Island
 Quebec
 Saskatchewan
 Yukon

HISTORY

The Fertile Crescent

About 10,000 years ago people living across a wide area of the Middle East began to live as farmers. They planted seeds that grew into crops and kept domestic animals to provide milk and meat. The lands where these people lived included Egypt, the valley of the Tigris and Euphrates rivers, and the Indus Valley. This area is known as the Fertile Crescent. It was here that the first towns and cities were built by early farmers.

○ The first great civilization was that of the Sumerians, who farmed irrigated land by the Euphrates c.5000 BC and lived in mud-brick houses.

○ About 3000 BC, a civilization developed from small farming communities in the Indus valley in Pakistan.

○ Indus cities were carefully planned, with straight streets, bath houses, and big granaries (grain stores).

○ By 1750 BC, the Indus civilization had declined. It finally vanished with the arrival of the Aryans c.1500 BC.

○ Only when Hammurabi became king in 1792 BC did Babylon become a powerful city. In his 42-year reign, Hammurabi built a huge empire.

○ Babylon was surrounded by walls 85 ft thick—faced with blue bricks, decorated with dragons, lions, and bulls.

▼ *Wealthy Assyrians strove to outdo each other with elaborate clothing and luxurious houses.*

Family shrine

Grand reception area where the official did his business for the pharaoh

Well

Central hall where the officials entertained friends

Bedrooms

Kitchen

Wine cellar

Servants' quarters

Stables

Grain stores

◄ *The prestigious officials of the pharaohs were building great houses like this one around 1200 BC.*

Find out more
Farming p. 333

◀ *Darius the Great ruled Persia from 521 until 486 BC.*

○ Egyptians believed that everyone was thought to have three souls: the ka, ba, and akh. For these to flourish, the body must survive intact, so the ancient Egyptians tried to preserve their dead bodies as well as they could.

River Nile

The Nile is the longest river in Africa, and its waters made farming possible for the people of hot, dry Egypt. Every year the Nile floods, as snow melts in mountains to the south raising the level of the water. As it floods, the river spreads fertile mud, which enables farmers to grow plentiful crops. The Egyptians sailed along the Nile to reach other farms and towns.

○ The grandest gate was the Ishtar Gate, which opened on to a paved avenue called the Processional Street.

○ The Assyrians were ruthless warriors who fought with bows, iron swords, spears, and chariots. They built up an empire covering all of Mesopotamia and Egypt by about the year 1100 BC. It was destroyed by the Persians in 612 BC.

Amazing

In 521 BC several men claimed the throne of Persia. Instead of fighting each other, the men decided that whoever's horse neighed first would be king. Darius won.

○ The Persian Empire reached its greatest extent around 490 BC under Darius I, who called himself Shahanshah ("King of kings").

Gilgamesh

The *Epic of Gilgamesh* was composed around 2000 BC. It tells the tale of Gilgamesh (right), a powerful and oppressive king in ancient Sumeria. When his people pray for help, the gods create Enkidu, who meets Gilgamesh in battle. But the two become friends and share many adventures. The poem includes an account of a great flood, which has been likened to the Bible story of Noah.

○ Pharaohs were the kings of ancient Egypt. They were also High Priest, head judge, and commander of the army.

○ There were 31 dynasties (families) of pharaohs, beginning with Menes around 3100 BC and ending in 323 BC.

▶ *Pharaohs were the rulers of ancient Egypt. The word "pharaoh" means great house. Egyptians thought of the pharaoh as both the god Horus and the son of the sun god Re. When he died he was transformed into the god Osiris, father of Horus. Since he was a god, anyone approaching him had to crawl. Here the pharaoh is holding the symbols of his rule, the hook and flail. Workers used these tools to separate grain from the stalks.*

▼ *The people of Mohenjo-Daro used ox-drawn carts. However, these would have been very slow and they probably relied on the river as their main source of transportation.*

Ancient Greece

Greek civilzation grew out of the earlier cultures of Minoan Cretians and the Myceneans—a race of people who lived in what became Greece. By about 800 BC, the ideas of Greek scholars started to spread throughout the ancient world. Ancient Greece was divided into small, self-governing city-states—the most powerful of which were Athens and Sparta.

○ From 1600 to 1100 BC, Greece was dominated by warrior people called the Mycenaeans. Mycenaeans lived in small kingdoms, each with a fortified city.

○ The early Greeks held four major athletic events. These were the Olympic, Pythian, Isthmian, and Nemean Games.

○ Ancient Greece was not a single country, but a collection of independent cities or city-states, called polis (plural poleis). There were hundreds of poleis. The largest were Athens and Sparta.

○ The great thinkers of Greece were called philosophers. The three greatest were Socrates, Plato, and Aristotle.

○ Greek mathematicians such as Euclid, Appolonius, Pythagoras, and Archimedes worked out the basic rules of math that are still used today.

○ In ancient Greece, there were thousands of sculptors, architects, painters, dramatists, and poets.

The Greek epic poems Iliad *and* Odyssey *are the principle sources for the story of the Trojan War. It is thought that they were composed in the second half of the 8th century BC, by the Greek poet Homer. During the war the Greeks trick the Trojans using a gigantic wooden horse.*

The Venus de Milo *was found on the Aegean island of Milos in* AD 1820. *It was carved in Greek Antioch (now in Turkey) c.150 BC and shows the goddess of love, Aphrodite.*

Famous people and their horses

Alexander the Great is known to have had a favorite horse, Bucephalus, but many other rulers had trusty steeds, too.

Alexander the Great	*Bucephalus*
Ulysses S Grant	*Cincinnati*
Duke of Wellington	*Copenhagen*
Richard the Lionheart	*Fauvel*
Caligula	*Incitatus*
Buffalo Bill	*Isham*
Buddha	*Kanthaka*
Stonewall Jackson	*Little Sorrel*
George Washington	*Magnolia*
Napoleon Bonaparte	*Marengo*
Robert E Lee	*Traveler*
General George Custer	*Vic*
Richard III	*White Surrey*

Find out more

Napoleon p. 355

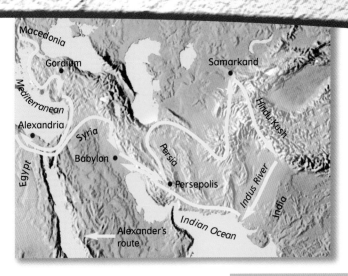

▲ **Alexander the Great was a young Macedonian king who united the Greek city-states, then led them on a vast invasion that created an empire that stretched from Greece to India.**

❍ A Tragedy is a grand drama doomed to end unhappily for the hero.

❍ Greek gods included Apollo the god of light, Demeter the goddess of crops, and Artemis the goddess of the Moon.

Amazing

The city of Sparta had the finest army in ancient Greece. The Spartans believed they could defeat any army that outnumbered them by four to one—and they usually did.

30 words derived from the Greek language

Alphabet	Asteroid	Amnesia
Bicycle	Category	Chaos
Dinosaur	Dynasty	Echo
Economy	Gorilla	Gymnasium
Harmony	Hymn	Hysteria
Idea	Mania	Mechanic
Monarchy	Nemesis	Ocean
Orgy	Panic	Parallel
Problem	Rhinoceros	Sarcasm
Statistic	Telephone	Zodiac

Grand statue

The Parthenon was the most splendid temple in Athens, which was the leading city-state in ancient Greece. During the 400s BC, the Athenians built temples and shrines to the gods on a hill called the Acropolis. The Parthenon was more than 230 ft long and about 60 ft high, and was built to house a magnificent 40 ft-tall statue of Athene, goddess of wisdom and guardian of Athens, made of gold and ivory.

Early money

Coins were first used by the Lydians (who lived in what is now Turkey) some time before 600 BC. The Greeks quickly adopted the use of coins for shopping and business. This one shows the head of Alexander.

▲ **Formal drama was developed in ancient Greece in the 5th and 6th centuries BC. Huge audiences watched plays in open-air arenas.**

The Seven Wonders of the World

The Tomb of King Mausolus —at Halicarnassus

The Statue of Zeus —at Olympia

The Pyramids at Giza—in Egypt

The Hanging Gardens of Babylon

The Colossus —at Rhodes

The Temple of Artemis —at Ephesus

The Lighthouse— at Alexandria

The Roman Empire

The Roman Empire was the greatest the world had ever seen at that time. By the first century AD, Roman rule extended over much of Europe, North Africa, and the Near East. The Romans took their way of life and government wherever they went. They used their skills of developing central heating and running water and introduced their food and language (Latin) to every country they conquered.

○ According to legend, Rome was founded in 753 BC by the twin boys Romulus and Remus, who were said to have been brought up by a wolf. By 550 BC, Rome was a large city that was ruled by Etruscan kings. In 509 BC, the Roman people drove out the kings and formed themselves into an independent republic.

○ In the 400s and 300s BC, Rome extended its power all over Italy, by both brute force and alliances. By 130 BC, Rome had built a mighty empire stretching from Spain to Turkey, and along the North African coast.

A *Roman gladiators trained to fight in the arena. Roman rulers staged lavish and often bloodthirsty entertainments to keep the people amused. Gladiators fought one another or wild animals. There were various types of gladiator—the netman wore hardly any armor, and his weapons were a net and a trident (three-pointed spear).*

○ Two popular generals, Pompey and Julius Caesar, used their armies to take over Rome and suspend the democratic, but corrupt, government of the Republic. Once in power, Caesar restored order and passed laws to reduce people's debts. Caesar was made dictator and ruled Rome without the Senate.

○ In 44 BC, a man called Brutus killed Caesar to restore the government of the Republic— but Caesar's place was taken by another general, Octavian, Caesar's adopted son. By 27 BC, Octavian was so powerful that he is recognized as the first Roman emperor. He took the name Augustus, which means "Exalted One."

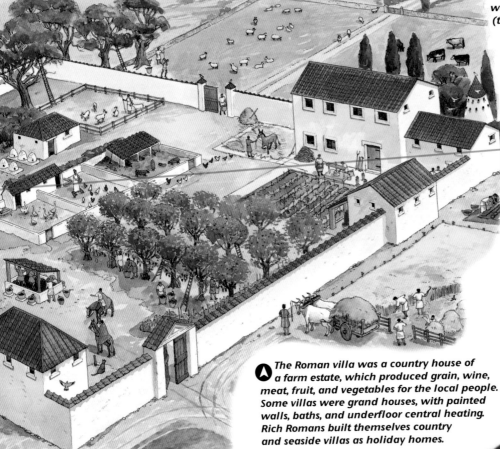

A *The Roman villa was a country house of a farm estate, which produced grain, wine, meat, fruit, and vegetables for the local people. Some villas were grand houses, with painted walls, baths, and underfloor central heating. Rich Romans built themselves country and seaside villas as holiday homes.*

Find out more

Aphrodite p. 316

O The bath houses (thermae) were places where people came to sit around and dip into hot and cold baths in magnificent surroundings.

▲ Roman towns were the biggest and most sophisticated the world had seen. There were blocks of flats, called Insulae, as well as luxurious houses.

O After the death of Emperor Marcus Aurelius, in AD 180, Rome was plagued by political struggles. The Praetorian Guard (the emperor's personal soldiers) chose or deposed emperors at will, and there were 60 emperors between AD 235 and 284 alone. The Empire was beset by famine, plague, and invasion.

Vast Empire

At its greatest, the Roman Empire ran from Britain in the west, as far as Africa in the south, and Babylon in the east. This map shows the Roman Empire in brown and the roads that they built in black.

Amazing

In AD 100 over a million people lived in Rome, the largest city on Earth. But plagues and wars meant that by AD 650 there were only 10,000 people left in the city.

Fearsome army

The Roman army was well trained and better disciplined than the enemies it faced. The best Roman units were the legions of about 5,000 foot soldiers, who went into battle throwing spears and then rushed in behind their shields using short, stabbing swords. Roman soldiers were trained to march all day, build roads and forts, and swim rivers. Roman officers were usually politicians. The testudo formation (right) proved itself highly effective for Roman foot soldiers.

O Roman roads were built by the army to make sure that troops on foot and supplies in wagons could be moved quickly around the Empire. Many Roman roads can still be seen today.

O In AD 410, Visigoths led by Alaric invaded Italy and sacked (burned and looted) Rome. In AD 455, Vandals sacked Rome again. In AD 476, the Western empire finally collapsed.

Roman and Greek gods

God of	Greek	Roman	Goddess of	Greek	Roman
Agriculture	Cronus	Saturn	Agriculture	Demeter	Ceres
The dead	Thanatos	Mors	The dawn	Eos	Aurora
Fire	Hephaestus	Vulcan	Flowers	Hestia	Flora
Love	Eros	Cupid	Health	Hygeia	Salus
The sea	Poseidon	Neptune	Hunting	Artemis	Diana
Sleep	Hypnos	Somnus	Love	Aphrodite	Venus
The Sun	Helios	Sol	The Moon	Selene	Luna
War	Ares	Mars	Motherhood	Rhea	Ops
Wine	Dionysus	Bacchus	Peace	Irene	Pax
The woods	Pan	Silvanus	Victory	Nike	Victoria
Messenger of the gods	Hermes	Mercury	Wisdom	Athene	Minerva
King of the gods	Zeus	Jupiter	Queen of the gods	Hera	Juno

China and Japan

*T**he first farming communities in China were formed about 7000 BC. The Chinese civilization developed separately from other early civilizations and had a quite different culture. By about 2000 BC all the Chinese were living under the control of a single emperor. Chinese technology and culture spread gradually to nearby lands. Around 300 BC, the Japanese began to farm their land and adopted skills from the Chinese.***

○ Early Chinese emperors are known of only by legend. Huang-Ti, the Yellow Emperor, was said to have become emperor in 2697 BC.

○ The Shangs were the first definitely known dynasty of emperors. They came to power in 1750 BC.

○ In 246 BC, Qin emperor Zheng expanded the empire and called himself Shi Huangdi, First Emperor. He had the 2,486 mi long Great Wall built to protect his empire from nomads from the north.

○ In 210 BC, the small Han kingdom was ruled over by Liu Bang. Liu Bang was a poor villager who had come to power as the Qin Empire broke down. In 202 BC, Liu Bang proclaimed himself to be the first Han emperor and took the name Gaozu.

○ Han cities were huge, crowded, and beautiful, and craftsmen made many exquisite things from wood, paint, and silk. Sadly, many of these lovely objects were destroyed when Han rule ended.

○ By AD 200, the Han emperors were weakened by their ambitious wives and eunuchs (guardians). Rebellions by a group called the Yellow Turbans, combined with attacks by warriors from the north, brought the empire down.

The great tomb of the Terracotta Army (or Warriors) is located near Xi'an, central China. In their underground chambers, the life-size figures are arranged in precise military formation.

Amazing

Shi Huangdi was buried with an army of 6,000 life-size clay soldiers, called the Terracotta Army when found in 1974. Certain parts of the tomb are said to be booby trapped and have not been opened.

Shinto priests believe that all things that inspire awe—from twisted trees to dead warriors—have kami (spirits).

Find out more

Clocks p. 350

Early clocks

Mechanical clocks were invented by the Chinese in AD 723–600 years earlier than Europe. This is Su Sung's "Cosmic Engine," an amazing 33 ft high clock built at Khaifeng in AD 1090.

◀ *Confucius believed that court officials should not plot for power but instead study music, poetry, and the history of their ancestors.*

○ Around 660 BC, Jimmu Tenno, the legendary first emperor of Japan, established power in Yamato.

○ From AD 200–645, the Yamato dynasty dominated Japan. Right up to today, Japanese emperors claim to be descended from the Yamato. The Yamato, in turn, claimed to be descended from the Shinto sun—goddess, Amaterasu.

○ Shotoku Taishi (AD 574–622) was a young regent for old Empress Suiko. He gave Japan organized, Chinese-style government and promoted both Buddhism and Confucianism.

Great Wall of China

Although today's brick and stone wall dates from the AD 1400s, the Great Wall of China was first built of earth bricks in 214 BC, under Shi Huangdi.

○ Shinto or "way of the gods" has been Japan's main religion since prehistoric times. It gained its name during the 6th century AD, to distinguish it from Buddhism and Confucianism.

▼ *The Shang emperors were warriors. Their soldiers fought in padded bamboo armor.*

The wisdom of Confucious

Never contract friendship with a man that is not better than thyself

The strength of a nation derives from the integrity of the home

Everything has beauty, but not everyone sees it

Silence is a friend who will never betray

Never give a sword to a man who can't dance

You cannot open a book without learning something

A journey of a thousand miles begins with a single step

The cautious seldom err

When anger rises, think of the consequences

It is better to light one small candle than to curse the darkness

If we don't know life, how can we know death?

To lead uninstructed people to war is to throw them away

When prosperity comes, do not use all of it

Real knowledge is to know the extent of one's ignorance

To know what is right and not to do it is the worst cowardice

Ignorance is the night of the mind, but a night without moon or star

The father who does not teach his son his duties is equally guilty with the son who neglects them

An oppressive government is more to be feared than a tiger

To see and listen to the wicked is already the beginning of wickedness

A man who has committed a mistake and does not correct it, is making another mistake

The Barbarians

After about AD 350 the ancient civilizations began to suffer problems caused by crop failure, disease, and economic decline. Uncivilized tribes attacked the weakening empires, looking for easy plunder and wealth. The old empires collapsed in the face of the attacks from these barbarians who could neither read nor write. Civilization was close to collapse as warfare spread rapidly and the population of the world declined suddenly.

❍ The Goths were German peoples divided into Ostrogoths in the east, near the Black Sea, and Visigoths on the Danube. It was the Visigoths who, under their king Alaric, took Rome in AD 476.

❍ The Vandals were a German tribe who took over Spain and North Africa in about AD 380. They gave us the word "vandal" for destructive troublemakers.

❍ The Huns were nomadic Mongols from eastern Asia who arrived in Europe AD c.370, driving everyone before them, until they were finally defeated in AD 455. The most feared Hun was their king, Attila.

Amazing

The barbarian wars caused massive bloodshed, starvation, and hardship. It is thought the population of the former Roman Empire may have fallen by 50 percent.

❍ In AD 476, Constantinople (now Istanbul in Turkey) became the capital of the Eastern Roman, or Byzantine, Empire. It was the center of Western civilization for a thousand years.

❍ The Byzantine Empire was under constant attack from tribes of barbarians, but it held out behind its massive defensive walls.

❍ When barbarians attacked, generals from Italy were sent to reorganize local defences. In some areas, power fell into the hands of local men like the British king, Vortigern (AD 425–50).

❍ Vortigern invited Anglo-Saxon warriors from Germany to help him against the invading Picts. But these men soon rebelled and defeated Vortigern. Thousands more Anglo-Saxons came to settle in Britain, becoming the English.

❍ In 318 the Chinese emperor Liu Yuën died. While his heirs fought for power, barbarians poured into China. All the cities north of the Yangtse River were destroyed. Not until 507 were the barbarian invasions halted in China.

▼ *At its height, Constantinople was graced by some of the ancient world's most magnificent buildings. This picture shows the tranquil palace quarter. The rest of the city was noisy and crowded.*

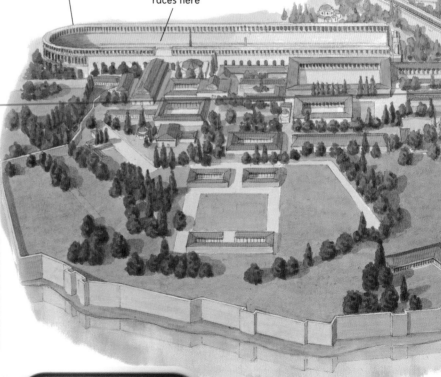

The Hippodrome was based on the Circus Maximus in Rome

60,000 spectators watched chariot races here

Find out more

Roman Empire p. 318

○ In 457 the Ye Ta, or Hephtha, barbarians invaded Persia. They massacred thousands of people and captured the cities of Merv and Herat.

○ In 475 the warrior Mehiragula led a group of tribes into India. For 50 years these tribes looted India. Then they fell back over the mountains to the north.

○ By about 550 the main barbarian invasions had come to an end. Apart from China, most of the old empires had been swept away. New kingdoms and nations had come into existence.

▶ *Anglo-Saxon villages were made from materials such as wood, thatch, and wattle (woven branches).*

The Hagia Sophia, now a museum, is the world's oldest Christian cathedral

Gothic leader

Alaric was the great Gothic leader who took Rome in 410. He looted the city but spared the churches. Alaric planned to settle in Africa, but a storm forced him to stop at Cozenza in southern Italy, where he died.

Justinian I

Justinian I was the greatest Byzantine emperor, although his general's secretary, Procopius, described him as "a demon incarnate." He ruled with his beautiful former actress wife, Theodora. Justinian relied on her for support and advice, and it was she who changed laws to improve the lives of women and the poor.

▲ *In 1939, the burial ship of the overlord Raedwald (died 625) was discovered at Sutton Hoo in East Anglia. This helmet is one of the treasures it held.*

New States

After about AD 550 the barbarian tribes stopped moving constantly in search of plunder and loot. They settled down to live as farmers and traders. Slowly the population began to grow once again as migrations of entire peoples came to an end. However, the old empires and civilizations had been destroyed or badly damaged. New kingdoms and states emerged from the chaos, and new ways of life were established.

○ Chinese emperor Yang Di was murdered by one of his 3,000 mistresses in AD 618. His minister Li Yuan seized power to found the Tang dynasty. Under the Tang trade grew, China became rich and the arts and sciences flourished.

○ By AD 800, the Tang dynasty was breaking up. Order was restored in AD 960, when the Song family began to rule from the city of Kaifeng. The Song lasted until AD 1276, when the Mongol Kublai Khan conquered China.

○ The Muslim religion began when the prophet Mohammed left Mecca in AD 622. The Muslim Arabs conquered Iraq (AD 637), Syria (640), Egypt (641), and Persia (650). By AD 661, their empire stretched from Tunisia to India. Its capital was at Damascus.

○ The Fujiwaras were the family who dominated Japan for five centuries from the 7th century AD. In 858, they married into the Imperial family. Fujiwara power peaked with Michinaga (966–1028).

○ The Angles, Saxons, and Jutes were peoples from Denmark and Germany who invaded Britain and settled there between AD 450 and 600. Each tribe had its own kingdom, yet by 600 most of these people thought of themselves as English.

▶ The Vikings' wooden ships, called longships, are masterpieces of boat-building—light and flat-bottomed enough to sail up shallow rivers, yet seaworthy in the open ocean.

Ships were driven along by a large, square sail made of woolen cloth

The ships often had a high prow, sometimes carved with a dragon's head

Shields were strapped in rows down each side

When the wind was still, they relied on banks of rowers each side

◀ This enamel and gold jewel was found near Athelney. It is inscribed with the words "Aelfred me ech eh t gewyrcan"—Old English for "Alfred ordered me to be made."

Amazing

The Vikings were the first seamen able to navigate out of sight of land. They used the stars and a primitive type of compass to find their way across the open ocean.

First New Zealanders

No human set foot on New Zealand before around 2,000 years ago. The first settlers in New Zealand were Polynesians known as Maori. The Maori came to New Zealand by canoe, from islands in the Pacific. The Maoris lived mostly near the coast.

Find out more
New Zealand p. 345

Not all Vikings were pirates. At home, they were farmers and fishermen, merchants, and craftworkers. Many went with the raiders and settled in the north of France, in northern England and in Dublin.

The ships were steered with a large paddle at the rear

○ The Vikings were from Norway, Sweden, and Denmark. Between AD 800 and 1100, they raided the coasts of northwest Europe in their longships, searching for plunder to carry away.

○ In AD 563, what is now Scotland was four kingdoms: the Scots in the west; the Picts in the north; the Britons in the southwest; and English in the east.

Viking voyages

This map shows some of the amazing voyages made by the Vikings, and their dates, with their Viking names.

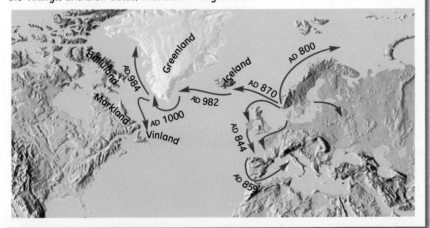

Alfred the Great (AD 849–899) was the greatest of the English kings. He defeated the Vikings by building forts, reorganizing the army and building England's first navy.

Viking weaponry included a spear, knife, and protective shield. Vikings held their weapons sacred.

Feudal Europe

By about AD **800** most of Europe was dominated by a new social system: feudalism. Land was owned by kings, who hired it out to nobles and knights in return for those men serving in the army or other government positions. The nobles hired the land out to peasants who farmed it. The peasants gave produce and some of their labor to the nobles. Each person in society had rights and duties that they owed to other people. Only a few, such as merchants or priests, lived outside the system.

○ The Magyars were a people who lived near Russia's river Don. In 889 AD, led by the legendary king Arpad, the Magyars moved into Hungary.

○ For 100 years, much of England was lost to the Vikings, but Alfred the Great's son Edward and his daughter Aethelflaed won back England by 918.

○ In the 900s and 1000s, many people fought to be king in Scotland, which was gradually becoming united as one country. King Duncan I was killed by his general, Macbeth. Macbeth was later killed by Malcolm III.

Kingdom of Denmark
Kingdom of England
Prussians
German Empire
Kingdom of Poland
Russia
Holy Roman Empire
Kingdom of Bohemia
Kingdom of France
Kingdom of Burgandy
Kingdom of Hungary
Kingdom of Italy
Kingdom of Aragon
Corsica
Papal States
Kingdom of Serbia
Kingdom of Bulgaria
Sardinia
Kingdom of the Two Sicilies
Epirus

A *In 1250 the Holy Roman Empire extended from the North to the Mediterranean Sea (highlighted in brown). The Papal states (yellow), separated the Kingdom of the Two Sicilies, which also belonged to the Emperor.*

Amazing

Knights had special designs, called coats of arms, painted on their shields and jackets so that they could recognize friend from foe in battle. Each knight had a different design.

Magna Carta

England's King John signed Magna Carta (Great Charter)—a list of rights requested by barons who felt that John was ruling badly. In 1215, they forced the king to put his seal (sign) to the Charter and promise to obey the rules within. Ever since, Magna Carta has been seen as a landmark in the development of modern government.

Find out more
Armor p. 319

> Knights practised fighting at special events called tournaments. Thousands of people watched famous knights.

○ Duke William of Normandy invaded England in 1066, believing that King Edward had promised him the throne. The English chose Harold Godwinson to be king, but William killed Harold at the Battle of Hastings.

○ The Holy Roman Empire lasted until 1806. It began in AD 800 when Pope Leo III gave King Charlemagne of the Franks, the title of the old Roman Empire.

○ The Hundred Years' War was fought between France and England, from 1337–1453. The war was caused by disputes over land in France.

Suit of armor

Ailettes	Small square shields protecting the shoulders
Aventail	Chainmail bib protecting the neck
Bascinet	Type of helmet
Beaver	Cup-shaped piece protecting the chin
Besagew	Small round plate protecting the armpits
Cervellaire	Skull cap
Chamfron	Metal plate protecting the head of a horse
Colf	Hooded chainmail protecting the head
Couter	Rounded cup protecting the elbow
Cuirass	The part of the armor that comprises the breastplate and backplate
Gauntlet	Large glove
Gorget	Metal plate protecting the neck
Grille	Metal visor protecting the face
Pauldron	Metal plate protecting the shoulders
Poleyn	Cup-shaped piece protecting the knee
Rerebrace	Metal plates protecting the upper arms
Sabaton	Armor for the feet
Surcoat	Cloth covering worn outside a suit of armor
Tasset	Metal plate protecting the hips
Vambrace	Rounded iron armor protecting the lower arms

Medieval monasteries

Monasteries played a key role in medieval life in Europe, reaching a peak in the 1200s. Most monasteries had a church called an abbey, some of which are among the greatest medieval buildings. Like most English monasteries, the great 12th-century Cistercian monastery at Tintern in Wales (seen here) was destroyed by Henry VIII.

○ The English won most battles during the Hundred Years War, but the French won the war because they had three times the resources.

○ The Crusades were wars fought for the control of Jerusalem. When the Turks prevented Christian pilgrims visiting Jerusalem, the Pope called the First Crusade in 1096. The Crusaders gained control of the Holy Land and kept it for about 200 years.

○ When Pope Gregory XI died in 1378, there was a Great Schism (split) in the Church. In 1417, the Great Schism was ended but the dispute had weakened the Church's authority fatally.

> The greatest knight of the war was Edward the Black Prince (1330–1376), hero of the Battles of Crécy, Poitiers, and Navarette.

Indian Empires

*T*he great subcontinent of India was almost cut off from other areas by the high Himalaya Mountains. The peoples of India developed their own cultures and ways of life. Throughout Indian history, powerful rulers have tried to unite the area into a single empire. Some of these empires were larger or lasted longer than others, but always the tendency for different areas to break away caused the collapse of even the strongest empire.

○ In 321 BC, the first great Indian empire was created by Chandragupta Maurya (c.325–297 BC). Its capital was Pataliputra on the Ganges.

○ The Mauryan Empire at its peak included most of modern Pakistan, Bangladesh and India—except for the very southern tip.

○ The most famous of the Mauryan emperors was Chandragupta's grandson, Asoka (c.265–238 BC).

○ Asoka's men dug wells and built reservoirs all over India to help the poor. They also provided comfortable rest-houses and planted shady banyan trees for travelers along the new roads.

○ The Hindu and Buddhist religions both began to develop and flourish during the great Gupta period.

○ Hindu mathematicians developed the decimal system (counting in tens) that we still use today.

○ Gupta power collapsed by about AD 500 under repeated attacks by Hun people from the north.

○ Akbar (1556–1605) was the greatest of the Mogul emperors—conquering most of India and setting up a highly efficient system of government.

○ Aurangzeb (1618–1707) was the last great Mogul ruler. He inspired rebellion by raising taxes and insisting on a strict Muslim code.

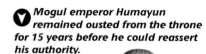

Mogul emperor Humayun remained ousted from the throne for 15 years before he could reassert his authority.

The first Mogul emperor was Babur (1483–1530), who invaded India on swift horses that completely outran the Indians' slower elephants. Babar founded the Mogul dynasty that was to dominate northern India for more than 200 years.

Amazing

Prince Gautama Siddhartha left his luxurious home and beautiful wife in Nepal to lead a life of poverty. He later founded the Buddhist religion and lived to be 80 years old.

Find out more

Empires p. 347

Stupas

During Asoka's reign, stupas—domed shrines said to contain relics of the Buddha—were built all over India.

▲ *The Moguls, or Mughals, were a family who ruled most of northern India from 1526–1748. The Mogul Empire reached its peak under Shah Jahan (1592–1666), when many magnificent, luxurious buildings were built—most notably the Taj Mahal, built as a tomb for his favorite wife. According to legend, Shah Jahan cut off the hands of the craftsmen involved in the construction of the Taj Mahal so that they could not make such a monument again.*

The Guptas

The Guptas were a family of rulers who reigned in northern India from AD 320–c.500. This was one of India's golden ages, with writing, sculpture, and other arts at their peak. The Hindu and Buddhist sculpture and painting of the Gupta period has been the model for Indian art down the centuries.

▲ *Buddhist shrine in Thailand, Asia. The various statues of the Buddha, or the enlightened one, as Prince Gautama Siddhartha became known, each gives a different gesture and stands or sits in a special way to emphasize one of the key teachings of the Buddhist religion.*

Medieval Asia

For six centuries from AD 618 China was unified, rich, and powerful under first the Tang Dynasty, then the Song dynasty. Chinese culture dominated neighboring peoples, such as the Thais, Tibetans, and Japanese and, at times, the Chinese emperor claimed to rule these areas as well as China itself. Then, in 1206, the barbarian tribes of Central Asia were united under the Mongol leader Genghis Khan. Within a few years the Mongols had devastated Asia, conquering vast areas and slaughtering millions of people.

○ In earlier times, only aristocrats tended to hold key posts in government, but under the Song, anyone could enter for the civil service exams. Competition to do well in the exams was intense, and the main yearly exams became major events in the calendar.

○ Under the Song, the Chinese population soared, trade prospered and all kinds of advances were made in science and technology—from the invention of gunpowder and the sailors' compass to paper and printing. Technologically, China was about 500 years ahead of Europe.

○ By 1275, Hangzhou was the world's largest city, with a population of a million. Its warm climate encouraged a lively, leisurely lifestyle. The city was full of luxury shops, bars, restaurants, tea-houses, and clubs where girls sang.

Chinese porcelain and pottery is famous for its beauty and delicacy, and the perfection of the covering glaze. It reached a peak in the Ming era (1368–1644).

Amazing

When Genghis Khan conquered northern China he turned the farmland into pasture for his horses. Almost 20 million Chinese were killed before he changed his mind.

Mongol horsemen swept into Russia, crushing resistance and conquering a huge area that extended almost as far north as the Arctic Ocean.

Find out more
Mongol horsemen p. 347

Genghis Khan

Of all the conquerors in history, few were more feared than 13th-century Mongol leader Genghis Khan, whose name means "lord of all."

❍ Often, people went out to stroll in the gardens by the West Lake or lazed over long meals on the lake's numerous floating restaurants. On the four islands in the lake there were gardens, statues, and temples.

❍ Genghis Khan's horsemen conquered a vast empire stretching across Asia from China as far west as the Danube River in Europe. He destroyed cities and massacred thousands, yet under his rule trade prospered and all beliefs were tolerated.

Samurai

Japan became dominated by samurai. The samurai warriors lived to fight and trained in fighting skills to an extraordinary degree. Bushido, the moral code that Samurai adopted, placed honor above life, so Samurai often preferred to kill themselves rather than surrender.

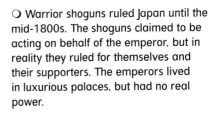

❍ Genghis's horse archers could kill at 60 ft while riding at full gallop. They once rode 273 mi in just three days.

❍ After Genghis Khan died, his son Ogodai ravaged Armenia, Hungary, and Poland.

❍ Genghis Khan's grandson—Kublai Khan—conquered the rest of China in 1265 and made himself the first of a line of Mongol emperors of China called Yuans. The Yuans lasted until 1368. Kublai Khan created a grand new capital called Ta-tu ("the Great Capital")—now Beijing. Kublai Khan adopted Chinese ways of government and ruled with such efficiency that China became very rich.

❍ In 1185, the Japanese nobleman Minamoto Yoritomo crushed the rival Taira clan and made himself ruler of Japan as sei-i-dai-shogun which means "barbarian-conquering great general."

❍ Warrior shoguns ruled Japan until the mid-1800s. The shoguns claimed to be acting on behalf of the emperor, but in reality they ruled for themselves and their supporters. The emperors lived in luxurious palaces, but had no real power.

▼ *When the Mongol Khans seized China from the Song, they made a new capital in the north at Beijing. At its center lies a walled area containing the emperor's palaces. It is called the Forbidden City because only the emperor and his servants could enter it.*

Mongol feats

Genghis Khan led an army of 250,000 men and more than one million horses.

Heavy catapults for sieges were carried in sections on ox carts and put together.

Mongol soldiers lived on a diet of smoked sheepmeat and dried milk.

Soldiers were armed with bows, swords, axes, and lances (long spears) with hooks for unseating enemy riders.

The Mongol Empire was the largest continuous land empire of all time.

Philosophers would travel from far away to talk to Genghis Khan about religion.

The Americas

People first reached North America, crossing a land bridge from Asia and traveling on foot and by boat, 15,000–20,000 years ago. They gradually spread across the continent. The great civilizations of the Americas were in Central America (around Mexico) and in South America (in Peru), where people built large cities. Much of this culture was destroyed by European invaders in the 1500s.

○ People began farming in Central America about 9,000 years ago, almost as long ago as in the Middle East.

○ Between 1200 and 400 BC, the Olmec culture developed in western Mexico. The Olmecs had a counting system and calendar, but no writing system, so little is known about them.

○ The Maya built cities such as Tikal (Guatemala). Each Mayan city had a tall pyramid-shaped temple in the center, with open courts around it. The Maya studied the Moon, Sun, and stars and had a number system based on 20.

○ Mayans traded far and wide. After about 1200, Mayan civilization broke up and the cities were abandoned.

○ Aztecs and other peoples of Central America sacrificed human victims in order to seek the favor of their gods. The Aztec people worshiped the Sun, and believed that unless they regularly offered human victims to the Sun god, then he would abandon them and their crops would fail.

▼ *The serpent was one of 20 creatures that gave its name to a day on the Aztec farmers' calendar. The Aztecs had two calendars: one for religious ceremonies, with 260 days, and another of 365 days, like ours, but with eight months, not 12.*

Amazing

Aztec priests sacrificed humans by cutting out their hearts with a stone knife. They aimed to lift the heart up to the sun god while it was still beating.

Find out more

Columbus p. 337

▶ *From AD 100 to 700, America's first true city developed at Teotihuacán, with vast pyramids and palaces. Teotihuacán may have been the world's biggest city in AD 300, with a population of more than 250,000 people. Spanish conquerors destroyed Teotihuacán and built a new city, now Mexico City.*

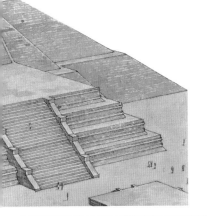

Early farmers

The first farming villages in the southwest were those of the Anasazi, Mogollon, and Hohokam peoples and dated from AD 100. They lived either in caves or in underground "pit houses" carved into the desert rock. About AD 700, the Anasazi began to build large stone villages called pueblos, which is why from this time they are also called Pueblo Indians.

○ Religion was so important to the Aztecs that they went to war to capture prisoners to be sacrificed to the gods.

○ The Aztecs did not use animals to carry loads or pull carts. They carried heavy loads on their backs or in canoes.

▶ *Aztec women made tortillas by hand and cooked them on a hot stone over a fire. The Aztecs called these cornmeal pancakes tlaxcalii.*

Olmecs

The Olmecs carved huge heads from basalt with enormous skill—apparently with only stone chisels, since they had no metal. The Olmec heads consist of huge blocks of volcanic rock that weigh up to 14 tons. The area identified as the source of the Olmec boulders lies in the Tuxtla Mountains over 100 mi away. No one knows how they were moved.

▼ *The Mayans began building large pyramids with small temples on top between 600 BC and AD 250. The Mayan pyramid at Chichén Itzá is in the Yucatán.*

Discovery of the Americas

	Explorer	Nationality	Work
1492–1504	Christopher Columbus	Italian	Working for the Spanish, Columbus discovered the Americas while trying to find a route to China. He made four voyages to the Caribbean and South America
1518–1521	Ferdinand Magellan	Portuguese	Discovered the straits through South America that still bear his name and explored much of the coast of South America
1519–1528	Hernan Cortés	Spanish	Explored most of Mexico and conquered the mighty Aztec Empire
1531–1541	Francisco Pizarro	Spanish	Explored the Andes Mountains of Peru, conquering the Inca Empire
1607–1611	Henry Hudson	English	Explored the northeast coast of North America, including Hudson Bay, which is named after him
1534–1537	Jacques Cartier	French	Sailed up St Lawrence River and founded French colonies

New Learning

From about 1350, scholars in Europe began to translate and copy books written by ancient scientists and historians. These books showed people that many of the things believed in the Medieval period were wrong. Exciting new theories and discoveries were written about and discussed. This period in European history is called the Renaissance, which means "a new birth." In the years after 1450, equipped with the new ideas of the Renaissance, Europeans had a huge cultural and scientific influence on the rest of the world.

❍ By the 1400s, kings relied on full-time soldiers paid with money. Kings turned to merchants to pay for their armies, so merchants gained power. The Italians invented banks to give loans to kings and merchants.

❍ Trading towns began to thrive across western Europe in the 1300s and 1400s —Antwerp, Flanders, Bruges, Bristol, Norwich, York, Florence, Venice, Milan, and many others. Trading towns grew powerful and some had self-rule.

Amazing

Michelangelo became the greatest artist of the Renaissance, but he started his career carving fake ancient Roman statues and selling them for cash.

❍ Artists in the Renaissance, inspired by classical examples, began to portray people and nature realistically rather than as religious symbols. In the 1400s brilliant artists like Donatello created startlingly realistic paintings and sculptures. The three greatest artists of the Renaissance were Michelangelo, Raphael, and Leonardo da Vinci.

❍ The Renaissance saw some of the world's greatest artistic and architectural masterpieces being created in Italian cities such as Florence and Padua.

❍ A spur to the Renaissance was the fall of Constantinople in 1453. This sent Greek scholars fleeing to Italy, where they set up academies in cities like Florence and Padua. Renaissance ideas later spread to northern Europe.

▲ *The ancient Italian city of Padua is full of masterpieces of Renaissance building and art, including paintings by Giotto and sculptures by Donatello.*

❍ The Medici family of Florence in Italy were one of the richest and most powerful families in Europe between 1400 and 1700. The Medici's fortunes began with the bank founded by Giovanni de' Medici in 1397. The bank was a success and the Medici family became staggeringly rich.

❍ The most famous Medici was Lorenzo (1449–1492). Under him, Florence became Europe's most spectacular city, full of great works of art and home to many artists.

◀ *This marble sculpture called David was made by Italian artist Michelangelo (1475–1564).*

Find out more

English monarchy p. 339

Renaissance warfare

Not all the new discoveries of the Renaissance were to do with arts and sciences. Warfare was revolutionized by adapting the Chinese invention of gunpowder to the new concept of the gun. From about 1460 large guns, called cannons, were used to batter down castle walls and smash apart town defenses. Soon after this, small guns were developed that could be carried into battle by individual soldiers. Warfare was never the same again.

◄ *Older artists took on apprentices in their studios so the younger generations of Renaissance artists could learn from them.*

Positions held in Henry VIII's household

Clerk of the Green Cloth
Clerk of the Poultry
Clerk of the Spicery
Falconer
Gentlemen of the Privy Chamber
Groom of the Privy Chamber
Marshall of the Hall
Master of the Children
Master of the Jewels
Minstrel
Officer of the Confectionary
Officer of the Vestry
Page of the King's Chambers
Purveyor of Ale
Purveyor of Sea Fish
Sergeant of the Bake House
Squire for the Body
Sergeant of the Larder
The King's Barber
Wardrober of the Robes
Yeoman of the Cellar
Yeoman of the Pastry

King Henry VIII

The Renaissance reached England during the reign of King Henry VIII (ruled 1509–1547). When he came to the throne Henry was handsome and athletic, spoke several languages, played the lute, and was keen on the new ideas of the Renaissance. He employed clever ministers such as Cardinal Wolsey and Thomas Cromwell. As he grew older, Henry was prone to savage tempers, ill health, and he became very fat. He married six times, divorcing two wives and having two others executed.

Age of Explorers

By about 1430, Europeans were building new types of ship that could sail through rough weather and carry enough food and drink for long voyages. Merchants were keen to find routes to rich nations such as India, China, and the Spice Islands. They hoped to become wealthy by trading with these countries.

Amazing

Many men died on voyages of discovery. The first voyage around the world set off in 1519 with five ships and 230 men. Only one ship and 18 men survived the journey.

○ Sailors were sent out to find routes across the seas. Sometimes they discovered what they were looking for, but sometimes they accidentally found completely different countries instead.

○ Many voyages were encouraged by Portugal's Prince Henry the Navigator (1394–1460), who set up a school for navigation skills at Sagres.

○ In 1488, Bartholomeu Dias sailed right round Africa into the Indian Ocean.

○ One of the greatest voyages was in 1492 when Christopher Columbus set out across the Atlantic. He hoped to reach China but found the Americas.

○ Within half a century of Columbus's voyage, the Spanish had conquered all the lands from California to Argentina.

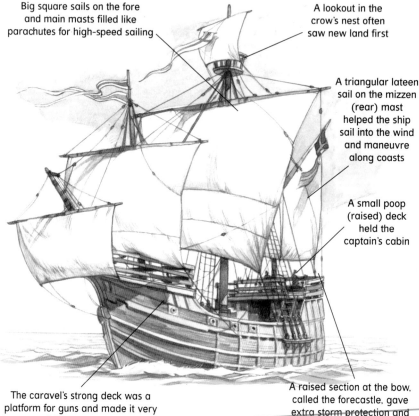

Big square sails on the fore and main masts filled like parachutes for high-speed sailing

A lookout in the crow's nest often saw new land first

A triangular lateen sail on the mizzen (rear) mast helped the ship sail into the wind and maneuvre along coasts

A small poop (raised) deck held the captain's cabin

The caravel's strong deck was a platform for guns and made it very storm-proof. The caravel had a deep, narrow hull and a strong, straight keel for speed and stability

A raised section at the bow, called the forecastle, gave extra storm protection and extra accommodation

○ By the Treaty of Tordesillas (1494) Portugal and Spain divided new discoveries along a line about 1,243 mi west of the Cape Verde Islands.

○ Thousands of Spaniards went to live in America in the 1500s, creating Spanish-style cities such as Cartagena in Colombia and Guayaqil in Ecuador.

▶ *Exploring the northeast coast of Canada, Martin Frobisher discovered the bay that bears his name, Frobisher Bay.*

▲ *Most of the explorers of the 1400s and 1500s sailed in a type of ship called a caravel. These were 98 ft long and could cope with the roughest seas.*

Greenland

Davis Strait

Great Britain

Hudson Strait

Iceland

North America

Frobisher Bay

ATLANTIC OCEAN

Find out more

Cook p. 344

The voyages of Portuguese navigator Vasco da Gama to India laid open the sea route to the East from Europe and helped Portugal to establish a flourishing trade. In 1497, Vasco da Gama sailed round Africa to Calicut in India, and returned laden with spices and jewels.

○ In 1553 English traders arrived in Nigeria to trade in gold and ivory.

○ In 1569 Flemish cartographer Gerardus Mercator introduced the Meracator Projection map, still used today for navigational chart making.

○ In 1580 the English explorer Francis Drake returned to Portsmouth after having sailed around the world.

Christopher Columbus

Columbus had three ships—the *Santa Maria, Nina*, and *Pinta*. Columbus persuaded King Ferdinand and Queen Isabella of Spain to pay for his voyage. He set sail on August 3, 1492 and sailed west into the unknown for three weeks, by which time the sailors were ready to mutiny with fear. On October 12, a lookout spotted the Bahamas. Columbus thought he was in the Indies (hence the "West Indies"). He called the natives Indians. Columbus left 40 men on a large island that he called Hispaniola and went back to Spain a hero.

In the course of his four voyages across the Atlantic, Christopher Columbus (1451–1596) explored much of the Americas. However, his original plan was to find a westward sea course to the East.

In 1534 French explorer Jacques Cartier (1491–1557) was commissioned by Francis I, king of France, on an expedition to North America. with the chief aim of finding spices, which were extremely precious at this time, as well as gold.

Ferdinand Magellan

Ferdinand Magellan was the first navigator to sail across the Pacific from east to west. In 1519–1522, Magellan's ship *Victoria* sailed across the Atlantic, round the southern tip of South America, across the Pacific and back round Africa to Spain. Although this Portuguese explorer was killed in the Philippines, his crew and ship went on to complete the first round-the-world voyage.

Sailors and ships

Roald Amundsen	*Fram*
Christopher Columbus	*Santa Maria*
Captain James Cook	*Endeavour*
Charles Darwin	HMS *Beagle*
Francis Drake	*Golden Hind* (originally *The Pelican*)
Ferdinand Magellan	*Victoria*
Walter Raleigh	*The Ark*
Robert Falcon Scott	*The Discovery*
Ernest Shackleton	*Endurance*

Religion and Wars

*I*n the early 1500s, many people in Europe were starting to question the teachings of the Catholic Church. They were angered by the excessive power of church leaders and the life of idleness that many monks seemed to lead. Many critics were especially annoyed by the huge amounts of money the Church made by selling "indulgences"—a pardon for sin bought with cash. People who protested against the Church were called "Protestants." Eventually some Protestants left the Catholic Church to set up their own churches, which followed a reformed style of Christianity. This movement became known as the Reformation.

○ In the 1500s the Roman Catholic church was determined to fight against the Protestant Reformation and other threats. Their fight is called the Counter-Reformation. In 1534, St Ignatius Loyola founded the Society of Jesus (Jesuits) to lead the Counter-Reformation.

○ Investigative bodies called Inquisitions were set up to seek out and punish heretics—anyone who held views that did not agree with the Catholic Church's.

Amazing

In 1547 the English had to be Protestants under Edward VI, in 1553 they were Catholic under Mary and in 1558 they had to be Protestant again under Elizabeth I.

○ From 1483, the Spanish Inquisition became a byword for terror, swooping on suspected heretics—Protestants and Jews alike—torturing them and burning them at the stake.

▲ *Thomas More (1478–1535) was executed when he refused to acknowledge Henry VIII as head of the English Church.*

Martin Luther

Martin Luther (1483–1546) was the monk at Wittenberg University, who earned a reputation for his great biblical knowledge. His radical views sparked off the great Reformation, which divided Christians in Europe into Catholics and Protestants. Luther attacked the sale of indulgences by Pope Leo X, who was selling them by the score to raise money to build St Peter's Church in Rome. In 1517, Luther nailed a list of 95 grievances on the door of Wittenberg Castle's chapel, hoping to start a debate. His action resulted in him being expelled by the Church in 1521. Other more extreme rebels joined the cause, such as John Calvin (1509–1564) and Ulrich Zwingli (1484–1531), and the movement gathered pace across northwest Europe.

Find out more
Henry VIII p. 335

Mary, Queen of Scots

Mary I (1542–1587) was the Catholic queen of Scotland held captive in England by Elizabeth I for 19 years, then beheaded. Mary was next in line to the English throne after Elizabeth. Many Catholics felt she was first in line, since they did not recognize Henry VIII's marriage to Anne Boleyn. Elizabeth's spymaster, Walsingham, trapped Mary into going along with a secret plot by Babington. Mary was found guilty of treason and beheaded at Fotheringay in 1587.

❍ The battle between Catholics and Protestants created many victims and many martyrs as they were persecuted in the late 1500s.

❍ In Germany, a terrible Thirty Years War was started in 1618 as the Catholic-Protestant rivalries flared up.

❍ Russians were Christians of the Eastern Church ruled from Constantinople. Constantinople had become the second focus of Christianity when Rome fell to barbarians in the AD 400s.

❍ When Constantinople fell to the Turks in 1453, Ivan III called for Moscow to be the Third Rome. He married a Byzantine princess, and his grandson Ivan IV took the title czar after the Roman caesars.

A *Elizabeth sent troops to Holland to help Protestants against the Spanish rulers, and secretly urged Francis Drake to raid Spanish treasure ships. In 1588 Spain sent an Armada to invade England. Elizabeth proved an inspiring leader and the Armada was repulsed.*

❍ In the St Bartholomew's Day massacre in 1571, up to 70,000 French Protestants, called Huguenots, were killed on the orders of the Catholic queen Catherine de' Medici.

❍ Many English Protestants were burned in Catholic Queen Mary's reign, earning her the name "Bloody Mary." Later, English Catholics, such as Edmund Campion (1540–1581), were killed in Protestant Queen Elizabeth I's reign.

❍ Catholic houses in England in the late 1500s had hiding places for priests called "priest holes."

▶ *Elizabeth I was daughter of Henry VIII and his wife Anne Boleyn, who was beheaded when Elizabeth was three. A brilliant scholar, Elizabeth was fluent in many languages by the time she was 12. She became queen in 1558, when her half-sister Mary died. At once Elizabeth strengthened the Protestant Church of England by the Act of Supremacy in 1559. She was expected to marry but she remained single, earning her the nickname "The Virgin Queen." Elizabeth's reign is famed for the poetry and plays of men like Spenser, Marlowe, and Shakespeare.*

Beyond Europe

uring the period 1400–1600 many different parts of the world began to make contact with each other. Sometimes the contact was a disaster—spreading deadly diseases or starting vicious wars. Other contacts were peaceful and profitable, with merchants swapping goods and ideas that benefited everybody. During these upheavals, some advanced European countries began to build empires in other parts of the world, but many countries remained independent of Europe.

○ Hernán Cortés (1485–1547) was a Spanish soldier and explorer who landed in Mexico with only 500 men in 1519. Perhaps thinking that Cortés was the god Quetzalcoatl, the Aztec leader Moctezuma let Cortés take him prisoner and become ruler in his place (see Aztec conqueror).

○ The Incas were South American people who created a remarkable empire in the Americas in the 1400s.

○ The Incas began as a tribe in highland Peru, but in 1438 Pachacuti Inca Yupanqui became their Sapa Inca (king) and they built a huge empire in an amazingly short time.

○ Francisco Pizarro (c.1478–1541) reached Peru when the Incas were hardly over a civil war between the Inca Atahualpa and his brother. The Incas, terrified of Pizarro's horses and guns, were easily slaughtered. Pizarro took Cuzco in 1533.

○ When the first European colonists arrived in North America, there were one and a half million Native Americans living in North America. There were hundreds of tribes in North America, each with its own language.

○ The first successful English colony was set up at Jamestown, Virginia on May 24, 1607, with 104 colonists. Many of the Jamestown colony died in "the starving time" of winter 1609.

Aztec conqueror

When Hernán Cortés landed in Mexico in 1519 he was treated like a god by the Aztecs. The Aztecs believed that the bearded Cortés was their god, known as Quetzalcoatl, returned to them. Their calendar told them it was a special year and so they welcomed Cortés and his army, even though they were terrified of the Spaniard soldiers' guns and horses. Within two years, Cortés had conquered Mexico.

◀ *Until Europeans arrived, Native Americans traveled around mainly on foot or by canoe. The Europeans introduced horses in the 1700s— and Indians quickly became skilled riders.*

○ Toyotomi Hideyoshi (1536–1581) was the great Japanese shogun who unified Japan under his rule. Hideyoshi proved himself a brilliant general in a series of wars with rival generals. After defeating his enemies, he kept warriors and peasants separated as classes.

Find out more

America p. 345

Pilgrimage

In 1620, 102 "Pilgrims" arrived in America from Plymouth, England, in the *Mayflower* and set up a new colony near Cape Cod. They survived, thanks to help from Wampanoag Indians. In November 1621 the Pilgrims invited the Wampanoags to celebrate their first harvest. This first Thanksgiving Day is now celebrated every year in the USA on November 25.

▼ *At its height the Inca empire stretched from northern Ecuador to central Chile. Machu Picchu was the Incas' last mountain stronghold in Peru. It was unknown to outsiders until rediscovered by an American archeologist in 1911.*

▲ *North American Indians wore clothes of buckskin (tanned deer hide). They adorned the costume with eagle feathers, which had special significance.*

Amazing

In 1539, a Spanish friar in Mexico heard about a city named Cibola, far to the north. Many men explored vast areas to find the city, but Cibola did not exist.

1600–1800

*A*fter the year 1600 the rate of progress began to speed up. Important new inventions and new ideas were developed. Mostly these led to people leading longer and healthier lives, but some people thought their traditional ways of life were under threat. There were uprisings and wars as people sought to adapt to the new realities of life. European countries with effective weapons continued to conquer other countries to build up empires.

1600 The British East India Company is formed and, over the next 250 years, becomes one of the most powerful commercial enterprises of its time. Most of its business is based in India, where it gains governmental and military authority.

1600 Tokugawa Ieyasu establishes himself as ruler of Japan after defeating many rivals for the throne in the Battle of Sekigahara.

1603 Queen Elizabeth I of England dies. On her deathbed she indicates that she wants the Protestant King James VI of Scotland to rule England after her. James becomes King James I of England. Although he rules both kingdoms, the two countries retain separate parliaments, legal systems, and finances.

1618 Roman Catholics of Bohemia shut down Protestant chapels.

1642 Tibet is formed as a religious state under the leadership of Ngawang Lobsang Gyatso, the fifth Dalai Lama.

1644 The Manchurians establish the Ch'ing dynasty, the last of the great Chinese dynasties. They later extend the boundaries of their kingdom to include Tibet, parts of Mongolia, Nepal, and Turkistan.

1646 The parliamentary forces of Oliver Cromwell defeat King Charles I's army, forcing the monarch to surrender and end the Civil War.

1648 The Peace of Westphalia ends the Eighty Years War between the Spaniards and the Dutch, and the Thirty Years War between Germany, France, and Sweden. About a third of the population of Germany die in the war.

Oliver Cromwell

1648 Charles I is arrested by the English Parliament for signing a secret treaty with the Scots. He is tried for treason against England, found guilty and beheaded the following year. The parliamentary leader Oliver Cromwell becomes "Lord Protector" of England and rules with the aid of Parliament and the army.

1660 After the death of Oliver Cromwell, Charles II, eldest son of

---

Bank of England

1694 The Bank of England is established in London. The bank introduces reforms that give England the world's first modern finance system, allowing the government to borrow money and thus be more stable than most others.

1695 The war between the League of Augsburg and France continues with France destroying Brussels, and England capturing Namur from France.

1695 Ottoman (Turkish Empire) sultan Ahmed II dies and his nephew Mustapha II ascendes the throne in his place. Mustapha II then renews the war against the predominantly Christian Austria.

1696 The English Parliament passes a new Navigation Act, which forbids the English American colonies from exporting goods directly to Ireland or Scotland.

1696 John III Sobieski, king of Poland, dies. Frederick, the elector of Saxony, is elected to the Polish throne the following year. He assumes the name of Augustus II and rules for 37 years. Augustus' invasion of Livonia starts the Second Northern War. During Augustus II's reign, Poland begins to decline from the position of a major European power and eventually becomes a protectorate of Russia.

1701 English agriculturist and inventor Jethro Tull revolutionizes farming by the invention of the horse-drawn hoe and seeding drill. He also stresses the use of manure and the importance of breaking-up the soil into small particles.

1709 Englishman Abraham Darby discovers that iron ore can be smelted using coke, to produce pig iron. He demonstrates that coke is

superior in cost and efficiency, by establishing furnaces that are much larger than is possible with using charcoal as fuel. Iron becomes much cheaper to produce and is a key factor in the Industrial Revolution.

1723–1790 Scottish philosopher and economist Adam Smith lives during this period. He is the author of *An Inquiry into the Nature and Causes of the Wealth of Nations*. This work

becomes a very important work in the field of economics.

1745 Charles Edward Stuart, also known as Bonnie Prince Charlie, leads the second Jacobite revolt. Although initially successful in capturing the English towns of Carlisle, Preston, and Manchester, he is defeated in the Battle of Culloden. The uprising is known as "The 45."

1757 In India, Bengal comes under British rule when forces of the East India Company, led by Robert Clive, defeat Siraj ud-Daula, the Nawab of Bengal, in the Battle of Plassey. The battle marks the first stage in the British conquest in India.

1767 English inventor James Hargreaves develops the spinning jenny. Recognized as one of the first mass-production industrial machines.

King James I

violating the rights that have been afforded to them by the late Holy Roman emperor Rudolf II. Angry Protestants throw two of Prague's governors from a window in Hradcany Palace. This incident, which is referred to as the "Defenestration of Prague," leads to the Thirty Years War, which is fought between France, Sweden, Spain, and the Holy Roman Empire, among other countries. The war devastates central Europe.

1626 French colonizers settle in Madagascar and begin to drive out the Hovas who had been on the island for 600 years.

1636 The Japanese people are forbidden from traveling abroad by the country's shogun (military leader). This begins an increasing policy of isolation (refusing to trade with other countries) by the Japanese that would last over 200 years.

1637–1709 A series of weak rulers leads to the decline of the Safavid dynasty of Persia (now Iran). Its end comes when the Ghalzai Afghans invade Persia and occupy the city of Kandahar.

1641–1652 Buryat Mongols from Lake Baikal are defeated and brought under the control of the Russians. This marks the end of the Mongols as a power in Asia.

Charles I's execution

Charles I, is crowned king of England after agreeing to accept key concessions to Parliament. England returns to peace as a constitutional monarchy.

1661 Louis XIV gains complete control of France after the death of his dominating prime minister, Cardinal Mazarin. The king decides not to appoint a new prime minister. Instead, he strips the nobles and all regional councils of their rights and political influence, concentrating all the power in his own hands.

1675 Native tribes in New England gather together under the leadership of King Philip—whose original name was Metacomet—to raid 52 settlements. They kill almost 600 colonists in a revolt against being forced to pay an annual tribute (tax) to the English settlers.

1680 Ietsuna, the Japanese Tokugawa shogun, dies and is succeeded by his brother Tsunayoshi. He promotes neoConfucianism and his reign is considered one of the most peaceful and prosperous in Japanese history.

1683 An Ottoman attack on Vienna fails due to German and Polish troops coming to the aid of the city. Viennese bakers invent a new pastry to celebrate: the croissant.

1696 Spaniards establish a colony at Pensacola in Florida.

1697 Charles XI of Sweden dies. His son Charles XII succeeds him. He promotes important domestic reforms. His disastrous invasion of Russia, however, marks the end of Sweden's status as a major power. Charles was shot dead in battle in 1718.

1697 The Ottoman Turks, led by Sultan Mustafa II, face a crushing defeat in the Battle of Zenta against Austria. This victory makes Austria the leading power in central Europe.

1697 The War of the League of Augsburg ends after 11 years with the Treaty of Ryswick.

1698 The London Stock Exchange is established. Although other European cities like Antwerp have organized trading houses, the exchange at London is the first of its kind in the world.

1698 The first steam engine is designed and made by English engineer Thomas Savery. The engine is made to pump out water from coal mines, though the idea is later adapted to other purposes.

Iron bridge

Bonnie Prince Charlie

1775 The American War of Independence begins with a fight between the British forces and the local militia at Concord in Massachusetts. France later joins the war on the side of the American colonies against Britain.

1783 The American Congress declares the end of the War of Independence and the continental army is disbanded.

1783 French brothers Joseph-Michel Montgolfier and Jacques-Étienne Montgolfier develop the first hot-air balloon. Their balloon rises to a height of 3,281 ft and remains aloft for ten minutes. Next, they send a sheep, a rooster, and a duck as passengers. The first manned flight takes place on November 21 when Francois de Rozier and the Marquis d'Arlandes fly over Paris.

Montgolfier balloon

Expanding World

In 1600 much of the world remained unexplored. Across the Pacific Ocean were vast areas of ocean and thousands of islands that were occupied by Polynesian and Melanesian peoples, but which had not been contacted by any ships. Australia and New Zealand were equally isolated from the outside world. Over the following two centuries, all these lands would be reached by outsiders.

○ In North America there were six kinds of tribal area: the Southwest, Great Plains, Far West Plateau, Northwest, Eastern Woodland, and Northern.

○ Southwest Native Americans like the Pueblo Indians lived by growing corn, beans, and squash.

○ Plains tribes like the Blackfoot, Comanche, and Cheyenne hunted buffalo on foot.

○ In Woodland tribes like the Delaware, the men hunted deer and fished while the women grew crops.

○ Plateau and Northwest Native Americans like the Nez Percé and the Kwakiutl lived by fishing and gathering berries. They are famous for their baskets.

○ Northern tribes like the Cree lived mainly by hunting caribou.

○ From 1500–1800, Europeans shipped 10–12 million black slaves from Africa to the Americas. A total of 40 percent went to Brazil, 30 percent to Cuba, Jamaica and Haiti, and 5 percent to the USA.

○ 1642 Dutch explorer Abel Janszoon Tasman became the first European to reach Tasmania. He named it Van Diemen's Land, in honor of Anton Van Diemen, the governor-general of the Dutch East Indies (later called Netherlands Indies).

○ 1768 the British navy asked English naval captain and explorer James Cook to go to the Pacific island of Tahiti, to make measurements and observations of the planet Venus passing in front of the Sun. He set out on this first Pacific expeditions, during which he also visited New Zealand and discovered the Great Barrier Reef, off Australia.

Captain Cook

Cook took with him scientists and artists to study and record the plants, animals, and peoples of the Pacific lands.

▼ Although French missionaries managed to settle in parts of North America, French colonization of the region was not a success.

Find out more

French colonies p. 333

New Zealand (shown in the map) was called Aotearoa by the native Maori. Aotearoa means "land of the long white cloud."

Amazing

An early British colonist in Australia asked an Aborigine the word for a local animal. The Aborigine replied "kangaroo," which means "I don't understand you."

○ Many people still believed there was an unknown continent in the south. So they sent Cook back to look for it again in 1772. He sailed further south than anyone had been before, until he found the sea was frozen solid. He sailed all the way around Antarctica, but it wasn't explored until 1820, 50 years later.

In southern USA many African slaves were field hands, picking cotton. Many tried to escape or protest, but they were in a minority—and there was no chance of a revolution like that led by Toussaint l'Ouverture (below) in Haiti.

Fighting for independence

In 1764–1765, British Prime Minister Grenville brought in three new taxes—the Sugar Tax on molasses, the Quartering Tax, and the Stamp Tax. Colonists tolerated sugar and quartering taxes, but the Stamp Tax provoked riots, such as the Boston Tea Party, when crates of tea were emptied into the Boston harbor. Delegates from nine colonies met in New York to demand a say in how they were taxed. A Congress of delegates from all the colonies except Georgia met to demand independence, and appointed George Washington to lead an army to fight their cause. In 1776, the colonists drew up a Declaration of Independence, written by Thomas Jefferson. The British recognized independence in 1783, and in 1787 the colonists drew up a Constitution to lay down how their Union should be run. In 1789, George Washington was elected as the first president of the United States of America and the capital city was later named after him.

American War of Independence

1765	American colonies object to the Stamp Act passed by British Parliament
1774	Boston Tea Party—American colonists throw chests of taxed tea into Boston harbor
1775	American troops fire on British troops at Lexington
1776	Second Continental Congress issues the Declaration of Independence
1778	France sends help to the American colonies in their war against Britain
1781	British lose the Battle of Yorktown
1783	Treaty of Paris—Britain recognizes American independence

Asia in Decline

The most powerful and sophisticated civilizations on Earth for centuries had been in Asia. Persia, China, Japan, and the Mongols had dominated the world. However, after about 1600 the Asian countries began to decline. Their economies faltered, so they did not have as much wealth as before, and they failed to invent or adopt the technological advances that were taking place in Europe. In many areas corrupt government made progress difficult and made everyday life miserable. Europeans took advantage of this to conquer more lands and add them to their growing empires.

○ In the 1600s, the Ming emperors of China were unpopular after three centuries in power. Rebellions became increasingly common.

○ In 1644, the last Ming emperor hanged himself as the bandit Li Zicheng and his men overran Beijing.

○ Guarding the Great Wall were Manchu troops, from Manchuria in the north. A desperate Ming general invited them to help get rid of Li Zicheng.

▶ *In 1757, 3,000 British soldiers, led by the East India Company's Robert Clive, defeated an army of over 50,000 French and Indian troops at the battle of Plassey. After Clive's victory, the British gradually gained control over much of India through a combination of bribes, bullying, and gaining well-placed allies.*

○ The Manchus marched into Beijing and proclaimed their own king as the "Son of Heaven" and set up the Qing dynasty of emperors.

○ In time, the Qing adopted Chinese ways, and even Manchu civil servants had to learn the classic works of Confucius, just like the Chinese.

○ In 1617 Mustafa I succeeded his brother Ahmed I to the Ottoman throne. He was deposed the very next year by the elite troops for his mental problems, but was restored to the throne in 1622. This marked the beginning of the decline in the power of the Ottoman emperor as power passed to bureaucrats and soldiers.

○ In 1700 the Mogul Empire in India was weakened by continuous rebellions against the emperor Aurangzeb and his corrupt reign.

○ In the 1700s, rebellions weakened the Mogul Empire in India. The French and British vied to gain control of the collapsing empire.

○ In 1774, the Turkish Ottoman Empire was defeated by the Russians after a six-year war, and was forced to allow Russian ships to pass through the Straits from the Black Sea to the Mediterranean.

Amazing

In 1758, the Nawab of Bengal thanked Robert Clive by showing him a vast pile of gold and jewelry. He told Clive he could keep anything he could carry at one time.

Find out more

China p. 320

> British rule lasted in India until 1947. British officials and their families moved to India during the period that is now referred to as the Raj. British rule was resented by many Indians. Hindus felt that the British were undermining their religion.

Mongol horsemen

For centuries the Mongol horse archers had been almost invincible in battle. The combination of speed and hitting power had been unchallenged. The Mongols defeated and ruled over many neighboring peoples. However, they were easily beaten by Europeans armed with guns in a series of wars after 1600. Mongolia became divided between Russia and China.

Chinese Empire

Under the Manchu rulers, the Chinese Empire was larger than it had ever been. The Manchu insisted that only the Emperor could make decisions. The administration of the vast empire soon became slow and corrupt as local governors refused to take decisions on their own. High taxes stopped merchants from making money. Although it was large, the Chinese Empire gradually grew poorer and weaker. The emperors of China ruled over a glittering court. They wore robes of silk, such as this one decorated with dragons.

A Europe of Ideas

Europe became a melting pot of new ideas and inventions after about 1600. Books were now cheap and easy to print, so people could read about discoveries more quickly and easily than before. Exciting new concepts about government, religion, and lifestyles swept across the continent. Some people wanted to adopt the new ideas, others preferred a traditional lifestyle. There were frequent disputes and arguments, which sometimes led to warfare. After 1750 ideas about democracy and human rights spread rapidly.

❍ The English Civil War (1642–1649) was the struggle between "Cavalier" supporters of King Charles I and "Roundheads," led by Oliver Cromwell, who supported Parliament.

❍ Many revolutionary groups emerged among poorer people, such as the "Diggers" and "Levellers."

❍ The war turned against the royalists when the parliamentarians formed the disciplined New Model Army. Oliver Cromwell was put in charge of the cavalry.

❍ After defeating the royal army, Parliament began talks with the king to establish a new, more democratic system of government. However, King Charles I broke his promises and tried to recruit a new army. He was beheaded in 1649.

◀ *Peter the Great (1672–1725) was the greatest of all the Russian czars (emperors). He built the city of St Petersburg and turned Russia from an inward-looking country to a major European power. Most earlier czars had bushy, traditional Russian beards. Peter shaved his off, in the modern European style.*

▲ *Charles II's rule coincided with the Great Plague and the Great Fire of London.*

❍ The successful parliamentarian general Oliver Cromwell (1599–1658) became the leader of the Roundheads and signed Charles I's death warrant. In 1653, he made himself Lord Protector —England's dictator. Cromwell supported the policies of the Puritans, groups of strict religious leaders.

❍ The Restoration of Charles II as king was in May 1660. Charles II proved a skilful ruler, tactfully easing tensions between rival religious groups. He introduced democratic reforms and reorganized the finances of government to make it more efficient.

Civil War

The Civil War in England was caused by a quarrel between King Charles I and his parliament over royal powers, religion, and taxation. The war was fought between 1642 and 1649.

Find out more

Religion p. 338

○ The Age of Reason is the time in the 1700s when many people began to believe that all-important questions about the world could be answered by reason.

○ The hero of the Age was Isaac Newton. His discovery of the Laws of Motion proposed that every single event in the Universe could be worked out mathematically.

○ In France, the great ideas were worked out by philosophers like Rousseau and Voltaire. People discussed the ideas earnestly when they met at fashionable "salons" (dinner parties).

The Hall of Mirrors in the Palais de Versailles, which is situated just outside Paris, France. The 17th-century palace was built by Louis XIX on the site of his father's chateau.

Famous books

1615   **Don Quixote**
Spanish writer Miguel de Cervantes writes about an adventurous knight

1637   **Discours de la Méthode**
French philosopher René Descartes writes: "I think, therefore I am"

1653   **The Compleat Angler**
English sportsman Izaak Walton writes the classic book about fishing

1659   **Diary**
English civil servant Samuel Pepys begins his diary

1719   **Robinson Crusoe**
English novelist Daniel Defoe's book about a shipwrecked sailor

1755   **Dictionary**
Writer Samuel Johnson lists thousands of English words

1776   **On the Wealth of Nations**
Adam Smith establishes economics as a science

1781   **Critique of Pure Reason**
German Immanuel Kant argues that humans cannot understand everything

Battle of Culloden

Fought in April 1746, the Battle of Culloden was the last stand of Charles Edward Stuart (known as "Bonnie Prince Charlie") to restore the Stuart monarchy in Britain. His highland army attempted to overthrow King George II, but it was beaten by the English army, which had many more men (9,000 against 5,000). Bonnie Prince Charlie had to flee into the hills before he eventually escaped by ship to France. The Stuart's hopes of regaining the throne had ended.

○ Charles II was known as the Merry Monarch, because his love of partying, theatre, horse-racing, and women was such a relief to the public after years of grim Puritan rule.

○ Charles II had many mistresses, and the most famous of them was Nell Gwyn. Previously an orange-seller, she became the most famous and highest paid actress in Europe.

Amazing

Charles II of England thanked those who had helped him escape execution during the Civil War by giving them pensions. Some are still being paid to their descendants.

The Industrial Revolution

Beginning in about 1700, a dramatic change swept over Britain and changed the way people lived. Before this time most people had lived in the countryside, where they farmed the land and produced only a bit more food than they needed for themselves. As the changes occurred, people began to live in towns where they worked in factories, producing goods that were sold for cash. This process is called the Industrial Revolution. It began with changes to farming techniques in Britain, that gradually spread out across the world.

❍ Before the 1700s, farmland was mostly wide open fields, cultivated in narrow strips by peasants growing food for themselves, using traditional, manual methods.

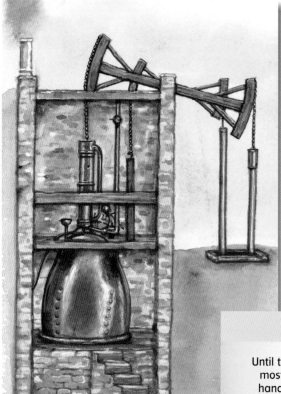

◀ British inventor Thomas Newcomen's (1663–1729) steam engine used atmospheric pressure and was a forerunner of James Watt's engine. Water was injected into a large metal cylinder that was filled with steam. This condensed the steam and created a vacuum. A piston was pushed to the bottom of the cylinder by the weight of the atmosphere, thus pulling up the pumps connected to the piston and raising the water.

Amazing

Until the Industrial Revolution most clocks had only hour hands. Minute hands were added so that people would know when to begin work exactly on time.

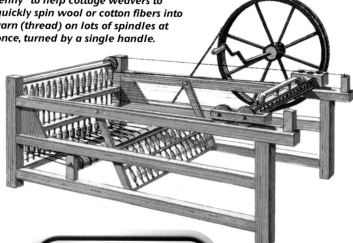

▼ In 1764, Lancashire weaver James Hargreaves created the "spinning jenny" to help cottage weavers to quickly spin wool or cotton fibers into yarn (thread) on lots of spindles at once, turned by a single handle.

❍ Crop-growing was improved by techniques such as the four-field crop rotation system. The four-field system of "Turnip" Townshend and Thomas Coke meant growing turnips, clover, barley, and wheat in successive years so land was used all the time.

❍ Livestock farmers learnt how to breed cattle, horses, and sheep to be larger, like Bakewell's Leicester sheep.

❍ The Farming Revolution created a pool of cheap labor, while the growth of European colonies created vast markets for things like clothing.

Find out more
Early farmers p. 314

Water wheel

Sir Richard Arkwright's spinning machine was a "water frame" that ran on water power. Arkwright had the machine set up at his cotton mill at Cromford in Derbyshire, England.

○ The Industrial Revolution began with the invention of machines for making cloth, like the spinning jenny.

○ In 1713, Abraham Darby found how to use coke, rather than wood charcoal, to make huge amounts of iron much more cheaply than ever before.

○ The turning point was the change from hand-turned machines like the jenny to machines driven by big water wheels—like Arkwright's "water (-powered spinning) frame" of 1766.

○ In 1771, Arkwright installed water frames at Crompton Mill, Derby, and created the world's first big factory.

○ In the 1780s, James Watt developed a steam engine to drive machines—and steam engines quickly replaced water as the main source of power in factories.

○ In 1784, Henry Cort found how to remove impurities from cast iron to make wrought iron—and iron became the key material of the Industrial Revolution.

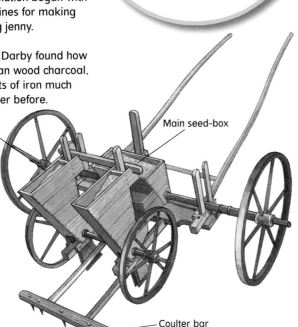

Side seed-box

Main seed-box

▶ *Jethro Tull's seed drill made holes and planted seeds in them, dramatically speeding up the planting process for farm workers.*

Coulter bar

James Watt

Between 1764 and 1790 the Scottish inventor James Watt made a series of improvements to the design of the steam engine. Among the more important changes he made was to develop a rotary motion and a double-acting engine. Taken together these made steam engines far more powerful and reliable than before. They began to be used in large numbers in factories and mines, and to power ships and railway locomotives.

Revolutionary ideas

1701	Jethro Tull	Mechanical seed drill improves arable farming
1705	Thomas Newcomen	First steam engine
1709	Abraham Darby	Produces coke and uses it to smelt iron ore
1733	John Kay	Flying shuttle improves quality of wool and cotton cloth
1764	James Hargreaves	Spinning jenny improves quality of cotton thread
1769	James Watt	Announces improvements to Newcomen's steam engine
1769	Richard Arkwright	Water-powered frame for spinning cotton
1770	Nicolas Cugnot	First self-propelled road vehicle
1776	Watt and Boulton	First commercial steam engine using steam pressure alone
1777	John Wilkinson	First boat with an iron hull launched in Yorkshire, England
1779	Samuel Crompton	Spinning mule produces several cotton threads at once
1783	Montgolfier Brothers	First successful flight of a hot air balloon
1785	Edmund Cartwright	Power loom weaves cotton cloth at high speed
1804	Richard Trevithick	First successful steam-powered locomotive

The Age of Revolutions

In 1789 France exploded in revolution. People were no longer willing to live in poverty under a corrupt and dictatorial government and a lavish monarchy. The French Revolution was only the first of many other democratic and nationalist uprisings that swept Europe in the decades that followed. Later came a wave of Communist and Fascist revolutions, and more democratic uprisings. The pace of technological and industrial change continued to increase.

1789 The French National Assembly make the reformist nobleman Marquis de Lafayette commander of the National Guards and Jean-Sylvain Bailly the Mayor of Paris. The "Declaration of the Rights of Man and of the Citizen" is made by the National Assembly to set out equal rights to all Frenchmen. Many areas of France collapse into violent anarchy.

1793 Louis XVI of France and his wife Marie Antoinette are accused of supporting foreign enemies of the new French Republic. They are tried, found guilty, and executed.

1793 The Reign of Terror starts in France, during which thousands of people are declared enemies of the Revolution and are executed. At least 17,000 people are killed during this period.

1789 ———

1852 Napoleon III, the grandson of Napoleon I, is elected to be the emperor of France. He is believed to be the first to lay the foundations for a family welfare system. During his reign, craftsmen and artists form associations to get finance for insurance.

1853 The Crimean War is fought between Russia and an alliance comprising the Ottoman Empire, the kingdom of Sardinia, Britain, and France. The war is best known for the futile and almost suicidal charge of the Light Brigade of British cavalry. The war ends in defeat for Russia.

1857–1858 The Sepoy Mutiny among Indian troops in British service spreads rapidly to military stations all over northern and western India. It is eventually suppressed by British troops.

1861 The American Civil War begins, with the Confederates making their first attack on Fort Sumter in South Carolina. The Confederate states break away from the United States of America to preserve their agricultural way of life, which is often based on slavery.

1865 In North Carolina, Confederate General J E Johnston surrenders to Union general William T Sherman.

1852 ———————————————→

Indian Mutiny 1857

December 17, 1903 The American inventors and pioneers, Wilbur Wright and Orville Wright, invent the first powered flying machine.

October 6, 1908 Austria announces its decision to make Bosnia-Herzegovina a part of the Austro-Hungarian Empire. This angers the Bosnia-Herzegovina natives, Serbia, and the Ottoman Turks, who both want to control the disputed area.

February 1912 The Qing monarchy of China gives up their claim to the throne. The politician Yuan Shikai becomes head of the Chinese republic.

June 28, 1914 Archduke Franz Ferdinand, heir to the throne of Austria–Hungary, is assassinated in Sarajevo by Gavrilo Princip, a Serbian activist from Bosnia-Herzegovina.

July 28, 1914 The Austrian emperor Franz Joseph declares war against Serbia, starting World War I.

July 1–November 13, 1916 Britain introduces the battle tank for the first time in the Battle of the Somme, an allied attack on German forces on the western front. The tanks can easily cross the muddy, uneven terrain, but suffer frequent mechanical failure. On July 1, 60,000 British soldiers were

killed in just a few hours. This long and expensive battle ends with no clear result.

March 8, 1917 Riots break out in St Petersburg. As soldiers join with the common people, a revolution against the monarchy begins to spread all over Russia. A provisional government takes power until elections can be held.

1903 ———

October 1, 1936 General Francisco Franco is declared the head of the nationalist forces in the town of Burgos. After winning a civil war, in which more than 500,000 people die, Franco becomes ruler of Spain in March 1938.

September 1, 1939 World War II begins with the German invasion of Poland by Hitler's army.

September 3, 1939 Britain and France declare war on Germany. Russia later joins the Allies against Germany.

December 7, 1941 Japanese aircraft attack Pearl Harbor in Hawaii. The United States declares war on Japan.

June 6, 1944 Allied Forces land on the Normandy coast in France on what is known as "D-Day."

April 30, 1945 Nazi leader Adolf Hitler kills himself.

May 7, 1945 Germany surrenders unconditionally to the Allied powers.

August 14, 1945 Japan announce its surrender from the war.

April 4, 1949 Belgium, Italy, Canada, the Netherlands, Portugal, Denmark, Britain, France, Iceland, Norway,

1936 ———————→ **Hitler invades Poland 1939**

1804 Napoleon Bonaparte becomes emperor of France. Two years earlier, Napoleon had instituted a new constitution whereby he secured for himself the position of First Consul—for life.

1815 Napoleon is defeated in the Battle of Waterloo by a British army under the Duke of Wellington, aided by the Prussians. Napoleon is exiled to the island of St Helena.

French Revolution 1793

1848 A series of revolutions starts in various parts of Europe, beginning with Sicily, and spreading to France, Germany, and Austria. They are mostly unsuccessful in bringing about any political change, and are all eventually suppressed.

1848 The February revolution in France forces King Louis-Philippe to give up his throne and France becomes a republic.

Battle of Waterloo 1815

The American Civil War ends with the Confederate states being forced to rejoin the United States.

1870 German states led by Prussia defeat France in the Franco-Prussian War. Victory signifies the end of France's domination in Europe, and the beginning of a unified Germany, led by Prussia. The new state is dubbed the Second Reich.

American Civil War 1861

1870 Napoleon III of France is forced to step down from the throne after losing the Franco-Prussian War. The Third French Republic is established.

1899–1902 British imperial forces defeat Boer settlers of South Africa after a long war that ends with the Treaty of Vereeniging, by which the Transvaal province and the Orange Free State become British colonies.

November 7, 1917 The Bolsheviks, led by Vladimir Iilych Lenin, overthrow the provisional Russian government and establish the Communist Soviet Republic. During the Russian Civil War that follows, Lenin launches a campaign called "Red Terror," which is aimed at eliminating his political opponents. He also launches a series of makor economic reforms to meet Russia's pressing economic needs.

November 11, 1918 Peace is declared and World War I ends.

1925–1927 Benito Mussolini, prime minister of Italy, passes laws to make himself dictator of Italy.

November 12, 1927 After Lenin's death, the Soviet Communist Party expel Leon Trotsky. Joseph Stalin gains undisputed control of the Soviet Union.

Lenin (left) with Stalin

August 2, 1934 Nazi party leader Adolf Hitler assumes the title of Führer (leader) of Germany. He now has dictatorial (total) power over Germany and begins a rapid build-up of military power. Hitler wants to reclaim the lands that Germany had lost after being defeated in World War I. He uses the enlarged army and air force to bully Austria and Czechoslovakia into giving him what he wants.

Luxembourg, and the United States form the North Atlantic Treaty Organization (NATO) to counter the the power of the Soviet Union.

October 1956 Hungarians revolt against Soviet rule, but the Russians suppress the uprising.

October 1962 United States President John F Kennedy discovers that the Soviet Union placed missiles

in Cuba, aimed at United States cities. Following a tense confrontation, Russia removes the missiles.

March 10, 1985 Mikahil Gorbachev becomes leader of the Soviet Union. His policy of modernizing the country leads to the break-up of the USSR.

May 10, 1994 Nelson Mandela becomes the first black president of the Republic of South Africa.

September 11, 2001 A group of Islamic extremists hijack four aircraft in the USA, crashing them into the World Trade Centre in New York and the Pentagon building in Washington, killing more than 3,000 people. Osama bin Laden, leader of the Al Qaeda terrorist group admits that he organized the attacks. US President George W Bush begins a worldwide campaign against terrorism.

March 19, 2003 American and British air forces attack Baghdad, Mosul and Basra in Iraq. Soon after this the land forces conquer Iraq in a lightning campaign.

December 26, 2004 An earthquake off the coast of Java sends a tsunami (tidal wave) across the Indian Ocean that kills over 130,000 people in India, Sri Lanka, Burma, Thailand, and Indonesia.

Europe in Revolution

France was one of the most powerful countries in the world, but years of incompetent government and expensive wars had made it almost bankrupt. In 1789 a revolution broke out that swept away the old monarchy and introduced a new republic. This led to war with the other monarchies in Europe. The French Revolutionary Wars would last until peace finally came in 1815. Later revolutions broke out in other countries to introduce democracy and human rights, but only some of them were successful.

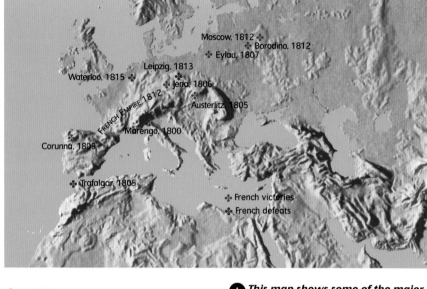

Moscow, 1812
Borodino, 1812
Eylau, 1807
Leipzig, 1813
Waterloo, 1815
Jena, 1806
FRENCH EMPIRE 1812
Austerlitz, 1805
Marengo, 1800
Corunna, 1809
Trafalgar, 1805
❖ French victories
❖ French defeats

○ In 1789, France was bankrupt, and King Louis XVI summoned Parliament for the first time in 175 years.

○ On July 14, 1789 the poor people of Paris, tired of debates, stormed the prison fortress of the Bastille.

○ The French Parliament became the National Assembly. It adopted radical policies, such as ending serfdom. Many nobles fled the country in panic.

◀ *Many nobles were sent to the guillotine and in 1793 King Louis XVI and his queen, Marie Antoinette, were themselves guillotined.*

▼ *The French Revolution, combined with Napoleon's ambitious plans to conquer Europe, caused the outbreak of wars all over Europe.*

▲ *This map shows some of the major battles of the Napoleonic Wars.*

○ French general Napoleon Bonaparte (1769–1821) set up a military government to bring order to France.

○ By 1804, Napoleon's conquests had made him a hero in France, and he elected himself as Emperor Napoleon I.

○ In 1805, Britain, Russia, and Austria allied against Napoleon. Napoleon crushed the Austrians and Russians at Austerlitz. But in 1805 the British Admiral Nelson destroyed the French and Spanish fleet at Trafalgar.

Find out more

Russia p. 360

Napolean retreats

Napoleon's retreat from Moscow in 1812 was one of the worst of all military disasters. The winter trek was so cold and food so scarce that only 30,000 of the original army of 695,000 that set out made it back to France alive.

Amazing

In 1848 Louis Napoleon, nephew of Emperor Napoleon, was elected President of France. In 1852 he made himself Emperor, just like his uncle.

○ In 1812, Napoleon invaded Russia and captured Moscow, but then had to retreat in the bitterest winter.

○ After the 1812 disaster, Napoleon's enemies forced him to abdicate and he was exiled to Elba.

○ Napoleon escaped from Elba in 1815 to raise another army, but this was defeated by Wellington's armies at Waterloo, Belgium.

○ The year 1848 saw revolutions break out across Europe—in France, Germany, Italy, Austria, and Hungary.

▶ *In 1860, the great hero Garibaldi led a rebellion and conquered all of southern Italy. In 1861, most of Italy was united under Victor Emmanuel. Venice was added in 1866 and Rome as capital in 1870. Garibaldi had landed in Sicily with just his thousand famous "Red Shirts." He went on to conquer all of southern Italy.*

▶ *Despite his extraordinary military resiliance, after his final defeat at Waterloo, Napoleon was banished by the British to the island of St Helena, where he died in 1821.*

Revolution

Simón Bolívar led the revolution against Spanish rule in New Granada. In 1819 revolutionary forces in South America defeated the Spanish army at the Battle of Boyaca. By 1828 nearly every country in Spanish America had become an independent republic, mostly with democratic constitutions and human rights well established in their systems of government.

○ Many revolutionaries—often nationalists—were angry at repressive foreign governments in which too few had a say, and at the poverty suffered by ordinary people in the new cities.

○ All but the new French Revolution were crushed—but the desire for change grew stronger over the century.

○ In 1857 Count Cavour, prime minister of Piedmont, asked France for help with evicting the Austrians. Italy became united as one country, except for Rome, which was ruled by the Pope.

○ After Napoleon's defeat in 1815, the new structure of Europe was decided at the Congress of Vienna, where the 1815 Vienna Settlement was signed by leading powers to prevent future territorial wars.

Europe Supreme

*T**he booming populations, great wealth, and many technological advances of Europe made this continent more powerful than any other in the 19th century. Several European countries used their power to build up large empires by conquering or taking over countries in other parts of the world. European factories dominated the world, while European ships carried trade between the nations. Later in the 19th century, America became wealthy and powerful, but could not yet rival Europe.*

Amazing

The world's shortest war was fought between Britain and Zanzibar in 1896. The battle lasted just 38 minutes and ended with a complete victory for Britain.

○ The British Empire began to build up in the 1600s, as British merchants started to extend their trading links throughout the world. The British won out over Dutch, Portuguese, French, and Belgian rivals through the success of their navy and also their reasonably efficient colonial government.

○ Britain gained control of India through the East India Company, between 1757 and 1858. In 1877, Queen Victoria was proclaimed Empress of India—the first time the word empire had been used in relation to the British possessions.

○ In 1788, the British sent a fleet of 11 ships, carrying convicts, to start a prison colony in Australia. About 160,000 convicts were sent to Australia over the next 80 years, but by 1810 British settlers were also arriving voluntarily.

○ In 1901, Australia became the independent Commonwealth of Australia, with its own parliament based at Melbourne.

○ At its height the British Empire covered a quarter of the world and ruled a quarter of the total world population.

○ After 1800, many Europeans wanted to explore the unknown interior of Africa in order to spread Christianity or to help combat the slave trade, run by Arab merchants. Some Europeans wanted to develop trade in products like minerals and palm oil.

○ In the 1880s, Europeans competed fiercely for African colonies. This was called "the scramble for Africa."

○ In some parts of Africa, colonial rule was established peacefully by agreement with the Africans.

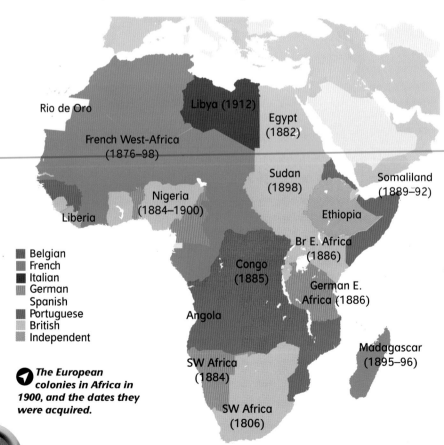

Rio de Oro

Libya (1912)

Egypt (1882)

French West-Africa (1876–98)

Sudan (1898)

Somaliland (1889–92)

Nigeria (1884–1900)

Liberia

Ethiopia

Br E. Africa (1886)

■ Belgian
■ French
■ Italian
■ German
  Spanish
■ Portuguese
  British
  Independent

Congo (1885)

German E. Africa (1886)

Angola

Madagascar (1895–96)

SW Africa (1884)

➤ *The European colonies in Africa in 1900, and the dates they were acquired.*

SW Africa (1806)

Find out more

Early vehicles p. 351

▼ *This map shows the British Empire in the 1930s, when it was already beginning to shrink. Egypt was given some independence in 1922, when Sultan Ahmed became King Fuad I. Iraq gained a similar independence when amir Ahd Allah Faisal became King Faisal I in 1921.*

▲ *In 1770, Captain James Cook landed on the east coast of Australia and claimed it for Britain. Eighteen years later, ships started to transport convicts there.*

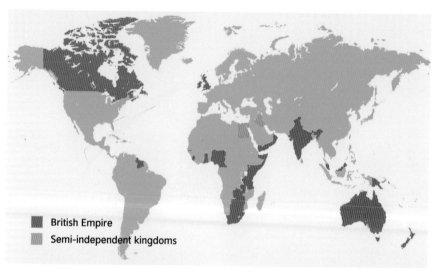

British Empire
Semi-independent kingdoms

○ In Nigeria and Ghana, the Africans fought hard against British rule, and in Tanzania and Namibia, they fought against German rule.

○ Until 1900, the USA played little part in world affairs. Bismarck said, "A special providence takes care of fools, drunkards, and the USA." But in 1898, the US battleship *Maine* was blown up off Cuba. Americans blamed the Spanish and in the war that followed, the USA easily defeated Spain. The USA then became more involved in world affairs.

Colonies in Africa in 1900

Belgium	Congo
Britain	Becuanaland, British Somaliland, Egypt, Gold Coast, Kenya, Nigeria, Nyasaland, Rhodesia, Sierra Leone, South Africa, Sudan, Uganda, Zanzibar
France	Chad, Djibouti, French West Africa, Gabon, Madagascar, Middle Congo, Shari Ubangi
Germany	Kamerun, Southwest Africa, Tanganyika, Togoland
Italy	Eritrea, Somaliland
Portugal	Angola, Guinea, Mozambique
Spain	Rio de Oro, Spanish Morocco, Spanish Sahara

Industrial power

In the late 1800s, the USA changed from a nation of farming pioneers and plantation owners to the world's biggest industrial powerhouse. American inventors and industrialists made products that changed the world—the typewriter (1867), the telephone (1876), the phonograph (1877), and electric light (1879). Then, in the early 1900s, Henry Ford pioneered the mass production of cars and made them affordable for millions of ordinary people.

World Wars

By 1914, Europe was divided into two armed camps as the empires and countries became rivals for power, territory, and wealth. When the European states went to war in 1914, fighting spread rapidly across the world, involving many other countries. This World War ended in 1918 with the defeat of Germany, Austria, and Turkey. The war was followed by economic hardship in many countries that had helped dictators to gain power. In Germany the dictator Adolf Hitler wanted to reverse the defeat of 1918. He invaded Poland in 1939, starting World War II, which would later involve more countries than World War I. When World War II ended in 1945, Europe was economically and physically ruined—millions had been killed.

○ World War I was caused by the intense rivalry between European powers in the early 1900s. When Archduke Franz Ferdinand was assassinated in June 1914, Austria started a war with Serbia, and Russia came to Serbia's defence. Germany declared war on Russia and Russia's ally, France, on August 3.

○ As the Germans invaded France, they marched through Belgium, which brought Britain into the war. Soon a line of trenches, the Western front, stretched from the English Channel across to Switzerland. The opposing armies dug trenches—and stayed facing each other in much the same place for the whole four years of the war.

○ The war also had an Eastern front, where the Central Powers (Austria and Germany) faced the Russians.

○ In the Alps the Central Powers were opposed by Italy, while in Turkey, British and Anzac (Australia and New Zealand) troops fought the Turks.

○ In 1917 the USA joined the Allies against the Central Powers, which precipitated the end of the war. At 11 o'clock on November 11, 1918, the Germans signed an armistice (peace).

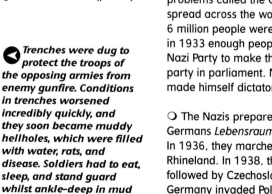

The Battle of Britain began in the late summer of 1940. By October, the British had defeated the Germans and won this battle for the skies.

Trenches were dug to protect the troops of the opposing armies from enemy gunfire. Conditions in trenches worsened incredibly quickly, and they soon became muddy hellholes, which were filled with water, rats, and disease. Soldiers had to eat, sleep, and stand guard whilst ankle-deep in mud and filth.

○ After World War I, economic problems called the Great Depression spread across the world. In Germany 6 million people were out of work, and in 1933 enough people voted for the Nazi Party to make them the strongest party in parliament. Nazi leader Hitler made himself dictator of Germany.

○ The Nazis prepared for war to give Germans *Lebensraum* ("living space"). In 1936, they marched into the Rhineland. In 1938, they took Austria, followed by Czechoslovakia. In 1939, Germany invaded Poland, which was allied to Britain and France. World War II had begun.

Find out more

World War II p. 360

U-Boats

German U-boats (submarines) were used during World Wars I and II to destroy warships and merchant ships belonging to the enemy.

Amazing

Britain's powerful warship HMS *Hood* had eight 15 in guns and 60 other guns. It was sunk in May 1941 by a single shell from German warship *Bismarck*.

USA enters the war

The Japanese attack on the United States fleet at Pearl Harbor, Hawaii, hastened the entry of the United States into World War II. American casualties included over 180 aircraft and more than 5,000 lives, from the military and the civilian population.

❍ After a lull, or "Phoney War," the Germans quickly overran Norway and Denmark, then Luxembourg, the Netherlands, Belgium, and France. By July 1940 only Britain was still at war with Germany.

❍ Italy joined the war on the German side, and Germany launched air raids on Britain to prepare for an invasion. This was the Battle of Britain. The British Royal Air Force won the battle, so Hitler called off the invasion of Britain.

❍ The USA joined the war when Japan bombed its fleet without warning in Pearl Harbor, Hawaii, on December 7, 1941.

❍ Germany, Italy, Japan, and six other nations joined forces as the "Axis." Britain, the USA, USSR, China, and 50 smaller countries formed the Allies. In 1942, the Allies halted the Axis in Africa, invading Italy in 1943 and France in 1944. Germany surrendered on May 7, 1945. Then the USA dropped atom bombs on the Japanese cities Hiroshima and Nagasaki. Japan surrendered on September 2, 1945.

❍ World War II (1939–1945) killed 17 million soldiers—compared to 10 million in World War I—and twice as many civilians, through starvation, bombings, and massacres.

▼ *Sir Winston Churchill (1874–1965) was the British prime minister whose courage and inspiring speeches helped the British withstand the German threat. He received a knighthood in 1953.*

Famous Quotes of Winston Churchill

I am easily satisfied with the very best

I have nothing to offer but blood, toil, tears, and sweat

Russia is a riddle wrapped in a mystery inside an enigma

Before Alamein we never had a victory. After Alamein we never had a defeat

A lie gets halfway around the world before the truth has the chance to get its pants on

Never in the field of human conflict was so much owed by so many to so few

If you are going through hell, keep going

This is not the end. It is not even the beginning of the end. But it is, perhaps, the end of the beginning

The Cold War

World War II left the USA and the Soviet Union as the two most powerful countries in the world. The Soviet Union thought that dictatorial Communism was the best way to run the world, while the USA believed in democracy and capitalism. Within a few years of the end of World War II the two powers had become hostile to each other. Other countries began to take sides in the dispute, and soon the world was divided into two opposing armed camps in a "Cold War"—a conflict in which neither side actually declares war. In 1990 the Communist bloc began to disintegrate due to economic problems, thus bringing the Cold War to an end.

○ Joseph Stalin (1879–1953) became dictator of the USSR after Lenin died in 1924, and remained so until he himself died, in 1953.

○ Stalin used terror to wipe out opposition and ensure the revolution survived. Russians lived in fear of the secret police NKVD (later the KGB), and millions went to their deaths in the Gulags (prison camps).

○ The USA and USSR waged an arms race to build up nuclear bombs and missiles one step ahead of their rival.

○ Real war loomed when US president Kennedy threatened the USSR as it tried to build missile bases on Cuba in 1962.

○ The Cold War was fought using both propaganda and art and by secret means such as spies and secret agents.

○ The Cold War thawed after 1985, when Soviet leader Mikhail Gorbachev introduced reforms in the USSR and began to cooperate with the West.

In 1989, the Berlin Wall, which divided east and west Berlin, was pulled down. For many, the tearing down of the Berlin Wall marked the end of the Cold War. Communist governments across Eastern Europe gave way to democracy in the following months.

Communism

Throughout the Cold War some people in the West supported Communism. The Argentinian Communist Ernesto "Che" Guevara fought with the Revolution in Cuba and encouraged students and radicals throughout the capitalist world to join the Communist cause. He was killed leading a Communist uprising in Peru in 1967.

Amazing

When the Soviets took over Poland, they arrested anyone who had a telephone. They thought that only rich people who opposed Communism would own a phone.

○ The republics within the USSR demanded independence too, and in 1991 the USSR was dissolved and replaced by a Commonwealth of Independent States (CIS).

Find out more

Communism p. 362

Mikhail Gorbachev

Mikhail Gorbachev was born in 1933 and worked his entire adult life for the Communist Party in the Soviet Union. In 1985 he became the head of the Soviet Union, and was faced by massive economic and social problems. He tried to solve these problems within a Communist framework, but his reforms served only to unleash democratic forces that brought down the Communist regime.

○ Gorbachev's reforms angered Communist Party leaders, who staged a coup and imprisoned Gorbachev, but he was freed and the coup was brought down by Boris Yeltsin, who became Russia's first president.

○ In 2000, the Russians elected Vladimir Putin as president, a strong leader who they hoped would see them out of the crisis.

○ Mao Zedong (1893–1976) led the communist takeover of China in 1949 and then ruled China as chairman of the republic. Chinese people hoped communism would end poverty and oppression. "We have stood up," Mao said. The Communist Party continued to rule China into the 21st century.

○ The Viet Cong started a rebellion in South Vietnam. They were supported by the Communist government of North Vietnam. In 1965, the USA began to bomb North Vietnam, while the USSR and China gave them arms. In 1975, the Viet Cong captured Saigon, the capital of the South, and the next year united North and South.

▲ *Fidel Castro was premier of Cuba from 1959 until 1976. He set up a one-party government to assume complete power.*

▼ *Following the establishment of the People's Republic of China, Mao ordered the redistribution of land and the elimination of rural landlords.*

End of Empires

African colony	Date of independence	African colony	Date of independence
Algeria	1962		
Angola	1975	Mali	1960
Benin formerly Dahomey	1960	Mauritania	1960
Burkina formerly Upper Volta	1960	Morocco	1956
Burundi	1962	Mozambique	1975
Cameroon	1961	Niger	1960
Central African Republic	1961	Nigeria	1960
Chad	1960	Rwanda	1962
Ethiopia	1941	Senegal	1960
Gabon	1968	Sierra Leone	1961
Gambia	1965	Somalia	1960
Guinea	1958	Sudan	1956
Guinea Bissau	1974	Tanzania	1964
Ivory Coast	1960	Tunisia	1956
Kenya	1963	Uganda	1962
Libya	1951	Zaire formerly Congo	1960
Madagascar	1960	Zambia	1964

The Changing World

The collapse of the Soviet Union ushered in a period of rapid change that is still continuing. Many countries that had previously supported communism abandoned left-wing dictatorships when they were no longer subsidized by Soviet money and weapons. The more repressive of the right-wing governments also collapsed in the wave of changes. However, some countries took advantage of the changes to begin wars or to attempt to bully their neighbors, which resulted in a series of small-scale wars in many areas.

A *The European Commission building in Strasbourg. The Parliament is in Brussels. The Court of Justice is in Luxembourg.*

○ In the 1970s and 1980s, opposition grew to the system of apartheid (or racial differentiation) in South Africa. Apartheid was supposed to allow the various peoples to develop their culture and exist economically separately within the one country, but in practice it was a racist system that discriminated against black people.

○ In the 1980s and 1990s, economic failure brought down most Latin American dictators, including the generals Galtieri in Argentina (1983) and Pinochet in Chile (1990) who were both replaced by democratically elected presidents.

○ On August 2, 1990 Iraqi forces made a surprise attack on Kuwait, which started the Persian Gulf War. The United States, NATO, and Arab forces from several countries joined together to try to free Kuwait from Saddam Hussein and his army.

○ The Hubble Space Telescope was launched in 1990 by NASA. It orbits around the Earth at 373 mi above the ground. Astronomers have used the telescope to obtain images of celestial objects and phenomena never before observed.

○ July 1, 1997 Hong Kong was handed over to China by Britain, ending more than 50 years of British control. It was made a special administrative region under the direct control of the Chinese government. Tung Chee-hwa was sworn in as Hong Kong's new leader.

Nelson Mandela

Nelson Mandela was imprisoned for 26 years for campaigning for the end of apartheid. Apartheid was a social system in place in South Africa that separated black and white citizens. Mandela was jailed in 1964 for being a senior member of the ANC (African National Congress). In 1990, South African president, F. W. de Klerk, released Mandela. In 1994, Mandela became the first black president of South Africa, and apartheid gradually began to break down.

Amazing

In 1999 a worldwide scare began about the "Millennium Bug" which was supposed to wreck computers at midnight on December 31, 1999. In fact, nothing happened.

○ On September 11, 2001, Islamic terrorists organized by Osama bin Laden's Al Qaeda organization flew hijacked airliners into the World Trade Center in New York and the Pentagon in Washington. This event sparked off a major campaign against terrorism led by US President George W. Bush.

○ In 2002 the US attacked Afghanistan, bombing bases of the Islamic government and of Al Qaeda in the country. American-backed rebels took control of the country and closed down all terrorist bases. Osama bin Laden went into hiding but his organization continued to organize terrorist attacks.

○ On April 4, 2003 American troops and tanks entered Baghdad, the capital of Iraq, and captured the airport. Hundreds of Iraqis fled the city. The next day, American and Kurdish forces jointly captured the Iraqi town of Mosul.

○ On January 4, 2004 *Spirit*, a six-wheeled robot made by the United States space agency NASA, landed on Mars.

○ On June, 27 2004 the American administration of Iraq ended and the governance of the country was given back to the Iraqis.

▲ *In April 1945, 50 nations met at San Francisco to draw up the Charter for the United Nations. Poland signed it shortly after, to create the first 51 Member States of the UN. In recent years, the UN peacekeeping force has been involved in keeping the peace in many places, including Somalia, Rwanda, Kosovo, Bosnia, Sierra Leone, and East Timor.*

European Union

The European Union is an organization of 15 European countries. The EU has four governing bodies: the Commission, Council of Ministers, Court of Justice, and Parliament. The 17 Commissioners submit laws for the Council to make and put into effect. Parliament is gaining more power each year. In 1999, the EU launched the euro, which is intended to become a single European currency. In 2004 the leaders of the European Union drew up a draft constitution that would change the EU from being an organization of independent countries to being a sovereign state in its own right. The move provoked controversy among those who preferred that the various member countries should remain independent states.

Find out more

Soviet Union p. 360

History Timeline

***c.*1,500,000 BC** In Africa, *Homo erectus* are the first people to use fire.

***c.*9000 BC** In what is now Iraq, the first farmers plant seeds of wheat and barley.

***c.*3000 BC** Stonehenge is built in England.

***c.*500–350 BC** The Greek Empire is at its most successful.

***c.*AD 500** Teotihuacán, in Mexico, is the largest city in the world.

1250 The Mongols rule Southern Russia.

1438 In Peru, the Incas start to build their Empire.

1492 In what is now the Caribbean, Columbus discovers the West Indies.

1700s The Agricultural Revolution takes place in Britain.

1770 Captain Cook reaches Australia.

1805 Nelson defeats Napoleon at the battle of Trafalgar, off the coast of Spain.

Find out more
Timelines pp. 312, 342, 352

*c.*2600 BC The pyramids at Giza are built in Egypt.

*c.*1200 BC The Phoenicians become successful sailors and traders in what is now Syria and Lebanon.

*c.*509 BC Rome, in Italy, becomes a republic.

*c.*AD 790 The Vikings begin raiding Europe.

1096 The Crusades begin in what is now Palestine.

1215 In England, Magna Carta is signed.

1519–1534 Spanish conquistadors conquer the Aztecs in Mexico.

1630s In Italy, Galileo proves that the Earth travels around the Sun.

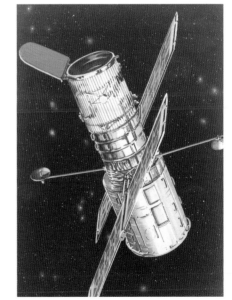

1854–1869 The Suez Canal is built in Egypt.

1914–1918 World War I
1939–1945 World War II

1990 Space exploration continues. The Hubble telescope is launched by NASA.

Glossary

Agricultural Revolution The period of time from 1700 to 1850 during which methods of farming changed dramatically. This allowed fewer farmers to grow more food on the same area of land.

Allies Generally, allies are countries that join together to try to achieve a specific purpose. Sometimes one side in a war will be called the Allies, as were Britain, the USA, the Soviet Union, and some other countries in World War II.

Anglo-Saxon The Germanic tribes who moved from Germany to Britain after the fall of the Roman Empire are known as the Anglo-Saxons. At first they were divided into a number of different kingdoms. They later became the English.

Apartheid A Boer word meaning "separate development." It was used to describe policies of the South African government that aimed to allow the different ethnic groups in the country to develop their culture, society, and economy along paths separate from each other. In practice, the government was dominated by Boers, who made sure that the Boers got the best out of the policy.

Armada A large and powerful fleet of warships that sets out on a voyage to conquer another country.

Armor A layer of special clothing to protect a person in battle. Most armor was made of metal, but some was formed from leather, horn, or wood.

Aztec A people who lived in what is now Mexico. They built up a large empire, but were conquered by the Spanish in the 16th century.

Bankrupt A person, organization, or country is said to be bankrupt if it is unable to pay its debts when they become due.

Barbarian Peoples and tribes that are uncivilized or behave in an uncivilized way. The word comes from ancient Greek and means "a person who cannot speak Greek."

Blockade A blockade happens when one side in a war tries to stop food and other supplies from entering a fortress, city, or even an entire country. It is usually hoped that a blockade will force the enemy to surrender without the need for serious fighting.

Boer A people living in South Africa who are descended from Dutch settlers who came to live there in the 16th and 17th centuries. They speak Boer, a language broadly similar to Dutch. The Boers are sometimes called Afrikaaners.

Byzantine The Eastern Roman Empire is known as the Byzantine Empire because it was based on the city of Constantinople, which had formerly been called Byzantine. The Empire lasted until 1453 when it was conquered by the Turks. Constantinople is now called Istanbul.

Caravel A type of ship used in Europe between about 1400 and 1600 that was small, but sturdy.

Charter A document issued by a king or other ruler that grants powers and rights to a group of people.

Civil War A civil war happens when the citizens of one country divide into two sides and fight each other.

Civilization People who live together in cities or towns and share a culture and way of life are said to form a civilization.

Cold war A cold war happens when two or more countries wage a campaign against each other without actually fighting. They may use propaganda, economic sanctions, or threats instead of weapons. The struggle of the USA and its allies against the Soviet Union and its allies is sometimes called The Cold War, and lasted from 1947 to 1990.

Colony The first colonies were small groups of people who went to live in another part of the world while keeping their own laws and ways of life. Later the word came to mean any territory ruled by another country that was located a distance away.

Commonwealth A country in which the wealth of the nation is held in common for the good of all the people. Often the word is used to describe a state that is not a dictatorship.

Communism A system of government under which all economic power is held by the government on behalf of all the people. In theory this means that all people have equal wealth and rights, but most communist governments have been run as dictatorships.

Conquistadors Spanish soldiers who conquered areas of the Americas in the 16th and 17th centuries and who often stole gold and spread Christianity. Conquistador is Spanish for "conqueror."

Convict A person who has been sentenced to prison for a number of years.

Coup An illegal seizure of power by a group of people. The term is often used to mean a violent event in which the army or part of the army replaces the existing government with army officers.

Crusade A military campaign fought to protect Christian pilgrims or to extend lands for Christian rulers. A series of crusades were fought between the Christians of Europe and the Moslems during the 11th–15th centuries.

Czar From about 1550–1917 the monarchs of Russia called themselves "czar," which is the Russian for "Caesar." They did this to compare themselves to the emperors of ancient Rome. Czar is sometimes spelled "tsar."

Democracy A Greek word meaning "people-power." Generally, a democracy is a country in which all or most of the people have a say in how the government is run.

Depression A period of time during which there are economic problems and great poverty. Some depressions last only a few months, others may continue for years or even decades.

Dictatorship From ancient Rome meaning "rule by speaking." Generally a dictatorship is a country in which one person, or a small group of people, decide how the government is run.

Dynasty A family of rulers, kings, or emperors. The history of some countries, such as China and Egypt, is divided into periods according to which dynasty was on the throne at the time.

Emperor Man who rules an empire. The word comes from ancient Latin and means "victorious commander."

Empire A territory in which members of one ethnic or national group rule over members of other ethnic or national groups.

Engine A machine that produces power to drive other machines. Engines may use one of several different sorts of fuel, such as coal, oil, or gas.

Epic A long poem or book that tells the story of a hero or a group of heroes. An epic is usually based on fact, but has been much exaggerated to make it more exciting.

Etruscan A people who lived in central Italy about 2,500 years ago. The Etruscans loved music and art, and were famous warriors. They were conquered by the Romans and lost their identity.

Explorer A person who travels to a place or area about which little is known by his own people, even if it is inhabited. Most explorers draw maps and write accounts of where they have been and what they have seen.

Felucca A boat used on the River Nile. It has a single triangular sail and a long, narrow hull.

Fertile Crescent An area of land reaching from Egypt, through the Middle East and along the valleys of the Indus and Euphrates rivers to the Indus Valley. The people who lived in this area were the first in the world to learn how to grow crops and raise livestock.

Franks A tribe of Germanic people who invaded the Roman province of Gaul around the year AD 500. They took over the land and named it after themselves—France.

Fundamentalism A belief that one form of a religion is absolutely correct and that all other religions, or even forms of the same religion, are not only wrong but evil. Many fundamentalists attempt peacefully to convert others to their belief, but a few resort to violence or terrorism.

Gladiator A man in the ancient Roman Empire who was trained to fight wild animals or other gladiators to the death, in order to entertain a crowd of spectators.

Guerrilla This Spanish word means "little war" and describes a military campaign during which no major battles take place. Instead the combatants attack each others supply lines, communications, and other small targets.

Guillotine This famous machine was designed to drop a heavy, sharp blade on to the neck of a condemned person. The blade sliced off the head instantly, so this was considered a painless and humane way to kill somebody. It was used to kill thousands of people during the French Revolution.

Hippodrome A horse racecourse surrounded by banks of seating. The word comes from ancient Greek and means "horse area."

Holy Roman Empire An empire covering much of modern Germany and parts of Italy, Poland, and nearby countries. The empire was usually weak as the nobles did not always do as the emperor instructed.

Inca A powerful people who lived in the Andes. The Inca Empire was conquered by the Spanish in the 16th century.

Indulgences Pieces of paper sold by the Catholic Church during the Middle Ages. The Church claimed that the indulgence cleansed the soul of the person to whom they were sold and allowed them to enter Heaven.

Industrial Revolution The dramatic change in the way industry was organized between 1700 and today. The Industrial Revolution saw the development of mass production using fewer workers to operate machines in factories, increasing productivity.

Knight In medieval Europe, a man who held land from a king or noble and, instead of paying rent, agreed to fight in an army.

Latin America Parts of the Americas where the inhabitants speak languages descended from Latin, mostly Spanish or Portuguese. Area covers most of South and Central America.

Legend A story that is passed on from generation to generation. Legends claim to be historical accounts of real events, but are often changed and confused as time passes.

Legion A unit in the army of ancient Rome. Each legion contained about 5,000 infantry and 200 cavalry, plus officers and engineers. Only citizens of Rome could join a legion.

Manchu A people who live in the province of Manchuria in northeastern China. The Manchu ruled all China from 1644–1908.

Maori The people who lived in New Zealand before it was discovered by Europeans. The Maori were divided into many different tribes. Maori still live in New Zealand today.

Minoan The people who lived in Crete more than 3,000 years ago are known as Minoans after their legendary king, Minos. They were probably a group of Greeks. their civilization ended around 1300 BC, perhaps after a volcanic eruption.

Missionary A person who seeks to convert other people to the religion in which he believes. Missionaries often travel to remote parts of the world to look for converts.

Mogul A people who ruled most of India from the 16th–19th centuries. The Moguls were Moslems, while most of the people they ruled were Hindus.

Monastery A religious institution in which monks live, dedicated to a life of prayer and learning. During the Middle Ages in Europe some monasteries owned vast estates and much wealth, and some monks led lives of scandal and luxury.

Mongol A tribe of nomadic horsemen who lived in what is now Mongolia and northern China. In the 13th century the Mongols were united with other nomads and set out to conquer surrounding lands.

Nazi A shortened name of the German "National Socialist Workers Party," led by Adolf Hitler during the 1920s–1940s. The Nazi Party wanted to restore the power of Germany by reforming society, building up its military, and invading neighboring countries.

Nomadic People who do not live in any one place, but who move from place to place. Some nomads follow a route each year between different places, but others simply wander wherever they think they should go.

Normans The Normans lived in what is now Normandy, northern France, in the 10th–13th centuries. They were descended from Viking settlers who arrived in the 9th century.

Olmecs The Olmec civilization prospered between c.1200–400 BC. The most important center for Olmec culture was on the Mexican Gulf coast. The Olmec lived in small thatched houses near rivers, fishing in the rivers and farming the lands made fertile by the river floods.

Ottoman The dynasty that ruled the Turkish people until the early 20th century. During the 15th and 16th centuries the Ottomans built up a powerful empire that covered much of southeastern Europe, North Africa, and the Middle East.

Peacekeeper A military force that is used to keep the peace between two other warring sides. Peacekeepers usually supervise agreements and may occupy disputed territory to stop either side gaining an advantage.

Philosopher A person who thinks about the meaning of life and ultimate reality. The word is Greek for "lover of knowledge" and the first philosophers lived in ancient Greece.

Picts People who lived in what is now northern Scotland before around AD 900. The Picts were famous as horsemen. The word means "painted man" and they got this name as they tattooed their skins. The Picts joined with the Scots to form Scotland before AD 900.

Pilgrimage A religious journey undertaken to reach a holy place or to meet a holy person.

Pirate A person who steals on the high seas. Often large numbers of pirates would use ships to attack other ships or coastal towns.

Pope The head of the Roman Catholic church and the bishop of Rome is known as the Pope. The first bishop of Rome was St Peter, appointed by Jesus Christ to lead the Christian Church. The popes claim that this makes them the most important of all the bishops.

Protestant A Christian who belongs to one of the various churches that were founded when their members protested against the corruption of the Catholic Church in the 15th and 16th centuries.

Quetzalcoatl The chief ancestral god of the Aztecs. The Aztecs believed that Quetzalcoatl would one day return to rule them with wisdom and justice.

Raj The period of time when the British ruled most of India. The word is sometimes used to mean the system of government used by the British in India.

Rebellion When a small group of people rise up against their rulers in protest against a specific problem or worry.

Redcoat British soldiers fighting between 1650 and 1890 were often called redcoats because they wore coats or jackets made of bright red woollen cloth.

Reformation A religious movement in western Europe which began in about 1500 and lasted about 100 years. During this time many people left the Catholic church to join 'reformed' churches which opposed what they saw as the corruption of the Catholic Church.

Renaissance A period of European history between about 1350 and 1550 when scholars rediscovered ancient Greece and Rome writings as well as developing new ideas and artistic styles.

Republic A country which is governed without a king or emperor. Some republics are democracies, which are run by their people, while others are run by a small group of people. The word comes from ancient Latin and means "in the name of the people."

Revolution A rebellion that spreads to include a significant number of the people in a country and is usually directed against a wide range of problems and complaints. A revolution may overthrow the entire system of government in a country.

Samurai Japanese warriors who trained continually to become highly skilled with both weapons and religion. The samurai were officially abolished in the 19th century.

Scots A tribe of people from northern Ireland who settled in what is now southwest Scotland around the year AD 400. The king of the Scots later inherited the kingdom of the Picts to create Scotland as it is today.

Serfdom A form of social status, close to slavery. Serfs were forced to farm a particular piece of land for a landlord. However, they did have rights under the law and there was a system to protect them from cruelty, unlike slaves.

Shogun This Japanese word means "military commander." It is usually used to refer to the military dictators who ruled Japan on behalf of the Emperor between the 12th and 19th centuries.

Slave A person who is owned by another person. Usually slaves have no human rights at all, they are forced to work without pay and may be punished or even killed by their owner. Slavery is illegal in most countries today.

Submarine A ship able to move below the water as well as on the surface. Some submarines are used by scientists to study sealife, but most are naval ships designed to sink other ships or to launch missiles.

Terrorist A fighter who seeks to inspire terror in his enemies. In recent years the word has come to mean a fighter who attacks and kills civilians rather than enemy soldiers.

Testudo A formation used by the Roman Army in which the shield of each man overlapped that of the next man, providing defence against arrows and spears. The word means "tortoise."

Tlatoani The Aztec name for their ruler.

Toltecs Mesoamerican people who lived in and around Tula, a city in central Mexico. Their civilization existed from around AD 950 to AD 1150.

Tournament A contest organized in medieval Europe so that knights could compete in events that tested their skills with weapons.

Vikings The people who lived in Scandinavia about a thousand years ago. The Vikings were fearless warriors who attacked many countries in western Europe. They were also highly skilled traders and seamen who traveled vast distances in their ships. The Vikings were the first Europeans known to have reached the Americas.

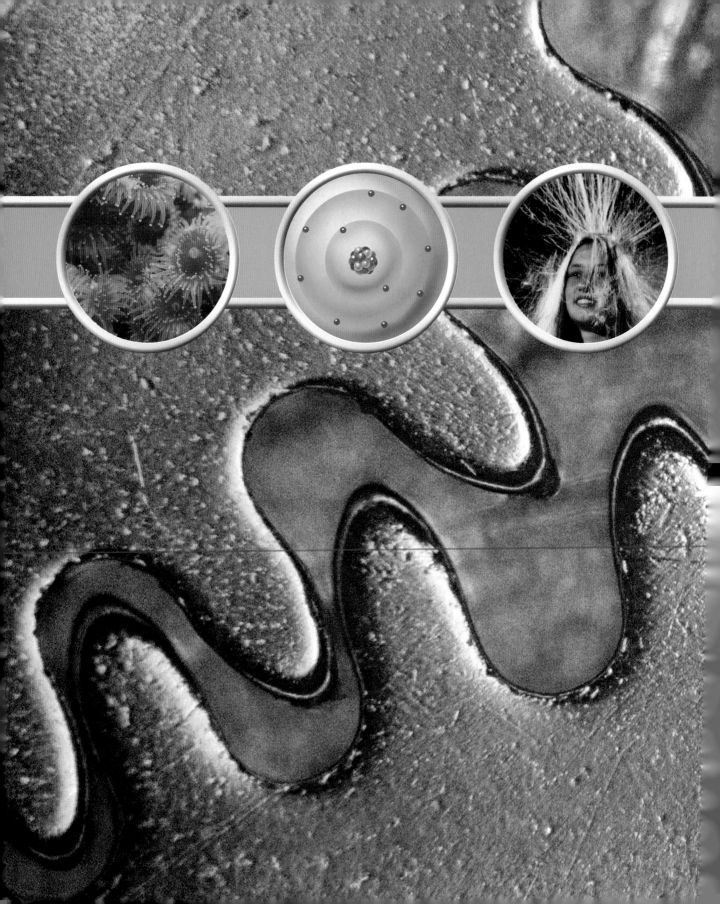

SCIENCE & TECHNOLOGY

Atoms and Molecules

***A**toms are the tiny bits, or particles, that build together to make every known substance. A substance made of only one type of atom is called a chemical element. A molecule is two or more atoms bonded together.*

❍ You could fit two billion atoms on the period after this sentence.

❍ Atoms are mostly empty space, dotted with a few even tinier particles called subatomic particles.

❍ In the center of each atom is a dense core, or nucleus, made from two kinds of particle: protons and neutrons. Protons have a positive electrical charge, and neutrons none.

❍ Around the nucleus orbit negatively-charged particles called electrons.

❍ The number of protons, neutrons, and electrons varies from element to element.

❍ Atoms and molecules are held together by chemical bonds.

❍ The shape of a molecule depends on the arrangement of bonds that hold its atoms together.

Inside an atom electrons (blue) whiz around a dense nucleus of protons (red) and neutrons (gray). There is always an equal number of negatively charged electrons and positively charged protons, so the atom has no overall charge.

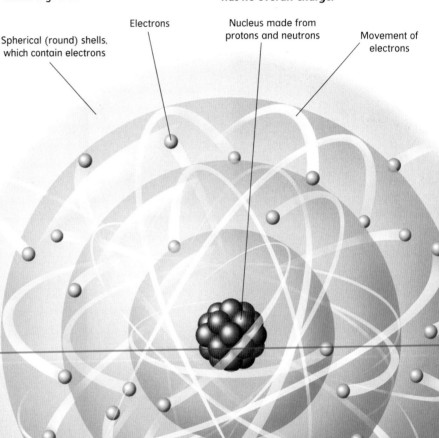

Spherical (round) shells, which contain electrons

Electrons

Nucleus made from protons and neutrons

Movement of electrons

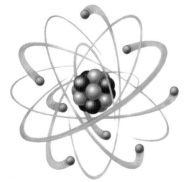

▲ *The protons and neutrons in the nucleus of an atom are held together by a powerful force. When the nucleus is split, as happens in a nuclear reactor, huge amounts of energy are released.*

Atom factfile

A typical atom measures about 0.2 to 0.3 nanometers across.

A nanometer is an incredibly small unit— one billionth of a meter. So 10 million atoms in a row would stretch just 2 mm!

The nucleus at the center of an atom is tiny compared to the size of the atom as a whole.

If the whole atom were the size of a massive sports stadium, the outermost electrons would be whizzing around the farthest seats, and the nucleus would be the size of a human thumb in the middle.

In a solid substance, the atoms are about 0.3 nanometers apart, so their outermost electrons almost touch.

Find out more

Periodic Table pp. 376–377

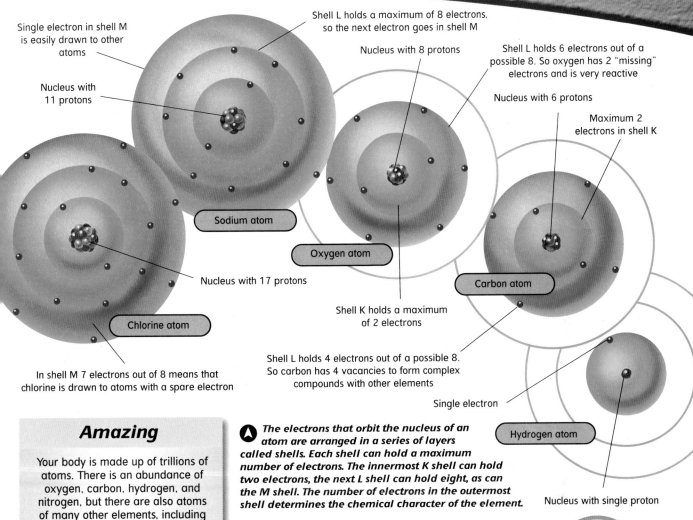

Single electron in shell M is easily drawn to other atoms

Nucleus with 11 protons

Shell L holds a maximum of 8 electrons, so the next electron goes in shell M

Nucleus with 8 protons

Shell L holds 6 electrons out of a possible 8. So oxygen has 2 "missing" electrons and is very reactive

Nucleus with 6 protons

Maximum 2 electrons in shell K

Sodium atom

Oxygen atom

Carbon atom

Nucleus with 17 protons

Shell K holds a maximum of 2 electrons

Chlorine atom

Single electron

In shell M 7 electrons out of 8 means that chlorine is drawn to atoms with a spare electron

Shell L holds 4 electrons out of a possible 8. So carbon has 4 vacancies to form complex compounds with other elements

Hydrogen atom

Nucleus with single proton

Amazing

Your body is made up of trillions of atoms. There is an abundance of oxygen, carbon, hydrogen, and nitrogen, but there are also atoms of many other elements, including iron, tin, silver, and even gold!

🅐 **The electrons that orbit the nucleus of an atom are arranged in a series of layers called shells. Each shell can hold a maximum number of electrons. The innermost K shell can hold two electrons, the next L shell can hold eight, as can the M shell. The number of electrons in the outermost shell determines the chemical character of the element.**

○ Chemical formulas use numbers and symbols to show the atoms in a molecule.

○ The formula for ammonia, a choking gas, is NH_3, because an ammonia molecule is made from one nitrogen (N) atom and three hydrogen atoms (H).

○ Compounds only exist as molecules. If the atoms in a compound's molecules were separated, the compound would cease to exist.

Simple hydrogen

The simplest and lightest atom of all is hydrogen. It has just one proton as the nucleus and one electron going around it.

Molecules

Atoms usually bond together in groups to form combinations called molecules. For example, a carbon dioxide molecule (a waste product when we breathe out) consists of one carbon atom linked to two oxygen atoms. Carbon dioxide has the chemical formula CO_2. When carbon joins with only one oxygen atom, it forms carbon monoxide, with the formula CO.

Solids, Liquids, and Gases

Nearly every substance in the Universe is either a solid, a liquid, or a gas. These are known as states of matter. Most substances can exist in all three states.

○ There is a fourth, less common state of matter called plasma, which is a bit like a gas but full of charged particles called electrons and ions.

○ Solids have strength and a definite shape. The molecules in a solid are firmly bonded together and locked into in a rigid framework.

Absolute zero

The lowest possible temperature is −459.67°F, known as absolute zero, at which atoms and molecules stop moving altogether. Scientists have come very close to achieving absolute zero in laboratories—within a millionth of a degree. There is no upper limit to temperature.

○ In a solid the molecules vibrate on the spot. The hotter the solid becomes, the more they vibrate. If it gets hot enough, the molecules vibrate so much that the framework breaks down and the solid melts and becomes a liquid.

○ A liquid has a fixed volume and flows and takes up the shape of any solid container into which it is poured.

○ A liquid flows because its molecules are less firmly bonded than those of a solid. The molecules in a liquid are not locked together, and can slide over each other without breaking away.

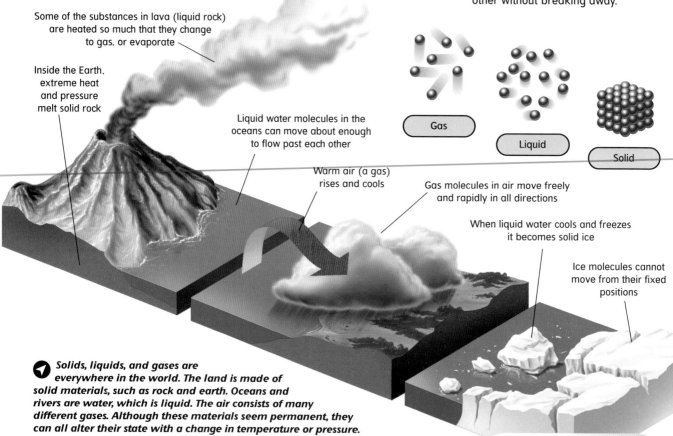

Some of the substances in lava (liquid rock) are heated so much that they change to gas, or evaporate

Inside the Earth, extreme heat and pressure melt solid rock

Liquid water molecules in the oceans can move about enough to flow past each other

Warm air (a gas) rises and cools

Gas molecules in air move freely and rapidly in all directions

When liquid water cools and freezes it becomes solid ice

Ice molecules cannot move from their fixed positions

Gas

Liquid

Solid

Solids, liquids, and gases are everywhere in the world. The land is made of solid materials, such as rock and earth. Oceans and rivers are water, which is liquid. The air consists of many different gases. Although these materials seem permanent, they can all alter their state with a change in temperature or pressure.

Find out more

Molecules p. 373

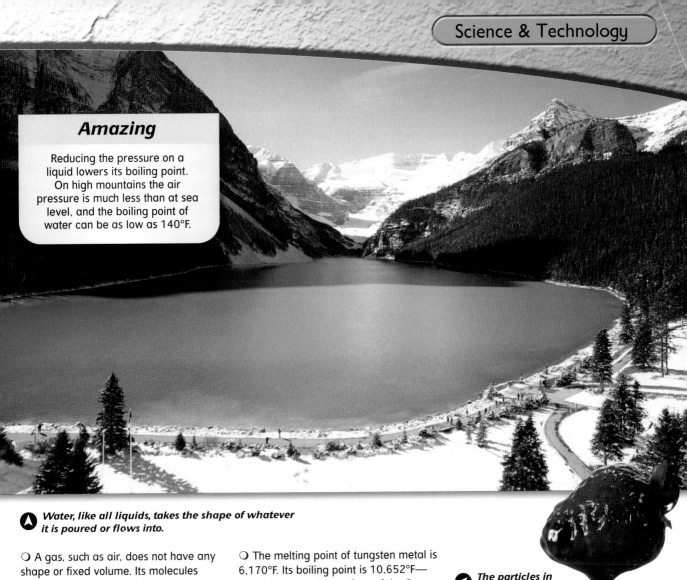

▲ *Water, like all liquids, takes the shape of whatever it is poured or flows into.*

❍ A gas, such as air, does not have any shape or fixed volume. Its molecules move too quickly for any bonds to hold them together, and the gas will spread out to fill any container it is put into.

❍ When a gas cools, its molecules slow down until bonds form between them to create drops of liquid. This process is called condensation.

❍ A substance can change state by gaining or losing energy.

❍ The melting point of tungsten metal is 6,170°F. Its boiling point is 10,652°F—about as hot as the surface of the Sun.

❍ The boiling point of the gas helium is −452.02°F, the lowest of any element.

◀ *The particles in solid chocolate gain energy as they are heated. They break away from each other as the solid melts.*

Melting and boiling points

The temperature at which a substance melts from a solid to a liquid is called its melting point. The highest temperature a liquid can reach before turning to a gas is called its boiling point. Each substance has its own melting and boiling point. Water melts at 32°F and boils at 212°F. When a gas cools down enough, it condenses to a liquid, such as when steam turns to water. When a liquid cools down enough, it turns solid or freezes, such as when water turns to ice.

Liquid elements

Only four elements are liquid at normal temperatures.

Mercury (Hg)	68°F–77°F
Bromine (Br)	68°F–77°F
Gallium (Ga)	86°F
Caesium (Cs)	83.3°F

The Periodic Table

Elements are the simplest possible substances. There are just over 100 elements, each of which is composed of its own unique type of atom. The Periodic Table is a chart that shows the similarities and differences between elements.

○ The Periodic Table arranges all the elements in order of their atomic number—the number of protons (positively charged articles) in their atoms—starting with hydrogen at 1.

○ Atoms usually contain the same number of electrons (negatively charged particles) as protons. So the atomic number also indicates the number of electrons in the atom.

○ The vertical columns in the periodic table are called groups. The horizontal rows are called periods.

○ Each group is made up of elements with same number of electrons in the outer shell of their atoms, so they all behave in a similar way chemically.

○ Each period begins with an alkali metal (which has one electron in its outer shell) on the left and ends with a noble gas (which has eight electrons in its outer shell) on the right.

Increasing electrons

The number of electrons in the atom's outer shell goes up one by one across each period.

Chemical symbol | Name of element

C Carbon 6 | N Nitrogen 7

Atomic number indicating number of protons in atom's nucleus

Amazing

In the 5th century BC Empedocles, a Greek philosopher, proposed that all matter was made from four elements—air, fire, water, and earth. Not until the 17th century was the true nature of elements realized.

Above the name for each element is its chemical symbol

Below the name for each element is the atomic number

As atomic numbers increase by one along each period, so chemical properties change

H Hydrogen 1								
Li Lithium 3	Be Beryllium 4							
Na Sodium 11	Mg Magnesium 12							
K Potassium 19	Ca Calcium 20	Sc Scandium 21	Ti Titanium 22	V Vanadium 23	Cr Chromium 24	Mn Manganese 25	Fe Iron 26	Co Cobalt 27
Rb Rubidium 37	Sr Strontium 38	Y Yttrium 39	Zr Zirconium 40	Nb Niobium 41	Mo Molybdenum 42	Tc Technetium 43	Ru Ruthenium 44	Rh Rhodium 45
Cs Caesium 55	Ba Barium 56		Hf Hafnium 72	Ta Tantalum 73	W Tungsten 74	Re Rhenium 75	Os Osmium 76	Ir Iridium 77
Fr Francium 87	Ra Radium 88		Rf Rutherfordium 104	Db Dubnium 105	Sg Seaborgium 106	Bh Bohrium 107	Hs Hassium 108	Mt Meitnerium 109
			La Lanthanum 57	Ce Cerium 58	Pr Praseodymium 59	Nd Neodymium 60	Pm Promethium 61	Sm Samarium 62
			Ac Actinium 89	Th Thorium 90	Pa Protactinium 91	U Uranium 92	Np Neptunium 93	Pu Plutonium 94

Group 1 elements are called alkali metals, which are all soft, very reactive metals

Group 2 elements, the alkaline-earth metals, occur naturally only in compounds

▶ As you move along a horizontal row in the Periodic Table the atomic weight of the elements increases. The lightest elements are upper left, the heaviest ones are lower right. The different colors represent elements with similar properties. Most of the elements are metals, although there are 15 nonmetal elements (the sand-colored block) on the right-hand side of the table.

Elements in the middle block (purple) are the transition metals, which include gold and copper

○ Scientists give each element a symbol. This is usually the first letter of its name, such as O for oxygen or C for carbon. If two or more elements begin with the same letter, a second small letter may be added. So hydrogen is H, and helium is He.

○ Only a few elements, such as gold, copper, and silver, can be found naturally in their pure state.

○ Most substances are made of two or more elements combined together chemically in a compound.

Noble gases

The elements in Group 18 (far right) of the periodic table are a very special group. They are extremely stable and unreactive. They are called the noble gases, because they stay "noble" (apart from) other chemicals and rarely form compounds. Noble gases such as argon and krypton are used in lightbulbs, because they are unreactive and will not burn out the filament—the thin, coiled wire inside the bulb. Neon is used to make neon lights for the same reason, because it can glow brightly without reacting.

○ Although there only about 100 elements, they can combine in so many different ways that they produce many millions of compounds.

○ The same combination of elements, such as carbon and hydrogen, can often react together to form a range of different compounds.

○ About 20 of the most recently identified elements were created artificially by scientists. These elements do not occur naturally.

○ Artificially created elements are often very unstable and last for only a fraction of a second before they break down.

○ New elements get temporary names from their atomic number. So the new element with atomic number 116 (not shown on this version of the Periodic Table) is called ununhexium. *Un* is the Latin word for one; *hex* is Latin for six.

○ Scientists have made three atoms of element 118, or ununoctium (not shown here), which is probably a colorless gas.

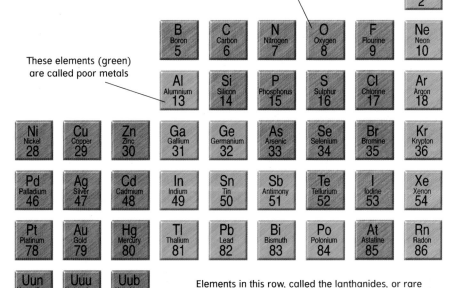

Elements in the final group (Group 18) on the right are called noble gases

These elements (sand-colored) are nonmetals

These elements (green) are called poor metals

Elements in this row, called the lanthanides, or rare earths, fit into Group 3, and are all shiny metals

Each left-to-right row is a period of elements with similar weights

This row, called the actinides, fits into Group 3, and includes radium and plutonium

Each top-to-bottom column is a group of elements with similar properties

Find out more

Atoms pp. 372–373

Chemicals and Materials

Compounds are substances formed when the atoms of two or more elements join together. The properties of a compound are usually very different from those of the elements it contains.

○ Compounds are different from mixtures. In a mixture, elements are combined loosely, but in a compound they are joined together chemically, and can only be separated by chemical reaction.

○ Every molecule of a compound contains exactly the same combination of atoms.

○ A compound's scientific name usually gives a clue to its components. Common salt, for example, is sodium chloride, indicating that it is made up of the elements sodium and chlorine.

Metals

Three out of four elements are metals. Most metals are shiny, hard substances that ring when you hit them. They are mostly tough, yet can often be easily shaped—either by hammering or by melting into molds. This makes metals good for making everything from spoons to space rockets. Metals are rarely pure. Most occur naturally in the ground in chemical compounds called ores, and the metal must be extracted by heating and other processes. Even then, metals usually contain some impurities. Sometimes impurities are added to create an "alloy," which gives the metal a particular quality. Carbon is added to iron to make an incredibly tough alloy called steel.

◐ *The substance called acetone, also known as propanone, is commonly used in nail varnish remover. Each molecule of acetone has three carbon atoms (orange), one oxygen (pink), and six hydrogen (light green). It is written as the formula* CH_3COCH_3.

○ The chemical formula of a compound summarizes which atoms its molecules are made of. The chemical formula for water is H_2O, because each water molecule has two hydrogen (H) atoms and one oxygen (O) atom.

○ Natural materials are found around us, as part of nature, rather than being artificial or manufactured.

◀ *Metals are excellent conductors of heat, which is why a hot drink soon warms a metal spoon.*

Find out more

Carbon chains and rings p. 381

○ Wood is an abundant natural material that is important in making furniture and utensils, as well as structures such as houses and bridges.

○ Various kinds of rock and stone are also widely used, especially in the construction of larger buildings.

Amazing

0.003 oz of gold can be drawn out into a thin wire 1.5 mi long.

○ Natural fibers, such as cotton, are woven into fabrics for clothes, drapes, and other items.

○ Glass is among the most useful of all materials. Various types of glass are made by heating the natural substances of sand (silica), limestone, and soda-ash with other ingredients.

○ Bulletproof vests are woven from an immensely strong material called Kevlar, which can withstand the impact of bullets. Kevlar threads are stronger than steel, but very light.

○ Composites are combinations of different materials. A composite combines the best features of each of its constituent materials.

Common compound

Citric acid, found in lemon juice, is a compound of hydrogen, oxygen, and carbon mixed with water.

When atoms join by covalent bonds, they share pairs of electrons. In this type of bonding an atom, with room in its outermost shell for an extra electron, gains such an electron by "sharing" it with another atom. The electron repeatedly flips to and fro, first in one atom and then in the other.

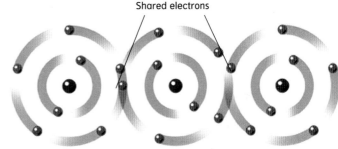

Shared electrons

Ionic bonding involves the movement of one or a few electrons in the outermost shell. The electron jumps across to another atom that has a space in its outermost shell. The atom that has lost the negative electron now has a positive charge; the one that gains has a negative charge. When atoms have charges, they are called ions. Ions of different charges, positive and negative, attract and bond to each other.

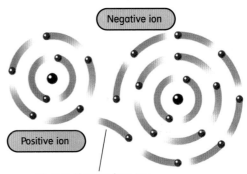

Negative ion

Positive ion

Electron "jumps" from one atom to the other

Chemical names for everyday items

Common name	Chemical name	Common name	Chemical name
Antifreeze	Ethylene glycol	**Laughing gas**	Nitrous oxide
Asbestos	Magnesium silicate	**Lime**	Calcium oxide
Aspirin	Acetylsalicyclic acid	**Mothballs**	Naphthalene
Baking powder	Sodium bicarbonate	**Plaster of Paris**	Calcium sulphate
Bleach	Sodium hypochlorite	**PVC**	Polyvinyl chloride
Carbolic acid	Phenol	**Rust**	Iron oxide
Caustic soda	Sodium hydroxide	**Salt**	Sodium chloride
Chalk	Calcium carbonate	**Saltpeter**	Potassium nitrate
Chloroform	Trichloromethane	**Sand**	Silicon dioxide
DDT	Dichlorodiphenyltrichloroethane	**Talcum powder**	Magnesium silicate hydroxide
Dry ice	Solid carbon dioxide	**TNT**	Trinitrotoluene
Epsom salts	Magnesium sulphate	**Vinegar**	Acetic acid
Fool's gold	Iron pyrites	**Vitamin C**	Ascorbic acid
Heavy water	Deuterium oxide	**Washing soda**	Sodium carbonate

Carbon Chemicals

Carbon is a very special element. The hardest known substance, diamond, is a form of carbon, as is coal and the graphite ("lead") in pencils. Carbon forms compounds easily because of its atomic structure.

○ Compounds are either organic (they contain carbon atoms) or inorganic.

○ There are more than one million known carbon compounds.

○ Pure carbon occurs in four natural forms: diamond, graphite, soot, and charcoal. There is also a special manufactured form called fullerene. Graphite can be stretched out into long fibers called carbon fibers.

○ Carbon fiber has four times more tensile strength than steel, It can be mixed with plastic resins to make strong, light composite materials.

Amazing

Scientists have suggested that some planets orbiting distant suns could be made largely of carbon, with atmospheres rich in carbon dioxide, liquid hydrocarbon seas, graphite crusts, and layers of diamond many miles thick.

○ Fullerenes are molecules containing between 32 and 600 carbon atoms linked together in a ball shape.

○ Plastics are made from carbon compounds with small molecules (mainly consisting of carbon and hydrogen atoms) that link up to form long chains.

Oils are organic liquids that burn easily and do not dissolve in water. Crude oil, or petroleum, is made mainly of hydrocarbons. These are compounds containing only hydrogen and carbon atoms, and are by far the largest group of carbon compounds. Crude oil formed from underground and undersea sediments provides over half the world's energy needs and is extracted by oil rigs erected in the sea. The oil is broken down into simpler substances in an oil refinery.

○ The small molecules are called monomers, and the long chains are called polymers. Different plastics are created using different monomers.

○ The plastic polythene is made by making thousands of ethene monomer molecules link up into polymer chains. Ethene is derived from petroleum.

Diamonds are forever

Diamond, made of carbon atoms linked together in a rigid structure, is the hardest naturally occurring material.

▶ *In some plastics, the chains are tangled together to make them strong yet flexible. These are ideal for making items such as parachutes, which need to be strong enough to support weight and yet flexible enough to glide in the air.*

○ Most carbon atoms have existed since the beginning of the Earth and, through a process called the carbon cycle, circulate continuously through animals, plants, and the air.

○ The leaves and stems of every plant are built largely from a natural material called cellulose. Like plastic, cellulose is a polymer—a long chain of carbon-based molecules. Plants put these chains together from sugar molecules called glucose, which they make with carbon dioxide from the air and water, using energy from the Sun.

▲ *Complex organic compounds are often made by mixing together two or more compounds so that a chemical reaction can take place. This can be done on a small scale in a laboratory.*

○ Plastic's durability makes it hard to dispose of, so scientists have developed types that can be degraded (broken down) by light or bacteria. However, the world still faces increasing problems with plastic waste.

▼ *All living things are based on carbon compounds. Over 90 percent of all compounds are organic.*

Carbon chains and rings

Carbon has an almost unique ability not only to form compounds with other elements, but also to join together with other carbon atoms as well to form complex chains and rings. Complex carbon chain and ring molecules are the basic chemicals that life itself depends on. For example, the proteins from which the body is built are all carbon compounds. There is such a huge variety of carbon compounds that there is an entire branch of chemistry, called organic chemistry, devoted to their study.

Find out more

Oil refinery p. 420

Electricity and Magnetism

*E*lectricity is one of the most useful of all forms of energy. Electricity is closely linked with magnetism —the invisible force between magnetic materials. When electricity moves, magnetism is created. When magnets move, electricity is created.

Amazing

Static electricity was discovered in the 6th century BC by the Ancient Greeks, who realized that amber (fossilized tree sap) will attract light objects when it is rubbed with wool or cloth.

○ Electricity is the movement or flow of the tiny parts of atoms called electrons, which have an electric charge.

○ Electric current only flows if it has a pathway or circuit of conductors from its source and back again.

○ Magnetism is the invisible force between materials such as iron and nickel. Magnetism attracts or repels.

○ A magnetic field is the area around a magnet inside which its magnetic force can be detected.

○ A magnet has two poles: a north pole and a south pole.

○ Like poles (e.g. two north poles) repel each other; unlike poles (e.g. a north pole and a south pole) attract each other.

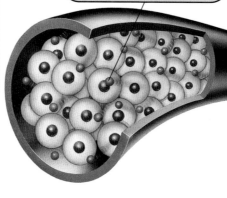

Electrons jump from atom to atom in conductor

Sheath or cover

○ Electrons move easily through materials called conductors. Metals are particularly good conductors— especially copper and gold, which are used for the wires and connectors in electric circuits.

○ Materials that are poor conductors of electricity are called insulators. Plastic and rubber are good insulators.

○ Batteries change chemical energy into electrical energy. The links or bonds between atoms in chemical substances contain energy. As these break down in a chemical reaction, their energy passes to the electrons in the atoms and makes them move.

○ DC is direct current electricity and AC is alternating current electricity. Direct current electricity flows steadily in the same direction. Alternating current electricity rapidly changes direction, flowing first one way and then the other.

▲ An electromagnet can lift a car into the air by attracting the iron-based steel of the car's body.

◀ Objects containing iron, such as nails or screwdrivers, are affected by magnetic fields.

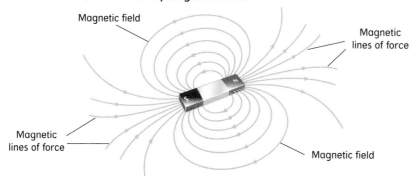

Magnetic field

Magnetic lines of force

Magnetic lines of force

Magnetic field

Find out more

Power stations p. 385

○ The Earth is a giant magnet. If a magnet is left to move freely, the Earth's magnetic field ensures that it always points with one end aimed at the North Pole and the other at the South Pole.

○ When an electric current flows through a wire, it produces a magnetic field around the wire. The magnetic field is stronger when the wire is coiled around a piece of iron. This "electric magnet" is called an electromagnet.

▼ *Electricity produced by generators in power stations travels as a current through power lines to our homes. Inside the power lines, millions of electrons jump between atoms in the conducting wires.*

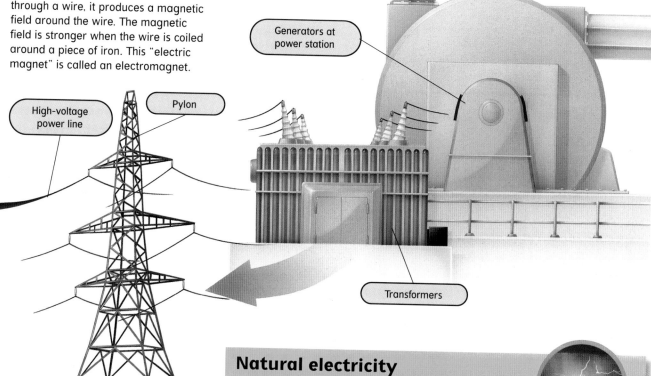

Generators at power station

High-voltage power line

Pylon

Transformers

Natural electricity

Lightning is the sudden release of a giant charge of static electricity that builds up inside storm clouds.

Static electricity

Electrons are negatively charged particles. When two materials rub together, electrons may transfer from one material onto the other. The material that gains extra electrons becomes negatively charged, and the material that loses electrons becomes positively charged. This is called static electricity, because the charges on the materials do not move—they are static (stationary). Like charges repel each other, while unlike charges attract. Static electricity can cause your hair to stand up on end.

How long?

Using the same amount of electricity, these gadgets would run for the following times:

"Instant" hot-water shower	10–15 min
Electric heater (convector)	1 hr
Hair-dryer on maximum setting	1–1 hr 15 min
Washing machine	2 hr
Large freezer	3 hr
Standard television	3–5 hr
Electric blanket	6 hr
100-watt lightbulb	10 hr
Electric shaver	70 hr

Energy

It takes energy to make something happen. Energy is not just the light that comes from the Sun, or the heat that comes from a fire. In science, energy is the ability or capacity to do work, or to cause change.

❍ Energy comes in many different forms, from the chemical energy locked in sugar to the mechanical energy in a speeding train.

❍ Potential energy is energy stored up ready for action—as in a squeezed spring or a stretched piece of elastic.

❍ Kinetic energy is energy that something has because it is moving, such as a rolling ball or a falling stone.

❍ Food is a store of chemical energy, and when eaten can be used to power the movements of the human body.

❍ Energy transfer is the movement of energy from one place to another, such as heat rising above a fire or a ball being thrown.

❍ Energy conversion is when energy changes from one form to another, for example when wind turbines generate electric power.

❍ Other forms of energy include heat, electricity, sound, and electromagnetic radiation.

❍ Light is type of electromagnetic radiation, as are microwaves, radio waves, X rays, ultraviolet, infrared, and gamma rays.

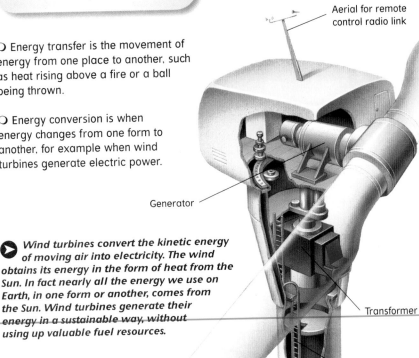

Aerial for remote control radio link

Generator

Transformer

Stairs inside pylon

Rotor blade

▶ Wind turbines convert the kinetic energy of moving air into electricity. The wind obtains its energy in the form of heat from the Sun. In fact nearly all the energy we use on Earth, in one form or another, comes from the Sun. Wind turbines generate their energy in a sustainable way, without using up valuable fuel resources.

▲ When something is lifted, it stores the energy that is used to lift it as potential energy.

Measuring energy

The main unit for measuring both energy and work is the joule (J).

An older unit was the calorie, which was used to measure heat energy and the chemical energy contained in foods.

One calorie equals 4.2 joules, and one kilocalorie or kcal (also written as "Calorie" with a capital "C") equals 4200 joules (4.2 kJ).

A 100-watt lightbulb requires one joule of electrical energy per second.

A typical lightbulb left on for 24 hours takes about 5 million joules.

A split-second bolt of lightning releases 2,000 million joules.

A large earthquake releases about 10 million million million joules in just a few seconds.

Spacecraft energy

About 100 billion joules of energy is needed to launch a spacecraft.

Power stations

Power stations are giant energy converters—they convert chemical or nuclear energy in a fuel into heat. The heat generated by power stations is transferred to water. This changes into steam, which is released out of large, concrete chimneys. The kinetic energy of the steam makes a turbine spin. The rotational (spinning) energy of the turbine drives a generator, which converts the rotational energy into electrical energy for us all to use.

▲ *For a split second, as runners move away from the starting blocks, they accelerate faster than a sports car. They convert chemical energy into muscle power to produce kinetic energy. At the end of a race, runners quickly lose their kinetic energy and come to a halt.*

❍ An average person needs 5 million to 10 million joules of energy from food each day to stay active and healthy.

❍ Energy is more concentrated in some foods than others. For example, 1 oz of butter gives the same amount of energy as 18 oz of peas.

❍ Nuclear energy is created in reactors inside nuclear power stations, nuclear-powered submarines, some spacecraft, and also in nuclear explosions. It is called nuclear energy because it comes from splitting the nucleus of an atom.

❍ Walking needs about five times as much energy as sitting still. Running needs about seven times more energy.

❍ Energy can never be created or destroyed—it can only be changed from one form to another. So all the energy in the Universe has always existed, no matter what form it is in now.

Find out more

Power pp. 420–421

Force and Motion

Forces are pushes and pulls. They change the speed, direction, or shape of things. Some forces act only when things touch each other, such as kicking a football. Other forces, including gravity and magnetism, act at a distance.

▶ *An object's mass makes it resist a force that tries to change its state of motion. This resistance is known as inertia. The more mass an object has, the greater is its inertia. The iron shot (ball) that athletes throw when they put the shot has a large mass, so it takes a lot of muscle power to overcome its inertia.*

○ Force is measured in newtons (N). One newton is the force needed to speed up a mass of 2 lb by 3 ft/sec every second.

◀ *Before Newton, no one knew why things fall to the ground or why planets go round the Sun. Newton said that the answer came to him while sitting in an orchard. As an apple fell nearby, he wondered if the apple was not simply falling but was being pulled down by an invisible force. From this simple idea, Newton developed his theory of gravity—a universal force that tries to pull all matter together.*

○ Everything that is standing still has inertia, which means that it will not move unless forced to.

○ Everything that moves has momentum—it will not slow down, speed up or change direction unless forced to.

○ When something moves there are usually several forces involved. When you throw a ball, the force of your throw hurls it forward, the force of gravity pulls it down, and the force of air resistance slows it down.

Newton's Laws of Motion

The Laws

1. An object keeps moving in a straight line in the same direction (or keeps still if it's already still), unless a force acts on it.

2. A force makes an object change its movement in the direction of the force, with an acceleration (increase in speed) that depends on the size of the force.

3. For every action caused by a force, there is an equal and opposite reaction.

Examples

A spacecraft heading into outer space will keep going straight, unless it is affected by gravity from a planet or star, and is pulled toward it.

Kick a football and it changes from being still to moving in the direction of the kick. Apply more force, which means a harder kick, and the ball gains speed faster and goes farther.

The engines of a jet-car blast hot gases backward, which is the action. The reaction is to push the car forward.

○ The direction and speed of movement depend on the combined effect of all the forces involved—this is called the resultant.

○ A force has magnitude (size) and works in a particular direction.

○ A force can be drawn on a diagram as an arrow called a vector. The way that the arrow points represents the direction of the force. The length of the arrow shows the force's strength.

Flea acceleration

A jumping flea can accelerate at up to 140 times the acceleration of gravity towards Earth, or 50 times the acceleration of a space shuttle taking off.

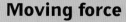

Moving force

To start moving, a skater uses the force of his muscles to push against the ground. As he or she pushes, the ground pushes back with equal force.

○ Friction is the force that acts between two things rubbing together. It stops them sliding past each other.

○ Drag is friction between air and an object. It slows a fast car, or any aircraft moving through the air.

▼ *The leverage of the bow string helps an archer to bend the bow so far that it has tremendous power as it snaps back into shape.*

○ Velocity is speed in a particular direction. Acceleration is the rate at which an object's velocity changes.

○ Every movement in the Universe seems to be governed by physical laws. These laws were explained by scientists such as Isaac Newton and Albert Einstein.

○ A force that misshapes material is called a stress.

Amazing

A space rocket taking off from the Earth's surface would have to achieve a velocity of more than 24,856 mi/h in order to escape the force of Earth's gravity.

Find out more

Machine power pp. 398–399

Heat and Temperature

Heat is another name for *"internal energy," or energy that is stored inside a substance. It is a form of energy that moves from one place to another when their temperatures are different.*

❍ Heat is not the same as temperature. Temperature is a measure of how fast molecules are moving. Heat is the movement energy of all the molecules added together.

❍ When you heat a substance its temperature rises because heat makes its molecules move faster.

❍ When objects heat up they expand because their molecules vibrate more and move further apart. When objects cool down, they contract because the molecules vibrate less and move closer together.

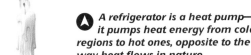

▶ *Radiation is one of the ways that heat spreads from a flame.*

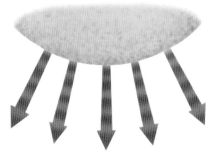

▲ *Radiation is rays of energy. The Sun's rays travel through space and reach us as heat and light energy.*

❍ Heat moves in three different ways: conduction, convection, and radiation.

❍ Conduction involves heat spreading from hot areas to cold areas by direct contact. It works a bit like a relay race. Energetic, rapidly moving or vibrating molecules cannon into their neighbors and set them moving too.

▲ *A refrigerator is a heat pump— it pumps heat energy from cold regions to hot ones, opposite to the way heat flows in nature.*

❍ Heat always spreads out from its source. It heats up its surroundings while cooling down itself.

❍ Every time energy changes from one form to another, some of it turns into heat, which then spreads to its surroundings.

▲ *A bimetallic strip is used in a thermostat to respond to a change in temperature. It consists of iron and copper bonded firmly together. The strip bends when heated, because the copper expands more than the iron.*

Iron

Copper

Heating element

Amazing

The temperature of the Big Bang, the explosion that created the Universe some 13 billion years ago, was more than 50 billion billion billion°F.

Trapped air

A hot-air balloon flies because the air trapped inside it is warmer (and thus less dense) than the surrounding air. The warm air floats upwards, carrying the balloon with it.

Find out more

Molecules p. 373

Center of Sun	Inside lightning bolt	Center of Earth	Lava from volcano	Oil in frying pan	Boiling water	Body temperature	Water freezes	Solid carbon dioxide ("dry ice")

27,000,032°F 54,032°F 9,032°F 1,832°F 392°F 212°F 99°F 32°F −109.3°F Absolute zero −459.67°F

There is no limit to how hot things can become. The hottest ever temperature achieved in a laboratory was 720,000,032°F. Scientists have reached the other extreme and have come close to reaching -459.6°F on the temperature scale.

Thermometers

Temperature is measured by a thermometer. When a thermometer is dipped in something hot, it quickly reaches the same temperature. A liquid (usually mercury or alcohol) inside the thermometer expands as it heats up and spreads out along a channel inside the thermometer. The hotter the liquid, the more it spreads.

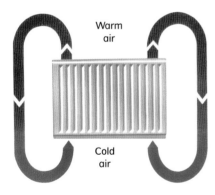

Warm air

Cold air

Air warmed by a radiator gets lighter and rises. Cold air moves in from below to replace it, and this is heated up too.

○ Radiation is the spread of heat as heat rays—that is, invisible waves of infrared radiation.

○ Convection is when warm air rises through cool air, like a hot-air balloon.

○ Convection currents are circulation patterns set up as warm air (or liquid) rises. Around the column of rising warmth, cool air continually sinks to replace it at the bottom. So the whole air turns over like a nonstop fountain.

○ The coldest temperature possible is absolute zero, or −459.67°F, when molecules stop moving.

Temperature conversions

Fahrenheit to Celsius
subtract 32, multiply by 5 and divide by 9

Celsius to Fahrenheit
multiply by 9, divide by 5 and add 32

10°C = 50°F
20°C = 68°F
30°C = 86°F
40°C = 104°F
50°C = 122°F

Absolute zero −273.15° = −459.6°F

When wood or coal is burnt on a fire, a chemical reaction starts that releases energy stored in the fuel. Flames are the area where substances in the fuel combine with oxygen in the air to release energy as heat and light.

Light

*L*ight is energy that we can see with our eyes. It is one of the forms of energy known as electromagnetic radiation, which also includes X rays, microwaves, radio waves, infrared, and ultraviolet.

○ For some purposes scientists view light as a continuous form of energy that moves in up-and-down waves. For other purposes, they view it as units of energy called photons. This is known in science as the "wave-particle duality" of light.

○ Although we are surrounded by light during the day, very few things give out light. The Sun and other stars and electric lights are light sources, but we see most things only because they reflect light. If something does not send out or reflect light, we cannot see it.

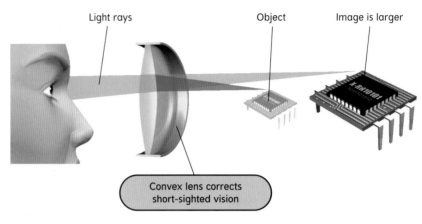

Light rays　　　Object　　　Image is larger

Convex lens corrects short-sighted vision

○ On a sunny day 1,000 billion photons fall on a pinhead every second.

○ Light travels in straight lines. The direction can be changed when light bounces off something or passes through it, but it is always straight. The straight path of light is called a ray.

○ When the path of a light ray is blocked altogether, it forms a shadow. Most shadows have two regions: the umbra and penumbra. The umbra is the dark part where light rays are blocked altogether. The penumbra is the lighter rim where some rays reach.

○ When light rays hit something, they bounce off, are soaked up or pass through. Anything that lets light through, such as glass, is transparent. If it mixes the light on the way through, such as frosted glass, it is translucent. If it stops light altogether, it is opaque.

○ When light strikes a surface, some or all of it is reflected. Most surfaces scatter light in all directions, and therefore all you see is the surface. But mirrors and other shiny surfaces reflect light in exactly the same pattern in which it arrives, so you therefore see a mirror-image.

Refraction

Refraction makes a straw look bent. It is not really bent—the light rays bend when they pass through the water.

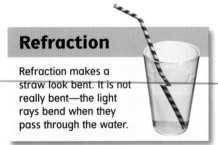

▶ *Light bounces or reflects off very smooth surfaces, in the same pattern and at the same angle as the rays hit the surface. This produces what we call a mirror-image. In this mirror-image, left and right are reversed. So in a mirror, we do not see our faces as other people see them.*

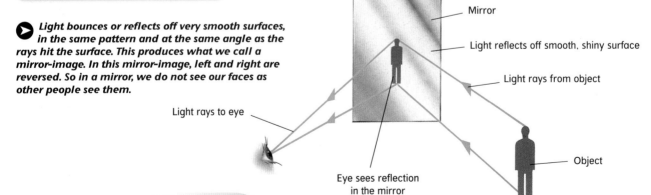

Mirror

Light reflects off smooth, shiny surface

Light rays from object

Light rays to eye

Object

Eye sees reflection in the mirror

Find out more

X rays p. 423

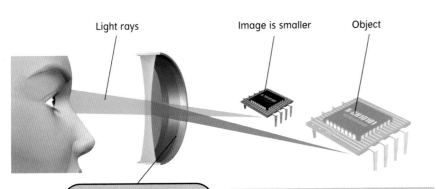

Light rays   Image is smaller   Object

Concave lens corrects long-sighted vision

Glass lenses are shaped to bend light rays in a particular way. Convex (outward-curving) lenses are fat in the middle and thin at the rim. Light rays passing through a convex lens bend inward, so they come together or converge. Concave (inward-curving) lenses are thin in the middle and thick around the rim. Light rays passing through a concave lens are bent outward, so they spread.

○ The emission of light by hot objects is called incandescence. Electric lightbulbs are incandescent—their light comes from a thin tungsten wire, or filament, that glows when it is heated by an electric current.

○ Fluorescent lights have a gas-filled glass tube coated on the inside with powders called phosphors. Electricity passing through the gas in the tube causes it to emit invisible ultraviolet (UV) rays. The UV rays hit the phosphors and make them glow, or "fluoresce."

Colors

When we see different colors, we are seeing different wavelengths of light. Sunlight appears colorless but it is called white light, which is actually a mixture of all colors. When it hits raindrops in the sky it can be split up into all the different colors to form a rainbow. They are split because the raindrop refracts (bends) each wavelength of light differently, fanning out the colors in a particular order, from red (the longest waves) at one end, to violet (the shortest) at the other.

Amazing

It takes 4.3 years for light from Alpha Centauri, the nearest star to the Sun, to reach the Earth.

○ In neon lights, a huge electric current makes the gas inside a tube electrically charged, causing it to glow.

Gas mixtures in neon lights glow different colors. Pure neon glows red.

Speed of light

The speed at which light travels depends on the medium through which it passes:

Vacuum	186,287 mi/sec
Air	186,230 mi/sec
Water	139,812 mi/sec
Window glass	121,171 mi/sec
Decorative glass (lead crystal)	99,422 mi/sec
Diamond	77,674 mi/sec

Sound

Most sounds you hear, from the whisper of the wind to the roar of a jet, are simply moving air. When any sound is made it makes the air vibrate, and these vibrations carry the sound to your ears.

○ The vibrations that carry sound through the air are called sound waves, which move by alternately squeezing air molecules together and then stretching them apart.

○ Sound waves travel faster through liquids and solids than through air because the molecules are more closely packed together in liquids and solids.

○ We cannot see sound waves in the air, but we can see big vibrations in solid objects that produce sounds, such as loudspeakers or engines.

○ We can also see the ripples on a liquid, such as water, through which sound passes.

▼ Military aircraft are built to perform in extreme circumstances and they are usually much noisier than civilian aircraft of comparable size—but the military also have the quietest planes. Stealth aircraft, such as this US B-2, have specially silenced engines to reduce their chances of being detected.

Amazing

Using only echolocation, bottlenose dolphins in captivity can distinguish between a tangerine and a small metal ball of the same size from a distance of 371 ft.

▶ The loudness (volume) of a sound depends on the energy of its sound waves. Loudness is measured on the decibel (dB) scale. Each rise of 10 dB represents a ten-fold increase in sound energy. For example, 60 dB represents ten times more sound than 50 dB. The quietest sounds we can hear, such as the ticking of a watch, are about 10 dB. Conversation varies between 40 and 60 dB.

Nuclear explosion more than 200 dB

Jet plane taking off 120–130 dB

Whispering 20 dB

Express train 80–90 dB

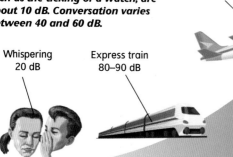

Mach

A supersonic jet plane flies faster than sound. Its speed is given as a Mach number. The Mach number is the speed of the plane divided by the speed of sound in the air the plane is flying through. Mach 1 is the speed of sound, Mach 2 is twice the speed of sound.

Using echoes

Whales and dolphins make high-pitched sounds that bounce off the seabed. The echo that returns to the whale or dolphin helps it to find food.

A bat's squeaks and clicks are mostly ultrasonic—too high for our ears to detect. The sounds reflect from objects nearby and the bat works out whether the echoes indicate leaves and twigs to be avoided when flying or prey to be caught. This system is called echolocation, and it allows the bat to fly and feed—even in total darkness.

Bat sends out ultrasonic clicks and squeaks

Bat's ears detect returning echoes

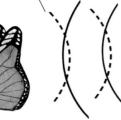

○ Since sound involves motion, it is a type of kinetic energy.

○ Sounds can be soft or loud, high-pitched, or low-pitched. It all depends on the energy and frequency of the sound waves.

○ Big, energetic waves move your eardrums a long way within the ear and sound loud. Small, low energy waves sound quieter. Loudness (volume) is measured in decibels (dB).

○ The pitch of a sound depends on the frequency of the sound waves (the number of waves that reach your ears every second). The greater the frequency, the higher the pitch of the sound. Frequency is measured in hertz (Hz); 1 Hz is one wave per second.

○ Sounds that are too loud can damage the ears. Sounds of 130 dB or over are painful, and prolonged exposure to sounds of between 90 and 100 dB can cause deafness.

○ Sound travels a million times more slowly than light, which is why you hear thunder after you see a flash of lightning, even though they both happen at the same time.

○ An echo is the reflection of a sound. You hear it a little while after the sound is made.

○ Acoustics is the study of how sounds are created, transmitted, and received.

○ The highest sound the average human can hear is 20,000 Hz; the lowest is 20 Hz.

Speed of sound

Sound can travel through any medium except a vacuum. It generally travels faster through liquids than gases, and more rapidly through solids than liquids. Its speed is measured in ft/sec.

Beryllium	42,290 ft/sec
Aluminum	21,.063 ft/sec
Stainless steel	18,996 ft/sec
Copper	15,617 ft/sec
Brick	11,975 ft/sec
Gold	10,630 ft/sec
Lead	7,087 ft/sec
Water, ocean (68°F)	5,023 ft/sec
Water, distilled (68°F)	4,911 ft/sec
Mercury	4,757 ft/sec
Hydrogen	4,213 ft/sec
Cork	1,640 ft/sec
Air (68°F)	1,125 ft/sec
Air (32°F)	1,086 ft/sec
Oxygen	1,037 ft/sec
Carbon dioxide	850 ft0/sec

Find out more

Sound and vision pp. 418–419

Air and Water

Air and water are the two most important substances in the world. Without air and water, life on Earth would be impossible. Air provides living creatures with the oxygen they need to breathe.

○ The air is a mixture of gases, dust, and moisture.

○ Water is a compound made of two hydrogen atoms and one oxygen atom. It has the chemical formula H_2O.

Amazing

Bacteria have been found alive in the air at an altitude of 10 mi, carried to that height by strong winds. Some scientists think that bacteria may even be able to survive in space.

▼ Antoine Lavoisier (1743–1794) was a brilliant French scientist who is regarded as the father of modern chemistry. He was the first person to realize that air is essentially a mixture of two gases: oxygen and nitrogen. Lavoisier also discovered that water is a compound of hydrogen and oxygen.

▲ The atmosphere—the blanket of air that surrounds the Earth—is about 435 mi deep. The atmosphere gets thinner with altitude.

○ Earth is the only known planet with a lot of water. In fact, three-quarters of the Earth's surface is covered by oceans.

○ Water is the only substance that can exist as a solid, a liquid, and a gas at normal temperatures. Water melts at 32°F and boils at 212°F.

▶ Plants and animals interact with each other in regions called ecosystems. Plants need water to grow and survive. Rainforests receive a lot of rain annually, and so are abundant with plant life and animals. In an ecosystem, each organism (living thing) is dependent on the other organisms living there. Plants are the primary producers in any ecosystem, using the energy of sunlight to convert carbon dioxide and water into carbohydrates, and giving off oxygen as a waste product.

▲ The liner Titanic was said to be unsinkable, but when an iceberg breached her hull and let in water to replace the air, she sank like a stone.

2005 hurricanes

Since 1953, hurricanes are given personal names that are revised every six years by the World Meteorological Organization.

Arlene	Harvey	Ophelia
Bret	Irene	Philippe
Cindy	Jose	Rita
Dennis	Katrina	Stan
Emily	Lee	Tammy
Franklin	Maria	Vince
Gert	Nate	Wilma

> *Things float because they are less dense in water, which is why you can lift quite a heavy person in a swimming pool. This loss of weight is called buoyancy. Buoyancy is created by the upward push, or upthrust, of the water. When you float in the water you will sink until your weight is exactly equal to the upthrust of the water, at which point you float.*

○ Water is one of the few substances that expands as it freezes, which is why pipes burst during cold weather.

○ When an object is placed in water, its weight pushes it down. At the same time the water pushes back with a force called upthrust, which is equal to the weight of water displaced (pushed out of the way).

> ▲ *An iceberg is a huge chunk of ice that has broken away from a glacier. Only the tip of an iceberg is visible above the ocean's surface. The rest of the ice (up to 90 percent) is submerged.*

Combining substances

A remarkable property of water is its ability to make solutions with other substances. A solution is formed when a substance is added to a liquid and instead of just floating in the liquid, the substance breaks up entirely, so that its atoms and molecules completely intermingle with those of the liquid. This happens when instant coffee is added to water. The substance dissolved is called the solute; the liquid is called the solvent.

○ An object will float if its weight is exactly equal to the upthrust of the water. This is called buoyancy.

○ The buoyancy of water reduces a swimmer's body weight by 90 percent.

Floating ice

Ice is less dense than water, which is why ice forms on the surface of ponds and why icebergs float.

○ Objects that are less dense than water float; those that are more dense sink.

○ Although steel is denser than water, steel ships float because their hulls are full of air. They sink until enough water is displaced to match the weight of steel and air in the hull.

○ People float because their lungs contain air, and because body fat is less dense than water (bone and muscle are denser).

○ About 2 percent of the world's water is frozen in ice caps and glaciers.

Find out more

Melting and boiling points p. 375

Early Inventions

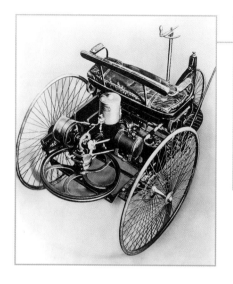

Karl Benz and his wife Berta were the German creators of the first successful gas-driven car in 1885. At the age of 16, Karl Benz dreamed of "a unit that could supplant the steam engine." Karl and Berta Benz began developing their own car in the 1870s, while trying to earn money from a tinmaking business. By 1880, they were so penniless they could barely afford to eat everyday.

Hammocks were used by Central American peoples 1,000 years ago. They were introduced to ships in the 18th century to make sleeping easier at sea.

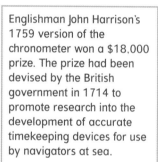

Englishman John Harrison's 1759 version of the chronometer won a $18,000 prize. The prize had been devised by the British government in 1714 to promote research into the development of accurate timekeeping devices for use by navigators at sea.

It is thought that Chinese navigators made the first compass-like device about 2,500 years ago. Early compasses were very simple. The navigators used lodestone, a naturally magnetic rock, to magnetize the needle. During the 1300s compasses became more detailed.

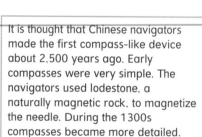

Rocket, a famous early locomotive built by English engineers George and Robert Stephenson, won the world's first locomotive speed trials in 1829.

France's Montgolfier brothers developed the first hot-air balloon. It was first launched in 1783.

Find out more

Early planes p. 411

Fireworks were invented by the Chinese about 1,000 years ago, after the invention of gunpowder. Original Chinese fireworks were only one color, yellow. However, new ingredients, such as magnesium and aluminum, were added in the 19th century to make a greater range of colors possible. The most popular form of firework, the rocket, is pushed high up into the sky by the jet of fire thrown out behind it when it burns rapidly.

The ancient Egyptians made sundials more than 3,000 years ago. The marks showed hours. The length of the hours varied with the seasons, but people were used to such an idea and called them "temporary hours."

The science of vibrating strings was first worked out by Pythagoras, a Greek mathematician and philosopher, 2,500 years ago.

Many early boats, like this Welsh coracle, were made by stretching animal skins over a wooden frame.

In 1887 German—American Emile Berliner invented the gramophone, which used a needle to play flat discs.

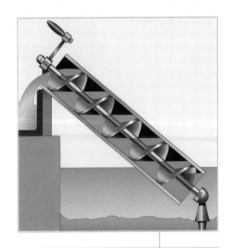

Archimedes' screw is a simple device for raising water. Devised by Archimedes, a mathematician and inventor of ancient Greece, Archimedes' screw scoops up water using a helical device that turns inside a tube. It is still used in the Middle East.

20 successful inventions and inventors

Year	Invention	Inventor
1595	Microscope	Zacharias Janssen
1620	Slide rule	William Oughtred
1709	Piano	Bartolomeo Cristofori
1798	Vaccination	Edward Jenner
1800	Electric battery	Alessandro Volta
1819	Stethoscope	Rene Laennec
1843	Typewriter	Charles Thurber
1853	Glider	George Cayley
1866	Dynamite	Alfred Noble
1872	Celluloid	John W Hyatt
1879	Cash register	James Ritty
1882	Electric fan	Schuyler Skatts Wheeler
1884	Fountain pen	Lewis Waterman
1885	Motorbike	Gottlieb Daimler
1888	Ballpoint pen	John Loud
1895	Diesel engine	Rudolf Diesel
1911	Cellophane	J Brandenburger
1922	Radar	Robert Watson-Watt
1928	Sliced bread	Otto Rohwedder
1939	Electronic computer	John Atanasoff

Machine Power

A *machine is a device that makes a task easier to do. There are two forces involved in every machine: the "load" (weight) that the machine has to move, and the "effort" used to move the load.*

○ There are six types of simple machine—the inclined plane (slope or ramp), lever, wedge, pulley, screw and the wheel, and axle. More elaborate machines, such as cranes, are made up of combinations of these simple machines linked to other mechanical components.

Inclined plane

Pulleys

▶ *An escalator combines the advantages of a pulley system and an inclined plane to carry passengers smoothly to the top. The steps are designed to swivel past each other as they go around the pulleys.*

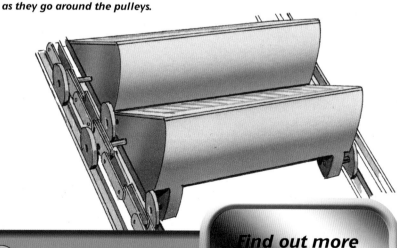

○ Mechanical advantage tells you how effective a machine is. It is calculated by dividing the load by the effort.

○ Work is done when a force moves an object and energy is converted from one form to another. The amount of work done is the effort multiplied by the distance through which the load moves.

○ Power is the rate at which work is done or energy changed from one form to another.

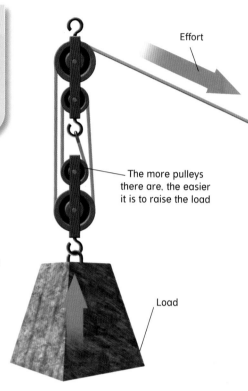

Effort

The more pulleys there are, the easier it is to raise the load

Load

▲ *Using a set of pulleys, or block and tackle, considerably decreases the amount of effort needed to lift a load, but proportionately increases the distance over which the effort must be applied.*

○ A pulley is a grooved wheel around which a rope passes to move a load.

○ A single pulley alters the direction through which the effort is applied, so by pulling downward on the rope a load can be moved upward.

Machine efficiency

Efficiency is how much work you get out of a machine compared to the energy you put into it. It is usually expressed as a percentage.

Airplane engine	10%
Steam locomotive	10%
Car gas engine	22%
Steam turbine	30%
Diesel engine	35%

Find out more
Force and motion pp. 386–387

➤ *A wheel and axle can reduce friction (resistance) between a load and the surface over which it moves. Pushing a load up a ramp, or inclined plane, is easier than lifting it vertically. The shallower the slope of the ramp, the less effort is required, but the further the load has to move.*

○ A wedge is a moving inclined plane. An axe head is a wedge that magnifies force and makes it possible to split logs with little effort.

○ A screw thread is an inclined plane wrapped around a shaft. Turning the screw moves it forward with more force than the effort used to turn it.

○ Gears are pairs of toothed wheels (cogs) that intermesh and turn together to transmit or change force and motion.

○ When an axle turns a wheel, the rim of the wheel turns with less force but travels a greater distance. Conversely, turning the wheel rim moves the axle a shorter distance but with more force.

○ A rope wrapped around a number of pulley wheels magnifies the force applied to the rope.

○ The inclined plane, or ramp, is a sloping surface that reduces the effort needed to raise a load.

○ A lever is a bar that moves round a pivot (the fulcrum) and uses turning force to make it easier to move a load.

Changing energy

A waterwheel changes the kinetic energy of running water into useful mechanical energy. This can be harnessed to drive machines such as millstones, which grind grain into flour.

Nutcracker

A nutcracker is a pair of levers. The fulcrum is the hinge between the levers. Squeezing the nutcracker applies force (the effort) to the levers and breaks the nut (the load).

▲ *A big cog (gear wheel) turns a smaller cog with less force but greater speed. A small cog turns a larger cog with greater force but more slowly. The gear ratio is the number of times that the wheel doing the driving turns the wheel being driven.*

▼ *A screwdriver used to prise the lid from a can of paint acts as a simple lever. The fulcrum is the rim of the can, the load is the lid, and the wrist provides the effort.*

Construction

It was once thought that all prehistoric humans lived in caves. We now know that most cave "dwellings" were actually used for religious rituals. The earliest houses were made of wood, leaves, grass, and mud. All traces of these have long since vanished.

❍ Early mudbrick houses dating from at least 9,500 years ago are found in Anatolia in the Middle East.

❍ Pyramids are huge monuments with a square base and triangular sides that taper to a point at the top. They were built by ancient peoples in many parts of the world—including Egypt, Iraq, Peru, and Mexico—as tombs or temples, and sometimes as a combination of the two.

Amazing

The Boeing Company's aircraft assembly plant at Everett, Washington, USA, has the largest capacity of any building in the world, with a total volume of 5,000,000 cu ft.

❍ The largest pyramid is the Great Pyramid at Giza in Egypt, built for the Pharaoh Khufu *c.*2551–2472 BC. This was once 482 ft high, but is now only 459 ft, because some of the upper stones have been lost.

▶ *The longest tunnels so far built are sub-sea rail tunnels that have a three-tube structure, with two large tunnels carrying the tracks separated by a smaller service tunnel for maintenance work.*

▲ *The world's biggest free-standing arch is the 630 ft high Gateway to the West arch in St Louis, Missouri, USA.*

❍ The Romans were the first to use round arches, so round arches are called Roman or Romanesque arches.

❍ Roman arches were built from blocks of stone called voussoirs. They were built up from each side on a semi-circular wooden frame (later removed). A central keystone (wedge) was slotted in at the top to hold them together.

Eiffel Tower

The Eiffel Tower in Paris was 1,024 ft high when it was first built. An antenna brings it up to 1,046 ft. There are 1,665 steps up to the top. It was made from 18,038 pieces of iron, held together by 2,500,000 rivets. It was built in 1889 for the exhibition celebrating the 100th anniversary of the French Revolution.

❍ Pointed arches were first brought to Europe from the Middle East by Crusader knights in the 1100s. They were used in churches, and become part of the gothic style of architecture.

❍ The first skyscrapers were built in Chicago and New York in the 1880s.

❍ A crucial step in the development of skyscrapers was the invention of the fast safety lift by American engineer Elisha Otis (1811–1861) in 1857.

❍ Manhattan in New York, USA, has more skyscrapers than any other city in the world.

❍ The Arab Gormaz Castle in the Castile region of Spain is western Europe's biggest and oldest castle. It was started in 956 AD by Caliph Al-Hakam II. It is 0.6 mi round and more than 1,312 ft across.

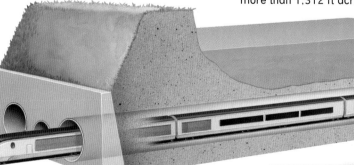

Find out more

Bridges pp. 402–403

Buildings or bridges erected on soft ground are supported by posts called piles. Usually made of steel or concrete, the piles are driven firmly into the ground by pile-drivers. Pile-drivers wind up a heavy weight called a pile hammer inside a frame, then drop it on the head of the pile to bash it into the ground.

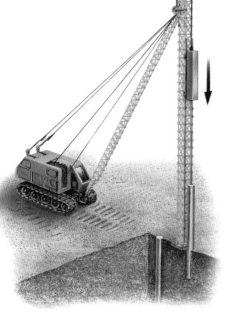

Leaning Tower

The Leaning Tower of Pisa in Italy is a 180 ft high belltower or "campanile." Building began in 1173, and it started to lean as workers built the third storey. It is now tilting 14 ft away from the perpendicular.

Deeper tunnels need to be bored out. Tunnels through soft rock or soil are dug with a powerful cutting machine called a shield. The shield's rotating cutting head is kept on a straight course by lasers. Ring-shaped steel and concrete supports are put in place to prevent the tunnel caving in again.

○ Horseshoe arches are used in Islamic buildings all round the world.

○ The world's biggest dam is the 837 ft high, 112 million cu m Kambaratinsk Dam in Russia.

A tall structure, such as a skyscraper, must have deep foundations (the part below ground) to support its height, made of massive concrete or steel piles sunk into the ground. The walls and floors are then attached to a skeleton of steel girders and beams.

Tallest buildings and structures

1	**The CN Tower** Toronto, Canada	1,820 ft
2	**Taipei 101** Taipei, Taiwan	1,669 ft
3	**Petronas Towers** Kuala Lumpur, Malaysia	1,483 ft
4	**Sears Tower** Chicago, USA	1,450 ft
5	**Jim Mao Building** Shanghai, China	1,381 ft
6	**Two International Finance Centre** Hong Kong	1,362 ft
7	**CITIC Plaza** Guangzhou, China	1,283 ft
8	**Shun Hing Square** Shenzhen, China	1,259 ft

Bridges

*T*he first bridges were probably logs and vines slung across rivers to help people across. Clapper bridges are ancient bridges in which large stone slabs rest on piers (supports) of stone.

Arch bridge

The Ponte Vecchio in Florence, built in 1345, is one of the oldest flattened arch bridges in Europe.

○ The first brick bridges were built by the Romans, such as the Alcántara bridge over the Tagus River in Spain, which was built around AD 100.

○ Long brick bridges could be made with a series of arches linked together. Each of these arches is called a span.

○ Roman arches were semi-circular, so each span was short. Chinese arches were flatter, so they could span greater distances.

○ Rope suspension bridges have been used for thousands of years. One of the first to use iron chains was the Lan Jin Bridge at Yunnan in China. It was built in AD 65.

○ The first all-iron bridge was built at Coalbrookdale, England, across the River Severn. It was designed by Thomas Pritchard and built in 1779 by Abraham Darby.

▼ **The first step in bridge-building is to build the piers and abutments.** To erect piers in the water, a steel wall or shuttering is built on the riverbed. The water is then pumped out while the pier is built, before the walls can be removed, and the spans laid between the piers.

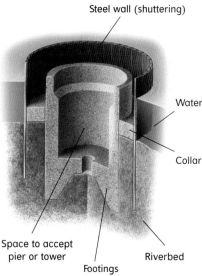

Steel wall (shuttering)

Water

Collar

Space to accept pier or tower

Footings

Riverbed

▶ **For wide or deep channels, a suspension bridge, with a span of up to 3,937 ft, is often used.** The deck (such as a roadway) is held up by steel cables hanging between tall towers. These cables are held in concrete blocks at both ends of the bridge. The deck may be supported by a framework to stop it swaying too much in the wind. The weight of the deck is transferred to the vertical cables over the towers and to the concrete blocks at either end.

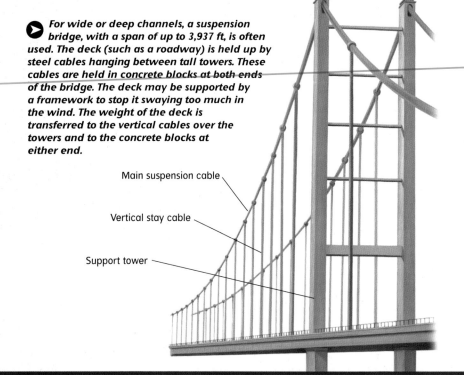

Main suspension cable

Vertical stay cable

Support tower

○ The Akashi-Kaikyo Bridge (1998), Japan, is the world's longest suspension bridge with a main span of 6,532 ft and two side spans of 3,149 ft.

Longest bridges

Steel-Arch

1	New River Gorge, USA	1,699 ft
2	Kill Van Kull (Bayonne), USA	1,654 ft
3	Sydney Harbor, Australia	1,650 ft
4	Fremont, USA	1,257 ft
5	Port Mann, Canada	1,200 ft

Cable-Stayed

1	Tatara Ohashi, Japan	2,919 ft
2	Pont de Normandie, France	2,808 ft
3	Qinghzhou Minjiang, China	1,985 ft
4	Yangpu, China	1,975 ft
5	Meiko-Chuo, Japan	1,936 ft

Suspension

1	Akashi-Kaiko, Japan	6,532 ft
2	Great Belt, Denmark	5,328 ft
3	Humber Estuary, Britain	4,626 ft
4	Jiangyin, China	4,544 ft
5	Tsing Ma, China	4,518 ft

Golden Gate Bridge

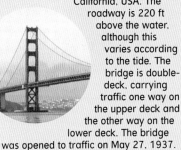

The Golden Gate Bridge spans the entrance to San Francisco Bay in California, USA. The roadway is 220 ft above the water, although this varies according to the tide. The bridge is double-deck, carrying traffic one way on the upper deck and the other way on the lower deck. The bridge was opened to traffic on May 27, 1937.

❍ In the early 1800s Scottish engineer Thomas Telford built superb iron bridges, such as Craigellachie over the Spey in Scotland (1814). He built Europe's first iron chain suspension bridge over the Menai Straits in Wales in 1826.

◗ *Most bridges are now built of concrete and steel. These are some of the main kinds. The longest are normally suspension bridges, usually carrying roads, but Hong Kong's 4,518 ft long Tsing Ma takes both road and rail.*

Amazing

An average of 274,000 vehicles per day used the San Francisco Oakland Bay Bridge in 1996, which works out at an astonishing 100 million vehicles per year!

❍ In 1940 the Tacoma suspension bridge in Washington, USA, was blown down by a moderate wind just months after its completion. The disaster forced engineers to make suspension bridges aerodynamic.

❍ Aerodynamic design played a major part in the design of Turkey's Bosphorus Bridge (1973) and the Humber Bridge in England (1983), for a while the longest bridge at 4,626 ft.

❍ The Akashi-Kaikyo Bridge (1998), Japan, is the world's longest suspension bridge, with a main span of 6,532 ft and two side spans of 3,149 ft.

❍ London Bridge was dismantled and reconstructed stone by stone in Arizona, USA, as a tourist attraction in 1971.

In cable-stayed bridges, the bridge hangs directly from steel cables

In suspension bridges, the bridge hangs on steel wires on a cable suspended between tall towers. They are light so can be very long

In cantilevered bridges, each half of the bridge is balanced on a support

Arch bridges are one of the oldest kinds and make very strong bridges

Steel or concrete beam bridges are carried on piers. The beam may be a hollow steel girder through which cars and trains can run

Bascule or lifting bridges like London's Tower Bridge swing up in the middle to allow tall ships through

Find out more
Construction pp. 400–401

History of Rail Transport

On September 15, 1830, the world's first major passenger railway opened between Liverpool and Manchester in England. By 1835 there were over 994 mi of railway in the USA. In Britain railway building became a mania in the 1840s.

Amazing

Indian Railways had nearly 1,600,000 staff in 1997, making it the world's largest employer.

❍ In 1831 the *Best Friend* started a regular train service between Charleston and Hamburg, South Carolina, in the USA.

❍ On May 10, 1869 railways from either side of the United States met at Promontory, Utah, giving North America the first transcontinental railway.

❍ Steam locomotives get their power by burning coal in a firebox. This heats up water in a boiler, making steam. The steam drives a piston to and fro and the piston turns the wheels via connecting rods and cranks.

▶ *This is a typical British diesel-electric locomotive from the 1960s. It has a cab at both ends so that it can be operated in either direction. This is one of the older generation of diesel-electrics that use DC (direct current) generators. DC generators give a current that flows in only one direction. Most newer engines take advantage of electronic devices called rectifiers to use the current from an AC (alternating current) generator. An AC generator gives a current that swaps direction many times a second. The rectifiers convert this into a direct current. AC generators are far more powerful and efficient.*

▶ *Track controllers use a '"block" system to stop a train entering a block of track that already has a train on it. Some routes in Europe and Japan use Advanced Train Protection (ATP), where the cab picks up signals from the track telling the driver what speed to travel. If the driver fails to respond, the train slows automatically. In the US, they are developing Advanced Train Control Systems (ACTS) that will rely on satellites and other high-tech links. Signals can also warn train crews of hazards on the track.*

❍ The *Flying Scotsman* was a famous loco designed by Sir Nigel Gresley (1876–1941). It pulled trains nonstop 391 mi from London to Edinburgh in under six hours.

❍ Diesel locomotives are electric locomotives that carry their own power plant. The wheels are driven by an electric motor, which is supplied with electricity by the locomotive's diesel engine.

❍ The first practical electric trains date from 1879, but they only became widespread in the 1920s.

❍ The first monorail was built in Wuppertal in Germany as long ago as 1901. Monorails have been seen as trains of the future ever since.

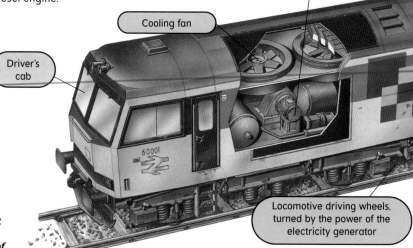

Direct Current (DC) electricity generator turned by the power of the diesel engine

Cooling fan

Driver's cab

Locomotive driving wheels, turned by the power of the electricity generator

Fastest train

The fastest recorded train speed is 320 mi/h by France's TGV between Courtalain and Tours on May 18, 1990.

Find out more

Early inventions pp. 396–397

Bullet train

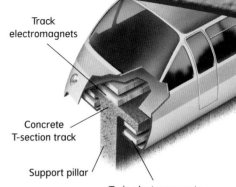

Japan's Shinkansen "bullet train" was the first of the modern high speed electric trains, regularly operating at speeds of more than 249 mi/h.

○ The heaviest trains ever pulled by a single locomotive were 250-truck trains that ran on the Erie Railroad in the USA from 1914 to 1929. They weighed over 15,000 tons.

○ Magnetic levitation or maglev trains do not have wheels but glide along supported by electromagnets.

○ A maglev is proposed in Japan to take passengers 320 mi from Tokyo to Osaka in under 60 minutes. Germany is planning a system called Transrapid.

○ Since 2000 the 149 mi/h tilting train *The American Flyer*—Washington to Baltimore—is the USA's fastest train.

○ The longest train was a 4.5-mi, 660-truck freight train that ran from Saldanha to Sishen in South Africa, on August 26, 1989.

○ The Trans-Siberian Express takes eight days to go right across Russia and Siberia, from Moscow to Vladivostok.

Track electromagnets

Concrete T-section track

Support pillar

Train electromagnets

🔺 **Maglev trains operate in many countries, including China, Japan, Germany, and the United States.**

○ Stretching for an incredible 5,865 mi, the Trans-Siberian Express is the world's longest train route.

○ The world's first underground was the cut-and-cover Metropolitan Line in London, opened on January 10, 1863, using steam engines.

○ New York City has the world's largest subway network, but unlike London's most of it is quite shallow. The first line opened on October 27, 1904.

🔻 **Switches are used to automatically change the direction of a train.**

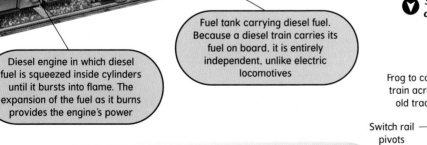

Fuel tank carrying diesel fuel. Because a diesel train carries its fuel on board, it is entirely independent, unlike electric locomotives

Diesel engine in which diesel fuel is squeezed inside cylinders until it bursts into flame. The expansion of the fuel as it burns provides the engine's power

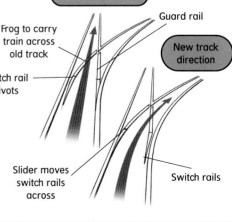

Old track direction

Guard rail

New track direction

Frog to carry train across old track

Switch rail pivots

Slider moves switch rails across

Switch rails

Longest metro systems

		Route (mi)	No. of stations	Year opened
1	London, UK	267	298	1863
2	New York, USA	244	469	1868
3	Paris, France	206	438	1900
4	Moscow, Russia	152	150	1935
5	Tokyo, Japan	152	216	1927
6	Mexico City, Mexico	111	154	1969
7	Chicago, USA	108	144	1892
8	Copenhagen, Denmark	106	61	1934
9	Washington DC, USA	89	74	1976
10	Berlin, Germany	88	166	1902

History of Road Transport

By 1904, the layouts of cars were starting to resemble those of modern vehicles, with an engine at the front, the driver and steering wheel on one side, a gas tank at the back, a shaft to drive the wheels and so on.

○ Early cars were "coach-built," which meant they were individually built by hand. This made them the costly toys of the rich only.

Mini car

The 1959 Mini, designed by Alec Issigonis, set a trend in small car design, with the engine mounted across the car driving the front wheels.

○ In 1906 an American steam-driven car, the Stanley Steamer, broke the land speed record at over 127 mi/h.

○ The first gas-engine motorbike was built by Gottlieb Daimler in Germany in 1885.

○ The first car for ordinary people was Ford's Model T. The Ford Company built their 10 millionth car in 1924 and produced their 50 millionth car in 1959.

○ The Model A Ford sold one million within 14 months of its launch in December 1927. The Ford Escort of 1980 sold one million in just 11 months.

○ In 1905 the first motor buses ran on New York's 5th Avenue. In 1928 the first transcontinental bus service crossed the USA.

Brake calliper

Brake fluid under pressure in brake pipe pushes on piston

Brake pads press on brake disc to create friction, thus slowing down wheel

Piston presses two brake pads together

Brake piston

◀ *Stopping a fast-moving car demands great force. When the driver presses the brake pedal, brake fluid is forced through narrow pipes to cylinders on each wheel. The pressure of the fluid presses special pads—brake pads—against the brake discs on the wheels, which slow it down by friction. Many cars have ABS (antilock braking systems) where a computer applies the brake automatically within a split second and prevents the car's wheels from locking up and the car from skidding to a halt.*

Amazing

The world's oldest known engineered roadway is the Sweet Track in England's Somerset Levels. Built in the 3800s BC, it ran for 6,500 ft across the marsh, and was made of oak plants supported by ash poles.

○ The first car speed record was achieved by an electric Jentaud car in 1898 at Acheres near Paris. Driven by the Comte de Chasseloup-Laubat, the car hit 39.23 mi/h. Camille Jenatzy vied with de Chasseloup-Laubat for the record, raising it to 65.77 mi/h in his car *Jamais Contente* in 1899.

○ In 1911 the governing body for the land speed record said that cars had to make two runs in opposite directions over a 0.5 mi course to get the record.

○ On October 13, 1997 a British jet car called *Thrust SSC*, driven by British fighter pilot Andy Green, broke the sound barrier for the first time. In two runs across Nevada's Black Rock desert it hit over 758 mi/h.

○ The Mercedes Benz 300SL of 1952 was one of the first supercars of the post-war years, famous for its stylish flip-up "Gullwing" doors.

First on the road

Steam coach	Trevithick, Britain	1801
Steam dredger	Evans, USA	1805
Gas carriage	Brown, Britain	1820s
Gas car	Benz, Germany	1885

Find out more

Early inventions p. 396

○ The Aston Martin DB6 was the classic supercar of the late 1960s, driven by fictional spy James Bond.

○ In 1861 French father and son Pierre and Ernest Michaux stuck the pedals directly on the front wheel to make the first successful bicycle, nicknamed "boneshaker."

○ In 1874 Englishman H. J. Lawson made the first chain-driven bicycle. This was called a "safety bicycle."

○ In 1885 John Starley made the Rover safety bicycle in England. Air-filled tyres were added in 1890, and the modern bicycle was born.

○ More people in China cycle today than in the rest of the world put together.

Donald Campbell took on the record-breaking mantle of his father—and the Bluebird name for his car. On July 17, 1964, Campbell's Bluebird hit a world record 429.323 mi/h on the salt flats at Lake Eyre in South Australia. At one moment he hit over 450 mi/h—faster than any wheel-driven car has ever been. The total weight of the car was 9,599 lb.

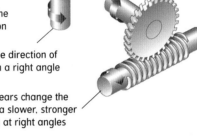

Simple cogs reverse the direction of rotation

Rack and pinion change the rotation to a sliding motion

Bevels move the direction of rotation through a right angle

Worm gears change the motion to a slower, stronger rotation at right angles

Gears are used to modify rotation —either the speed, as in the link between an engine and wheels, or the direction, or the angle.

Juggernauts

Big trucks are sometimes called "juggernauts." The word comes from Jagannath, a form of the Hindu god Vishnu. A statue of the god is annually carried in procession on a large chariot in Puri, Orissa, India.

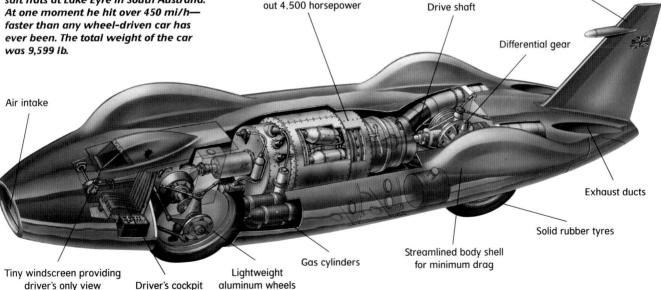

Bristol-Siddeley Proteus 705 gas-turbine engine pushing out 4,500 horsepower

Drive shaft

Tail-plane for stability

Differential gear

Air intake

Exhaust ducts

Solid rubber tyres

Streamlined body shell for minimum drag

Gas cylinders

Lightweight aluminum wheels

Driver's cockpit

Tiny windscreen providing driver's only view

History of Water Transport

*T*he ancient Egyptians made ships by a process of interlocking planks of wood and lashing them together with rope. Wooden sailing boats have been used for the last 4,000 years.

○ Sailors used to be called "tars," after the tarpaulins used for making sails. Tarpaulin is canvas and tar.

Amazing

The world's smallest submarine, the *Water Beatle*, measures 9.68 ft long, 3.77 ft wide and 4.66 ft high. Built by Englishman William Smith, it can dive to 100 ft and stay submerged for four hours.

○ Sailors' lavatories on old ships were simply holes overhanging the sea called "jardines," from the French word for garden.

Hydrofoils

By lifting themselves out of the water and almost flying across the surface, hydrofoils achieve very high speeds.

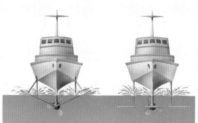

Surface-piercing hydrofoil

Fully submerged hydrofoil

○ In 1807 American Robert Fulton made the first steam passenger boats, running 150 mi up the Hudson River from New York.

○ Early steamships were propelled by paddles, but in 1835 Swede John Ericsson invented a screw propeller. In 1845 a screw-driven boat won a tug of war with a paddle steamer.

○ In 1843 British engineer Isambard Kingdom Brunel launched the first all-iron hull steamship, the *Great Britain*.

○ In 1858 Brunel launched *Great Eastern*, the biggest ship of the 19th century, 692 ft long and weighing 30,000 tons.

▼ Hovercrafts, or "air-cushion" vehicles, use a huge fan to blow air downward and lift the craft above the water.

Find out more

Air and water pp. 394–395

○ The great age of ocean liners lasted from the early 1900s to the 1950s.

○ The *Titanic* was the largest ship ever built at 46,329 tons when launched in 1912—but it sank on its maiden (first) voyage.

○ The *Queen Elizabeth* launched in 1938 was the largest passenger ship ever built—1,030 ft long and 83,673 tons. It burned and sank during refitting in Hong Kong in 1972.

○ Navies of the 21st century have five main classes of surface warship, listed here in descending size order: aircraft carriers, landing craft, cruisers, destroyers, and frigates.

○ The world's biggest warships are the 1,092 ft-long US aircraft carriers *Nimitz*, *Dwight D. Eisenhower*, *Carl Vinson*, *Abraham Lincoln*, *John C. Stennis*, *George Washington*, and *Harry S. Truman*.

Submarines

To gain weight for a dive, submarines fill their "ballast" tanks with water. To surface, they empty the tanks.

○ The first workable submarine was a rowing boat covered with waterproofed skins, built by Dutch scientist Cornelius van Drebbel in 1620.

○ On January 23, 1960, the bathyscaphe *Trieste*, controlled by Swiss oceanic engineer Jacques Piccard, descended a record 35,814 ft into the Marianas Trench in the Pacific.

○ The world's busiest ports are Rotterdam, Singapore, and Hong Kong.

○ The world's busiest canal is the Kiel in northern Germany, through which 45,000 ships a year travel from the North Sea to the Baltic. It reduces the distance of the journey around Denmark by over 298 mi.

◀ *Most ships are driven under the water by a screw propeller with slowly turning blades to force (thrust) the ship forward. This system is powerful, but the resistance of the water slows down the boat (drag). Small powerboats use high-speed jets of water instead to push themselves along faster.*

Metal blades or screws slice through water, propelling boat forward

Rudder steers boat left or right

▲ *Sailing ships rely on wind power to drive them along and can sail in almost any direction except directly into the wind—because the wind does not push the sails but sucks them. As the wind blows across the curve of the sail, it speeds up and its pressure drops, creating suction in the same way that an airplane's wings create lift. However, the sail must be kept at exactly the right angle. Sailors let the sail swing round until the angle is right then hold it taut (tight) with ropes.*

Emergency signals

The following signals indicate an emergency at sea and a request for help:

1. Parachute flare or hand flare showing a red light
2. Rockets that throw off red stars at intervals
3. Smoke signals emitting large volumes of orange smoke
4. Signal by radio in the Morse Code group SOS or the spoken word MAYDAY (only used in life-threatening emergencies)
5. Slowly raising and lowering hands repeatedly
6. Continuous sounding of whistle or siren
7. Flames on the vessel (for example, from the burning of an oily rag)
8. Flying the International Flag code signal NC
9. Flying a square flag with a ball above or below it
10. An ensign (flag) flown upside down
11. A coat or article of clothing on an oar or mast

History of Air Transport

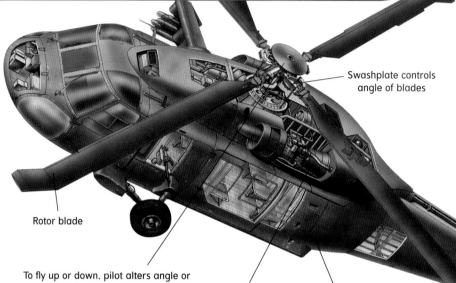

An aircraft's wings are lifted by the air flowing above and beneath them as they slice through the air. The amount of lift depends on the angle of the wing and its shape, and also how fast it is moving through the air.

▶ *A helicopter's rotor blades are really long, thin wings. The engine whirls them round so that they cut through the air and provide lift just like conventional wings. But rotor blades are also like huge propellers, hauling the helicopter up just as a propeller pulls a plane.*

Swashplate controls angle of blades

Rotor blade

Jet turbine engine

To fly up or down, pilot alters angle or "pitch" of main rotor blades with "collective pitch" control. When blades cut through the air almost flat, they give no lift and helicopter sinks. To climb, pilot steepens pitch to increase lift

To fly forward or backward, pilot uses "cyclic pitch" control to vary rotor pitch as blades go around from one side to the other

Amazing

The first controlled, powered flight was made by American Orville Wright in 1903. His plane, the *Flyer*, traveled just 118 ft!

○ The first jet engines were built at the same time in the 1930s by Pabst von Ohain in Germany and Frank Whittle in Britain—though neither knew of the other's work.

○ Turbojets are the original form of jet engine. Air is scooped in at the front of the engine and squeezed by spinning "compressor" blades. Fuel sprayed into the squeezed air in the middle of the engine burns, causing the mixture to expand dramatically. The expanding air not only pushes round turbines, which drive the compressor, but also sends out a high-speed jet of hot air to propel the plane. This high-speed jet is noisy but good for ultra-fast warplanes and supersonic aircraft.

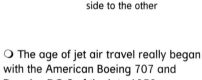

▲ *The four-engined Boeing 747 flies at 32,800–42,600 ft, well above most storms, and it can fly nonstop from New York to Tokyo.*

○ Turboprops are turbojets that use most of their power to turn a propeller rather than force out a hot air jet.

○ Turbofans are used by most airliners because they are quieter and cheaper to run. In these, extra turbines turn a huge fan at the front. Air driven by this fan bypasses the engine core and gives a huge extra boost at low speeds.

○ The age of jet air travel really began with the American Boeing 707 and Douglas DC-8 of the late 1950s.

○ Four-engined jets, such as the 747, can fly 6,214 mi nonstop at speeds of up to 621 mi/h. Two- and three-engine jets, such as the DC-10, make shorter flights.

Rocket launch

Only powerful rockets can give the thrust to overcome gravity and launch spacecraft into space. They fall away in stages once the spacecraft is traveling fast enough.

Find out more

Mach p. 392

In 1937 German designer Heinrich Focke built an aircraft with two huge variable pitch rotors instead of wings and achieved a controlled hover. Months later, German Anton Flettner built the first true helicopter.

Because the top of the wing is curved, air pushed over the wing speeds up and stretches out. The stretching of the air reduces its pressure. Underneath the wing, air slows down and bunches up, so air pressure here rises. The wing gains "lift" as the wing is sucked from above and pushed from below.

Drag

Lift

Thrust

Weight

Spar

Flap

Aileron

Trailing edge

Leading edge

Tip

Tail rotor drive shaft

The world's first airport was built at Croydon near London in 1928. Many early airports, such as Berlin's, were social centers, attracting thousands of visitors and sightseers each year.

The world's largest airport is King Abdul Aziz in Saudi Arabia. It covers 22,464 hectares. The USA's biggest is Dallas. Europe's biggest is Paris's Charles de Gaulle.

Supersonic planes travel faster than the speed of sound, about 758 mi/h at sea level at 59°F. A plane flying at supersonic speeds builds up shock waves in front and behind because it keeps catching up and compressing the sound waves in front of it.

On March 20, 1999 Bertran Piccard of Switzerland and Brian Jones of Britain made the first round-the-world hot-air balloon flight.

The first human parachute drop was made by Jacques Garnerin from a balloon over Paris in 1797.

Modern hang-gliding began with the fabric delta (triangular) wing design developed by the American Francis Rogallo in the 1940s.

Early planes

Most early planes were biplanes (double-wingers) or even triplanes (triple-wingers). Biplane wings were strong because struts and wires linked the small, light wings to combine their strength. In the years after World War I, huge biplane airliners were built including the Handley Page Heracles of the 1930s.

Busiest airports

	No. of passengers handled each year (millions)
Atlanta	79.09
Chicago O'Hare	69.35
London Heathrow	63.47
Tokyo Haneda	63.17
Los Angeles	54.97
Dallas/Fort Worth	53.24
Frankfurt	48.35
Paris Charles de Gaulle	48.12
Amsterdam Schiphol	39.96
Denver	37.46

Computers

*A*t the heart of every computer is a powerful microchip called the central processing unit (CPU). The CPU works things out, within the guidelines set by the computer's operating system (basic working instructions).

● Computers have come a long way since 1823 when English mathematician Charles Babbage invented the first type of computer—the "difference engine." It proved too complex to complete and in 1834 Babbage began constructing his "analytical engine" in which data was fed into the engine by punched cards. The results were designed to be printed out. Though it was never built in full, as it would have been the size of a small train, Babbage's idea helped others to invent the first practical computers.

○ A microchip is a slice of a semiconductor material such as silicon. "Micro" means that all the components and connections of the integrated circuit on the chip are microscopic in size.

○ Information is fed into the CPU as patterns of millions of tiny electrical signals per second.

● Computers can sometimes fool us into thinking something is real using virtual reality (VR) systems. VR sends data (information) to our senses that closely mimic real scenes or events. In the VR tennis game below, pressure and flex (bending) sensors in the glove detect wrist, hand and finger movements and send signals to a computer. The computer analyses these movements to determine if the player had moved in the correct way to hit the "virtual" ball, which can only be seen through the eyepieces.

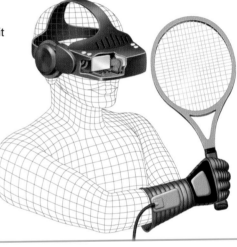

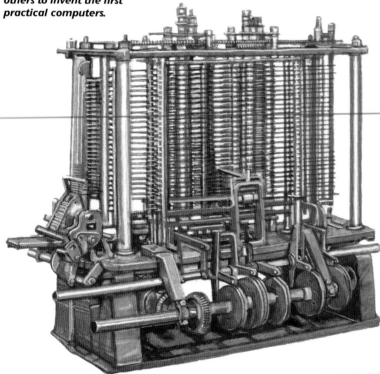

○ The microcircuits in the CPU analyse or process the signals and "decide" what to do according to a set of rules built into the circuit design. The results are fed out as more electrical signals to various other parts of the computer.

○ RAM (random-access memory) consists of microchips that receive new data and instructions when needed.

○ The circuit can be made up of thousands of individual components. The components, such as switches, resistors, capacitors, and transistors, are connected by wires or metal strips on the circuit board.

Find out more
The Internet pp. 416–417

Computer hygiene

Electronic components must be made in extremely clean conditions. A few specks of dust could get inside the components and ruin the manufacture of microchips and electrical circuit boards.

○ In general, computing ability doubles in speed and power every 18 months. This is called Moore's law, named after Gordon Moore who suggested it would happen in 1965.

○ Some microprocessors can handle billions of bits of data every second.

Microchips

Microchips and other components are connected by inserting their metal "legs" into sockets.

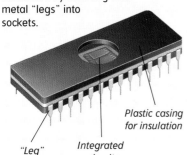

"Leg" connecting pins

Integrated circuit

Plastic casing for insulation

○ Computers store information in bits (binary digits), either as 0 or 1.

○ The bits 0 and 1 are equivalent to the OFF (0) and ON (1) of electric current flow. Eight bits make a byte.

▶ *The latest personal computers (PCs) are flat-screened. A liquid crystal display (LCD) produces images on a flat screen by using electric current to control the path of light through liquid crystals and colored filters. The mouse and keyboard are connected by a short-range wireless system (bluetooth®).*

Computer abbreviations

AAC	Advanced Audio Coding
AGP	Accelerated Graphics Port
AI	Artificial Intelligence
AMD	Advanced Micro Devices
API	Application Programming Interface
BASIC	Beginners All-Purpose Symbolic Instruction Code
BBS	Bulletin Board System
CAD	Computer Aided Design
CPU	Central Processing Unit
DOS	Disc Operating System
FAQ	Frequently Asked Questions
GIGO	Garbage In Garbage Out
HTML	Hypertext Markup Language
HTTP	Hypertext Transport Protocol
ICT	Information Communication Technology
LAN	Local Area Network
MMU	Memory Management Unit
PC	Personal Computer
RAM	Random-Access Memory
ROM	Read Only Memory
WAN	Wide Area Network
WAP	Wireless Application Protocol
WYSIWYG	What You See Is What You Get
WWW	World Wide Web

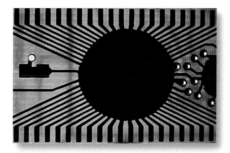

◀ *Transistors are electronic switches. They are made of materials called semiconductors that change their ability to conduct electricity. In the early 1970s, the CPUs or microprocessor chips inside the first home computers contained about 8,000 transistors each. By the early 21st century, more than 40 million transistors can be found in the same-sized chip, working a thousand times faster than the first ones.*

Telecommunications

*T*elecommunications is the transmission of sounds, words, pictures, data, and other forms of information by electronic means. In order to function, every telecommunication system needs three things: a transmitter, a communications link, and a receiver.

○ Transmitters can be telephones or computers with modems. They change the words, pictures, data, or sounds into an electrical signal and send it. Similar receivers pick up the signal and change it back into the right form.

Amazing

FLAG (Fiber-optic Link Around the Globe) is a submarine telephone cable that runs for 16,777 mi from Japan to the UK. FLAG links 11 countries in Europe, Africa, and Asia via the Mediterranean, the Indian Ocean, and the South China Sea. The cable can support 600,000 simultaneous telephone calls.

○ Telecommunications links carry the signal from the transmitter to the receiver in two main ways. Some give a direct link through telephone lines and other cables. Some are carried on radio waves through the air, via satellite, or microwave links.

○ Telephone lines used to be mainly electric cables, which carried the signal as pulses of electricity. More and more fiber optics are used, which carry the signal as coded pulses of light.

○ Single-mode fibers are very narrow and the light bounces very little from side-to-side. These fibers are suitable for long-distance transmissions.

○ The largest cables can carry hundreds of thousands of phone calls or hundreds of different television channels.

○ Microwave links use very short radio waves to transmit telephone and other signals from one dish to another. The signals travel between the dishes in a straight line across Earth's surface.

Broadcast communications satellites send radio signals direct to many receivers over a wide area, for radio programs and television channels.

Mobile phones

Mobile or cell phones use low-power radio waves to send messages. Areas across the world are divided into many small sectors called cells, each with an antenna that picks up signals from phones and sends them out. Because there are so many antennae spread across the world, millions of people can use mobile phones at once.

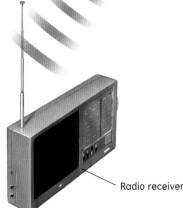

Communications satellite

Broadcast radio signals

Uplink dish

Radio receiver

Radio lingo

A	Alpha	N	November
B	Bravo	O	Oscar
C	Charlie	P	Papa
D	Delta	Q	Quebec
E	Echo	R	Romeo
F	Foxtrot	S	Sierra
G	Golf	T	Tango
H	Hotel	U	Uniform
I	India	V	Victor
J	Juliet	W	Whisky
K	Kilo	X	X-ray
L	Lima	Y	Yankee
M	Mike	Z	Zulu

Fax

Fax is short for "facsimile," which means "copy." A fax machine scans a document under a light past a line of sensors. The white parts of the document reflect light so switch on the sensors; the dark parts do not reflect light so switch off the sensors. Thus, a pattern of ons and offs is created and sent to the receiving fax. The receiving fax machine uses heat sensors that pick up the pattern of electrical signals coming through and creates the same pattern on the heat-sensitive paper. More modern machines print on plain paper, using charges of static electricity to attract the toner powder to the paper.

Telephone

Image to be sent is fed through a scanner

Phone socket that enables fax to connect to a phone line and send and receive messages

Image received is printed on paper from internal roll

Scanner sensors

Dial pad for typing in fax number

Drive rollers, to run document under scanner

○ Communications satellites are satellites orbiting the Earth in space. Telephone calls are beamed up on radio waves to the satellite, which beams them back down to the recipient, in the right part of the world.

○ Calls across the ocean go one way by satellite and the other by undersea cable to avoid delays.

Small loudspeaker in earpiece

Mode or function keys

Small microphone in mouthpiece

Numerical keys

○ Most of the 5,000 satellites circling the Earth in space are used for telecommunications. Communications satellites use a special orbit, called a geo-stationary orbit, which ensures that they are always in the same place above the Earth's surface.

○ A fast and convenient form of contact today is electronic mail or e-mail. The message is typed up on a computer or even on some mobile phones and is sent to another e-mail address. The message is stored until the recipient "logs in" to receive it.

Telephones convert sound into an electrical signal. When you speak into a phone, the vibrations of your voice move a tiny microphone that alters an electrical current in strength. This creates an electrical signal, which is sent to the receiving phone. In the receiver the varying signal works a loudspeaker, which vibrates the air and recreates the sound of your voice. Today, many signals are sent as pulses of laser light along special glass threads called optical fibers. Signals are also sent as radio waves or microwaves through the air—bouncing off satellites in space.

Find out more
The Internet pp. 416–417

The Internet

The Internet is a vast network linking millions of computers around the world. The Internet began in the 1960s when the US Army developed a network called ARPAnet to link computers.

○ The World Wide Web is a way of finding your way to the data in sites on all the computers linked to the Internet.

○ A hyperlink is a fast link to another Internet site.

○ The World Wide Web was invented in 1989 by Englishman Tim Berners-Lee of the CERN laboratories in Switzerland.

○ The information superhighway is the network of high-speed links that might be achieved by combining telephone systems, cable TV, and computer networks. Television programs, movies, data, direct video links, and the Internet could all enter the home in this way.

The Internet consists of the global telecommunications network and all the computers that are connected to the network at any particular time. Web sites and web pages are often said to exist in "cyberspace," because they have no physical existence. In fact, the various components of a web page (headings, text, pictures, etc.) may be stored on different computers that are thousands of miles apart.

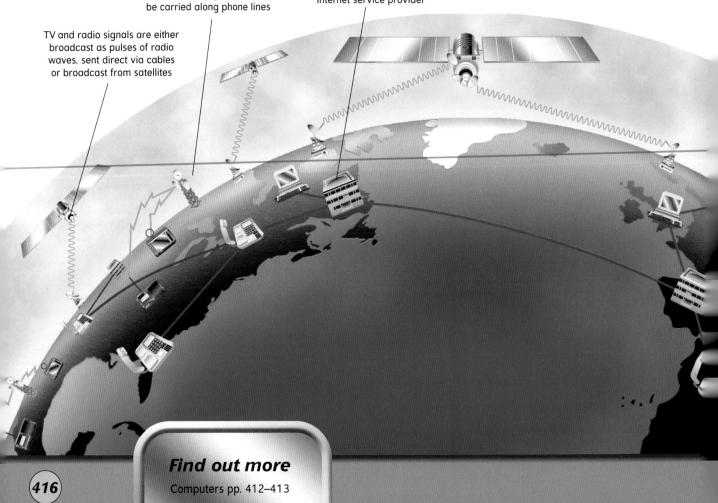

Computer data is translated by a modem into signals that can be carried along phone lines

Signals from individual transmitters are sent on from a telephone exchange or an Internet service provider

TV and radio signals are either broadcast as pulses of radio waves, sent direct via cables or broadcast from satellites

Find out more

Computers pp. 412–413

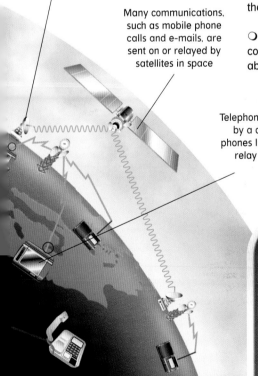

A *Portable laptop computers can be moved around easily so they can be linked to the Internet at various locations.*

Games consoles

Games consoles become more realistic every year, with faster action and better graphics, as well as more imaginative challenges. Some games can be played "live" over the Internet with people anywhere in the world.

Main unit feeds images to monitor

Hand console with controls

Internet phones

Internet phones allow people to "surf" (browse) the Internet from all over the world.

○ For the Internet a computer's output is translated into a form that can be sent by phone lines with a modem (short for modulator/demodulator).

○ Computers access the Internet via a local phone to a large computer called the Internet Service Provider (ISP).

○ Each ISP is connected to a giant computer called a main hub. There are about 100 linked main hubs worldwide.

Communications travel via satellites and are beamed up and down from antenna dishes on ground

Many communications, such as mobile phone calls and e-mails, are sent on or relayed by satellites in space

Telephones link into phone network by a direct cable link. Mobile phones link through the air to local relay towers by radio waves

○ Some links between hubs are made via telephone lines, while others are made via satellite.

○ Web pages are viewed using a piece of software called a browser. The browser creates a virtual machine on the computer screen with its own cursor-operated controls and features.

○ A plug-in is a piece of software that extends the capabilities of a browser—for example, by allowing it to play cartoons with sound.

○ HTML stands for hypertext mark-up language—a series of symbols that tells browsers how to display the words and pictures on a web page.

○ There are billions of different pages on the web—people can find the pages they want by entering keywords into a search engine.

○ A broadband Internet connection can be up to ten times faster than a dial-up connection, which uses an ordinary telephone line.

What can you use the Internet for?

1. View pictures
2. Read text
3. See movies
4. Have "realtime" conversations with friends using audio software and web cameras (webcams)
5. Listen to sounds and music
6. Shop and buy products
7. Send messages by e-mail
8. Send files to other people by file transfer protocol (FTP)
9. Join newsgroups and e-distribution lists
10. Take part in live, on-line discussions

Sound and Vision

*T*echnology is frequently updated, making existing versions out-of-date. For example, vinyl discs were used to play back recorded sound for more than 50 years. Cassette tapes also became popular for about 30 years. About 20 years later, CDs took over. Some ten years after that, MP3-players arrived, storing sounds in electronic microchips.

○ Most sound recording today is digital, which means that sound vibrations are broken into tiny electrical chunks.

Amazing

The first ever sound recording was made in 1877 by American inventor Thomas Edison. He recorded the words "Mary had a little lamb," on to tin foil using a device called a phonograph.

Wire coil electromagnet

Permanent magnet

Cone

▲ *A loudspeaker converts a changing electric current into sound. Electrical signals flow through a wire coil and turn it into an electromagnet, which pushes and pulls against a permanent magnet to vibrate a cone and produce sound.*

○ To make a digital recording a device called an analogue-to-digital converter divides the sound vibrations into 44,100 segments for each second.

○ On a CD (compact disc) the pattern of electrical pulses is burned by laser as a pattern of pits on the disc surface.

○ Television relies on the photoelectric effect—the emission of electrons by a substance when struck by photons of light. Light-sensitive photocells in cameras work like this.

○ Television cameras have three sets of tubes with photocells (reacting to red, green, and blue light) to convert the picture into electrical signals.

○ Most TV sets are based on glass tubes shaped like giant lightbulbs, called cathode-ray tubes. The narrow end contains a cathode, which is a negative electrical terminal. The wide end is the TV screen.

▼ *A powerful microscope reveals the bowl-like pits and flat areas between them, in the surface of a CD (compact disc).*

Milestones

1936	First regular TV broadcasts in UK
1948	First vinyl discs produced
1951	First color TV broadcasts in USA
1962	International relay of TV pictures by *Telstar* satellite
1964	Cassette tapes become available
1967	UK begins color TV broadcasts
1975	Flat liquid crystal display (LCD) TV screen developed
1977	Pocket TVs go on sale
1982	Compact discs widely available
1984	Camcorders introduced
1993	Early videophones created
2000	DVDs introduced commercially

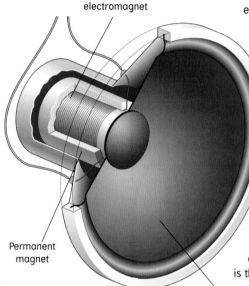

▲ *Personal music players can store sounds on tape, compact disc (like this version), minidisc (similar to CD but smaller), or electronic microchip.*

Find out more

Sound pp. 392–393

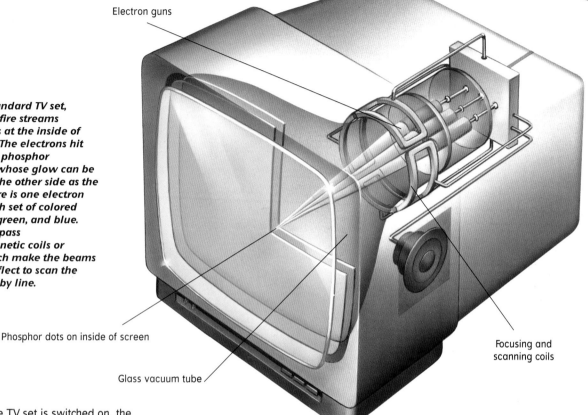

Electron guns

▶ *In a standard TV set, "guns" fire streams of electrons at the inside of the screen. The electrons hit tiny dots of phosphor chemicals whose glow can be seen from the other side as the image. There is one electron gun for each set of colored dots—red, green, and blue. The beams pass electromagnetic coils or plates, which make the beams bend or deflect to scan the screen line by line.*

Phosphor dots on inside of screen

Focusing and scanning coils

Glass vacuum tube

○ When the TV set is switched on, the cathode fires a nonstop stream of electrons at the inside of the TV screen.

○ Wherever electrons hit the screen, the screen glows as its coating of phosphors heats up.

○ To build up the picture the electron beam scans quickly back-and-forth across the screen, making it glow in certain places. This happens so quickly that it looks as if the screen is glowing.

○ The picture quality of a TV depends on the number of lines the electron guns scans the screen. Most TVs use about 600 lines, but high-definition TVs use twice that number.

○ In a CD there are over 3,000 million pits in a spiral path or track about 3 mi long. They can store about 70 minutes of high-quality music, over 700 megabytes (MB) of computer data or similar amounts of information.

Camcorder

The camcorder is a personal movie camera and videotape recorder. Some easy-to-use models can now fit in the palm of the hand.

Laser beam

The amazingly intense light beam produced by a laser is used in a huge number of devices, from CD players to satellite guidance systems.

○ A DVD has more pits than a CD. The pits are smaller and arranged in different vertical layers. A DVD stores 4.7 gigabytes (GB)—which is equal to 4,700 megabytes—enough for a full-length movie and its soundtrack. These pits are "read" by a laser beam.

Power

O ur world is driven by energy. Without energy the world would be dark, cold, still, and silent. We use it in many forms, including movement, sound, chemical bonds, electricity, heat, light, waves, and rays. Energy is needed to power thousands of devices and machines.

❍ Engines are devices that convert fuel into movement.

❍ Engines that burn fuel to generate power are called heat engines. The burning is called combustion.

❍ An internal combustion engine, as used in a car, a jet, or a rocket, burns its fuel on the inside.

❍ In four-stroke engines, such as those in most cars, the pistons go up-and-down four times for each time they are thrust down by the hot gases.

❍ In jets and rockets, hot gases swell and push against the engine as they shoot out of the back.

▶ Electricity is brought to homes and factories through a network of high-tension cables. Some cables are buried underground, some are suspended high in the air from metal towers called pylons.

Oil refinery

In an oil refinery, crude oil is broken down into an enormous range of different hydrocarbons. Crude oil is separated by distillation into various substances, such as aviation fuel, gasoline and paraffin. As the oil is heated in a distillation column, a mixture of gases evaporates. Each gas cools and condenses at a different height into a liquid, or fraction, which is then drawn off.

❍ About 60 percent of the world's electricity is "thermal electricity," which is produced in power stations by burning coal, oil, and natural gas. Peat, alcohol, and biomass (firewood) are also used, but to a lesser extent.

❍ The other 40 percent of the world's electricity is generated using nuclear energy, or by harnessing the energy of river water (hydro-electricity), sunlight (solar electricity), or the wind and tides.

❍ France is the most nuclear-electric country in the world—about 80 percent of French electricity is generated in nuclear power stations.

Amazing

One pound of deuterium (a type of hydrogen) can give the same amount of energy as 6,600,000 lb of coal.

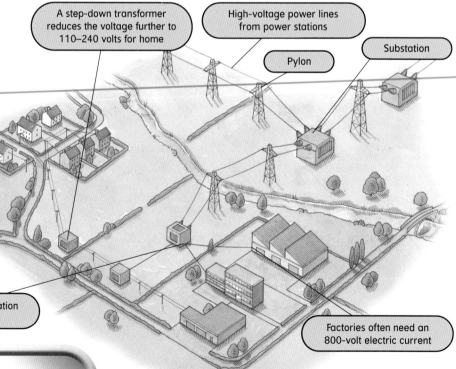

A step-down transformer reduces the voltage further to 110–240 volts for home

High-voltage power lines from power stations

Pylon

Substation

A step-down transformer at the substation reduces the voltage to 800 volts

Factories often need an 800-volt electric current

Find out more

Power stations p. 385

Common fuels

Common fuels we burn for energy include oil, coal and gas. These were formed by the fossilization of decayed plants and other life-forms long ago. Their energy came as light from the Sun. Oil and coal are extracted from deep in the ground, formed beneath rock layers.

○ In thermal power stations fuels are burned to make heat. The heat is used to boil water into steam, which blasts past the fan-shaped blades or rotors of a turbine and makes them spin. The turbine is linked to a generator. Inside the generator is a magnetic field, which rotates near a coil of wire, and this makes electricity flow through the wire.

○ In hydroelectric power stations, running water spins the turbine blades.

○ Electricity from power stations is distributed around a country in a network of cables known as the grid.

○ Power station generators push out 25,000 volts or more. This voltage is too much to use in people's homes, but not enough to transmit over long distances.

○ To transmit electricity over long distances, the voltage is boosted from 25,000 to 400,000 volts by step-up transformers. It is fed through high-voltage cables. Near its destination the electricity's voltage is reduced by step-down transformers at substations for distribution to homes, shops, offices, and factories.

Electricity is distributed across the country through high-voltage power lines

A "moderator" such as graphite slows down the neutrons so that they hit more nuclei, making the most of the fuel

Control rods slow the process down by absorbing neutrons

Hot air from the reactor turns water in the pipe into steam

Steam is blasted over turbines, driving them round

Uranium fuel rods give off heat

Concrete surrounds the reactor

Transformer boosts the voltage ready for transmission

As the turbines spin, they drive magnets round inside electric coils to generate electricity

Steam is cooled to water and cycled back to the reactor

Like coal- and oil-fired power stations, nuclear power stations use steam to drive turbines to generate electricity. The difference is that nuclear power stations obtain the heat by splitting uranium atoms, not by burning coal or oil. When the atom is split, it sends out gamma rays, neutrons, and immense heat. In a nuclear bomb this happens in a split second. In a nuclear power plant, control rods soak up some of the neutrons and slow the process down.

Medicine

Technology is vital in many aspects of medicine today. Doctors can see inside the body using various kinds of scanners, or directly by looking through an "endoscope."

○ An endoscope is a flexible tube that can be inserted into the body to view internal organs and achieve a more detailed and accurate diagnosis of a problem. Light to illuminate the interior of the body is carried to the tip of the endoscope along optical fibers.

Before an operation, patients are given anesthetics, which either cause a loss of feeling in the body to numb the pain, or send them to sleep. English chemist Humphrey Davey noted the anesthetic effects of nitrous oxide (laughing gas) in 1799, and in 1844 it was used by American dentist Horace Wells for tooth extractions. Later, other substances such as chloroform and ether were used. An operating theater is kept extremely clean to prevent infection. Surgeons wear masks, hats, and coats to avoid spreading germs through breathing and from cuts on the skin.

Amazing

Trepanning was an ancient practice that involved drilling a hole in the skull to relieve severe headaches, or release "evil spirits" that were believed to cause mental illness. If the person survived, the bone eventually grew back over the hole.

Find out more

Atoms pp. 372–373

○ The natural background radiation you receive over a year is about 100 times what you receive from a single ordinary chest X ray.

PET scans

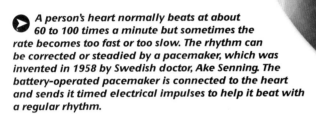

PET scans can show a living brain in action. This scan shows a monkey's brain from above.

▶ *A person's heart normally beats at about 60 to 100 times a minute but sometimes the rate becomes too fast or too slow. The rhythm can be corrected or steadied by a pacemaker, which was invented in 1958 by Swedish doctor, Ake Senning. The battery-operated pacemaker is connected to the heart and sends it timed electrical impulses to help it beat with a regular rhythm.*

○ Various complex scanners are used in medicine to give pictures of the inside of the body and help doctors diagnose problems. They include PET scanners, CT scanners, and MRI scanners.

○ PET stands for Positron Emission Tomography. The scanner picks up positrons (positively charged electrons) sent out by radioactive substances injected into the blood.

○ CT stands for computerized tomography. An X ray beam rotates around the patient and is picked up by detectors on the far side to build up a three-dimensional (3-D) picture.

○ MRI stands for Magnetic Resonance Imaging. An MRI scan works like a CT scan but it uses magnetism, not X rays. The patient is surrounded by such powerful magnets that all the body's protons line up.

○ Genes are found in every living cell on special molecules called DNA (deoxyribonucleic acid). Scientists alter genes by snipping them from the DNA of one organism and inserting them into the DNA of another. This process is known as gene splicing.

X rays

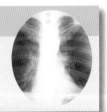

X rays pass through most body tissues except bones, which show up white on medical X rays.

○ By splicing new genes into the DNA of bacteria, scientists can turn them into factories for making valuable natural chemicals. One protein made like this is interferon, a natural body chemical that protects humans against certain viruses. Enzymes for detergents and melanin for suntan lotion can also be made in this way.

○ Gene therapy means altering the genes to cure diseases that are inherited from parents or caused by faulty genes.

Doctors and diseases

Doctor	Specializes In
Cardiologist	Heart disease
Dermatologist	Skin
Gynecologist	Female reproduction
Hematologist	Blood
Histologist	Cells and tissue
Nephrologist	Kidney
Neurologist	Nervous system
Ophthalmologist	Eyes
Otologist	Ear
Pediatrician	Children
Proctologist	Rectum and lower intestine

Disease	Affects
Athritis	Joints
Bursitis	Joints
Cirrhosis	Liver
Conjunctivitis	Eyes
Cystitus	Bladder
Dermatitis	Skin
Gingivitis	Gums
Glossitis	Tongue
Hepatitis	Liver
Meningitis	Brain
Phlebitis	Veins
Pneumonia	Lungs

Numbers and Shapes

Numbers are used for counting, calculating, and measuring quantities and sizes. Number symbols are also used for identification and to establish a sequence, as in the page numbers in this book.

○ Throughout history people have used 10 as the basis for their numbers because we have ten fingers and thumbs on our hands.

○ More than 4,000 years ago the ancient Egyptians had a number system that used just four symbols to write all the numbers smaller than 10,000. The symbols they used were for 1, 10, 100, and 1,000. So 365 was written as 100+100+100+10+10+10+10+10+10 +1+1+1+1+1.

○ Despite having such a cumbersome number system, the ancient Egyptians were able to calculate well enough to build the giant stone pyramids at Giza.

○ The ancient Sumerians used a 10-based system that was similar to the Egyptian system, but the Sumerians also considered the number 6 to be important because 10 x 6 x 6 = 360, which is nearly the exact number of days in a year (365).

Amazing

The word plus is short for surplus. The symbol + was originally written on sacks and boxes that were overweight. The symbol – (minus) was written on those that were underweight.

○ It is because of the ancient Sumerians that hours are divided into 60 (10 x 6) minutes, each with 60 seconds; and that a circle is divided into 360°.

Binary numbers

Computers and other electronic devices operate using the binary system of numbers that has just two symbols, 1 and 0. These two symbols correspond to an electronic switch being either on (1) or off (0). Binary numbers are difficult to read without a lot of practice. The number 10 is written in binary as 1010, 23 is written as 10111, and 55 is written as 110111.

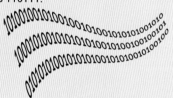

○ The ancient Romans had a number system that used seven letter symbols to write all the numbers below 10,000. The symbols they used were: I (1), V (5), X (10), L (50), C (100), D (500), and M (1,000). So 365 was written as CCCLXV (100+100+100+50+10+5).

○ The Mayans of Mexico used a base-20 number system 1,500 years ago.

○ Most Roman numbers were written by adding together smaller numbers like the Egyptians did, but some Roman numbers were written using subtraction instead. The number 4 was written as IV (5–1), 9 was written as IX (10–1), and 99 was written as IC (100–1).

○ Roman numbers are still sometimes used to give the date at the end of a motion picture, for example MMV (2005).

Round the world

Many civilizations invented systems of numbers. Most ancient systems did not use the number zero. This made counting difficult. Arabic numbers are now the main system, because they are so easy to use.

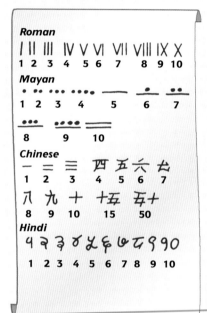

○ The numbers we use today are based on Arabic numbers that were first used nearly 1,500 years ago.

○ The decimal system that is now used around the world was not possible until the Arabs invented a symbol for the number 0 (zero).

○ The Arabs took the ancient Indian numbers for 1–9 and added the number 0 (zero), so that large numbers such as 500 and 1,000 did not need their own special symbols.

Find out more

Computers pp. 412–413

Regular polygons

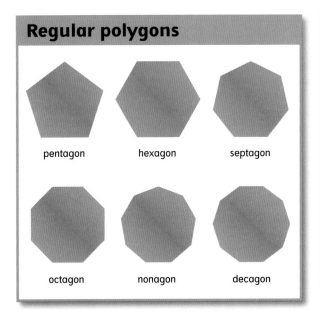

pentagon hexagon septagon

octagon nonagon decagon

Regular polyhedrons

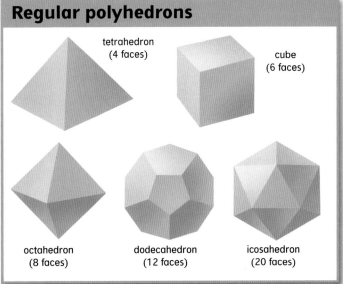

tetrahedron
(4 faces)

cube
(6 faces)

octahedron
(8 faces)

dodecahedron
(12 faces)

icosahedron
(20 faces)

Areas of 2-D (flat or plane) shapes

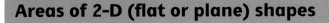

area of a **rectangle**
= length x height
= $l \times h$

area of a **parallelogram**
= base length x right-angle height
= $l \times h$

area of a **triangle**
= ½ base length x right-angle height
= $\frac{1}{2}l \times h$

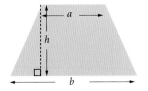

area of a **trapezium**
= ½ (sum of parallel sides) x right-angle height
= $\frac{1}{2}(a + b) \times h$

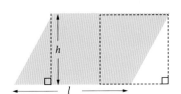

area of a **circle**
= π x radius²
= πr^2

area of a **sector**
= $\dfrac{\text{angle of sector}}{360}$ x π x radius

= $\dfrac{x}{360}$ x πr^2

Surface area of common 3-D shapes

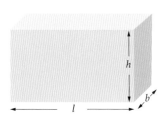

surface area of a cube
(faces are identical)
= 6 x area of each surface
= $6l^2$

surface area of a cone
= area of a curved surface + area of base
= π x (radius of cross section x slant height)
+ π(radius of cross section)^2
= $\pi rl + \pi r^2$
= $\pi r(l + r)$

surface area of a cuboid
(opposite faces are identical)
= area of two end faces + area of two sides
+ area of top and base
= $2lh + 2hb + 2lb$
= $2(lh + hb + lb)$

surface area of a sphere
= 4π x radius^2
= $4\pi r^2$

surface area of a cylinder
= area of a curved surface + area of top and base
= 2π x (radius of cross section x height)
+ 2π x (radius of cross section)^2
= $2\pi rh + 2\pi r^2$
= $2\pi r(h + r)$

Volume of common 3-D shapes

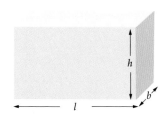

volume of a cone
= $\frac{1}{3}$π x (radius of cross section)^2
x slant height
= $\frac{1}{3}\pi r^2 l$

volume of a cube
= length^3
= l^3

volume of a cuboid
= length x breadth x height
= $l \times b \times h$

volume of a cylinder
= π x (radius of cross section)^2
x height
= $\pi r^2 h$

volume of a sphere
= $\frac{4}{3}$π x radius^3
= $\frac{4}{3}\pi r^3$

Find out more

Numbers/shapes pp. 424–425

Types of triangles

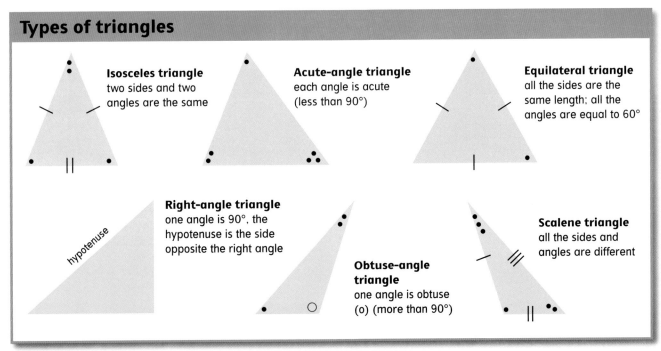

Isosceles triangle
two sides and two
angles are the same

Acute-angle triangle
each angle is acute
(less than 90°)

Equilateral triangle
all the sides are the
same length; all the
angles are equal to 60°

Right-angle triangle
one angle is 90°, the
hypotenuse is the side
opposite the right angle

hypotenuse

**Obtuse-angle
triangle**
one angle is obtuse
(o) (more than 90°)

Scalene triangle
all the sides and
angles are different

Trigonometry

For any right-angled triangle with angle u as shown the
trigonometric ratios are:

$$\text{sine } u = \frac{BC}{AB} = \frac{\text{opposite}}{\text{hypotenuse}}$$

$$\cos u = \frac{AC}{AB} = \frac{\text{adjacent}}{\text{hypotenuse}}$$

$$\tan u = \frac{BC}{AC} = \frac{\text{opposite}}{\text{adjacent}}$$

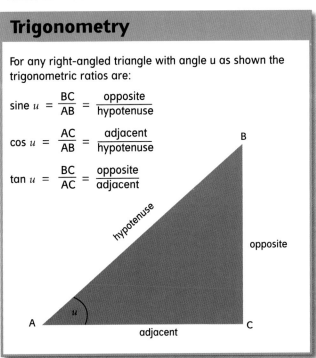

hypotenuse

opposite

A

u

adjacent

C

B

Pythagoras' theorem

Pythagoras' theorem $a^2 = b^2 + c^2$
i.e. the square of the hypotenuse is equal to the sum of
the squares on the other two sides.

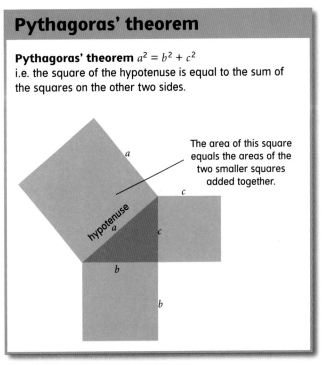

The area of this square
equals the areas of the
two smaller squares
added together.

hypotenuse
a

a

b

b

c

c

Glossary

Absolute zero the lowest temperature possible (−459.67° Farenheit).

Acceleration a change in velocity.

Air the mixture of gases that makes up Earth's atmosphere.

Alloy a type of metal made by adding other substances to a pure metal element.

Angle the relative position, measured in degrees (°), between two lines that meet or intersect.

Artificial manufactured or otherwise produced by human beings.

Atom the tiniest particle of any pure substance or chemical.

Bacteria single-celled organisms that live in a wide variety of environments, from hot springs to the human body.

Binary number a number written using just two symbols: 0 and 1.

Biplane an aircraft that has two wings, one above the other.

Boil to turn from a liquid into a gas.

Bond a close attachment formed by atoms and molecules.

CPU Central Processing Unit, the microchip that does most of the work in a computer.

Carbon an element that forms millions of compounds with other elements.

Carbon dioxide an invisible gas that is naturally present in air in small quantities.

Chemical formula a description of the number and type of atoms in a single molecule of a substance.

Circle a flat geometric shape in which every point around the edge is the same distance from the center.

Circuit a pathway around which electricity flows.

Circumference the distance around the edge of a circle.

Compound a combination of two or more elements.

Conductor a material through which heat or electricity can flow.

DNA Deoxyribonucleic acid. DNA carries genetic information in the body.

Data information, usually expressed in electronic form.

Decibel the unit used to measure the loudness of sounds.

Diameter any line across a circle that passes through the center.

Digital describes information that has been converted into binary numbers.

Electricity energy involving the flow of electrons through substances.

Electromagnetic radiation energy that travels as waves through space and matter.

Electron a subatomic particle that orbits the nucleus of an atom.

Element one of the pure substances that make up materials and compounds.

Fax (facsimile) machine a device for sending written documents along telephone wires.

Freeze to turn from a liquid into a solid.

Friction the force that acts between two objects rubbing together.

Fulcrum the point on which a lever (a type of simple machine) pivots.

Gas any substance that flows and varies in volume to fit into a container.

Gene splicing the process of modifying DNA.

Heat the internal energy stored in an object or substance.

Hydrogen an element that is normally a gas. Hydrogen combines with oxygen to make water.

Insulator a material that resists the flow of heat or electricity.

ISP Internet Service Provider, a company that provides access to the Internet.

Internal combustion engine a gasoline (petrol) or diesel engine that produces rotary power.

Jet engine an engine that blasts out hot gas to provide forward motion for airplanes.

Laser a device that produces very strong, amplified light of a particular wavelength.

Lever a simple machine that uses turning force to reduce the effort needed to move objects.

Light a form of energy that we can see with our eyes.

Liquid describes any substance that flows and has a fixed volume.

Machine a device that makes doing work easier.

Magnetic field the area around a magnet in which it exerts its force.

Magnetism an invisible force that attracts or repels magnetic materials, and which has electromagnetic effects.

Metal one of a group of elements with similar characteristics. Most metals are hard, have a shiny appearance, and are good conductors of heat and electricity.

Microchip a tiny electronic device that contains thousands of electrical circuits.

Modem (modulator/demodulator) a device that converts sounds into digital signals.

Molecule two or more atoms held together by chemical bonds.

Mouse a device used to control the cursor on a computer screen.

Natural made entirely by nature without human assistance.

Neutron a subatomic particle without electric charge that forms part of the nucleus of an atom.

Noble gas one of the five gaseous elements that are almost totally unreactive.

Nucleus the central core of an atom.

Optical fiber a thin glass thread, along which light rays can pass. Optical fibers are used to transmit data in communications cables.

Organic chemistry the study of compounds that contain carbon.

Oxygen an element that is normally a gas. Oxygen is one of the components of air, and it is essential for living things.

Periodic Table an organized arrangement of chemical elements.

Plasma a substance that consists of electrically charged gas atoms.

Plastic an artificial substance made from crude oil.

Polymer a long chainlike molecule composed mainly of carbon and hydrogen atoms.

Proton a positively charged particle that forms part of the nucleus of an atom.

Radius the distance between the edge of a circle and the center.

Rhombus a flat geometric shape that has four sides and two pairs of equal angles.

Right angle the relative position of two lines that meet or intersect at 90°.

Rocket a very powerful type of engine used in missiles and space vehicles.

Scanner a device that produces an electronic picture of something.

Shell one of the regions of space around the nucleus of an atom that is occupied by electrons.

Solid describes any substance that has strength and a fixed shape and volume.

Sphere a solid geometric shape in which every point on the surface is the same distance from the center.

Square a flat geometric shape with four straight sides of equal length and four right angles.

Steam water in the form of a gas.

Steam engine a device that is driven by steam given off by boiling water.

Steel an alloy composed mainly of iron, together with a small amount of carbon. Other substances are also added.

Subatomic smaller than an atom.

Submersible small craft designed to operate underwater.

Temperature a measurement of an object's internal energy (heat).

Transparent allows light to pass through.

Trapezium a flat geometric shape that has four sides, two of which are parallel.

Triangle a flat geometric shape that has three straight sides.

Turbine a device that converts horizontal motion into rotation.

Water a liquid that is a chemical compound of hydrogen and oxygen.

Web the part of the Internet that is available to public access.

X rays high-energy light beams that can pass through skin and muscles.

ARTS & CULTURE

The First Artists

Many thousands of years ago, artists began to decorate the world in which they lived. There are many reasons why artists painted—personal, social, religious, and magical. They also wanted to make their surroundings more interesting and more beautiful. Painting is clearly a natural instinct of human beings.

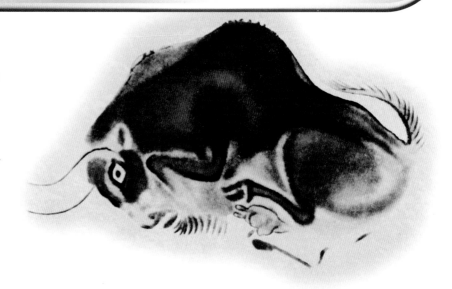

○ The oldest known works of art are small sculptures of bone and stone made in Europe around 25,000 BC. The most famous of these is the *Willendorf Venus*, found in Austria. It portrays a plump, seminaked female figure, who was probably a fertility goddess.

○ Many wonderful paintings, on rocks hidden deep inside caves, survive from around 20,000 to 15,000 years ago. They mostly show bison, deer, and horses. These may have been holy animals that protected tribes of prehistoric people. Or they may have been painted by hunters, to give them magical power over their prey.

○ The beauty of the natural world was the inspiration for many early artists. They created patterns and designs based on plants and living creatures.

◀ The bright colors and varied shapes of flowers, birds, and insects fascinated early craftworkers. They used dried plants, feathers, and insect wings as raw materials, and created images of wild creatures to decorate their pottery, textiles, jewelry, and stone carvings.

▲ This dramatic picture of a bison, with head lowered ready to charge, was painted deep inside a cave at Lascaux, southern France, around 17,000 years ago. It was discovered by four French boys searching for treasure. Many more fine paintings, mostly of wild animals, have been found in caves nearby.

○ Egyptians decorated mummies' tombs with wall paintings, showing happy scenes in the afterlife. They believed that art had magic powers to help keep a dead person's spirit alive.

○ For thousands of years, artists have created beautiful objects to honor dead ancestors. They have shaped containers for sacrifices (offerings) to ancestor spirits, and carved memorials recording ancestors' lives.

Amazing

Many murals (wall paintings) were discovered in the Roman city of Pompeii, preserved under tons of ash from the eruption of Mount Vesuvius in AD 79.

○ Much early art was made for use in religious ceremonies. Around 2,000 years ago, Nazca artists in South America made pottery drums and played them to chants and dances.

▼ Artists who came from many early civilizations, from South America to Siberia, made works of art to help dead people's spirits survive. The best known are ancient Egyptian mummies—dried-out, bandaged bodies, protected by beautifully decorated containers.

Find out more

Art techniques pp. 436–437

Pottery

For thousands of years, pottery has been beautifully painted with patterns and pictures, ranging from simple geometric designs to elaborate and complex scenes, including figures and landscapes. These Roman pots would have been used as kitchenware.

▼ *Square bronze vessels were used to offer food and drink to ancestor spirits in China over 3,000 years ago. They were decorated with faces of "taotie"—fierce monsters with claws and horns. Taotie may have originated as pictures of male ancestors but became monsters over time.*

◄ *The Romans followed the Greek approach to sculpture, and many Greek sculptors went to work in Rome. This life-size sculpture of Augusto di Proma Porta can be seen today in the Vatican Museum, Rome, Italy.*

○ Gods and spirits feature in many early works of art. Long-haired nature goddesses were pictured on statues, carvings and metalwork made by Celtic peoples living in Europe between around 800 BC and AD 100.

○ Early Christian artists painted icons (holy images) of Christian saints. Worshipers believed that honoring these icons helped them to communicate with God.

Carefully planned

Ancient Egyptian artists, who worked between c.3100–30 BC, planned their tomb-paintings very carefully. First, they marked out the design on the tomb wall using a grid (pattern of squares) to help them. Then they sketched the outlines of human figures, plants, and animals. Finally, they filled in the outlines with colored paints.

Earliest art

c.30,000 BC	Small sculptures of stone and bone, Europe
c.20,000–15,000 BC	Many cave paintings, Europe
c.11,000 BC	Earliest-known pottery, Japan
c.10,000 BC	Rock-art pictures of human figures, Australia
c.8500 BC	Rock-art pictures of animals, North Africa
c.7000 BC	First copper jewelry, Middle East
c.6500 BC	First known woven cloth, Turkey
c.4800 BC	First engraved seals, used to stamp pictures on clay, Mesopotamia
c.4500 BC	First gold jewelry made, eastern Europe
c.3500 BC	Picture-writing invented, Mesopotamia
c.3000 BC	First jade jewelry made, China
c.2750 BC	First decorated bronze-castings, China
c.2700 BC	First silk made, China
c.2600 BC	Glass-making invented, Mesopotamia

○ Between around 600 BC and AD 100, artists in ancient Greece and Rome created works of art portraying beautiful human bodies. Many of their greatest works show men and women naked, or wearing very few clothes. Artists often asked famous athletes to be their models, since they were fit, healthy, and strong.

Old Masters, New Ideas

*I*n Europe, from around AD 300, most art was based on Christian religious themes. But after around 1,000 years, great changes took place in art and design. Artists began to copy ancient Greek and Roman works, and to observe the world around them with scientific curiosity. After another 500 years, fashions in art changed dramatically once again, as artists experimented with exciting new painting styles.

○ Christian monks painted tiny, brilliant "illuminations" (images) to illustrate religious books they had carefully written by hand. They were not just for decoration, but helped the reader to find particular passages of text faster.

▼ *In the 18th and early 19th centuries, artists in France were trained to paint in schools called academies. The teachers were often very gifted artists who could paint with technical brilliance, however the strict teaching rules of these schools tended to stifle personal flair. This meant artists who trained in them often produced technically correct but dull work.*

○ Monks did not try to make the people in their pictures look lifelike. Instead, they aimed to convey a religious message in their work.

○ In medieval times most art was paid for by the Church but, during the Renaissance, rulers paid artists to work for them and preferred nonreligious subjects for paintings, such as battles and Greek and Roman mythology.

○ Artists in Italy were the first to study ancient Greek and Roman designs, from around AD 1300. Historians gave the art they created a new name, the "Renaissance." It meant the "rebirth" of ancient civilization.

▲ *Before the printing press was invented in the 1440s, manuscripts (handwritten books) were written out by monks. Their pages were decorated with beautiful small "illuminations," or paintings. The early skills of European painting were learned by illumination. It could take a year to copy out and illuminate (illustrate) a medieval manuscript. For this reason, they were very valuable.*

Amazing

In Medieval Europe, books were written out on vellum, a very fine kind of parchment made from the skin of a lamb, kid, or calf.

▶ *Dutch painter Vincent van Gogh (1853–1890) was influenced by Impressionist painting techniques, but developed them in his own style. He created images, like this portrait of his friend, Dr Gachet, by using thick layers of oil paint, brushed onto canvas in swirling lines. This created striking images, and may have reflected Van Gogh's troubled mind.*

Find out more

Printing/Publishing pp. 468–469

○ In France, around 1874, a group of artists pioneered a new painting style. They tried to convey their "impression" of scenes, rather than create detailed copies. They experimented with ways of dabbing paint onto canvas to create movement, light, and shade, and became known as the "Impressionists."

○ The Impressionists painted using vibrant colors, rapid brush-strokes, and swirls of paint. They painted outdoors to capture a sense of immediacy.

 A painting by Auguste Renoir (1841–1919). He tried to capture a lazy atmosphere and the relaxed feeling of friends sharing a meal. Renoir was an Impressionist and built up pictures using dabs of color, rather than strong shapes and lines.

○ Renaissance artists discovered "perspective." This is a way of painting that shows three dimensions on a flat surface. It transformed the way buildings, landscapes, and crowds of people were portrayed.

○ The best artists became known as "Masters" or "Old Masters." They ran special "academies" (schools) to teach students to paint and let them help in their studios.

Pointillism

Impressionist paintings inspired later arists to develop new techniques. They included Pointillism (painting with tiny "points," of paint) to create fascinating 3-D effects without the use of hard line. This detail from a Pointillist painting, by French artist Georges Seurat (1859-1891), shows swimmers by a river on a sunny day.

○ Around 1700, artists developed new painting skills. In "Still Life" pictures, they copied flowers and animals in precise, realistic detail. They painted portraits that showed people's inner feelings as well as their outer appearance. With landscapes, they created dramatic effects of light and shade.

Leonardo da Vinci

The greatest Renaissance artists were not just painters and sculptors, but also gifted architects, engineers, poets, and musicians. One of the most famous is the Italian Leonardo da Vinci (1452–1519). Although celebrated as a painter, he only completed about 25 paintings. He spent much of his time making drawings of his inventions—such as this flying machine, multibarrelled guns, a parachute, and even a tank.

European artists

1266–1337	**Giotto** Italian, his pictures showed people in a more lifelike way
1452–1519	**Leonardo da Vinci** Italian, painter, sculptor, and architect, famous for the *Mona Lisa*
1475–1564	**Michelangelo Buionarotti** Italian, painted Rome's Sistine Chapel ceiling
1483–1520	**Raphael** Italian, famous for portraits of women and children, and biblical scenes
1541–1614	**El Greco** Spanish, painted many religious scenes
1606–1669	**Rembrandt von Rijn** Dutch, master of portraits
1775–1851	**J M W Turner** English, painted mostly landscapes
1776–1837	**John Constable** English, famous for his landscapes
1840–1926	**Claude Monet** French, Impressionist, famous for paintings of his garden and various landscape scenes
1853–1890	**Vincent van Gogh** Dutch, landscapes and portraits
1881–1973	**Pablo Picasso** Spanish, styles included abstract Cubism

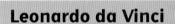

Art Techniques

Artists use many different methods to create visual images and present important ideas. Whatever technique they use, they all hope to make us see the world in a new way—and to think about what we see.

Pottery (also called ceramics) is the art of making objects from clay. Wet clay is shaped by hand or by using a potter's wheel. Then it is dried, fired at high temperatures, cooled, and painted or covered with a glaze (thin layer of glass). This vase was made in ancient Greece around 400 BC.

A fresco is a picture painted directly on to fresh, wet plaster covering a ceiling or a wall. As the plaster dries, the paint bonds to it, creating an image. This is an Egyptian fresco.

Sculptors carve stone or mold clay to create statues and small figurines (model figures). This baked clay figure comes from the Bahia culture of Ecuador, South America, and is over 1,500 years old.

Oil paints were invented in Europe around AD 1400. They could be blended smoothly together. This allowed artists to create subtle effects of light and shade, as in this painting by John Constable (1776–1837).

Watercolors are paints made of pigments (solid colors) mixed with water. They are used to create delicate, transparent "washes" of color on fine paper. This watercolor is by British artist Samuel Prout (1783–1852).

Since medieval times in Europe (C.AD 500–1500), colored glass has been used to decorate churches and other buildings. Stained glass windows are made from pieces of glass cut to shape then joined by strips of lead.

Find out more

Modern art pp. 440–441

Lithography is a way of creating multiple copies of a picture. An image is drawn on stone with wax. Oil and water are poured over the stone. Ink runs off but sticks to the wax image. Sheets of paper are pressed on top of the stone. They pick up a layer of ink. Machines use a similar technique to print newspapers and magazines, but use curved metal rollers instead of a flat stone.

The technique of collage takes its name from a French word, coller, which means "to stick." To create a collage, artists glue scraps of paper, fabric, and many other materials onto wood, canvas, or paper, to make an attractive design.

Casting is a method of making metal objects. Ores (rocks containing metal) were crushed and baked to release the metal. This was melted, then poured into molds. As the metal cooled, it hardened into the shape of the mold.

Illustration is the art of adding pictures to words on a page. Sometimes, illustrations give the reader extra information. Sometimes, they excite the imagination or create a special mood.

Amazing

Lithography was invented in 1798. French painter Henri de Toulouse-Lautrec (1841–1901) used lithography to create his famous posters.

The color wheel

The three primary colors are red, yellow, and blue. These can be mixed together to form orange, green, and purple. On a color wheel, one primary color will appear opposite the mixture of the two other primary colors (for example, red will appear opposite green, which is a mixture of yellow and blue). These opposites are called complementary colors.

Making colors

In the past, the pigment (color) of paints was taken from naturally occurring substances, such as extracts of plants. Today, many pigments are made using synthetic chemical dyes, such as the phthalocyanine, used to make phthalo green. Modern paints are manufactured in many shades based on mixing primary colors, as well as black and white. These can be mixed together to produce just about any color found in nature.

Art around the World

Art is important, all round the world. It can be amusing, entertaining, informative, and inspiring. Or it can be threatening, disturbing, and challenging. It can strengthen traditional values, spread new ideas, or preserve a treasured heritage from past times.

This totem pole comes from the northwest of North America. It is carved with images of totem (guardian) animals, together with the faces of dead ancestors. Both watch over living family members, and symbolize their importance. Only the wealthiest families could afford fine totem poles such as this one.

○ The ancient Greeks were the greatest sculptors of the ancient world. They used sculpture to decorate their temples. The Greeks were experts at turning stone into lifelike imitations of real people.

○ Traditionally, Native Americans carved tall tree-trunks into towering totem poles, and stood them outside the homes of powerful families. They were signs of high rank, and records of family history. They were sometimes also thought to have protective powers.

○ In Tibet, painted canvas cloths called *tankas* hang in Buddhist temples. They show gods, spirits, and sacred symbols, and help Buddhist worshipers pray. The artists who create *tankas* follow strict rules and use traditional patterns and colors when composing their designs.

○ The Inca civilization flourished in the Andes Mountains of South America around 500 years ago. Inca artists used gold and other precious metals to create statues of their gods, and fabulous jewelry worn by emperors, queens, and priests.

Amazing

In Islam, it is forbidden to paint pictures of people or animals. So artists decorate mosques and holy books with beautiful and intricate geometric patterns.

Japanese art

Japanese artists are skilled at making woodblock prints. They carve their designs on to wooden blocks, which are covered in ink and pressed against paper. Some prints require 20 separate blocks, one for each color.

Find out more

Art techniques pp. 436–437

○ Muslim designers in North Africa, Central Asia, India, Southeast Asia, and the Middle East use beautiful abstract patterns to decorate buildings, pottery, glassware, and textiles. They blend Muslim holy designs, based on Arabic lettering, with local artistic traditions and techniques.

○ Folk arts or ethnic arts are names given to art and crafts created by ordinary people. They include wood carving, wall paintings, basket making, weaving, and embroidery, and are often used to decorate homes, clothes, and other everyday objects. Their designs and patterns may reflect religious beliefs, historic events, or local wildlife.

○ Powerful kings and queens are portrayed in art from many different lands. Royal portraits often show them wearing crowns, jewelry, or other symbols of wealth and power. In West Africa, rulers were traditionally portrayed seated on ancient sacred stools or thrones.

▲ This mosque (meeting place for prayers) in Isfahan, Iran, is covered with patterned pottery tiles. Glazed tiles were generally used on the inside walls and floors of buildings. However, in Isfahan, tiles also cover the domes of the mosques. The blue colored tiles are also typically used for pottery made in the region.

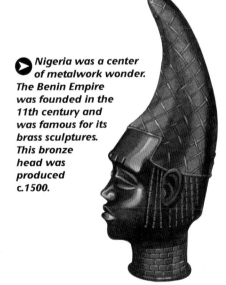

► Nigeria was a center of metalwork wonder. The Benin Empire was founded in the 11th century and was famous for its brass sculptures. This bronze head was produced c.1500.

Festival of lights

Diwali is the Hindu festival of lights. It celebrates the victory of good over evil, light over darkness, and knowledge over ignorance. Houses and shops are decorated with small earthenware lamps, fuelled by mustard oil. Patterns called *rangoli* are traditionally drawn on houses and floors.

Modern Art

In the early 20th century, young European artists began to explore new ways of painting. They stopped trying to imitate the real world in their pictures. Instead, they experimented with colors and shapes to create powerful images that startled, and sometimes shocked, their viewers.

○ Cubists painted pictures showing the world from several different viewpoints, all at the same time. Their pictures looked as if they were made out of jagged geometric shapes, blocks, or cubes.

○ The style of painting known as Expressionism began in Germany and France around 1905. Expressionists used strong colors, wild brush-strokes, and distorted images to express powerful, anguished feelings.

○ Abstract artists did not try to show people, places, or things in their work. They arranged shapes and colors to create striking images.

▶ *This landscape painting by Spanish artist Juan Gris (1887–1927) was created in 1913 in typical Cubist style. It shows a view of houses, trees, and fields split into angular shapes then rearranged. By painting with these Cubist techniques, the artist has managed to show three-dimensional space on the picture's flat surface.*

○ Early 20th-century artists were inspired by science and technology, especially photography. They were excited to find out about different styles of art from all around the world.

◀ *Expressionist painters often chose dramatic subjects for their pictures, or tried to show energy, movement, or dramatic action. This painting of stacks of corn, by Belgian Expressionist Constant Permeke (1885–1952), suggests the frantic movements of busy farmworkers at harvest time.*

Amazing

The Spanish painter Salvador Dali (1904–1989) is famous for his strange, dreamlike paintings with oddly extended bodies, melting watches, and half open drawers set in desert landscapes.

Find out more

New ideas pp. 434–435

Surrealism

During the 1920s, a group of European artists set out to paint images of the unconscious mind, creating bizarre, dreamlike pictures, often in lifelike detail. One of these "surrealists" was the Belgian painter René Magritte (1898-1967), who enjoyed tricks and puzzles. His picture of a pipe (right) was labelled "This is not a pipe."

○ After around 1950, the USA replaced Europe as the world centre of modern art. American artists pioneered huge paintings in bold bright colors, reflecting the vast American "Wild West" landscape and dramatic modern American architecture.

○ Other American artists copied techniques used in film and advertising to create multiple images. The most famous was Andy Warhol (1929–1987). His printed pictures of all kinds of objects, from soup cans to movie stars, became known as Pop Art.

○ Photographs were seen as a new kind of art by the late 20th century. Memorable images ranged from glamorous fashion shots to grim war scenes.

○ Many artists design fashions, cars, furniture, and also posters and logos. The best logos are simple but instantly recognizable.

○ In the early 21st century, artists in Britain and Europe experimented with art that did not need pictures. They created "installations," showing preserved dead animals or crumpled beds. Some people said that displaying objects in this way was a new kind of creativity, called Conceptual Art.

▶ *The most famous 20th-century artist was Pablo Picasso (1881–1973). Born in Spain, he spent most of his working life in France. During his long career, he experimented with many exciting new artistic styles.*

Computer art

Computers are powerful tools for artists. They can alter the shape, size, color, and content of images, at the click of a mouse. They can add special effects— bending and stretching features, adding "soft focus" effects, or blurring and shading to make a photograph look like a painting. Computers also allow artists to combine multiple images to create home-grown cartoons or movies, and to add music or other sounds.

Modern artists

Alexander Calder (1898–1976) American sculptor of mobiles

Christo (born 1935) Bulgarian-born Belgian, famous for wrapping buildings and sections of coastline in plastic

Salvador Dali (1904–89) Spanish Surrealist painter

Barbara Hepworth (1903–75) British sculptor

David Hockney (born 1937) British painter

Roy Lichtenstein (1923–97) American pop artist

Henry Moore (1898–1986) British sculptor

Piet Mondrian (1872–1944) Dutch painter of abstracts

Gilbert and George (Gilbert Proesch born 1943 and George Passmore born 1942) British avant-garde artists known for their Performance Art

Andy Warhol (1928–87) American painter and graphic artist famous for prints of soup cans and Marilyn Monroe

▶ *In the late 20th century, the focus of modern art shifted from Europe to the United States. A leading figure was Jackson Pollock (1912–56) who created large, abstract pictures by splashing paint onto a canvas laid on the floor —a style known as Abstract Expressionism.*

Making Music

Many thousands of years ago, early humans discovered that certain objects—for example, hollow tree trunks, different kinds of stone, and the bones of large animals—made interesting sounds when struck. Gradually, they invented new kinds of instruments to make an exciting range of new and different sounds.

○ Early people jangled small bones as rattles, made drums from animal skins and blew into hollow bamboo canes and bones to produce notes.

○ Expert players taught other people the skills needed to make music. Instrumentalists and singers began to perform together.

○ The oldest surviving instrument is a set of mammoth bones, trimmed and decorated around 20,000 years ago in Ukraine. Tunes were played by tapping them. Modern xylophones are still played the same way.

The Aztec people, who ruled an empire in Mexico around AD 1400, made a drum. Aztec drums were used to accompany dancing at religious festivals, and to summon soldiers to fight in wars.

Aboriginal people have lived in Australia for at least 50,000 years. One of their best known instruments is the didgeridoo—a long hollow tree-trunk, played by blowing. It makes a deep droning sound, that carries for long distances. Players use a technique, called "circular breathing" to produce the drone continuously.

○ Since prehistoric times, music has formed an essential part of many religious ceremonies. It can express hope and happiness, for example at a wedding, or echo the miserable cries of mourners at funerals. Many priests and priestesses were also musicians. They sang, chanted, or played instruments to honor the gods.

Ancient Egyptians played bow-shaped harps at funeral ceremonies. The top of this harp is decorated with an image of Maat, the goddess of truth and justice who judged dead peoples' actions and decided their fate in the afterlife.

○ Until the 20th century, musical instruments were made of natural materials. Some, like rams-horn trumpets, were played almost unchanged. Others, like brass trumpets, fine violins (made of carved wood) or piano-keys (made of ivory) were carefully shaped by craft workers. In the 20th century, new, artificial materials, such as plastic and nylon, were used by instrument-makers to mass-produce instruments more cheaply than ever before.

Instrument inventions

c.4000 BC	Flute, harp, trumpet
3500 BC	Bells
AD 1500	Trombone
c.1545	Violin
1709	Piano
1821	Harmonica
1822	Accordion
1832	Modern flute
1840	Saxophone

Find out more
Musical instruments pp. 446–447

This musician from the Andes region of South America is playing a set of wooden panpipes. In the late 20th century, haunting panpipe tunes from the high, remote Andes Mountains became popular worldwide.

The first instrument?

Luciano Pavarotti, born in Italy in 1935, is famous for his fine tenor (high male) voice. The oldest instrument of all is the human voice. From the beginning of human existence, human beings made calls to communicate (as do many other living creatures). Later, no one knows precisely when, they also began to sing, and speak separate words.

Amazing

The giant of the violin family is the double bass. Its four thick strings can be plucked or played with a bow. The deep sounds are amplified by the huge wooden sound box.

This Etruscan wall painting, made about 2,500 years ago, shows a young man playing a double flute. The Etruscans lived in central Italy. Like other ancient Mediterranean peoples, they used music in religious ceremonies, as well as for entertainment.

○ Panpipes have been popular for at least 3,000 years. They are made of tubes, such as hollow plant stalks, of different lengths fastened together. Players blow across the top of the tubes. Panpipes are named after the ancient Greek god, Pan, who lived in wild countryside. Greek legends told how he made the first set of panpipes, by binding riverside reed stalks together.

○ The first flutes were made of hollow bones. Later, they were made from wood. Ancient Greek and Italian flute players were very clever—they could play two flutes at the same time.

○ Early instrument makers were not afraid to think big. For example, the Japanese koto had strings 6 ft long. It produce a loud, deep, humming sound. Musicians had to kneel on the floor to play it.

Griots are traditional West African singers and storytellers. They entertain crowds in streets and market places. In places where some people cannot read or write, their songs are vital in preserving and passing on historical information.

Musical notes

In medieval Europe, composers devised a way of writing music on parchment, so it could be read by other musicians. They invented a musical "scale" based on a pattern of dots (or squares) combined with five horizontal lines. The shape and size of each dot indicated the length of each note. The position of each dot in relation to the lines showed its pitch. Today, a modern version of this notation is used all round the world. But traditional, local ways of writing music still survive.

whole note   quarter note

half note   eighth note

sixteenth note

Classical Music

*T*he music created in Europe between around 1600 and 1950 is often called "classical." It developed from chants, religious songs, and instrumental pieces played in Christian churches from around AD 500.

○ Church musicians tried to create a richer, more complicated sound by building better instruments, and finding new ways to use singers' voices. To write down their works, they began to use a musical scale that contained eight notes (still sung today; it begins, "do, ray, mee").

○ Church musicians were supported by rich people who paid them to write religious music. After about 1400, kings and other powerful people paid these composers to write nonreligious pieces for them as well.

○ Classical music developed still further once composers started to have their music printed, after around 1500. This meant that new compositions could easily be carried to performers in many different countries.

A *German composer Johann Sebastian Bach (1685–1750) wrote music to be played on organs and sung by church choirs. He also composed chamber music. He was musical director at the church of St Thomas in Leipzig, north Germany. Bach's works are still performed, and greatly admired, today.*

Amazing

Mozart mastered his first piano piece before his fifth birthday, and in the space of just 30 minutes.

○ Written or printed music was given a new name, a score. Each page showed all the parts played by different instruments, and performed by singers.

○ Top classical composers became very famous, and attracted crowds of devoted fans. But people could never agree on which composer was best. Today, many music lovers rank Johann Sebastian Bach (1685–1750), Wolfgang Amadeus Mozart (1756–1791), and Ludwig van Beethoven (1770–1827) among the greatest composers who ever lived.

○ From around 1600, many classical composers wrote music for operas. These are plays in which a complete story is sung by actors and singers, accompanied by an orchestra.

V *Ludwig van Beethoven (1770–1827), who lived and worked in Germany, was the greatest composer of his day. He composed many passionate works for solo piano and for the orchestra. Extra players were needed to perform many of his compositions, which were considered very advanced and difficult for their time. Tragically, Beethoven went deaf and had to stop performing, but he went on composing until the end of his life.*

◄ *Born in Austria, Wolfgang Amadeus Mozart (1756–1791) was a child prodigy who began composing when he was only five years old. Soon, he began to write concertos (pieces for solo instrumentalist plus orchestra), symphonies (works for full orchestra), church music, and operas. Mozart became famous throughout Europe, but died aged only 35, in poverty.*

Find out more

Musical instruments pp. 446–447

Conductor

The job of the conductor is to rehearse and direct the musicians. He or she shows them the speed and rhythm (often using a baton), and how to obtain the right balance in sound. Since the 19th century, great conductors have become classical music superstars, traveling all over the world to direct performances by top orchestras.

▲ *Richard Wagner (1818–1883) wrote the world's longest operas. Each one runs for over five hours. To stage them, Wagner built a huge opera house in his home town, Bayreuth, in Bavaria (southern Germany). He also founded an annual opera festival there that is still held today.*

○ Various new musical styles evolved during the 19th century. These included program music (a wordless composition in which the music tells a story) and orchestral and instrumental pieces with increasingly experimental and complex melodies and harmonies. Leading composers of this period include Schubert, Chopin, and Liszt.

The symphony orchestra

The instruments of the symphony orchestra are arranged in groups in an arc in front of the conductor—strings at the front, then wind, and percussion at the back. The modern orchestra has about 100 musicians. Orchestras have four main sections: strings (violins, violas, cellos, and double basses), woodwind (clarinets, flutes, oboes, and bassoons), brass (horns and trumpets), and percussion (drums, cymbals, and bells).

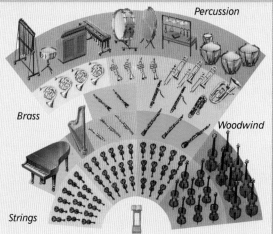

Percussion

Brass

Woodwind

Strings

Great classical composers

Johann Sebastian Bach (1685–1750)	German composer
Ludwig van Beethoven (1770–1827)	German composer
Johannes Brahms (1833–1897)	German composer
Benjamin Britten (1913–1976)	British 20th-century composer
Frederick Chopin (1841–1904)	Polish composer
Edward Elgar (1857–1934)	British composer
George Gershwin (1898–1937)	American 20th-century composer
Edvard Grieg (1843–1907)	Norwegian 19th-century composer
George Frideric Handel (1685–1759)	German/British composer
Joseph Haydn (1732–1809)	Austrian composer
Wolfgang Amadeus Mozart (1756–1791)	Austrian composer, who wrote more than 40 symphonies
Franz Peter Schubert (1797–1828)	Austrian composer
Igor Stravinsky (1882–1971)	Russian 20th-century composer, most celebrated work was *The Rite of Spring*
Peter Ilyich Tchaikovsky (1840–1893)	Russian composer, famous for symphonies and ballet scores
Giuseppe Verdi (1813–1901)	Italian 19th-century opera composer
Richard Wagner (1818–1883)	German composer

○ In the early 20th century, composers began to experiment with new and different ways of writing music. One of the pioneers of this modern style was the Austrian composer Arnold Schoenberg (1874–1951). He abandoned the classical eight-note musical scale, creating an entirely new sound, called atonal music.

○ A few years ago, many people thought that classical music had lost its popular appeal. But with the help of CDs, television, and music radio stations, a new generation of talented performers have found a fresh audience.

Musical Instruments

*T*he four main groups of instruments are called strings, woodwind, brass, and percussion. Stringed instruments, such as violins and guitars, have strings stretched over a shaped hollow box. The strings produce a sound when they are rubbed with a bow or plucked by the fingers or a plectrum. Percussion instruments, such as drums or cymbals, make a sound when hit by sticks or fingertips. Woodwind and brass instruments are hollow tubes, made of wood or brass. Both are played by blowing. Players can open or close holes on the tubes to produce various notes.

Keyboards

Today, many instruments can be connected to electronic amplifiers, to make a much louder sound than was previously possible. For example, electronic keyboards have keys that look similar to a piano. But these produce a sound by sending an electric signal through an amplifier and loudspeakers. Keyboard players can also use electronics to change the type of sound they produce. By switching on electronic devices fitted to the keyboard, players can add "special effects."

Strings

Cello

Violin

Double bass

Guitar

Sitar

Woodwind

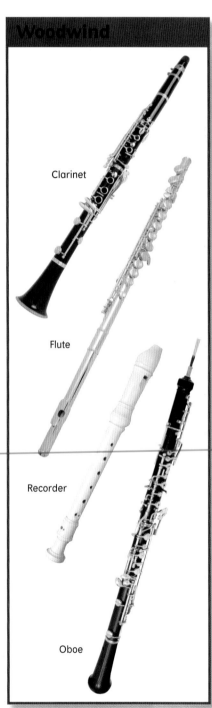

Clarinet

Flute

Recorder

Oboe

Find out more

The first instrument p. 443

Brass

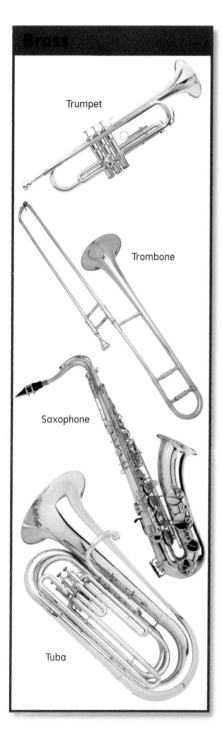

Trumpet

Trombone

Saxophone

Tuba

Percussion

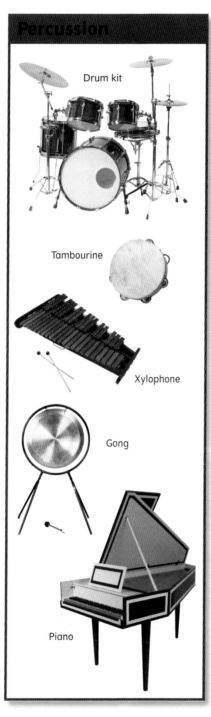

Drum kit

Tambourine

Xylophone

Gong

Piano

Piano

Pianos were invented in Europe in the early 1700s. Their name came from two Italian words: *piano* soft and *forte* (loud), because they could produce a very wide range of sounds, from quiet and gentle to very noisy. The first pianos were made of wood, but today most piano frames are made of metal. Old or new, all pianos produce sound in the same way. When the player presses a key with their finger, a set of levers moves a wooden hammer. This hits a wire and makes it vibrate to sound a note. The longer the wire, the lower the note that is played. Players can increase the sound made by the piano, or make each note last longer, by pressing pedals, connected to the wires by more levers, with their feet.

Amazing

An advantage of the keyboard is that players can accompany themselves as they sing. This is why many songwriters use the piano both to compose and perform.

Popular Music

There has always been popular music. But, until the 20th century, people could only hear popular tunes when musicians sang or played them "live." Sound recording, invented in 1878, changed the way people listened to music —forever.

○ The first records, made from wax or plastic, let people hear their favorite music at home and in clubs and bars.

○ Three of the most popular styles of 20th-century music were created by African–Americans in southern USA. Jazz music, played on brass and wind instruments, accompanied dancing and street processions. Soulful blues music told of love and suffering. Gospel music, performed by church choirs, combined hymn tunes with jazz and blues.

○ Blues and gospel music, originally sung by African slaves, became popular with church choirs. Its energetic sound influenced rock and pop. Blues and jazz merged into R & B (rhythm and blues).

▶ *One of the greatest blues musicians was the guitarist B B King, born in 1925, in the southern US state of Mississippi. He began his career as a singer, but later became famous for his own special style of guitar playing that influenced many younger musicians. His 1981 recording, "There Must Be A Better World Somewhere," won international awards.*

▶ *One of the greatest jazz musicians was Louis "Satchmo" Armstrong (1900–1971). He was a gifted trumpet player, who also pioneered "scat" singing—a type of jazz performance in which the singer's voice is used like an instrument—and appeared in over 50 films.*

○ In the 1950s, young musicians in the USA mixed White American country-and-western music with African-American rhythm and blues to create an exciting new sound—rock 'n' roll. Played on guitars backed by drums, rock 'n' roll's pounding beat made it great for dancing. Rock 'n' roll songs also put in words how many teenagers were feeling—they were bold, defiant, angry, sexy, anxious, happy, and sad—sometimes all at the same time.

○ In the late 1960s, bands started to mix rock 'n' roll, jazz and blues, amplified it electronically and created the style now known as "rock."

○ Radio stations and record shops compiled charts of the most popular songs. Selling records became competitive between pop performers as they tried to get more publicity and enter the charts with bestselling records.

○ In the 1990s record producers created a new phenomenon—girl and boy bands, advised by marketing experts. Some band members were not necessarily good musicians but the band's image was the main factor in selling records.

10 bestselling songs

Bestselling 20th-century songs

1	**Candle in the Wind**	Elton John
2	**White Christmas**	Bing Crosby
3	**Rock around the Clock**	Bill Haley
4	**I Want to Hold Your Hand**	The Beatles
5	**Hey Jude**	The Beatles
6	**It's Now or Never**	Elvis Presley
7	**I Will Always Love You**	Whitney Houston
8	**Hound Dog**	Elvis Presley
9	**Diana**	Paul Anka
10	**I'm a Believer**	The Monkees

Find out more

Hip-hop p. 461

◀ *The most famous rock 'n' roll performer was the American Elvis Presley (1935–1977)—known to his fans as "the King." Elvis became famous for his moody good looks, amazing stage clothes, and provocative style of dancing, as well as for his singing. He became the first global rock music star. Thousands of screaming fans mobbed him whenever he appeared.*

▶ *Reggae is a type of dance music from Jamaica, noted for its use of a heavy, offbeat rhythm. It was made world famous in the 1970s by Bob Marley (1945–1981) and his group The Wailers. Reggae was one of the first alternative music styles to have a major impact on pop music.*

Recorded music

The first machine to play recorded sound was the phonograph, designed by American inventor Thomas Edison in 1877. It used a stylus (needle) to draw sound waves on a spinning tinfoil (or wax) cylinder, then play them back through a horn. In 1887, German designer Emile Berliner invented the gramophone (right). It used a stylus to play sound recorded on flat wax discs.

The Beatles

The world's most successful recording group of the 1960s was the British band The Beatles. The "Fab Four" were Paul McCartney (born 1942), John Lennon (1940–1980), George Harrison (1943–2002), and Ringo Starr (born 1940).

10 bestselling albums

Bestselling 20th-century albums with sales over 30 million copies

1	*Thriller*	Michael Jackson
2	*Back in Black*	AC/DC
3	*The Eagles Greatest Hits 1971–1975*	The Eagles
4	*Saturday Night Fever*	Soundtrack album featuring The Bee Gees
5	*The Bodyguard*	Soundtrack album featuring Whitney Houston
6	*Bat out of Hell*	Meat Loaf
7	*Dark Side of the Moon*	Pink Floyd
8	*Come on Over*	Shania Twain
9	*Sergeant Pepper's Lonely Hearts Club Band*	The Beatles
10	*Dirty Dancing*	Soundtrack album featuring various artists

❍ By the late 20th century, CDs, pop videos, personal music players, and the Internet had made popular music a multimillion dollar industry.

❍ By the year 2000, popular music had "gone global." "World Music" from developing countries, especially Africa and the Caribbean, became popular with western listeners.

Amazing

The first popular singer to sell one million records was Italian tenor Enrico Caruso (1873–1921) who recorded passionate opera arias.

The Origins of Drama

Performing is very much a part of our lives. We all perform when we tell a joke or recount a story. Some people are especially good at performing and can hold an audience spellbound. For thousands of years, professional storytellers, actors, clowns, acrobats, and dancers have earned a living by their skills.

○ Early drama had a religious purpose. Kings, queens, priests, and priestesses took part in holy rituals, acting out myths and legends about the gods.

○ The first-known people to watch plays were the ancient Greeks. They gathered in large crowds on sloping hillsides to watch actors perform on level ground below.

○ After around 500 BC, the Greeks began to build theaters. They arranged rows of stone seats in semicircle shapes, looking down on a stage called an orchestra.

▲ *Ancient Greek and Roman theaters were built in the open air. Actors performed in front of painted wooden scenery. This hid cranes or lifts that helped actors make dramatic appearances. Musicians stood nearby, playing music to accompany singing and dancing on stage.*

▼ *In ancient Greece, all actors wore masks. They wore different masks for happy, fierce, or sad characters. By changing them, actors could have many varied roles in the same play. Masks also helped audiences sitting at the back of large theaters, far away from the stage, see the actors' expressions. For this reason, they were made with deliberately exaggerated features, and often painted in bright colors. Some had hair or hats attached.*

○ Ancient Greek plays were written for religious festivals in honor of the god Dionysus. Authors entered their plays in festival competitions. The winners had their plays performed.

○ Greek actors were all men. The Greeks believed it was indecent for women to appear on stage. So young men and boys played women's roles.

○ Greek actors spoke in verse and used mime. A "chorus" (group) of singers and dancers commented on the events being acted.

○ Greek drama was of two kinds: amusing comedies or serious, sad tragedies. "Comic" and "tragic" are terms still used to describe plays today.

Shakespeare

English poet and dramatist William Shakespeare (1564–1616) is one of the most famous and respected playwrights of all time. He wrote around 37 plays and hundreds of poems. Some of his plays are tragedies, for example *Romeo and Juliet* or *Hamlet*. Some are comedies, such as *A Midsummer Night's Dream*. Some are historical epics, like *Henry V*. Shakespeare worked as an actor, and ran his own theater, called the Globe. Shakespeare's plays have been made into numerous films and translated into many different languages.

Find out more

World theater pp. 452–453

Ballad singers

Ballads are traditional songs that tell a story, often about the adventures of ordinary people. They were usually sung by one or two people, perhaps with guitars. Printed copies of the songs were often sold in the street.

○ In medieval times, traveling poets, actors, and minstrels entertained crowds in streets, at markets and fairs. They acted out stories about heroes, monsters and other traditional tales. They sang ballads telling of battles, love-stories and exciting adventures.

○ Medieval craft-workers presented open-air plays based on biblical stories. They acted out stories of Jesus Christ's life, from his birth to his crucifixion.

○ In Tudor times (1485–1603), top playwrights, such as Shakespeare, trained troops of actors to perform their plays. Shakespeare also built an open-air theater in London called the Globe.

○ Medieval and Tudor kings employed "jesters" to entertain in their courts. Jesters told jokes, performed tricks, sang, and danced. If they were too rude they lost their jobs or were put in gaol.

Amazing

The first purpose-built theater with a stage was built in Italy in 1618. It seated 3,000 people and was almost completely destroyed during World War II.

▼ *Mime is a specialized kind of acting performed entirely without words. Mime artists use movements and gestures to indicate an imaginary world around them. The world's best-known mime artist is Frenchman Marcel Marceau (born 1923).*

Famous playwrights

Aristophanes (c.445–385 BC) Greek, wrote comedies such as *The Frogs*.

Alan Ayckbourne (born 1939) British, prolific author of successful comedies of modern life, including *The Norman Conquests*.

Samuel Becket (1906–1989) Irish, wrote *Waiting for Godot*.

Anton Chekhov (1860–1904) Russian, wrote *The Cherry Orchard*.

William Congreve (1670–1729) English, author of *The Way of the World*, a comedy.

Johann Wolfgang von Goethe (1749–1832) German, playwright and scientist, his most famous work is *Faust*, in which a scholar sells his soul to the devil.

Henrik Ibsen (1828–1906) Norwegian, wrote *A Doll's House* and *Hedda Gabbler*.

Molière (Jean-Baptiste Poquelin) (1622–1673) French, wrote comedies including *The Misanthropist* and *The Miser*.

Eugene O'Neill (1888–1953) American, wrote *The Iceman Cometh* and other plays.

William Shakespeare (1564–1616) English, greatest dramatist whose plays include tragedies *King Lear*, comedies *Much Ado About Nothing*, and histories *Julius Caesar*.

George Bernard Shaw (1856–1950) Irish, wrote *St Joan*, *Major Barbara* and other plays, usually from a satirical viewpoint.

Richard Brinsley Sheridan (1751–1816) Irish, wrote *The Rivals*, one of the most enduring comedies.

Sophocles (about 496–406 BC) Greek, wrote tragedies, including *Oedipus the King*.

Tom Stoppard (Thomas Straussler, b. 1937) Czech-born British writer, whose plays include *Travesties* and *Jumpers*.

World Theater

Over the centuries, cultures all around the world developed their own distinctive forms of drama. In each country, drama was shaped by local beliefs, customs, myths, legends, and living conditions. Everywhere, plays reflected the society in which they were performed.

○ The south Indian tradition of theater called Kathakali is at least 2,000 years old. It was originally performed in temple ceremonies. The actors, dressed in rich costumes and dramatic make-up, act out stories from Hindu mythology. They use vivid facial expressions and elaborate arm and hand movements.

○ In Japan, there are three traditional types of drama: Noh ("accomplished" plays), Kabuki (popular dramas), and Jojuri (puppet plays). Noh drama is the oldest. It originated around AD 1375, and is based on ancient Japanese literature. Each Noh performance contains five separate plays. Kabuki and Jojuri plays were first performed around 1700. They feature loud music, athletic dancing, and spectacular costumes.

▶ Noh actors are all men. They wear stiff, formal costumes, and heavy make-up. They chant their words, and use stately, stylized gestures to express their emotions. Their performances are accompanied by music on flute and drums.

◀ Kathakli performers use intricate movements to express their devotion to the gods. Keeping the top half of their body still and balanced, they take tiny, rapid steps, making complicated patterns with their feet as they twirl round and round. As performers move, hundreds of tiny bells, worn round their ankles, create jingling music.

○ Carnival was originally a religious festival, marking the beginning of the Christian fasting season, called Lent. Its name meant "goodbye to meat." People held parties, sang, and danced as they used up all the rich foods in their homes, and prepared to eat only plain, simple meals for 40 days. Over the years, these celebrations became more elaborate. Today, carnival is celebrated in Europe and America with music, dancing, processions, and actors dressed in the most amazing costumes.

○ In many parts of the world, shamans (magicians, priests, and healers) use drama, singing, and dancing to try and persuade the unseen spirits they believe in to help and heal.

○ Priests from the Hopi people, who live in the southwest of North America, dress up as Kachinas (ancestor spirits) to perform ritual dramas. They visit Hopi villages, dancing and singing, to bless them. Traditionally, Hopi people believe this will help make the rain fall, and encourage their food crops to grow.

Find out more
Modern theater pp. 454–455

The circus

The name "circus" originated in ancient Rome. Originally it referred to a curved arena, where chariot races took place. Around 1700, European showmen used the name to describe shows by performing horses. After around 1800, other performers, such as acrobats, lion-tamers, and clowns, started to take part in shows as well.

▲ *This Kachina (spirit figure) is made from natural materials: clay and plaited maize straw. According to Hopi legends, there are 335 different Kachinas. Each has its own special character and appearance.*

○ During the 18th and 19th centuries, lively, colorful shows that combined singing, dancing, loud music, clowning, acrobatics, and mock battles were a popular form of entertainment in China. They became known as Beijing Opera.

Amazing

In 1924 over 16,700 people packed into a big top in Kansas, USA, to see the Ringling Brothers and Barnum & Bailey Circus.

▲ *This shaman from West Africa is completely hidden by his costume of woven grass. Shamans put on disguises to help communicate with nature spirits, and ask them to use their magic powers.*

▼ *In Indonesia, shadow-puppets perform after dark from behind a brightly-lit screen. The puppets are cut out of sheets of leather, and moved by long sticks held by a dalang (puppet master).*

Punch and Judy

Punch and Judy is a puppet show, performed at English fairgrounds and seaside resorts. Characters include Punch (a clown), his wife Judy, their dog, their baby, a crocodile, and a policeman. Punch and Judy stories range from funny and silly (stealing sausages) to cruel and violent (murder!). They are based on old, traditional drama, first performed for adults. This originated in Italy around 1500, where it was known as *Commedia dell'Arte* (Comedy of the Arts).

Modern Theater

Until the late 19th century, most plays described dramatic historical or mythological events, or made fun of the way powerful people lived. But after around 1850, writers began to create dramas about the modern, everyday world, using situations that audiences might recognize from their own lives. Styles of acting changed as well, from loud and exaggerated to quieter, more lifelike, words and movements on stage.

▶ Marie Lloyd (1870–1922) was a music hall star, famous for her sometimes suggestive, witty, cheerful, songs. In the late 19th and early 20th centuries, music halls had twice–nightly shows of about 20 turns (acts) including conjuring, telling jokes, reciting monologues, and dancing. Many top performers were women.

❍ In the 18th and 19th centuries, actors had to perform in huge, crowded theaters or noisy music halls. They had no microphones or electronic amplifiers to help them. So they shouted—or spoke in very loud, strong voices—and used grand, dramatic gestures to catch the audience's attention. This was called "barnstorming" because traveling actors often performed in barns during the 19th century.

❍ The Norwegian playwright Henrik Ibsen (1828–1906) was the first major dramatist to write about the problems of modern society. Later, 20th-century writers copied his ideas.

❍ The Russian actor and director Constantin Stanislavsky (1863–1938) revolutionized the way many plays were performed. He encouraged actors to think and feel like the characters they were playing, rather than just pretend to experience emotions on stage. This is called "method acting."

❍ Many 20th-century playwrights aimed to spread a political message. For example, in Soviet Russia (1917–1989), the government paid actors to put on plays that praised Communist society.

❍ In Europe and the USA, many playwrights portrayed depressing or violent scenes from modern life. A few wrote plays that seemed to be nonsense. By shocking their audiences, these writers hoped to make people think, and maybe change society.

❍ Directors in the 20th century borrowed ideas from traditional theater, especially ancient Greece and Japan, and copied circus skills. They changed theatre layouts and created "theater in the round" by seating the audience on all sides of the stage. They used the latest technology to produce dramatic lighting effects and astonishing scenery.

❍ After 1950, directors staged "modern dress" versions of ancient masterpieces. They showed how old plays can still be relevant to the modern world. They also presented old works in new, fresh ways, by adding singing, music, or dancing.

Scripts

Any moveable object, such as a gun, used by actors in stage or screen performances is called a "prop" (short for "property"). It is the job of the assistant stage manager (in a theater) or continuity staff (on a movie set) to make sure that all props are in the right place at the right time.

Amazing

The Reduced Shakespeare Company is famous for performing the entire catalog of Shakespeare's works—37 plays, and 154 sonnets—in just 97 minutes.

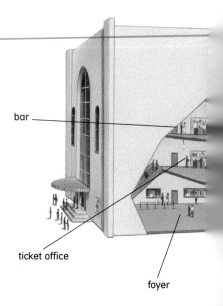

bar

ticket office

foyer

Find out more

Making movies pp. 476–477

A *Many new theaters are modern looking buildings, like the National Theatre in Ghana, Africa. The architecture of this building helps to create a national center for the performing arts.*

○ Today, audiences can choose from an amazing variety of performing styles and plays. Playgoers might enjoy realistic dramas showing a "slice of life" or they may like lighthearted comedies, passionate romances, charming fantasies, bitter tragedies, well-known classics, or controversial new works.

"Kitchen sink" drama

In the mid 20th-century, British and American writers experimented with new kinds of plays about ordinary peoples' lives. Known as "kitchen sink dramas," these plays described life in the raw, and often reproduced unhappy or unpleasant situations on stage. Their scripts included slang, swearing, quarrels, and sometimes fights. Actors wore drab, everyday clothes instead of glamorous theatrical costumes, and were encouraged to speak in rough regional accents, rather than the refined, polished speech taught at traditional drama schools. One of the best-known kitchen-sink dramas, *Look Back in Anger*, by British writer John Osborne (1929–1994) caused outrage when it was first performed in 1956. Osborne (right) and his fellow-dramatists were nicknamed "Angry Young Men."

▼ *A big theater is a highly complex building. The audience sees only a small part of it as they enter through the foyer and find their seat in the auditorium. Behind the stage, which is in the middle of the building, are large areas used for storing scenery, wardrobe rooms for storing costumes, dressing and make-up rooms, rehearsal areas, and a canteen for the actors and stage crew.*

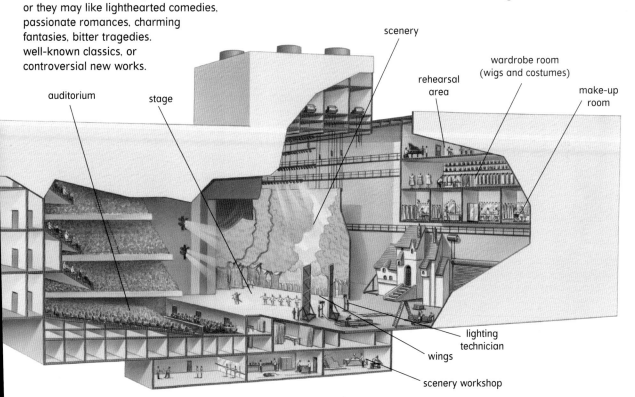

scenery

rehearsal area

wardrobe room (wigs and costumes)

make-up room

auditorium

stage

lighting technician

wings

scenery workshop

Moving to Music

Dance is one of the oldest of all the performing arts. Originally, everyone took part, moving to music made by singing, clapping hands, or beating sticks and stones. But before long, the best dancers began to attract an audience. Other people stopped what they were doing to watch them perform.

▶ *This wall painting, from the tomb of an Egyptian scribe c.1360 BC, shows musicians playing for dancers at a royal feast. The girl on the right is plucking a harp, while her companion strums a lute (an instrument rather like a guitar). Egyptian musicians also played flutes, drums, and tambourines.*

○ Some of the first dances were performed for special occasions such as weddings, or at harvest-time. Dancers jumped and ran around to show their joyful feelings. Often, they sang and shouted at the same time.

○ Early dancing was often very energetic. The best dancers could leap high, walk on their hands, and turn cartwheels, and somersaults.

○ Dancers often began to train at an early age. Young girls were sent to Hindu temples in south and east Asia when they were around five years old. They learned very graceful, complicated movements, and how to wear elaborate costumes. They were said to give their best performances when they were around 12 years old.

○ Traditional dancers tried to change the weather. In Japan, for example, rain-dancers made rapid movements and chanted words to encourage rain to fall and crops to grow. In South America, they shook rattles that sounded like raindrops on leaves.

○ Many dances had a religious purpose. For example, in Australia aboriginal people danced to try to bring themselves closer to nature spirits. As they danced, they copied the movements of wild animals or birds.

▶ *A young girl takes part in an ancient religious dance at a Hindu temple in Bali, Indonesia. Her performance includes elegant hand movements and tiny running steps that make her look as if she is gliding across the floor. Nearby, a gamelan (an orchestra of metal gongs) plays a beautiful tune to accompany her dance.*

Amazing

The Inuit of Canada and Greenland perform a traditional dance to the beat of a large, caribou-skin drum. The dances often act out a story, told in the singing, usually about hunting or animals.

○ In North Africa and the Middle East, Sufis (a group of Muslim mystics) danced to worship God. They chanted God's name to rhythmic music and clapping, and began to turn round and round in a trancelike state. They forgot the everyday world around them, and instead concentrated all their thoughts on heaven.

Find out more

Ballet pp. 458–459

Ghost dancers

In the late 19th-century, Native American warriors joined the "Ghost Dance" movement to try to save their homelands. Before fighting against US government troops, farmers, and settlers, they sang, danced, and put on magical "Ghost Shirts." They believed these would all help protect them from bullet wounds.

▼ *These folk dancers are from Brittany, a region in northwest France. They are wearing traditional costume, including caps made from lace—a local craft speciality. Dances from Brittany feature fast, neat footwork, and are often accompanied by bagpipes, accordions, fiddles, and drums.*

▲ *Wearing long, traditional robes and tall felt (pressed-wool) hats, a group of Surfi men from Turkey begin their solemn religious dance. Turkey was home to the most famous community of Surfi dancers. They became known as the "whirling dervishes."*

○ Many African traditions tell how the spirits of dead ancestors can protect their living descendants, frighten enemies, drive out demons and keep harmful spirits away from houses and fields. Dancing often forms part of ceremonies designed to please the ancestors, and summon their power.

○ Vigorous dances helped fighting men build up courage and team spirit before a battle, or celebrated victories after battle. African warriors, and Cossacks from Russia, became especially famous for their dancing skills.

▲ *This rain-dancer from northern Japan is wearing a kimono (a long robe) and broad-brimmed hat. Hats like this were traditionally worn by farmers working in the fields, to keep their head and shoulders dry in wet weather. The hat is trimmed with a fringe that looks like falling rain.*

Cossack dancers

A Cossack dancer from Ukraine leaps high in the air, showing off his agility. Cossacks were famous for their bravery and horse-riding skills, and the men traditionally expressed their warlike energy in dramatic dances.

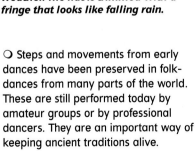

○ Steps and movements from early dances have been preserved in folk-dances from many parts of the world. These are still performed today by amateur groups or by professional dancers. They are an important way of keeping ancient traditions alive.

Ballet

Ballet originated in Italy and France about 300 years ago in stage performances that told stories through music and movement. Until around 1900, most dancers performed in a strict "classical" style. Since then, some dancers have chosen new styles, such as jazz ballet and modern dance that allow them to move more freely.

❍ In classical ballet, all movements are planned and rehearsed in great detail. Dancers must develop great strength and control of their bodies, and learn how to dance on the tips of their toes.

❍ Classical ballet became an international success after the first performance of *La Syphide* in 1832. In this ballet, based on a Scottish folk-story, a peasant leaves his bride to follow an enchanting female spirit. She is a symbol of perfect happiness, which he can never possess.

❍ In the 19th century, large theaters were built in many European cities to house companies (teams) of the very best dancers. One for the most famous ballet theaters, the Bolshoi in Moscow, Russia, opened in 1856. Its dancers became famous for their daring feats on stage, and still attract large audiences today.

❍ All ballet dancers use their technical skills to create an artistic interpretation of music. They have to try to convey thoughts and feelings through movement and sound, and the results can be powerfully dramatic.

❍ Modern ballet was developed by an American dancer, Isadora Duncan (1875–1927). She invented a new way of dancing, inspired by ancient Greek styles. Like the ancient Greeks, she performed barefoot in flowing robes, and used wild, free movements to express her feelings on stage.

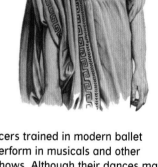

Isadora Duncan, pictured in one of her favorite costumes, which were inspired by voluminous ancient Greek clothes. Compare what she is wearing with the more traditionally dressed ballet dancer shown below-left. Classical ballet steps would not be possible in Isadora's clothes.

❍ Dancers trained in modern ballet often perform in musicals and other stage shows. Although their dances may look easy, and are often comical, they still involve a great deal of practice and technical skill.

❍ Female ballet dancers wear slippers of thin satin, with padding in the toes. In 1948, a pair of ballet slippers featured in a successful film, *The Red Shoes*. It told the story of a girl who became obsessed by ballet-dancing.

◀ *These dancers are performing a dramatic pas de deux (dance for two). Dances like this are very popular in most classical ballets. All classical ballet relies on close partnerships between male and female dancers. They have to trust each other completely in order to perform daring, complicated moves.*

Amazing

Leading ballerinas put such a strain on their shoes during performances that they will often wear out two pairs of shoes in a single night.

Find out more

World theater pp. 452–453

Ballet positions

In classical ballet, all movements made by male and female dancers begin and end in one of five positions. These originated around 1700, probably as a way of making dancers' feet look elegant. Each foot position is accompanied by a special way of holding the arms, from the simplest and most relaxed (1) to the most difficult and strenuous (5).

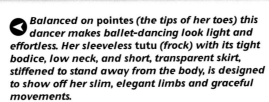

A *The famous Bolshoi Ballet was founded in Moscow as a dance school in 1773. The Bolshoi Theater was built in 1856. The ballet school is famous for the athletic skills of its dancers, and its large-scale performances, such as the 1907 ballet* Les Sylphides, *originally choreographed by Mikhail Fokine (1880–1942).*

◄ *Balanced on pointes (the tips of her toes) this dancer makes ballet-dancing look light and effortless. Her sleeveless* tutu *(frock) with its tight bodice, low neck, and short, transparent skirt, stiffened to stand away from the body, is designed to show off her slim, elegant limbs and graceful movements.*

Stravinsky

Ballet pioneer Sergei Diaghilev asked some of the leading young composers of his time to write music for his new ballets. They included fellow-Russian Igor Stravinsky (1882–1971). Stravinsky's brilliant compositions included *Firebird* (based on a Russian folk-tale) and *Rite of Spring* (based on ancient, pagan Russian dances). They created great excitement when they were first performed.

Classical ballet steps

Arabesque	Balanced on one leg with the other leg extended behind
(en)Arriere	Backward step
(en)Avant	Forward
Ballone	A broad leap with a kick
Cote	To the side
Etendre	To stretch
Glissade	A gliding step
Grand jete	A long jump
Pirouette	Spinning on one foot
Plie	Bending at the knees
Sissone	Jumping from both feet to one foot
Temps leve	Leaping in the air from one leg

► *The Russian Vaslav Nijinsky (1890–1950) was one of the most celebrated ballet dancers of all time. He became famous for his dancing with the Ballets Russes. Roles included* L'Aprés-midi d'un faune *("A faun's afternoon") in 1912. His career was cut short when he became mentally unwell in 1919.*

◯ The other great pioneer of modern ballet was Russian company manager, Sergei Diagilev (1872–1929). He commissioned new music, and combined this with dances that used bold, dramatic movements. This new style of dancing shocked many audiences.

◯ Russian dancer Vaslav Nijinsky wore a skin-tight costume to perform his most famous role. Here, he is standing in a twisted position, with his knees bent and his arms held stiffly by his sides. Movements like this were a complete change from the smooth, poised steps of classical ballet.

Dance

Ballet performances are still popular worldwide. So are many folk-dances. But new forms of dancing are developing all the time. They are based on the kinds of music people like to listen to and the ways they choose to entertain themselves.

○ Dancers perform at weddings and parties, in bars and clubs, and at open air venues. Their lively movements, combined with cheerful music, create a feeling of celebration and encourage everyone watching to relax and have a good time.

○ Dance is also an important part of many stage entertainments, such as British pantomime or Chinese Beijing Opera. In both, dance is used to show the character of heroes and villains, to create tender love scenes, or add extra interest to the plot.

○ In many countries, people perform traditional dances to entertain tourists and display their local culture. Dancers wear traditional dress, and move to music performed on traditional instruments.

○ At carnival time, in South America and Europe, dancers wearing fantastic costumes lead crowds to sing and dance through city streets.

○ Among young people, many new styles of dancing developed in the late 20th century. Most were closely linked to popular music. In the 1950s, dancers "jived" to rock and roll. In the 1960s, they danced the "twist" to pop music played by The Beatles. In the 1970s, they "pogoed" to raw, rebellious sounds played by punk rock bands.

▲ *Dressed in a bright and beautiful costume, this African entertainer performs an energetic, high-stepping dance to the beat of a goatskin drum. Behind her, fellow dancers, wearing face-paint, leopard-skins and ankle decorations join in.*

▶ *Stars of Beijing Opera— a traditional Chinese entertainment that combines words and music with dance—perform a daring acrobatic feat. These dancers have spent many years training to develop their skills. They need strong muscles, very flexible bodies and excellent balance.*

○ Breakdancing is a dynamic and very acrobatic style of dance that is part of hip-hop culture. It emerged gradually out of the hip-hop movement in the South Bronx of New York City, USA, during the late 20th century.

Find out more

Moving to music pp. 456–457

Ballroom dancing

In 19th-century Europe, dances and balls gave young men and women a rare opportunity to meet. They learned formal dances, such as the waltz or the polka. The tango is a racier and more daring type of ballroom dancing that developed in Argentina in the early 1900s.

Breakdancing involved much more energetic movements than previous dance styles, and greater use of the hands and body on the floor, with spinning and gymnastic floor movements. For greater ease of movement, and to look fashionable, break-dancers often wear clothing that is influenced by sportswear.

Fancy footwork

During the 1920s, a new dance called the Charleston caused a sensation. Invented by African–Americans in Charleston, South Carolina, USA, and danced to a jazzy rhythm, it featured fast, high-kicking, backward steps that made women's skirts fly high above the knees.

This dancer is performing at the world-famous Rio carnival in Brazil. Originally, carnival was a Christian festival held at the beginning of Lent, a period of fasting in February or March. The word carnival means "farewell to meat." People held special meals so that they could eat up all the meat that was forbidden in Lent. During carnival time normal life is suspended and the daily worries are forgotten for as long as the festival lasts.

Amazing

On May 24, 1998, the greatest ever number of tap dancers gathered for a single routine at the Stuttgart City Square, Germany—6,952 dancers tapped away for 2 min 15 sec.

Popular dances

Country Dances (origins 16th–19th century Europe)	Reel, Jig, Circle Dance, Morris Dance
Ballroom Dances (origins 19th century Europe)	Waltz, Quadrille, Polka
Ragtime Dances (origins 20th century USA)	Foxtrot, Bunny Hug, Turkey Trot, Quickstep
Latin American Dances (origins 20th century African-Caribbean-American fusion)	Cha-cha-cha, Samba, Rhumba, Tango, Lambada

○ Dance can express joy at achievements of all kinds. Sportsmen and women dance with delight when they have won a race, or scored an important point.

Words and Writing

Words have played a key part in the development of civilization. Spoken language, picture symbols, and written alphabets based on sounds have all been used to communicate ideas, beliefs, histories, technologies, and laws. Just as importantly, they have also been used to educate and entertain.

○ Stories were told for thousands of years before they were written down. They were memorized, then passed on from one generation to the next by word of mouth.

○ Some of the earliest stories were epics—long tales, recited as poetry that told the adventures of revered heroes and leaders from the distant past. Other stories were based on religious beliefs, or gave a warning against possible dangers, or passed on a moral message.

○ To hold listeners' attention, spoken tales were full of exciting events, strong characters, practical wisdom, humor, romance, and suspense. Storytellers would sing, dance, use gestures and make dramatic sounds, to make their recitals even more entertaining.

▶ *Ancient legends from Britain and France tell of King Arthur and his knights. These tales of heroic deeds, love and Christian values are not just exciting stories. First written down in medieval times, they may have been based on much older, Celtic, tales from England, Wales, and France.*

○ Many early stories aimed to give young people guidelines as to how they should behave. For example, epics about soldiers and knights taught young boys to grow up as fighters, and to be brave when in battle. They also encouraged adults who heard them to live up to the great exploits of the heroes in epic tales.

○ Writing allowed stories and many other kinds of information to be stored and learned by others. It also made it much easier to send information from one place to another.

◀ *The Vikings of Scandinavia and Iceland told sagas—long, exciting tales of warriors that mixed legend with true history. The sagas were created by poets called skalds, who made a living by telling the tales as entertainment. The sagas were not written down until long after Viking times.*

○ The world's earliest writing was invented in Mesopotamia (now Iraq), around 3400 BC. At first, it was used to make lists, recording goods handed over to government tax collectors, and stocks stored by merchants.

○ Early writing used picture symbols. Each symbol stood for one item, such as a cow or a tree. Later, around 1000 BC, scribes in Phoenicia (now Syria and Lebanon) invented an alphabet—a system of writing in which each symbol stood for a separate sound. Today, most languages use alphabets. However, Chinese and Japanese languages both still use picture symbols.

Viking runes

There were 16 letters, called runes, in the Viking alphabet. They were used for labeling valuable items with the owner's name, recording accounts, keeping calendars and for sending messages. From top left, these symbols stand for the sounds: F U Th A R K H N I A S T B M L R

Find out more

Words and pictures p. 465

▶ *North-European legends told how Thor, the mighty thunder god, rode angrily through the clouds, brandishing a great thunderbolt. Stories like this were entertaining, and they may also have helped to explain to early farmers how and why natural disasters, such as thunderstorms, took place, causing terrible damage to their crops.*

▲ *The poem* Beowulf *was originally performed aloud. Set in 6th century Scandinavia, part of the story tells how the hero Beowulf dives into a lake to battle the monster Grendel's mother (shown above) in an underwater cave. Beowulf and his exploits are paralleled in other northern mythologies.*

▼ *The ancient Egyptians invented a system of writing that used more than 800 picture symbols. It was called hieroglyphs, or sacred writing, because it was used to write religious texts on temple walls.*

❍ Alphabets were simpler to use than picture writing, and easier to learn. Instead of memorizing thousands of different picture symbols, readers and writers only had to learn the sound of each letter of the alphabet. Most alphabets contained around 30. By combining these, they could produce the sound of each word.

Letters and characters

Sound-based alphabets can be traced back to the Phoenicians, who lived in Lebanon in ancient times. Japanese writing is based on the Chinese system, the oldest form of writing in use today.

▼ *Ancient legends from Japan tell the story of Susano, god of storms and seas. He was one of three children of Izanagi, the great father god. One day, Izanagi decided to divide the world among his children, and gave all the seas to Susano. But Susano was not satisfied and quarreled with his father, who banished him from heaven. Susano went to live in the Underworld, stealing a wife from an eight-headed dragon he met on the way.*

Amazing

Sometimes, Viking runes were used to write messages in secret code, or even magic spells. These supposedly gave the objects they were carved on special power.

❍ Over the centuries, people have used many different writing materials. The first scribes (trained writers) in Mesopotamia used pointed sticks to make marks in wet clay slabs and cylinders. Ancient Egyptians made sheets of papyrus (an early kind of paper) from reed plants that grew by the River Nile. Chinese and Japanese people wrote with delicate brushes.

Scriptures and Sacred Writing

Originally, the word "scripture" just meant "writing." But over the years, its meaning changed. Today, it is used to describe holy books from many different faiths. All around the world, believers rely on scriptures to teach and guide them. Scriptures tell millions of men, women, and children how to worship, what to think, and how to live their lives. They inspire people to create great art or do brave and noble deeds, and comfort them when they face death, despair, or disaster.

○ Creation myths, preserved in many scriptures, offer answers to important questions, such as "Who made us?" or "How did we get here?." The answers are often religious, involving a powerful god or gods. In most creation myths, the gods lay down holy laws for people to obey. These are often strict but give meaning and purpose to peoples' lives and reassure them that the world has an underlying order, and that nothing happens by chance.

▼ *For centuries, Demotic (Egyptian writing using symbols) hieroglyphs were a mystery. But in 1799 a stone was found near Rosetta, in Egypt, inscribed in Egyptian, Greek and hieroglyphs. By comparing them, scholars were able to work out what the hieroglyphs meant.*

▲ *In some civilizations, the symbols used to write holy texts were also considered to be holy. For example, in ancient Egypt, picture symbols, which were known as hieroglyphs (holy writing), were used for writing gods' names and other religious words. The hieroglyphs were respected and feared, because people thought they shared the gods' powers.*

○ The Veda (poems praising Hindu gods and goddesses) are some of the oldest holy scriptures to survive, dating from around 1500 BC. At first, they were memorized and passed on by word of mouth. Later, they were written down in the holy Hindu language, Sanskrit. Other Hindu scriptures include the Upanishads (teachings of religious leaders) and the Mahabharata and Ramayana (religious poems about the adventures of Hindu heroes and gods).

> *Most scriptures were first written down many hundreds of years ago. In times of danger they were hidden away for safety. About 2,000 years ago, when ancient Romans occupied the Jewish homeland, Jewish people hid copies of their scriptures in pottery jars (right), and stored them in caves near the Dead Sea (now in Israel). These Dead Sea Scrolls were found again in 1947, and are some of the oldest-known scriptures to survive.*

○ Buddhist holy scriptures are called the "Tripitaka" (Three Baskets) because they were originally written on palm leaves and stored in three baskets. In the first were rules on how Buddhist monks should live. Stories of the Buddha's life were stored in the second and Buddha's teachings of the right way to live were kept in the third basket.

○ The world's first-known printed book is a Buddhist holy scripture, called the Diamond Sutra ("Precious Verse"), made in China around AD 800.

○ Muslims believe that their scripture— the Holy Koran—contains the actual words of Allah (God). They believe that the text of the Koran was revealed to the Prophet Muhammad, who lived in Arabia from AD 570–632. Muslims respect and honor Arabic, the language in which it is written.

○ *Tao-te Ching/Daode jing* (The Book of the Way and its Power) was written by Chinese religious teacher Lao-tzu around 400 BC. His book taught people to lead good lives. By doing this, they would be following a great power, called Tao (the Way).

Find out more
Words and writing pp. 462–463

A *The Sikh religion was founded in Punjab (now part of India and Pakistan) by Guru (wise leader) Nanak, in 1499. He preached purity, self-control, charity, and tolerance. Followers of the Sikh religion are guided by the teachings of their holy scriptures, the Guru Granth Sahib. Copies of this book are handled with great reverence. In Sikh gurdwaras (temples), they are placed on a cushion, and covered with a cloth, to protect their pages. At night, they are carefully put away in a special room.*

David and Goliath

Many scriptures contain stories about heroes who have fought for their religion. The Jewish Tenakah and the Christian Old Testament both describe how Jewish hero David fought bravely against the enemy giant Goliath to defend his people, their homeland, and their traditional faith. Goliath belonged to an ancient people, called the Philistines. Since the time David killed him, "philistine" has been used to mean "people who attack religion or culture."

Amazing

Followers of Judaism, Christianity and Islam all respect the same scriptures and are sometimes known as the "People of the Book"

❍ The religious philosopher Confucius lived in China from 551 to 479 BC and taught people how to live in peace by practising five "virtues:" goodness, kindness, wisdom, modesty, and trustworthiness. His teachings were written in a book called the *Analects* ("conversations") Many people in China and East Asia still follow his teachings.

A *St Paul (who lived around AD 60) was one of the first Christian preachers. He traveled to many parts of the Roman Empire, teaching the Christian faith. He also wrote Epistles (letters) to guide new Christian communities.*

Words and pictures

Until the 20th century, many people could not read. So stories from many different holy scriptures were portrayed in religious art. In Christian countries, they were often painted on church walls, where worshipers could see them. This church wall-painting is from Ethiopia, the first African country to make Christianity its official religion (AD 321).

▶ *Many Buddhist men and women decide to spend some time as monks or nuns, to learn more about their faith. This bhikkhu, or Buddhist monk, is studying holy scriptures.*

Major world scriptures

	Religion	Date first written down
Veda	Hindu	c.1500 BC
Upanishads	Hindu	c.500 BC
Mahabharata	Hindu	c.400 BC–AD 400
Ramayana	Hindu	c.400 BC–AD 400
Tenakah	Jewish	c.1200 BC onwards
Torah		
Nevi'im (Books of Prophets)		
Ketuvim (Books of Histories)		
Talmud (writings of Jewish religious teachers)		c.AD 200–500
Tripitaka	Buddhist	c.386–349 BC
Bible		
Old Testament (the Jewish Tenakah)	Christian	c.1200 BC onwards
New Testament	Christian	c.AD 300 (as a collection)
Koran	Muslim	c.AD 632 (as a collection)

Poems and Novels

*P*oets have held a special place in society since ancient times. In each civilization, they have won praise for their special ways of seeing the world, as well as for their skill at creating word patterns. Playwrights (since around 500 BC) and novelists (since around AD 1500) have also become famous for creating works that provoke, protest, inspire, and amuse.

○ We do not know the names of many early poets. The first well-known poet was a Greek, later called Homer. His epic stories, the *Iliad* (about war between Greeks and the city of Troy) and the *Odyssey* (about the travels of Greek hero Odysseus), were based on older traditions, and were first written down about 800 BC.

Haiku

"Breaking the silence of an ancient pond, A frog jumped into water… A deep echo." Those words are a translation of a Japanese poem, known as haiku. Each haiku is very short. In its original Japanese, it has only 17 syllables (separate sounds). Haiku poems are often inspired by natural sights and sounds, and describe a moment of insight or understanding— or perhaps a glimpse of eternity.

○ Homer may never have existed. He may have been a name given to a group of poets working in Greece to retell stories at the same time.

○ One of the most famous episodes in Homer's epic poem, *Iliad*, tells how a wooden horse helped the Greeks to capture the enemy city of Troy. They built the huge horse outside the city walls, then pretended to go away. Curious to find out more, the men of Troy dragged the horse into their city. They were horrified when fully armed Greek soldiers leaped out from inside the horse, where they had been hiding, opened the city gates, and let the rest of the Greek army march in.

◀ *The* **Rhymes of Robin Hood,** *first written down around AD 1350, describe the adventures of an English outlaw hero who hid in the woods. With his band of merry men and girlfriend, Maid Marian, Robin Hood robbed the rich and helped the poor.*

○ Many popular poems tell stories in verse. Originally composed to be recited out loud, they feature dramatic characters, strong rhythms and catchy rhymes. One famous series of story poems, about Anansi the spider, has traveled all around the world.

○ Early poets also told tales of brave knights and noble ladies. Their poems were based on ancient folk-tales, that combined Celtic or Germanic legends with the Christian faith.

○ In the past, poems were often very long, and followed various complicated rhyming word patterns. Today, many are short, and do not rhyme at all. Old or new, most poets share the same aim —to use language to say something new and memorable about the world.

○ After around AD 1400, collections of stories became popular in Europe. They were called "novels," from the Italian word *novella*, which means "new things," or "news." By around 1700, novels had taken the form they still have today—a long, imaginary story with powerful central characters.

○ Novels did not become popular until after around AD 1700. But as more people learned to read, and public lending libraries opened, novels slowly attracted a much larger readership.

Amazing

When the first part of *Don Quixote de la Mancha* was published in 1605, it was a bestseller. It is said to be the first modern novel. It was written by Spanish author Miguel de Cervantes (1547–1616).

Find out more

Words and writing pp. 462–463

A In the late 18th century, a group of British poets gathered in the Lake District of northwest England and wrote about their feelings for nature. Robert Southey (1774–1843), William Wordsworth (1770–1850) and Samuel Taylor Coleridge (1772–1834) became known as the "Lake Poets." They used poems about nature as a way of exploring their deepest feelings, and commenting on events in their world.

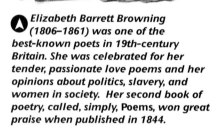

A Elizabeth Barrett Browning (1806–1861) was one of the best-known poets in 19th-century Britain. She was celebrated for her tender, passionate love poems and her opinions about politics, slavery, and women in society. Her second book of poetry, called, simply, Poems, won great praise when published in 1844.

○ Novels do not have to tell of great events or adventures. Jane Austen (1775–1817) was a genius at portraying the lives of ordinary people in a carefully observed way and with wry humor. Her novels include Sense and Sensibility, Emma, and Pride and Prejudice.

○ Some of the most famous works of literature in the 19th and 20th centuries were written by adults for children. Their text was often combined with illustrations. Together, text and pictures created magical, imaginary worlds.

○ Writers of the 19th century created books showing how new discoveries in science and technology might change the world. This kind of work has now developed into a special kind of literature, known as science fiction, or sci-fi. In recent years, fiction writers with expert scientific knowledge, such as Isaac Azimov (1920–1992) and Arthur C Clarke (born 1917), have created complex but believable science-fiction adventures.

▶ One of Britain's best-loved poets is John Keats (1792–1821). In 1818 and 1819, Keats produced a series of brilliant poems including "Ode to a Nightingale," "To Autumn," and "The Eve of St Agnes." However, he was already seriously ill with tuberculosis. In 1820, Keats left England to escape the cold weather. He died in Italy, aged only 25.

Famous characters

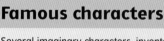

Several imaginary characters, invented by novelists, have become extremely well-known. A few people think that they once really existed. Quasimodo, a tragic figure who lived in cathedral bell tower, was created by French writer Victor Hugo (1802–1885) in his novel The Hunchback of Notre Dame. One-legged pirate Long John Silver, famous for his cry of "Yo Ho, my hearties!" appeared in Treasure Island, a novel by Scottish writer Robert Louis Stevenson (1850–1894). Brilliant detective Sherlock Holmes—together with his great friend, Dr Watson —starred in novels and short stories by Scottish doctor Sir Arthur Conan Doyle (1859–1830).

▶ The adventures of shipwrecked sailor Robinson Crusoe on a tropical island, were described in a novel by English writer Daniel Defoe, published in 1719. Defoe based his book on the true story of Scottish sailor Alexander Selkirk, who spent five years alone on an island off South America.

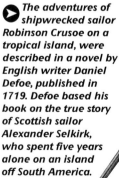

Printing and Publishing

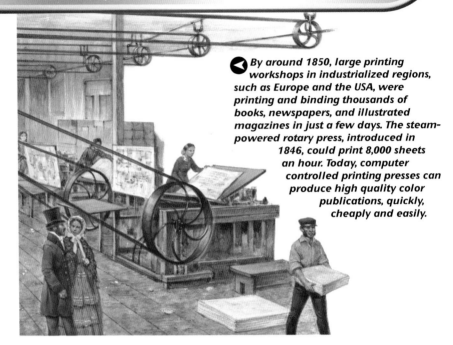

By around 1850, large printing workshops in industrialized regions, such as Europe and the USA, were printing and binding thousands of books, newspapers, and illustrated magazines in just a few days. The steam-powered rotary press, introduced in 1846, could print 8,000 sheets an hour. Today, computer controlled printing presses can produce high quality color publications, quickly, cheaply and easily.

*U*ntil around 500 years ago, there were very few books. Most were written by hand, and all were very expensive. But around AD 1440, a German inventor, Johannes Gutenberg, built a machine that could print books in large numbers. This revolutionized the way books were produced, and made them available, cheaply, to many more readers. Printed books remain an important source of information and entertainment in our world, today. Hundreds of thousands of new titles are published every year.

○ Gutenberg's machine—called a printing press—used moveable type. Skilled workers assembled individual letters to make words and sentences, then locked these into place in a wooden frame called a "forme." They covered the forme with a thin layer of ink, laid a sheet of paper on top, pressed down hard with a wooden

pad, removed the sheet (now covered with inky type, or letters) and hung it up to dry.

○ Printing was not a new invention. The first printed pages were produced in China soon after AD 800. But the writing for each page was carved as a whole from a single wooden block. Gutenberg's moveable type was much easier, quicker, and more flexible to use.

○ Once printed books became widely available, after around AD 1600, more people learned to read (and write). To satisfy this mass-market, soon newspapers, pamphlets, posters, and song sheets were printed in large numbers.

The bestselling book of all time is the Bible. Over the centuries, about six billion copies of the Bible have been sold. The aim of most publishers is to create bestsellers.

Gutenberg printer

In about 1438 the German, Johannes Gutenberg, developed a way of printing using movable type. First he cast hundreds of individual metal letters in molds. Then he arranged these letters into pages of text, which he printed on a press—a far quicker method than woodblock printing.

Find out more

Words and writing pp. 462–463

A *Some authors write books out by hand, others use a computer, and they often make many revisions along the way.*

A *At the publisher, editors go through the author's text and designers plan how the pages will look. They choose the size and style for the type, and for illustrated books work out where to position the pictures and text so that they are closely linked. The designer also briefs the illustrator on what the pictures need to show.*

A *Following the designer's instructions, the illustrator usually produces pencil sketches (called roughs) first, for approval, before painting the final illustrations, or in the case of digital artwork, creating them in a software package on the computer.*

○ Books, newspapers, and magazines are produced by businesses known as publishing (or media) companies. They select the best books and articles from among those sent by authors to them, or commission specially written work.

○ Authors are the starting point for most books—fiction or nonfiction. Before starting writing, they may spend many weeks researching a subject and making notes on how to shape the content of the book.

○ Book illustrators are artists who specialize in turning ideas into visual images. They generally work on books of one particular kind, for example storybooks or reference books. Specialist photographers also provide photos to use in books, to illustrate a particular point, or inspire a special mood.

○ At a publisher's office, editors go through an author's text, correcting any errors, making suggestions for changes, and questioning anything that is not clear. They works closely with a designer, who plans how the finished pages of a book will look.

○ Once the text and pictures are ready, the finished pages (prepared by a designer) are sent in electronic form to a reproduction house. There, they are

Electronic books

Novels and other electronic books (e-books) can be downloaded from the Internet to your home computer Soon it may be possible to read them on portable, booklike screens. We may be on the threshold of an entirely new age of literature.

A *Newspapers today are printed on machines called web presses. Paper is fed from huge rolls through the press at a rate of up to 3,000 ft a minute. The pages are then folded and cut, ready for distribution.*

made into color film, or processed by special computers linked directly to color printers. Modern printers are very fast, and usually print eight pages at a time on huge rolls of paper. The paper is then folded, cut, stitched, and bound to produce a finished book.

○ Finished books and magazines are stored in a publisher's warehouse. Bookshops and libraries order the titles they want from publishers.

Amazing

The longest novel ever written was *A la Recherche du Temps Perdu* by Marcel Proust with an estimated 9,609,000 characters.

Beginnings of Broadcasting

O ver the last 100 years, broadcast media have spread news, views, arts, sports, music, and drama worldwide. The first broadcasting system to be invented was radio. By the mid-1920s, there were more than 1,500 licensed radio transmitters, and over 4 million radio receiver sets in peoples' homes.

Amazing

Nowadays, we have MP3 devices that play files of music and radio broadcasts downloaded from the Internet. There are also hand-held televisions.

Italian scientist Guglielmo Marconi pioneered the use of radio waves as a means of communication. He constructed his first radio apparatus in 1895. At first it was only used to transmit simple messages in Morse Code. But by 1897, Marconi was able to send long-distance messages by radio, over a distance of 12 mi. In 1901, he made the first "wireless" radio transmission across the Atlantic Ocean.

The radio was designed only to transmit simple messages, but in 1906 music was broadcast. By the time this picture was taken in the 1940s, many households in Europe and America had a radio. It was the most popular family entertainment before the arrival of television.

○ Radio systems contain several separate elements. Microphones convert sounds into electrical signals (electromagnetic waves that move at the speed of light). Valves or transistors amplify (magnify) them. Transmitters send them out into the world. Aerials receive them, and carry them to more amplifiers. Then they pass to loudspeakers, tuning and volume controls in each radio.

○ Early radio sets were huge and heavy, with massive wooden cases, wide loudspeakers, and fragile glass valves (electrical components that magnified sound) inside. The first portable radio receiver was made in 1923. Car radios were invented in 1929.

○ Television works by scanning images, converting them into electric signals and sending these along a cable or through the air on radio waves. A television receiver collects the signals, turns them back into images and displays them on a screen. Several different television systems have been invented since 1925. Baird's system is no longer used.

○ By 1901, radio messages could be sent across the Atlantic Ocean. The first, experimental, music broadcast was made in 1906. By 1916, radio stations made regular broadcasts, playing "concerts" of gramophone recordings, or live performances by musicians in studios.

○ By 1916, radio states in Europe and the USA made regular broadcasts, playing "concerts" of gramophone recordings, or live performances by musicians in radio broadcast studios.

Camcorders

Camcorders (video recorders) allow people to make their own films easily. The films have a special hand-held quality that is now sometimes imitated in Hollywood movies to mimic live reportage. They are also used by television reporters making live news broadcasts, and by reporters working in remote, war-torn areas where it is too difficult or dangerous to send a full camera and sound-recording crew.

Find out more

Home entertainment pp. 472–473

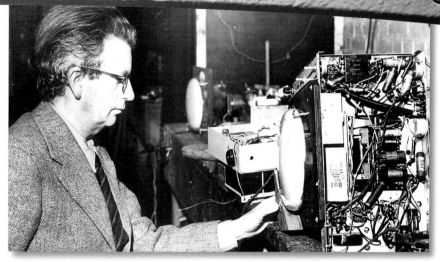

○ Color television broadcasts began in the USA in 1951. Videotape recording of TV broadcasts was invented in 1956.

○ In the USA, scientists made a broadcasting breakthrough in 1969 when their spacecraft sent back live pictures of the first person to walk on the Moon. The moonwalk pictures were shown on television all round the world.

○ In 1979, Japanese businessman Akio Morita, head of the Sony Corporation, invented a battery-powered portable personal stereo cassette tape player. He called it a Walkman. Later broadcasting inventions include personal radios and CD players.

A *The British inventor John Logie Baird (1888–1946) gave the first demonstration of a television in 1925. His apparatus included a cookie tin and darning needles. The system remained basic until the 1950s. Broadcasts were in black and white, and usually performed live. Color was introduced in 1953, but was only used widely from the 1960s.*

○ Radios were revolutionized in the late 1950s and 1960s when transistors (miniature switches and amplifiers) and microchips (tiny electrical circuits made of layers of silicon) were invented. Radios became smaller, lighter and easy to carry around.

○ Outside broadcasts of sports events, church services and important royal occasions began in the 1920s and 1930s. In Britain, King George V gave the first royal Christmas broadcast by radio in 1934. This began a tradition that still continues today.

○ The scientist who invented the first reliable television camera, in the 1930s, feared that television would become "the biggest time waster of all time." He warned, "Use it well."

○ The world's first regular television broadcasts were made in London by the British Broadcasting Corporation (BBC) in 1936 and 1937. Announcers wore formal evening dress to introduce the programs.

Broadcasting satellites

TV pictures and sound waves can be sent around the world. They are sent from one location up to satellites floating in space and transmitted to a receiver at another location. This means that live news pictures can be broadcast immediately from any trouble spots, making the world seem a smaller place. Global broadcasts mean viewers and listeners can now choose the latest international productions, instead of their own local or traditional media. Some people fear that this might weaken local cultures, or make them disappear completely.

A *The first television broadcasts were made in 1929. Early sets were disguised as pieces of decorative furniture. By 1949, when this "Predicta" set was made, television was still a rare and expensive luxury, but the design of the "Predicta" was streamlined and modern, rather than functional and hidden away. Today, there are television sets in most homes in the developed world.*

Home Entertainment

ince they were first invented, radio and television have had an enormous impact on home entertainment. Broadcasting has created thousands of new jobs, from camera operators to newsreaders, and has allowed information to be accessible to millions of people as news, entertainment and education. Today, online broadcasts via the Internet keep people up-to-date with events, sports, music and celebrities, all round the world, 24 hours every day.

Television

A TV set receives signals broadcast at a very fast rate. Each signal represents a tiny amount of light. When these signals reach the TV set, they enter a cathode-ray tube—a long funnel with a cathode (electrical contact) at one end, and a glass screen at the other. The cathode converts the signals into particles of energy and directs them at the screen. When each electron hits the inner coating of the screen it glows. This creates pictures made of tiny patches of color and light.

○ Before television sets became affordable in the 1950s, radio plays were popular home entertainment. In 1938, Orson Welles caused a sensation by broadcasting a science-fiction play. Called *War of the Worlds*, it described an invasion by aliens. It was so realistic that many listeners fled from their homes in terror.

○ Since the 1960s, broadcasts on television have both entertained and informed audiences. Programs about distant countries, exotic wildlife, art, archeology and ancient monuments have all allowed audiences to view wonderful things that they might otherwise not have seen.

Amazing

Jerry Seinfeld earned an estimated $267 million for the show *Seinfeld* in 1998—the highest annual earnings ever by a television or film actor.

▼ *Today, many radio and television broadcasts can be seen and heard on computers, or downloaded on to personal media players using formats such as MP3. Most broadcasts are now also interactive. Broadcasters invite audiences to take part in favourite programs by sending e-mails, joining in Internet debates, and even making their own programs.*

▲ *In the late 20th century, television presented classic dramas filming works of literature, such as* **Pride and Prejudice** *by Jane Austen, to a vast new audience. Most of these costume dramas were made in Britain, and exported, with translated dialogue, to different parts of the world.*

Find out more
Broadcasting pp. 470–471

Television has revolutionized political campaigns. Politicians who are skilled television performers have a better chance of winning elections.

Television broadcasts of live music—from opera to rock festivals—bring pleasure to millions who cannot travel to concerts or buy tickets for live shows. However, some music fans say that watching television can never replace the thrill of being at a live performance.

Television producers make serials that they can sell to as many TV networks as possible. These serials are then shown as repeats in later years to earn extra fees.

Soap operas originated in the 1920s and 1930s as daytime radio broadcasts designed to appeal to housewives. They were sponsored by the makers of soap, and cosmetic products. They describe the daily lives of ordinary people—who lead extraordinarily eventful lives. Today, soaps are some of the most popular television programs.

Fashions in broadcasting often lead to complaints, as program makers take part in ratings wars to attract the most viewers. This leads to many similar programs, all on popular topics such as cookery or gardening, being shown at the same time.

A DVDs (Digital Versatile Discs) were developed from CDs (Compact Discs) in the late 1990s. Like CDs, they are made of plastic with a thin metal coating and read by laser-beams. Each DVD can store an enormous amount of data—words, music, and very high quality images—in digital form. The first DVD recorders went on sale in 2000. Today, they have replaced video players for recording TV broadcasts and for showing movies in many homes.

Telecommunications is the almost instantaneous transmission of sounds, words, pictures, and information by electronic means. At present, TV, radio and phone links are all carried separately, but increasingly they will all be carried the same way. They will be split up only when they arrive at their destination.

This Play Station portable (PSP) brought out in 2005 took game playing to new heights with the small handheld screen and controls. In 2005 the Ridge Racer game (above) was one of the fastest graphics contained within a portable device.

Home cinema

Until videotape recorders were invented, viewers had only once chance to see a program—at the time it was scheduled to be broadcast. The first videotape recording was made in 1956, but home video recorders and players were not available until 1972. Videos were a breakthrough in broadcasting. They turned each TV set into a "home cinema," allowing viewers to watch what they wanted, at a time that they could choose.

Video games originated in the late 1960s. Several different systems were invented, but all used a console that could be loaded with computer programs and linked to a TV set. These early games were revolutionized by the Game Boy, invented by Japanese company Nintendo in 1989. Each set had a tiny screen and console that could easily be carried around, and offered players many different adventure games and puzzles.

Game Boy was followed by Play Station, launched by Japanese electronics giant Sony in 1995. The games feature advanced graphics, realistic feedback, and fast, sensitive controls.

The First Films

Films are one of the world's youngest and most profitable art forms. The first film was shown to the public in 1895. By the 1930s, millions of people in Europe and North America were visiting the cinema every week. Today, videos, DVDs (digital versatile disks), and other electronic media mean that people all round the world can watch movies whenever they like, at home.

○ Today's film industry would not exist without three 19th-century inventions: photography, lantern-slide projectors, and the zoopraxiscope.

○ The oldest surviving photograph was taken in 1827. It was produced after spreading a mixture of chemicals on a glass plate, reflecting an image on to them, then exposing the plate to light.

Celluloid film

The cinematographe machine, invented by the Lumière brothers, worked by passing a continuous strip of film printed with photographic images in front of a bright light and a magnifying lens. This produced a large, moving picture on a screen. From around 1889, cinema films were made of celluloid—a kind of plastic manufactured from wood pulp, acid, and alcohol. Celluloid film was flexible and transparent—but also dangerously explosive! Many early films were destroyed when they caught fire.

○ Early photographers discovered that by shining a light through finished glass-plate photographs, images could be projected onto another surface. They gave magic lantern shows, in which the audience sat in a darkened room and watched photos projected on to a wall.

Amazing

The first movie in Three-Color Technicolor was *Becky Sharp* (1935), starring Miriam Hopkins.

○ In the 1880s, American Eadweard Muybridge (1830–1904) set up groups of cameras with threads attached to the shutters, so that dozens of photos could be taken in quick succession. Muybridge's aim was to study movement, but he realized that by showing his photos one after the other, very fast, he could produce pictures that appeared to move.

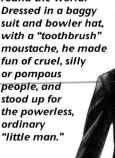

Charlie Chaplin (1889–1977) was one of the first, and most famous, movie stars. He began his career as a comedian in English music halls, but moved to America, where he soon became a great success in early silent films. A brilliant mime, with great comic timing, he developed an instantly recognizable image, popular with fans all round the world. Dressed in a baggy suit and bowler hat, with a "toothbrush" moustache, he made fun of cruel, silly or pompous people, and stood up for the powerless, ordinary "little man."

In France, two brothers, Auguste (1862–1954) and Louis Lumière (1864–1948) had the brilliant idea of combining a camera and a projector. In 1895, they perfected the cinematographe machine. It took pictures on a continuous strip of film, and replayed them on a screen. They had invented movies.

Find out more
Making movies pp. 476–477

Movie sound

In the early days of cinema, movie shows were accompanied by live performances of piano music, or by recorded tunes played on gramophones. In 1911, the Wurlitzer company in the USA began to make huge organs—known as "Mighty Wurlitzers"—for cinemas, to provide loud, dramatic music, and many sound-effects, for movies. The first movie with a built-in soundtrack (recorded speech that was played at the same time as the film) was not produced until 1927.

○ The earliest movies were silent. Actors told the story in mime. This meant that performances could be enjoyed by audiences in many different countries. Movie shows were usually accompanied by mood music, played in the cinema on a piano or organ.

○ The first movie with sound—known as a talkie—was produced in 1927. It was very successful with audiences, but disastrous for some movie stars. Although they were clever at movement and mime, they did not have pleasant speaking voices. They were replaced by actors who looked attractive and could also speak their lines well.

○ Many of the first movies were comedies. But, by the 1920s, dramatic adventure stories, historical epics, and classics from world literature were also made into movies.

○ Muybridge invented a machine called a zoopraxiscope to show his moving pictures. It was made of a large hollow cylinder, which turned around and around. Images were pasted on the inside; as the drum turned, viewers could not see where one image ended and the next began. They blurred together and seemed to move.

○ Also in America, Thomas Edison (1847–1931), helped by William Dickson, built a kinetograph—a very fast camera that could take 40 photos a second. They also designed a special machine, called a kinetoscope, for viewing kineotgraph film. Viewers looked down a pair of lenses—rather like binoculars—in a darkened booth.

Movie firsts

1927	First "talkie"	The Jazz Singer
1928	First movie to win Best Film Oscar	Wings
1937	First feature-length Walt Disney animation	Snow White and the Seven Dwarfs
1939	First color movie to win Best Film Oscar	Gone With the Wind
1939	First African American to win an Oscar	Hattie McDaniel (Best Supporting Actress for Gone With the Wind)
1940	First movie in stereosound	Fantasia
1942	First twins to win an Oscar	Julius and Philip Epstein (Best Screenplay for Casablanca)
1948	First British movie to win Best Film Oscar	Hamlet
1953	First movie to be released in Cinemascope	The Robe
1963	First African American to win a Best Actor Oscar	Sidney Poitier for Lilies of the Field
1964	First James Bond movie to win an Oscar	Goldfinger for Best Effects and Sound Effects
1969	First X-rated movie to win Best Movie Oscar	Midnight Cowboy
1970	First actor to refuse a Best Actor Oscar	George C Scott for Patton
1974	First sequel to win Best Movie Oscar	The Godfather Part II
1975	First movie released in Sensurround	Earthquake
1976	First woman to be nominated for Best Director Oscar	Linda Wertmuller for Seven Beauties
1976	First posthumous winner of Best Actor Oscar	Peter Finch for Network
1991	First animated movie to be nominated for Best Film Oscar	Beauty and the Beast
1995	First wholly computer-generated movie	Toy Story
2001	First African American woman to win Best Actress Oscar	Halle Berry for Monsters Ball

A *Buildings, known as movie theaters or cinemas, were designed to house the large audiences who wanted to watch new movies. Cinemas soon became a popular—and much cheaper—alternative to the theater. Like music halls, they became favorites with ordinary people, as well as wealthy, educated theatergoers.*

Making Movies

Making a movie is a complicated and very expensive process. Visual images, spoken words, sound effects, music, studio sets, outside locations, and action sequences all have to be very carefully planned and rehearsed, before shooting (photography) can start.

British director Sir Alfred Hitchcock (1899–1980) became known as the master of suspense, after he created many chilling horror movies. In the movie industry, a producer raises money to make a new movie and organizes the financial side of movie making, while the director is in charge of the more creative elements. The director tells the camera crews how to set up their cameras, and directs the actors to act the way the script is written.

On the set of Lord of the Rings: The Fellowship of the Ring (2001). Producer Barrie Osbourne and Viggo Mortensen playing Aragorn check a take.

○ As well as having creative responsibility for the concept behind each movie, directors are also responsible for writing, or checking, the script, directing the actors' speech and movement on the movie set, giving instructions to lighting and camera crews, checking on how each scene looks through the camera, and choosing the "cut" (final selection of images) for each movie.

○ Many directors uses a storyboard to work out how to shoot a movie. This is a sequence of sketches that show roughly how each scene will look. This visual planning also helps to ensure that small details of costume or background remain the same from scene to scene throughout the filming.

Movie lighting is a very skilled profession. The level of light on each movie set, or in the open air, can affect the overall color of the finished file. Lighting can also be used for dramatic effect, for example to create a stormy, threatening mood, or to suggest that characters are harmless.

○ Lighting plays a major part in creating the look of a movie, whether it's shot outdoors on location, or indoors on a studio set. Lighting can create cosy, gloomy, frightening, or very dramatic effects.

Hollywood

In 1911, movie makers went to a remote settlement called Hollywood, near Los Angeles, to film westerns. Hollywood had a dry, scrubby landscape, very much like parts of the American Wild West. Within two years it had become the center of American movie making and it has dominated the industry worldwide ever since.

Find out more
Special effects pp. 478–479

SHREK

Clapperboard

A clapperboard is used in a movie or TV studio to mark the beginning or end of a take (a short section of movie). Details of each take are filled in on the clapperboard, which is held up in front of the camera before filming begins. Movies are not usually made in the order of a story. Director, scriptwriters, camera crew, and actors work on the scenes in whatever order is convenient, for example when the actors are available or the weather is right. Several takes may be needed before a scene is filmed properly. The final takes are put together in order by an editor and, if necessary, cut to create the finished movie.

○ Sometimes movie makers build sets—lifelike mock rooms, buildings, landscapes, fantasy environments, or moving models of monsters. It is often cheaper, easier, and visually more effective to film on location out in the real world.

○ Once shooting has finished, each movie has to be edited. Most directors shoot more material than they need. The final visual images

▲ *Completed films are marketed to the public. Big posters outside cinemas show dramatic scenes from each film or glamorous pictures of its stars. Directors and actors give interviews to press and TV journalists, or appear at film festivals and awards ceremonies.*

are chosen by the director and a team of editors. They are then combined with a soundtrack of voices, music, and sound effects.

◀ *Bollywood movies, made in Bombay, India, are lavish song and dance spectacles that tell exciting adventure stories or passionate tales of love. Male and female stars are chosen for their good looks, and attract vast numbers of fans. They use facial expressions, mime and dance to express powerful emotions without breaking the Indian movie industry's strict no kissing code.*

Special Effects and Superstars

Throughout the 20th century, new technology helped movie makers create fantastic visions of reality. Color photography made scenes on screen seem more dramatic and lifelike. Special effects and computer-generated images allowed directors to create visual impressions that could never exist in real life.

○ All early movies were shot (photographed) in black and white, although a few had faint color added after shooting by technicians at film studios. The first full color movie, made using a process called "Technicolor," was produced in 1935.

○ Movie makers use models and computer technology to create stunning visual effects, such as earthquakes, floods, or invasions from outer space. Pioneered in the 1960s and 1970s, these SFX (special effects) are now extremely accomplished and realistic.

○ From the 1930s to the 1950s, cowboy adventures, crime thrillers, and wartime hero stories were popular, together with cartoons. In the 1950s and 1960s, light romances and historical epics were a favorites with audiences. In the late 1960s and 1970s, many movies began to feature the latest fashions in pop and rock music and dancing.

○ Serious "art" films, inspired by writers and philosophers, asked questions about the meaning of life. Many were made, using experimental techniques, in France and Scandinavia between 1950 and 1980.

○ Since the early days of movie making, directors from many countries made films designed to make a political protest, or spread their political ideas. The most outspoken films were often banned by governments whose ideas were criticized in the film.

Amazing

Andy Serkis, who played the character of Gollum in *The Lord of the Rings* film trilogy, was ruled ineligible for an Oscar nomination because his onscreen character was computer generated.

▼ *Technology developed by scientists at the US government's National Aeronautics and Space Administration (NASA) helped create special effects for the action movie* Terminator 3: Rise of the Machines *(2003). Engineers and movie makers relied on NASA robotics to design terrifying robot monsters that moved in a menacing way to threaten human heroes on screen. Since the mid- 20th century, growing expertise in robotics and photography have raised expectations among moviegoers. Viewers now expect robots to be slick, smart and extremely lifelike. Old-fashioned monsters that look homemade are no longer so appealing.*

Superstars

Marilyn Monroe

Audrey Hepburn

Rudolf Valentino

Elizabeth Taylor

Boris Karloff (as Frankenstein's Monster)

Nicole Kidman

Tom Cruise

Samuel L Jackson

George Clooney

Nicholas Cage

Find out more

Hollywood p. 477

Awards record

The Oscars are the gold-plated awards presented each year by the US Academy of Motion Picture Arts and Sciences. US actress, Katharine Hepburn (1907–2003), is the only actor to have won four Oscars.

In **The Matrix Reloaded** *(2003) movie makers pioneered a new technique, known as "Bullet Time," to create extraordinary scenes. They arranged still cameras in a circle around the actors, then used them to take photos in a carefully-timed sequence. When linked together, copied on to movie film, and played through a movie projector, the photos showed events happening in hyperslow motion, or let viewers see the actors from front, back and sides, all at the same time. These stunning images had a startling visual impact on audiences in the cinema.*

Movie makers use costumes and make-up to create a character's look. Dressing an actor can take hours and may include prosthetics (false body parts), wigs as well as make-up effects. Shown here, the face of Frankenstein's monster in Curse of Frankenstein *(1957) featured blisters and scars. Many effects can be added using computers.*

○ Modern movie acting is very different to acting on stage. Actors use subtle changes of facial expression and small movements to show thoughts and feelings. Directors shoot actors' faces in close-up with high-powered lenses, allowing viewers to share each character's emotions.

○ Leading actors cannot risk getting hurt in action scenes so directors hire specialist stunt actors to take their place. Male and female stunt actors are trained to crash cars, climb mountains, jump from moving trains or leap through fire, all as safely as possible, to avoid injury.

Animatronic techniques create special effects that would be impossible in real life. For example, in Lord of the Rings: The Two Towers *(2002), the character of Gollum was made by filming a live actor's movements and combining them on computers with scanned images. When refined using "morphing" software, this created a creature with unsettling traces of human behavior.*

Academy Award winners

Best actor

1994	Tom Hanks
1995	Nicholas Cage
1996	Geoffrey Rush
1997	Jack Nicholson
1998	Roberto Benigni
1999	Kevin Spacey
2000	Russell Crowe
2001	Denzel Washington
2002	Adrian Brody
2003	Sean Penn
2004	Denzel Washington
2005	Jamie Foxx

Best actress

1994	Holly Hunter
1995	Susan Sarandon
1996	Frances McDormand
1997	Helen Hunt
1998	Gwyneth Paltrow
1999	Hilary Swank
2000	Julia Roberts
2001	Halle Berry
2002	Nicole Kidman
2003	Charlize Theron
2004	Halle Berry
2005	Hilary Swank

Buildings Great and Small

Architecture is the art and science of designing buildings. Before starting each new project, an architect has to consider the purpose of the building, the site where it will stand, the money needed to pay for it, and the materials available. In the past, almost all big buildings were designed for rich and powerful people. They paid for fine palaces, temples, and tombs. Ordinary people built their own smaller, simpler shops, workplaces, and homes. In each civilization, buildings for rich and poor reflected local beliefs and traditions, plus local environmental and climatic conditions.

Some of the very first homes were shelters of brushwood and branches, built inside caves or under overhanging rocks around 50,000 years ago. This stone house in Portugal makes use of the space underneath large boulders in the same way.

The trading town of Çatal Hüyük in Turkey dates from around 6000 BC. Its houses, made of sundried clay bricks, were built joined together, side by side. They had no windows. Access was through a trapdoor in the roof.

Stonehenge, in southwest England was built in phases between 2800 and 1500 BC. Its stones are arranged in circles around an open space. They align with the rising Sun at midsummer. Stonehenge may be a temple or observatory.

The ancient Egyptians built pyramids as tombs for important people, especially their pharaohs. The Great Pyramid, at Giza, built around 2500 BC, is the largest pyramid. It is over 486 ft tall, and its base measures 755 ft on each side.

The ancient Greeks and Romans built temples as homes for gods. They believed that the gods' spirits might live there. The Parthenon temple (of the goddess Athena, built in the 5th century BC) in Athens is the most famous Greek temple of all.

Water wheels were invented in the Middle East 2,000 years ago. They were designed to carry water for drinking and to water crops. As the wheel turned, buckets dipped into a river and filled with water. Water was then poured into ditches.

The Colosseum was a vast amphitheater (circular arena) in Rome, Italy. It was built of wood, concrete and stone by the ancient Romans around AD 80. It seated almost 50,000 spectators, who flocked there to watch gladiator fights.

This Buddhist pagoda at Pagan, Burma, is one of many holy temples built for King Anawrahata (ruled 1044–1077) and his family. Each layer of the pagoda represents a different stage in a human soul's journey toward nirvana (peace and blessedness).

Find out more

Modern architecture pp. 482–483

This temple in Qufu City, in the Shandong province of China, was built in 1302 to honor the ancient Chinese philosopher, Confucius. Like many Chinese buildings, it has a wide, heavy roof, decorated with elaborate carvings.

The Forbidden City—a huge network of temples, palaces, and gardens, built between 1421 and 1911—lies within the Chinese capital, Beijing. This is the Temple of Heaven, where the emperor went every year to make sacrifices to the sky gods.

These onion-shaped domes decorate the roof of the Russian Orthodox Cathedral in Moscow, Russia. Like other cathedrals, it is cared for by a bishop (Christian leader). Each Christian country has cathedrals built in its own local style.

In regions with plentiful timber, such as Canada, Russia, and northern Europe, many traditional homes are built of wood—a cheaper material than imported brick or stone.

This stone-walled, straw-thatched house in Peru is built to a design used by the Incas, who ruled the Andes over 500 years ago. Like Inca houses, it has a walled courtyard. Many traditional building styles are hundreds of years old.

In crowded cities there is not much space for building, and houses are often several storeys high, closely packed together, to fit lots of people in one place. These tall merchants' houses in Amsterdam, in the Netherlands, were designed about 1650.

This house on the prairies (grasslands) of western USA is made of sods—slabs of earth with the grass roots attached. In the 19th century, migrant families that settled on the prairies could not afford expensive timber, bricks or stone.

The Potala Palace in Llasa, Tibet, is built of clay, bricks and stone. It is perched high on a cliffside for safety. First designed as a fortress between AD 1000–1500, the palace later became home to the Tibetan Buddhist leader, the Dalai Lama.

Mobile homes

Nomadic peoples, like the Mongols of Central Asia, live in homes that are easy to move. The Mongols take their gers—domed tents made of thick felt—with them when they go in search of new grazing land for their flocks.

Master masons

Castles were among the biggest buildings in the world before around AD 1500. The first castles were small and made of wood. After around 1100, they became splendid forts and homes, built of stone. By around AD 1500, there over 20,000 castles in England, Wales, France, Spain, and Germany.

Modern Architecture

*T*oday, buildings are bigger, taller and more complex than ever before. Many also feature "intelligent" computer-controlled systems to manage the environment inside.

○ Modern architecture developed as a rebellion against cluttered, heavy, and dull 19th-century designs. Most modern buildings have clean-cut lines, simple shapes and few decorative details.

○ After around 1900, architects began experimenting with exciting new styles, including Art Nouveau, using flowing shapes inspired by nature. Arts and Crafts is based on traditional buildings. Art Deco is glamorous and streamlined. Functionalism is based on practical needs while Brutalism uses massive shapes. Modernism and High Tech uses new engineering.

▶ *Air-conditioned shopping malls have everything under one roof, including many shops, services, and often a food hall. Architecture varies from one mall to another, however they are all similar. Critics say they are "consumerist machines" lacking the social aspect of outdoor markets.*

▶ *Some designers win fame for their personal style. The Spanish architect Antonio Gaudi (1853-1926) is famous for his original and unusual building designs. Most of his buildings are in the city of Barcelona in Spain. In an attempt to break away from historical styles, he used flowing curves in many of his buildings, which he decorated with brightly colored ceramics or mosaics of glass.*

○ Architects used industrial technology to create the first modern buildings. Instead of old-style load-bearing walls, they constructed frames of strong steel girders (beams) to support the weight of floors, windows, roofs, ceilings and the people living or working inside. Buildings were "clad" (covered) by thin "skins" of clay tiles, concrete blocks, bricks, timber, metal, glass, or stone.

▶ *Bridges are some of the biggest and most beautiful structures in the world. But their graceful curves and arches are the result of careful mathematical calculations, not simply artistic design. Their strength and safety are more important than their appearance.*

Find out more

Buldings pp. 480–481

At 1,821 ft, the CN Tower in Toronto, Canada, is the tallest structure in the world. Built in 1976, it is a communications mast, designed to send telephone, radio and TV signals over long distances.

The Opera House at Sydney, Australia, was designed by Danish-born architect Jorn Utzon. The Opera House stands on the edge of Sydney Harbour, so Utzorn based its design on curving ships' sails.

Skyscrapers

Steel-frame construction technology was first used to build 19th-century factories, then skyscrapers in the USA. The world's earliest skyscrapers were built in the 1880s in Chicago, USA, after a fire destroyed many old wooden houses. The first to be completed was the Home Insurance Building with ten storeys in 1883. Electricity-powered elevators (lifts) were invented to carry people to the upper floors. Nowadays many skyscrapers have more than 200 storeys.

❍ By the mid-20th century, many buildings were made of solid concrete poured into wooden molds and reinforced (strengthened) by steel rods inside. Big dark gray concrete buildings were tough and often forbidding.

❍ Buildings in the 20th century were inspired by ideas of how people should live. Architects wanted to replace slums with bright modern buildings and create healthier environments. In wealthy countries, the standards of housing rose but in spite of modern architects' achievements, many ordinary people in poor countries still live in homes without sanitation or clean water.

❍ Top 20th-century architects win prizes for their designs. But some people blame them for wrecking cities with new developments that overpower older buildings nearby. Supporters of modern buildings admire architects' imagination, daring, and skill.

Amazing

Some skyscrapers sway in the wind. They are sometimes fitted with weights at the top that are moved from side to side to make the building lean into the wind—cancelling out the effect.

The Atomium

Modern engineering techniques have allowed artchitects to create exciting structures on a huge scale. The Atomium, shown here, was built for the international fair held in Brussels in 1958. It represents a giant model of an atom with nine huge steel balls rising to 394 ft.

The Gateway to the West is a massive arch in the city of St Louis, Missouri, USA. It was designed to honor pioneers who set out from St Louis after 1893 to settle in western USA. Completed in 1965, the arch is covered in shining steel plate and is 630 ft high. There are two theaters and a museum at the base, and an elevator takes visitors to an observation room right at the top.

History of Culture

*T*he word "culture" is often used to describe art forms that are enjoyed by only a few people—such as opera or ballet. But culture can mean much more than that. It can describe someone's upbringing and education, their religious faith, their community's traditions, and their nation's language, literature and art. It can also describe how a person lives, their political ideas, and how they identify themselves. Usually, culture refers to all these things together, and is used to describe a unique civilization of a particular time or people.

○ Within each society or civilization, culture has many separate functions. It can amuse and entertain, or be thought provoking. It can reinforce traditional values, or inspire people with unsettling new ideas.

○ All around the world different cultures have developed special ceremonies to mark the important stages of each person's life. For example, new babies are traditionally welcomed with naming rituals. Older children take part in initiation ceremonies, which show they are leaving childhood behind and becoming young adults.

○ In many cultures, marriages traditionally involve the bride moving home, and gifts of food or property to the newly married couple. Almost everywhere they are an excuse for joyful celebrations.

○ Often people are laid to rest with funeral prayers. Usually these express hope in a new life after death. In many cultures, dead family members are honored with tombstones or similar memorials, while important, powerful people are commemorated by grand public monuments.

○ National costumes are a symbol of pride, closely linked to local culture. People dress to conform to their cultural beliefs. Flesh-revealing clothes are unacceptable in certain cultures, Clothes reflect local climates and products (wool or silk) as well.

○ Today many people work in food industries—farming, fishing, or working in factories and supermarkets. Global distribution allows people in richer countries to eat foods from all over the world, but in poor regions some people starve. Natural disasters or too much or too little rainfall result in famines. Other countries can send emergency supplies to aid those people in need.

○ People who belong to a particular faith use holy signs. For Christians, the cross is a holy sign. It reminds them of the wooden frame on which Jesus Christ was executed in about AD 30. Muslims use a crescent moon to symbolize Islam and Jewish people use a six-pointed Star of David.

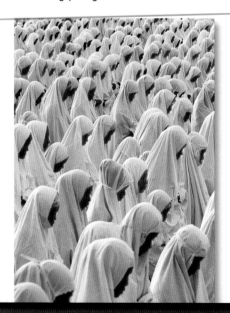

Many different faiths teach that men and women should be modestly dressed in public, and that they should wear special clothes when performing religious rituals, as a sign of respect. These Muslim women, who are on holy pilgrimage, have covered their heads and shoulders with a simple white garment. Jewish men also cover their heads and shoulders while reading from holy scriptures.

Flags originated as banners, carried to help soldiers follow their leaders into battle. Now they are important national symbols, carried in processions at international events and flown on public holidays.

Find out more

Buldings pp. 480–481

> Clothes can reflect religious beliefs, wealth, occupation, and status, as well as ethnic or national identity. This young Masai woman, from Kenya, East Africa, wears a traditional beaded collar. Her large metal earrings are a sign of wealth, and her beaded necklace will be individual to just her.

▲ Depending on where they live or what they believe, people may prize some foods as delicacies, or refuse to eat them at all. For centuries, growing and catching food have been important occupations. Many people are also employed in food-based industries, such as driving refrigerated lorries or stacking fruit on shop shelves.

Birthday celebrations

People celebrate birthdays in different ways across the world. In Europe and America, birthdays are celebrated by offering gifts and cards, and by sharing a cake decorated with candles. Each candle stands for one year of the birthday person's age. It is considered good luck to blow them all out in one go.

Changing eating habits

Sharing a meal is one of the oldest pleasures known to civilized human beings. In many cultures, hospitality (offering food and drink) is a sacred duty. But in the 20th century new fast foods, such as takeaway burgers and fries, seemed likely to change these ancient cultural traditions in many parts of the world.

▼ In many countries mothers are the head of the family. Many mothers work to support their children and also manage the home. Some companies provide childcare. To prevent overpopulation in China, the government made a law forbidding people to have more than one child. This has helped to slow down the population growth.

◀ A Jewish bride and groom sip wine together during their wedding ceremony as a symbol of the joys and sorrows they will share together in the years ahead.

○ People in the armed forces and public services, such as police, wear uniforms as a sign of belonging and to encourage discipline and self-respect. Members of national or local sports teams show their loyalty to each other and are united by the same clothes.

Glossary

Abstract art Paintings that have no obvious similarity to real objects, made by arranging shapes and colors in a purely imaginary way, which may be hard to understand.

Alloy A metallic substance made from a mixture of two or more metals, or from a metal mixed with other nonmetallic elements, examples being brass, bronze, and steel.

Amphitheater A circular or oval building that contains rows of seats rising from an arena, where performances take place for an audience.

Amplify To make louder. Sounds can be amplified by sound boxes or resonators, or electronically by turning them into electrical signals using a microphone, and passing the signals through an electronic amplifier into loudspeakers.

Animatronics The techniques of designing, building, and operating lifelike machines or robots that are worked by electronics, assisted by computers and controlled remotely, to mimic real people, animals, or aliens.

Architect A person who designs buildings.

Art nouveau French phrase meaning "new art," an elegant design style of natural flowing or swirling lines, fashionable at the beginning of the 20th century.

Atonal music A form of modern music composition where the notes or sounds are not arranged in the traditional order of scales and harmonies, but in a more abstract way.

Audition An interview to find suitable performers for roles in a play or musical performance. It usually involves candidates reading from a script, singing or giving a short performance, watched by the director.

Auditorium The main part of a theater, cinema, or public performance venue where the audience sits to view the stage. It may consist of a floor area, with seats called stalls, and layers called circles and balconies above, also with seats.

Bass The very low sounds or musical notes, played by large instruments such as a double bass or a tuba, or sung by a man with a very deep voice.

Baton A stick waved by the conductor of an orchestra to emphasize the rhythm and pattern of the music, so that everyone plays or sings the notes in the correct way at the correct time.

Biographies Accounts of a person's life, written or told by someone else.

Brass A shiny, yellowish metal that is an alloy, or mixture, of the pure metals copper and zinc. It is used to make wind instruments such as cornets, trumpets, trombones, and horns, which form the brass section of an orchestra.

Broadcast To scatter or spread something over a wide area—today this word usually refers to the spreading of information, news, or knowledge usually by radio or television.

Camera obscura A windowless room or box with a small hole in one wall, through which light passes from outside, to produce on the wall opposite inside, an upside-down (inverted) image of the scene outside.

Cast A list of characters in a play, opera, or similar production, and the names of the actors who play them. Decisions by the director and others about which actor suits each role is called casting.

Celluloid An early synthetic plastic, used for billiard balls, dentures, combs and photographic film. It is highly flammable and has been replaced by less flammable cellulose acetate for movie film, but the term "celluloid" is still used generally to mean movies or films in the cinema.

Ceramics Objects that are made by shaping and firing (heating) clay or similar materials, at very high temperatures, so they become hard and brittle.

Ceremony A formal act, convention, or event carried out according to custom or traditional rules, usually performed to honor and continue some kind of past ritual, rite, or anniversary.

Choreographer The person who decides which dance steps and movements should be used by people during a ballet, musical, or similar production. The choreographer then instructs and directs the performance of the dancers.

Civilization A people, their society and culture that have developed in a social, political, and technological sense, and are refined in interests and tastes.

Commission To order a piece of work to be created, often especially for and to the instructions of the person making the order. The person making the order will usually make a payment to whoever is completing the piece.

Cubism A 20th-century painting technique where the image is broken down into geometric shapes like circles, squares, and cubes, which are then rearranged in the picture.

Cue Words or actions of a performer that alert other performers that it is their turn to speak or carry out certain actions.

Culture A way of life of a group of people who share certain customs, beliefs, technology, and ideas. People who speak the same language may share the same culture (the Japanese, for example) but not necessarily.

Custom A traditional practice, usually established by a particular community of people.

Dialogue A conversation or discussion between two actors in a play or production, or possibly between two representatives of groups with different ideas.

Digital Digital sound is recorded, not as continuous up-and-down waves, but as codes of numbers or digits, which usually results in a clearer, purer, more accurate recording.

Engraving A printing technique where a pattern or image is cut, or engraved, into a metal or wooden plate. Ink is then rubbed on, and the plate is pressed onto paper to make an impression.

Epic A very long story, poem, or tale, told in an elevated style, which relates many great and magnificent deeds, especially involving a hero or heroine.

Etching A printing technique where a pattern or image is cut into an acid-proof coating on a metal plate, and acid is applied that etches, or erodes, the image into the metal. Then the coating is removed and the plate is used to make prints.

Expressionism A style of drama, music, or painting where the artist or performer tries to illustrate or express emotions and feelings, rather than real images of the actual world.

Fables Short stories, often based on animal characters, which teach lessons especially to children, to show them how they can lead better lives.

Folk dance The traditional dance of a group of people or a country. Its movements and steps are passed down from generation to generation, and dances are often performed in traditional costume.

Foyer The entrance hall of a theater, cinema, or performance venue, where the audience enters the building, perhaps meet in groups, and buy tickets, programs, refreshments, and merchandise. Also known as "front of house."

Fresco From the Italian word for "fresh," a painting done on the plaster or render (coating) of a wall or ceiling using water-based paints, which are applied while the plaster is still wet.

Frets The series of small metal bars found on a fingerboard or fretboard of a stringed instrument, such as a guitar. When a string is pressed down onto a fret and made to vibrate, a certain note is played.

Guilds Associations often dating from medieval times, formed by craftspeople, traders, or merchants engaged in a particular skill or occupation, to protect their work and maintain standards. Guilds usually provided apprenticeships to train young people.

Hieroglyphs The system of writing that uses small pictures to represent words, syllables, or sounds, and which was invented and used by, for example, the ancient Egyptians for religious scripts and texts.

Hit A song or a type of recording that is extremely popular, often selling many copies so that it enters the weekly bestseller charts or "hit parade."

Icons Sacred images from Christianity such as Christ, Mary, one of the saints or a scene from the Bible—sculpted or painted onto wooden panels and used as a centerpiece for prayer and worship.

Illuminations Paintings of characters, especially those made by medieval monks, to illustrate handwritten books, often to emphasize the first letter on a page.

Impasto A technique of applying oil or acrylic paint so thickly, with a brush or a palette knife, that the texture and thickness of the strokes remain in the paint.

Impressionism A technique developed by French artists in the 19th century, who painted very quickly outside, using tiny dabs of paint to give an idea of the subject, rather than a detailed and realistic image.

Jazz A form of popular music, originating from African Americans, often with a fast or syncopated rhythm, complicated musical pattern and tunes, and improvised words. (made up at the time).

Legend A popular traditional story or myth, about historical characters and past events, for which there is no modern proof that it is true.

Lithography A printing technique where an image is drawn in wax or oil onto a slab of stone or metal, and after treatment with chemicals such as acid and water, ink sticks only to the waxed or oiled areas and can then be transferred to paper.

Location A site outside a movie studio, where actors and crew film parts of a movie that need specialized backgrounds, scenery, and real places or buildings.

Logo An emblem, design, or symbol used by an organization, which appears on things concerned with that organization, such as buildings, vehicles, and clothing.

Manuscript The original handwritten (or more recently, typed) version of a book or document.

Mason A person who builds or works with stone.

Mass media The method by which information and news are communicated to the general public, usually by way of television, radio, and the press.

Melody A sequence of musical notes that travel up and down the scales, usually producing a recognizable and pleasant tune.

Mosaics Decorative patterns or pictures made by arranging pieces of coloured glass, tiles, or stones, often bedding them into cement or mortar to be firmly held.

Mural A painting made to decorate a wall, which may be applied directly to the surface such as the rock of a cave, or the plaster of a wall, or to canvas, which is then stuck onto the wall.

Music hall Usually a type of theater or concert hall, in which musical entertainment can be seen.

Neoclassicism A grand 19th-century style of painting that tried to recreate the formal artistic glory or classical tradition of ancient Greece and Rome.

Nobel Prizes Six international awards given annually to people who have made great achievements in physics, chemistry, physiology or medicine, literature, economics, and the promotion of peace. They are named after Swedish industrialist Alfred Nobel.

Opera A dramatic play in which the words are sung, accompanied by an orchestra. The play usually tells a story of great tragedy or love.

Oral culture Oral culture is passed on by speech, not by being written. In this way many of the world's epic tales, for example Homer's *Iliad* and *Odyssey* were told and retold by generations of Greeks before they were written down.

Patron A rich person, or benefactor, who pays, gives gifts to, or otherwise assists a poorer but talented person such as a musician, artist, or composer.

Perspective The technique of illustrating the three-dimensional space of the real world on a two-dimensional flat surface such as paper, for example, by showing things farther away as smaller, and making horizontal lines of walls, buildings and fences lead away toward a single point on the horizon.

Pigment A chemical that gives color to whatever contains it, for example, paints are made of finely ground crystalline pigments mixed with a base such as an oil.

Pioneer Someone who does things that no one has done before, such as exploring unknown lands, or developing new musical styles or playing techniques.

Porcelain A type of pottery invented in China more than 2,000 years ago, made from fine, white clay and ground glass, to produce delicate, thin-walled, translucent (almost see-through) pieces of china.

Primary colors Red, yellow, and blue pigments, from which all other colors can be made by mixing them—but which cannot be made by mixing other colors.

Projector A machine, such as a movie projector, that casts an enlarged image, either still or moving, onto a screen, wall, or some other smooth surface.

Prose The ordinary form of written language composed of phrases, sentences, and paragraphs, rather than broken up into lines or verses, as in songs or poems.

Quartet Any group of four. In music, the term usually refers to a group of singers, or musicians who play instruments from the same category, such as a string quartet.

Realism The 19th-century paintings of the real world, especially those of ordinary working people and their lives and hardships, which were subjects that previously had not been considered worthy of art.

Rehearsal Preparation for a public performance, such as playing a piece of music or acting in a play, by repeating and practising over and over again.

Renaissance "Rebirth," the period in history after the medieval time of the Dark Ages, when European artists and scholars began to rediscover and extend the classical knowledge of ancient Greeks and Romans; it generally dates from about AD 1400.

Resonate When the vibrations of a sound produce further vibrations in nearby objects or air spaces, which enhance or amplify (make louder) the original sound.

Ritual A ceremony or event that is always carried out in the same way, according to strict rules.

Romanticism Early 19th-century paintings and literature that illustrate powerful feelings and emotions, often suggesting a sentimental ideal but unrealistic view of reality.

Scribe A person who writes. Long ago, when few people could write and there was no printing, scribes copied out important documents and books.

Scriptures The writings of a particular religion. For example, the scriptures of the Christian religion in the Bible.

Scroll A long piece of paper or parchment (dried animal skin used like paper), with writing on it, which is rolled up for storage.

Surrealism A 20th-century painting style with strange, bizarre, unreal, often dreamlike images, which may be inspired by deep thoughts or the unconscious mind.

Symbolism An artistic style of the late 19th century where painters used symbols, or representations, to suggest ideas, which are inspired by the imagination rather than by reality.

Synchronized When things happen at the same time or in a set pattern. For example, in films, the sound recording runs alongside the film so that the actors' words are heard precisely when their lips move—words and movements are "in synch."

Synthesize To make artificially or put together from various sources. In music, the synthesizer is a machine that can make a huge variety of sounds electronically, which can resemble other instruments and even produce sound effects such as the wind, thunder, and lightning.

Take Part of a scene with words and action, shot without interruption during filming in a scene from a movie.

Tapestry A thick piece of fabric on which a picture or pattern is created, either during the original weaving process, or by embroidery stitches added afterward.

Textiles A term originally used only for cloth made by weaving (passing crosswise threads, or weft, between lengthways threads, or warp), but now used for fabric made by any different methods.

Theory A set or system of ideas or proposals, which tries to explain how something works or happens. Theories are tested by observing and doing experiments, to find out if they are true.

Tradition The passing on of the culture of a group of people from old to young, including their customs, stories, history, and beliefs.

Tragedy A very sad event, such as an unhappy love affair or an appalling crime or a disaster. In theater, the term refers to a play about a sequence of unhappy events which usually end for the worst.

Transmission The transferring or moving of something from one place to another. Nowadays the term usually refers to the sending out or broadcasting of the radio signals for a radio or television.

TV network A large group of broadcasting stations, operated by a single organization, which are linked so that they can send out, or broadcast, the same programs over a large area, such as an entire country or continent.

Vibrations Regular, repeated, often rapid movements, to and fro. Musical instruments work by vibrating particles or molecules in the air, which are called sound waves and pass through the air to the ears.

Western movies Films about people exploring and settling in western North America, mainly in the 19th and early 20th centuries, especially people descended from the European arrivals in North America, their struggles against the elements and their dealings with the Native North American peoples (Indians).

Zoepraxiscope A device that gives the illusion of a moving image, when a series of pictures on the inside of a spinning cylinder are viewed through vertical slits in the cylinder.

Index

Page numbers in *italics* refer to illustrations.

A

Aaron 83
aborigines 192, *192*, 217, 274, 276, 277, *277*, 313, 345
  dance 456
  music 442, *442*
Abraham 204
absolute zero 374, 389, *389*, 428
abstract art 440
Abu Simbel, Egypt 312, 313, *313*
abyssal plain 106, *106*
AC/DC current electricity 382
Academy Awards 479
acceleration 387, 428
acetone 378, *378*
Achernar 15
Achilles 211
Aconcagua, Argentina 98
acoustics 393
acrobats 450, 453
actors 450–451, *450–451*, 452, 475, 478–479, *478–479*
Adams, John Couch 46
Adirondacks, USA 98
Aeneid 212, 213
aerodynamics 411, *411*
  bridge construction 403
aerosols 123
Afghanistan 280
Africa 86, *86*, 87, 90, *90*, 91, 252, 253, *253*, 262–263, *262–263*, 336, 337
  art 439, *439*
  colonization 356–357, *356–357*, 361
  dance 456, 460, *460*
  deserts 110
  factfile 263
  music 443, *443*
  people and places 264–265, *264–265*
  tectonic plate 91
African clawed toad 156, *156*
African rock python 160
aftershocks 95
Age of Reason 349
ages 76

agriculture 144, *144*, 145, *145*, 312–313, 314, 315, 320, 332, 333
  Agricultural Revolution 350–351, *350–351*, *364*, 366
air 29, 114, 124, 394–395, *394–395*, 428
  air pressure 115, *115*, 375
  hot-air balloons 388, *388*
  mountains 99
  radiators 389, *389*
  resistance 386
  transport 410–411, *410–411*
aircraft 117
  aluminum 82
  military 392, *392*
airports 411
Akashi-Kaikyo Bridge, Japan 268, *268*, 402, 403
Akbar 328
Akhenaten (Amenhotep IV) 195, *195*
Akkad dynasty 312
Al Qaeda 353, 363
alan (mythical creature) 217
Alaric the Visigoth 313, 319, 322, 323
Alaska, USA 254
Albania 280
albatrosses 150
Alcántara Bridge, Spain 402
Alcock, Sir John 230, *230*
Aldrin, Buzz 62, 63, *63*
Aleutian Islands, USA 95
Aleutian Mountains 99
Alexander the Great 313, *313*, 317
Alfred the Great 230, 325, *325*, 326
algae 134, *134*, 141, 145
algebra 298
Algeria 265, 280
alimentary canal 181
Allies 366
alligators 160
alloys 428
Alpha Centauri 391
Alpha stars 15, 16
alphabets 462, 463, *463*
Alps 270, 271
Altacama Desert, Chile 110
Altiplano, Bolivia 261
altostratus clouds 118, *118*
aluminum 81, 82, 125
alveoli 178, *178*, 188, 189
Amazon 259, 260

Amazon River 87, 103, 112, 258, *258*
amber 82, 85, 382
American football 220, 221, *221*, 228
America *see* Central America; Latin America; North America; South America; United States of America (USA)
American Civil War 352–353, *353*
American Falls, USA 254, *254*
American War of Independence 343, 345
amethyst 82, 83, *83*
ammonia 40, 42, 72
  molecules 373
ammonites 77, *77*, 85, *85*
amphibians 76, 147, *147*, 156–157, *156–157*
  reptiles 160
Amsterdam, Netherlands 481, *481*
amulets 194, *194*, 195, *195*
Amundsen, Roald 278
Amundsen-Scott base, Antarctica 278
Anansi the Spider 466
ancestor worship 432, 433, 452, 453, *453*
Anderson, Elizabeth, Garrett 230
Andes 98, 99, *99*, 105, 112, 258, 261
Andorra 280
Andromeda Galaxy 18, 19
anesthetics 422
Angel Falls, Venezuela 103
angel sharks 153, *153*
angiosperms 135, 137, 141
Angkor Wat, Cambodia 209, *209*
anglerfish 152
angles 425, *425*, 427, *427*, 428
Anglo-Saxons 322, 323, *323*, 366
  invasion of Britain 324
Angola 280
animals 73, 76, 114, 132, 146–147, *146–147*, 394
  Africa 262
  Antarctica 278, 279, *279*
  brain weights 164
  caves 108

communication 164–165, *164–165*
  deserts 111
  endangered species 170–171, *170–171*
  fastest lan d animals 150
  feeding 154–155, *154–155*
  fossils 77, 84–85, *84–85*
  most farm animals, by country 281
  North America 254
  Oceania 274
  movement 150–151, *150–151*
  rainforests 112
  record breakers 147
  reef formation 88, 89
  reproduction 158–159, *158–159*
  rock formation 80
  seed germination 141
  South America 259
  trade 170
  young animals 158
animatronics 479, *479*
Annapurna 99
annual plants 140, 188
Antarctic Ocean *see* Southern Ocean
Antarctica 86, *86*, 87, 90, 90, 91, 121, 123, 253, *253*, 278–279, *278–279*
  Antarctic Circle 87
  Antarctic Treaty 87, 278
  icebergs 101
  factfile 279
  mineral wealth 278
  tectonic plate 91
Antares 15
antelopes 111
anthers 136, *136*, 188
antimatter 12, 68
Antigua 280
ants 146
Anubis 207, *207*
anus 181
anvil lightning 119
apartheid 362, 366
apes 159, 168
aphelion 29
Apollo 62–63, *62–63*
Appleton, Sir Edward 230
aquamarine 82, 83, *83*
Arabian Desert 110, 111
Arabian Sea 107
Arabic numbers 424, *424*
arachnids 146

Aral Sea, Asia 105
Archaeopteryx 77, 77, 133, 133, 166
archery 387, 387
arches 400, 400
   bridges 402, 402, 403, 403
   horseshoe arches 401
Archimedes 230, 230
   Archimedes' screw 387, 397
archipelagos 88, 89
architecture 316, 480–481, 480–481
   modern 482–483, 482–483
Arctic 86, 88
   Arctic Circle 87
   Arctic Institute Glacier, Antarctica 101
   Arctic Ocean 106, 107, 253, 253
   icebergs 101
Arcturus 15
Argentina 75, 98, 260, 261, 280
argon 377
Aristophanes 451
Aristotle 230, 316
Arkwright, Sir Richard 230, 351
Armada, Spanish 339, 338–339, 366
Armenia 280
armies 312, 313, 334
   Roman 319, 319
   Spartan 317
armor 327, 366
Armstrong, Louis "Satchmo" 448, 448
Armstrong, Neil 62, 63, 63
art 438–439, 439–438
   earliest 432–433, 432–432
   Europe 434–435, 434–435, 440–441, 440–441
   modern art 440–441, 440–441
   movies 478
   royalty 439
   techniques 436–437, 436–437
art academies 434, 434, 435
Art Deco 482
Art Nouveau 482
Arthur, King 462, 462
artists 432, 435
Arts and Crafts 482
arteries 173, 173, 182, 183,

183, 188
Arthur, King 214, 215, 230
artificial materials 377, 428
artists 334, 335, 335
arum lily frog 156, 156
Aryans 314
asexual reproduction 158
Asia 86, 86, 87, 90, 90, 91, 98, 253, 253, 266–267, 266–267
   decline 346–347, 346–347
   factfile 267
   people and places 268–269, 268–269
   medieval 330–331, 330–331
Asimov, Isaac 467
Asoka Mourya 328, 329
aspirin 145
Assyria 314, 315
asteroids 26, 31, 49, 52–53, 52–53, 68
   Asteroid Belt 52, 53, 53
asthenosphere 78, 78
Aston Martin cars 407
astrological signs 55, 55
astronauts 62–63, 62–63, 64, 65
astronomers 13, 15, 16, 23, 26, 28, 29, 37
astronomy 54, 54, 362
Atacama Desert, South America 258
Athelney treasure 324, 324
Athens 316, 317
athletics 218, 224–225, 224–225
Atlantic Ocean 88, 103, 106, 107
Atlas 197, 197
atmosphere 68, 392
   Earth 15, 30, 72, 73, 76, 114–115, 114–115
   Mercury 34
   Moon 32
   Neptune 46
   Uranus 45
   Venus 36
atolls 89, 89
Atomium, Brussels 483, 483
atoms 12, 15, 68, 77, 372–373, 372–373, 428
   atom bombs 15, 359
   compounds 378, 379
   electricity 372
   electrons 379, 379
   elements 373
   molecules 378

nuclear power 421
Periodic Table 376–377, 376–377, 429
Attila the Hun 322
Attlee, Clement 230–231, 231
Auckland, New Zealand 75
Aurigae constellation 15
Aurora Borealis 115, 115
Augustus Caesar 213
Augustus 312, 318
Aurangzeb 328, 346
Austen, Jane 231, 467, 472
Australia 75, 81, 86, 86, 89, 90, 90, 91, 280, 344, 345, 356, 357, 364
   aborigines 274, 276, 277, 277
   Australian Desert 111
   desert 274, 274
   mineral wealth 277
   satellites 61
   world's longest fence 281
Austria 280, 342, 343, 352
   music 444, 445
axis of the Earth 75, 75
axles 398, 399
axons 184, 184
Ayckbourne, Alan 451
Ayers Rock, Australia 274, 274
Azerbaijan 281
Aztecs 207, 215, 221, 256, 332, 333, 333, 365, 366
   music 442

B
B-2 stealth aircraft 392, 392
Baba Yaga 215, 412, 463
Babbage, Charles 231
babies 175, 186–187, 186–187, 252, 484, 485
Babur 328, 328
Babylonia 16, 127, 192, 314
Bach, Johann Sebastian 444, 444, 445
backbones 77, 175
bacteria 105, 132, 145, 183, 394, 428
badminton 218, 219, 222
Baffin Island 88, 101
Bahamas 281
Baird, John Logie 231, 471, 471
Bali 214, 456
ball lightning 119
ballad singers 451, 451
ballet 458–459, 458–459

positions and steps 459
ballroom dancing 461, 461
balls 220, 223
Baltic Sea 106
bamboo 136
Bangladesh 119, 123
Bangkok, Thailand 269, 269
Bangladesh 266, 281
banking 334
   Bank of England 342, 342
bankruptcy 366
banshees 215, 215
Bantus 313
Barbados 281
barbarians 322–323, 322–323, 366
   new states 324–325, 324–325
Barbuda 280
Barcelona, Spain 482, 482
bark 137, 137, 143, 143
barnstorming 454
Barnum & Bailey Circus 453
Barnum, Phileas T 214
barons 326
Barrett Browning, Elizabeth 467, 467
barred spiral galaxies 18, 18
baseball 218, 220, 220
basilisks 217
basketball 221
Bastet 194, 194
bath houses (thermae) 318
bathyscapes 409
bats 108, 108, 150, 154, 168, 169, 393, 393
batteries 382
bauxite 82, 82, 125
Bayeux Tapestry 51, 51
Bayreuth Festival, Germany 445
beach volleyball 221
beaches, coral 89
bead lightning 119
beans 142, 142
bears 150, 151, 151
Beatles, The 231, 449, 449
Beaufort Scale 119, 119
Becket, St Thomas (à) 231, 231
Becket, Samuel 451
Becky Sharp 475
Bede, St 231
bees 146, 149
   honeybees 164
Beethoven, Ludvig von 231,

444, *444*, 445
beetles 146, 148
Beijing, China 75, 269, *269*, 331
Beijing Opera 453, 460, *460*
Belarus 281
belemnites 85
Belgium 281
Belize 281–282
Bell, Alexander Graham 231
Benin 282, 439
Benz, Karl and Berto 396
Beowulf 210, *210*, 463, *463*
Bering Sea 107
Berliner, Emile 397, 449
Berlin Wall, Germany 360, *360*
Berners-Lee, Tim 232, 414
beryl 82, *82*
Bes 195, *195*
Beta stars 15, 16
Bhutan 282
Bhutan glory butterfly 149, *149*
Bible 83, 204, 206, 217, 315, 451, 465
bicycles 407
biennial plants 140, 188
Big Bang 12–13, *12–13*, 68, 388
Big Crunch 13
Big Dipper constellation 16, *16*
biggest planet 26, 40
Bin Laden, Osama 353, 363
binary numbers 424, *424*, 428
binoculars 17, 20
biosphere 30
biplanes 411, *411*, 428
bipolar "butterfly" nebulae 23, *23*
birds 76, 84, 111, 147, *147*, 166–167, *166–167*
anatomy 166, *166*
Archaeopteryx 77, *77*, 133, *133*, 166
birds of prey 155, 159, 167
display 159, *159*
fastest flier 150
birthdays 484, 485
birthstones 82, 83, *83*
Bismarck 359
Bismarck, Otto 357
bison 173
bits (binary digits) 413
black holes 18, 24–25, *24–25*, 68
Milky Way 20, 21

black ice 118
Black Prince 327, *327*
black smokers 107
bladder 172, *172*, 181, 188
Blake, William 232, *232*
block and tackle 398, *398*
block printing 438, *438*, 468
blockades 366
blood 182–183, *182–183*
blubber 278
blues 448
blue stars 14, 15
board games 218
Boeing aircraft 410, *410*
Boeing Company plant, USA 400
Boeing Delta II 25, *25*, 35, *35*
Boers 353, 366
boiling point 375, 428
Bolivar, Simón 355
Bolivia 261, 282, 283
Bollywood 477, *477*
Bolshoi Ballet 459
Bonaparte, Napoleon 244, *244*, 353, 354–355, *354–355*
bonds 372, 428
covalent bonds 379, *379*
ionic bonds 379, *379*
bones 174–175, *174–175*, 395
fossils 76, 84, 85
Bonnie Prince Charlie *see* Stuart, Charles Edward
books 348, 349, 434
printing 468–469, *468–469*
Bootis constellation 15
boreal forests 266
boreholes into the Earth's crust 79
Borneo 88
Bosphorus Bridge, Turkey 403
Botswana 282
Boudicca 232
boxing 222, 228, 229
Boyle, Robert 232
brachiopods 85
Brachiosaurus 163
Bradman, Sir Donald 229
Brahma 202, *202*, 203
Brahms, Johannes 445
brain 184–185, *184–185*
Brashnahan, George 225
brass 446
breakdancing 460, 461, *461*
Brazil 109, 261, 282, 284
Brazilian Coastal Range 99
breathing 178–179, *178–179*

breeding *see* reproduction
brick 402
bridges 379, 402–403, *402–403*, 482, *482*
bascule bridges 403, *403*
beam bridges 403, *403*
cable-stayed bridges 403, *403*
cantilevered bridges 403, *403*
clapper bridges 402
longest bridges 268, 291, 402
piers 402, *402*
suspension bridges 402, *402*, 403, *403*
brightest stars 15
bristlecone pines 143, *143*
Britain 256, 270, 324, 347, 352
Battle of Britain 358, *358–359*, 359
Industrial Revolution 350–351, *350–351*
world wars 358, 359
British Broadcasting Corporation (BBC) 471
British East India Company 342
British Isles 88
Britons, ancient 313, 322
Brittany 457, *457*
Britten, Benjamin 445
Britten, Benjamin 232
broadband 417
broadcasting 448, 470–471, *470–471*
broadleaved plants 135, *135*, 188
bronchi 178, *178*, 179
Brontë sisters 232, *232*
Bronze Age 197, 198
Brown, Lancelot 'Capability' 232
browsers 417
browsing animals 155
Bruce, Robert the (Robert I) 232–233
Brunei 282
Brunel, Isambard Kingdom 233, *233*
Bruno, Frank 229
Brutalism 482
bryophytes 141
Buddhism 204, 205, 208, 209, 321, 328, 329, *329*
art 438

scriptures 464, 465, *465*
Buenos Aires, Argentina 75, 260, *260*
buildings 125, 379, 480–481, *480–481*, 482–483, *482–483*
construction 400–401, *400–401*
world's tallest buildings 401
bulbs 138, *138*, 139
Bulgaria 252, 282, 285
bulge of the Earth 75
bullet-proof vests 379
bunyip 217, *217*
buoyancy 395
Burkino Faso 282
Burma 282–283
Burney, Venetia 48
Burns, Robert 233, *233*
Burundi 283
buses 406
Bush, George W 353, 363
bushes 135
butterflies 146, 149, *149*
bytes 413
Byzantium 322, 323, 366

C

cables 414, 420, 421
cacti 137, *137*
Caerlaverock Castle, Scotland 272
Cage, Nicholas 478, *478*
Cairo, Egypt 264, *264*
calcium 81
calcium carbonate 108, 109
calculus 298
calderas 93
calendars 75
Aztecs 332, 340
California, USA 87
Callisto 41, *41*
Caloris Basin, Mercury 34
Cambodia 283
Cambrian Period 76
camcorders 419, *419*, 470, *470*
camels 111
camouflage 188
newts and salamanders 157
Campbell, Donald 407
Bluebird 407, *407*
Campion, Edmund 339
Canada 81, 256, 258, 283, 336, *336*

forests 254
Nunavut 257
water 105
canals, Mars 38
canals, world's busiest 409
cane toad 157
Canis Major constellation 15
Canis Minoris constellation 15
cannons 335, *335*
canopic jars 207
Canopus 15
canyons 96, *96*, 97
Cape Canaveral, USA 25
Cape Town, South Africa 264, *264*
Cape Verde Islands 283, 336
Capella 15
capillaries 182, 183, 188
capitalism 360
caracals 151, *151*, 169, *169*
caravels 336, *336*, 366
carbon 82
carbon dioxide 36, 73, 92, 114, 115, 138, 139, 188, 373, 428
carbon cycle 381
breathing 178, 179
chemicals 380–381, *380–381*
compounds 380, 381
global warming 122
carbon dioxide 428
Carboniferous Period 76, 124
cards 218, *218*
Caribbean 254, 255, *255*, 256, *256*, 364
Caribbean Sea 107
Carinae constellation 15
Carlsbad Cavern, USA 109
Carnera, Primo 228
Carnival 452, 460, 461, *461*
carnivores 154, 155, 157, 188
carpels 141, 188
Carroll, Lewis 233
carrots 136, *136*
cars 122, 123, 357, *357*, 406–407, *406–407*
engines 420
invention 396
Oakland Bay Bridge, San Francisco, USA 402
Carthage 313
Cartier, Jacques 337, *337*
cartilage 147, 152, 175, 188
Caruso, Enrico 449
Caspian Sea 105

Casseiopia constellation 16
cassette tapes 418
Cassini 42, 59
casting 272, 437, *437*
castles 481, *481*
Castro, Fidel 361, *361*
cat sharks 158, *158*
Çatal Hüyük, Turkey 480, *480*
cathedrals 481, *481*
cathode-ray tubes 418, 419
Catholicism 338–339
cats 133, 151, 155, 164, 168, 169, *169*, 195
cattle 123, *123*, 155
Caucasus 270
cave paintings 109, *109*, 432, *432*
caves 108–109, *108–109*
deepest 109
longest systems 108, 109
Cavour, Camillo Benso di, Count 355
Caxton, William 233
CDs (compact discs) 418, *418*, 419, 449, 471
celery 137, *137*
cells 138, 188
anatomy 172, *172*
blood cells 182–183, *182–183*
sperm 186, *186*
celluloid 474, *474*
cellulose 381
Celsius 389
Celts 433
mythology 206, 207, *207*, 213, *213*
cement 125
Cenozoic Era 76
Centauri constellation 15
centaurs 217
centaury 145, *145*
Central African Republic 283
Central America 254, 256, 312–313, 332–333, *332–333*, 340
central heating 318
central processing units (CPUs) 412, 413
cephalopds 146, 148
Cerberus 217, *217*
Ceres 52, 53
Cervantes, Miguel de 467
CFCs (chlorofluorocarbons) 123, *123*
chalcopyrite 125

chalk 80, 81, *81*
chameleons 161, *161*
Chandra X Ray Observatory 21
Chandragupta Mourya 328
Chao Meng Fu Crater, Mercury 35, *35*
Chaplin, Charlie 233, 474, *474*
charcoal 380
Charge Coupled Devices (CCDs) 56, 57, 68
chariot racing 218
Charlemagne 233, 327
Charles I 342, 343, *343*, 348
Charles II 233, 342–343, 348, *348*, 349
Charles de Gaulle Airport, Paris, France 411
Charleston (dance) 461, *461*
Charon 48, 49
Chasmosaurus 163, *163*
Chaucer, Geoffrey 234
cheetahs 150, *150*
Chekhov, Anton 451
chemicals 80, 82, 378–379, *378–379*
chemical bonds 372
chemical elements 81, *81*
chemical formula 372, 428
names for everyday items 379
chess 298
Chichén Itzá 256, *256*
chicks 167, *167*
children 484, 485
children's literature 466, 467
Chile 260, 261, 283, 289, 341
chimaera 217
China 75, 87, 91, 95, 206, 268, 269, 283, 335, 336, 342, 346
ancestor worship 433, *433*
ancient China 313, 320–321, *320–321*
barbarian invasions 322, 323
bicycles 407
block printing 468
clocks 321, *321*
Communism 361
compasses 397, *397*
fireworks 397, *397*
medieval 330–331
myths 193, *193*, 216, 217
numbers 424, *424*
playing cards 218, *218*
population 485

satellites 61
theater 453
zoos 282
Ch'ing dynasty 342
Chippendale, Thomas 234
chlorine 378
chlorophyll 138, 139, 188
Cho Oyu 99
chocolate 375
consumption of 285
Chopin, Frederick 445
Christ the Redeemer, Rio de Janeiro, Brazil 261, *261*
Christianity 204, 205, 207, 208, 312, 356, 433, 434, 452
drama 451
religious wars 338–339, *338–339*
scriptures 465, *465*
Christmas 205, 471
Christo 441
Christy, James 48
chrome 278
chromosomes 188
chromosphere 28, *28*, 68
chronometers 396, *396*
chrons 76
Chuquicamata, Chile 260
churches 208
Churchill, John "Duke of Marlborough" 234, *234*
Churchill, Sir Winston 234, 359, *359*
chyme 181
Cibola 341
cinema 474–475, *474–475*
home entertainment 473, *473*
making movies 476–477, *476–477*
special effects and superstars 478–479, *478–479*
circles 424, 425, *425*, 428
circulatory system 173, *173*
circumference 428
circus 453, 455
cirques 100, *100*
cirrus clouds 116, *116*, 117, *117*, 118, *118*
cities 252
citric acid 379
civil wars 342, 343, 348, 352–353, *353*, 366
civilization 268, 313, 314, 315, *315*, 322, 366, 484

Middle East 314–315, *314–315*
clapperboards 477, *477*
clarinets 446, *446*
Clarke, Arthur C 467
classical mythology 196–197, *196–197*, 210, *210*, 213, *213*, 216, *216*, 217, *217*
classical music 444–445, *444–445*
claws 77, 85
clay 125
cleaner wrasse 153, *153*
climate 120–121, *120–121*
  continental 121
  forests 112–113, *112–113*
  global warming 122–123, *122–123*
  oceanic 121
Clive, Robert 342–343, 346, 347
clones 188
Clooney, George 478, *478*
cloth 351
clothing 484–485, *484–485*
cloud to air lightning 119
cloud to ground lightning 119
clouded leopards 169, *169*
clouds 72, 116–117, *116–117*
  appearance of Earth 31, *31*
  Jupiter 40
  Neptune 46
  Venus 36
clowns 450, 453, *453*
clusters 68
  galaxies 18
  stars 15, 17
CN Tower, Canada 483, *483*
coal 122, 124, 278, 380
  seam formation 124, *124*
  world's largest reserves 298
Coalbrookdale Iron Bridge, England 402
coats of arms 326
cobras 161, 164, 165, *165*
cockatrices 217
cockroaches 77
coconuts 142
cod 278
coffee 261
coins 317, *317*
coke 342, 351
cold 87, 97, 120, 121
  planets 40, 42, 44
cold-blooded animals 160, 161

Cold War 360–361, *360–361*, 366
Coleridge, Samuel Taylor 467
collage 437, *437*
collagen 174
Colombia 283–284
Colorado River, USA 96, *96*, 97
Colosseum, Rome 480, *480*
colonization 366
  Africa 356–357, *356–357*, 361
  India 342–343, 346, 347
  North America 340, 341, 342, 343
color 119, 391
  animal communication 164
  color wheel 437, *437*
  gemstones 82
  minerals 81, *81*
  pigments 437
  sky 115
  stars 14
  Venus 37
Columbia Glacier, USA 101
Columbus, Christopher 234, 336, 337, *337*, 364
Comaneci, Nadia 228
comets 26, 50–51, *50–51*, 68
Commedia dell'Arte 453
Commodus 312
Commonwealth 366
communications 414–415, *414–415*
  computers 416
Communism 353, 360, 361, 362, 366
Comoros 284
compasses 397, *397*
composers 444–445, *444–445*
composites 379
compounds 378, 379, 428
  carbon 380, 381
computers 412–413, *412–413*
  abbreviations 413
  art 441
  buildings 482
  central processing units (CPUs) 412, 413
  Internet 416–417, *416–417*
  laptops 417, *417*
  Millennium Bug 363
  personal computers (PCs) 413
  publishing 469, *469*
  viruses 415

world's most powerful 412
Conceptual Art 441
condensation 375
conduction 388
conductors 378, *378*, 382, 428, 445, *445*
cones 426, *426*
Confucius 205, 234, 321, *321*, 346, 465, 481
Congo Brazzaville 284
Congo, Democratic Republic of 284
Congress of Vienna 355
Congreve, William 451
conifers 76, 113, 135, 137, 188
  coniferous forest 143
conquistadors *365*, 366
Constable, John 234, 435, 436
Constantine the Great 313, *313*
Constantinople 322, *322*, 334, 339
constellations 16–17, *16–17*, 68
  brightest stars 15
construction 400–401, *400–401*
  world's tallest buildings 401
continents 72, 86–87, *86–87*, 252, *252*, 253, *253*
  climate 121
  continental crust 78, *78*, 79
  continental drift 90–91, *90–91*
  continental shelf 106, *106*
  farmworkers 287
contrails 117
convection 388, 389
convection currents 78
convicts 356, 357, 366
Coober Pedy, Australia 277
Cook, Captain James 234, *234*, 278, 344, *344*, 357, *357*, 364
Cooper, Anthony Ashley (Lord Shaftesbury) 234–235
Cooper, Charlotte 227
Copernicus, Nicolaus 30, 235
copper 260, 261, 276, 278, 377, 382
coprolites 162
coracles 397, *397*
corals 133, *133*
  coral reefs 88, 89, 148, *148*
core of Earth 30–31, *30–31*, 72, 78, *78*, 79

core of Jupiter 40
core of Mercury 34
core of Sun 28, *28*
corries 100
corona 28, *28*, 68
corn 145
Cort, Henry 351
Cortés, Hernan 340
cortex 185, *185*, 188
corundum 82
Cossacks 456, 457, *457*
Costa Rica 284
cotton 144, 145
cotyledons 143
countries 252
  flags 306–309
  largest by area 391
  most farm animals, by country 281
  most populated countries 292
country and western music 448
coups 361, 367
courtship 159
covalent bonds 379, *379*
coyotes 201, *201*
Crab Nebula 22
crabs 107, 146
crafts 439
Craigellachie Bridge, Scotland 403
cranes 398
Crater Lake, USA 105
craters 73, *73*
  Chao Meng Fu Crater, Mercury 35, *35*
  crater lakes 105
  Kulper Crater, Mercury 35, *35*
  Mercury 34
  Meteor Crater, Arizona, USA 52, *52*
  Moon 32, 33
creation myths 192–193, *192–193*, 204, *204*, 206, *206*, 464
  Native Americans 200
crescent Moon 32, 33, *33*
Cretaceous Period 76
crevasses 100, *100*
cricket 218, *218*, 220, 229
Crimean War 352
crinoids 85
Croatia 284
crocodiles 147, 159, 160, 161
Cromwell, Oliver 235, 342,

342, 348, *348*
crop production 145
crows 165
Cruise, Tom 478, *478*
Crusades 327, *365*, 367, 400
crust of the Earth 72, 78, *78*, 79
crustaceans 146
crystals 80, 81, 82, *82*
  birthstones 83, *83*
Cuba 284, 361
Cuban Missile Crisis 353, 360
cubes 425, *425*, 426, *426*
Cubism 440, *440*
Cuchulain 213, *213*
Culloden, Battle of 342, 349, *349*
cultures 83, 252, 272, 334, 484–485, *484–485*
cumulonimbus clouds 116, *116*, 118, *118*
cumulus clouds 116, *116*, 117, *117*
cuneiform 192
Cuquenan Falls, Venezuela 103
Curie, Marie and Pierre 235, *235*
Curse of Frankenstein 479, *479*
cycads 135, 137
cycling 219
Cyclops 197, *197*
Cygnus constellation 16, *16*
cylinders 426, *426*
cymbals 446
Cyprus 284
Czars 339, 348, 367
Czech Republic 284

D

Daedalus 210, *210*
Daimler, Gottlieb 406
daisies 141, *141*
Dalai Lama 342, 481
Dali, Salvador 440, 441
Dallas Airport, USA 411
Dallol, Ethiopia 110, 121
Damascus, Syria 324
dams 261
  world's biggest 401
  world's highest 295
dance 450, 460–461, *460–461*
  ballet 458–459, *458–459*
  popular dances 461
Darby, Abraham 342, 351, 402

Darius the Great 315, *315*
dark nebulae 22, 23
dark side of the Moon 32
darkness 74, 119
darts 219
Darwin, Charles Robert 235
data 428
David and Goliath 465, *465*
da Vinci, Leonardo 241, 334, 435
Davies, Emily 235
Davy, Sir Humphry 235
day 74, 75
Dead Sea, Israel 104, *104*, 105
Dead Sea Scrolls 464, *464*
death 252, 294
death's head hawkmoth 149, *149*
Death Valley, USA 87, 254
decibels 392, 428
deciduous trees and plants 113, 143, 188
decimal system 328, 424
deer 155
Defoe, Daniel 467
deforestation 113, *113*, 123
Deimos 38, *38*, 39
deltas 103
de 'Medici, Catherine 339
democracy 348, 360, 367
Denmark 89, 256, 284
dependencies 302–305
depression, economic 358, 367
Descartes, René 235
deserts 76, 86, 97, 110–111, *110–111*, 252, 255, 258, 266, 274
  mountains 98
  plants 137, *137*
  world's largest 110, 111, 282
design 441, 469
deuterium 420
Devonian Period 76
Diadectid fossil insect 91
Diaghilev, Serge 459
diameter 428
diamonds 82, 83, *83*, 380
Dias, Bartholomeu 336
dice 218
Dickens, Charles 235
Dickson, William 475
dictatorships 367
didgeridoos 442, *442*
diesel locomotives 404–405,

404–405
digital information 428
digital recording 418
digestion 180–181, *180–181*, 188
dinosaurs 53, 81, 84, 148, 162–163, *162–163*
  biggest 162
  extinction 76
  footprints 85, *85*
  names 163
Diplodocus 163
discovery of planets 26, 27, 45
Discovery Rupes Scarp, Mercury 35, *35*
discus 224, 225
diseases
  insects 149
  top global causes of death 294
Disney World, Florida, USA 257
Disraeli, Benjamin 235–236
distance of planets from Sun 27
Diwali 439, *439*
Djibouti 284
DNA (deoxyribonucleic acid) 187, 188, 423, 428
doctors 252, 423
dodos 170, *170*
dogs 133, 154
dolphins 151, 168, 170, *170–171*, 392, 393, *393*
Dome of the Rock, Jerusalem 208, *208*
Dominica 284–285
Dominican Republic 285
dominoes 218
Don Quixote 467
Donatello 334
double bass 443, 446, *446*
Doyle, Arthur Conan 467
Dracula 297
drag 387
dragonflies 77, *77*, 146, 154
dragons 216, *216*
Drake, Sir Francis 236, *236*, 336, 339
drama 316, 450–451, *450–451*, 452–453, *452–453*
  ancient Greece 317, *317*
  modern 454–455, *454–455*

world theater 452–453, *452–453*
drought 119
drums 442, *442*, 446
  drum kits 447, *447*
dryness 87
duck-billed platypus 168, *168*
Duncan, Isadora 458, *458*
dust 14, 15, 20, 22, 26, 72, 92, *92*, 114, 115, 121
  Earth's formation 30
  Saturn's rings 43, *43*
DVDs 419, 473
dynasties 312, 313, 321, 328, 329, 367
  China 320, 324, 330, 331, 342, 346, 352

E

e-mail 415
ears 168
  sound 392–393, *392–393*
eagles 154, 167
Earth 27, *27*, 30–31, *30–31*
  ages of 76–77, *76–77*
  appearance of 31, *31*
  asteroid collision 31, 52, *52*, 53
  atmosphere 114–115, *114–115*
  caves 108–109, *108–109*
  climate 120–121, *120–121*
  compared to Mars 38
  constellations 16, 17
  continental drift 90–91, *90–91*
  deserts 110–111, *110–111*
  distance from Sun 27, 29
  driest place 110
  earthquakes 94–95, *94–95*
  forests 112–113, *112–113*
  formation of 72–73, *72–73*
  galaxies visible from 18, 19
  glaciers 100–101, *100–101*
  global warming 122–123, *122–123*
  hottest place 110
  interior of 78–79, *78–79*
  islands 88–89, *88–89*
  lakes 104–105, *104–105*
  landscapes 96–97, *96–97*
  magnetism 383
  Mariner 35
  mountains 98–99, *98–99*
  oceans 106–107, *106–107*
  resources 124–125,

124–125
rivers 102–103, *102–103*
seas 106–107, *106–107*
spinning 74–75, *74–75*, 107, 127
Sun 29
Venus 26, 37
volcanoes 92–93, *92–93*
weather 116–119, *116–119*
wettest place 121
earthquakes 78, 94–95, *94–95*, 258
earthquake waves 79, *79*, 94, *94*
major 95
Richter Scale 95, *95*
San Andreas Fault, USA 254
tectonic plates 91
earthworms 150, 151, *151*
earwigs 146
east 74, 75
East China Sea 107
East Timor 285
Easter Island, Polynesia 276, *276*
eating 180–181, *180–181*, 485
echinoderms 149
echoes 393
echolocation 392, 393, *393*
eclipses 29, *29*, 68
lunar eclipses 32
ecliptic 30
ecotourism 171
economics 342, 346
Great Depression 358
ecosystems 394
Ecuador 285, 341
Edison, Thomas Alva 236, *236*, 418, 449, 475
Edward III 236
eels 153
eggs 85, 166, 167, *167*
dinosaurs 163
human reproduction 186, *186*, 187
eggs 85
Egypt 127, 285
Suez Canal *365*
Egypt, ancient 206, 312, 313, *313*
astronomy 16, 54
creation myths 193
dance 456, *456*
gods 194–195, *194–195*, 207, *207*
hieroglyphs 463, *463*
music 442

numbers 424
pharaohs 314, 315, *315*
pyramids *365*, 480, *480*
ships 408
sundials 397, *397*
tomb paintings 432, 433, *433*
Eiffel Tower, Paris, France 400, *400*
Eighty Years War 342
Einstein, Albert 236, 387
El Greco 435
El Salvador 285
electricity 12, 82, 122, 382–383, *382–383*, 384, 420, 428
black holes 24, 25, *25*
computers 412, 413
distribution 420, *420*, 421, *421*
household appliances 383
wind turbines 125, *125*
electromagnetism 382, *382*, 383
electromagnetic radiation 56, 384, 428
light 390
electrons 15, 382, 428
atoms 379, *379*
Periodic Table 376–377, *376–377*, 429
television 418, 419
elements 72, 81, *81*, 428
compounds 378, 379
liquid 375
Periodic Table 376–377, *376–377*, 429
elephants 77, 154, *154*, 155, 159, 168, 328
Elgar, Sir Edward 236, 435
Eliot, George (Mary Anne Evans) 236
Elizabeth I 236–237, *237*, 338, 339, *339*, 342
Elizabeth II 237
elliptical galaxies 18, *18*
emeralds 82, 83, *83*
emergency signals at sea 409
Empedocles 376
emperor penguins 87, 279, *279*
emperors 367
China 320, 321, 324, 346, 347, *347*
India 328, 329, 346
Japan 313, 321, 324,

330
Rome 312, 313, 318, 319
empires 356, 361, 367
Austro-Hungarian 352
British 347, 356–357, *356–357*
Chinese 347
Holy Roman 326, *326*, 327, 367
Ottoman 342, 343, 346, 367
Roman 318–319, *318–319*
Empty Quarter (Rub'al-khali) 110
emus 166
endangered species 188
endocrine glands 181, *181*
endoscopes 422
energy 12, 384–385, *384–385*
energy consumption 257
energy conversion 384
energy transfer 384
heat 384, 388–389, *388–389*, 428
light 384, 390
measuring 384
power 420–421, *420–421*
sound 384
engines 367, 420
internal combustion engine 420, 428
jet engines 410, 428
steam engines 343, 350, *350*, 351, *351*, 404, 429
England 322, 323, 324, 325, 326
American colonies 340, 341, 342, 343
Civil War 342, 343, 348
Magna Carta *365*
Norman Conquest 327
Reformation 338, 339
trade 336
Enuma Elish 192, *192*
environments 124
enzymes 181, 188
eons 76
epaulette sharks 153, *153*
epicenters 94, *94*
epics 210–211, *210–211*, 316, 367, 462
Gilgamesh 315, *315*
epochs 76
Equator 17, 30, 74, 75, 120, *120*, 262
latitude 126

Equatorial Guinea 285
eras 76
ergs 110
Encke Comet 50
Ericsson, John 408
Eridani constellation 15
Eritrea 285
erosion 81, 84
landscapes 96–97, *96–97*
escalators 398, *398*
Espelands Falls, Norway 103
Estonia 285
eternal life 206–207, *206–207*
ethene 380
Ethiopia 264, 286, 465
Etruscans 318, 367, 443, *443*
Eugene Onegin 467
Euphrates River 192, 314
Eurasia 86
tectonic plate 91
Europa 41, *41*
Europe 86, *86*, 87, 90, *90*, 91, 253, *253*, 264, 268, 270–271, *270–271*
art 434–435, *434–435*, 440–441, *440–441*
factfile 271
Enlightenment 348–349, *348–349*
feudal Europe 326–327, *326–327*
Ice Age 101
maps 126, *126*
people and places 272–273, *272–273*
Renaissance 334–335, *334–335*, 367
revolution 354–355, *354–355*
world power 356–357, *356–357*
European Commission 362, *362*, 363
European Union 272
countries joining in 2004 273
Evening Star 36
Everest 38, 98, 266
evergreens 143, 188
forest 113
evolution 133, 188
dinosaurs 162
Excalibur 215, *215*
excretion 181, 188
exoskeletons 148, 188
exosphere 114, *114*
expanding Universe 12, 13

exploration 336–337,
    336–337, 344–345,
    344–345, 367
  discovery of the Americas
    333, 337, 340
explosions 21
Expressionism 440, *440*
external fertilization 159
extinction 170–171, *170–171*,
    188
  dinosaurs 163
  mass extinction 170
eyes
  corrective lenses 390–391,
    390–391
  Sun 29

F

fabrics 379
factories 122, 123, 351, 356
Faery Queen 215, *215*
Fahrenheit 389
fall 74
familiars 215
famine 484
Fangio, Juan Manuel 229
Faraday, Michael 237
farming 252, 276, *364*
  farmworkers 287
  most farm animals, by
    country 281
  New Zealand 277
fault block mountains 98, *98*
Fawkes, Guy 237, *237*
fax (facsimile) machines 415,
    415, 428
feathers 77, 166
feluccas 367
ferns 76, 84, 135
Fertile Crescent 314–315,
    314–315, 367
fertilization 141, 188
  external fertilization 159
feudalism 326–327, *326–327*
Fiji 274, *274*, 286
fingernails 91, 173, *173*
fingers 77
Finland 286
Finn McCool 212, *213*
fire 113, *113*, 389, *389*
fireworks 397, *397*
firn 100, *100*
firs 113
fish 76, 84, 147, *147*, 148,
    150, 151, 152–153,
    152–153

biggest 153, *153*
coral reefs 88
Dead Sea 105
  schooling 152, *152*
fishing 276
Fitzimmons, Bob 229
fjords 270, *270*
FLAG (Fibre-optic Link Around
    the Globe) 414
flags 484, *484*
  countries 306–309, *306–309*
fleas 146, 387, *387*
Fleming, Alexander 237
Flettner, Anton 411
flies 146, 149, *149*
flight 77, 150, 151
  world's first powered 410
floating 395
floods 118, *118*, 315
  global warming 123
Florence, Italy 334
flowers 76, 135, 136, *136*
  meanings 144
fluorescent light 391
flutes 443, 446, *446*
Flying Scotsman 404
Focke, Heinrich 411
Fokine, Mikhail 459
fold mountains 98, *98*, 99, *99*
folk art 439
food 384, 385, 484, 485, *485*
  digestion 180–181, *180–181*
  invertebrates 149
  plants 144–145, *144–145*
Food and Agriculture
    Organization (FAO) 253
football 218, 228, 229
  American football 220, 221,
    221, 228
  Brazil 220
  referees 218
  World Cup winners 221
Forbidden City, Beijing 269,
    269, 331, 481, *481*
force 386–387, *386–387*
  diagram representation 387
Ford, Henry 357
  Ford cars 406
foreshocks 95
forests 76, 112–113, *112–113*,
    124, 143, 171, 189, 254,
    255
  fires 113, *113*
forked lightning 119
fossils 76, 77, 84–85, *84–85*,
    188
  bacteria 132

continental drift 90, 91
dinosaurs 85, *85*, 162
fossil fuels 124, 421
Mars 38
resin 82
foxes 111
France 273, 286
  nuclear power 420
  satellites 61
France 327, 338, 342, 343, 344
  art 434, 435, 440
  ballet 458
  French Revolution 352–353,
    353, 354, *354*
  Napoleonic Wars 354–355,
    354–355
  world wars 358, 359
Francis I of France 337
Franco, General Francisco 352
Franklin, Benjamin 237
Franks 367
Franz Ferdinand, Archduke
    352, 358
freezing 395, 428
frequency 393
fresco 436, *436*
freshwater 104
freshwater habitats 152
  birds 167
freshwater islands 89
Freud, Sigmund 237
Freyja 199, *199*
friction 387, 399, 428
frigatebirds 159, *159*
fringe-toed lizards 150
Frobisher, Martin 336
frogs 147, 154, 156–157,
    156–157, 159
  deserts 111
  poisonous 156, *156*, 164,
    164
  rain 118
fronts 117, 118
frost 97
fruit 141
Fry, Elizabeth 237
fuels 124, 125, 420, 421
Fujiwara dynasty 324
fulcrum 399, *399*, 428
Full Moon 32, 33, *33*
fullerene 380
Fulton, Robert 408
Functionalism 482
fundamentalism 367
funerals 484
fungi 134, *134*
furniture 379

G

Gabon 286
Gagarin, Yuri 65
Gaia 197
galaxies 12, 13, 17, 18–19,
    18–19, 20, 21, 68
  black holes 24
  Local Group 19, 68
  NGC4438 25
galena 125
Galileo Galilei 41, 56, *56*,
    237–238
Galileo 52, 58, *365*
gall bladder 180, *180*
Gama, Vasco da 337, *337*
Gambia 286
game birds 167
games 218
  key dates 219
games consoles 417, *417*,
    473, *473*
gamma-rays 25, 384
Gandhi, Mohandas 238, *238*
Ganesha 203, *203*
Ganges River 266, *266*
Ganymede 41, *41*
Garibaldi, Giuseppe 355, *355*
Garnerin, Jacques 411
garnet 82, 83, *83*
gas giants 31, 41, *42*
gases 12, 23, 24, 25, *25*, 26,
    72, 73, 374–375,
    374–375, 428
  Earth's atmosphere
    114–115
  gas clouds 12, 13, 14, 20,
    22
  greenhouse gases 122, *122*,
    123
  natural gas 122, 124
gases (*continued*)
  Sun 28
  volcanoes 92, *92*, 93
gastropods 148
Gates, Bill 238
Gateway to the West Arch,
    Missouri, USA 400, *400*,
    483, *483*
gauchos 261
Gaudi, Antonio 482
Gautama Siddhartha 328,
    329
gazelles 154, *154*, 155
gears 399, *399*, 407, *407*
Gemini 63
gemstones 82–83, *82–83*
genes 187, 188

gene splicing 423, 428
gene therapy 423
generators 383, *383*, 421
Genghis Khan 238, 330, 331, *331*
geographers 126
geology 76–77
  geological column 76, *76*, 77
  geologists 76, 77, 90
George III 238
George V 471
Georgia 286
geosphere 30
geostationary orbit 60, 68, 415
Germanic peoples 313, 322, 324
Germany 286, 338, 339, 342, 352, 353
  art 440
  music 444, 445
  railways 404, *405*
  world wars 358, 359
germination 141, 142, *142*, 188
Gershwin, George 445
geysers 93, *93*, 254, *254*
  world's highest 274
Ghana 286
giant pandas 170, *170*
gibbous Moon 33, *33*
Gibraltar 106, 270, *270*
Gilbert and George 441
Gilgamesh 315, *315*
gills 152, 188
gingkos 135, *137*
Giotto 334, 435
giraffes 154, *154*, 155, 168, 262, *262*, 395
glaciers 30, 97, 97, 100–101, *100–101*, 259, *259*
  fastest flowing 101
  Patagonian Ice Field 259
  longest 101, 284
gladiators 318, *318*, 367
Gladstone, William Ewart 238
glass 125, 379
Glossopteris fossil fern 91
Glendower, Owen 238
Global Positioning System (GPS) 60, 61, 127
global warming 122–123, *122–123*, 145, 278
glowing nebulae 22, *22*
glow worms 165

glucose 181, 188
Gobi Desert 111
Godwinson, Harold 327
Goethe, Johann Wolfgang von 451
gold 82, *82*, 337, 373, 377, 379, 382
  Witwatersrand, South Africa 264
Golden Gate Bridge, San Francisco, USA 403, *403*
golden lion tamarind 171, *171*
Golden Temple, Amritsar 208, *208*
golden tree snake 151
golf 219, *219*, 222, 229
Goliath frog 157
Gondwanaland 90, *90*
gongs 447, *447*
Gopaljang, Bangladesh 119
Gorbachev, Mikhail 353, 361, *361*
Gorgon 217
gorillas 165
Gormaz Castle, Castile, Spain 400
Gospel music 448
Goths 313, 322
government 346, 348, 354, 355
grain farming 144, *144*
gramophones 397, *397*, 449, *449*
Gran Chaco, Argentina 258
Grand Canyon, USA 39, 96, *96*, 97
granules 29
graphite 380
graptolites 85
grass 137
grasslands 76, 252, 255, 258, 262, 266
grasshoppers 146, 149, *149*
gravel 125
gravity 12, 15, 23, 72, 74, 107, 386
  black holes 24
  Moon 33
  Sir Isaac Newton 346, *346*
  spacecraft 64, 65
grazing animals 155
Great Barrier Reef, Australia 89, *89*, 148, 275, *275*, 344
Great Bear constellation 16, *16*
Great Britain *see* Britain

Great Comet 50–51, *50–51*
Great Dark Spot, Neptune 46, *46*, 47, *47*
Great Dividing Range 99
Great Dog constellation 17, *17*
Great Lakes, North America 104, 105, *105*
Great Nebula of Orion 22, 23, *23*
Great Pyramid, Giza, Egypt 400, 424, 480, *480*
Great Red Spot, Jupiter 40, *40*
Great Wall of China 320, 321, *321*
great white shark 153, *153*, 171
Greece 93, 273, *273*, 287, 312–313, 316–317, *316–317*, 364, 434, 435
Greece, ancient 272
  astronomy 16, 17, 21, 40, 44, 46
  drama 450–451, *450–451*, 455
  epics 210, 211, *211*
  gods and godesses 317, 319
  myths 196–197, *196–197*, 210, *210*, 213, *213*, 216, *216*, 217, *217*
  Olympic Games 218, 219, 224, 226
  sculpture 433, *433*, 438
  static electricity 382
green 119
Green, Andy 406
green tree frog 156, *156*
greenhouse effect 122, *122*, 123
  Venus 36
Greenland 88, 89, 127, 254, 256
Greenwich, London, UK 127
Grenada 287
Grenadines 295
Gresley, Sir Nigel 404
Grieg, Edvard 445
Grigg-Skjellerup Comet 50
griots 443, *443*
Gris, Juan 440
gryphons 217
Guatemala 287, 332
guerillas 367
Guevara, Che 360, *360*
Guinea 287
Guinea-Bissau 287
Guinevere 214

guitars 446, *446*
Gulf of Mexico 107
gulper eels 153
gunpowder 335
Gunung Mulu caves, Borneo 109
Gupta dynasty 328, 329
Guru Nanak 204, 208, 465
Gutenberg, Johannes 468
  printing press 468, *468*
Guyana 287
Gwyn, Nell 349
gymnastics 226, 227, *227*, 228
gymnosperms 135, 137, 141

H

habitats 188
  destruction 170–171, *170–171*
Hadrian 312
haiku 466
hailstones 117, 119, *119*
Haiti 257, 287, 345
Hale Bopp Comet 50, 51
Halley's Comet 50, *50*, 51
Halley, Edmund 51, 238
hamburger consumption 257
hammocks 396, *396*
Hammurabi of Babylon 314
Han dynasty 320
Handel, George Frederic 445
Handley Page aircraft 411
hang-gliding 411
Hanging Gardens of Babylon 312, 317, *317*
Hangzhou, China 330–331
Hannibal 313
Hanuman 203, *203*
"Happy Birthday To You" 484
Harappan civilization 313
Hargreaves, James 238, 350, 351
Hargreaves, Jenny 342
Harold II 327
Harrison, John 396
Harry Potter 214, *214*, 217
Harvey, William 238
Hastings, Battle of 327
Hawaii 92, 93
  Ice Age 101
Hawking, Stephen 239
hawks 154, 155
Haydn, Joseph 445
heart 182–183, *182–183*
  beats per minutes 423

heartwood 137, *137*, 143, *143*
heat 74, 78, 79, 80, 82, 120,
   121, 384, 388–389,
   388–389, 428
   Death Valley, USA 87
   Sahara Desert, Africa 86
   stars 14, 15
   Sun 28
heaviest planet 26
Hecate 215
helicopters 410–411, *410–411*
helium 12, 15, 22, 28, 42, 44,
   46
   boiling point 375
Hellenism 313
hellodor 82
hematite 125
Henry the Navigator 336
Henry VIII 239, *239*, 335, *335*,
   339
   household staff 335
Hepburn, Audrey 478, *478*
Hepburn, Katherine 479, *479*
Hepworth, Barbara 441
herbivores 154, 155, 188
herbs 135
Hercules (Heracles) 287, 291
   labors of 213, 217
Hermitage Museum, St
   Petersburg, Russia 273
heroes 212–213, *212–213*
Herschel, Sir William 44, 45
Hideyoshi, Toyotomi 340
hieroglyphs 193, *193*, 463,
   463
high jump 224, *224*, 225
High Tech 482
Highland Games 224, *224*
hills 97, *97*
Himalayas 98, 99, *99*, 266, 328
Hinduism 204, 208, 209, 266,
   328, 329, 347, 439, 452,
   452
   dance 456, *456*
   deities 202–203, *202–203*
   epics 210, 211, *211*
   scriptures 464
Hine, Jim 225
Hippocrates 239
hippodromes 322, *322*, 367
hippopotamuses 155
history
   ancient world 312–313,
      312–313, 314–315,
      314–315
   Earth 73
   medieval 326–327,

326–327, 330–331,
   330–331
1600–1800 342–343,
   342–343
present day 362–363,
   362–363
Hitchcock, Alfred 239, 476,
   476
Hitler, Adolf 239, *239*, 352,
   352, 353, 358, 359
HMS *Hood* 359
Hobbes, Thomas 239
hockey 221, *221*
Hockney, David 441
Hodgkin, Dorothy 239
Holland 339, 342, 343
Hollywood, California, USA
   477, *477*
Holy Roman Empire 326, *326*,
   327, 367
home entertainment 472–473,
   472–473
Homer 210, 316, 466
homes 299, 480, *480*
   wood 481, *481*
Homo erectus 364
Homo sapiens 133, *133*
Honduras 287
Hong Kong 252, *252*, 362, 409
Hooke, Robert 40, 239
Hopi 452
hormones 181, 188
horse flies 149, *149*
Horsehead Nebula 23, *23*
horses 155, 328, 340
   famous owners 315, 316
   horse racing 219
Horseshoe Falls, Canada 254,
   254
horsetails 135
Horus 194, *194*, 195
hot-air balloons 343, *343*,
   388, *388*, 396, *396*
   first around-the-world flight
   411
hot ball 12, *12*
hot spots 79
hottest planet 27, 36
hours 74, 75, 424
houses 400, 480, *480*
   ancient world 314, *314*
   mud 481, *481*
   Rome 318, *318*, 319, *319*
   wood 481, *481*
   underground 277
hovercraft 408, *408*
hsigo 217

HTML (hypertext mark-up
   language) 417
Huang-Ti 320
Hubble Space Telescope 23,
   45, 46, 48, 61, *61*, 362,
   365
Hudson Bay, Canada 107
Hugo, Victor 467
Huguenots 339
human evolution 312
human rights 348
human sacrifice 332, 333
humans 73, 76, 133, 168
   atoms 373
   body 172–172, *172–173*
   bones and joints 174–175,
      174–175
   eating and digestion
      180–181, *180–181*
   heart and blood 182–183,
      182–183
   lungs and breathing
      178–179, *178–179*
   muscles and moving
      176–177, *176–177*
   nervous system 184–185,
      184–185
   reproduction 186–187,
      186–187
Humayun 328, *328*
Humber Bridge, UK 403
hummingbirds 150
Hundred Years War 327
Hungary 287
Huns 313, 322
hurdling 225
hurricanes 118, *118*, 254, 394
Huygens 59
hydro-electric power stations
   421
hydrocarbons (CHs) 380
hydrofoils 408, *408*
hydrogen 12, 15, 22, 28, 42,
   44, 46, 72, 188, 373, 428
   atoms 373
   deuterium 420
   plants 139
hypocenters 94, *94*

I

IBM computers 412
Ibsen, Henrik 451, 454
Icarus 210, *210*
ice 76, 86, 87, 96, 97, 123,
   374, 395
   Antarctica 278–279,

278–279
   black ice 118
   clouds 116, 117
   glaciers 97, *97*, 100–101,
      100–101
   Greenland 89
   Ice Ages 100, 101, 121
   icebergs 101, *101*, 278,
      278, 394, 395, *395*
   Io 41
   Saturn's rings 43, *43*
ice hockey 221
ice skating 223, *223*, 227
Iceland 88, 288
icons 433
Ieyasu, Tokugawa 342
igneous rock 77, 80, *80*
Iguacu Falls, South America
   87, *87*, 258, *258*
Iliad 210, 211, *211*, 213, 316,
   466
illustration 437, *437*, 469
Impressionism 435, *435*
incandescence 391
Incas 260, 261, 340, 341,
   364, 367
   art 438
   houses 481, *481*
index fossils 85
India 87, 90, *90*, 91, 95, 121,
   269, 288, 298, 336, 337,
   407, 424
   ancient India 313,
      328–329, *328–329*
   barbarian invasions 323
   Bollywood 477, *477*
   colonization 342–343, 346,
      347
   Indian Mutiny 352, *352*
   Indian Railways 404
   religion 202, 203
   satellites 61
   snakes 161
   tectonic plate 91
   theater 452, *452*
Indian Ocean 88, 89, 106,
   107, 253, *253*, 336
indigo 119
Indonesia 88, 93, 266, 288,
   299
   Islam 299
   shadow-puppets 453, *453*
Indricatherium 77, *77*
"indulgences" 338, 368
Indus Valley civilization 268,
   313, 314
Industrial Revolution 272, 342,

350–351, *350–351*, 368
inertia 386
inflation 12
infrared rays 384, 390
inorganic compounds 380
Inquisition 338
insects 76, 77, 84, 111, 146, *146*, 148–149, *148–149*
  communication 164, *164*, 165
  facts 148
  fossils 85, 91
  mimicry 164, *164*
installations 441
instruments, musical 442–443, *442–443*, 445, 446–447, *446–447*
insulators 382, 428
International Space Station (ISS) 65, 66–67, *66–67*
internal combustion engine 420, 428
Internet 416–417, *416–417*, 449, 470
intestines 180, *180*, 181
Inuit 257
  dance 457
inventions 396–397, *396–397*
  inventors 397
invertebrates 146, 148–149, *148–149*, 188
Io 41, *41*
ionic bonds 379, *379*
Iran 288, 343
Iraq 127, 288, 353, 362, 363, *364*
Ireland, Republic of 288
iron 30, 34, 72, 78, 81, 82, 125, 312, 373, 382
  bridges 402
  magnetic poles 127
  Mars 38
  smelting 342, 351
Iroquois 200, *200*
irregular galaxies 18, *18*, 19
irrigation 105
Isis 195
Islam 204, 205, 206, 207, 208, 209, 253, 324, 328, 401, 465
  dress 484, *484*
  Indonesia 299
  religious art 437, 438, 439, *439*
  scriptures 464
islands 88–89, *88–89*, 267
  biggest 89, 285, 286

largest 88
newest 89
  Oceania 274
isoseismic lines 94, *94*
ISP (Internet Service Provider) 417, 428
Israel 288
  satellites 61
Israelites 83
Istanbul, Turkey 259, 269, 322
Itaipú Dam, Brazil 261
Italy 252, 288, 334, 353, 355
  ballet 458
  Renaissance 435
Ivory Coast 288–289

J

Jackson, Samuel L 478, *478*
Jacobite rebellions 342, 349
jade 82
jaguars 169, *169*
Jajuri drama 452, *452*
Jamaica 289
James I and VI 240, 342, 343, *343*
Jamestown, Virginia, USA 340
Janus 207
Japan 75, 95, 209, 266, 268, 269, 289, 340, 342, 343, 346, 352
  ancient 313, 320, 321, *321*
  art 438, *438*
  dance 456, 457, *457*
  legends 463, *463*
  medieval 330, 331
  music 443
  myths 207
  poetry 466
  satellites 61
  theater 452, *452*, 455
  trains 405, *405*
  World War II 359
javelins 224, 225, *225*
jaws 77
jazz 448
Jefferson, Thomas 257, 345
jellyfish 133, 148, 151, 152
Jenner, Edward 240
Jerusalem 312, 327
jesters 451
Jesus Christ 204, 205, 207, 312, *312*
jets
  astronomy 23, 24, 68
  jet engines 410, 428
jewels 82, 337, 346

Jimmu Tenno 321
Joan of Arc, St 240, *240*
John, King 240, 326, *326*
Johnson, Samuel 240
joints 174–175, *174–175*, 188
Jones, Brian 411
Jordan 289
Jordan River 105
Jormungand 216, *216*
Judaism 204, 205, 208
  dress 484, 485, *485*
  scriptures 464, 465
judo 222, 223, *223*
juggernauts 407
Julius Caesar 240, 312–313, 318
Jupiter 26, 27, *27*, 40–41, *40–41*
  distance from Sun 27, 40
  Shoemaker-Levy Comet 51
  Trojan asteroids 52
Jurassic Period 76
Justinian I 323, *323*

K

K2 99
Kabuki drama 452, *452*
Kachinas 452, 453, *453*
Kalahari Desert, Africa 111, 262, 263, *263*
Kambaratinsk Dam, Russia 401
Kangchenjunga 99
kangaroos 169, *169*
Karachi, Pakistan 75
Karloff, Boris 478, *478*
karst landscape 266, *266*
Kathakali 452, *452*
Kazakhstan 289
Keats, John 240, 467, *467*
Kelvin, Lord *see* Thomson, Sir William
Kennedy, John F 240, 353, 360
Kenneth MacAlpine 240
Kenya 289
Kevlar™ 379
keyboards 446, *446*, 447
Kidman, Nicole 478, *478*
kidneys 181, *181*
Kiel Canal, Germany 409
Kilimanjaro, Kenya 262, *262*
Kilanea, Hawaii 92
killer whales 154
kinetic energy 384, 385, 393, 399
kinetographs 475

King Abdul Aziz Airport, Saudi Arabia 411
King, B B 448, *448*
King, Martin Luther 242
Kingsley, Mary 241
Kipling, J Rudyard 241, *241*
Kiribati 289
kitchen foil 82
kitchen sink drama 455
kiwis 166
knights 326, 327, *327*, 368
komodo dragon 161, *161*
Kongfuzi *see* Confucius
Kooris 276
Koran 205, 464
Korea, North 289
Korea, South 289
Korowai people 266
Kohoutek comet 50, *50*
Kohoutek; Lous 50
kotos 443
Krakatoa, Indonesia 93
krill 278
Krubera Caves, Georgia 109
krypton 377
Kublai Khan 324, *324*, 331
Kulper Crater, Mercury 35, *35*
Kuwait 289–290
Kyrgyzstan 290

L

labor 187
Lady of the Lake 215
Lagoon Nebula 22, *22*
Lake Baikal, Siberia 104, 105, 266
Lake Erie, North America 105, *105*
Lake Great Bear, Canada 105
Lake Huron, North America 105, *105*
Lake Malawi, Africa 105
Lake Maracaiba, Venezuela 261
Lake Michigan, North America 105, *105*
Lake Ontario, North America 105, *105*
Lake Poets, the 467
Lake Superior, North America 105, *105*
Lake Tanganyika, Africa 104, 105
Lake Titicaca, Peru 105, *105*, 294
Lake Victoria Nyanza 105

lakes 104–105, *104–105*, 255, 262
  deepest 104, 266, 298
  glacial 97, 104
  highest navigable 105, 294
  islands 89
  largest 105, 300
  North America 254
Lambert–Fisher Glacier, Antarctica 101
Lan Jin Bridge, Yunnan, China 402
Lancelot 214
land 73, 76
landscapes 96–97, *96–97*
  ocean bed 106, *106*
languages 256, 260, 264
  most speakers 297
  Papua New Guinea 277
lantern-slide projectors 474
Lao-Tzu 204, *204*, 464
lapis lazuli 82
Large Magellanic Clouds 18, 68
larynx 179, *179*
Lascaux caves, France 109, *109*
lasers 419, 428
Latin 16, 318, 377
Latin America 336, 340, 341, 355, 362, 368
latitude 126, 127
Latvia 290
laughing gas *see* nitrous oxide
Laurasia 90, *90*
lava 73, 80, *80*, 92, *92*, 93, *93*
  crystals 82
Lavoisier, Antoine 241, 394, *394*
Lawson, H J 407
League of Augsburg 342, 343
Leakey, Louis 241
Leaning Tower of Pisa, Italy 401, *401*
leap years 75
leaves 136, *136*, 137
  cells 138, 139, *139*
Lebanon 290
legends 318, 368
legions 319, *319*, 368
leisure 218–219, *218–219*
lemurs 165
Lenin, Vladimir 241, *241*, 353, *353*
leopard seals 279, *279*
leopards 154, *154*

Lesotho 290
Leverrier, Urbain 46
levers 398, 399, 428
  leverage 387, *387*
Lewis, Lennox 229
Lhotse 99
Li River, China 266, *266*
Liberia 264, 290
Libya 110, 264, 290
lichens 134, *134*
Liechtenstein 290
Lichtenstein, Roy 441
life 30, 31, 394
  conditions on Earth 31, 73
  eternal life 206–207, *206–207*
  Europa 41
  Mars 38, 39
  origins 132–133, *132–133*
  plant lifecycles 140, *140*
  taxonomy 132, *132*, 133
  theories 133
lifts (elevators) 400
ligaments 175, *175*, 189
light 13, 15, 22, 74, 75, 139, 390–391, *390–391*, 429
  black holes 24, 25
  color 119
  Earth 44
  Jupiter 41
  light years 13, 20, 21, 23, 68
  Moon 32, 33
  Uranus 44
  Venus 36
lightning 119, 383, *383*
light bulbs 357, 391
limestone 80
  cave systems 108, *108*
Lincoln, Abraham 241, 257
lions 168, 169, *169*
liquids 374–375, *374–375*, 429
Lister, Lord Joseph 242, *242*
Liszt, Franz 445
literature 466–467, *466–467*
  famous characters 467
  publishing 468–469, *468–469*
lithography 437, *437*
lithosphere 78, *78*
Lithuania 290–291
Liu Bang 320
liver 77, 84, 172, *172*, 180, *180*, 181
Livingstone, David 242
lizards 147, 150, 160, *160*,

161
  biggest 161, *161*
lizards 77, 84
llanos 258
Lloyd, Marie 454, *454*
Lloyd George, David 242
Llywelyn the Great 242
lobsters 146, *146*
Local Group 19, 68
locomotives 404–405, *404–405*
  Rocket 396, *396*
lodestone 397
Loki 199
London, UK 75, 101
London Bridge, Arizona, USA 403
London Stock Exchange 343
longitude 126, 127
longships 324–325, *324–325*
Look Back in Anger 455
Lord of the Rings: The Fellowship of the Ring 476
Lord of the Rings: The Two Towers 479, *479*
Los Angeles, USA 75
Love waves 79
loudness 392, *392*, 393
loudspeakers 418, *418*
Louis XIV 343
Lowell, Percival 38
Lumière, Auguste and Louis 474, *474*
Lunar 9 62
lunar eclipses 32
lungs 178–179, *178–179*, 189, 395
Luther King, Martin 242, 338
Luxembourg 291
Lydians 317
Lyra constellation 15
  Ring Nebula 23, *23*
Lystrosaurus 91

M

M80 (Nac 6093) 15
Maat Mons, Venus 37, *37*
MacArthur, Ellen 229, *229*
Macedonia 291
Mach speed 392
machines 398–399, *398–399*, 429
  Industrial Revolution 350, *350*, 351, *351*
  machine efficiency 398
Machu Picchu, Peru 261, *261*,

341, *341*
Mackintosh, Charles Rennie 242–243
Madagascar 88, 291
Magellan, Ferdinand 242–243, *242*, 337
Magellanic Clouds 19, *19*, 68
magic 214–215, *214–215*
magma 80, *80*, 91, 92, *92*, 93, *93*
Magna Carta 240, 326, *365*
magnesium 30
magnetic field 382, 383, 429
magnetism 382–383, *382–383*, 429
  Jupiter 40
  Neptune 47
  Uranus 47
magnets 127
Magritte, René 441
Magyars 326
Maiasaura 162, *162*
main sequence stars 28
Makalu 99
malaria 149
Malawi 291
Malaysia 288, 291
Malaysian horned frog 156, *156*
Maldives 291
Malleus maleficarum 215
Malta 290, 291
mammals 76, 84, 147, 150, 168–169, *168–169*
  record-breaking 169
Mammoth Caves, USA 109
mammoths 85, 442
Manaslu 99
Manchester United FC 229
Manchus 342, 346, 368
Mandela, Nelson 243, 353, 362, *362*
mandrake 214, *214*
Manhattan, New York City, USA 257, *257*, 400
manticores 217
mantle of the Earth 72, 78, *78*, 79
  continental drift 90, 91
manufacturing industries 268
manuscripts, illuminated 434, *434*
Mao Ze Dong (Mao Tse-Tung) 361, *361*
Maoris 276, 277, 325, *325*, 345, 368
maps and mapmaking

126–127, *126–127*
conic projection 127, *127*
Mercator projection 126, 127, *127*
Mara Valley Falls, Norway 103
marathon racing 225
marble 80
Marceau, Marcel 451, *451*
Marconi, Guglielmo 470, *470*
Marcus Aurelius 319
marganite 82
Marley, Bob 449, *449*
Marianas Trench 409
Mariner 34, 35, *35*, 59
Marlowe, Christopher 243
marriage 484, 485, *485*
marrow 174, *174*, 189
Mars 26, 27, *27*, 38–39, *38–39*
    compared to Earth 38
    distance from Sun 27, 38
    Mars 3 58
    Mars landings 38
Marshall Islands 291
marsupials 168
Martinique 93
Marx, Karl Heinrich 243
Mary I 339
Mary, Queen of Scots 243, 339, *339*
Masai tribe 264, *264*, 485, *485*
masks 450, *450*
mass 15, 386
Masters 435
materials 378–379, *378–379*
mathematics 424
    ancient Greece 316
    calculating area 425, *425*, 426, *426*
    calculating volume 426, *426*
matter 12, 24
    black holes 25, *25*
Matrix Reloaded 479, *479*
Matses tribe 260
Matterhorn, Switzerland 271, *271*
Mauna Kea, Hawaii 99
Mauna Loo, Hawaii 93
Mauritania 292
Mauritius 292
Maxwell, James Clark 243
Mayans 208, 256, 332, 333
    numbers 424, *424*
McMurdo, Antarctica 278
meanders 102, *102*, 103

measuring energy 384
measuring force 386
measuring space and time 13
mechanical advantage 398
medicine 422–423, *422–423*
    plants 144
medicine men *see* shamans
Medicis 334
Mediterranean Sea 106, 107
Medusa 217
Megazostrodon 77, *77*
Melanesia 274, 344
melting points 375
Menai Straits Bridge, UK 403
Menes of Egypt 313, *315*
Mercalli Scale 95
Mercator, Gerardus 127, 336
Mercedes Benz cars 406
merchants 326, 334, 336, 340
Mercury 26, 27, *27*, 34–35, *34–35*
    craters 34
    distance from Sun 26, 27, 34
    South Pole 35, *35*
    sunrise and sunset 34
Merlin 214, 215
mermaids 216, 217, *217*
mesocyclones 119, *119*
Mesopotamia 312
    writing 462, 463
mesosphere 78, *78*, 114, *114*
Mesozoic Era 76, 162
Messenger 35, *35*
metals 72, 81, 82, 124, 429
    metallurgy 312, 342
    processing 378
    recyling 125
metamorphic rock 80
metamorphosis 157
Meteor Crater, Arizona, USA 52, *52*
meteorologists 117
meteoroids 52, 68
meteors 52–53, *52–53*, 68
    meteorite ALH84001 39
    meteorites 30, 68
methane gas 39, 44, 46, 72, 123, 145
metro systems 405
Mexico 254, 256, 257, 292, 332, 333, 340, *364*
Mexico City, Mexico 75
mice 155
Michaux, Pierre and Ernest 407

Michelangelo Buonarotti 334, 435
    David 334, *334*
microchips 412, 413, *413*, 429
micrometeoroids 68
microorganisms 76, 77
microprocessors 413
Micronesia 274, 292, 313
microwave background radiation 13, 68
microwaves 384, 390, 415
Middle East 192
migration 167, 189
militarism *see* warfare
Milky Way 15, 18, 19, 20–21, *20–21*, 68
Mill, John Stuart 243
millet 264
Milne, A A 466
Milton, John 243–244
mime 451, *451*
mimicry 164, *164*, 189
Minamoto Yoritomo 331
minerals 80, 84, 108, 124, 125
    Antarctica 278
    Australia 277
    color 81, *81*
Ming dynasty 330, 346
Mini car 406, *406*
mining 124, 276, 277
    world's biggest mine 260
Minoans 313, 316, 368
Minotaur 213, *213*
minus 424
Mir 66, 67
mirrors 390, *390*
missionaries 344, 356, 368
Mississippi–Missouri river 103
mist 117
mitochondria 172, *172*
mobile phones 414, *414*
modems 415, 429
Modernism 482
Mogul dynasty 328, 329, 346
Moguls 368
Mohenjo-Daro civilization 315, *315*
Moldava 292
molecules 372–373, *372–373*, 429
    gases 374, 375
    heat 388
    liquids 374
    solids 374–375
    sound 392
moles 150

Molière, Jean-Baptiste Poquelin 451
molluscs 85, 146
molting 148
momentum 386
Monaco 292
monasteries 327, 368, 434
Mondrian, Piet 441
Monet, Claude 435
money 317
Monge Falls, Norway 103
Mongolia 292
Mongols 322, 324, 330–331, *330–331*, 343, 346, 347, *364*, 368, 481, *481*
monkeys 150
monomers 380
monorails 404
Monroe, Marilyn 478, *478*
monsoons 121, *121*
Mont Blanc, Switzerland 270
Montenegro 296
Montezuma 340
Montgolfier, Joseph-Michel and Jacques-Étienne 343, 396
Montréal, Canada 286, 293
Monument Valley, USA 110–111, *110–111*
Moon 31, 32–33, *32–33*, 72, 73, *73*
    craters 32, 33
    distance from Earth 62
    formation 32, *32*
    Mariner 35
    Moon landings 62–63, *62–63*, 471
    seas 32, 33
    solar eclipses 29, *29*
    tides 107, *107*
moons (satellites) 68, 69
    Jupiter 40, 41, *41*
    Mars 38, *38*, 39
    Pluto 48, 49
    Saturn 43
    Solar System 26, 27
    Uranus 44, 45, *45*
Moore's Law 413
Moore, Gordon 413
Moore, Henry 441
moraine 97, 100, *100*
More, Sir Thomas, St 244, *244*, 338, *338*
Morgon, William George 221
Morita, Akio 471
Morocco 292
Mortensen, Viggo 476
Moscow, Russia 75

Moses 205, *205*
mosques 208, 209, *209*, 439, *439*
mosquitoes 149
mosses 76, 134, *134*
mother of pearl clouds 117
moths 146, 149, *149*
motion 386–387, *386–387*
    Newton's laws 386
motor racing 222, 223, *223*, 229
motorcycling 406, 222, *222*
Mount Elbrus, Caucasus 270
Mount Everest, China/Nepal 38, 98, 266
Mount Fuji, Japan 207, *207*
Mount Goldsworthy Mine, Australia 277
Mount Kilimanjaro, Kenya 262, *262*
Mount Machhapuchhare, Nepal 266, *266*
Mount Pelée, Martinique 93
Mount Pinatubo, Philippines 93
    climate change 121
Mount Rushmore, USA 257
Mount St Helens, Washington State, USA 93, 98
Mount Vesuvius 432
mountains 88, 97, 98–99, *98–99*, 252, 255, 258, 266, 375
    climate 120
    glaciers 100, *100*
    highest 98, 99, 266, 300
    longest ranges 98, 99
    Moon 73
    rivers 102, *102*
    seamounts 106, *106*
Mourya dynasty 328
mouse 429
movies 474–475, *474–475*
    directors 476, *476*
    lighting 476, *476*
    making 476–477, *476–477*
    marketing 477
    special effects and superstars 478–479, *478–479*
Mozambique 292
Mozart, Wolfgang Amadeus 244, 444, *444*, 445
MP3-players 418, 470
MRI (Magnetic Resonance Imaging) scanners 185
mud 80, 84

Muhammad 205, 208, 324
mummification 194, 206, 207, 432, *432*
    cats 195
murals 432
muscles 151, *151*, 395
    body's biggest 177
    body's smallest 177
    brain 185
    breathing 178, *178*
    humans 176–177, *176–177*
music 448–449, *448–449*
    ballet 458–459, *458–459*
    classical 444–445, *444–445*
    dance 456–457, *456–457*
    instruments 446–447, *446–447*
    notation 443, *443*, 444
    popular 448–449, *448–449*, 460
    sound recordings 418
music hall 454
Muslims *see* Islam
Mussolini, Benito 244, 353
Mutarazi Falls, Zimbabwe 103
Muybridge, Eadweard 474
Myceneans 312–313, 316
myths 192–193, *192–193*
    Egypt 194–195, *194–195*
    Greece 196–197, *196–197*, 210, *210*, 213, *213*, 216, *216*, 217, *217*
    mythical creatures 216–217, *216–217*
    Native Americans 200–201, *200–201*
    Norse 198–199, *198–199*
    paradise 206–207, *206–207*

N

nacreous clouds 117
Naismith, James 221
Namgyal, Sir Tashi 214
Namib Desert, Africa 87, *87*, 262, 263, *263*
Namibia 292
Nanga Parbat 99
NASA (National Aeronautics and Space Administration) 362, 363, 365, 478
Natal ghost frog 156, *156*
National Aeronautical and Space Administration (NASA) 54, 59, 61
Native Americans 256, 257, 340–341, *340–341*, 343

drama 452, 453, *453*
    Ghost Dance 457, *457*
    myths 200–201, *200–201*
    totem poles 438, *438*
    tribes 344
natural materials 378, 379, 429
NATO (North Atlantic Treaty Organization) 352–353, 362
Nauru 293
navies 409
navigation 396, 397
    satellites 60, 61
Nazcas 432
Nazism 358, 368
Near Earth Objects (NEOs) 52, 68
Nebuchadnezzar II 312, 313, *313*
nebulae 17, 22–23, *22–23*, 68
    star formation 14, 22, 23
Nelson, Admiral Horatio 244, *244*, 354, *364*
neon 377, 391, *391*
Nepal 293
Neptune 26, *26*, 46–47, *46–47*
    distance from Sun 27, 46
    rings 46, *46*, 47
nerves 184–185, *184–185*
netball 221
Netherlands 270, 293
neurons 184–185, *184–185*, 189
neutrons 372, 429
Nevada, USA 87
névé 100, *100*
New Guinea 88
New Guinea Range 99
New Horizons 49
new Moon 32, 33, *33*
New York, USA 75
New Zealand 75, 86, 93, 274, 275, 277, 293, 325, 344, 345, *345*
    Ice Age 101
Newcomen, Thomas 350, 351, 244
newspapers 468, *468*, 469, *469*
Newton, Sir Isaac 244–245, 349, 386, *386*, 387
newtons (N) 386
newts 147, 156, 157
Niagara Falls 254, *254*
Nicaragua 293
nickel 30, 72, 78, 81
Niger 293

Nigeria 265, 293
night 74, 75
Nightingale, Florence 245, *245*
nightshade, deadly 137
Nijinsky, Vaslav 459, *459*
Nile crocodiles 159
Nile River 103, 262, *262*, 263, *263*, 265, 315, *315*
nimbostratus clouds 116, *116*, 118, *118*
Nineveh 192
nitrogen 30, 47, 114, 115, 373
nitrous oxide 123
noble gases 377, 429
nobles 326
nocturnal creatures 155, 189
Noh drama 452, *452*
Nohoch Nah Chich cave system, Mexico 108
nomadic peoples 322, 368, 481, *481*
noon 75
Normans 368
Norse myths 198–199, *198–199*
North America 86, *86*, 87, 90, *90*, 91, 127, 253, *253*, 254–255, *254–255*
    colonization 340, 341, 342, 343
    history 332–333, *332–333*, 340–341, *340–341*
    factfile 255
    Ice Age 101
    people and places 256–257, *256–257*
    tectonic plate 91
North Atlantic Ocean 253, *253*
North Pole 75, *75*, 127
Northern Hemisphere 15, 16, *16*, 74, *74*, 115
Northern Lights 115, *115*
Norway 270, 293, 300
    A (village name) 272
nose 179, *179*
novels 466–467, *466–467*, 469
nucleus 172, *172*, 186, *186*, 189
Nunavut 257
Novaya Zemlya Glacier, Russia 101
nuclear
    power 385, 420
    reaction 14, 15, 28
    weapons 359, 360, 368

nucleus 372, 373, 429
numbers 424, *424*

O

Oakland Bay Bridge, San
    Francisco, USA 402
oases 111
oboes 446, *446*
observatories 56–57, *56–57*,
    69
ocean habitats 152, 153
ocean liners 409
    Queen Elizabeth 409
    Titanic 394, *394*, 409
Oceania 86, *86*, 87, 253, *253*,
    274–275, *274–275*
    factfile 275
    people and places
      276–277, *276–277*
oceanic crust 78, *78*, 79
oceans 31, 72, 73, 86, *86*, 90,
    106–107, *106–107*, 252,
    253, *253*
    climate 120
    depths 107
    Panthalassa 90, *90*
    trenches 91, 106, *106*
octopuses 146, *146*, 148
Odin 198, *198*
Odyssey 210, 212, *212*, 213,
    316, 466
Offa 245
oil 122, 261, 268, 278, 380
    refineries 380, 420
    reserves 288
    rigs 125, *125*
oil paints 436, *436*
Okavango River, Africa 262
Old Faithful, Yellowstone, USA
    254, *254*
Old Masters 435
Olmecs 312–313, 332, 333,
    333
Olympic Games 218, 219,
    224, 226–227, *226–227*
    ancient Greece 316
    modern venues 227
    most gold medal winners
      228
Olympus Mons, Mars 38
Oman 293–294
O'Neill, Eugene 451
opals 82, 83, *83*
opera 444, 445, 467
Opportunity 38
optical fibers 414, 415, 429

optical telescopes 56
orange 119
orangutans 164
orbits 26, 69
    comets 50
    Earth 30
    geostationary orbit 60, 68,
      415
    Jupiter 40
    Mars 38
    Mercury 34
    Moon 32
    Neptune 46
    Pluto 48
    retrograde 69
    satellites 60, 61
    Saturn 42
    Venus 36
orchestras 445
orchids 141
Ordovician Period 76
ores 82, *82*, 125
organic chemistry 381, 429
organic compounds 380, 381
organisms 134, 189
organs 172, *172*, 189
Orion constellation 15, 16
    Great Nebula 22, 23, *23*
    Horsehead Nebula 23, *23*
Ornithischians 163, *163*
Orwell, George (Eric Blair)
    245
Osborne, John 455, *455*
Oscars 475, 478, 479
Osiris 195
ostriches 151, 166, 167
Otis, Elisha 400
Ottoman Empire 342, 343,
    346, 368
oval galaxies 18
ovaries 141, *141*, 186, *186*,
    189
ovules 141, *141*, 189
Owen, Robert 245
Owen, Wilfred 245
owls 155, 166
oxbow lakes 102, *102*, 103
oxygen 30, 73, 76, 81, 114,
    115, 189, 373, 429
    algae 145
    fish 152
    human body 178, 179, 182,
      183
    plants 138, 139
oysters 82, 83, *83*
ozone layer 115
    global warming 123

P

pacemakers 423
Pacific Ocean 86, 106, 107,
    253, *253*, 274, 344
    coral islands 88, 89
    Ring of Fire 93
    tectonic plates 91
packaging 123
Padua, Italy 334, *334–335*
painting 316, 334
Pakistan 75, 294, 314
palaces 480, 481, *481*
Palaeozoic Era 76
paleontologists 162, *162*
Palau 294
Palestine *365*
pampas 258, 261
Panama 294
    Panama Canal 257, *257*
pancreas 180, *180*, 181, *181*
Pangaea 90, *90*
Pankhurst, Emmeline 245
panpipes 443, *443*
panspermia theory 132
Panthalassa 90, *90*
paper 125
Papua New Guinea 274, 276,
    277, 294
parachutes 381, *381*
    first parachute drop 411
paradise 206–207, *206–207*
Paraguay 294
parasites 149
parsecs 13, 69
parthenogenesis 158
Parthenon, Athens, Greece
    317, *317*, 480, *480*
pas-de-deux 458, *458*
Pasteur, Louis 245
Patagonia 259
Pathfinder 39
Pavarotti, Luciano 443, *443*
peacekeepers 368
peacocks 159, *159*
Pearl Harbor, Hawaii, USA
    352, 359, *359*
pearls 82, 83, *83*
peasants 326
peat 124, *124*
Peel, Sir Robert 245
Peking *see* Beijing
Peloponnesian Wars 312–313
penguins 87, 151, 166, 278
pensions 349
People of the Book 465
Pepys, Samuel 245
perching birds 167

percussion 446
peregrine falcon 150, *150*
perennial plants 189
peridot 82, 83, *83*
perihelion 29
Periodic Table 376–377,
    376–377, 429
Periods 76
Perito Moreno Glacier,
    Argentina 259, *259*
permafrost 85
Permeke, Constant 440
Permian Period 76
Perry, Fred 228, *228*
Perseus constellation 16
Persia 312, 313, 315, 343,
    346
    barbarian invasions 323
personal music players 449,
    471
Perth, Australia 81
Peru 294, 332, 341, 360, *364*
PET (Positive Emission
    Tomography) scans 423,
    423
Peter the Great 348
petroleum 380
pharaohs 195, 314, 315, *315*
phases of the Moon 32, 33, 69
pheromones 165
Philippines 93, 121, 217, 294,
    296
philosophers 316, 349, 368
phloem vessels 137, *137*
Phobos 38, *38*, 39
Phoenicia *365*, 462, 463
phoenix 217
phones 414–415, *414–415*,
    416, 417
phonographs 357, 449
photography 440, 441
    cinema 474–475, *474–475*
    space probes 35, 39, 43
photons 390
photosphere 28, *28*, 69
photosynthesis 114, 138–139,
    138–139, 189
physics 25
phytoplankton 134, *134*
pianos 442, 447, *447*
Piazzi, Giuseppe 52
Picasso, Pablo 435, 441, *441*
Piccard, Bertran 411
Piccard, Jacques 409
Picts 322, 325, 368
pigments 437
pike 152, *152*

piles (construction) 401, *401*
Pilgrim Fathers 340, *340*
pilgrimages 369
pines 113
Pinnacle Desert, Australia 274, *274*
pirates 369
pitch 393
Pitch Lake, Trinidad 255
Pitt, William ("Pitt the Younger") 246
Pizarro, Francisco 340, *340*
planes *see* aircraft
planes, inclined 398, *398*, 399
planetary nebulae 22, 23, *23*
planetary rings 43, *43*, 45, *45*, 46, *46*, 47, 69
planetesemals 72
planets 14, 69, 72
  carbon 380
  Solar System 26–27, *26–27*
plankton 155, 189
plants 73, 76, 90, 119, 124, 125, 133, 134–135, *134–135*, 394
  Asia 266
  cellulose 381
  deserts 111
  Earth's atmosphere 30
  giant plants 142
  growth 142–143, *142–143*
  human uses 144–145, *144–145*
  medicine 144
  parts 136–137, *136–137*
  photosynthesis 114, 138–139, *138–139*
  plant families 141
  poisonous 137
  rainforests 112
  record plants 138
  reproduction 140–141, *140–141*
plasma, gas 15, 374, 429
plasma, human body 182, 189
Plassey, Battle of 342–343, 346–347, 347
plastics 380, 381, 429
Plato 316
playing cards 218, *218*
playwrights 450, 451, 468
Pleistocene Ice Age 101
plesiosaurs 163
Plow constellation 16, *16*
plug-ins 417
plus 424

Pluto 26, *26*, 48–49, *48–49*
  distance from Sun 27, 48
poetry 316, 466–467, *466–467*
Pointillism 435, *435*
Poland 343, 358, 360
polar regions 75, 87, 120, 121, 123
Polyakov, Valery 66
Pohutu Geyser, New Zealand 274
Poland 294
polar regions 255
pole-vaulting 224, 225
poles, magnetic 382, 383
politics 473, 484
pollen 141, *141*, 189
pollination 140, 141, 189
  insects 149
Pollock, Jackson 441, *441*
polo 220
Polo, Marco 243, *243*
polygons 425, *425*
polyhedrons 425, *425*
polymers 380, 429
Polynesia 274, 313, 325, 344
  creation myths 193
polyps 88, 133, 148
polythene 380
Pompeii 432
Pompey 318
Ponte Vecchio, Florence, Italy 402, *402*
pop videos 449
popes 327, 355, 369
Popocatepetl, Mexico 257
poppies 139, *139*
population 87, 252, 253, 333, 356
  Africa 265
  China 269, 485
  density 273
  most populated countries 292
  Oceania 274
  Rome 319, 322
porcelain 330, *330*
porpoises 168
ports, world's busiest 409
Portugal 260, 261, 294–295, 336, 337
Potala Palace, Tibet 481, *481*
pottery 433, *433*, 436, *436*
potential energy 384
poverty 170, 171, 252, 260, 261, 272, 483
power 420–421, *420–421*

power stations 383, *383*, 420
  nuclear power 385, *385*, 421, *421*
  pollution 171
prairies 255
Precambrian Time 76
precipitation 116
predators 150, 151, 154, 189
  birds of prey 155, 159, 167
  great white shark 153, *153*, 171
Presley, Elvis 449, 449
pressure 28, 30, 78, 80
  air pressure 115, *115*, 375
  Jupiter 40
  Saturn 42
  Venus 37
prey 154, 189
Pride and Prejudice 472, *472*
prime meridian 127
Príncipe 295–296
printing 468–469, *468–469*
Pritchard, Thomas 402
Procyan 15
progress 342–343, *342–343*
prominences 28, *28*, 29, 69
props 454, *454*
Protestantism 338–339, 369
proton-proton chain 15
protons 372, 373, 429
Prout, Samuel 436
pteridophtes 141
pterosaurs 163
Pueblo Indians 333, 344
pulleys 398, *398*, 399
pulse 182
pumas 169, *169*
Punch and Judy 453
Punic Wars 313
puppets 452, 453, *453*
Purcell, Henry 246
Pushkin, Aleksandr Sergeevich 467
Putin, Vladimir 361
putting the shot 386, *386*
pylons 383, *383*, 420, *420*
pythons 160, *160*
pyramids *365*, 400, 424
  Egyptisn 16, 54
  Mayans 333, *333*
Pythagoras 396
  theorem 427, *427*

Q
Q-waves 79

Qatar 295
Qing dynasty 320, 346, 352
quarks 12
quarters of the Moon 33, *33*
quartz 82, *82*
quasars 18, *18*, 24, 69
Quaternary Period 76
Queen Elizabeth 409
Quetzalcoatl 340, 369
Qu'ran *see* Koran

R
rabbits 168, *168*
race
  Africa 264
  South America 260, 261
radar 69
radiation 22, 69, 388, 389, 390
radiators 389, *389*
radio 414, *414*, 448, 470–471, *470–471*
  home entertainment 472–473, *472–473*
  radio lingo 414
  radio waves 384, 390, 415
radio telescopes 57, 69
radioactivity 77
radiocarbon dating 77
radius 429
Raedwald of Anglia 323
Ragnarok 199, *199*
rain 72, 87, 97, 121
  clouds 116–117, *116–117*
  deserts 110–111, *110–111*
  monsoons 121, *121*
  mountains 98
  water cycle 103
rain dances 452, 456, 457, *457*
rainbows 118, 119, *119*
rainforest 97, 112–113, *112–113*, 121, 252, 255, 258, 259, 262, 266
  Amazon 258, *258*, 259, 260
  global warming 123
Raj 347, 369
Raleigh, Sir Walter 246, *246*
rallying 223
RAM (random access memory) 412
Ramayana 210, 211, *211*
ramps 398, *398*, 399
Ramses II of Egypt 312
Raphael 334, 435
raptors *see* birds of prey

ratites 166
rats 155
rays (fish) 153
Rayleigh waves 79
Re-Atum 194, 195
rebellions 369
receivers 415
recorders 446, *446*
records 448
  best sellers 448, 449
recycling 125
red 119
Red Crescent 253
Red Cross 253, 273
red giants 15, 28
red planet 38
Red Rum 219
Red Shoes 458
redcoats 369
red stars 14, 15
Redgrave, Sir Steve 229
redwood trees 254
reefs 88
  Great Barrier Reef, Australia
    89, *89*
Rees, Leighton 219
reflection nebulae 22
reflections 390
Reformation 338, 369
refracting telescopes 56
refraction 390, *390*
refrigerators 123, 388, *388*
reggae 449
relay racing 225, *225*
religions 83, 348, 432, 433
  buildings 208–209, *208–209*
  drama 450, 451, 452, *452*
  founders 204–205, *204–205*
  most followers 296
  music 442, 444
  South America 261
  symbols 485
  wars 338–339, *338–339*,
    342–343
  writing 464–465, *464–465*
Rembrandt van Rijn 435
Renaissance 334–335,
  334–335, 369, 434, 435
Renoir, Auguste 435
reproduction 158–159,
  158–159, 189
  humans 186–187, *186–187*
reptiles 76, 90, 91, 147, *147*,
  160–161, *160–161*
  amphibians 160
republics 369
  Rome 318

Reseu Jean Bernard caves,
  France 109
resources of the Earth
  124–125, *124–125*
respiration 139, 178–179,
  178–179, 189
resultant 387
retrograde 69
revolution 352–353, *352–353*,
  369
  Europe 354–355, *354–355*
rhinoceroses 155, 165, *165*
rhombus 429
rhyme 466
rhythm and blues 448
ribbon lightning 119
Richter Scale 95, *95*
rice 142, 144, 145
  growing 145, *145*
  terraces 266, *266*
Rigel 15
right angles 425, *425*, 427,
  427, 429
rime 118
Ring Nebula 23, *23*
Ring of Fire, Pacific Ocean 93
Ringling Brothers Circus 453
Rio de Janeiro, Brazil 261, *261*
river dolphins 170, *170–171*
rivers 76, 80, 84, 102–103,
  102–103, 252, 255, 258,
  262
  islands 89
  landscape formation 96, *96*,
    97, *97*
  longest 103, 293
Robin Hood 466, *466*
rock 'n' roll 448
roads 319
  oldest 406
robots 66
rock 30, 72, 73, 76, 80–81,
  80–81, 114, 379
  fossils 77
  gemstones 82–83, *82–83*
  interior of the Earth 78
  lava 73
  Mars 39
  oldest 81, 86, 87
  rock cycle 80, *80*, 81
  Saturn 42, 43
  volcanic bombs 92, *92*
  waterfalls 103, *103*
rockets 25, *25*, 35, *35*, 387,
  410, *410*, 429
  Space Shuttle 64–65, *64–65*
Rocky Mountains, North

America 98, 99, 254, *254*
rodents 111, 155
Rogalla, Francis 411
Romania 295
Rome, ancient 196, 213, 272,
  273, 290, 312, 313,
  318–319, *318–319*, 434,
  435
  astronomy 34, 36, 38, 40,
    42, 48
  bridges 402
  drama 450
  gods and goddesses 319
  myths 207, 212
  numbers 424, *424*
  population 319, 322
  pottery 433, *433*
Romulus and Remus 212, *212*
Rontgen, Wilhelm 175
Rooney, Wayne 228, *228*
Roosevelt, Franklin Delano
  246, *246*
Roosevelt, Theodore 257
roots 136, *136*, 137, *137*
  seedlings 142, *142*, 143
  vegetables 137
Rosetta Stone 193, *193*, 464,
  464
Rotterdam, Netherlands 409
Rousseau, Jean-Jacques 349
rovers 38, 39, *39*
rowing 229
Rowling, J K 214, 217
Rub'al-khali (Empty Quarter)
  110
rubber 144, 145
rubidium 77
rubies 82, 83, *83*
rugby 218, 219, 221
runes 462, *462*, 463
running 385, *385*
Russia 75, 79, 87, 127, 326,
  330, 343, 346, 362
  ballet 459
  Cold War 360–361,
    360–361
  Napoleon Bonaparte 355
  Peter the Great 348
  railways 405
  religion 339
  Russian Federation 295
  Russian Revolution 352–353
  satellites 61
  space exploration 58, 60,
    61, 62, 66, 67
  theater 454

S

S-waves 79, *79*
sagas 462
Sagittarius 21
Sahara Desert, Africa 76, 86,
  110, 111, 121, 262, 263,
  263, 280
Sahel, Africa 262
sailing 229
sailors 408, 409
sailors and ships, famous 337
salamanders 147, 156, 157
saliva 181
salmon 152
Salt Lake City, USA 85
salt water 104, 105
Salyut 1 66
Samoa 295
Sampras, Pete 229, *229*
samurai 331, *331*, 369
San Andreas Fault, USA 254
San Marino 295
San Francisco, USA 95, *95*
sand 80, 81, 84, 103
  sand dunes 110, 111, *111*,
    263
sand tiger sharks 153, *153*
sandstone 80
Santorini, Greece 93
São Tomé 295–296
sap 137, 189
sapphires 82, 83, *83*
sapwood 137, *137*, 143, *143*
Sarawak Chamber caves,
  Malaysia 109
Sargon of Mesopotamia 312
Sassanid dynasty 313
satellites (artificial) 60–61,
  60–61, 69, 123
  broadcasting 471, *471*
  communications 414–415,
    414–415, 416–417,
    416–417
  global positioning system
    (GPS) 127
  lasers 419
  Space Shuttle 64, 65
  WMAP 54
Saturn 26, *26*, 42–43, *42–43*
  distance from Sun 27, 42
Saturnalia 42
Saudi Arabia 296
Saurischians 163, *163*
savannah 86, 112
Savery, Thomas 343
saxophones 447, *447*
Scandinavia 270, 462, 463

epics 210, *210*
myths 198–199, *198–199*, 216, *216*, 217
scanners 422, 423, *423*, 429
scarab beetles 195
Schoenberg, Arnold 445
Schubert, Franz Peter 445
science 334, 440
science fiction 467
scientific research
Antarctica 87
scientists 12, 13, 24, 25, 30, 79, 81, 85, 122
Scooter, Uranus 47
Scorpion constellation 17, *17*
Scotland 325, 326
Jacobite rebellions 342, 349
Scots 369
Scott, Sir Robert Falcon 246, 278
screw propellors 408, 409
screws 398, 399
scripts 454
scriptures 464–465, *464–465*
sculpture 316, 334, *334*, 436, *436*
sea anemones 154
sea creatures facts 153
Sea of Japan 107
Sea of Okhotsk 107
seals 87, 107, *107*, 151, 278
seamounts 106, *106*
seas 80, *80*, 81, 84, 88, 106–107, *106–107*, 252
Antarctica 278, 279, *279*
Europe 271, *271*
icebergs 101, *101*
inland seas 300
largest 107
Moon 32, 33
rivers 102, 103
sea levels 89
tsunamis 95, *95*
seasons 74, 112, 113
seconds 75
sediment 102, 103
sedimentary rock 80, *80*, 81
fossils 84
seeds 76, 134, 135, 141, 189
germination 142, *142*, 143
Seinfeld, Herry 472
seismologists 95
seismometers 95
Seismosaurus 163
Selkirk, Alexander 467

Senegal 296
Senning, Ake 423
senses 184, *184*, 185
sepals 189
Serbia 296
serfdom 369
Serkis, Andy 478
Seth 195
Seurat, Georges 435
Seven Wonders of the World 312, 317, *317*
sexual intercourse 187
Seychelles 296
shadows 390
Shaftesbury, Lord *see* Cooper, Anthony Ashley
Shah Jahan 329
Shakespeare, William 45, 246, *246*, 450, *450*
Reduced Shakespeare Company 454
the Globe 451
Shakta Pantuhijina caves, Georgia 109
shale 80
shamans 201, 452, 453, *453*
Shangs 320, 321, *321*
shape of Earth 30
shapes 425–427, *425–427*
calculating area 425–426, *425–426*
calculating volume 426, *426*
Shark Bay, Australia 274
sharks 147, 152, 153, *153*, 154, 171
eggs 158, *158*
Shaw, George Bernard 451
sheep 276, 277
sheet lightning 119
shellfish 76, 82
ammonites 77, *77*, 85, *85*
fossils 84
shells (atoms) 373, *373*, 429
Sheridan, Richard Brinsley 451
Shi Huangdi 320
shield volcanoes 93
Shintoism 207, 209, 320, *320*, 321
ships 324–325, *324–325*, 336, *336*, 356, 369, 395, 396, 408–409, *408–409*
battleships 359
famous sailors and ships 337
sailing ships 409, *409*
Shiva 203

Shoemaker-Levy Comet 51
shoes, ballet 458, 459
shoguns 331, 340, 342, 343, 369
shooting stars 69
shopping malls 482, *482*
Shotoku Taishi 321
Shrek 477
shrews 77, *77*, 154
Siberia 85
Siddhartha Gautama 204
Sidney, Australia 75
Sierra Leone 296
Sikhism 204, 208
scriptures 465, *465*
Sikkim 214
silicon 30, 81, 412
silt 84, 103
Silurian Period 76
silver 82, *82*, 373, 377
Simpson, Sir James 246–247
Singapore 296, 409
singing 442, 443
singularity 24, 69
Sirius 15
Sistema Huautla caves, Mexico 109
sitars 446, *446*
size of
Earth 27
galaxies 18, 19
Jupiter 26, 27, 40
Mars 27, 38
Mercury 27, 34
Moon 32
Neptune 27, 46
Pluto 27, 48
Saturn 26, 27, 42
Solar System 27
stars 15
Uranus 27, 44, 45
Venus 26, 27
skating 387, *387*
skeleton 174–175, *174–175*
skiing 219, 222, 223, 227, *227*
skin 173, *173*
skull 174, *174*
trepanning 422
skunks 164, *164*
sky 115
Skylab 66, 67
skyscrapers 257, *257*, 400, 401, *401*, 483, *483*
slavery 344, 345, *345*, 356, 369
sloths 258

sloughing 161
Slovakia 109, 296
Slovenia 296
Small Magellanic Clouds 18, 68
SMEC Earthmover 398
smell
animal communication 164, 165
Smith, Adam 247
The Wealth of Nations 342
snails and slugs 146, *146*, 148, 159
snakes 147, 151, 160, 161, 165, *165*
biggest 160
constrictors 161
poisonous 161
snooker 218, *218*, 219
snout 100, *100*
snow 87, 119, *119*
glaciers 100
snowflake crystals 101
snow leopards 169, *169*
soap operas 473
Sobek 198, *194*
soccer *see* football
Socrates 247, *247*, 316
sodium 378
sodium chloride 78
solar eclipses 29, *29*
Solar System 18, 26–27, *26–27*, 69, 73, *73*
air 395
formation 26
solar wind 115
solids 374–375, *374–375*, 429
Solomon Islands 296
solutions 395, *395*
Somalia 252, 296–297
Song dynasty 324, 330
song thrushes 167, *167*
Sony 473
Sophocles 451
sound 392–393, *392–393*
animal communication 164
sound recording 418, *418*, 419, 448
bestsellers 448, 449
cinema 475, *475*
radio stations 448
South Africa 264, 265, 297, 362
South America 86, *86*, 87, 90, *90*, 91, 98, 253, *253*, 258–259, *258–259*
ancient 312, 313

dance 456
factfile 259
history 322–333, *322–333*,
  340–341, *340–341*
people and places
  260–261, *260–261*
tectonic plate 91
South American frog 159
South Atlantic Ocean 253, *253*
South China Sea 107
South Pole 75, *75*, 87, 127
Antarctica 278–279,
  278–279
Southern Cross constellation
  17, *17*
Southern Hemisphere 16, 17,
  17, 74, *74*, 115
Southern Ocean 87, 106
Southey, Robert 467
Soviet Union (USSR) *see* Russia
space 73, 114, 115
exploration *365*
space firsts 65
space probes 58–59, *58–59*,
  69
Mars 38, 39, *39*
Pluto 49
Venus 36, 37
Space Shuttle 64–65, *64–65*,
  69
space stations 66–67, *66–67*,
  69
space telescopes 56, 69
Hubble Space Telescope 23,
  45, 46, 48, 61, *61*
spacecraft 385, *385*
rockets 387, 410, *410*, 429
Spain 256, 260, 261, 270,
  297, 333, 337, 343
England 339
General Franco 352
Inquisition 338
Latin America 336, 340,
  341, 355
Sparta 316, 317
species 146, 189
endangered 170–171,
  170–171
fish 152
frogs and toads 156
invertebrates 148
numbers 133
speed of aircraft 410
speed of cars 406, 407
speed of Earth 74, 75
speed of light 12, 391
speed of planets 40, 42

speed of sound 392, 393
sperm 186, *186*
sphalerite 125
spheres 426, *426*, 429
sphinxes 216, *216*
Spice Islands 336
spices 337
spicules 28, *28*
spiders 146, *146*, 148, 154
spinal cord 185, *185*
spinning machines 350, *350*,
  351, *351*
spiral galaxies 18, *18*, 19
Spirit 38, 363
spitting spiders 155, *155*
spittlebugs 149, *149*
Spitz, Mark 228
sponges 133
spores 142, *142*, 189
sport 218–219, *218–219*
key dates 219
key motor sport dates 223
record-breakers 228–229,
  228–229
solo sports 222–223,
  222–223
team sports 220–221,
  220–221
spring 74, 107
springtails 149, *149*
sprinting 225
Sputnik 1 60, 61, *61*
squares 429
squash 223
squid 146
squirrels 155
Sri Lanka 297
St Bartholomew's Day
  massacre 339
St Basil's Cathedral, Moscow,
  Russia 273, *273*
St Kitts-Nevis 295
St Lucia 295
St Paul 465, *465*
St Paul's Cathedral, London
  208, *208*
St Peter's Basilica, Rome 209,
  209
St Petersburg, Russia 273
staccato lightning 119
stained glass 436, *436*
stalactites 109, *109*
stalagmites 109, *109*
Stalin, Joseph 247, 353, *353*,
  360
stamens 141, 189
Stanislavsky, Constanti 454

Stardust 25
starfish 149, 154
Starley, John 407
stars 12, 13, 14–15, *14–15*,
  69
black holes 24
life cycle 15
Milky Way 20, 21
Northern Hemisphere 15,
  16, *16*
number of stars 15
Southern Hemisphere 17, *17*
swarms 15
starting blocks 225
static electricity 382, 383, *383*
statistics
Earth 30
International Space Station
  66
Jupiter 41
Mars 38
Mercury 35
Neptune 46
Pluto 48
Saturn 43
Sun 28
Uranus 45
Venus 37
steam 92, 93, *93*, 429
power stations 421, *421*
steam engines 343, 350,
  350, 351, *351*, 404, 429
steamships 408
Steamboat Geyser, Yellowstone
  Park, USA 93
steel 395, 429
stems 136, *136*, 137, *137*
Stephenson, George 247, 396
Stephenson, Robert Louis 467
steppes 266
stick insects 158, *158*
stigmas 136, *136*, 141, *141*,
  189
still life 435
stomach 180, *180*, 181
stomata 139, *139*, 189
Stonehenge, UK 273, *273*,
  312, *312*, *364*, 480, *480*
Stoppard, Tom 451
storms 121, 123, 254
Jupiter 40, 41
Saturn 43
storyboards 476
storytellers 450, 462, *462*,
  466–467, *466–467*
Strait of Gibraltar 106
strata 124, *124*

stratosphere 114, *114*
stratus clouds 116, *116*, 117
Stravinsky, Igor 459
stress 387
stromatolites 274
strings 446
Stuart, Charles Edward 342,
  349
stukas 329, 328
stunts 479
Styracosaurus 163
Su Sung 321
subatomic particles 372, 429
subduction 91
submarines 359, *359*, 369,
  385, 409
world's smallest 408
submersibles 429
subtropics 86
subways 405
Sudan 293, 297
Suez Canal *365*
Sufis 456, 457, *457*
sugar 138
sugar cane 139
sulfur 81
sulfuric acid 36
Sumerians 192, 314, 424
summer 74, 75, 87, 121
sumo 219
Sun 15, 26, 28–29, *28–29*, 69,
  72, 73, 74, 75, 107, 114,
  115, 120
Antarctica 278
distance from Earth 28
energy 124, 125
global warming 122, 123
gods 194, 195
nearest planet 27
plants 138, 139
position in galaxy 20, 21
radiation 388, *388*
rays 114, 115, 123
sunspots 29, 69
winter 118
sundials 397, *397*
supergiants 15
supernovae 15, 22, 69, 384
supersonic aircraft 411, *411*
surface of the Earth 72, 73, 78
surgeons 422, *422*
Suriname 297
Surrealism 441, *441*
Surtsey Island, Iceland 88
Sutton Hoo treasure 323, *323*
swamps 76, 124
swans 159, 159

Swaziland 297
Sweden 343
Sweet Track, Somerset, UK 406
Swift Observatory 25
swifts 166
swimming 150, 151, 219, 222, *222*, 223, 228
Switzerland 252, 273, 297
swordfish 153
Sydney Opera House, Australia 277, *277*, 483, *483*
Sylphides, Les 458, 459
symphony orchestras 445
synagogues 208
synapses 184, *184*, 189
Syria 297

T

Tacama Bridge, Washington, USA 403
tadpoles 157, *157*
    South American frog 159
tails 77
Taj Mahal, India 269, *269*, 329, *329*
Tajikistan 298
talkies 475
Tambora, Indonesia 93
tambourines 447, *447*
Tang dynasty 324, 330
tankas 438
tanks 352
Tanzania 298
Taoism 204, 207
    Tao-te-Ching 464
tap dancing 461
tapeworms 149
tar 255
tarpaulin 408
Tasman, Abel Janszoon 344
Tasmania 344
    Ice Age 101
taxonomy 132, *132*, 133
Taylor, Elizabeth 478, *478*
Tchaikovsky, Peter Illyich 445
Technicolor 475, 478
technology 346, 356, 440
    buildings 482, 483
    Industrial Revolution 342, 350–351, *350–351*, 369
tectonic plates 90, 91, *91*, 98
    earthquakes 94
teeth 7, 85, 168
    extraction 422

human body 181, *181*
    predators 155, *155*
    rodents 155
telecommunications 414–415, *414–415*, 473
    cable 414
    computers 416
    fiberoptics 414, 415
telephones 357, 360, 414–415, *414–415*, 416, 417
telescopes 42, 54, 56–57, *56–57*, 69
television 418, 419, *419*, 470–471, *470–471*
    home entertainment 472–473, *472–473*
    television set ownership 257
Telford, Thomas 403
temperate forest 143, 189
temperate zone 120, 121
temperature 120, 121, 388–389, *388–389*, 429
    Africa 86, 110
    Antarctica 87, 278
    Arctic Ocean 107
    Asia 266
    conversion 389, *389*
    deserts 111
    global warming 122–123, *122–123*
    interior of the Earth 78, 79, 80
    mountains 99
    stars 14, 15
    Sun 28
temples 208
    Buddhist 480, *480*
    Chinese 481, *481*
    Egyptian 312, 313, *313*
    Greek 197, *197*, 208, *208*, 317, *317*, 480, *480*
    Hindu 202, *202*, 209, *209*
    Mayan 208, *208*, 332
    Roman 480, *480*
tendons 175, *175*, 189
tennis 218, 222, 223, *223*, 228, 229
tenpin bowling 219, *219*
Teotihuacán 332–333, 333, 364
tephra 92, *92*
Terminator 3: Rise of the Machines 478, *478*
Terracotta Army, China 320, *320*

Terrestrial Planet Finder (TPF) 59
territories 159, 189, 302–305
    disputed 305
terrorism 353, 363, 369
Tertiary Period 76
Tethys Sea 90, *90*
Thanksgiving 340
theater 450–451, *450–451*
    modern 454–455, *454–455*
    theater layout 455, *455*
    theater staff 454
    world theater 452–453, *452–453*
thecodonts 162
thermometers 389, *389*
thermosphere 114, *114*
thermostats 388, *388*
Theseus 213, *213*
Thirty Years War 339, 342–343
Thomson, Sir William 247
Thor 199, *199*, 463, *463*
Thoth 194, *194*
thunder 116, 117, 121
Thunderbird 201, *201*
Thursday 199
Tibet 342
tides 107, *107*
Tien Shan 99
tigers 170
Tigris–Euphrates civilization 268
Tigris River 192, 314
tilt of the Earth 29, 30, 74, *74*, 75, *75*
tilt of Uranus 44
timber 276, 481, *481*
time 13, 76
    time travel 25
    time zones 75, *75*, 252
tin 373
Tintern Abbey, UK 327, *327*
tissues 173, *173*, 189
Titan 43, 59
Titan III/Centaur 59, *59*
Titanic 394, *394*, 409
Titans 197, *197*
toads 147, 156–157, *156–157*
Tobago 298
Togo 298
Tokyo, Japan 75
Tombaugh, Clyde 49
Tongan Islands, Pacific 89, 298
topaz 82, 83, *83*
tornadoes 118, 119, *119*

tortoises 147, 160, 161
totems 200, *200*
tourism 276
tourmaline 82
tournaments 327, *327*, 369
Toussaint l'Ouverture, François Dominique 345
Tower Bridge, London, UK 403, *403*
towns 252
trace fossils 85, 85
trade 252, *252*, 334, 336, 337, 356
Trafalgar, Battle of 354, *364*
tragedy 317
trains 404–405, *404–405*
    bullet train 405, *405*
    heaviest 405
    longest 405
    maglev trains 405, *405*
    Rocket 396
    track control 404, *404*, 405, *405*
Trans-Siberian Express, Russia 405
Transantarctic Range 99
transistors 413, *413*
transits of Venus 37
transmitters 414
transparency 429
transport
    air 410–411, *410–411*
    rail 404–405, *404–405*
    road 406–407, *406–407*
    water 408–409, *408–409*
trapeziums 425, *425*, 429
Treaty of Tordesillas 336
treehouses 266
trees 76, 84, 85, 114, 124, 135, *135*, 188
    forestry 125
    forests 112–113, *112–113*
    growth rings 143, *143*
    Namib Desert, Africa 87, *87*
    structure 137, *137*
trench warfare 358, *358*
trenches, ocean bed 91, 106, *106*
Trevithick, Richard 247
triangles 425, *425*, 429
Triangulum galaxy 19
Triassic Period 76
tributaries 102
Triceratops 163, *163*
trilobites 85
Trinidad 298
triplanes 411

triple jump 226, *226*
Triton 46, 47, *47*
Trojan asteroids 52
Trojan Horse 211, *211*, 316, *316*
trolls 217
trombones 447, *447*
tropical forests 86, 112–113, *112–113*, 143, 171, 189
tropics 86, 112, 113, 117, 121, 127
  storms 121
  Tropic of Cancer 127
  Tropic of Capricorn 127
  wind 118
troposphere 114, *114*, 115
trucks 407
trumpets 442, 447, *447*
trunks 137, *137*
Tsing Ma Bridge, Hong Kong 403
tsunamis 95, *95*, 353
tubas 447, *447*
tube worms 107
Tugela Falls, South Africa 103
Tull, Jethro 247, 342–343, 351
tundra 266
tungsten 375
Tunisia 298
tunnels 400, *400*
  construction 401, *401*
  world's longest 288
turbines 421, *421*, 429
turbofans 410
turbojets 410
turboprops 410
Turing, Alan 247
Turkey 292, 298
Turkmenistan 299
Turner, Joseph Mallard William 247, 435
turquoises 82, 83, *83*
turtles 147, 160, 161, *161*
Tuttle, William 225
Tutunendo, Colombia 121
Tuvalu 299
typewriters 357
Tyrannosaurus rex 85, *85*, 163
Tyssestrengene, Norway 103

U

U-boats 359, *359*
UFO sightings 31
Uganda 299
Ukraine 299
ultrasonic sound 393

ultrasound scans 187, *187*
ultraviolet rays 114, 115, 123, 384, 390, 391
unconformities 77
underground railways 405
UNESCO 253
UNICEF 253
unicorns 216, 217, *217*
uniforms 484
United Arab Emirates (UAE) 299
United Kingdom (UK) 75, 299
  railways 404, 405
  satellites 61
United Nations (UN) 253, 363, *363*
United States of America (USA) 75, 85, 87, 127, 254, 256, 299, 356
  aircraft carriers 409
  art 441
  Civil War 352–353, *353*
  Cold War 360–361, *360–361*
  flag 342, *342*
  industrial power 357
  popular music 448, 449
  railways 404, 405
  satellites 61
  space exploration 58–59, 62–63, 64–65, 66–67
  states and zip codes 257
  War of Independence 343, *345*
  world wars 358, 359
Universe 12–13, *12–13*, 69
  age of 12
  brightest objects in 24
  history 13
  measuring 13
ununoctium 377
uranium 77, 421
Uranus 26, *26*, 44–45, *44–45*
  distance from Sun 27, 44
  rings 45, *45*
urinary system 181, *181*
Uruguay 260, 299
USS *Glacier* 101
Utigord Falls, Norway 103
Uzbekistan 299–300

V

Valentino, Rudolf 478, *478*
Valkyries 199
Valles Marineris, Mars 39
valleys 97, *97*, 102, *102*

van Drebbel, Cornelius 409
van Gogh, Vincent 434, 435
van Ohain, Pabst 410
Vandals 313, 319, 322
Vanuatu 300
Vatican City, Rome 209, *209*, 300, 301
Vedas 202, 464
vegetables 135, 137, 145
vegetation zones 112
veins 173, *173*, 182, 183, *183*, 189
vellum 434
Velociraptor 163
velocity 387
Venezuela 261, 300
vents, volcanic 92, 92
Venus 26, 27, *27*, 36–37, *36–37*
  clockwise spin 37
  craters 36
  day 37
  distance from Sun 27
  Mariner 35
Venus de Milo 316, *316*, 433, *433*
Vercors caves, France 109
Verdi, Giuseppe 445
Versailles, France 349, *349*
vertebrates 146, 147, 189
Vesuvius 432
Victoria Falls, Africa 262
Victoria, Queen 248, *248*
video games 473
videotapes 473
Vietnam 300
Vietnam War 361
Viking 38, *38*, 58
Vikings 198, 199
Vikings 198, 199, 324–325, *324–325*, 326, *365*, 369
  runes 462, *462*, 463
villi 180, *180*
vineyards 270, *270*
vinyl discs 418
violet 119
violins 442, 446, *446*
Virgil 212, 213, *213*
virtual reality 412
viruses 183
Vishnu 203
Visigoths 313, 319, 322
vitamins 137
Vlad the Impaler 297
vocal cords 179, *179*
voice 443
volcanoes 72, 73, *73*, 78, 79,

79, *258*
  biggest 93
  earthquakes 94
  eruptions 92–93, *92–93*, 121
  Io 41
  island formation 88–89, *88–89*
  Mars 38
  Moon 32, 33
  most active 92
  Ring of Fire 266
  rock cycle 80, *80*, 81
  tectonic plates 91, 93
  Venus 36, 37, *37*
  volcanic mountains 98, *98*
  volcano records 289
  Yellowstone, USA 254
volleyball 221
Volsunga Saga 210
Voltaire, François-Marie Arouet 349
Vortigern 322
Vostok science station, Antarctica 87
Voyager 42, 43, 44, 58, 59, *59*

W

Wagner, Richard 445, *445*
walking 385
Walkmans 471
Wallace, Sir William 248
Wallis, Sir Barnes 248
Walpole, Sir Robert 248
Walsh, Stella 224
waning and waxing Moon 32, 33, *33*
War of the Worlds 472
warfare 312, 315
  Renaissance 335
  trench warfare 358, *358*
Warhol, Andy 441
warships, world's biggest 409
Washington, George 248, 257, 345
Washington, USA 101
wasps 146, 149
water 12, 29, 30, 72, 73, 80, 84, 114, 124, 394–395, *394–395*, 429
  ancient Rome 318
  cave formation 108–109, *108–109*
  chemical formula 378
  clouds 116–117, *116–117*
  deserts 110, 111

Europa 41
human body 180
hydroelectric power stations 421
lakes 104–105, *104–105*
landscapes 96–97, *96–97*
life on Earth 31
Mars 39
movement 150, 151
oceans and seas 106–107, *106–107*
rivers 102–103, *102–103*
transport 408–409, *408–409*
water cycle 103, *103*, 104
water vapor 123
water boatmen 149, *149*
watercolors 436, *436*
waterfalls 87, *87*, 254, *254*, 258, *258*, 262
highest 103, 290
Waterloo, Battle of 353, *353*, 355
waterwheels 399, *399*, 480, *480*
Watts, James 248, 350, 351
wave-particle duality 390
waves 96
tsunamis 95, *95*
wealth 252, 260, 262, 268, 272
weapons 325, *325*
weather 80, 118–119, *118–119*, 252
clouds 116–117, *116–117*
erosion 81, 84, 96, *96*
troposphere 115
weather records 283
wedges 398, 399
Wednesday 199
weight of
Earth 28, 79
Jupiter 26, 40
Sun 28
weightlessness 66, 69
Welles, Orson 472
Wellington, Duke of (Arthur Wellesley) 248, 355
Wells, Horace 422
Wesley, John 248
West Indies *364*
Western Wall, Jerusalem 208, *208*
whale shark 153, *153*
whales 145, 154, 155, 168, 278
wheels 398, 399
whirling dervishes 457, *457*

white dwarfs 15
white holes 25
white stars 14, 15
Whitten, Sir Arthur 230
Whittle, Frank 410
Wilberforce, William 249
wildlife parks 171
Willendorf Venus 432
William I, the Conqueror 249, *249*, 327
willow 145, *145*
wind 80, 87, 96, 97, 115, 117
Neptune 46
renewable energy 125, *125*
Saturn 42
tropics 118
Uranus 44
Venus 36
wind turbines 384, *384*
windmills 270, *270*
wings 167, *167*
winter 74, 75, 118, 120, 121
witchcraft 214–215, *214–215*
Witwatersrand, South Africa 264
wizards 214, *214*
Wolsey, Thomas 249
wolves 165, *165*
wood 143, 144, 145, 379
Woods, Tiger 229, *229*
woodwind 446
words 462–463, *462–463*
words derived from Greek 317
Wordsworth, William 249, 467
work 398
world 252–253, *252–253*
biggest
cities 280
dams 295
goldfield 264
mines 260
deepest lake 298
driest places 258
highest
capital city 283
dams 295
geyser 274
navigable lake 294
languages 297
largest
coal reserves 298
deserts 282
inland seas 300
islands 285
lakes 300
oil reserves 288

longest
bridges 268, 291
fence 281
glaciers 284
tunnels 288
most southerly city 289
population 253
religions 296
tallest
buildings 281, 483
living thing 254
World Health Organization (WHO) 253, 272
World Trade Organization 252
World War I 272, 352, 353, 358–359, *358–359*, 365, 411
World War II 272, 352, 358–359, *358–359*, 365
World Wide Web 416, 417, 429
wormholes in space 25, *25*
worms 146, *146*
Wren, Sir Christopher 208, 249
wrestling 218
Wright, Orville and Wilbur 249, *249*, 410, 352
writing 462–463, *462–463*, 466–467, *466–467*
publishing 468–469, *468–469*
religions 464–465, *464–465*

X
X rays 15, 56, 175, *175*, 185, 384, 390, 423, *423*, 429
xylem vessels 137, *137*
xylophones 442, 447, *447*

Y
Yamato dynasty 321
Yanomami tribe 260
Yangtze-Kiang river 103
yawning 179
years 75
Yeats, W B 249
yellow 119
yellow stars 15
Yellowstone Park, USA 93, 254, *254*
Yeltsin, Boris 361
Yemen 300
Yenisey/Angara River 103
Yevgeny Onegin 467

Yosemite Falls, USA 103
Yosemite National Park, USA 254
Yuan dynasty 331

Z
Zambesi River, Africa 262
Zambia 300
Zanzibar 356
zebras 155
zero 424
absolute zero 374, 389, *389*, 428
Zeta Puppis 15
Zeus 196, *196*, 197, *197*, 226
ziggurats 192, *192*
Zimbabwe 300
zinc 125
zircon 81, 82
Zodiac 55, *55*
Zoff, Dino 229
zoopraxiscopes 474, 475
zoos 171, 282
Zoroaster 204

Acknowledgments

All artworks are from MKP Archives

The Publisher would like to thank the following picture sources whose photographs appear in this book:

page 81 (CL) Jeremy Horner/CORBIS
page 88 (C) Yann Arthus-Bertrand/CORBIS
page 104 (TR) Roger Tidman/FLPA
page 113 (TL) Michael and Patricia Fogden/Minden Pictures/FLPA
page 214 (TR) Warner Bros/pictorialpress.com
page 227 (TL) Duomo/CORBIS
page 228 (BR) Reuters/Ian Hodgson
page 229 (TR) Reuters/Marc Serota; (BR) Reuters/ Kieran Doherty
page 281 (TL) Reuters/Simon Kwong
pages 334–335 (C) Yann Arthus-Bertrand/CORBIS
page 349 (TL) Archivo Iconografico, S.A./CORBIS
page 387 (B) photolibrary
page 413 (TC) Richard T. Nowitz/CORBIS; (CR) Courtesy of Apple
page 414 (TR) Nokia
page 417 (TL) Courtesy of Apple; (TR) Sony Computer Entertainment
page 439 (BR) Archivo Iconografico, S.A./CORBIS
page 440 (TR) The Art Archive / Moderna Museet Stockholm / Dagli Orti;
        (BL) The Art Archive / Constant Permeke Museum, Jabbeke / Dagli Orti (A)
page 455 (TR) pictorialpress.com
page 472 (BL) BBC/pictorialpress.com; (BR) Stewart Cohen/photolibrary.com
page 473 (CR) Sony; (BL) Sony Computer Entertainment
Page 476 (TC) New World/pictorialpress.com
page 477 (TL) DreamWorks/pictorialpress.com; (BL) NRI/Pictorial Press
page 478 (BC) Hemdale/pictorialpress.com; (BR) Volkswagen
page 479 (TL) Warner Bros/pictorialpress.com; (C) Hammer/pictorialpress.com;
        (BR) New Line/pictorialpress.com
page 482 (TR) Matt Seaber

All other photographs from:
Castrol, Corbis, Corel, digitalSTOCK, digitalvision. Hemera
ILN, Nasa, PhotoAlto, PhotoDisc, PhotoEssentials, Stockbyte